# GERMAN QUESTION/

# JEWISH QUESTION

## REVOLUTIONARY

## ANTISEMITISM

## FROM KANT TO WAGNER

# GERMAN QUESTION/

# JEWISH QUESTION

## REVOLUTIONARY

## ANTISEMITISM

## FROM KANT TO WAGNER

*PAUL LAWRENCE ROSE*

PRINCETON UNIVERSITY PRESS · PRINCETON, NEW JERSEY

Published by Princeton University Press, 41 William Street,
Princeton, New Jersey 08540
In the United Kingdom: Princeton University Press,
Chichester, West Sussex

*Library of Congress Cataloging-in-Publication Data*

Rose, Paul Lawrence.
[Revolutionary antisemitism in Germany from Kant to Wagner]
German question/Jewish question: revolutionary antisemitism
from Kant to Wagner / Paul Lawrence Rose.
p. cm.
Originally published: Revolutionary antisemitism in Germany from
Kant to Wagner. Princeton, N.J.: Princeton University Press, © 1990.
Includes bibliographical references and index.
ISBN 0-691-00890-6
1. Antisemitism—Germany—History—19th century. 2. Philosophy,
German—19th century. 3. Germany—Intellectual life—19th century.
4. Germany—Ethnic relations. I. Title.
[DS146.G4R64   1993]
305.892'4043'09034—dc20        92-27142

Originally published as *Revolutionary Antisemitism in Germany
from Kant to Wagner* .
First Princeton Paperback printing, with a new title and a
new afterword, 1992

This book has been composed in Linotron Baskerville

Princeton University Press books are printed on acid-free paper
and meet the guidelines for permanence and durability of the
Committee on Production Guidelines for Book Longevity
of the Council on Library Resources

1   2   3   4   5   6   7   8   9   10

Printed in the United States of America

To the memory of the

**ROSENBAUM FAMILY 1942**

and for their great-grandchildren,

**Alexander, Livy, Zoe, and Ariel**

# CONTENTS

# ACKNOWLEDGMENTS

Much of the research for this book was done at James Cook University of North Queensland, Australia, and it is a pleasure to thank my former head of department, Professor Brian Dalton, for his encouragement of the work from its inception, and indeed for steering me from my earlier exclusive concern with Renaissance history into modern fields. My thanks also are due to the Australian Research Grants Committee for its funding of several research visits both within the country and overseas.

To Professor R. B. Rose of the University of Tasmania, I am most grateful for his hospitality, which enabled me to consult the Henry Handel Richardson Collection of Wagneriana at Hobart in 1982–83. A fellowship from the Humanities Research Centre of the Australian National University in 1980 allowed me to undertake at Canberra the initial spadework and to present a first report on the subject in the framework of the Centre's Romantic Nationalism seminar.

My move to the University of Haifa in 1985 gave me the benefit of many stimulating conversations on the themes of antisemitism and Jewish history with colleagues there, especially Professor Myriam Yardeni (whose own book on early modern antisemitism is to appear soon) and Professor Dan Segre, whose enthusiasm for new ideas is infectious. Their comments, as well as pointed questions from Haifa students, greatly helped me to refine some of the analytical ideas in the book. Dr. Reuben Hecht also kindly read several sections, and his remarks on the text—as well as on many kindred subjects—proved most valuable.

Professor Sir Geoffrey Elton's generous encouragement of my work in an area not his own primary interest deserves my warmest recognition. And to Professor Aryeh Dvoretzky, then head of the Institute of Advanced Studies at the Hebrew University of Jerusalem, I am deeply indebted for his invitation to work there on this material in 1984 and 1985.

For convincing me that the original prolix manuscript would not make its points as clearly as a revision of reasonable length, I would like to thank Joanna Hitchcock and Deborah Tegarden of Princeton University Press. And for actually carrying out the major abridgement required and for soothing the author's apprehension at losing so many golden words—as well as for giving so many other things— my greatest thanks of all go to my wife, Susan Rose.

# ABBREVIATIONS

CWD   *Cosima Wagner's Diaries*, trans. G. Skelton (London, 1978–80)

GF   H. H. Houben, *Gutzkow-Funde* (Berlin, 1901)

HAS   L. Poliakov, *The History of Anti-Semitism*, trans. R. Howard et al. (London, 1974–85)

LBIY   *Leo Baeck Institute Yearbook*

MLE   Richard Wagner, *My Life*, trans. (New York, 1936)

PW   *Richard Wagner's Prose Works*, trans. W. A. Ellis (London, 1892–99)

SB   Richard Wagner, *Sämtliche Briefe*, ed. G. Strobel et al. (Leipzig, 1967–   )

# The German Revolution and Antisemitism

THIS book seeks to reinterpret both the "German revolution" and German antisemitism in more authentic terms than has usually been the case. A great deal of sterile controversy has arisen as a result of the tendency of historians to view the German revolutionary movement, German antisemitism, and Jewish emancipation in Germany through modern Western liberal spectacles. One thinks of the endless futile arguments over whether Fichte was a universal revolutionary or a nationalist reactionary, whether Herder was "pro-" or "anti-Jewish," whether either of them was a "proto-Nazi" or a free spirit. In these disputations, one school of historians naively lines up its selection of suitable quotations supporting a humane Fichte, while the opposition marshals against them an array of Fichte's nastier remarks. The problem, however, with this kind of crude argument is that it disregards the crucial problem of historical context on several different levels: individual statements are torn from their original context; the context of a given thinker's overall view of the world is ignored; and the general context of the political debate and its language is excluded. Reflection suggests that simply quoting one set of statements against another will never resolve the historical problems of German revolutionary and antisemitic thought. Such a procedure merely generates a series of false paradoxes, false alternatives, false contradictions. And it totally fails to explain how a German "revolutionary" author is able in his own mind, or within the confines of one essay, or even indeed within a single sentence, to combine support for Jewish civil emancipation with expressions of intense disgust for Jews and Judaism.

Most of these unresolvable debates and controversies actually originate in a fundamental misunderstanding of the nature of German mentality and culture. In the German context, it is misconceived to demand whether a particular thinker such as Fichte or Wagner is "left" or "right," "pro-" or "anti-Jewish," revolutionary or nationalist. What is needed instead is a higher and more embracing context of analysis within which the contradictions typical of German thinking will be perceived to be merely false paradoxes, and in which apparent contradictions are merely single but complementary aspects of a unitary whole, two sides of a single coin. Such a solvent context is supplied by what this book calls "German revolution," or "German revolutionism," a phenomenon quite distinct from Western "liberal" varieties of revolutionary thought. In this context the German revolution is simultaneously revolutionary *and* national, "left" *and* "right"; it is not a liberal revolutionary faith at all. It is rather an outlook, a mood, a sensibility shared by disparate thinkers despite their wide differences of formal ideological opinion. Fichte and Kant, Humboldt and Hegel, Marx and Feuerbach, Börne and Marr, Frantz and Bauer, Heine and Wagner were all imbued with the faith of the *German* revolution—not necessarily a nationalist or racist revolution, but one founded ultimately on a new vision of freedom and emancipated humanity that had been vouchsafed especially to men raised in German culture.

This book, therefore, seeks to demonstrate what is specifically "German," firstly, about the German revolutionary mentality, and secondly, about German antisemitism, as distinct from other antisemitisms. It uses the problem of the German revolution to throw light on the nature of German antisemitism, and at the same time it elucidates the problem of German antisemitism as a key to understanding the character of the German revolutionary movement.

Such a specifically German contextual approach is not without its dangers. Above all, it carries with it the temptation to lose sight of the more general problem of antisemitism. Despite the proliferation of specific antisemitisms—pagan, Christian, rationalist, economic, moral, racist, French, Russian, American, anti-Zionist, liberal, Arab and even Jewish antisemitism—it is obvious that there is a universal essence of "antisemitism" that prevades all its various manifestations.[1] It seems to me that the constant factor in all these different antisemitisms is a resentment of the Jews for being "a nation apart," "a chosen race," separated from the rest of humanity. This concept was always a dual one in that it fused a religious concept of the chosen people with a secular one of Jewish ethnicity. The idea of a Jewish ethnic identity—often defined in negative vicious terms—had been familiar since antiquity, but it achieved new force in an age of growing nationalism when it was redefined as Jewish "national character." The German philosophical revolution equipped this notion with a theoretical framework which held that the Jews were not only ethnically "apart" from other peoples, but somehow morally "against humanity" because they suffered from a defect of truly human moral feelings, notably love and freedom. The Jews were a people that

[1] Universal and particular aspects are investigated in L. Poliakov's brilliant synthesis, *The History of Anti-Semitism*, trans. R. Howard et al. (London, 1974–85). For a succinct survey, see B. Lewis, *Semites and Anti-Semites* (London, 1986). Useful essays are in S. Almog, ed., *Antisemitism through the Ages* (Oxford, 1988).

needed still to be "redeemed into full humanity" by emancipation or assimilation; if this gentle dissolution of Judaism were not thought feasible, then harder measures were recommended. In both cases, the "destruction of Judaism" was the objective.

This prejudice about the need to eradicate Jewish identity became the central pillar of a European "revolutionary antisemitism," fostered by "right" and "left" alike, which reached its most intensive development in nineteenth-century Germany with twentieth-century results known to everyone. But its capacity for evil has not yet been exhausted. Thanks in large part to the influence of its left-wing exponents such as Marx (who identified Judaism with capitalism), the assumption of a base Jewish national character opposed to revolutionary freedom has come to dominate recent antisemitic mentalities, especially since the discrediting of "reactionary" racist antisemitism after 1945.[2]

It may seem that placing such an emphasis on revolutionary antisemitism ignores the prominence of racial ideology in German thought. But again, the frequent opposition of "racist" to "revolutionary" thought appears to be misconceived. To a large degree, the idea of race was but a late development that tied up some loose ends in earlier thinking about the "national character" of the Jews and lent it a pseudoscientific basis. That "race" and "revolution" were not mutually opposed categories is clear from the careers of many of the leading antisemitic theorists who began with a revolutionary attitude to the Jewish Question and only later enhanced it with racial elements as they became available in the 1850s and after. Richard Wagner, Bruno Bauer, and Wilhelm Marr, for example, are often mistakenly categorized as "nationalist-racist" antisemites of the "right," simply because their later racist ideas have obscured the fact that they were all primarily and permanently revolutionary antisemites.

In a book that sets such store on the uniqueness and strangeness of the German revolutionary tradition, the lack of adequate English terms to translate the crucial German word *Judentum* has been a serious difficulty. The German carries at least three meanings, variously rendered in English as (1) Judaism (the religion); (2) Jewry (the community or nation of Jews); and (3) Jewishness (the specifically Jewish qualities inhering in Jews and Judaism). In some contexts, it is obvious that an author intends only one of the English meanings, but frequently this is not the case. One of the most important features of

[2] See especially Lewis, *Semites*, chap. 9. *Antisemitism in the Contemporary World*, ed. M. Curtis (Boulder, Colo., 1986). Y. Manor, "The New Anti-Zionism," *Jerusalem Quarterly* 35 (1985): 125–44.

German antisemitic writing is that this seemingly innocuous term *Judentum* possesses a polyvalence of meaning that fluctuates constantly without precise definition. It is this unfixed quality in the German that gives apparently rational discussions a highly emotional character, making them almost dreamlike at times in their fluidity. A German writer can move unconsciously and imperceptibly between the different levels of meaning in the word *Judentum* in a way of which the precise-minded English reader remains totally unaware. This dynamic instability in the German word remains a major block to the English reader's understanding of German antisemitism.

Finally, some readers may be put out by the use of the term "antisemitism" to denote anti-Jewish mentalities that existed before the term was launched properly in the 1870s. Sometimes, in order to be more faithful linguistically, I have used the much older word "Jew-hatred" (a term that might well be reinstated to describe some very recent forms of antisemitism). The justification for this rather free usage is that continuities do exist between earlier and later varieties of anti-Jewish mentality. It is these continuities that provide one of the unifying themes of the book and so render the interchangeability of terms less anachronistic than might be expected. It seemed worth incurring the risk of a technical anachronism in order to bring out some of the constants of anti-Jewish prejudice.

# PART ONE

# Genealogy and Mythology of Revolutionary Antisemitism

C H A P T E R   1

# The Genealogy of Modern Antisemitism:
# National Character, Race, and Revolution

## NATIONAL CHARACTER

TRADITIONAL Christian hostility to the Jews and Judaism revolved around a cluster of related theological and social themes. The first and earliest of these was the conception of Judaism as a super-seded religion that was essentially national, and based on the Law, and thus merely a precursor of Christianity, the new universal religion of Love. This basic critique of Judaism is clearly expressed in St. Paul's Epistle to the Romans (Rom. 8–11) in the framework of a relatively benign attitude toward the Jews themselves. But with the destruction of the Second Temple and the Jewish Commonwealth, a bitter, punitive view of the supersession of Judaism emerged. The Jews now stood accused as the deicidal nation that had murdered Christ. Christians were to find corroboration in pagan sources for a hateful Jewish national character that had driven the Jews to deicide. In the large commercial cities of the Roman Empire, social and religious rivalries between Jews and pagans had long been intense, and these engendered the resentful national critique of Judaism summed up in Tacitus's indictment of the Jews as a nation driven by their "hatred of the rest of humanity." The writings of the church fathers, most notably St. John Chrysostom, expanded this charge into a repertoire of anti-Jewish clichés: the Jews are full of hatred for the rest of mankind and are the enemies of all gentiles; they are parasites on the gentile societies that harbor them; they are addicted to money, and through the power of money, they aspire to be rulers of the world even though they have, by their innate quarrelsomeness, lost their own state.[1]

It is often said that this pagan and Christian conception of the Jews as a hateful nation was not racial in the modern sense. Individual

[1] In general, see *HAS*, vol. 1; C. Klein, *Anti-Judaism in Christian Theology* (Philadelphia, 1978); J. C. Gager, *The Origins of Anti-Semitism: Attitudes toward Judaism in Pagan and Christian Antiquity* (New York, 1983); F. H. Littell, *The Crucifixion of the Jews* (New York, 1975); N. Ravitch, "The Problem of Christian Anti-Semitism," *Commentary* (April 1982): 41–52; P. Richardson and D. Granskou, eds., *Anti-Judaism in Early Christianity* (Waterloo, Ont., 1986), vol. 1, "Paul and the Gospels." For pagan attitudes, see M. Stern, ed., *Greek and Latin Authors on Jews and Judaism* (Jerusalem, 1974–84).

Jews might share the ugly national character of their people, but conversion to paganism or to Christianity signified their abandoning of that national character. Nevertheless, many Christian thinkers remained skeptical of the Jews' capacity for redemptive conversion. The sixteenth-century Christian humanist Erasmus would charge that the converted Jews among his opponents had not purged themselves of the hateful spite of their nation. In any event, the question of the efficacy of conversion in changing national character was of marginal importance, since most Jews obstinately refused to convert. And here another thematic justification of Jew-hatred emerges—the notorious "stubbornness" of the Jews. It was their inexplicable refusal to accept the self-evident truth of triumphant Christianity that perplexed and infuriated Christian observers of Judaism—and worried them too. For it was not just a matter of Jewish redemption, of forcing the Jews to become free, nor even a question of punishing them for their deicide. Rather it was Christian redemption itself that was at stake; the Jews held Christendom itself hostage, since Christ could not return in the Second Coming until they should be converted.

From this Christian notion of the Jews' role as frustrators of redemption grew a new theme that was to be of central importance for the later history of a specifically German antisemitism. In 1543 Martin Luther denounced the Jews as a special affliction of the German people. The Jews (in league with the papacy) were blocking the Germans' need to fulfill themselves in achieving both their "Christian freedom" and their political "freedom." In Luther—and in modern German antisemitism—this perception was fed by the older theme of the Jews as Christ-killers, but the murderous instincts of the Jews had taken on a new form. Having crucified Jesus, they were currently intent on crucifying the German people.

This attack was being carried forward on two levels. Materially, the Jews were extorting money from an exploited German nation. Luther's bogeyman, the indulgence-hawker Tetzel, was a converted Jew and Jewish money was enabling the Emperor Charles V to proceed against those German princes who had embraced evangelical truth. Morally, the Jews were the worldly agents of the devil, deadly menaces to the truth of the Gospel as preached by Luther. The spirituality of the German people and the purity of Lutheran doctrine were threatened by contamination with "Jewishness" and with "Judaizing." Thus, Luther, the molder of so much of German culture, launched the essential myth of *Verjudung*, or "Jewification," which was to dominate modern German antisemitism. It is a myth that is at once social and moral, spiritual and political, a myth that pervades Luther's later writings against the Jews and by means of which he "Germanized" the traditional universal themes of Christian Jew-hatred.[2]

The often contradictory nature of German antisemitism, which oscillates between a sort of suspicious benevolence and hatred, was personified in Luther.[3] In his early writings of 1510–20 the reformer had adopted a traditionally hostile attitude toward the Jews. The Jews had been exiled as punishment for rejecting Christ; Jewish stubbornness rendered them enemies still, and they were not to be tolerated. In 1523, however, Luther allowed himself to be swayed by charity into temporarily modifying this harsh stereotype. The tract, "Jesus Christ Was Born a Jew," sought the conversion of the Jews through kindness and at times anticipated the views of some later Enlightenment thinkers that the evil national character of the Jews was not the result of any intrinsic badness or hatred of humanity, but rather was the product of centuries of Christian oppression and ostracism of the Jew from the brotherhood of mankind. Thus, Jewish usury was not an expression of innate greed, but rather was something into which the Jews had been forced by Christian rulers. The Jews were deserving of love rather than punishment.

Luther's apparently benevolent attitude was not in any meaningful sense "pro-Jewish"; he was moved to act as a "friend of the Jews" not out of respect for Judaism, but from a thirst to redeem them by destroying Judaism. This idea of redeeming the Jews from being Jews had long been a feature of Christian thought; Luther now engraved it obsessively and permanently on modern German culture. Even after its Christian context had fallen away, the destructionist ideal of Jewish redemption survived the Enlightenment to become a fixture in the secular mentality of later German thinkers.

[2] See S. Aschheim, " 'The Jew Within': The Myth of 'Judaization' in Germany," in *The Jewish Response to German Culture*, ed. J. Reinharz and W. Schatzberg (Hanover, N.H., 1985), pp. 212–41. "Judaizing" was, of course, a term of some antiquity in Christian thought and was revived widely in the sixteenth century, notably by Calvin. But Calvin did not attempt to give it any national or social significance, restricting it rather to a theological context. Luther, in contrast, saw it as a specific threat to the German nation. Cf. A. G. Dickens, *The German Nation and Martin Luther* (London, 1974).

For the early role of the charge of "Judaizing" in antisemitic conceptions, see St. John Chrysostom, *Discourses against Judaizing Christians*, trans. (Washington, D.C., 1979).

[3] The best accounts of Luther's Jew-hatred are H. A. Oberman, *The Roots of Anti-Semitism in the Age of Renaissance and Reformation* (Philadelphia, 1984); R. Lewin, *Luthers Stellung zu den Juden* (Berlin, 1911; repr., Aalen, 1973); *HAS*, 1:216–26; Mark U. Edwards, Jr., *Luther's Last Battles: Politics and Polemics 1531–1546* (Ithaca, N.Y., 1983), chap. 6; S. Stern, *Josel of Rosheim in the Holy Roman Empire of the German Nation* (Philadelphia, 1965), pp. 157–62, 186–200; H. Kremers, ed., *Die Juden und Martin Luther* (Neukirchen, 1985).

However, the soft invitation to conversion did not work and so—
again setting a pattern for German antisemitism, this time its fluctu-
ation between "soft" and "hard" views of "destruction"—Luther
swung in later years to a vehement conviction that the Jews were an
active principle of evil, "children of the devil, who have perverted
everything."[4] In 1539 he told his congregation, "I cannot convert the
Jews. Our Lord Jesus Christ did not succeed in doing so; but I can
close their mouths so that there will be nothing for them to do but lie
upon the ground."[5] This is a seminal example of what was to become
a salient and recurring characteristic of later German antisemitism—
the use of ambiguous terms that may seem purely metaphorical but
are also open to a physical interpretation. "Close their mouths" (*das
Maul . . . ihnen zustopfen*) and "lie upon the ground" (*herniederlegen
muessen*) have a vagueness and at the same time a potential brutality
that will be met with again in modern exponents of Jew-hatred, most
notably Wagner, Dühring, and Hitler himself.

The pose of the "disappointed friend" was yet another syndrome
of Jew-hatred that Luther bequeathed to subsequent German thinkers. Like many of the figures analyzed in this book, Luther had once
entertained hopes that Jews might be redeemed into Christianity (or
into "full humanity" in secular language)—only to be disappointed.
He was forced to conclude that any hope of Jewish redemption was
rendered vain by the irremediable evil of Jewish national character,
and that consequently the only solution was to take practical measures of German self-defense against the Jews. In his furious invec-
tive of 1543, "Against the Jews and Their Lies," Luther accused the
Jews of being the bloodthirsty murderers not only of Christianity but
specifically of the German people, who are held captive in their own
country, tortured, and robbed. In an uninhibited rehearsal of the
paranoid themes of later German antisemitism, Luther explodes that

> the Jews are lords of the world and all the gentiles flock to them . . .
> giving the noble princes and lords of Israel all they have, while the
> Jews curse, spit on and malign the Germans. . . . They say that God
> is to kill and exterminate all of us Germans through their messiah,
> so that they can lay their hands on the land, the goods and the gov-
> ernment of the whole world. . . . They let us work with the sweat of

---

[4] *Last Words of David* (1543), in *Luther's Works* (Philadelphia, 1955–76), 15:344 (one
of many such demonic descriptions of the Jews). More concretely, Luther in his *Genesis
Lectures* of 1538–39 insisted that the Jews were no longer a "true Nation, but bands of
brigands without law and government, without a leader"; they are no longer the people of God (*Luther's Works*, 3:113).

[5] Quoted in Lewin, *Luthers Stellung*, p. 77.

-gation of

our brow . . . while they stuff themselves, guzzle and live in luxury from our hard-earned goods. With their accursed usury they hold us and our property captive. . . . They are our masters and we their servants. . . .

We are at fault in not avenging all this innocent blood of our Lord and Churches and . . . the blood of the children which they have shed since then, and which still shines forth from their Jewish eyes and skin. We are at fault in not slaying them.

Luther hysterically spells out the practical measures he has in mind for the destruction of Judaism and the protection of Germany: burn the houses and synagogues of the Jews; ban their rabbis under pain of death; withdraw Jewish safe-conduct on the highways; prohibit usury; institute manual labor for young Jews; and finally, confiscate their wealth and expel them from Germany. Let them clear off back to Jerusalem where they can murder and cheat to their heart's content. The governments of Germany must be like a physician in using a "sharp mercy" to cut out gangrene; the princes must "deal harshly with them . . . and drive them out like mad dogs." For fourteen hundred years (he says, anticipating a later slogan), the Jews "have been and still are our plague, our pestilence, our *misfortune!*"[6]

Lutheran apologists have often tried to dismiss these outpourings as an unfortunate aberration, but clearly the case is not simply one of a young "pro-Jewish" Luther *versus* an old "anti-Jewish" Luther. Throughout his life Luther longed for the destruction of Judaism; it was simply that in his later years the emotion had modulated into a hysterical but nonetheless still related key.[7] Luther all along felt his antagonism to Judaism to be central to his personality, to his faith, and to his mission to save his "beloved German nation." The first great national prophet of Germany and the forger of the German language itself, Luther himself shaped the overwhelmingly pejorative, indeed demonic, significance of the word *Jude*. Through the in-

---

[6] *Against the Jews and Their Lies*, in *Luther's Works*, 47:121–306. Luther did not shrink from countenancing the actual murder of Jews. When one of his friends expressed regret that Jews were being maimed and killed, Luther retorted that though this was certainly wrong where Jews were protected by a prince's safe-conduct, the tribe of the Jews was so stubborn as to merit such punishments (*Tischreden*, cited by H. G. Haile, *Luther: An Experiment in Biography* [Princeton, 1980], p. 291).

The Jews are the subject of Luther's very last sermon of February 1546. If the Jews would abandon usury and convert *genuinely* to Christianity, he would welcome them. But otherwise they are to be seen as the enemies of all Christians. "If they could kill us all they'd gladly do it—and do so often enough." Those who will not reform, then, "we shall not pardon or pity." (Quoted in Lewin, *Luthers Stellung*, pp. 108ff.).

[7] For the "destruction of Judaism" and for the views of another ostensibly "pro-Jewish" contemporary of Luther's—Johannes Reuchlin—see below, chap. 2, n. 17.

fluence of Luther's language and tracts, a hysterical and demonizing mentality entered the mainstream of German thought and discourse; Luther in fact legitimated hysteria and paranoia in a major European culture.

Luther laid down the distinctive features of a Jew-hatred that is specifically German though it retains Christian and pagan aspects. Thus, to the traditional stereotype of the Jews as parasites, pariahs, and human forms of the devil, Luther adds German lineaments— self-pity, feelings of victimization, xenophobia, paranoia, the condemnation of the hated as the haters. The honest and true German nation, the new Chosen Race of Europe, is now being crucified by foreigners, Italians, Catholics, all of them instigated by the Jews. Here in Luther is first announced the principle that Germany's redemption means her redemption *from* the Jews and Judaism.

Thomas Mann's profound allegory of German history, *Doktor Faustus*, connected the demonized psychological universe of Luther with that of Hitler. Despite all the historical and religious distance between them, Luther and Hitler remain uniquely, characteristically German figures. They were both charismatics in whom revolutionary and reactionary impulses flowed together; and they both provoked revolutions—one religious and the other secular—in which the issues of "Germanness" and "Jewishness" and national redemption stood to the fore. It will not do to dismiss these parallels as pure accidents or as the delusory inventions of the "Luther to Hitler" school of German history.

Luther's Germanized Christian critique of Judaism combined German social resentment with Christian theological hostility. This adaptation of Christian Jew-hatred was amplified in eighteenth-century Germany by the notorious Jew-hater Johann Andreas Eisenmenger, whose *Judaism Unmasked* (*Entdecktes Judenthum*) appeared under Prussian royal patronage in 1711. Eisenmenger cleverly mixed the different emotional elements of the Lutheran approach into a form that would appeal not only to devout Christians, but also to the free-thinking secular public that was now growing. Canting that he intended his book to promote the conversion of those honest Jews who would be shocked by its revelations, Eisenmenger proceeded to amass quotations from the Talmud and other Hebrew sources revealing to all how the Jewish religion was barbarous, superstitious, and even murderous. All this was done in an apparently scholarly and reasonable way that belied the author's evident preoccupation (like Luther) with tales of Jewish ritual murder of Christian children and poisoning of wells. While piously insisting that the Jews must not be converted by cruel methods, Eisenmenger blithely recommended abolishing their present "freedom in trade," which was making them "lords" over the Germans. He demanded too an immediate ban on their synagogues, public worship, and communal leaders and rabbis. The contradiction in Eisenmenger's approach is more obvious to us than it would have been to his contemporary readers.[8]

This slightly modernized Lutheran Jew-hatred, though fueled socially by the rising prominence of the "court-Jew" financiers in Germany, was nevertheless combated by the universalism of the Enlightenment, and by the spread of ideals of religious toleration such as those celebrated in Lessing's great drama *Nathan the Wise* (1779). But the Enlightenment was not to be as beneficial to the Jews as Lessing and his Jewish friends hoped, for it carried within it the structure of a new kind of "enlightened" Jew-hatred.

No less a figure than Voltaire himself was preeminent in engineering the transition from Christian to enlightened antisemitism. Drawing on the ancient pagan testimonies to the evil national character of the Jews as enemies of humanity and reason, the patron of enlightened religious toleration was able to write without intellectual embarrassment in his *Dictionnaire philosophique* that

> this [Jewish] nation is only an ignorant and barbarous people who have long united the most sordid avarice with the most detestable superstition and the most invincible hatred for every people by whom they are tolerated and enriched.[9]

[8] See Johann Andreas Eisenmenger, *Entdecktes Judenthum* (Königsberg, 1711), 2:993–97, 1019–26, for his anti-Jewish policies. Both Luther and Eisenmenger were cautious about actually asserting the truth of the Blood Libel, preferring instead to affect a bogus scholarly detachment that pretended to suspend final judgment while faithfully retelling the stories. On Eisenmenger, see J. Katz, *From Prejudice to Destruction: Anti-Semitism 1700–1933* (Cambridge, Mass., 1980), chap. 1, which seems to me to underrate the hatred beneath the reasonable surface and to be somewhat too lenient in accepting the good intentions of the author. (For a Catholic counterpart of Eisenmenger—Abraham a Sancta Clara—see R. Kann, *A Study in Austrian Intellectual History* [New York, 1960], pp. 76–79.) More recently, Heidegger also found attitudes in Abraham that could fuel his own now increasingly patent antisemitism. See R. L. Rubenstein, "The Philosopher and the Jews: The Case of Martin Heidegger," *Modern Judaism* 9 (1989): 179–96, at p. 182.

[9] Voltaire, *A Philosophical Dictionary*, trans. E. R. Dumont (New York, 1932), s.v. "Jews" (2:99–116). (This article appears in very few of the French texts and English translations.) Cf. Katz, *From Prejudice to Destruction*, chap. 3. *HAS*, 3:86–99. A. Hertzberg, *The French Enlightenment and the Jews* (New York, 1968), pp. 299–308. For comments on Voltaire's attack on the Jews as Molochists, see below, chap. 3.

A great deal of fascinating material on how pre-Voltairean French authors conceived Jewish "race" and "nationality" and how they redefined Jewish "domination" and

Notwithstanding Voltaire's antagonism to Christianity, his critique of Judaism was still constructed around a Christian framework, albeit an updated, secularized one. The old patristic and medieval Christian deprecations of Jewish greed and addiction to money were trotted out without apology as secular social truths, but now embellished with intimations of a Jewish conspiracy to dominate the world by finance. Instead of crucifying Christ with nails and cross, the Jews were currently murdering European man (personified in poor Voltaire himself) by their usury and infamy. In this new age the Jews were deemed to be holding hostage all rational and moral humanity, not just superstitious Christendom; they did so, not by refusing to convert to an obsolescent Christianity, but by refusing to disappear as a nation and a religion through the gentle means of assimilation into European society and submission to reason. Though the new era of freedom and reason no longer believed in the Second Coming of Christ, it could still blame Jewish stubbornness for frustrating the advent of the heavenly reign of universal love and humanity. When Voltaire and the *philosophes* excoriated the Jews' refusal to be redeemed by giving up both their separate national identity and their unenlightened religion, they were merely putting a secular gloss on the old Christian theme of the stubbornness of the Jewish nation. There existed underneath these secular transformations deep continuities between the themes of the old Christian and the new secular Jew-hatreds.[10] Soon, however, the picture would be complicated by the appearance of new concepts of "race" and "revolution" that were quite unknown to the old pagan and Christian views of the world.

RACE

The idea of a "Jewish nation" possessing a specifically hateful national character had been well established since antiquity and predates the appearance of the modern concept of "race" in the mid-nineteenth century. This historical accident—the fact that it was pos-

"stubbornness" is to be found in Myriam Yardeni, *Anti-Jewish Mentalities in Early Modern Europe* (Washington, D.C., 1990). See also E. Barker, *National Character and the Factors in its Formation* (New York, 1927), and the useful analysis in H. Ritter, *Dictionary of Concepts in History* (Westport, Conn., 1986), pp. 289–94.

[10] S. Ettinger, "The Young Hegelians—A Source of Modern Anti-Semitism?" *Jerusalem Quarterly* 28 (Summer 1983): 73–82, remarks on these continuities. It will be clear that the thrust of the present book is related to the ideas of political messianism and secular redemption argued in the writings of J. L. Talmon, especially *Political Messianism* (London, 1960), and *The Myth of the Nation and the Vision of Revolution* (London, 1981). Curiously enough, Talmon never tried to incorporate an analysis of the Jewish Question into his general interpretation. I have tried here to fill this strange lacuna.

sible to speak of an evil Jewish "nation" before one could strictly
speak of a Jewish "race"—has led to fundamental misconceptions
about the nature of antisemitism. This is especially true with respect
to the attitudes on the Jewish Question held by major German thinkers of the transitional period when nationalist thought was evolving
into racist conceptions, the years running roughly from 1780 to 1860.
In Kant, Fichte, and Herder, for example, we encounter an apparent
paradox that is mystifying unless we understand that they are thinking in terms of what nowadays would be called "ethnic" character
rather than "race." These thinkers condemned the "animal" theory
that human *racial* characteristics were as biologically inherited and
immutable as the physical and mental characteristics of those of
horses or dogs—and yet at the same time they wanted to deny civil
rights to Jews on the ground that the Jewish nation was irreducibly
alien to "German" life. The key to resolving this paradox lies in the
concept of national character and culture that was extensively developed not only by such romantic nationalists as Herder and Fichte in
the 1790s but even by such rationalist cosmopolitans as Kant himself,
much of whose *Anthropologie* of 1798 is an anecdotal compilation of
national quirks.

For all sorts of anti-Jewish thinkers, the national character of the
Jews had been so long and so clearly established in both their religious and social habits that there was no need for a biological explanation; it was reasonably assumed to be something passed on by "tradition" and "religion" from generation to generation in an automatic
process. The Jews proudly "dwelt as a nation apart," maintaining
themselves in ritual and social "separation" and "isolation" from the
gentile nations. It was easy for Germans resentful of the Jewish claim
to be the "Chosen Nation apart" to show how the differences between
Jewish and German national character were exposed in the social institutions, religious and moral sensibilities, cultural achievements,
and social behaviors of the two nations. Herder might take pains to
disavow "animal racism," but in practice he believed that Jewish national character was so entrenched in the Jews by their traditions that
it might just as well be racially inherited. Despite recent efforts to
deny it, Herder's belief in "national character" contains a racial concept, though he believed "race" to be culturally rather than biologically determined.

This central role of national character in the conceptual structure
of Jew-hatred has a considerable significance for the historiography
of modern antisemitism. It is often postulated that modern antisemitism differs primarily from traditional Christian Jew-hatred in es-
pousing a materialist biological theory of race. According to this view,

any Jew-hatred that lacks a genuinely racial dimension does not deserve to be classified as being in the mainstream development of modern antisemitism. This scheme does, it is true, allow for the inclusion of sundry German nationalist thinkers of the early nineteenth century on the ground that their "animal-breeding" analogies makes them "proto-racists." But where is the idealistic anti-Judaism of Kant and Herder to be fitted into this scheme? Almost invariably no meaningful historical category can be found for this kind of Jew-hatred and it is usually written off as a personal biographical oddity.

This failure to integrate Kant and Herder and Fichte into the historiography of modern German antisemitism is merely symptomatic of a more general flaw in the conventional histories of both antisemitism and of German thought that have adopted a rather arbitrary and unhistorical conception of "German nationalism." Kant, Fichte, and Herder certainly cannot be fitted into the school of "German nationalists" and "proto-racists" as it is currently conceived. But neither can they be left outside the mainstreams of German thought as isolated anomalies. Fichte was not the crude right-wing nationalist fanatic he is often portrayed to be; his nationalism was far more complicated and idealistic. He was, in truth, a German revolutionist and his hostility to Jews must be placed in this context. Fichte, together with Kant and Herder, laid the intellectual foundations of "German revolutionism," a movement at once nationalistic and cosmopolitan in its aspiration to be the messenger of a universal "revolution of humanity." It is the response of this German revolutionism to the Jewish Question—"revolutionary antisemitism"—that forms the subject of this book.

If we try to impose biological racism (or indeed any rigid concept of race) as the criterion for defining authentic modern German antisemitism, then we exclude what is here argued to be the most fundamental source of that antisemitism. That source is highly fluid in character and overflows the formal barriers of ideology. It consists in the redemption-seeking mentality of the German revolutionists of the left and right alike that could embody, without paradox, a sharp consciousness of the key role of "national character" in the "human" as well as the "German" revolution.

The misconceived categories of the conventional history of both German antisemitism and German nationalism have, not surprisingly, created false paradoxes of which the most basic is that constructed between "revolution" and "national character." There are, for instance, the sterile debates over whether Fichte was a right-wing nationalist *or* a left-wing revolutionary; there is too the progressivist paradox which runs that, since the revolution was by definition progressive, it could not have produced the most unprogressive phe-

nomenon of antisemitism. The key to dissolving these false paradoxes is to recognize that such essentially *historical* phenomena as
"revolution" and "race" are not incompatible categories, no matter
how mutually exclusive they may seem when defined in purely logical
or philosophical terms drained of historical content. On the one
hand, German nationalist thinking was imbued with revolutionary
idealism. The quest of the nationalists for the elusive essence of national identity was an expression of their urge for redemption;
through the nation redeemed would come the individual's redemption. On the other hand, German revolutionists of all stripes accepted
the implicit racial prejudice that there existed a virtually unchanging
Jewish—as well as a German—national character. German revolutionism was therefore embedded in a pattern of thought that was essentially racial and potentially anti-Jewish.[11]

*Potentially* . . . These notions of race and national character did not
necessarily have to be anti-Jewish. In France in the 1850s, for instance, a cultural anthropology of race emerged under the aegis of
Joseph-Arthur Gobineau and Ernest Renan that lacked any animus
against the Jews. While it is true that Gobineau in the 1870s developed a hostile attitude towards Judaism under the influence of Wagner, Renan, in contrast, chose in later life explicitly to repudiate any
social or political interpretation of his philological theory of the "Semitic" and "Aryan" races.[12] Again, even in the case of the physical
anthropologists and biologists, there was no inevitably anti-Jewish
charge to their racial ideas. Johann Friedrich Blumenbach and Dar-

[11] Cf. the interesting comments by M. Zimmermann, "From Radicalism to Anti-Semitism," *Jerusalem Quarterly* 23 (Spring 1982): 114–28; R. Wistrich, "Antisemitism as a
'Radical' Ideology in the Nineteenth Century," *Jerusalem Quarterly*, 28 (Summer 1983):
83–94.

"Revolutionary antisemitism" does not figure in the survey by I. Schorsch, "German
Antisemitism in the Light of Post-War Historiography," *LBIY* 19 (1974): 257–71.

[12] M. Biddiss, *Father of Racist Ideology: The Social and Political Thought of Count Gobineau* (London, 1970), points out that Gobineau never argued for the adoption of anti-
Jewish policies. L. Poliakov, *The Aryan Myth* (New York, 1977), pp. 206ff, is somewhat
too harsh on Renan. In the aftermath of the French defeat of 1870, Renan took pains
to refute racist interpretations of his "ethnographical" distinctions between the Aryan
and Semitic races. In any case, Renan always regarded Jewish civil and political rights
in France as automatic and without relevance to racial origins or national character.
Nor did he desire the disappearance of what he called the "assimilated" Jewish race,
which he hoped would continue to collaborate with "all the liberal forces of Europe
for the social progress of humanity." For Renan's racial thought, see the texts in Renan,
*Judaisme et Christianisme*, ed. J. Gaulmier (Paris, 1977). Cf. I. Goldkorn, "Renan and
Racism," *Midstream* (Nov. 1986): 40–43; R. M. Chadbourne, *Ernest Renan* (New York,
1978).

For a provocative treatment of the impact of racist theory on the historiography of
ancient "Aryan" Greece, see M. Bernal, *Black Athena: I. The Fabrication of Ancient Greece
1785–1985* (London, 1987).

win, for example, had a great impact on German racist antisemitism, but they themselves were not at all anti-Jewish in their opinions. Indeed, Blumenbach explicitly rejected the drawing of racist conclusions from his racial anthropology.[13]

Racist theory itself, therefore, was not the crucial factor in the development of German antisemitism, but merely represented a particular ideology of Jew-hatred that lent antisemitism a pseudoscientific basis.[14] Biological theories of race and genetics were welcomed by antisemites because they conferred a systematic "modern" logic on an original intuition that Jewish national character could not be changed. By the time of Kant and Fichte, the concept of Jewish national character had sufficed to demonstrate that for all practical purposes the "Jewish Nation" was the Jewish biological race. The lack of the biological element in this early German antisemitic thinking only became problematic in the case of a Jew converting to Christianity who would thereby (in theory) lose his Jewish national characteristics. But, in practice, conversion made little difference for it was frequently remarked by Christian critics that baptismal water failed to wash away the unpleasantly Jewish character of converts.[15]

[13] Blumenbach (1752–1840) treats the Jews as a distinctive people within the Caucasian race, which he regarded as the finest of the five races (though he refused to accept the slavery lobby's view that the blacks were genetically inferior). See *The Anthropological Treatises of Johann Friedrich Blumenbach*, trans. (London, 1865), pp. 9, 234, 265. Cf. A. Kelly, *The Descent of Darwin: The Popularization of Darwinism in Germany 1860–1914* (Chapel Hill, N.C., 1981); G. L. Mosse, *Toward the Final Solution* (London, 1978).

W. Petersen rightly points out ("Jews as a Race," *Midstream* [February 1988]: 35–37, and in his forthcoming book *Ethnicity*) that the nineteenth-century concept of race as a perfected prototype is quite different from the modern biological and anthropological idea of race as a probabilistic aggregate.

[14] See J. Katz, "Misreadings of Anti-Semitism," *Commentary* (July 1983): 39–44, for this point. Katz seems to use "racial" to denote racial theories hostile to Judaism, but I have adopted the current English usage of employing "racist" to denote such hostile theories, "racialist" to signify hostile acts and policies, and "racial" to mean neutral theories of race (insofar as any such theories can be neutral).

[15] See the brilliant lecture by Y. H. Yerushalmi, *Assimilation and Racial Anti-Semitism: The Iberian and the German Models*, Leo Baeck Memorial Lecture 26 (New York, 1982). This is to my mind the most fertile critical discussion of the nature of racial antisemitism. Against the conventional scholarly wisdom, Yerushalmi searches for a "latent racial antisemitism" in Spain and elsewhere—including Germany—before the official arrival of racial antisemitism in the 1870s. I believe that the concept of "national character" used in the present book is in fact Yerushalmi's "latent racial antisemitism"; at any rate, some of the proto-racist content that Yerushalmi finds in early nineteenth-century German thinkers is better explained in terms of a traditionally transmitted national character than biologically. Certainly, using "national character" as a technical term will avoid the anachronistic problems that arise (as Yerushalmi is well aware) when the word "racial" is applied to anti-Jewish thought, German or otherwise, before about 1860. The most important study of these proto-racist German thinkers of the

"Race" may have become the basic frame of argument for modern Jew-hatred, but its overwhelming currency conceals the fact that racist thinking was predicated on the notion of "national character" that is central to the evolution of modern antisemitism. For between 1780 and 1860 there occurred in German thinking a shift in the conceptualization of national character; the ethnic idea of national character was refined into a racial idea.

Upon these two successive phases were superimposed the principles of revolutionary antisemitism. It is these revolutionary principles that created modern antisemitism. What modernized the old Jew-hatred was not the application of biological theories, but the advent of the new vision of revolution and redemption. In this vision—shared by Kant and Fichte—there was no real need at all for a biological racism because the established doctrine of national character performed very well indeed the function of discovering "Germanness"— German national identity and the German mission for the redemption of humanity. In the passion play of this new world of revolution the sufferings of Christ were replaced by the sufferings of Germany and humanity—but the Jews still remained the villains of the piece, the obstacles to redemption.

## REVOLUTION

The Revolution, redeemer and creator of a new world blessing . . . I,

the Revolution, am the ever-rejuvenating, ever-fashioning Life. . . .

For I am Revolution, I am the ever-fashioning Life, I am the only

God. . . . The incarnated Revolution, the God become Man, . . . pro-

claiming to all the world the new Gospel of Happiness.

—Wagner, *The Revolution* (1849), *PW*, 8:234, 238

---

period before 1860 is E. Sterling, *Judenhass: Die Anfänge des politischen Antisemitismus in Deutschland 1815–1850* (Frankfurt, 1969), a book that draws on a wealth of original material. For the phenomenon of conversion during the emancipation see J. Katz, *Out of the Ghetto* (Cambridge, Mass., 1973), chap. 7, especially p. 123 for the remark of Karl Grattenauer that baptismal water cannot cleanse the immoral character of the Jew. (A recent article by J. Friedman, "Jewish Conversion, the Spanish Pure Blood Laws, and Reformation: A Revisionist View of Racial and Religious Antisemitism," *Sixteenth Century Journal* 18 (1987): 3–29, follows Yerushalmi and also argues that it was precisely the phenomenon of large-scale conversion that provoked not only the Pure Blood Laws but also Luther's attacks on the Jews. There may be a parallel here with the role played by the conversions of the German emancipation period in the intensification of antisemitism.)

The music that underlies the varying libretti of nineteenth-century antisemitism is the great ground bass of the "revolution." Not "revolution" in the narrowly political sense, but rather the urgent need for human redemption and freedom that found expression in the French Revolution, as well as in the failed German revolutions in politics and the more successful ones in philosophy and literature. The quest for liberation of the human spirit was more than just a secular version of the powerful religious movements that had swept over Europe during the Reformation. It was itself a religious instinct that happened, it is true, to take a secularized form. During the Reformation the need for redemption had driven men to forsake family and to destroy established forms of belief and government; so now, men experienced conversion to the new truths and passions of the redeeming revolution. Earnest young German students made as existential a commitment to Hegelianism as their sixteenth-century predecessors had to Protestantism.[16]

In German culture, the political revolution was seen as merely the epiphenomenon of a much more profound philosophical revolution. Kant and Fichte and their disciples envisioned the power of reason revolutionizing the state, making it rational and so, in the most profound sense, "free." This belief in the rational, free, revolutionized state was not exclusively a liberal or left-wing program; the conservative administrators of Prussia and the German states also pursued it in their development of a rationally organized bureaucratic, "well-policed" state.[17] Moralists and statists, philosophers and statesmen, left and right, together contributed to the ethos of "revolutionism" that was emerging in Germany well before the outbreak of the French Revolution.[18]

[16] D. R. Kelley, *The Beginning of Ideology: Consciousness and Society in the French Reformation* (Cambridge, 1981); J. E. Toews, *Hegelianism: The Path toward Dialectical Humanism 1805–1840* (Cambridge, 1980); M. J. Lasky, *Utopia and Revolution: On the Origins of a Metaphor . . .* (Chicago, 1976); J. H. Billington, *Fire in the Minds of Men: Origins of the Revolutionary Faith* (New York, 1980).

[17] M. Raeff, *The Well-Ordered Police State: Social and Intellectual Change through Law in the Germanies and Russia 1600–1800* (New Haven, 1983).

[18] Some confusion may arise here from my use of "revolutionary" as both noun and adjective but in two different senses. I have tended to use "revolutionary" as a noun to signify a participant in political revolutions, whereas "revolutionist" refers to someone who is sympathetic to revolutions or who, being in exile, cannot participate directly (such as Ludwig Börne). I have extended "revolutionist" also to mean someone who has a revolutionary temperament, whether in philosophy or in politics or in literature. I have not been wholly consistent in these usages but it will usually be clear from the context which meaning is to be inferred. However, the adjective "revolutionary" presents more difficulty since it carries both an active political meaning (deriving from the French coinage of the 1790s) as well as a neutral sense simply of "pertaining to revo-

From the beginning, the Jewish Question was necessarily involved in this "revolutionary" discussion; indeed, the new ethos worked often to benefit the Jews. The "outsider," victimized status of the Jews was a glaring anomaly in the rational bureaucratic state, calling out for regularization and the removal of irrational discrimination. There was a need in Enlightened Prussia and Austria to show that the modern state with its rational ideology could cope with the problem of the Jews more satisfactorily than had the old policies inspired by Christian theology. Yet there were deep continuities between the old and new creeds. They shared the belief that, to be complete, the final redemption of mankind—whether Christian or revolutionary— required the redemption of the anomalous Jews. And, in turn, the redemption of the Jews entailed their becoming fully moral members of the human race. Previously the Jews had to join the church; now they had to join the state and humanity itself. Ultimately, the belief that the Jews were possessed of an immoral national character in need of reform integrates Christian consciousness with that of the Enlightenment and its offspring, the revolution.

The moral and statist revolutionism of the eighteenth century was the matrix of revolutionary antisemitism. As the philosophical revolution itself rapidly developed and as political revolutionism became rampant in Germany in the wake of the French Revolution and Napoleonic invasions, so too revolutionary antisemitism underwent a spectacular evolution, ramifying along several main branches that superficially may seem unrelated, but that all stemmed from the same trunk.

The first of these was the German nationalist antisemitism of the Fichte school. With Fichte's notorious "internationalist Jacobin" defense of the French Revolution in 1793, revolutionary antisemitism made, as we shall see, its formal debut. Later, during the Napoleonic invasions, Fichte channeled his revolutionary idealism into a patriotic exaltation of the Prussian spirit as the spirit of German *and* human freedom. But although this heightening of German national consciousness also entailed a sharpening of the awareness of the alien nationality of the Jews, Fichte himself refrained from developing a "nationalist" antisemitism. Few of his sympathizers, however, were so inhibited and the result was the rapid growth of the fierce nationalist Jew-hatred of Arndt, Jahn, and the other "Christian-German" patriots, a nationalism inflamed with Germanic romanticism. Romantic

lution." Thus, the term "revolutionary antisemitism" should not be construed purely as meaning antisemitism that is associated solely with political revolutionaries, but rather has the broader meaning of an antisemitism that stems from visions of a new world and new man and from intellectual as well as political revolution.

nationalist antisemitism was at its height from 1800 to 1848, but it often found itself reverting to its inner revolutionary nature, most of all when it emerged as a movement of student revolt during the Metternich years. Nationalist antisemitism was never, in fact, independent of its revolutionary aspect even if many of its proponents seem to have belonged to the right. As we shall show, to impose such modern categories of left and right on the German nationalism of this period is historically misconceived. Neither nationalism nor antisemitism at this time were so narrowly political as to be classifiable in purely political terms. "Left" and "right" ideologies were rather aspects of an outlook that envisaged the moral regeneration of the German people, to be achieved variously by means of politics, or culture, or a crusade to rediscover the authentic German national character through the removal of "Judaism."

A second branch of revolutionary antisemitism originated in the self-criticism, often violent to the point of self-hatred, of radical Jews themselves.[19] Here again there was an interest in a double redemption—that of the Germans and humanity on the one hand, and that of the Jews on the other. Börne and Heine deployed metaphors of emancipation and liberation that insisted that the Jewish Question was, in fact, the microcosm of the whole question of European freedom, and supremely, that of Germany. For Börne indeed, the German revolution came to mean the redemption of the Jews. On account of these views, Börne and Heine are often regarded as exponents of a revolutionary liberal perception of the Jewish Question. But they also popularized a more sinister interpretation of the question when they cemented the foundations of one of the most powerful elements of revolutionary antisemitism, namely, the image of the Jew as the embodiment of capitalism. Thanks to them, the old resentment of Jewish moneylending and commerce that had long fomented socioeconomic antisemitism now found a solid theoretical structure with which to justify itself as high-minded morality rather than as mere envy.

The basic theory of this new anticapitalist Jew-hatred had been adumbrated by Kant and Fichte. It revolved again around the concept of Jewish national character and the fact that the Jews were an alien "Palestinian" race who lived as parasites among their host European peoples. This parasitism was economic in that their exile and disper-

---

[19] See H. Liebeschütz, "German Radicalism and the Formation of Jewish Political Attitudes during the Earlier Part of the Nineteenth Century," in *Studies in Nineteenth-Century Jewish Intellectual History*, ed. A. Altmann (Cambridge, Mass., 1964), pp. 141–70; Sander L. Gilman, *Jewish Self-Hatred: Anti-Semitism and the Hidden Language of the Jews* (Baltimore, 1986).

sal had caused the Jews to develop a power based no longer on territory, but on commerce and money; they were no longer a national state, but rather a supranational power. This immersion in "money" faithfully reflected their egoism and self-interest, which stemmed from a rooted ignorance of true moral freedom, as evidenced in their enslaving religion of "obedience to the Law."

These ideas, implicit in the thought and writings of Kant and other idealists, were to be elaborated systematically in the writings of the "critical" Young Hegelians of the 1830s and 1840s.[20] The interests and political attitudes of these Young Hegelians varied richly. Some, such as Laube and Gutzkow (the founders of the Young German literary school), appeared to be "liberals," but in truth they were not seriously interested in politics. Their main object was, in imitation of Heine, to rediscover the "flesh" and to liberate an alienated mankind into an era of human "love." They were happy to support the movement for Jewish political emancipation while at the same time denouncing Judaism as the symbol of a loveless and calculating capitalism, and exhorting Jews to free themselves from their "lovelessness" and greed to become true human beings, true Germans.

Other Young Hegelians were more rigorously philosophical in their attitudes towards Judaism. Feuerbach, for instance, spelled out a critique of Jewish religion that had also been implicit in Kant and Hegel, but which was now in his *Essence of Christianity* (1841) reduced to simplistic and obvious axioms: the Judeo-Christian idea of God was nothing but a projection of man's fears and powers onto an alien fetish of his own imagining; Judaism represented a more primitive—and more egoistic—version of this process than did Christianity, which, at least, had tried to restore divine power to man by conceiving of an incarnation myth wherein Jesus the man was raised to godhood.

It was this sort of reductionism that Karl Marx and Moses Hess were to apply to more concrete political thinking. Drawing on Feuerbach's philosophical critique as well as Börne's and Heine's savage indictment of Jewish "moneyness," the two critical philosophers in the 1840s sketched out a socialist critique of Judaism as the religion of egoistic capitalism and human alienation. Judaism and Jews became for them not just a metaphor for the corruption of the modern bourgeois world, but were also seen as the practical promoters of that

---

[20] Cf. L. Poliakov, *La causalité diabolique* (Paris, 1980), chap. 6, "Philosophie allemande; la diabolectique." For a refutation of this alluringly plausible philosophical critique of Judaism, see E. L. Fackenheim, *Encounters between Judaism and Modern Philosophy* (New York, 1973), especially pp. 145–53.

"beast of prey world" in which real Jews from the peddler to the banker functioned as its financial agents.[21]

The years 1840–43, the years between the Damascus Affair and Bruno Bauer's provocative essay *The Jewish Question*, are the precise years when these radical critiques of Judaism crystallized.[22] In 1840–41, the new king of Prussia, Frederick William IV, devised a ghetto-like arrangement for the Jews as part of his general plan to restore the "old regime." This provoked an outcry not just from the Jews, but from those liberals who had no wish to lose their own gains to the king's romantic desire to turn back the political clock. Radical Young Hegelian philosophers were also stirred to theorize, but rarely in a way favorable to Jewish rights. Feuerbach's book, published in 1841, promoted a hostile picture of Judaism and this was developed in 1843 by Bruno Bauer and others into a radical analysis of "the free state" in which both Frederick William IV's reactionary policies and Jewry alike were excoriated. Most ominous, however, was the way in which the thoroughly modern humanist-radicals took up the Damascus Affair, the notorious event of 1840 that seemed to mark a return to the most superstitious Jew-hatred of the Middle Ages. This revival of the Blood Libel against the Jews was a turning point in the histories of Jewish emancipation and European antisemitism alike. It forced European liberals to stamp Jew-hatred definitively as barbaric and illiberal, but at the same time encouraged the new revolutionary antisemites to think that their enlightened "critical" explanations vin-

---

[21] On this embarrassed Jewish tendency to condemn Jewish involvement in capitalism, see M. Friedman, "Capitalism and the Jews: Confronting a Paradox," *Encounter* (June 1984): 74–79. In general, see the two books by R. Wistrich, *Socialism and the Jews*, (Rutherford, N.J., 1982) and *Revolutionary Jews from Marx to Trotsky* (London, 1976). Also E. Silberner, *Sozialisten zur Judenfrage* (Berlin, 1962). There was, of course, also a strong vein of antisemitism in French socialists. Alphonse Toussenel's *Les Juifs, rois de l'époque* (Paris, 1845) popularized the notion of an international Jewish conspiracy, but he insisted that he only meant "Jew" in a figurative sense denoting the mercantile or banking mentality and he stressed his admiration for "the superior character" of the Jewish nation. "The Jewish people holds an immense place in the history of humanity." All the same, Toussenel approved the practice of subjugating the Jews. "The universal repulsion which the Jew has inspired for so long is but the just suppression of his implacable pride and requires from us those legitimate reprisals for that hatred which they seem to bear towards the rest of humanity." Like Marx and other radicals, Toussenel moves easily from the Jew as a metaphor of capitalism to the Jew as the real-life capitalist. This influential book was reviewed and excerpted in Germany, for instance, in the *Allgemeine Zeitung*, Beilage, 1845, 2801–2, and *Minerva* 217 (1846): 259–342. Cited by V. Eichstädt, *Bibliographie zur Geschichte der Judenfrage* (Hamburg, 1938)—for all its Nazi genesis, still a fundamental work of reference, alas.

[22] For background, see J. Carlebach, *Karl Marx and the Radical Critique of Judaism* (London, 1978).

dicated a popular instinct of Jew-hatred that otherwise stood in danger of being disgraced by its hopelessly primitive religious themes. Despite its rationalistic jargon, however, much of the critical debate on the Jewish Question in the 1840s was, in fact, stoked by the powerful emotional signal of "blood," whether actual Christian sacrificial blood or the figurative blood of money—"social coagulated blood" as Hess called it. The blood of Christ Himself, spilled by ancient Jews, had now found a modern secular parallel in the crucifixion of modern mankind by Jewish capitalism.

By 1848, therefore, we find that revolutionary antisemitism had undergone a half-century of rapid development in various directions—moralist, nationalist, critical-philosophical, Jewish self-critical, economic, socialist. At this point, the ground was fertile for its great systematizing transmutation into racial and biological antisemitism. The actual theory of race itself flowed from several sources: from the concept of national character; from Renan's and Max Müller's notions of philologically and culturally defined Semitic and Aryan races; from Gobineau's unbreakable nexus between physical race and culture; from Blumenbach's physical anthropology and comparative anatomy. In the 1850s these fragmented insights acquired a cumulative power sufficient to persuade even universalist believers in revolution of the potency of race.

Marx and Engels engaged in only random racial speculations about blacks, but former comrades of theirs in Germany seized upon the new racial theories to rethink the idea of the German revolution. This shift from the critical to the racial concept of revolution entailed a reinterpretation of the Jewish Question among radicals that is vividly illustrated in the intellectual careers of Bruno Bauer and Wilhelm Marr, who veered from radical politics to racial antisemitic ideology in the 1850s.[23] The revolution that each preached was not *politically* the same. Bauer belonged, in conventional party terms, to the Prussian right during the 1850s, Marr to the communist left. But they shared the same revolutionary impulse towards a radical realization of human freedom that would essentially be "German" in character and whose antithesis was "Judaism."

Revolution and race were thus inextricable elements in the "German revolution." Among the few Jewish observers to recognize the significance of this connection was Moses Hess, who by 1860 came to understand that in Germany the prevalence of the concept of race

[23] The continuity of race and revolution in radical thought is missed by Ettinger, "The Young Hegelians," pp. 8of., but noticed by Zimmermann, "From Radicalism to Anti-Semitism" with reference to the career of Wilhelm Marr.

meant that no conventional solution to the Jewish Question was possible. The German revolution, Hess belatedly recognized, was not the beacon of hope for the Jews that Börne and Marx thought it to be; the true nature of the German revolution was actually to be found in its racial aspect. Sadly admitting this truth after years of self-delusion, Moses Hess in *Rome and Jerusalem* (1862) proposed the first real Zionist—at once ethnic and revolutionary—solution to the Jewish Question. The "racial domination" idea of German revolutionary thought was at last rejected in favor of an evaluation of Jewish national character that held it to be worth preserving, and saw "Judaism" as a valid revolutionary form instead of one that had to be destroyed by revolution.[24]

[24] For a modern statement that German exclusiveness meant that the idealized "German-Jewish symbiosis" had never been a real possibility and, as far as the Jews were concerned, had always been a one-sided bargain that the Germans had no intention of keeping, see G. Scholem, "Against the Myth of the German-Jewish Dialogue," in his *On Jews and Judaism in Crisis: Selected Essays* (New York, 1976), pp. 71–92. Also D. Sorkin, *The Transformation of German Jewry 1780–1840* (Oxford, 1988).

CHAPTER 2

# Ahasverus and the Destruction of Judaism

THE ORIGINAL Christian mythology of Jew-hatred that had co-
alesced out of the New Testament formed a repertoire of intellectual and emotional signals. In later centuries these were amplified
by a mythogenic process as the European imagination created new
icons, above all, the myth of Ahasverus, the Wandering, Eternal Jew.
An allusive, plastic myth, comprehending themes of death, eternal
Jewish character, and final redemption, Ahasverus supplied the most
potent vehicle for the secular mythology of the "destruction of Judaism" that came to dominate German revolutionary antisemitism in
the nineteenth century.[1]

Far from being a Gospel story, the Wandering Jew is in fact a late
medieval invention. Its details were fixed and the name Ahasverus
determined only in 1542, when the suggestible Lutheran cleric Pau-

[1] The most extensive survey of the tradition is G. K. Anderson, *The Legend of the
Wandering Jew* (Providence, R.I., 1965). Cf. J. Gaer, *The Legend of the Wandering Jew*
(New York, 1961). Bibliographies are L. Neubaur, "Bibliographie der Sage vom
Ewigen Juden," *Centralblatt für Bibliothekswesen* 10 (1893): 249–67, 297–316; A. Soergel,
*Ahasver-Dichtungen seit Goethe* (Leipzig, 1905); W. Zirus, *Ahasverus, der Ewige Jude* (Leip-
zig, 1930).

For interpretations, see A. Leschnitzer, "Der Gestaltwandel Ahasvers," in *Zwei Welten:
Siegfried Moses zum fünfundsiebzigsten Geburtstag*, ed. H. Tramer (Jerusalem, 1962), pp.
470–505 (summarized in his paper "The Wandering Jew: The Alienation of the Jewish
Image in Christian Consciousness," *Viator* 2 [1971]: 391–96); L. Poliakov, *The History of
Anti-Semitism* (London, 1974–84), 1:242, 3:352ff.; H. Maccoby, "The Legend of the
Wandering Jew: A New Interpretation," *Jewish Quarterly* 20 (1972): 3–8; idem, *The Sa-
cred Executioner* (London, 1982), pp. 166–71; A. Bein, *Die Judenfrage* (Stuttgart, 1980),
2:75–79; E. A. Rappaport, *Anti-Judaism: A Psychohistory* (Chicago, 1975), chap. 5;
H. Mayer, *Outsiders* (Cambridge, Mass., 1982), pp. 269–71 (which, however, misses the
shift of Ahasverus from a Christian to a secular figure of Jew-hatred and argues that
in the process of secularization he lost his anti-Jewish content); G. Hasan-Rokem and
A. Dundes, eds., *The Wandering Jew: Essays in the Interpretation of a Christian Legend*
(Bloomington, Ind., 1986), appeared after the completion of this chapter. It contains
an excellent study by R. Edelmann, "Ahasverus, the Wandering Jew. Origin and Background," pp. 1–10, which argues that the two cities most involved in the propagation
of the legend were experiencing a social "Jewish problem" with the appearance of
Marrano merchants and local Christian efforts to exclude them. Hamburg, where
Ahasverus was seen in 1542 by von Eitzen, was the scene of a group of Marranos'
alleged relapse into Judaism, while at Danzig, where the legend was first published in
1602, a struggle was then under way to expel the Jews. The Jewish Question was thus
embedded in the Ahasverus myth from its first modern formulation. Edelmann also
asserts a personal connection between von Eitzen and Luther.

lus von Eitzen encountered a bearded vagrant of this name in a Hamburg church. Ahasverus turned out to be the Jew who had jeered at Christ on the way to Golgotha and consequently had been cursed by the Redeemer with eternal wandering and joyless life until death should finally redeem him at the Last Judgment. When the tale was eventually published in 1602 as the *Brief Description and Account of a Jew Named Ahasverus* it struck a chord in the European Christian mind and ran through nearly fifty editions within a few years.[2]

Much of the reason for this success was the myth's capacity to open up new vistas into Jewish guilt while assuaging Christian anxieties. A living, Wandering Jew was a far more pregnant emblem of enduring Jewish wickedness than a dead Judas Iscariot. No longer was the guilt of the Crucifixion seen as something personal and expiable like Judas's crime; instead, Ahasverus represented now a collective guilt inherent in the wandering, homeless Jewish nation.[3] Each individual Jew lay under a curse from which he had to redeem himself and his race, a curse symbolizing inherited ethnic guilt. This explained to bewildered Christians why it was that the Jewish nation was still inexplicably present long after it should either have been redeemed or destroyed. The Jews were actually being punished by being allowed to survive in agony and in servitude. Herein lies the symbolic essence of Ahasverus: his punitive, homeless wandering must continue until he is at last redeemed by "death." Thus explained, the persistence of the Jewish nation—the epitome of "Jewish stubbornness"—should cease to trouble the Christian mind.

However, when Christian mentality gave way to the secular sensibility of the nineteenth century, the myth of the redemptive death of Ahasverus and of the Jews had to change accordingly. This shift is visible in the changed meaning of Ahasverus's epithet, the *Ewiger Jude* or "Eternal Jew."[4] Until the nineteenth century it was the eternally unending character of Ahasverus's punishment that made him the Eternal Jew; but by the time of Ludwig Börne's *Der ewige Jude* (1821), the label had changed its point. It now referred to those guiltful traits that were commonly regarded as eternally stamped on the

[2] *Kurze Beschreybung und Erzählung von einem Juden mit Namen Ahasverus*, 1602, with false "Leiden" imprint, reprinted by L. Neubaur, *Die Sage vom Ewigen Juden* (Leipzig, 1884), pp. 59ff.

[3] Ahasverus is apparently first identified explicitly with the Jewish race as a whole in J. Schudt, *Jüdische Merckwürdigkeiten* (Frankfurt, 1714–17), according to Bein, *Judenfrage*, 2:77.

[4] The first occurrence of the German epithet "Ewiger Jude" is in a tract of 1694 entitled *Neue Zeitung von demsogenennten Ewigen Jud*. In England, France, and Italy he was known as the "Wandering Jew."

Jewish national character and demanded redemption. (In this book I translate *Ewiger Jude*, following English usage, as "Wandering Jew," but the German emphasis on his unredeemed eternity of life has always to be kept in mind.)

This was, however, not the only way in which the myth was secularized. Between 1770 and 1850, Ahasverus emerged as a powerful myth of Promethean revolutionism, and a major topos in non-Christian romantic literature and humanist philosophy alike. Ahasverus was transformed from theological legend into secular vision of human liberation and revolutionary redemption. He even lost for a time his Jewish significance. Shelley celebrated him as a new Prometheus in messianic revolt against political and religious tyranny.[5] Byron did retain the Jewish identity of Ahasverus but characteristically took his eternal Jewish wanderings and Jewish stubbornness as a living refutation of the charge that the Jews were unprincipled. In France, Edgar Quinet's epic of 1833 made the Wandering Jew into a Faustian symbol of suffering mankind's progress, and inspired Alexandre Dumas to attempt a universal and supernatural history of humanity centered on the figure of Ahasverus.[6] One of Gustave Doré's famous engravings of the Wandering Jew shows him portentously crossing the Rhine into Germany, and Ahasverus did indeed become a literary obsession there. He appeared ubiquitously in the writings of Goethe, Schiller, and Heine as well as in the works of a host of lesser authors.[7] As in France, his transformation into a Promethean figure often camouflaged the original Jewish content of the myth. Wagner, for instance, referred to his eminently *non-Jewish* personification of redemption through love, the Flying Dutchman, as an "Ahasverus of the Ocean."

But the generic anti-Jewish animus of the myth was never really lost. The two leading Christian-German romantics of the early nineteenth century, Achim von Arnim and Clemens Brentano, included

[5] Shelley, "The Wandering Jew's Soliloquy" and also "Queen Mab." See Anderson, *Legend*, pp. 185ff., for other romantic portrayals. Between 1774 and 1930 no less than 1,460 literary works on the Ahasverus theme appeared in numerous European languages.

[6] Anderson, *Legend*, pp. 201–14, for French interpretations. Cf. G. Pradal, *La dimension historique de l'homme. Le mythe du Juif-errant dans la pensée d'Edgar Quinet* (Paris, 1961). E. Fromentin and P. Bataillard, *Sur l'Ahasverus d'Edgar Quinet* (Geneva, 1982). For Dumas see *HAS*, 3:351–54.

[7] Goethe attempted a treatment in 1774 (not published until 1836). Schubart's *Der ewige Jude* dates from 1783. For the German tradition, easily the most luxuriant in the nineteenth century, see Anderson, *Legend*, pp. 169–200; Soergel, *Ahasver-Dichtungen*; Zirus, *Ahasverus*. Cf. A. Low, *Jews in the Eyes of the Germans: From the Enlightenment to Imperial Germany* (Philadelphia, 1979), p. 44.

in their famous *The Boy's Magic Horn* (1806) the poem, "The Suffer-ing of the Lord," which represented Ahasverus in a conventionally anti-Jewish light.[8] Arnim's labored verse epic, *Halle und Jerusalem* (1809–11), deployed Ahasverus as its central character to express both the old and the newer kinds of Jew-hatred. Confessing the fer-vent hope of medieval Christian Jew-hatred that the Jews would be redeemed by conversion to Christianity, Achim portrayed Ahasverus as a convert whose full redemption must await the general conversion of the Jewish people. "Until you Jews have all been converted, I shall not find rest. I must wander through all countries, must see *you* mar-tyred, tormented, flayed. How thus are *you* made ridiculous."[9] De-spite individual conversion, therefore, the old Jewish guilt seems to inhere. It inhibits Ahasverus from approaching the Holy Sepulchre and it manifests itself even in converts in the form of Mammonism. The Jew Nathan rejects Ahasverus's pleas for money to ransom other captive Jews and is delighted to see that his own converted grand-children have made up a banking game. "You merciful God whose blessing rests upon the seed of your people! Conversion cannot wash it away!"[10] To the medieval Christian idea of Jewish guilt, Arnim has added a keynote of the revolutionary Jew-hatred of the nineteenth century: the charge that the Jews are guilty of a loveless, egoistic, and well-nigh ineradicable devotion to money.

In 1811 Arnim and his friend Brentano put these literary preju-dices into social practice with the creation of the "Christian-German Dining Club" at Berlin whose statutes barred from membership "Jews, converted Jews, and the descendents of converted Jews." To this group Brentano read a notorious paper, *The Philistine*, that estab-lished a connection between Judaism and Philistinism as cold, barren forms of rationalism shot through with a commercial spirit injurious to humanity in art and social life alike. Thus, the pernicious Jewish influence on art was damned with a word that emphasized the geo-graphical origin of that alien *Judentum*—"Palestine" of the Philis-tines.[11]

[8] *Des Knaben Wunderhorn* (Heidelberg, 1806), 1:143. Cf. Anderson, *Legend*, pp. 192ff. For the Christian-German romantics and the Jews, see Low, *Jews*, pp. 171, 190–207; Soergel, *Ahasver-Dichtungen*, pp. 43ff. See below, chap. 13, n. 16.

[9] Arnim, *Halle und Jerusalem*, in his *Sämtliche Werke* (Berlin, 1857), quoted by Low, *Jews*, p. 207 (cf. p. 174). Cf. E. Knecht, *Le mythe du Juif-errant: Essai de mythologie litteraire et de sociologie religieuse* (Grenoble, 1977), pp. 144ff.

[10] Quoted by C. A. Lea, *Emancipation, Assimilation, and Stereotype: The Image of the Jew in German and Austrian Drama 1800–1850* (Bonn, 1978), pp. 11–16.

[11] For *Der Philister*, see Brentano's *Gesammelte Schriften* (Frankfurt, 1852–55), vol. 5.
The attitudes of the club's members to the Jews are quite complicated on the surface. Kleist was not overtly hostile, while Fichte, who could be bitter on the subject, objected

The real potential of the Ahasverus myth to function as an anti-semitic image was inadequately realized in the quaintly medieval romanticism of Arnim and Brentano. The full transformation of the Wandering Jew into an emblem of the Jewish Question was brought about by the "modern" philosophical humanism that dominated German intellectual life by the 1830s, extending into the realm of literature as well as philosophy itself. At first the anti-Jewish meaning of the new humanist Ahasverus was not evident, masked as it was by his refinement from the flamboyant Promethean figure of the romantics into a universal symbol of human alienation. Many of the progressively minded German novelists and philosophers of the 1830s, who tried to tame the wilder excesses of romantic feeling within the limits of a precise vocabulary, still embraced a romantic urge to "freedom." But now they looked to a general emancipation of humanity from such sophisticated notions as "destructive self-love," rather than from the old-fashioned, external political and religious tyrannies denounced by Shelley and company. To this self-love the German revolutionary philosophizers gave the label "egoism." Ahasverus was swiftly reinterpreted as the personification of this egoism: his lack of love for others, his essential failing of "lovelessness," were taken to symbolize the generally alienated condition or *Zerrissenheit* of European—and especially German—man, a personal alienation reflected in an unhealthy "inorganic" political society. This universalist interpretation of a loveless Ahasverus, symbolic of the general human need for redemption, barely veiled, however, what was in effect a specifically anti-Jewish theme not so different from the original Christian content of the myth.

To the literary and philosophical revolutionists of the period 1815–48 Jewish lovelessness was really the other side of the old Jewish stub-

strongly to Brentano's reading of *Der Philister* (not because he was pro-Jewish but because he was offended by Brentano's sanctimoniousness). Arnim's hopes for the conversion of the Jews, on the other hand, prevented him from supporting the clause against *converted* Jews that Brentano had framed. Arnim was married to Brentano's fervently pro-Jewish sister, Bettina, but that did not lead him into following in his friend's footsteps in later years and abandoning his prejudices against the Jews. In the 1820s Brentano suppressed *Der Philister*, and in a poem of 1830 he even portrayed Ahasverus as mindless of money, an object of compassion, and an emblem of personal tragedy rather than of Jewish guilt (*Blätter aus dem Tagebuch einer Ahnfrau*, in *Gesammelte Schriften*, 4:121ff., quoted by Low, *Jews*, p. 194. Cf. Anderson, *Legend*, pp. 195f.). Arnim, however, remained obsessed: "I feel well in Wiepersdorf and am disturbed only by the loveliness of the place and by thoughts about Jews," runs one letter (quoted by Low, *Jews*, p. 194). Cf. below, chap. 6, n. 25, and chap. 8, n. 8.

Nikolas Lenau and A. von Platten-Hallemünde were among those Christian romantic poets who wrote sympathetically on Ahasverus. (See Low, *Jews*, pp. 212, 225; Anderson, *Legend*, pp. 199, 220f., 445.)

bornness (*Verstocktheit*). Both qualities were now secularized, but they still were understood in terms of a basic quest for Jewish "redemption." No longer was Ahasverus's sin the rejection of Christ; in keeping with a new vision of humanity, his sin was the rejection of love itself. Consequently, the redemption that the Jews had earlier spurned from Christ they were now seen as continuing to rebuff in a modern enlightened age by refusing to become truly human through embracing authentic love; they preferred to cling to money and self-love. Thus, Jewish sin and redemption had secularized their formal expressions, but their deeper emotional meanings had not really changed at all.

Primary among these emotions were the resentment and fear aroused by Jewish resistance to joining the rest of mankind. Jewish stubbornness was now reinterpreted to fit the prejudices of philosophy. The Jews had formerly resisted Christ; now they resisted love and humanity. But at the root of this formal shift was the anthropological fear of "the other" that refuses to be absorbed into the organic whole. This was linked to a profound anxiety that the Jews were alien in some way to the human race itself. In medieval Europe, membership of Christendom had defined authentic humanity. Conversion had afforded the Jews the sole means of becoming truly human, even though unconverted Jews might continue to live on in a strange, incompletely human sort of existence. Thus, the achievement of full humanity was correlated to the extinction of Judaism and Jews. What happened in the nineteenth century was that the definition of "humanity" became secularized. It was redefined in terms of the possession of moral autonomous freedom; nevertheless, the original religious experience, the act of entering into the truly human community, was carried over. Jewish redemption, in German secular revolutionism as much as in medieval Christianity, meant the disappearance of Judaism and the absorption of Jews into the organic whole of humanity, specifically, German humanity. This emotional ideal of the extinction and "destruction" of Judaism constitutes the very essence of revolutionary antisemitism.

For the German revolutionists Ahasverus became the archsymbol of the "destruction" (*Untergang*) of Judaism. Karl Gutzkow's feverish *Plan for an Ahasverus* (1838) exclaimed that "there is a metaphysics in the Wandering Jew legend and therein the whole fate of Judaism lies expressed." Ahasverus was declared to be emblematic of the Jewish Question because he will not be saved and the question not solved until the Jews make a "loving surrender" into full humanity by "emancipating themselves." This is the truly human emancipation into love that no mere civil emancipation can assure. Gutzkow explained how the redemption of Ahasverus and the Jews had to be pursued along two avenues. One was the destruction of Jewish egoism:

> Ahasverus's crime was the basest lovelessness. He offended not as a
> Jew but as an egoist. . . . The Jews were damned to wander over the
> earth, not because they were not Christians, but because they lacked
> the stirrings of moral, noble, beautiful, human feeling, because they
> lacked love. . . . Ahasverus is the Jew in his futile materialism.

When Ahasverus and the Jews renounce loveless egoism, they will no longer be Jews and Judaism will have been destroyed.

Gutzkow's second avenue to the "destruction" of Judaism was the disappearance of the Jews as a nation—their Hegelian emancipation into "history." The curse of Ahasverus and the Jews is their refusal to have died at the appointed hour, hanging on instead in a sterile, restless immortality that excludes them from the organic flow of history. "Ahasverus is the Jew in that he has been excluded from taking part in the call of history, the Jew precisely in his incapacity to have a mission." Ahasverus, uselessly present in all the great ages of European history, persists into the present age of universal emancipation, but cannot be part of the "modern" as long as he remains a Jew. The Wandering Jew represents the inability of the Jewish nation to have "died" when their historical mission had been completed with the death of Christ; now is the time for them to rejoin the stream of living European history and to abandon their ghostlike existence:

> The stubborn clinging to life by the Jews is a tragedy among their
> misfortunes. A messianic hope that cannot be relinquished by even
> the most enlightened and purified Jews tethers them to a bleak exis-
> tence. . . . Ahasverus's tragic fate . . . is his exhausted dusk-watch, his
> outliving of himself, his obsolescence.

The real redemption of Ahasverus and the Jews is, according to Gutzkow, "self-destruction" (*Selbstvernichtung*).[12]

The explicit antagonism of Gutzkow to Judaism is notable because he was prominently identified with liberal causes and was even denounced for his outspoken advocacy of Jewish civil emancipation. The fact that an apparent contradiction exists in Gutzkow's attitude should alert us to a possible misconception about the nature of his liberalism and that of other German "liberals." Clearly, Gutzkow's conception of the Jewish Question was not liberal in any modern Western sense of the word, for his support of Jewish emancipation

---

[12] For these quotations from Gutzkow, see below, chap. 11.

really turned on the radical notion of the "destruction" of Judaism rather than upon properly liberal ideas of individual rights. Moreover, many so-called German "liberals" like Gutzkow based their arguments on the national character of the Jews. Unlike reactionary Jew-haters, these "liberals" believed that the Jews were capable of reforming their bad national characteristics, above all, their instinct for hateful "separation" from the Christian peoples around them. Such "liberals" rather illiberally demanded the national and spiritual suicide of Jewish identity. Since this was also the prejudice that underlaid the German edicts of emancipation, it was easy for Gutzkow and his friends to lend their support to the cause of civil emancipation.[13]

Nor did it seem unreasonable for these "liberal" supporters of emancipation to adopt the principle that at least some "reform" of Judaism should be required as an immediate quid pro quo for these edicts. In 1831 the progressive theologian Heinrich Paulus, arguing against the genuinely liberal Gabriel Riesser, was troubled by the "enigmatic contradiction" for such liberals as himself in seeming to discriminate against a group of subjects on account of their religion. He resolved the difficulty by insisting that it was not Jewish religion to which he objected, but Jewish "separation" from their hosts, a separation encouraged by religion.[14] The leading liberal jurist and publicist Karl Rotteck was not embarrassed to explain in 1833 that the real source of Jewish legal disabilities was the Jews' own hostility to other peoples, which contrasted with the universal brotherhood preached by Christianity.[15] So ridden was much of German liberal thinking by this kind of prejudice against Jewish "separation" that even such a public defender of Jewish rights as Theodor Mommsen, writing in 1880, felt impelled to decry the persistence of self-consciously Jewish institutions and society in Germany, and he called upon the Jews to abolish the separation between themselves and the Germans. "Entry into a great nation costs a price," he averred.[16] The price was the validity of Jewish identity in Germany.

There may indeed be a programmatic logic operating here. In

[13] See R. Rürup, "The Tortuous and Thorny Path to Legal Equality: Jews and Emancipatory Legislation in Germany from the Later Eighteenth Century," *LBIY* 31 (1986): 3–33. Also below, chap. 5.

[14] Heinrich Paulus, *Die jüdische Nationalabsonderung . . .* (Heidelberg, 1831). Cf. R. Rürup, *Emanzipation und Antisemitismus: Studien zur Judenfrage der bürgerlichen Gesellschaft* (Göttingen, 1975), pp. 56, 152; Low, *Jews*, pp. 245f.; J. Katz, "A State within a State: The History of an Anti-Semitic Slogan," in his *Emancipation and Assimilation: Studies in Modern Jewish History* (Farnborough, Hants., Eng., 1972), pp. 44–76, especially p. 67.

[15] Quoted by Rürup, *Emanzipation*, p. 61.

[16] Mommsen, "Auch ein Wort über unser Judenthum" (1880), in *Der Berliner Antisemitismusstreit*, ed. W. Böhlich (Frankfurt, 1965), p. 225.

other times of revolutionary renewal—during the Crusades and the Reformation—there were similar calls for the destruction of Judaism; and they gave rise to paradoxes of a similar kind as here. Reuchlin, for example, in the sixteenth century anticipated Gutzkow in accusing the Jews of "persecuting us with undying hatred," while also pleading for the Jews to be treated fairly as "fellow-citizens."[17] As with Gutzkow, emancipation was only an interim solution; the real solution was the destruction of Judaism.

If the friends of the Jews could write thus, it is not surprising that the reactionary opponents of emancipation also used Jewish national character as grounds for denying rights to the Jews. Frederick William IV and his Prussian kindred spirits were convinced that Jewish peculiarities could never be shed and that this fact permanently debarred Jews from emancipation as Germans. The whole debate on Jewish emancipation, therefore, revolved around the almost metaphysical question of whether Judaism could or could not commit suicide by abandoning its national character: the friends of the Jews were optimistic that it could, their enemies thought it quite irredeemable. But the Jews lost by both sides. The offer of rights was poisoned by the condition that they effectively cease to be Jews and become "real Germans," a notion that may have been clothed in practical political language but which was curiously mystical for all that. In the end, therefore, the very premise of the emancipation debate turned out to be profoundly anti-Jewish.[18]

The classic call for the "destruction of Judaism" is uttered in Richard Wagner's *Judaism in Music* (1850). "Only one thing can redeem you from the burden of your curse—the redemption of Ahasverus—*destruction* [*Untergang*]!" But what exactly did "destruction" mean here? Wagner's later advice to his Jewish conductor Hermann Levi that "as a Jew, all you have to learn to do is die" is equally obscure.[19] It simply extends the ambiguity to the meaning of the word "die." Was it meant literally or metaphorically?

[17] See H. A. Oberman, *The Roots of Anti-Semitism in the Age of Renaissance and Reformation* (Philadelphia, 1984), pp. 30f., 53, for the need to escape false modern categories in the case of Reuchlin, and also *passim* for interesting comments on the deeper currents beneath the surface of Christian antisemitism. There are parallels between Reuchlin and the later Protestant Jew-hater Eisenmenger, as in their apparent dislike for "cruel" methods for converting the Jews, while still advocating harsh policies now or in the future.

[18] J. Katz, "Misreadings of Anti-Semitism," *Commentary* (July 1983): 39–44, points out that rights were usually conditioned on the negation of Jewish existence (p. 43).

[19] The quotation concerning Ahasverus forms the concluding words of *Judaism in*

A dictionary is of little help here, or with understanding the meaning of other key words used in connection with the Jewish Question: *Ausrottung* (extermination), *Vernichtung* (annihilation), *Vertilgung* (extirpation) recur in the nineteenth-century revolutionary discussion and chillingly reappear in the Nazi discussion of the Final Solution. But even in their genocidal context, whether in Hitler's speeches or in the documents of the SS, such words continue to be shrouded in ambiguity. A cryptic, oracular quality seems always to be present.[20]

Most historians have adopted a simple approach to the problem of meaning. Some have argued that the words are meant to be taken literally, that when an antisemite speaks of exterminating the Jews or Judaism, he means it practically. Others have explained that the words carry a purely metaphorical or allegorical meaning.[21] It seems, however, that to formulate the problem in such an either/or fashion is misconceived, for it distorts the psychological complexity of the issue. Indeed, it misses the whole significance of this ambiguity in German thought—which is, that the ambiguity is intentional and central, and rooted in both the German language and the German mentality. To reduce this fundamentally characteristic ambivalence to a simple opposition of "metaphor versus reality" in effect destroys the essence of German antisemitic thought. Luther's "making the Jews lie upon the ground," Fichte's "cutting off Jewish heads" to get rid of their ideas, Wagner's Ahasverian redemption of "destruction," Hitler's "end of the Jewish race in Europe," are all manifestations of the tradition of ambiguity in German antisemitism.

The intricacy of the problem was well understood by early nineteenth-century writers. *Ausrottung*, for example, had first been applied to the Jewish Question by Luther, who used it to translate the Hebrew precept in Genesis that the uncircumcized Jew should be cast out from Israel; the implication was that the circumcized Jews of

---

*Music* (1850), *PW*, 3:100. The advice to Levi appears in *Cosima Wagners Tagebücher* (Munich, 1976), entry of 12 November 1880.

*Untergang* was used by Ludwig Börne in 1807 to signify the dialectical striving between Judaism and Christianity for each other's destruction (Börne, *Sämtliche Schriften*, ed. I. and P. Rippmann [Dreieich-Düsseldorf, 1964], 1:12: "Der Hass zwischen Judentum und Christentum ist notwendig; denn jedes, um sein höchstes Leben zu erreichen, erfordert, den Untergang des andern" [*14 Sätze*, 1807, no. 8]). But according to Jakob and Wilhelm Grimm, *Deutsches Wörterbuch* (Leipzig, 1854–1965), XI/4, cols. 1558ff., the word was widely used in the nineteenth century in both metaphorical and concrete senses.

[20] For Nazi ambiguity, see the quotations in Y. Bauer, *The Holocaust in Historical Perspective* (Seattle, 1978), pp. 8–12.

[21] E.g., J. Katz, *Richard Wagner: Vorbote des Antisemitismus* (Königstein, 1985), pp. 201ff., accepts Wagner's use of *Untergang* as purely metaphorical.

modern times should be cast out from the "New Israel" (that is, Christianity).[22] The sense here was more expulsion than murder, but in the nineteenth century *Ausrottung* came frequently to be used in conjunction with the removal of parasites (such as the Jews) and here the idea crept in of killing the parasites once they were removed.[23] So clearly understood in Germany was the usefulness of this ambiguity that it took a satirist to expose the wickedness of the unspoken assumptions in the literature. Mocking the discrete formulae of the antisemites, an author of 1804 proposed that the "total extermination [*Vertilgung*] of the Jews would be incomparably easier than relocating them on the moon. . . . The total massacre [*Niedermetzelung*] of Jewry could be used to improve the soil."[24] During the Hep-Hep pogroms of 1819 another author, Hundt-Radowsky, suggested the extermination (*Vertilgung*) of the Jews within Germany as a possible policy, but, out of conscience, settled instead "for hounding them out of the country" after confiscating all their goods. "With a thousand cannon the vermin can be driven across to the Turks . . . and perhaps in this way they can be exterminated [*vertilgt*] completely from the earth."[25]

The only sure guide to understanding the meanings of the keywords of the Jewish Question is a knowledge of the contemporary context, that is, of the revolutionary discussion itself. We have to be aware of the assumptions permeating the language of contemporary debate on the Jewish Question, and the key to this debate is to be found in the German perception of "Judaism." To understand the

[22] Luther uses *ausrotten* in his *Lectures on Genesis*, 17:14, and *Against the Jews and Their Lies*, quoted by C. Cobet, *Der Wortschatz des Antisemitismus in der Bismarckzeit* (Munich, 1973), p. 213, who notes that it had a similar meaning in an 1830 Brockhaus dictionary. I have not been able to consult N. Hortzitz, *Früh-Antisemitismus in Deutschland (1789–1871/72): Strukturelle Untersuchungen zu Wortschatz* (1988).

[23] A. Bein, "The Jewish *Parasite*," *LBIY* 10 (1964): 3–41.

[24] "Dominicus Haman Epiphanes," *Unumstösslicher Beweis . . . [der] schleunigste Niedermetzelung aller Juden* (Königsberg, 1804), written in refutation of the Jew-hater C. von Grattenauer. The "Jerusalem" 1833 edition is quoted by P. Mendes-Flohr and J. Reinharz, *The Jew in the Modern World* (New York, 1980), pp. 261f., who seem to take the satire as genuinely anti-Jewish and attribute it to Friedrich von Holzschuher, but the early Königsberg edition (noticed by V. Eichstädt, *Bibliographie zur Geschichte der Judenfrage* [Hamburg, 1938], no. 420) renders this unlikely.

[25] H. von Hundt-Radowsky, "Betrachtungen über Verbesserung, Ausrottung und Vertreibung der Juden," in his *Judenspiegel* (Würzburg, 1819), pp. 141–48. *Ausrottung* was thus used here in the sense of rooting out the Jewish parasites, but it can be seen that it led easily to the notion of their subsequent murder (*Vertilgung*). In his subsequent *Neuer Judenspiegel oder Apologie der Kinder Israels* (Cannstadt, 1828), Hundt-Radowsky proposed the gentler solution of conversion. He now admitted that Christian oppression had contributed largely to Jewish vice. Cf. Low, *Jews*, p. 111; Mendes-Flohr and Reinharz, *Jew in the Modern World*, pp. 260f.

meaning of *Ausrottung* and *Untergang*, we must really first understand the meaning of *Judentum*.

In the German *Judentum*, several concepts and allusions are layered in the one word which in English require quite distinct words for their expression. For *Judentum* contains the various ideas of Judaism as a religion ("Judaism"), Judaism as a community or nation ("Jewry"), and Judaism as Jewish ways of behaving and thinking ("Jewishness"). A "Jew" therefore is anyone who fits any one of these definitions of "Judaism." He can be a religious, "sabbath Jew," or a nonreligious person of Jewish descent, or a wholly assimilated convert who nevertheless retains a distinctive Jewishness about his artistic outlook or his economic behavior, his way of speaking, or even of thinking. It is this plasticity of "Jewishness" that renders the myth of *Judentum* endlessly fertile. Thus, in the course of the nineteenth century the allusive, pregnant term "Jewishness" replaced the older comparatively rational concept of "Jewish national character," though both ultimately referred to the same thing.

The multiplicity of meaning in *Judentum* made the German debate on the Jewish Question especially volatile, for it enabled German authors to fluctuate ambiguously and easily between speaking of the Jews as metaphors and as real people, between implying a destruction that is purely figurative and one that must necessarily in part be physical. The "Jews," like "Judaism," are at once myth and practical reality. Authors like Marx oscillated, sometimes within the same sentence, between referring to Jews as reprehensible real people engaged in the dirty business of capitalism and understanding "Jews" as abstract symbols of capitalist society and the capitalist spirit. This polyvalence of meaning renders the reader always uncertain of which precise sense an author has in mind, and it often strikes a Western reader as intellectually dishonest. But it explains the fascination and persuasiveness of many antisemitic writings of the nineteenth century. For the reader can respond intellectually and emotionally to as many meanings of *Judentum* as he wants. The imprecision, the polyvalence, of *Judentum*, like *Untergang*, was ideally suited to a discourse that was fundamentally irrational and founded on emotion despite its wealth of overly rational argumentation.

When interpreted in the framework of *Judentum*, the complex meanings of *Ausrottung* and *Untergang* unfold themselves. Take, for example, the case of the revolutionary Jena professor, Jakob Fries.[26] This is a classic example of the way in which Jew-haters have exploited the ambiguity of *Ausrottung* and *Judentum*, claiming that they

---

[26] For Fries, see below, chap. 8.

only wished to exterminate "Judaism" and not "Jews." In 1819, while under investigation for his role in inciting the Hep-Hep riots, Fries told the police that his inflammatory utterances had only advocated the *Ausrottung* of the "commercial caste of Judaism" and had not at all been meant to instigate attacks on individual Jews. The flaw in this argument is that it is not possible to disengage the "Jews" from "Judaism," whether Judaism is understood as a commercial caste or as a religious community. For "Jews" are the bearers of "Judaism" and only if these Jews shall redeem themselves from their bad national character can "Judaism"—their religion, their economic behavior, or whatever—*die*. The sophistical distinction between even the metaphorical death of "Jews" and of "Judaism" cannot in practice be sustained. Yet, for Fries and most of his fellows, it is extremely difficult for the Jews to "die" spiritually. What is to happen to those Jews who remain "Jewish"? At some point, a practical, and not just a metaphorical, sanction must be imposed on the Jews.[27]

There is always an unavoidably practical, concrete meaning to the destruction of "Judaism," no matter how metaphorically one may try to speak either about that destruction or about "Judaism." Judaism in Germany undoubtedly was composed of institutional and other communal bonds and cannot be exclusively described in metaphorical terms. Even those writers who inveighed most abstractly about Judaism as a "spirit" or "mental frame" understood that Judaism is also formed of real Jews and institutions. The destruction of Judaism must always entail a real living or social element. *Untergang* is simultaneously concrete and metaphorical, a fluctuating dynamic feeling and idea, rather than a mere metaphor or a practical plan.

———

How precisely was the "destruction of Judaism" to be achieved? Here there was a division of opinion as to whether the means of destruction should be gentle or severe. Too often this division is taken to be one between "pro-Jewish" and "anti-Jewish" camps, but in reality both were united in seeking the negation of Jews and Judaism. In any case, the apparent contrast between hard and soft lines was not as sharp as it might seem. The means proposed were very often ranged on a single sliding scale, rather than against one another. Thus the softer school believed in positive assimilation as the best destruction, and they supported legal emancipation as a means to this painless death of Judaism. To this school belonged such contrasting

[27] For the extremity of this destruction of Jewish *Gemeinschaft*, see E. Gellner, "Accounting for the Horror," *Times Literary Supplement* (6 August 1982): 843–45.

figures as the Young German "liberals" Gutzkow and Laube, Jewish radicals such as Börne and for a time Heine, and socialist revolutionists like Marx and Hess. The first objective here was not just the moral death of Jewishness but the physical death of the Jews as a nation. This practicality may be seen even in the treatments of the Ahasverus myth by two of the least practically minded members of the soft school, Jacoby and Schopenhauer.

In his *Lament of a Jew* of 1837, Joel Jacoby mourned the tragic obsolescence of Judaism. Even if the Jews were to join the revolutionaries and liberals and become emancipated, says Jacoby presciently, the next day they would be guillotined as capitalists. Their only hope of an extinction that would not entail their physical execution lies in a national death and their spiritual extinction as Jews. Whereas the other nations are young, Ahasverus, longing for youth, is moribund: "Lord, let us go hence. We are weak, we are tired, we yearn for the burial vault." Let the Jews be completely assimilated into Germany and thus be reborn.[28]

With Schopenhauer, whose ideas of annihilation of the self and the will were so mystically felt, the unapprized reader might expect to find purely mystical attitudes also applied to the annihilation of Judaism. But Schopenhauer was quite practical in his solution to the Ahasverus enigma. Indeed, he even accepted for this purpose ideas that he scorned philosophically, including the Hegelian concept of historical anomaly and the doctrine of the "Christian-German state" that excluded Jews on "medieval" grounds:

> Ahasverus, the Wandering Jew, is nothing but the personification of the whole Jewish race. . . . This pettifogging little nation, this John Lackland among the nations, is to be found all over the globe, nowhere at home and nowhere strangers. . . . It asserts its Jewish nationality with unprecedented stubbornness . . . [but] lives parasitically on other nations. . . . To bring an end in the gentlest manner to the tragicomedy, the best way is for marriages . . . between Jews and gentiles. . . . Then in the course of a century there will be only a very few Jews left and soon the ghost will be exorcized. Ahasverus will be buried and the chosen people will not know where their abode was. . . . They are and remain a foreign oriental race.[29]

[28] *Klagen eines Juden*, published anonymously in 1837. See S. Liptzin, *Germany's Stepchildren* (Philadelphia, 1944), pp. 49ff. Jacoby later converted to Christianity and also spied for the police on his former Young German friends. (See below, chap. 11, n. 26, and chap. 18, n. 2).

[29] Arthur Schopenhauer, *Parerga and Paralipomena*, trans. E. F. J. Payne (Oxford, 1974), 2:261–64. Schopenhauer condemned the expulsion of the Jews from Spain and he insisted on the granting of civil—but not political—rights to German Jews. Cf.

This ardent desire for the assimilation of the Jews, however, often envisaged expulsion as an alternative; Laube and Wagner spoke of "assimilation or expulsion" as the issue. This almost irresistible tendency may be seen in the development of Paul de Lagarde's thinking. In 1853 Lagarde wanted to "make this nation disappear by having to fuse with us Germans," and he felt it wrong to deny the Jews civil and political rights on the reasoning of the "Christian-German state." Here and elsewhere he repudiated racial biological theories that barred the way to a fusion between Jews and Germans, but he still confessed himself doubtful as to the success of assimilation given the "tenacity of the Jewish religion which makes them a nation." They must give up their *Judentum* and their religion "so that they are no longer recognizable as Jews. . . . It is up to God's will whether we shall completely enter the door with them, or stand apart."[30] Already then, in an assimilationist argument, there is implicit a threat of a final parting of the ways. In later years Lagarde slid further along the scale, first to expulsion, and then to extermination. "With bacilli . . . one does not negotiate, nor try to educate them. . . . They are exterminated as quickly and as thoroughly as possible."[31]

A member of the softer school of assimilation—and a repudiator of biological racism—could from the outset envisage the forcible separation of the Jews from the Germans should the gentler means of assimilation fail, and then move on to propose extermination. This phenomenon suggests an inherent lethal logic in the whole idea of the destruction of Judaism that, once begun, was compelled to work itself out.

In the writings of the "hard" school we find a similar sliding from comparatively moderate measures to rather sterner ones. Constantin Frantz's early *Ahasverus or the Jewish Question* (1844) advanced a curious argument based on Christian religious idealism. Frantz offered a new revolutionary twist to old Christian notions about the perpetual servitude and the final conversion of the Jews at the Last Judgment, and he rejected any possibility of converting them before then. Assimilation into German Christianity was impossible; civil exclusion of the Jews was the only proper policy:

H. W. Brann, *Schopenhauer und das Judentum* (Bonn, 1975); Low, *Jews*, pp. 321–27. N. Rotenstreich, *Jews and German Philosophy* (New York, 1984), pp. 179–200, points out the fundamental importance of Schopenhauer's hatred of Judaism for his whole philosophy.

[30] Paul de Lagarde, "Über die gegenwärtigen Aufgaben der deutschen Politik" (1853), reprinted in his *Deutsche Schriften*, 4th ed. (Göttingen, 1903), 1:24ff., 35.

[31] Quoted by F. Stern, *The Politics of Cultural Despair* (Berkeley, Calif., 1963), pp. 61–63.

> Now the Jews are incapable of forming either a people or a state nor
> can they decompose themselves through mixture into the Christian
> peoples and states. They can neither live nor die, and from this fate
> no earthly power can redeem them. . . . Emancipation is an empty
> word . . . inadmissible and unsuccessful. Jews always remain Jews and
> are thereby in their innermost being excluded from Christian history.
> . . . But through the world-historical penance that has been imposed
> on them, they will gradually be softened and confess their infidelity
> on the last day.[32]

In his later works, Frantz saw this revolutionary German-Christianity
as the basis of a new federated order of Europe in which there would
be no place for the Jews. Frantz moved from exclusion to expulsion,
predicting now a great

> popular rage . . . the tragically sad way of solving the Jewish Question.
> . . . Where the first blow would be struck, the place from where the
> movement will rapidly spread abroad, is the German Empire. . . . The
> great Jewish catastrophe in prospect for central Europe will strike. . . .
> Out of the whole of Europe a huge exodus of Jews will take place be-
> cause no one will put up with them any longer. Who knows where
> they will be scattered. . . . Is it not a premonition that from their earli-
> est history the Jews have been wandering. . . . They themselves are
> Ahasverus to whom no peace is granted, not even the peace of the
> grave, because they cannot die. That myth assuredly has profound
> meanings.[33]

A disastrous potential was always implicit in the mode of thinking
about the "destruction of Judaism." Only time, social and political
changes, and a growing personal obsessiveness were required to
bring it forth.

Frantz sanctimoniously refrained from calling for the actual murder of Jews, but others were less cautious. As early as 1865, the revolutionary anti-Marxist socialist Eugen Dühring insisted that "killing
and extermination" (*Ertötung und Ausrottung*) were the only ways to
destroy *Judentum*.[34] Dühring became one of the most rabid enthusi-

---

[32] C. Frantz, *Ahasverus oder die Judenfrage* (Berlin, 1844), pp. 27f. (also p. 47). He
befriended Wagner in the 1860s. See below, chap. 19.

[33] Frantz, *Die Weltpolitik* (Chemnitz, 1882–83), pp. 115–18.

[34] According to the *Encyclopaedia Judaica, s.v.* "Dühring," this phrase about *Ertötung*
appears in the 1865 edition of Dühring's *Wert des Lebens*. However, according to
E. Silberner, *Sozialisten zur Judenfrage* (Berlin, 1962), pp. 152, 327, the term seems to
appear only in the later fifth edition of 1894, at p. 9. Though I have not been able to
see either the first or fifth editions, I would think that 1865 is likely to be its first
occurrence.

Cf. B. Mogge, *Rhetorik des Hasses: Eugen Dühring und die Genese seines antisemitische*

asts for the new racial biology; he recognized it immediately as the missing intellectual link that would finally explain—scientifically and rigorously—the necessity of Jew-hatred. Racial biology would also dictate once and for all the solution of the Jewish Question: physical extinction. But even this most crazed of Jew-haters found it politic to cloak some of his utterances in ambiguity and for this he resorted to Ahasverus. "The Jews remain collectively a single Wandering Jew [*Ewiger Jude*] who persistently defies all nobler things by reason of his inherited nature," he wrote in his monomaniacal *The Jewish Question as Racial, Moral, and Cultural Question* (1881). "The Wandering Jew, who cannot aspire to higher and nobler nature and restlessly drives himself ever lower through world history, is the whole race [*Volk*] itself, laden down with the curse of nature." Dühring demanded a "Carthaginian" solution, but preferred to remain vague about the details, apart from wanting a ban on intermarriage. Ominously, he insisted on the need for "outward restriction, penning up , and a final settlement of accounts [*Abschliessung*]."³⁵ The fifth edition of 1901 demanded the "annihilation [*Vernichtung*] of Jewish nationality."³⁶ Revising this in 1920 in the light of Versailles, Dühring menaced:

> Whereas in the first edition of this book only incomplete means were recommended and discussed because they alone seemed to be possible, such half measures appear now after so many experiences quite out of place. The world must settle its account with the Hebrew people in a radical manner.

Only "terror and brute force" would work with the Jews; the old Carthaginian image was no longer adequate for dealing with these "antihuman attacks of foreign parasites." There was "no room on earth for Hebrew existence."³⁷ In sum, "the murder of races" was "the higher law of history."³⁸ Was this a metaphor?

---

*Wortschatz* (Neuse, 1977). Cobet, *Der Wortschatz des Antisemitismus*, also deals primarily with Dühring's language. G.-K. Kaltenbrunner, "Eugen Dühring," *Zeitschrift für Religions- und Geistesgeschichte* 22 (1970): 58–79. G. L. Mosse, *The Crisis of German Ideology* (New York, 1964), pp. 131ff., and *Toward the Final Solution: A History of European Racism* (London, 1978), pp. 164ff.; L. Poliakov, *The Aryan Myth* (New York, 1974), p. 294.

³⁵ Dühring, *Die Judenfrage als Racen-, Sitten- und Culturfrage*, 2d ed. (Leipzig, 1881), pp. 113f. (Title varies slightly in later editions.) Reading this abominably written book, Theodor Herzl felt that "its effect on me was as though I had suddenly been hit on the head" (Herzl, *Zionist Writings* [New York, 1973–75], 2:111).

³⁶ *Die Judenfrage*, 5th ed. (Leipzig, 1901), pp. 113, 126.

³⁷ *Die Judenfrage*, 6th ed. (Leipzig, 1930; Dühring had actually revised it in 1920), pp. 114, 136, 139f., 142.

³⁸ Quoted by Kaltenbrunner, "Eugen Dühring," pp. 76f. Cf. Dühring's aptly titled autobiography *Sache, Leben und Feinde*, 2d ed. (Leipzig, 1903), pp. 507ff.

J. Katz, "Was the Holocaust Predictable?" in *The Holocaust as Historical Experience*, ed.

Ahasverus was the myth of *Jewish* redemption. To convey mythologically the need for *German* redemption from Judaism another emblem was needed. This was to be the allegory of *Verjudung* and *Entjudung*, of "Jewification" and "de-Jewification." It depicted how Germans had become Jewified and now stood in need of a redemption that entailed the "de-Jewifying" of German life and culture and its restoration to an authentic "Germanness."[39] Whereas Ahasverian *Untergang* could symbolize Jewish assimilation into Germany, *Verjudung* was the allegory of the reverse process in which the Germans were being assimilated into "Jewishness."

Why did *Verjudung*—the word was coined by Wagner in 1850 but the idea is as old as Luther—become such an obsessive parable in German culture?[40] The answer is likely to be threefold. In the first place, *Verjudung* represented how the Jewish Question, far from being a merely particular matter of Jewish redemption, had transmogrified into the problem of how the Jews were parasitically attacking their German host. The German mind seemed unable to live with an unassimilated social entity that dwelt symbiotically on the same territory (though for many Jews such a coexistence was to become an article of faith). Such an alien entity as *Judentum* must assimilate (that is, destroy itself), consume its host, or be ejected or destroyed by that host. If Germany did not absorb Judaism, then Judaism must absorb Germany and indeed it seemed to the Germans that this process of "Jewification" was already well under way. A de-Jewification was, therefore, an urgent priority if "Germany" was to survive; the destruction of Judaism thus became the ultimate source of German redemption.

To subscribe to this pessimistic view did not mean that one had to be necessarily a "right-wing" nationalist or racist. Given the inculcation of "German" ways of thinking and feeling by the educational,

---

Y. Bauer and N. Rotenstreich (New York, 1981), pp. 23–41 fails to appreciate the significance of such mythological concepts as "destruction" and "extermination" for the question of the continuity of nineteenth-century German antisemitism and the extermination policy of Hitler. He seems to argue, for example (pp. 37ff.), that Dühring's concept of extermination only becomes important or meaningful because of the rise of Hitler. The point, surely, should be that Hitler's antisemitism is only *possible* in the context of a mythological tradition of antisemitism. (This is not to say that Hitler was *inevitable*, which is a different question altogether).

[39] See S. Aschheim, " 'The Jew Within.' The Myth of *Judaization* in Germany," in *The Jewish Response to German Culture*, ed. J. Reinharz and W. Schatzberg (Hanover, N.H., 1985), pp. 212–41.

[40] *PW*, 3:82.

the cultural, and the religious system, it was easy for German "liberals" to take alarm at the pace of Jewish emancipation and draw the wrong conclusions from it. From the debate on the Jewish Question, it is all too clear that the prevailing habit of thought in Germany was to assume that only two alternatives existed—"Jewishness" or "Germanness"—and then to press each of these to their logical conclusions. In a less closed, not to say less hysterical mentality, it would have been more obvious that two possibilities could and did exist, and, furthermore, that it is not always necessary or inevitable to force things to logical conclusions. But *Verjudung*, with its polarized schema of good and evil, was far too much in tune with German sensibility to be passed over in favor of a more nuanced and complex attitude to the Jewish Question.

A second attraction of the *Verjudung* frame of mind was the central preoccupation of Germans with the nature of their own national identity. "What is German?" is the perennial inquiry of German culture. It was urged by Fichte, by Wagner, by Thomas Mann; it is a question whose very asking presupposes an insecure sense of national identity. For nineteenth-century Germans, so unsure of their own "Germanness," the Jewish Question was ultimately the German Question. It was, in effect, another way of asking "What is German?" and receiving the satisfying answer—"whatever is not Jewish."[41] If Germans could de-Jewify themselves, then the German Question would be solved along with the Jewish Question. As Lagarde put it, "to the degree that we [Germans] become *ourselves*, the Jews will cease being Jews."[42]

The urgent search for German authenticity, for German redemption, helps to explain the strange intensity of the debate on the Jewish Question. This quasi-religious need for salvation drew for its psychological fervor on the messianic notion of the Germans as a new Chosen Race. And here we come to the third resonance evoked by the *Verjudung* allegory. The Jews were, of course, by tradition the Chosen Race, but the Germans had also a very long history of self-awareness of their own election as a race apart. They had resisted the Roman colonization of Europe and preserved faithfully their own unique national culture and character; with the Lutheran Reformation they had given expression to a rejuvenated and higher spirit of human— not just German—freedom that had been reformulated anew as pure philosophical truth by the German Enlightenment. Germany's sacred

[41] See H. Glaser, *The Cultural Roots of National Socialism (Spiesser-Ideologie)*, trans. E. A. Menze (London, 1978), for historically based insights into German national character that cannot be dismissed as mere stereotyping.

[42] Quoted by Aschheim, " 'The Jew Within,' " pp. 235f.

mission for humanity was confirmed by Luther, by philosophy, by her defeat of Napoleon, by the rational German state, through to the current concept of a special German role in Europe (*Sonderweg*). Frantz openly declared that "in place of the Jews, the Germans have become the people of God."

Endowed with such a lofty awareness of their own mission as the new Chosen Race, it is hardly surprising that the Germans should have felt particularly vexed by the more ancient pretensions of the Jews. At the same time, there was present a strong self-pitying tendency to regard Germany as the perennial "victim" of foreign machinations. This combination of grievances gave rise to a resentment of the Jews not just as rivals, but also as persecutors of the Germans. The Jews were a living reproach to them, a reminder of German weakness and sinfulness, a challenge to German self-esteem. Above all, the Jews seemed to possess an effortless natural ability to remain a "people" endowed with its own national culture and consciousness, an ability envied as well as hated by the less-than-secure Germans.

In understanding German antisemitism, it is this unpleasing psychology—the prevailing emotional climate—that is important rather than the various formal rearrangements of its ideological components. Luther had set the tone for the *Verjudung* mentality: the paranoid feeling that Germany was being devoured by foreigners, whether papists or Jews, all of them agents of the devil; the hysterical conviction that no compromise was possible, that the worst evil must transpire unless drastic measures were taken. In the minds of the secular Jew-haters of the nineteenth century, that same psychology persisted. It was masked only by a new set of formal, secular themes and unspoken assumptions that were necessitated, firstly, by the intellectual changes of the Enlightenment and the German philosophical revolution, and, secondly, by the political and social changes of the German wars and Jewish emancipation.

Perhaps what more than anything was bound to rack up German insecurity and resentment to fever pitch was the outrageous fact that Jews had escaped from the ghetto, becoming "German" in appearance but still remaining Jews either in a religious, or, more insidiously, in a social or psychological sense. With emancipation, it was no longer possible to distinguish sharply and unambiguously between "German" and "Jew." Jews were not really Germans, but they were admitted as such by the state. When primal existential categories became blurred like this, the whole order of the world is thrown into doubt, assurance fails, and the hysterical temperament runs free. Under these conditions—created by a mixture of novel political, social, and intellectual factors—the Jewish Question rose to an uncomfortable and enervating prominence in the early nineteenth century.

Only when the psychology of the debate is appreciated may one begin to comprehend one of the strangest features of modern German antisemitism, namely the easy assent of so many apparently civilized authors to the most monstrous premises and proposals about the Jewish Question. There is a perplexing psychological willingness to *believe* in both the absurd allegations and the cruel measures to be applied against the Jews. The Ahasverus myth's *Leitmotiv* of "destruction" had helped to attune the German mind to envisaging only extreme solutions to the Jewish Question, whether metaphorical or physical solutions, whether motivated by goodwill or malice. So natural and so reasonable, so self-evident, are the expressions, modest proposals, and mental states of German antisemitism, that it is often necessary to remind oneself just how bizarre a mental universe it was in which so many respectable German writers moved. This mythological universe, this state of mind, did not make Hitlerism inevitable—but it made it possible.

# CHAPTER 3

# "Against Humanity": Moloch, Mammon, and the Secularization of the Blood Libel

*VERJUDUNG*—"Jewification"—was an allegory of German redemption from the Jews, but it was really a special case of a more universal allegory—Molochism and Mammonism—which spoke for the redemption, not just of the Germans, but of all humanity from Judaism.

The *Verjudung* of Germany manifested itself abrasively in the spread of a "Jewish" materialism, based on "money," that was corroding the spiritual substance of Germanness. This theme of Jewish "money" united the whole spectrum of hostile—and sometimes even friendly—opinion on the Jewish Question, whether conservative or radical. Of course, the precise ideological explanations varied. Those on the right saw the rise of Jewish money and its associated capitalist values as corrupting the honest old order of things and undermining the properly hierarchical government of Germany. To combat the menace of bourgeois capitalism appeal was made to the well-established refrains of traditional social Jew-hatred, that is, Jewish exploitativeness, greed, and ambition. The enemies of the Jews on the left, however, were more inventive and developed a revolutionary critique of Judaism and Jewishness built on two interconnected notions: that the human failing of "egoism" was embodied for the modern era in the economic system of bourgeois capitalism; and that "money" was the supreme expression of a self-interest and self-seeking that impeded the final emancipation of humanity and the emergence of a genuinely social "new man."[1]

The basic idea was hardly new. In the guise of amour propre it had been a central theme in Rousseau, but in Germany the insight was seized upon and systematized with a grim determination that drained it of its original spontaneity and turned it instead into a mechanical ideology, a set of clumsy conceptual building blocks. More sinisterly, it was in Germany that a specifically Jewish significance was injected into the general idea that humanity was being alienated from its true loving social nature by an egoism that was seen as essentially Jewish,

[1] Cf. E. Silberner, *Sozialisten zur Judenfrage* (Berlin, 1962); J. Carlebach, *Karl Marx and the Radical Critique of Judaism* (London, 1978); R. Wistrich, *Socialism and the Jews* (Rutherford, N.J., 1982).

being intrinsic to Jewish national character. Kant and Fichte had launched this theory with their remarks on the economic parasitism of the Jews; the revolutionary discussion of the Jewish Question between 1830 and 1850 turned on the elaboration by the next generation of philosophers of the notion of Jewish egoism. The mythology generated in this discussion reveals that the German revolution did not see the Jewish Question as a marginal issue, but rather as an exemplar of human redemption in general. German revolutionary thinkers of both "left" and "right" looked to redeem not just Germans from "Judaism," but all mankind from the modern disease of Jewishness.

This crusade may have appeared secular, yet actually it was appealing to the same emotional core as the original call of Christianity itself. Thus, Judaism could conveniently continue to figure as the villain of the piece; it was both the actual and metaphorical evil from which men needed to redeem themselves. The new mythology, however, had to be able to convey the specific idea that capitalistic Judaism was antihuman, and that money played a special role in this equation. The best mythological vehicles for the understanding of a capitalistic, inhuman Judaism were discovered to be Moloch, the semitic god of human sacrifice, and Mammon, the god of money.

The cult of Moloch has a long religious history, alluded to in various passages of the Bible that severely prohibit its practice. It is usually assumed to have been a Phoenician-Carthaginian cult of child sacrifice, though it has been argued that it was in fact merely a symbolic rite of initiation.[2] In any event the details of the Crucifixion made it easy for Christians to see the Jews reverting to a Molochism from which their prophets had warned them so many times: the Jews were the killers of Christ, and in the Christian period could be seen as constantly reenacting that crime in their ritual murders of Christians. In the secular modern period this mythological framework was readily updated, so that the old Jewish tradition of human sacrifice was now expressed metaphorically by the Jewish sacrifice of mankind and of love to the interests of egoism and money. In a way this was also a return to the old pagan reproach that the Jews were animated by "hatred of mankind"; Voltaire, for instance, showed himself aware of the connection when he juxtaposed his attacks on the tradition of human sacrifice with his harsh criticism of their love of money.

Mammon too has a long ancestry but one more specifically Christian. In fact, "Mammon" was not originally a god at all but simply a

[2] See the *Encyclopaedia Judaica*, vol. 12, *s.v.* "Moloch." The cult is banned in Lev. 18:21 and elsewhere.

Hellenized Aramaic word meaning "riches." In the Sermon on the Mount, Christ insisted that "Ye cannot serve God and Mammon" (Luke 16:13; Matt. 6:24). Thanks to the financial "parasitism" typical of Jewry, it did not take long for the European Christian mind to see in Christ's words an intimation that the Jews were the demonic servants of a false devil-god of money opposed to God and the truly human. St. John Chrysostom demonized the Jews by associating them both with this Mammonist devil and with Molochism: "The Jews are the plague of the universe. . . . Possessed of the devil, they murder their offspring and offer themselves to the devil." This is typical of the tendency of medieval Christian Jew-haters to fuse the devil and Moloch by seeing them both as gods of ritual murder; in the Middle Ages, Moloch is one of the names given to the devil.[3]

Onto this Molochist foundation was grafted the later medieval Blood Libel—the allegation that the Jews required human blood for their Passover rituals.[4] Yet, ironically enough, the thinker who did most to ensure that these Christian delusions persisted into modern European consciousness was also the archenemy of Christian infamy. Voltaire's anti-Jewish articles in his *Dictionnaire philosophique* combined attacks on Jewish Mammonism with an assault on their Molochism, gleefully recounting those parts of the Hebrew Bible in which human sacrifice was endorsed. The article "Jephtha or Human Blood Sacrifices" noted that

> the Jewish Law expressly ordered the immolation of men dedicated to the Lord (Lev. 27:29). . . . Human blood sacrifices were thus clearly established. No historical detail is better attested. A nation can only be judged by its own archives.[5]

The article "Jews" (frequently omitted from modern editions) stated that

> it is then too true that the Jews, according to their Law, sacrificed human victims. This act of religion was in accordance with their manners. . . .
>
> Did the Jews eat human flesh? Among your calamities which have so often made me shudder, I have always reckoned your misfortune in having eaten human flesh. You say that this happened only on

[3] For Chrysostom, see above, chap. 1. For Moloch as the devil, see J. B. Russell, *Lucifer: The Devil in the Middle Ages* (Ithaca, N.Y., 1984), p. 249.

[4] J. Trachtenberg, *The Devil and the Jews* (New Haven, 1943), chaps. 9 and 10, though the Molochist background is not sketched. Cf. Russell, *Lucifer*, p. 192, for recent bibliography.

[5] Voltaire, *Philosophical Dictionary*, ed. T. Besterman (Harmondsworth, 1971), pp. 256f. See also above, chap. 1.

great occasions. . . . Either renounce your sacred books . . . or acknowledge that your forefathers offered up to God rivers of human blood unparalleled by any people on earth.[6]

Those biblical passages prohibiting the Moloch cult were taken by Voltaire merely to be evidence of its widespread existence among Jews. Most of this onslaught is well in tune with Voltaire's anti-Christian sentiments, and he readily confesses that the Christians too had their ritual of human sacrifice in the form of the Inquisition. But for Voltaire, of course, that only proved the double guilt of the Jews, for they had engendered Christianity and staffed the new cult with converted Jews.

This promising line, at once anti-Christian and anti-Jewish, was followed up enthusiastically by German revolutionists of all stripes in the aftermath of the Damascus Blood Libel of 1840, undoubtedly a major turning point in the history of modern Jew-hatred. This anachronistically "medieval" incident, in which the Jews of Damascus were accused of murdering a Christian friar to obtain blood for their rituals, anticipated the Dreyfus trial as a *cause célèbre* and litmus test of liberalism. Though the French consul approved the libel, it was repudiated by most educated French opinion. In Germany, however, some of the most advanced thinkers found it a not improbable charge; they welcomed it as confirming—albeit rather crudely—their secular theory that Judaism was the religion of human sacrifice.[7]

The new secularized Blood Libel developed rapidly along two main lines. The first of these was the literalist allegation that some Jews had remained acolytes of Moloch and, furthermore, passed the cult on to the early Christians. The second line was the radical socialist revelation that the Jews had transformed their religion of actual blood sacrifice into a metaphorical shedding of blood—that is, they had transformed the cult of Moloch into Mammon.

The major proponent of the charge that the Jews were literal Molochists was the well-known crackpot Georg Friedrich Daumer, who, in 1839, deduced that the sabbath was instituted as the day of sacrifice to a Moloch disguised as Jehovah. But it was the Damascus Affair that really got him going, exploring old cellars in Nuremberg for human bones and mapping the spread of cannibal Jews to the shores of Tahiti and Australia. Daumer's grotesque work *The Fire and Moloch Cult of the Ancient Hebrews* of 1842 claimed that the efforts of Moses and the prophets to replace the sacrifice of the firstborn by the Pass-

---

[6] See Voltaire, *A Philosophical Dictionary.* trans. E. R. Drumont (New York, 1932), 2:99–115.

[7] For the Damascus Affair, see below, chap. 9 (Heine).

over offering had been resisted by King Solomon and that the ritual had survived in different guises until the present, as the Damascus Affair proved.

Daumer's works also influenced Feuerbach's famous attacks on Christianity. Even though Feuerbach had the sense to break with this "slave of a sick imagination" in 1844, he had earlier used Daumer's erudition to elaborate in the second edition of the *Essence of Christianity* a historical basis for his philosophical view that Judaism was a religion of egoism, and ultimately one of the stomach. In the notes to this edition Feuerbach stated:

> Human sacrifice belongs to the very idea of religion. Bloody human sacrifices only dramatize this idea. . . . On the human sacrifices in the Jewish religion, we refer the reader to the works of Daumer and Ghillany.

Daumer was not at all interested in the political aspects of the Jewish Question. In the course of the "Bruno Bauer controversy" of 1843, however, his follower Friedrich Wilhelm Ghillany applied Daumer's esoteric Blood Libel to the politics of the Jewish Question, citing it as evidence that the Jews were too depraved to receive civil and political rights.[8]

The second main line taken by the secular Blood Libel after 1840— the socialist—was spelled out by Marx and Moses Hess in two notorious articles of 1843–44.[9] Marx's piece on *The Jewish Question* did not quite descend to the use of the blood metaphor, but Mammon is triumphantly present as the modern form of Moloch:

> The god of practical need and egoism is money. . . . Money is the jealous God of Israel. . . . Money debases all the gods of mankind and turns them into commodities. . . . Money is the alienated essence of man's labor and life.

Behind this theorizing lay an undoubted acquaintance with the more lurid imagery of his then close associate Moses Hess. In his Zionistic *Rome and Jerusalem* (1862) Hess recalled how the Damascus Affair had shaken him into trying to find a guarantee of a better life for the

---

[8] Daumer was successively a Protestant, Hegelian, and Catholic, and also tried to become a Reform Jew. He was the guardian of the famous foundling Caspar Häuser. For Daumer, Ghillany, and Feuerbach, see below, chap. 14.

[9] For the following references to Marx and Hess, see below, chaps. 17 and 18. Among some French socialists, particularly the Blanquists, the Moloch theme was given a strongly racist tinge, as in Gustave Tridon's *Du Molochisme Juif* (Paris, 1884; written in 1866–68), which draws on Gobineau and Renan. Cf. Silberner, *Sozialisten*, pp. 66ff.

Jews. His early *European Triarchy* of 1841 had called upon his fellow Jews to redeem themselves from the sterile existence of Ahasverus by joining through intermarriage the progressive forces of the new Europe. But in his "Philosophy of Action" of 1843, Hess grew more radical and hostile, equating for the first time bourgeois society and egoism with Judaism, and setting his critique in the context of Molochism. Following Daumer and Ghillany, Hess now identified the Jewish Jehovah with the egoistic god Moloch who dominates society:

> The essence of religion and politics consists in absorbing the real life of the real individual. . . . Moloch is the archetype. Human sacrifices form everywhere the keynote of divine and state service. . . . The Christian God is an imitation of the Jewish Jehovah-Moloch to whom was sacrificed the firstborn. The *juste-milieu* age came to terms with this God by means of money, the firstborn being redeemed by money and animals being sacrificed in their place. The original slaughtered sacrifice was everywhere man—and he remains so sacrificed in a figurative sense.

Here Moloch has become God, who has, in turn, metamorphosed into Mammon.

In *The Essence of Money*, written in 1843 but not published until 1845, Hess took the "money = blood" theme to extremes. This article began by advancing a Rousseauesque morality, though in somewhat gruesome terms:

> What God is for theoretical life, money is for practical life. . . . Money is the hallmark of our slavery, the brand of our servitude. . . . Money is the coagulated blood and sweat of those who market their inalienable property, their real wealth—namely, their life activity—in exchange for something called capital in order to feed cannibalistically off their own fat. . . . Make no mistake; not only we proletarians but also we capitalists are the victims who suck our own blood, consume our own flesh. . . . The money we consume, for which we work, is our own flesh and blood—acquired, looted and consumed by us in its alienated form. We are all, to be honest, cannibals, beasts of prey, bloodsuckers.

The host to this mass of alienated egoistic people living off the metaphorical blood of money is the "Christian world" of bourgeois Europe. But Hess is so seduced by the logic of the radical critique of Judaism that he must go on, via a congealed series of metaphors about carnivorous animals, to characterize Christian Europe as essentially "Jewish":

We find ourselves at the apex of the social animal world; we are now social beasts of prey. . . . We are no longer herbivores like our gentle ancestors. . . . We are bloodsuckers. . . . Man enjoys his life in the form of money in a brutal, bestial, cannibalistic way. Money is social blood, but alienated spilled blood.

In the natural history of the social animal world the Jews had the world-historical mission of developing the beast of prey in mankind and they have now completed their task. The mystery of Judaism and Christianity has been revealed in the modern Jewish-Christian peddler-world. The mystery of the blood of Christ, like that of the ancient Jewish reverence for blood, appears now finally unveiled as the mystery of the beast of prey.

Hess was in this essay doubtless trying to rescue Jews from the concrete Blood Libel of the Damascus Affair by cleverly showing that the interest of modern Jews was directed towards the metaphorical blood of money rather than human sacrifice. Better educated in Judaism than was Marx, Hess might have happened upon his idea of a metaphorical approach to "blood" through an awareness that in Hebrew the plural of the word for blood also signifies "money" (*dam, damim*), a fact full of allegorical potential. Unfortunately, Hess seems to have been quite blind to the possibility that he was invoking a powerful emotional anti-Jewish image that was deeply embedded in Christian consciousness. And even if he intended his thrust to be as much against Christian as against Jewish capitalism he was flagrantly careless in his singling out the Jewish denizens of the "social animal world." He lists its inhabitants as "beasts of prey, bloodsuckers, Jews, money-wolves." The secularized, universal Blood Libel of capitalism thus remains specifically Jewish. In later years, Hess sought to combat this impression by emphasizing how the Jewish Jehovah represented the genuinely social ethics of justice and humanity. But it was too late to be of avail in the dismantling of the mythology of the new Blood Libel constructed by the German revolution.

# Myth and Reality in Antisemitic Mentalities

AHASVERUS, Moloch, and Mammon were the mythological figures conjured up in the early nineteenth century to express a secular vision of the need for a revolutionary change both in Judaism and in humanity. For the new secularized religions these figures personified the evil from which mankind had to be redeemed by a revolution of the spirit as well as of society. It was essentially a "Jewish" evil, taking the forms of lovelessness, egoism, and Mammonism. Through such distortions, modern Jews now sacrificed humanity just as their ancestors had crucified Christ. Ahasverus lived on into the present as an eternal reminder of that archetypal human sacrifice, and was modernized as the symbol of the loveless crucifixion of humanity. The Jewish devotees of Moloch and Mammon were continuing the sacrifice by means of money and egoism. By 1840, thanks to this paralleling and interweaving of meanings, the Ahasverus, Moloch, and Mammon myths all had fused psychologically into a general image of the sacrifice of human beings.

This confluence of Ahasverus and Moloch is not, however, unique to the nineteenth century, for a deep symbolic and mythogenic connection had always existed between Moloch and Ahasverus. It is a connection that is able to throw a powerful light on some of the most fundamental problems of the phenomenon of antisemitism. What is the relationship between a universal "antisemitism" and its multitude of special forms or "antisemitisms"? Is there a specific and permanent core of antisemitic emotion that is always present beneath these varying forms? Is there an inner unity to all forms of antisemitism, despite the shaping effect that varying social or intellectual circumstances have on its precise form of expression? While fully granting the significance of these various forms or antisemitisms, might there be more to be gained in insight and analysis by assuming that antisemitism is a universal mental structure, responding to an emotional imperative, rather than being simply a set of responses to a particular social, economic, political, or doctrinal condition? Without an approach of such explanatory power, we are all too often left with a chaotic set of phenomena—a miscellaneous collection of different antisemitisms—that have no common factor other than that they are directed against Jews (and even that is not really a common factor since extreme anti-Zionists claim that they are not anti-Jewish).[1]

The riddle of antisemitic mentality, then, is this: Why is it that the Jews have been seen by so many disparate thinkers and groups as being the archetypal enemies of love and freedom and indeed of the whole human race? The historian here is not faced with the usual transient antagonism that every minority is liable to encounter. Anti-Jewish feeling has been one of the most abiding emotions of European, and indeed, now world history, and it requires from the historian some sort of interpretation that is at once general and specific. A clue to such an interpretation may be found in the profound psychological and symbolic relationship between the loveless Wandering Jew and the dread cult of Moloch.[2]

In European culture the Jews have always occupied a unique position as the sacred executioners of Christ. The Crucifixion, which, for the sake of argument, may be reduced anthropologically to the type of a human sacrifice designed to relieve the social guilt of the community, might have remained an internal Jewish affair had it not been for one thing—that Christ was believed to be the Son of God.[3] This belief raised the event to cosmic significance since it was now seen as bringing redemption to the whole world. The problem was that the Jews refused to become part of the new Christian universal

[1] See H. Mayer, *Outsiders* (Cambridge, Mass., 1982), pp. 338f., 394, 397: "A somewhat awkward terminology that speaks of Zionists instead of Jews, ostensibly not wishing to eliminate the Jewish outsider but the state of Israel and ostensible Jewish imperialism, has added nothing new. . . . Whoever attacks 'Zionism' but under no circumstances means to say anything against 'Jews' is deceiving himself or others. . . . The hindrances that embarrassed the unfolding of anti-Semitism after Auschwitz have in the meantime fallen by the wayside, if Shylock is seen as the state of Israel . . . an outsider state. . . . It can virtually signify the new genocide." In 1981 a German Evangelical Church group issued a declaration defining the "New Anti-Semitism" as nothing more than the old antisemitism hiding behind criticism of Israel. "It is anti-Semitism when erroneous actions by the Israeli government are judged one-sidedly, without regard for the actions of Israel's enemies, and are pointed out and judged more sharply than similar actions by other governments," quoted in *Commentary* (Oct., 1982), p. 66. Using this criterion, it is instructive to compare the international media outcry that greeted the Israeli siege of Beirut in 1982 with the muted response a year later to the similar siege by the PLO of the Lebanese city of Tripoli.

[2] For the connection I am indebted to Hyam Maccoby's intriguing analyses *The Sacred Executioner* and "The Legend of the Wandering Jew" (see above, chap. 2, n. 1). The association of the Ahasverus and Moloch myths in many nineteenth-century writings had struck me before Maccoby's work suggested that the two subjects were mythopoeically intertwined.

[3] This reductionist argument is outlined here only for the sake of explaining a particular aspect of the Crucifixion. Christianity—like any other religion—is, of course, much more than anthropological reductionists would like to allow.

human community and, unlike the Roman participants in the sacred execution, they conspicuously survived to bear the guilt not only of the sacrifice of a man, but of a God.

The guilt that attaches in many cultures to the ritual sacrificer of human beings is a peculiar one and the ancient Jews were well aware of its nature. There is an intimation of the accursed character of the sacred executioner in the wandering punishment inflicted on Cain for the murder of his brother Abel. The Jews had sought to abolish Molochist human sacrifice, first by commuting it to animal sacrifice (as in the story of Abraham's frustrated sacrifice of Isaac) and subsequently (in their later prophetic and rabbinical literature) to prayer. While the Temple stood, the executioner as well as his victim had found substitutes in the Day of Atonement ritual of the High Priest and the scapegoat; one goat was sacrificed and another sent laden with the sins of the people into the wilderness. In Hebrew culture, therefore, the practice of human sacrifice had long ceased, even if an archaic memory of it endured.

For Christians, however, the solution was not so easy: the sacrifice of Christ as they saw it raised the question of what should be done with his sacred executioners. Like Cain, the Jews held a peculiarly ambiguous position, accursed as murderers, yet under a divine protection that was also a punishment in itself. In the Middle Ages, this was mirrored in the institution of the ghetto as a social "mark of Cain"; here the accursed Jews bought themselves a protection that kept them apart from Christian humanity. In 1208 Innocent III had dramatically linked the wandering Jews to the sacred executioner, and signaled this extension of the symbolic into the realm of social practice:

> God made Cain into a vagabond and a fugitive upon the earth. . . .
> Thus, the Jews, against whom the blood of Jesus Christ calls out, although they are not to be killed lest Christian people forget the divine law, must remain vagabonds upon the earth until their faces be covered with shame and they seek the name of Jesus Christ the Lord.[4]

The connection was thus fixed in the Christian mind—simultaneously on a formal, psychological, and social level—between the role of the Jews as human sacrificers and their wanderings in Europe. The symbolism of the Ahasverus and Moloch myths had fused.

What produced the sudden clarification of the Ahasverus myth during the Reformation? One major reason may be that the explo-

[4] For the Bull of 17 January 1208, see *HAS*, 1:242, citing Migne, *Patrologia Latina*, vol. 215, p. 1291, no. 190. Cf. R. Mellinkoff, *The Mark of Cain* (Berkeley, Calif., 1981).

sion of social violence in the religious wars, which was focused in the ritualized murders ordered by the heresy and witchcraft trials, imposed a fresh heavy burden of guilt on Christian communities. As the religious literature of the sixteenth century testifies, Christians were more anxious than ever to reassure themselves that Christ had died to remove *their* guilt. It was natural, therefore, that a corresponding psychological need grew to have the Jews relieve this general guilt besetting Christendom by acting out their proper role as scapegoats for the communal guilt of an age of brutalism. This need for redemption stimulated Christians to invent a particular but symbolic Jew who testified voluntarily to the deicidal, sacrificial guilt that the stubborn Jews had so far refused to admit. Previously ill-defined and lacking even an agreed name for its hero, the legend of the Wandering Jew suddenly sprang into sharp relief, with sightings reported all over Europe, to remind Christians that the Jews were indeed the sacred executioners and must shoulder the guilt of all sinning humanity.

If 1542 marks the clear resolution of the features of the Christian myth of the Ahasverus out of its blurred medieval lineaments, then 1840 is the critical year for the emergence of the Molochist myth of the Jews as the sacred executioners of mankind. Yet the 1830s and 1840s were also the decades when a new, secularized, non-Christian myth of Ahasverus was being formed. In these critical decades, then, we find the confluence of various mythological currents—the Wandering Jew, the Damascus Blood Libel, the revival of the charge of Molochism, the stamping of the Jews as loveless, egoistic worshipers, and the makers of an inhuman capitalistic society—all flowing together into a broad new river of modern antisemitism. It was, however, a river that followed an older channel marked out by the most ancient theme of the wandering guilt of the sacred executioner. The mythopoeic expressions of this theme, Ahasverus and Moloch-Mammon, are truly the psychological engines of the revolutionary Jew-hatred of the nineteenth century.

---

Much of the symbolic power of Ahasverus and Moloch in the nineteenth century derived from their plasticity, from their ability to fuse and intertwine according to the contexts into which they were summoned forth. Thus, the significance of these archetypal myths in the history of antisemitism lies in their indefiniteness and their permutability rather than merely in their particular representation of individual themes. In fact, these twin myths are invested with an enormous psychic energy that transcends any restrictive specific meaning.

Of course, it is useful to analyze the intellectual or ideological function of the myths, but their real power is to be seen in the dimensions
of emotion and psychology, where they act as dynamic agents that
serve to unify the history of European Jew-hatred.

This powerful unifying function may be seen in various contexts.
Above all, Ahasverus leaps across the gulf between the two great
movements of Christian and secular antisemitism. In both mentalities
is found lurking his symbolic essence—namely, inherited collective
Jewish guilt. But secularization brought new possibilities for anti-Jewish theorizing that were ultimately to be more perilous for Jews than
the old Christian framework. With the rise of a secular philosophy,
Ahasverus mutated to become the symbol of an enlightened "noble-
minded" Jew-hatred, which preached human redemption as the
greatest good of mankind. In Germany, reason and revolution were
conscripted into the service of the new secular antisemitism. Ahasverus retained his status as the emblem of Jewish stubbornness, but
now his symbolic qualities were translated into the enlightened modern terminology of human freedom and moral enslavement, egoism
and lovelessness, reconciliation to nature and to history. In revolutionary and rationalist discourses Ahasverus frequently makes personal appearances, but sometimes he is represented only by his qualities and attributes. Incognito or no, the Wandering Jew is a
perennial protagonist in the revolutionary debate, not only on the
Jewish Question in particular, but on the nature of German and human freedom and history in general.

There is more than just a continuity involved here. The question
must be faced of whether there is a unitary psychological structure to
antisemitism. This may be put into terms of the relative merits of
"analogy" versus "morphology" as means of historically understanding the various phenomena of antisemitism. An analogical interpretation would allow that interesting parallels exist between the antisemitisms of different historical periods, but that these parallels—as
with the forms of the Ahasverus myth—are very limited and indeed
accidental. A morphological approach, on the other hand, implies
that Christian and revolutionary antisemitisms both reflect the same
kind of inner psychological structure, albeit one whose formal expression mutates as intellectual and religious systems change.

Moreover, a morphological interpretation implies a dynamic potential—an inner developmental logic—within the systems of ideas
themselves, which drives them to change and transformation. Morphology, therefore, has the double advantage of understanding
antisemitism as a universal and at the same time admitting the historical conditioning of the various antisemitisms. It avoids the tendency

of the analogical approach simply to accept the proliferation of antisemitisms as a chaotic mystery.

The Ahasverus myth thus unifies Christian and secular antisemitisms. It also acts as a unifying theme within the flux of new ideas and
ideologies that constitute the German revolutionary movement of the
nineteenth century, pointing to a deeper unity existing beneath the
superficial welter of formal disputes between right and left. It is, for
instance, generally assumed that the "left-wing" antisemitism of Marx
had nothing in common with the racial antisemitism of his erstwhile
Young Hegelian comrades Bruno Bauer and Wilhelm Marr. Certainly, German antisemitism, like the interpretation of Ahasverus,
modulated in the mid-nineteenth century into new racial keys; but
the basic essence of Ahasverus, and of revolutionary antisemitism, remained the same. Just as in the old Christian and the more recent
"enlightened" contexts, so in the new racist setting Ahasverus signified the immutable character of the Jewish people.[5] Of course, a biological explanation was now given by the racists for the persistence of
Jewish national characteristics, but these were still the very same unpleasing traits that had disturbed traditional Christians, "enlightened" philosophers, and revolutionary Germans alike. The Ahasverus myth may have changed its vocabulary, but its essential
meaning had not altered.

A third aspect of the unifying power of the Ahasverus and Moloch
myths—and perhaps the most dangerous—is their capacity to fuse
together symbol and reality, so that the ordinary Jews of the social
environment were imbued with a supernatural demonic significance.
Christianity had seen in Jews a frightening combination of social de-
viance and cosmic religious guilt, as the devil's accomplices.[6] Yet,
though often persecuted, expelled, and massacred, at least the possibility of their social existence had not been totally rejected. On a *social*
level, somewhere, the Jews might be allowed to exist. There were
many specific reasons offered for this permitted survival: the Jews
were necessary for economic reasons; they might serve as living re-
minders of the peril of rejecting Christ; and so forth. Yet it is the
mental structure that underlies these various justifications that really
matters. Despite its frequent intrusion into the political and social
world, Christianity was ultimately a religious mythology and it was

[5] It is no accident that the most virulent of all Nazi antisemitic films was *Der ewige
Jude.* Curiously, A. Leschnitzer, "Der Gestaltwandel Ahasvers," in *Zwei Welten*, ed.
H. Tramer (Jerusalem, 1962), thinks that the Third Reich made no use of the Wandering Jew theme in its propaganda; yet, apart from the film, a major antisemitic ex-
hibition was held in 1938–39 under the title of *Der ewige Jude.*

[6] Cf. J. Trachtenberg, *The Devil and the Jews* (New Haven, 1943).

because of this that the Christian negation of Judaism in the end took place on a theological plane. Consequently, on the worldly social level, Christianity was often able to tolerate and coexist with its mythological antithesis of Judaism. There was a fortunate discrepancy between social reality and religious mythology, which could sometimes protect the Jews from social, as opposed to mythological, "destruction."

The real danger began when Christianity was superseded by a new secular mythology of reason and revolution that claimed dominion over the whole territory of society, a territory that had never been the primary concern of Christianity, no matter how successful it had been in acquiring temporal power. In the new revolutionary epoch, the mythological and the social were no longer two distinct worlds as in the Christian mental structure, but had now fused together. The revolution demanded jurisdiction over both the realm of mythology and of society. The result was that there was no longer permitted any autonomous social space for Jews to live within. Secular revolutionary mythology not only negated Judaism on a mythological level as had Christianity, but also negated the future existence of Judaism on the social level that had always been theoretically independent of Christian religious mythology. The Jews must sooner or later disappear, either through assimilation or less pleasant means. This was the revolutionary demand, a demand that was at once mythological and social. Paradoxically, the rise of secularism in Germany meant that the Jews lost the secular space in which they so long found refuge.

All this may seem rather abstract, but it helps to explain how in Hitler's political vision we find present—along with an awful practicality—a dreamlike quality that seems to belong to the realm of the religious and the supernatural. In Hitlerism, the barrier that normally exists between mythologizing fantasy and social reality seems to have been abolished. Much of the theoretical foundation for this process had been laid down by the Christian construction of the Jewish people as the *symbol* of everything that obstructs redemption and, at the same time, as the actual *practical* obstacles to that redemption. This view had been carried forward by the German philosophers and secularists for whom the Jews both *symbolized* and actually *were* the forces opposing reason, freedom, and love. Symbol and reality increasingly became one and the same as the distinction dwindled between secular mythology and the real world in which it operated. The twin paths of the evolution of nineteenth-century German antisemitism intertwined—the mythological path producing such new ideological forms as racial biology, the social and political path engendering the antisemitic parties of the 1880s. Thus, more and more, a dream-

like symbolic perception of the Jews was being applied without me-
diation of any sort to the real world, so that in the increasingly bizarre
world of German antisemitism, practical politics assumed the nature
of a phantasm. And since the mythological world of dreams and the
real world of society were now congruent, there remained nothing in
the end to stop the dreadful excesses of dream and fantasy from being enacted in political life and imposed on real, living Jews. In Nazi
Germany, the world of nightmares in the end completely took over
the world of everyday political life. The drive to unite the symbolic
and the real attained its final fulfillment in the death camps. A mythological hell had become real.[7] This was the ultimate practical
achievement of a century and a half of the mythogenic development
of German revolutionary antisemitism.

[7] See T. Des Près, *The Survivor: An Anatomy of Life in the Death Camps* (New York,
1976) for the transformation of nightmares into reality.

For the interaction of the twin processes of the secularization of religion and the
sacralization of politics, see U. Tal, "On Structures of Political Theology and Myth in
Germany prior to the Holocaust," in *The Holocaust as Historical Experience*, ed. Y. Bauer
and N. Rotenstreich (New York, 1981), pp. 43–74.

# PART TWO

# Archaeology of Revolutionary Antisemitism

# CHAPTER 5

# The Jewish Question: Conceptions and Misconceptions

A GREAT deal of modern scholarship on the Jewish Question in Germany in the first half of the nineteenth century has been undermined by a number of misconceptions. Chief among these has been a liberal prejudice that sees the debate as revolving around the central issue of Jewish emancipation, meaning the granting of civil and political rights to the Jews of Germany. Historians have been rather too quick to accept the views of Gabriel Riesser (1806–63) and his liberal contemporaries who at the time—admittedly for the best of moral reasons—reduced the Jewish Question to one simply of Jewish rights. This approach, however, leads immediately to paradoxes and contradictions where the critical historian is concerned. For instance, it renders unintelligible the attitudes of those many thinkers ranging from Hegel to Gutzkow, Laube, and Marx who combined support for the granting of Jewish rights with a profound and often fervent hostility to Judaism and "Jewishness." Such problematic cases as these—and indeed the whole tortuous evolution of Jewish-German relations—must create a strong suspicion that any interpretation that sees the essence of the Jewish Question before 1850 as residing purely in equality of rights is not only anachronistic but historically forgetful of the central issues of the debate.[1]

---

[1] Useful narratives and documentation of the Jewish Question are S. Dubnow, *History of the Jews*, trans. (London, 1973), vols. 4 and 5; R. Mahler, *A History of Modern Jewry 1780–1815* (New York, 1971); idem, *Jewish Emancipation: Selected Documents* (New York, 1941); I. Freund, *Die Emanzipation der Juden in Preussen* (Berlin, 1912); A. Bein, *Die Judenfrage* (Stuttgart, 1980); J. Carlebach, *Karl Marx and the Radical Critique of Judaism* (London, 1978), pp. 9–90. A large body of useful material has been brought together by A. Low, *Jews in the Eyes of the Germans: From the Enlightenment to Imperial Germany* (Philadelphia, 1979), although its analysis is conducted in excessively liberal terms. The three best accounts—each very different—of the role of antisemitism in the Jewish Question are E. Sterling, *Judenhass: Die Anfänge des politischen Antisemitismus in Deutschland 1815–1850* (Frankfurt, 1969); L. Poliakov, *The History of Anti-Semitism* (London, 1975), vol. 3; J. Katz, *From Prejudice to Destruction: Anti-Semitism 1700–1933* (Cambridge, Mass.), 1980.

Recent analytical treatments include the important essay by J. Katz, "The Term 'Jewish Emancipation': Its Origin and Historical Impact," in his *Emancipation and Assimilation: Studies in Modern Jewish History* (Farnborough, Hamps., Eng., 1972), pp. 21–45. (Cf. his *Jewish Emancipation and Self-Emancipation* [Philadelphia, 1986].) R. Rürup,

The fundamental theme that divided opinion in the period before 1850 was not rights, but Jewish "national character" and its relation to German national character. It was a theme that dominated several distinct phases of the argument. During the Enlightenment phase of the 1780s the "improvability" of Jewish national character had been seen by rationalist and statist commentators as vital to making the Jews useful to the state and so justifying them "in the eyes of reason." When rationalism yielded to nationalism two decades later, the "unimprovability" of Jewish character—as evidenced in its permanent "alienness" from German character—became a central theme across the spectrum of German public opinion from right to left. Even though Jewish national character figured in the hotheaded antisemi-

---

*Emanzipation und Antisemitismus: Studien zur Judenfrage der bürgerlichen Gesellschaft* (Göttingen, 1975); idem, "Emanzipationsgeschichte und Antisemitismusforschung," in *Antisemitismus und Jüdische Geschichte: Studien zu Ehren von Herbert A. Strauss*, ed. R. Erb et al. (Berlin, 1987), pp. 467–78; idem, "Emancipation and Antisemitism: Some Connecting Links," in *The Antisemitism in Our Time*, ed. L. Eitinger (Oslo, 1984), pp. 28–37; idem, "Emanzipation und Antisemitismus: Historische Verbindungslinien," in *Antisemitismus: Von der Judenfeindschaft zu Holocaust*, ed. H. A. Strauss and N. Kampe (Frankfurt, 1985), pp. 88–89. J. Toury, "The 'Jewish Question': A Semantic Approach," *LBIY* 11 (1966): 85–106; H. D. Schmidt, "The Terms of the Emancipation: The Public Debate . . . ," *LBIY* 1 (1956): 28–47; S. W. Baron, "Étapes de l'émancipation juive," *Diogenes* 29 (1960): 56–81, and his article on "Jewish Emancipation" in the *Encyclopaedia of the Social Sciences* (New York, 1963), 8:394–99. Several of these accounts tend to reduce the Jewish Question to equality of rights. Moreover, there is often a lack of precision as to exactly which rights were in question and to whom exactly they were to be granted. For the restricted nature of apparently generous grants to the Jews, see the important article by H. Arendt, "Privileged Jews," in *Emancipation and Counter-Emancipation*, ed. A. G. Duker and M. Ben-Horin (New York, 1974), pp. 56–87.

On the "social facts" of Polish-Jewish immigration, see S. A. Aschheim, *Brothers and Strangers: The East European Jew in German and German-Jewish Consciousness 1800–1923* (Madison, Wis., 1982), chap. 1. There are also two provocative articles by H. Brunschwig, "L'Aufklärung et le mouvement philosémite en Prusse à la fin du dix-huitième siècle," and "La lutte de l'Aufklärung contre les orthodoxes juifs en Prusse à la fin du dix-huitième siècle," in *Annales Historiques de la Revolution Francaise* 12 (1935): 385–415, and 13 (1936): 436–59. These have been translated and expanded in his *Enlightenment and Romanticism in Eighteenth-Century Prussia* (Chicago, 1974), pp. 249–92. Brunschwig argues from a rationalist prejudice that sees the obvious orthodoxy and differentness of the mass of Jews as posing a real problem not only for enlightened Prussian administrators but also enlightened Jewish reformers. I have tried here to take the social facts into account without uncritically accepting (as does Brunschwig) that the enlightened officials were entirely objective about their assessment of Jewish character. There is nevertheless a real problem here that, if one excepts the horde of antisemitic writers on the subject, seems to have been discussed frankly only by Brunschwig and Schmidt ("The Terms") and most recently, Aschheim, *Brothers and Strangers*, chap. 1. (The tone of some of Brunschwig's comments is unfortunate.) By contrast, Katz's liberal treatment does not attempt to assess how far "peddling" and pauperization adversely affected Jewish character (*Out of the Ghetto* [Cambridge, Mass., 1973], pp. 68f., 186).

tism of the crudest German nationalists, the same basic notions about its unimprovability and alienness were to be found in numerous thinkers of an idealist and revolutionary cast of mind, beginning with Kant and Fichte, who were by no means empty-headed chauvinists. Riesser might dismiss "national character" as irrelevant to the Jewish Question, but for many "pro-Jewish" as well as antisemitic authors, Jewish national character was indeed the crux of the matter—without it there was nothing much to discuss. It can only be written off by modern historians because of a now automatic sympathy with Riesser's political views.

This is not, of course, to say that "national character" was or is necessarily a valid *political* category, but it is certainly a *historical* category that needs to be taken very seriously by any critical historian seeking to understand the lost intellectual and social world of nineteenth-century Germany. Nor, it should be emphasized, must national character as a historical category be reduced anachronistically to "race" as has become the common practice in the last fifty years of historical writing. Some of the most ardent German believers in national character rejected explicitly the notion that it was racial by nature. Admittedly, most nationalists tended to see national character as racially determined and immutable, and this subsequently became the dominant way of understanding national character in the twentieth century. But this does not mean that Kant, Fichte, and Herder were "racists," intensely hostile to Judaism as they were. The historical reality is far too complex to be interpreted as a crude polemic over race. So again, we should beware of being unhistorical and of imposing rigid categories of post-1850 thinking upon an earlier, more fluid period of German perceptions of the Jewish Question.

The conceptual framework of the Jewish Question before 1850— by which date it had become simplified and consolidated into well-defined liberal, nationalist, and revolutionary elements—was indisputably richer and subtler than it has appeared to most modern writers. During this formative age of the new enlightened secular criticism of the Jews, it even appeared for a time that anti-Jewish feelings could be seen as quite compatible with a certain measure of support for Jewish rights, and indeed even with a certain friendliness towards the Jews. By the second half of the nineteenth century, however, such diverse inclinations were no longer reconcilable; by then, antisemites were by definition opposed to Jewish equality of rights. From this time on, feeling against Judaism was logically identified with antagonism to Jewish emancipation, so that the former combination of hostility to Judaism and support for Jewish rights was no longer comprehensible and could only be understood as some kind of bewildering paradox. Henceforth, the basic categories for discussing the Jewish Question become the straightforwardly opposed ones of "liberal" and "antisemite." The age of that strange combination, the "liberal antisemite," had passed—at least in theory.

---

The confusion caused by partisan and often anachronistic preference for a liberal conception of the Jewish Question has been worsened by a number of basic analytical failures surprising in so well-examined a subject.

The first of these has been a failure to clarify and define the precise rights involved in the contemporary discussion of the Jewish Question. These were variously described in writings of the time as human, natural, civil, and political rights.[2] There was no agreement at that time on the precise meanings of these terms, and because modern scholars and readers alike have imported their own personal understandings of these labels into the discussion, most later accounts of "Jewish emancipation" have proven somewhat idiosyncratic. "Human," "civil," and "political" rights have by now become freely interchangeable and hence meaningless terms. Despite this semantic fog, however, some effort has to be made to clarify the terms in a way that does not do violence to their common usage during the pre-1850 phase of the debate on the Jewish Question.

By "human rights," most German authors of that early period understood the rights of the Jews to follow their own religion and to live protected from the arbitrary violence of their Christian enemies. Except on the part of those who demanded the expulsion or murder of the Jews, these human rights were generally conceded (at least in theory) to the Jews of Germany.

"Civil rights" were also conceded by many German public figures and governments in the course of the first half of the nineteenth century, despite widespread social resistance to this policy. At the time, it was the process of granting these civil rights that was popularly understood as "Jewish emancipation," but the rights were complicated, and there was immense variation across Germany over precisely which rights were to be conceded. Basically, these rights consisted in the repeal of medieval and later Christian laws discriminating against the Jews, including special taxation and levies; bans on landholding and agriculture on the part of Jews; forced res-

---

[2] M. Stolleis, "Untertan-Bürger-Staatsbürger," in *Bürger und Bürgerlichkeit im Zeitalter der Aufklärung* (Wolfenbütteler Studien zur Aufklärung, Bd. 7, Heidelberg, 1981), pp. 65–99, which, however, neglects the significance of the Jewish Question for the whole conception of political and civil rights in the period.

idence in ghettoes; limits on the number of Jewish marriages; laws closing honest trades and professions to Jews; and the consequent compulsion, legislated or not, for Jews to pursue marginal and less than wholesome trades such as moneylending and peddling. Seen positively, the repeal of these discriminatory laws meant the conferring of *municipal* citizenship (*Bürgertum*) and free residential rights upon the Jews and the opening to them of landownership and access to the professions.

"Political rights," however, though nowadays regarded as the essence of emancipation, were rarely seen (except by liberals) as legitimate concessions to the Jews and took longer in coming. These amounted mainly to the right to hold political and public office, to act as judges and civil and legal officials, to be a full *state* citizen (*Staatsbürger*) in the most complete sense.

During the century between Joseph II's Edict of Toleration in 1782 and Bismarck's final promulgation of universal equal Jewish rights in the Second Empire in 1871, the history, even the very sequence, of the award of these various rights in the different German-speaking states is very complicated indeed and difficult to reconstruct. Too often accounts of Jewish emancipation blur and confuse the different types of rights, leaving the reader mystified about particular rights conferred by particular legislation in the individual German states. Only if we bear clearly in mind the specific rights under discussion in each particular context may we expect to be able to understand the views of an individual author or any school of thinkers on the Jewish Question. And we must, too, always remember that for the very heterogeneous group of thinkers outside the properly liberal camp (some of them in favor of the Jews, others opposed), the essence of the matter was not the rights themselves, but the moral, alien character of the Jewish people.

A second major failure of the analysis of Jewish rights has been the absence of any serious effort to discover precisely which Jews were to receive such rights as were offered on occasion. The liberal prejudice is to see "Jews" as meaning the totality of the Jewish community within the borders of the state. But in the eyes of many administrators, the "Jews" to be granted rights consisted only of a small select class of the Jewish population.[3] Moreover, it was not always the inten-

---

[3] R. Rürup's useful survey, "The Tortuous and Thorny Path to Legal Equality: 'Jew Laws' and Emancipatory Legislation in Germany from the Late Eighteenth Century," *LBIY* 31 (1986): 3–33, may mislead less-informed readers when it says (p. 14) that the "Edict conferred on all Prussian Jews [state-citizenship] . . . unless specifically excluded by other provisions." The phrase "all Prussian Jews" suggests that only a few Jews were excluded under such provisions.

tion of emancipatory legislation to absorb in a liberal fashion the Jews into Christian society; very often the "emancipated" Jews remained constitutionally a caste or a *Stand* apart from their Christian fellow citizens.

This suggests a third aspect of the Jewish Question that has yet to be analyzed—that beneath the surface of the political argument, the real issue was administrative and turned on conceptions of naturalization and immigration law. It should be remembered that the mere fact of birth within a German state did not confer citizenship as it does in some modern liberal states. There are, in fact, two distinct traditions of citizenship law. One is the Roman idea of citizenship by consent, that is, consent of the state as well as of the subject, whereby the actual place of birth is immaterial; what matters here is the citizenship status of one's parents. The other tradition is that of citizenship by ascription, in which the place of birth is all important; this concept of *jus soli* is embodied in United States citizenship law.[4] In Germany, where the Roman law tradition prevailed, Jews were rather in the position of modern *Gastarbeiter*, whose children born in their temporary country of domicile do not as a rule acquire West German citizenship. Accordingly, most of the debate on Jewish rights in Germany took place on the level of modern immigration and citizenship law, that is administrative law, rather than on the level of present-day civil and political rights legislation as is so often erroneously assumed.

Here again one must be very careful of imposing anachronistic modern liberal categories of thinking on the German reality of the nineteenth century. What often looks like a liberal granting of rights frequently amounts instead to a notable restriction of rights to a small group, once the administrative definitions of the various edicts are understood. The edicts of emancipation are, in fact, all too often misread as political documents, whereas they are actually very precise administrative legal documents whose definitions must be understood with exactitude. Of course, Riesser and contemporary liberals would have liked very much to transfer the debate to properly political ground, and indeed they tried very hard to do so. But that is no reason for a critical historian to assume that the views of one

[4] Citizenship by ascription or place of birth is feudal in origin, whereas modern citizenship by consent has not only a Roman but also a modern liberal ancestry in that it was proposed by Locke and figures in current British immigration law (cf. the British Nationality Act, 1983). In contrast, the revolutionary liberalism of the United States and France inclines to citizenship by place of birth (*jus soli*), as in the Fourteenth Amendment to the U.S. Constitution. But this principle is now under great pressure in the United States and is likely to be changed. Cf. P. H. Schuck and R. M. Smith, *Citizenship without Consent: Illegal Aliens in the American Polity* (New Haven, 1986).

group of participants in the debate reflected those of all the other participants. One must be extremely wary of mistaking the apparently political forms of the great debate for its administrative and legal substance as it appeared, not only to the opponents of emancipation, but even to many of the leading, nonliberal emancipationists.

Indeed, as a fourth and final failure of analysis, one may instance the tendency to regard all positions favorable to the award of Jewish rights as "liberal." Actually, there were some very diverse justifications given for Jewish emancipation; some were indeed "liberal," but others were "revolutionary," others "tolerationist," yet others "Prussian" or "statist." Only by bearing all these analytical factors in mind can the Jewish Question begin to be understood historically in terms of what it really meant to contemporaries. Only thus may the historian begin to remove what seem to be illogical contradictions and paradoxes in the thought of so many intelligent commentators. What is really needed now is to reconstruct the views on the Jewish Question of such thinkers as Dohm, Kant, Fichte, Herder, and Hegel in a way that will not judge them in liberal terms solely by their attitude to the particular issue of Jewish rights, but rather by their feelings towards "Jewishness" and "Jewish national character." Only then will any sense be made of their—to modern minds—rather peculiar and confused thoughts on the Jewish Question.

---

Any candid discussion of the Jewish Question in German thought must begin with a social fact: Jews were a distinct social group in Germany with customs very different from those of Christian Germans; a different religion; a different language; different family attitudes and values; different ways of life; even a different and noticeable physiognomy. The inevitable problem faced by the Germans was how to deal with this "foreign" nation that lived symbiotically within German society. That the Germans felt this problem to be so overwhelming and central a political issue, that they reacted so hysterically, that so many persuasive rational arguments were advanced all too often in a spirit of essential bad faith masquerading as concern for humanity—all this must ultimately be explained by deep-rooted elements in German culture, German tradition, and the German psyche that cannot be investigated here. But to deny that the phenomenon of German national character is a real category of explanation, to deny the specificity of the various national political and cultural traditions of the European peoples, is to react in a spirit of liberal prejudice which, while it may be morally inspired, is scarcely objective or respectful of historical reality. There is clearly such a thing as German national character, just as there is Jewish national character. These historical concepts begin to be morally dangerous only when they are inadequately analyzed and presented, when, for instance, only the unfavorable aspects of national character are insisted upon in a spirit of bad faith and with intellectual dishonesty. And this is precisely what happened in nineteenth-century Germany.[5]

To the large and varied collection of thinkers who took the national character of the Jews to be the essence of the Jewish Question, two salient features of that character revealed themselves. The first of these was the evident alienness of the Jews. That the Jews formed a separate nation or people seemed beyond doubt, a people of quite marked difference from the German people, although opinions might vary widely on the reason for this difference. Some argued that it came about through an inherited racial character, while others saw it as merely the result of cultural or religious identity. Yet again, others sympathetically inclined to the Jews blamed it on the persecutions practiced against them by Christians over the centuries. But all agreed that Jewish national character was somehow alien, foreign, different from that of the Germans.

The other constituent of Jewish national character was seen as having to do with morality—or rather, the Jewish lack of morality. Many writers, who might otherwise be easily mistaken for Riesserian liberals, began from this position, denouncing the vices of past and contemporary Judaism, but going on sometimes to argue forcefully in favor of Jewish emancipation. To those Jews of the time who wrote in defense of both Judaism and of Jewish emancipation, this strange mixture of prejudice and sympathy on the part of such apparent allies as Dohm, Hegel, and Gutzkow seemed paradoxical; but it need not be so to the modern historian who looks at it through the right conceptual lenses. For these seemingly inconsistent German thinkers, civil rights were really a secondary matter. For them, the primary problem was to how improve morally the national character of the Jews so as to render it compatible with living in a modern European state. Civil rights might certainly be a necessary and desirable means

---

[5] J. Katz, "German Culture and the Jews," *Commentary* (Feb. 1984): 54–59, refers to "factual observations [of Jewish character] which may or may not have been accurate. . . . It is obvious that there are certain qualities which may be called characteristically Jewish, and which would crop up in the work of Jewish artists even after they have assimilated into a non-Jewish culture." Emancipated Jews did not really become "Germans," but rather created for themselves a new "German-Jewish" national character. See D. Sorkin, *The Transformation of German Jewry 1780–1840* (Oxford, 1987).

of moralizing the Jews, but were most definitely not the true heart of the matter.

The imperative of improving Jewish national character produced a general solution to the Jewish Question that was essentially moral: the Jew must be made into a fully moral, free human being. The Jew must be "humanly" emancipated and thus truly redeemed, rather than being simply emancipated politically as the liberals preached. Though the term "Jewish emancipation" was modeled on "Catholic emancipation" and, in fact, gained currency only after the English Catholics won their emancipation in 1828, the two emancipations were not at all the same thing. Catholics were never regarded as "alien," or as politically "immoral" as a *people* or as a *nation*: Catholic emancipation had been a purely political question. But when it came to the Jews, even such a well-intentioned advocate of giving them civil equality as Dohm saw the matter as one of improving the moral character of Jewry for the benefit of the state, rather than of acknowledging the equal rights of the Jews as legally and morally indisputable and self-evident.

Naturally opinion divided on the prospects for this "human" emancipation of the Jews. Dohm insisted that it would come automatically with the removal of discriminatory laws against them, whereas Fichte believed it well-nigh impossible to humanize the Jews since Jewish vice was so embedded in Jewish heads that it would disappear only when those heads were replaced with new ones. Cruder German nationalistic minds did not take long to develop this belief—that the Jews were nationally and unimprovably immoral—into the properly racist theories with which the present century is so well acquainted. What is less well known is that the basic conceptual structure upon which these racist ideas stand was shared with apparently less dangerous, and sometimes even benevolent attitudes, that saw the Jewish Question as rooted in Jewish national character. Such deceptively benign views, favorable though they might be to Jewish civil rights, were predicated upon the alienness and the immorality of the Jewish nation and upon the necessity of improving the Jews' moral character and humanly emancipating them into moral rather than just political freedom. The easy descent into this particular racist Avernus was paved with what purported to be the best of moral intentions.

# CHAPTER 6

# The German Statists and the Jewish Question, 1781–1812: Dohm, Humboldt, and Hardenberg

## DOHM

THE BEGINNING of modern, formal political discussion of the Jewish Question in Germany may be dated to 1781, the year when the Prussian administrator Christian Wilhelm von Dohm (1751–1820) published his book on *The Civil Improvement of the Jews*.[1] It was the first serious attempt to shift the discussion of the Jewish Question from the terms of medieval Christianity into quite new categories typical of secular enlightened thought. In it, Dohm blended arguments taken from the rationalist and humanitarian currents of the Enlightenment with principles of Prussian constitutionalist and raison d'état doctrine. Humanity and politics alike led Dohm to reject the old religious Jew-hatred as medieval, irrational, and unenlightened, and to argue eloquently for granting "equality" (*Gleichmachung*) to the Jews. On the humanitarian side, Dohm invoked the ideas of toleration and liberty of conscience so as to award the Jews not only human rights, but also a wider equality.

[1] Christian Wilhelm von Dohm, *Über die bürgerliche Verbesserung der Juden* (Berlin, 1781–83; repr. Hildesheim, 1973). Page references in text are to this edition. The first part has been translated as *Concerning the Amelioration of the Civil Status of the Jews* (Cincinnati, 1957). The contemporary French translation has been reissued as *De la réforme politique des Juifs*, ed. D. Bourel (Paris, 1984). See now R. Liberles, "Dohm's Treatise on the Jews: A Defense of the Enlightenment," *LBIY* 33 (1988): 29–42; H. Möller, "Aufklärung, Judenemanzipation und Staat: Ursprung und Wirkung von Dohms Schrift . . . ," in *Deutsche Aufklärung und Judenemanzipation*, ed. W. Grab (Tel Aviv, 1980), pp. 119–53; I. Dambacher, *Christian Wilhelm von Dohm: Ein Beitrag zur Geschichte des Preussischen aufgeklärten Beamtentums . . .* (Bern, 1974); *Judentum im Zeitalter der Aufklärung* (Wolfenbütteler Studien zur Aufklärung, Bd. 4) (Heidelberg, 1977). (I have not seen the article by R. Vierhaus, "C. W. von Dohm [1751–1820]," in *Begegnung von Deutschen und Juden in der Geistesgeschichte des 18. Jahrhunderts* [Wolfenbütteler Studien zur Aufklärung] [Heidelberg, 1984].)

For policy under Frederick II, see S. Stern, *Die Preussische Staat und die Juden* (Tübingen, 1962–71), vol. 3. Official papers on the "Jewish Question" are in I. Freund, *Die Emanzipation der Juden in Preussen* (Berlin, 1912). H. Brunschwig, *Enlightenment and Romanticism in Eighteenth-Century Prussia*, trans. (Chicago, 1974), pp. 249–92, overstates the rationalism of the Prussian officials at the expense of the statist element that dominates their public attitudes.

For the Russian bureaucratic approach, see J. Klier, *Russia Gathers Her Jews: The Origins of the "Jewish Question" in Russia 1772–1825* (DeKalb, Ill., 1986).

Dohm's central theme, however, was statist in character and founded on the utility of the Jews to the Prussian government. "Should a number of industrious and law-abiding citizens," he asks, "be less useful to the state because they stem from Asia and differ from others . . . by a special way of worshiping the Supreme Being?" And he answers by demonstrating that the Jewish *religion* in itself is not antisocial enough to "keep the Jews from fulfilling their duty to the state." For Dohm, the Jews are a potential class of productive citizens whose acceptance into Prussia will benefit the state's prosperity and security. The Jewish Question is thus reduced to the basic principle of raison d'état (pp. 4–8).

Dohm accepted it as self-evident that these potential productive citizens were, as a nation, corrupt. The "objective" facts of Jewish life in Prussia proved it—66 percent of the Jews were petty traders and peddlers, while 84 percent of the Jewish population lived in official poverty.[2] Their moral status corresponded to this material wretchedness, both being the result of Christian oppression.

> I may concede that the Jews may be more morally corrupt than other nations, but I must add that this supposed greater moral corruption of the Jews is a necessary and natural consequence of the oppressed condition in which they have been living for so many centuries. . . . Everything the Jews are blamed for is caused by the political conditions under which they now live. (pp. 31ff., 34f.)

This twist enables Dohm to introduce a new note into the official bureaucratic discussions of the Jewish Question with which he was clearly familiar. He now takes the demonstrably corrupt character of the Jews and inverts it from being a reason for denying them admittance to German society into being instead a deformation produced by those oppressive laws that bar the Jews from participating in German life. Jewish corruption thus proves the need for enlightened reform, rather than being an argument against it!

Dohm's civil emancipation would allow the Jews of Prussia to enter all guilds, trades, and professions, to receive the right to own land, to gain entry to education, and to participate in military service from which they had previously been barred. No prior reform of Jewish character nor of the Jewish religion itself was required, and in this respect Dohm showed himself markedly more sympathetic to the Jews than most of his contemporaries. But there were definite limits

---

[2] J. Carlebach, *Karl Marx and the Radical Critique of Judaism* (London, 1978), p. 56; Brunschwig, *Enlightenment*, p. 281; J. E. Küster, *Beiträge zur Preussischen Staatskunde* (Berlin, 1806), pp. 237ff. (I have not been able to check this last source.) For Hoffmann's later statistics of 1837–42 see below, n. 28.

to his sympathies, though his apparently strongly liberal language may suggest otherwise. One needs to look critically at what Dohm means when he speaks of granting a full "equality" to the Jews in such statements as, for example:

> Why would the Jew hate those men from whom he is no longer divided by humiliating prerogatives and with whom he shares equal rights and duties? (p. 29)
>
> When the Jews shall enjoy wholly the advantages of political society . . . (p. 87)
>
> If it please our governors to grant soon to the Jews equality . . . (p. 108)
>
> To improve the Jews it is necessary first of all that they receive completely equal rights with all other subjects [*Unterthanen*]. (p. 110)

Instead of being taken at their liberal face value, these passages must be understood in the context of the distinction made in this period between the rights of a *Bürger* and a *Staatsbürger*, that is, between civil or resident rights and the full political rights of a citizen. What Dohm had in mind in talking here about equality of rights amounts only to the civil rights of the *Bürger*; he wishes the Jew to be fully equal in civil rights to the Christian *Bürger* (for instance, in enjoying freedom from discriminatory taxation). This crucial distinction between Jewish civil rights and the full political rights of a *Staatsbürger* is evident in the following observation:

> Another question is whether in our states Jews may be admitted to public office. To be sure, it appears that if the Jews enjoy all the rights of the *Bürger*, they cannot be forbidden from aspiring to the glory of serving the state.

But then Dohm, nevertheless, concludes that this must, in fact, be done and he recommends that Jews be barred from public office, that is, from full state-citizenship and political rights!

It must be emphasized that in the context of the eighteenth-century Prussian state, the right to public office is the most fundamental *political* right. One should not fall into the anachronistic error of thinking that Prussian political rights in this period were the same as, say, English ones, which turned on the right to vote. The concept of a political "citizen" in absolutist Prussia was remote not only from that current in England, but also from the idea of citizenship that reigned in the Prussia of the nineteenth century. Dohm's grant of rights to the Jews would, therefore, not have matched the political expectations of the emancipationists of the 1840s since he proposed essentially the granting of *Bürger* civil rights, not *Staatsbürger* political rights. Note such careful phrasing as "It would assuredly be useful if every new Jewish artisan might be treated as a newly won *Bürger* for the state" (p. 113).

In other respects, too, Dohm's concept of "equality" is not at all liberal in any meaningful sense:

> If a Jew compete at the same time with a Christian, each of equal merit, the latter has to be preferred. This prerogative seems to belong by right to the most numerous nation, at least until a more equitable treatment shall have transformed the Jews into fully equal *Bürger* [!] and all distinctions have been abolished. (p. 120)

Dohm does not believe that the Jews are like all other subjects *entitled* to equality. Rather, they are granted a limited equality of certain rights (at the *Bürger* level only) purely by grace of the state. For this reason, it cannot be assumed that Dohm intended his grant of even limited civil rights to be allotted to *all* the Jews in Prussia; they had no legitimate claim as *individuals* to these rights, and, given Dohm's statist argument, they could receive these rights only as members of a particular group of Jews, that is, as "useful" Jews (2:159ff.). Certainly, Dohm speaks nowhere of a universal grant of rights to all the Jews in Prussia, and without such a clear statement, there is no justification for jumping to the conclusion that he was a modern liberal, intending his benevolence to apply to more than just a select number of Jews.

It was only natural for a Prussian constitutionalist believer in a state formed of *Stände* (estates) to regard the Jews as a special *Stand* defined by religion and national character, rather than viewing them as individual subjects with entitlement to full political rights. For Dohm, the "citizen" was an entity owing service to the state, not someone to whom the state was *obliged* to grant rights. In consequence, the fact that Dohm's case is essentially statist permits him to prescribe the restriction of rights in a way quite incompatible with the theories of an authentically liberal thinker, whether German or otherwise.

Dohm's book, however, has often been taken as the classic German liberal argument for Jewish civil rights; his notion, for instance, that religion should be a matter of indifference to the state has been misinterpreted as being close to Riesser's idea of the separation of church and state. Actually, it is only an expression of his fundamental principle of raison d'état. For Dohm, all rights exist at the discretion of the state. There is no axiom or principle in Dohm that Jews have by right exactly the same rights as other Germans—only the quite different proposal that in a prudent state a class of useful Jews should be made equal with German Christians.[3] Jewish equality is always determined according to the interests of the state. That is the meaning of his "separation" of state and religion.

There is no denying Dohm's genuine humanitarian feelings for the oppressed Jews, whom he insisted were first of all "human beings" endowed with human rights. But a humanitarian reading of Dohm cannot override his statist preconceptions. Thus, Dohm's remark about the validity of a continuing discrimination (to last for three or four generations: p. 87) against Jews in competition for posts raises one of the most problematic aspects of his book for the modern liberal reader. Are the Jews (for him as for Riesser) really nothing more than Germans of "Mosaic confession"? Or is there some essential difference between Jews and Germans, which certainly should not prevent the Jews' expedient and humanitarian admission into the Prussian state, but which is nonetheless so considerable as to warrant a continuing distinction between "Jews" and "Germans"?

Dohm regarded the Jews as originally "Asiatic refugees" from their own homeland, and he attributed to them an individual, though alterable, national character:

> Those common traits of thought, opinions, and passions that are to be found in the majority of people belonging to one nation and that are called its individual character are not unchangeable and distinctive qualities stamping them as a unique modification of human nature. As has been clearly recognized in our time, these are influenced by the climate, the food, and most of all the political conditions under which a nation lives. (pp. 35f.)

He was no more a "racist" than was Moses Mendelssohn, who also acknowledged that the Jews would never "coalesce" entirely with the Germans, but would remain a separate "nation."[4]

Yet Dohm somehow believed that the Jews would continue to be different from the Germans. How is this to be understood? Essentially, Dohm's conception of the Jewish Question was circumscribed by the basic assumption of a Prussian administrator that the Prussian state consisted of an association of corporate interests or estates (*Stände*), in which Jews formed a corporation like those of the nobles,

---

[3] As in Dohm, *Verbesserung*, 2:153, 171, which require a careful reading.

[4] Thus Mendelssohn seems to accept the contention of Michaelis (one of Dohm's anti-Jewish critics) that the Jews will never really coalesce with the Germans, but then insists, like Riesser, that this point is entirely irrelevant to the matter of civil rights. The important point here is that for Dohm, Michaelis, and Mendelssohn, there remains an uncomfortable sense of "difference" between Jews and Germans. (The Mendelssohn and Michaelis texts are printed in Dohm, *Verbesserung*, 2:41ff., 72–77.)

farmers, scholars, merchants or, for that matter, Catholics.[5] The Jews were expected to go on doing so even after their emancipation as *Bürger*, just as did the farmers and the academics. Later, Dohm wrote that "those principles that pertain only to the *moral* and *social* status of the Israelites will *not* aim at destroying their *nationality* and will leave them full power to follow their religic ."[6] The Jews, then, would remain a separate *nation* as well as a separate religion within Prussia.

Dohm's constitutionalist outlook permitted him to view with equanimity this future Jewish symbiosis within Prussia. But it proved a disturbingly unresolvable problem to Herder and Fichte, and it became for other frankly racist writers an intolerable and illogical living arrangement. Within a few decades, Dohm's statist solution of a symbiotic Jewish *Stand* had itself become a new variation of the Jewish Question.

---

While well intentioned towards the Jews, Dohm introduced potentially dangerous themes into his discussion that were afterwards to figure in the growth of a new kind of moral and revolutionary Jew-hatred that he himself never countenanced. For example, Dohm domesticated into the political discussion the idea that the Jews had a national character that was blatantly bad. His friend Moses Mendelssohn protested in vain against this labeling.[7] Dohm continued to insist that his book was not meant to be an apology for the Jews, but one designed to draw attention to their vices so that the Jewish nation might be improved. Certainly Dohm was on the side of the angels in his optimism about Jewish capacity for improvement. He stated baldly that he would not descend to debate with those who made the wicked assumption that the Jews were wholly incapable of improvement; he would engage in discussion only with those who differed with him over the best means of improvement.[8] Still, the idea of "improving" the Jews morally and not just civically (the title of his book had this double meaning) was two-edged, for it suggested the major theme of the new moral Jew-hatred that the Jews were somehow lack-

---

[5] "The great and noble purpose of government is to integrate the mutually exclusive principles of all these varied corporations, so that the single notes are dissolved in the great harmony of the state" (pp. 25f.).

[6] Dohm's memorandum of 1818, printed in M. Kohler, *Jewish Rights at the Congresses of Vienna 1814–15 and Aix-la-Chapelle 1818* (New York, 1918), p. 55.

[7] Ibid., 2:152. Also, Dohm's *Denkwürdigkeiten meiner Zeit* (Lemgo, 1815), 2:284ff. For Mendelssohn, see below chap. 7, n. 1f.

[8] Dohm, *Verbesserung*, 2:22.

ing the inner morality of truly free and moral human beings. Passages in Dohm that might strike the modern liberal reader as commendably repentant for Christian sinning against the Jews need, therefore, to be read with some care.

To take two examples. As the climax to a long argument that the Jews are corrupt as both human beings and citizens, Dohm urges:

> The Jews have been corrupt as human beings and as citizens because they have been denied the rights of both. . . . It is up to us to instill in the Jews human feelings by giving them proofs of our own. We have to rid ourselves of our own prejudices to cure the Jews of their prejudices against us. If these today still deter the Jew from being a good citizen, a sociable human being, if he feels dislike and hatred towards Christianity, if he believes himself not bound towards Christians by the same laws of honesty, then this is all our work.[9]
>
> The Jews have been given by nature the same capability to become better, more useful [!] members of society; only oppression, unworthy of our age, has corrupted them. It is in accordance with humanity, justice, and enlightened politics for us to banish that oppression and improve the lot of the Jews to their own benefit and that of the state.[10]

We should now recognize in these passages an ambivalence that cannot be swept away by their undoubted eloquence and nobility of expression. But if, regardless, the phrases are taken at their face value and out of context, the unwary reader will be puzzled to find them juxtaposed with comments that seem to belong to an anti-Jewish tract. For instance, commenting on the national character of the Jews, Dohm notes:

> In contrast to the finer traits of the Jewish character is the exaggerated love of that nation for every kind of profit, usury, and crooked practices, a fault nourished in many by their exclusive religious principles and rabbinic sophistries, and more still by Christian oppression. . . . But as I remarked, all these crimes do not stem from their national character [that is, *their genetic character*], but from the oppressed state in which they live. . . . The mercantile spirit of most Jews will probably be broken more easily by heavy physical labor than by the sedentary work of the public servant.[11]

This unsettling combination of concern for the Jews and a certain callousness towards them appears paradoxical only when it is read in

[9] Ibid., 1:28–39.
[10] Ibid., p. 130.
[11] Ibid., pp. 96, 119.

terms of the categories of liberal thought, as opposed to its original statist context.

The same may be said of the general framework of Dohm's book, which is, as he stipulated, as much about the improvement of Jewish moral character as it is about the improvement of their civil status. This dual concern leads in the book to a perfectly consistent argument. But if one tries to read it in the light of liberal categories, then the picture immediately becomes contradictory and incoherent. Dohm seems to be muddling liberal conceptions with Prussian statist ones, and fogging matters first with sympathetic murmurings about the Jews, and then with condemnations of Jewish national character, especially its economic and financial aspects.[12] Dohm had brought into the mainstream of respectable discussion of the Jewish Question a theoretical beast that was not to prove as easily tamed as he expected.

The particular danger of many German "pro-Jewish" writings lies in the fact that their virtues are often only the manifest aspect of a general system of argument, of which unseen vices are an integral part. When Dohm set out so laudably his argument for Jewish rights, he did so in terms that implicitly accepted deep-seated German perceptions of Jewish "alienness." The only counter to this was the dogmatic liberalism of the Riesser school, which resolutely stamped such prejudices as utterly irrelevant to questions of state.

Dohm's views were not merely idiosyncratic, advanced views, but rather represented a significant current of official thinking in various German states. This was quickly demonstrated by the appearance of Joseph II's Austrian Edict of Toleration within a few months of the publication of Dohm's tract.[13] Though the edict is remarkable as the first modern grant to the Jews of the civil right of residence in a German city, and though it opened most trades to them, it still incorpo-

---

[12] See Dohm's attacks on Jewish control of Polish commerce in *Denkwürdigkeiten*, 2:286n.

[13] Printed in A. Pribram, *Urkunden und Akten zur Geschichte der Juden in Wien* (Vienna, 1918), 1:494ff., trans. R. Mahler as *Jewish Emancipation: Selected Documents* (New York, 1941), pp. 18ff.

The analysis of this and other edicts of emancipation given by J. Katz, *Out of the Ghetto* (Cambridge, Mass., 1973), chap. 10, pp. 161–75, seems to me to fail to account for the "contradictory features" noticed in the legislation. This is because no attention is given to the legal terminology of "citizen," "resident," "alien," "privileged/tolerated Jew," and "Jew." Thus, Katz speaks of "Jews" indiscriminately and creates what are essentially false "contradictions." A closer reading of these edicts as immigration laws would have obviated the problem. (Katz's recent *Jewish Emancipation and Self-Emancipation* [Philadelphia, 1986], p. 76, does note that the edict granted residency and not equal rights, but he does not pursue the point.)

rated (according to textbook accounts) apparently anomalous illiberal features. Certain professions and businesses remained closed to Jews, who were explicitly denied the political right of citizenship. Moreover, the edict applied solely to Jews "once they have been admitted and tolerated in our states," that is, it was restricted to officially "tolerated" Jews who had been permitted to immigrate but whose children born in Austria were not on a par with those of Christian native subjects. In clause 18, for example, it is expressly only the class of "tolerated Jews" who have the right to establish free residence in the cities. The "Jewish nation," therefore, remains apart politically and socially from the Christian nation, as in Dohm. And, as with Dohm, the edict is essentially statist in its whole attitude to the Jewish Question: the preamble declares that "it is our goal to make the Jewish nation useful and serviceable to the state."

Dohm later complained that both his book and Joseph II's edict had been mistaken for apologetic pro-Jewish acts. Yet their purpose had not been to increase the number of Jews, but simply to make them "civil" (moral) and "useful."[14] Thus, the edict contains the same ambivalence about "equality" of Jews and Christians as does Dohm's book. There is no question of political rights being granted, despite the preamble's fine words:

> All our subjects, without distinction of nationality and religion, once they have been admitted and tolerated in our states [*note here the key juridical restriction*], shall participate in common in public welfare [and] shall enjoy legal freedom and not find any obstacles in any honest ways of gaining their livelihood.

And the edict retains a keen sense of the persisting difference between Jewish and Christian subjects, as may be seen graphically in the nice use of "almost" in speaking of equality in clause 25:

> By these favors we almost place the Jewish nation on an equal level with adherents of other religious associations in respect to trade and enjoyment of civil and domestic facilities.

The dangerous assumption of Joseph II and Dohm that the Jew was somehow in need of moral redemption appealed widely to contemporaries. Klopstock's "Ode to the Emperor" acclaimed Joseph's various enlightened reforms thus:

> You summon the priest back to the discipleship of Christ the founder,
> You make a subject of the yoke-laden peasant,

[14] Dohm, *Verbesserung*, 2:283–88 (also for the absence of any direct connection between his book and the edict).

You make of the Jew a human being . . .
Who is not seized by the shudder of compassion when he sees
How our mob dehumanizes [*entmenscht*] the people of Canaan?[15]

It was this alleged moral defect of the alien Jews, this lack of "humanity" in them, whether caused by their own innate evil or Christian persecution, that was soon to form the kernel of a revolutionary antisemitism unintended by statists like Dohm and Joseph II.

## HUMBOLDT

The facility with which the statist argument could present itself in liberal clothing is well illustrated by a celebrated official memorandum prepared in 1809 by the prominent Prussian minister Wilhelm von Humboldt (1767–1835). A friend and student of Dohm's since 1785, Humboldt had been asked to comment on a proposed Prussian edict of emancipation, and he now did so in a spirit that genuinely sought a diminution of German hatred of the Jews.[16] What gives his report a startlingly liberal appearance is its language of universal equality:

I favor only a legislative system which places Jews and Christians on an absolute equality. (p. 74)

Should we tolerate the presence of aliens possessing only such limited rights in a state? (p. 72)

Only a sudden grant of equal and full rights is just, politic and consistent. (p. 72)

Humboldt indeed goes even further than Dohm in requiring an immediate grant of all political rights to Jewish citizens (p. 78). And coupled with this is the apparent outright rejection of national character as a factor in discussing the Jewish Question. Granted that the Jews do have a national character, says Humboldt, national character is still an extremely difficult thing to define and "a conscientious man

[15] F. G. Klopstock, "An den Kaiser," *Sämtliche Werke* (Leipzig, 1823), 2:45f.

[16] Humboldt, "Über den Entwurf zu einer neuen Konstitution für die Juden," July 1809, trans. in Kohler, *Jewish Rights*, pp. 71–83 (pages cited in text). The German is in Wilhelm von Humboldt, *Gesammelte Schriften*, ed. B. Gebhardt (Berlin, 1903), 10:97–115; *Werke*, ed. A. Flitner and K. Giel, 2d ed. (Darmstadt, 1964), 4:95–112; Freund, *Emanzipation*, 2:269–82, also includes the edict under comment. Cf. P. R. Sweet, *Wilhelm von Humboldt: A Biography* (Columbus, Ohio, 1978) 2:71–76; Katz, *Out of the Ghetto*, pp. 76ff.; W. Grau, *Wilhelm von Humboldt und das Problem des Judens* (Hamburg, 1935). Cf. P. Honigmann, "Alexander von Humboldt's Verhältnis zu Juden," *Bulletin des Leo Baeck Instituts* (Frankfurt) 76, (1987): 3–34. In general, see H. A. Strauss, "The Prussian Emancipation Policies toward the Jews 1815–1847," *LBIY* 11 (1966): 107–36.

will never predicate upon it the granting or withholding of rights" (p. 73). To be consistent, the state would also have to institute a moral and cultural test for its Christian citizens! And, adds Humboldt, "does experience justify anyone in casting such obloquy upon a whole nation?" (p. 73). Taken together, these straightforward remarks seem to prove Humboldt to have been a wholly modern Western liberal.

But, as with Dohm, it is vital that these liberal and humane sentiments be read in the context of Humboldt's thinking as a whole, and, at the same time, be interpreted in their specific context within the document in question. Read thus, Humboldt's rejection of national character is not as total as it might seem. He is very much in agreement with Dohm when he avers that

> oppression is breeding now a really appreciable immorality among a number of Jews. . . . [This oppression] evinces a lack of moral esteem for Jews . . . and expresses a moral depreciation of them in an almost repelling fashion. . . . It robs them of all reliance on their probity, loyalty, and truthfulness. (p. 76)

It may be the fault of Christian oppression, but the Jews are nevertheless immoral.

In any case, Humboldt insists that there is a need for administrators to consider this immoral national character of the Jews as a political factor in emancipation:

> The point at which legislation must certainly take into account a thorough understanding of the race is not as to the purpose of the state itself, but as to the selection of means for carrying out plans based on universal principles. For this purpose even an incomplete knowledge—and no other is possible—of character will serve. (p. 74)

To translate, "universal principles" of state dictate the granting of Jewish rights, but one must have an eye to Jewish national character in arranging this. The purpose of emancipation is not to *acknowledge* the fact that the Jews are equal to Christians in Germany, but rather to remove administrative anomalies that present problems to the smooth and rational functioning of the Prussian state. When Humboldt says "no real human intercourse is possible where one side by reason of its descent inspires suspicion in the other as to its elemental moral attributes, namely its truthfulness" (p. 79), the context shows he is commenting on the difficulty of living in a state deeply divided by hatred and mistrust. It is a statement that must, therefore, be read in its functionalist context rather than as purely humanitarian aspiration.

Humboldt's memorandum is thoroughly statist, then, but it has another characteristic that belies its seemingly liberal and humanitarian analysis of the Jewish Question. The memorandum is based on rigorous categories and concepts of administrative immigration law. Thus, Humboldt accepts the first clause of the proposed edict restricting the grant of rights to the *Stand* of "privileged Jews" (p. 76, clause 1). These official Jews have the right to be full Prussian citizens (*Staatsbürger*) and—this is Humboldt's central point—they should have the same unfettered rights as the Christian "citizens" of Prussia, including the right to hold public office (p. 78, clauses 9–10). But while Humboldt gives with one hand, he takes away with the other; he tightens up the immigration laws and expects the "state to determine accurately who is in fact an alien [and] who a resident." Humboldt establishes a rigidly controlled three-tier system of immigration categories for Jews: *alien-* ("traveller"), *resident-* and *citizen-Jew*. Acquisition of citizenship, as we have seen, is restricted to the last category, and in his additional comments on the proposed edict Humboldt seeks to be even more stringent than the original text by insisting that citizenship for those not already "privileged Jews" should in future be only obtainable "upon the express authorization of the king," so as to keep numbers within reason. With this safeguard about citizenship, Humboldt is able to be quite relaxed about admitting to Prussia a reasonable immigration of *resident-* or *alien-Jews* whose commercial activities may easily be policed; but the magic door to citizenship is kept barely ajar. When Humboldt says that immigration is in his opinion "not so dangerous" (p. 79, clauses 23–26), he is not liberally welcoming the kind of open immigration of *Ostjuden* that took place in late nineteenth-century Imperial Germany and Austria where full political citizenship accompanied the influx. Rather he is referring to a *noncitizen* immigration where the immigrants have no entitlement to political rights and so may easily be controlled without danger to the state.

This context allows us to reread Humboldt's remarks on Jewish rights quoted above in a quite different light. For instance, placing "Jews and Christians on an absolute equality" means that Jews and Christians of similar administrative status, or in the same immigration categories, are to be treated equally in the eyes of the law. A Jewish citizen should have the same rights as a Christian citizen, a Jewish resident as a Christian resident, a Jewish alien as a Christian alien. It does not mean that a Jewish *resident* should have the same rights as a Christian *citizen*. The trouble, *liberally* speaking, is that the administrative laws discriminate against Jews, since even after many generations of domicile in Prussia, Prussian Jews remain (except for the official "tolerated and privileged Jews") a class who are presumed, unlike their Christian neighbors, to be at best merely residents, and not citizens. Again, when Humboldt deprecates the "presence of aliens possessing only limited rights," he refers not to all the Jewish subjects, residents, and "aliens" living in Prussia, but simply to the small class of *citizen-* or "privileged Jews" who were formerly aliens. These *citizens* are now to have the same rights as their "Christian fellow citizens." As to the "sudden grant of equal and full rights," this is to be made only to the select body of privileged/citizen-Jews, not to the whole Jewish population of Prussia.

It may seem that this kind of close interpretation is going against a natural and commonsense reading of Humboldt. Yet it is the only kind of reading that is consonant with the legal and constitutional framework within which Humboldt was acting and writing at this period. If we do not accept the present interpretation, how else is sense to be made of Humboldt's tacit acceptance of the first clause of the proposed edict, which expressly extends Prussian citizenship *only* to those Jews in Prussia "holding letters of protection and concessions"? If Humboldt really had had in mind a general grant of citizenship to the Jewish population ("privileged" and "unprivileged" alike), then he should have been forced to take sharp exception to this crucial clause—and he does not. Moreover, as a statist, Humboldt can without contradiction impose a quota on the number of Jewish "citizens." Humboldt's position is simply that of a rationalist administrator determined to make things tidier bureaucratically by removing the irrational anomalies of citizenship status that obstruct the efficient functioning of the rational Prussian state. Perhaps no single case proves the need for a contextual and close legal reading of the various emancipation tracts than does this remarkable, coldly rational memorandum of Humboldt's of 1809.

In three major respects, then, we must be careful not to misconstrue Humboldt's views. Firstly, although he and Riesser seem to arrive at the same position vis-à-vis the state's "indifference" to the Judaism and Christianity of its subjects, the convergence is only apparent, for they hold to entirely opposed conceptions of the state. Humboldt speaks always as an administrator believing in the need for a rational bureaucratic state that will be free of irrational religious attachments that would unnecessarily complicate its operations; Riesser, however, sees the state's purpose as guaranteeing the rights of its individual subjects, whatever their religion might be. Between these ideas of the state as "blind to religion" there is a world of difference.

Secondly, it is of fundamental importance not to misread Humboldt's idea of *Humanität* in a Western liberal way. *Humanität* is here not a matter of feeling, of compassion and respect for the individual's life and beliefs; rather it relates to the abstract principle of the rational development of the individual and of the state. Humboldt's concern for the Jews exists only on a rational, high-minded level.

Thirdly, there has always been a wishful tendency to see Humboldt as a philosemite. Despite his advocacy of emancipation and his friendly acquaintance with certain Jews, Humboldt (like Dohm) maintained a certain coolness towards both Jews and Judaism. Behind the favorable stance on Jewish rights lay a basic denial of the validity of Jewish existence. The ultimate achievement of Jewish emancipation was envisaged by Humboldt to be the destruction of Judaism by the soft means of assimilation. Nor did Humboldt even consider himself as a "friend of the Jews"; this is obvious in his ambivalent correspondence with his fiercely anti-Jewish wife Karoline. These exchanges—with Humboldt wryly disclaiming his popular reputation as a friend of the Jews but still urging a soft line on his wife—present a perplexing picture to readers bent on preserving his philosemitic image. Certainly, in the letters there is a debate for and against emancipation, but the differences between the couple are only superficial. Karoline thinks that since Jews are awful, they must not be given rights; Wilhelm agrees that the Jews are repellent, but argues that raison d'état and *Humanität* require that Jews be emancipated. Humboldt never really disagreed with his wife's hope that "in fifty years, the Jews will be exterminated as Jews."[17]

## HARDENBERG AND THE 1812 EDICT OF EMANCIPATION

Humboldt was a close advisor to the reforming Prussian chancellor Karl August von Hardenberg (1750–1822), who shared with him a desire to resolve the Jewish Question by means of civil emancipation. In 1812 Hardenberg succeeded in passing the first genuine Prussian Edict of Emancipation, although, owing to resistance within government circles, it realized only imperfectly his and Humboldt's ideas.

Often seen as a positive response to the spread of the emancipatory ideas of the French Revolution in Germany, the edict is much more an expression of that influential current of Prussian reformist admin-

[17] See *Wilhelm und Karoline von Humboldt in ihren Briefen*, ed. A. von Sydow (Berlin, 1907–13). This intriguing correspondence needs to be reexamined carefully, as *HAS*, 3:293–96, points out. Cf. Sweet, *Humboldt*, 2:203–8.

Katz, *Jewish Emancipation*, p. 80, reads Humboldt as intending that the Jews should eventually abandon Judaism for Humanity rather than for Christianity.

For the antisemitism of the Berlin Jewish salon visitors, see now D. Hertz, *Jewish High Society in Old Regime Berlin* (New Haven, 1988).

istrative thinking that we have traced back to Dohm's tract of 1781. In 1792 Hardenberg had proposed in typically Dohmian phrases the improvement of Jewish "civil and moral circumstances" in the duchies of Bayreuth and Ansbach. He wrote to the king of Prussia:

> Politics and love of humanity strongly demand relief of that unfortunate group of people. . . . The lowering of their civil status has worsened their moral character. . . . With the political ennoblement of their civil status must begin again their moral improvement. Only a raising of their civil status can alter their character for the better.

Though approved by the king, the proposals were allowed to lapse. Hardenberg revived his efforts to "ennoble" the immoral national character of the Jews of Bayreuth in 1797, again without much success.[18] In 1806–7, however, Napoleon threatened "to take hold of the Jews by calling a Great Sanhedrin," an initiative followed up by the Bonaparte king of Westphalia's sponsorship of the emancipation of the Frankfurt Jews in 1808. This alarmed the Prussian government enough for it to take Hardenberg's suggestions seriously, which he now resubmitted in the framework of a general reform plan for the Prussian state.[19] If there were indeed a French inspiration for the Prussian emancipation, it was one that chimed with Hardenberg's statist outlook rather than with any putative "liberal" instincts.

Statist principles permeate the edict of 1812, which Hardenberg intended to be based on the precept of "equal duties, equal rights."[20]

[18] Hardenberg's letter of 16 April 1792 to the king is printed in F. Morgenstern, "Hardenberg and the Emancipation of Franconian Jewry," *Jewish Social Studies* 15 (1953): 253–74, at p. 268. For the 1797 proposal see L. Ranke, *Denkwürdigkeiten des Staatskanzlers Fürsten von Hardenberg* (Leipzig, 1877), vol. 4, appendix, p. 57.

[19] Hardenberg's plan of September 1807 is printed in G. Winter, *Die Reorganisation des preussischen Staates unter Stein und Hardenberg* (Leipzig, 1931), 1:302ff.; see p. 336 for the remarks on the "ennobling" of the Jews through education and the statist hope of being able to make use of the Jews' international contacts and influence as Napoleon is threatening to do through the summoning of the Great Sanhedrin. R. Dukas, *Die Motive der preussischen Judenemanzipation von 1812* (Berlin, 1912), demonstrates the importance for the edict of 1812 of the Prussian statist context over that of the French Revolution. Cf. H. Haussherr, *Hardenberg: Eine politische Biographie*, 2d ed. (Cologne, 1963–65), 3:202–23; P. C. Thielen, *Karl August von Hardenberg 1750–1822* (Cologne, 1967), p. 277; S. Schwarzfuchs, *Napoleon, the Jews, and the Sanhedrin* (London, 1978); *HAS*, 3:226–30. Also below, n. 21, and chap. 8, n. 4.

[20] The edict of March 1812 is in Freund, *Emanzipation*, 2:455–59. English trans. is in Mahler, *Documents*, p. 32 (repr. in P. Mendes-Flohr and J. Reinharz, *The Jew in the Modern World* [New York, 1980], p. 127). Cf. S. Dubnow, *History of the Jews*, trans. (London, 1973), 5:60ff.; R. Mahler, *A History of Modern Jewry 1780–1815* (New York, 1971), pp. 200ff.; Carlebach, *Karl Marx*, pp. 123ff.

This, it must be stressed, was no universal emancipation of the Prussian Jews, but one again restricted to a well-defined class of Jews who were to assume "equal duties" with their fellow Prussian *Staatsbürger*. Naturally Hardenberg follows Humboldt in restricting the grant of citizenship and political rights to the official *Stand* of "privileged Jews" (clause 1). In two respects, however, Hardenberg has to retreat from the more radical positions of his colleague. Firstly, he abandons the immigration category of "resident" Jews by now "forbidding foreign Jews to take up residence in these states as long as they have not acquired Prussian state-citizenship"; this means that the only categories of Jews allowed in Prussia are "citizens" and "traveling aliens" (clauses 31 and 36). Secondly, while the edict granted a full range of civil rights to the Jews, including landownership and entry to the professions, the political right of eligibility for government office was to be deferred until the administration should determine a suitable time for it (clause 9). This was, of course, also Dohm's view and in essence the edict should be seen as the long-delayed victory of Dohm's proposals of 1781 for the civil emancipation of the Jews.

Though the initiatives of Dohm, Humboldt, and Hardenberg were welcome to liberals and Jews alike at the time, hindsight allows us to see that their statist and constitutionalist approach to the Jewish Question had its dangers. Chief among these was the fact that the award of rights was done purely by government fiat for state purposes. What the state has given, however, the state can also take away when its own perceived needs change. This granting of rights from "above" rendered the position of the Jews in Germany peculiarly vulnerable and subject to political debate for the next century, until finally the rights *were* taken away in 1933. Rights won by the assent of a larger public or representative assembly—as they were in England and France and the United States—might have proved more secure.[21] Moreover, the constitutionalist tendency to think of the Jews—even when emancipated—as a separate *Stand* or a nation of

---

[21] Though the emancipation laws of the French Revolution are also ambivalent. The French emancipation was carried out in stages similar in some respects to the Prussian process of extending rights to defined categories of Jews (e.g., Spanish and Portuguese Jews, Alsatian Jews). The final emancipation law of 28 September 1791 implies also that Jews have no guaranteed right of free religious association as a community. See Mahler, *Documents*, pp. 25f.; A. Feuerwerker, *L'Émancipation des Juifs en France de l'Ancien Régime à la fin du Second Empire* (Paris, 1976); P. Neher-Bernheim, ed., *Documents inédits sur l'entrée des Juifs dans la société française 1750–1850* (Tel Aviv, 1977). Also above, n. 19, and below, chap. 8, n. 4.

emancipated aliens, placed them in a continually exposed position, so that they were always forced to argue defensively.

The fragility of the enlightened statist approach to the Jewish Question became evident in practice very soon indeed. At the Congress of Vienna in 1815 and during the years that followed, Hardenberg proved powerless to prevent Frankfurt and the free cities from rescinding their imposed emancipation of the Jews; Dohm's intervention at the Congress of Aachen in 1818 was just as unavailing.[22] The deaths of Dohm in 1820 and of Hardenberg two years later, along with Humboldt's retirement from politics, meant the end of effective statist support for Jewish emancipation in the government, a change sealed in 1822 by the repeal of the edict's clauses permitting Jews to teach and to hold municipal office. With the accession of the romantic Frederick William IV in 1840, the clock was very nearly turned back as rapidly as it had gone forward under the enlightened statists. For the benefit of his beloved Jewish subjects, the new king proposed the restoration of the comfortably medieval protected ghetto. The draft law of 1841 proposing this measure was, however, withdrawn after widespread public protest.[23] The king's idea of a medieval Christian "corporate" realm did find support from a conservative group of statists, who, unlike Humboldt and company, felt that the nature of Prussian society demanded the cohering bond of both Christianity and Germanness among its members. The philosophy here was "generally to keep Jews and Judaism totally outside the [Christian] state while benevolently protecting them."[24] This attitude had been expounded at the Christian-German Dining Club of Berlin in 1811, but there it had been tainted for being pushed by such romantic Jew-haters as Arnim and Brentano.[25] By the 1840s, however, a respectably conservative legal theory had evolved to justify this prejudice in the doctrine of the "Christian-German state." The chief

[22] Kohler, *Jewish Rights*, p. 56; Dubnow, *History*, 5:36ff., for the reaction.

[23] Amusingly, Frederick William IV was skeptical about the rising "modern" force of German nationalism, which he saw as part of "the Teutonic fury of the Jews, which completely lacks support in northern Germany." Quoted by A. Low, *Jews in the Eyes of the Germans: From the Enlightenment to Imperial Germany* (Philadelphia, 1979), p. 297. Cf. Carlebach, *Karl Marx*, pp. 65ff.; Dubnow, *History*, 5:47ff.; I. Jost, *Neuere Geschichte der Israeliten 1815–1845* (Berlin, 1846).

[24] See Wolfart's Finance Ministry memorandum of November 1816, referring to "our Christian, German, Prussian people" and barring Jews from political office though allowing a restricted class of respectable Jews to hold civil rights (Freund, *Emanzipation*, 2:482f.).

[25] For Arnim and the Christian-Germans see above chap. 2, n. 11, and below, chap. 8, n. 8.

spokesman of this school, the converted Jew F. J. Stahl, held that as the German states were constitutionally, historically, and socially "Christian," conformity to Christianity was legally required for the enjoyment of full citizenship.[26]

## THE "SOCIAL FACTS" OF THE JEWISH QUESTION AND THE PRUSSIAN ADMINISTRATIVE MIND

In the eyes of rationalist Prussian administrators, "social facts" amply demonstrated the irrationality and immorality of the Jews. The ferocious quarrels between the "enlightened" and "orthodox" Jewish factions reinforced this Prussian prejudice. For instance, it took twenty-seven years (from 1772 to 1799) for the Jewish community to accept the state's demand that the time required between death and burial be changed from four hours to three days. The delay was not so much due to religious resistance against the state as to internal Jewish feuds. The religious Talmudic law itself was not inflexible on the precept that burial take place on the same day as death, but several reforming Prussian Jews loudly alleged that the actual practice had become unreasonably rigid owing to the influence of the more traditionally minded Polish rabbis.[27] (Unfortunately for the enlightened party, some of the reformers subsequently converted to Christianity and so vindicated their opponents' charges that they had really been seeking all along to destroy Judaism.)

This stubborn traditionalism of the majority of Jews was perceived by the Prussian statists as part of the general problem of immigration, which was bringing large numbers of impoverished and backward Polish Jews into Prussian lands. By 1806 the Jews there numbered a quarter of million (about 2.5 percent of the general population) and perhaps four-fifths of this number were classed as "poor" and orthodox.[28] The question that troubled the administrators was whether

[26] On Stahl, see below, chaps. 14 and 19.

[27] Brunschwig, *Enlightenment*, pp. 277, 281.

[28] Cited by Carlebach, *Karl Marx*, p. 56. Brunschwig, *Enlightenment*, pp. 277, 281, reads these administrative opinions as "rationalist" rather than statist. Brunschwig's rationalistic bias also leads him to favor strongly the party of the "enlightened" Jews over their "orthodox" rivals.

A great deal of interesting material on Jewish social history is contained in Katz, *Out of the Ghetto*, though most of it pertains to the small minority of comfortably off Jews; the vast impoverished majority do not come into either analytical or descriptive focus (e.g., in the discussions of peddling at pp. 68f., 186).

For the social facts of the 1830s see Johann Gottfried Hoffmann's compilations *Die Bevölkerung des preussischen Staates nach dem Ergebnisse der zu Ende des Jahres 1837 amt-*

this mass of "immoral" and "irrational" immigrants so alien in nationality and customs could be absorbed into Prussian society. Not surprisingly, most of the officials urged the need for restriction of immigration and for the strict regulation of Jewish subjects.

Put this way, the case of the Jews in Prussia might not seem so different from that of other foreign minorities in modern European industrialized countries; it is a fact of life that no country, however liberal, can sustain unrestricted immigration. Moreover, then as now, it is a universal truth that foreign minorities attract prejudice simply by virtue of their being "different." But the case of the Jews is a special one that involves more than the usual factors making for prejudice. In this case, reasonable statists were led to a discriminatory policy against the Jews coinciding remarkably closely with widespread popular anti-Jewish feelings that fed upon centuries of Christian and socioeconomic hatreds of the Jews. It might well have been the case that the restrictive measures against Jewish commercial and public activity were dictated merely by political prudence; but in the context of the period, these measures are difficult to disengage from the public prejudices that they seemed to gratify, and that erupted so brutally in the Hep-Hep riots of 1819. Indeed, one may wonder to what extent the calm, measured statist language of the various official memoranda are a psychological disguise for an ingrained emotional hostility towards the Jews.

At times in these documents the irritation of an official shows through even when he may be recommending an emancipatory policy. One bureaucrat opting in 1816 for the award of Jewish civil rights wrote:

> There are only two ways, since the matter cannot remain in the present position: Either the Jews must be rooted out by force [*gewaltsam auszurotten*] or they must be educated. The former course does not seem to me to be grounded in law [note here the term "law" rather than "humanity"]. . . . But we must rightly recognize that
>
> 1. It would be desirable if we had no Jews in the country;
>
> 2. Once we have them, we must endure it but unceasingly strive to render them as harmless as possible;

*lichen aufgenommenen Nachrichten in staatswirtschaftlichen, gewerblichen und sittlichen Beziehung* (Berlin, 1839), pp. 81ff., and *Zur Judenfrage: Statistische Erörterungen* (Berlin, 1842). As Katz, *Out of the Ghetto*, p. 255, points out, the attack on Hoffmann's findings by Ludwig Philippson was unconvincing, modern work tending to substantiate them. Cf. S. Kuznets, "Economic Structure and Life of the Jews," in *The Jews*, ed. L. Finkelstein (Philadelphia, 1960), 2:1597–1666 (see above, n. 2).

3. The immigration of foreign Jews whom we have as yet no duty to tolerate must be made more difficult where it is not wholly stopped.[29]

On the other hand, sometimes a dire alternative is spelled out, not so much in wishful thinking as to demonstrate vividly just what anti-Jewish prejudice entails in practical terms. Thus one official opinion of 1808:

> Either the Jews are really dangerous and are beyond any hope of being raised out of their corruption . . . or through humanity, reason, and politics, they can share the rights of other dwellers in the state. If the former is decided, then total extermination of the Jews [*gänzliche Vertilgung*] is, on every assumption, the end for which the state must strive.[30]

The tone of this last quotation suggests that there is good reason to beware of accepting as objective the "social facts" reported by Prussian officials. The "facts" themselves were often very likely to have been perceived, perhaps unconsciously, through the distorting spectacles of prejudice, whether anti-Jewish prejudice, or merely bureaucratic or rationalist prejudice. Nevertheless, one is struck by the fact that so many of the reports seem to be reasonable enough responses to what was (or was seen to be) a very difficult and growing social problem. This comparative reasonableness is characteristic of a phase of government attitudes to the Jewish Question that lasted from the 1780s until the eve of the 1848 revolutions, and it was reflected in the enlightened press of the time. By 1848, however, the limitations of a statist policy were becoming felt, especially in the slow and erratic rate at which emancipation was proceeding. There was also increasing appreciation of the danger of relying on the fiat of authority for achieving what was coming now to be seen in some quarters as a revolution in attitude that should arise instead out of social and moral imperatives. By contrast, Gabriel Riesser had promoted successfully a more cogent and logical case for Jewish emancipation, one that was ideological rather than vaguely empirical.[31] The emancipationist case was shifting on to higher and firmer ground, no longer statist but liberal—and sometimes socialist. We should not, therefore, be sur-

[29] "Votum des Finanzministeriums," November 1816, in Freund, *Emanzipation*, 2:482f.

[30] Troschel's report, in Freund, *Emanzipation*, pp. 193f. Brunschwig, *Enlightenment*, p. 289, seems to misquote this source, which is not cited in his original French articles.

[31] On Riesser, see below chap. 9, nn. 26, 52; chap. 10, nn. 22ff.; chap. 11, n. 41; F. Friedländer, *Das Leben Gabriel Riessers* (Berlin, 1926); Dubnow, *History*, 5:43ff.; Katz, *Out of the Ghetto*, pp. 194–97.

prised to find that the anti-emancipationists had also been busily staking out fresh ground, and that new radical ideologies of Jew-hatred—moral, revolutionary, and nationalist—had emerged. The matrix of these novel ideologies was supplied unintentionally by the Prussian statists themselves. It consisted in the premise that the Jews had a national character that was morally corrupt and alien to that of the Germans.[32]

[32] Bismarck's emancipation of 1871 marks the culmination of the statist approach to the Jewish Question. But even though the Jews had now obtained full citizenship rights and were no longer considered a *Stand*, the discrimination against them did not fade away. Informal barriers were implemented by the government to block them from university professorships and judgeships, for instance. Fueled by the new increase of Jewish immigration from the east, this discrimination became fairly intense. It could have been legally justified in the earlier period when the Jews officially lacked full rights; but for such quasi-legal discrimination to continue to exist in a modern emancipated state where the Jews were now officially full citizens only signified the fatal flaws in the Jewish position in Germany.

The statist matrix continued to exert its influence in the 1880s, as Heinrich Treitschke's thinking shows. Treitschke was willing to confer civil rights on the Jews though still insisting (like Dohm) on continuing a certain measure of administrative discrimination against them in such areas as the holding of public office and university posts. The justification for this was that the price Jews must pay for rights was the destruction of their Jewish identity. As long as this identity persisted, a proportionate degree of discrimination was necessary and deserved. At bottom, however, there was a certain dishonesty to this position: Treitschke seems to have believed that Jewish characteristics could never become dilute or invisible enough for the Jews to become pure and indistinguishable *German* citizens. See A. Dorpalen, *Heinrich von Treitschke* (New Haven, 1957), pp. 241–47, 266ff., for an excellent account of the historian's antisemitism, and more extensively, S. Herz, "The Jewish Problem in the Works of Heinrich von Treitschke," Ph.D. dissertation, University of Melbourne, 1970.

# CHAPTER 7

# The German Moralists and the Jewish Question: Kant, Herder, and Hegel

So PERSUASIVE was the assumption of Jewish immorality in Dohm's tract of 1781 that only two critics found it questionable. Moses Mendelssohn rejected the tendency of his friend Dohm to say that Jews were morally inferior to Christians "at present," while Heinrich Diez confessed his amazement that in speaking of the depravity of the Jews Dohm had forgotten the same degree of depravity existed among Christians![1]

The danger of this well-intentioned prejudice was to emerge clearly in the following revolutionary decade, but even in 1782 Moses Mendelssohn was warning how the shift from a Christian to a secular morality had introduced new possibilities for Jew-hatred:

> It is strange to see how prejudice changes its form in successive centuries in order to suppress us and place obstacles in the way of our civil admission. . . . In those superstitious times it was said of us that we desecrated wafers, . . . required Christian blood for Passover, poisoned wells. . . . Now times have changed. These defamations no longer produce the desired effect. Now it is superstition and stupidity—of all things!—with which we are charged: lack of moral feeling, taste, good manners; an incapacity for the arts, sciences, and useful occupations, especially for military and civil service; an irrepressible inclination towards fraudulence, usury, and lawlessness.[2]

The danger of this moralizing against the Jews went deeper than perhaps Mendelssohn was prepared to admit. It was more than just a matter of civil acceptance. In the 1780s Friedrich Traugott Hartmann used an enlightened moral argument to exclude the Jews, not just from the German state, but from humanity as a whole.

[1] Mendelssohn, preface to Manasseh ben Israel's *Rettung der Juden*, in *Gesammelte Schriften: Jubiläumsausgabe*, ed. A. Altmann et al. (Stuttgart, 1971–85), 8:3–25. Cf. Heinrich Diez, *Über Juden* (Dessau, 1783).

[2] Mendelssohn, preface to *Rettung der Juden*, 8:6f., writing against Michaelis and others rather than Dohm who, of course, regards these Jewish defects as removable. Cf. A. Altmann, *Moses Mendelssohn: A Biographical Study* (University, Ala., 1973), pp. 466–74.

Man is always a man; he is always entitled to expect help from his
brother. All national hatred is therefore unjustified, for it springs
from poisonous pride—*unless* [!] a nation has attracted to itself by its
moral vices the absolute contempt of mankind and unless it itself de-
liberately opposes all enlightenment of heart and mind. Is this not the
case with the Jews?[3]

In 1791 C. W. Grattenauer popularized these views in a notorious
polemic, which in enlightened fashion denounced the national and
religious morality of the Jews for infringing all universal moral principles, such as were "respected even by the savage, the Red Indian
and the Negro."[4]

Grattenauer's vicious conception of the Jews reflected a new moralist hostility to Jews and Judaism that had sprung up in the 1790s in
the most advanced circles of German philosophy under the aegis of
Kant himself.[5] This moralist Jew-hatred of the philosophers was a
quite different animal from the relatively fair-minded criticisms of
Jewry offered by the statists, whose assumption of Jewish immorality
was at least arguably taken from empirical observation of "social
facts." Moreover, Dohm and Hardenberg regarded the Jewish national character as improvable and attributed much of its present corruption to Christian oppression. But the moralists made their assumption of Jewish viciousness on a priori grounds, insisting that
such viciousness was rooted in the Jewish religion, which actually defined "Jews" and so rendered delusory any hopes of improvement in
the national character of Jews as long as they remained Jews.

The powerful new moralist critique of Judaism nevertheless followed the statists in rejecting "Jew-hatred" as medieval, fanatical, irrational—"un-enlightened." *Their* modern critique, maintained Kant,
Herder, Fichte, and the young Hegel, would be cool and detached
from Christian religious superstition; it would be objective, moral

[3] Quoted from H. Brunschwig, *Enlightenment and Romanticism in Eighteenth-Century
Prussia*, trans. (Chicago, 1974), p. 285, apparently from Hartmann's articles in *Hiero-
glyphen* (1780) or his *Untersuchungen ob die bürgerliche Freiheit den Juden zu gestatten sei*
(Berlin, 1783). The quotation does not appear in Brunschwig's original French version
and I have not been able to verify it.

[4] "Stimme eines Kosmopoliten" [C. W. Grattenauer], *Über die physische und moralische
Verfassung der heutigen Juden* (Germanien, 1791), quoted by Brunschwig, *Enlightenment*,
p. 285, who finds puzzling the fact that the tract is permeated with the spirit of Enlightenment (which must be by definition opposed to Jew-hatred)!

[5] See N. Rotenstreich, *The Recurring Pattern: Studies in Anti-Judaism in Modern Thought*
(London, 1963); E. L. Fackenheim, *Encounters between Judaism and Modern Philosophy*
(New York, 1971), pp. 37ff., 50ff.; J. Carlebach, *Karl Marx and the Radical Critique of
Judaism* (London, 1978); *HAS*, vol. 3.

and, above all, "freedom"-seeking. Revolutionary antisemitism was thus born of the idealist, revolutionary vision of a newly redeemed, emancipated, "free" mankind.

## KANT AND THE "EUTHANASIA OF JUDAISM"

Like the statists, the moralists offer many apparently liberal opinions on the Jewish Question that are apt to mislead the modern reader innocent of the historical and conceptual contexts of the arguments. Ideals of the brotherhood and freedom of humanity seem commendable; it is only under a detailed contextual analysis that the sinister meaning of this altruistic vision emerges, especially in the case of Kant.

To the unwary reader, the contradictions in Kant's attitude to the Jewish Question usually appear mystifying. How is it possible to understand the apparent contradiction between Kant's crude remarks in his writings against Jews and Judaism, and his vision of a universal peace and a just society where the Jew would be welcome?[6] That Kant's friend Herder also presents the same sort of paradoxical thinking suggests we are dealing here with a basic conceptual framework that is alien and perplexing to the modern reader, but that was quite natural and uncomplicated in its own context.

Kant starts unequivocally from a position of extreme hostility to Jewish religion. His *Religion within the Limits of Reason Alone* of 1793 announced that "the Jewish religion is not really a religion at all, but merely a community of a mass of men of one tribe [*Stamm*]," that is, Judaism was nothing but a national community shaped by a miscellaneous set of pseudoreligious statutes. This he deduced by applying the critical principle that a true religion must be founded on "pure moral belief." Judaism completely lacked moral content, being based

---

[6] See A. Low, *Jews in the Eyes of the Germans: From the Enlightenment to Imperial Germany* (Philadelphia, 1979), pp. 93–99. Brunschwig, *Enlightenment*, p. 281, associates Kant with the Dohmian rationalists and so finds him incapable ("liberal to the core") of true anti-Jewish feeling! The paradox extends to Kant's personal relations. Personally he had warm relations with some of his Jewish friends and students, yet he also wrote snidely in private about one such friend evincing the characteristic Jewish tendency of "trying to give themselves an air of importance at someone else's expense." See letter of 28 March 1794, in Kant, *Gesamtausgabe* (Leipzig, 1842), 10:530f. The Jew in question was Solomon Maimon.

The account of Kantian revolutionism in B. Yack, *The Longing for Total Revolution* (Princeton, 1986), does not consider the Jewish problem in Kant and also confuses "revolutionary" with "left-wing" attitudes.

on obedience to an externally imposed law that testified to the absence of an inner moral imperative—that is to say, of "freedom."[7]

That Kant was well aware of the practical meaning of his critique of Judaism is clear from his *Anthropology*, published in 1798. While Dohm had insisted that there was nothing intrinsically "harmful" in Judaism and that the evident corruption of Jewish character stemmed from Christian oppression, Kant invidiously extended his own philosophical principle of the immorality of Judaism to explain the perpetual immorality of the Jews:

> The Palestinians who live among us owe their not undeserved reputation for cheating (at least the majority of them) to their spirit of usury which has possessed them ever since their exile. Certainly it seems strange to conceive of a nation of cheats, but it is just as strange to conceive of a nation of traders, most of whom—tied by an ancient superstition—seek no civil honor from the state where they live, but rather to restore their loss at the expense of those who grant them protection as well as from one another. . . . Instead of vain plans to make this people moral . . . I prefer to give my opinion on the origin of this peculiar constitution of a nation of traders. . . . [Kant argues that ancient Israel lay on the crossroads of commerce and that after their exile the Jews carried their trading habits across the globe.] . . . The religious and linguistic unity of this people was not a curse but a blessing. . . . The wealth of this people, calculated per capita, exceeds probably the wealth of every other people of equal numbers.[8]

What Kant has done here is first to assume the immorality of the Jews as a nation of cheaters and usurers, and then to link this with the plausible charge that they are a nation of traders. At the same time, he stresses their enduring unity and alienness as a Palestinian nation. Taken together, these claims amount to the basic elements of a new secularized form of Jew-hatred—the idea of the Jews as an alien nation, the conviction they are almost intrinsically immoral, and the labeling of them as a nation dedicated to the winning of money. Tempting though it may be to excuse Kant by interpreting the passage as objective comment, this cannot really survive a reading of the original, which carries an unmistakable hostility of tone that we shall meet again in Herder.

One particular point that exposes Kant's lack of integrity in his general approach to Judaism is the question of the afterlife. He

---

[7] Kant, *Die Religion innerhalb der Grenzen der blossen Vernunft*, in *Werke*, 12 vols., ed. W. Weischedel (Frankfurt, 1964), 8:789–93.

[8] Kant, *Anthropologie*, in *Werke*, 12:517ff.

praises the Christian belief in the afterlife as a moral belief of the highest excellence and at the same time condemns the Jews for neglecting the doctrine of human immortality and paradise. Here Kant was trying to have things both ways at the Jews' expense: Jews obey the Ten Commandments out of self-interest and "un-freely" and are reprimanded for doing so, while Christians who follow their religion out of an essentially self-interested desire for an eternal reward are lauded!

Written in the same years as the *Anthropology* and also published in 1798, Kant's *Dispute of the Faculties* has been taken to be his most "pro-Jewish" work. Looking forward to a rapprochement of belief between enlightened Catholics and Protestants, Kant hoped that

> even in regard to the Jews, this [rapprochement] is possible without the dream of a general conversion of the Jews to Christianity as a messianic faith if, as happens now, purified religious conceptions awaken among them and they discard the old rites.[9]

Kant has rejected the old Christian dream of converting the Jews, but in its place he envisages something far more insidiously destructive of Judaism, namely moral and human purification. The first step to this is to reform Judaism into a rational and moral religion of human freedom that will accept the validity of Christianity:

> The idea of a very keen mind of this nation, Lazarus Bendavid, to accept publicly the religion of Jesus—probably with its vehicle, the Gospel—is not only very fortunate but it is also the only proposal whose realization would soon turn this people, even without merging with others in matters of belief, into an educated, moral people, one capable of all the rights of civil status.

Notice here how Dohm's grant of civil rights without prior moral improvement of the Jews has now been conditioned on such a moral reform. No longer need the granting of rights require conversion to Christianity, allows Kant; instead rights now require religious and moral reform, something that is altogether more elusive to fulfill.

Some Jews were naive enough to accept this fundamental shift and willingly yielded up Dohm's crucial principle of unconditionality. Thus, Bendavid began the work to which Kant refers with the abject question: "What must the Jews do to make themselves fit for a civil reform?"[10] Even such a defender of Jewish rights as Saul Ascher suggested that some orthodox Jews were too benighted to be emanci-

---

[9] Kant, *Streit der Fakultäten*, in *Werke*, 11:320f.

[10] L. Bendavid, *Etwas zur Charakteristik der Juden* (Leipzig, 1793).

pated and that some rational reform of Jewish ceremonial law should precede the general award of civil rights.[11]

The most sinister implication of Kant's critique of Judaism was that it acknowledged no validity or even right to an independent existence of Judaism, which was seen not only as immoral, but obsolete in the modern world. "The euthanasia of Judaism," he confidently affirmed, "is the pure moral religion!"[12] Of course, this was in effect nothing more than a secularization of the old Christian idea that the Old Testament and the Jewish religion had been superseded by the New Testament and Christianity. But in the context of the German philosophical revolution and the revolutionary excitement of the 1790s, such a crude transformation fell upon receptive ears as a stunning revelation.

Again, Kant's persuasively moral vision of a future world governed by peace and humanity in which freedom shall reign is often assumed to be part of a fixed constellation of progressive, humanitarian, liberal opinions. If Kant is concerned to maintain the independence of the European nations so as to prevent the emergence of a "universal despotism without a soul," *and* if he holds that moral duties are not contingent on race and religion, *then* he is also assumed to subscribe to universal rights for all citizens—including the Jews—as part of the package. But this reasoning entails obvious logical and historical fallacies. Moreover, it is not supported by any explicit statements in Kant about the granting of Jewish rights. Certainly, Kant holds out hope that at some date in the future the Jews will be accommodated in his moral commonwealth; but it is clear from his statements about Jewish immorality, as well as from the logical shape of his argument, that only the most enlightened Jews are capable for the present of being admitted into German public and intellectual life. This was the meaning of his public embrace of that obviously exceptional enlightened Jew, Moses Mendelssohn. For the present, however, Jews as a group are not morally—and for that reason should not be *politically*— equal to Germans. The absence of any explicit statement in Kant in favor of the immediate granting of civil and political rights to the Jews is not an accident or an oversight; it stems from the very nature of his argument.

In Kant, therefore, we find a collection of potent anti-Jewish concepts: Judaism is an *immoral* and *obsolete* religion; the Jews are an *alien*

[11] Cf. E. Navon, "The Encounter of German Idealists and Jewish Enlighteners 1760–1800," in *Deutsche Aufklärung und Judenemanzipation*, ed. W. Grab (Tel Aviv, 1980) (Beiheft 3, Jahrbuch des Instituts für deutsche Geschichte), pp. 225–41. See above, chap. 6, n. 28, for Jewish reforms.

[12] Kant, *Streit*, in *Werke*, 11:321.

nation; the Jews are a nation of *traders* devoted to *money*. Unifying all
these themes is the central Kantian revolutionary idea of moral freedom that sees the Jews as refusing to be free: they chain themselves
to an external, irrational Law that reduces them in the end to being
slaves of their own unenlightened egoism. It was this implicit notion
of "egoism" that was to receive an extraordinary elaboration and currency in subsequent philosophical critiques of Judaism.

## HERDER: "HUMANITY" AND THE JEWISH QUESTION

The complex attitude to the Jewish Question of Kant's friend,
Johann Gottfried von Herder (1744–1803), has often been simplified
into a "pro-Jewish" position reflecting what purports to be his generally humanitarian—even liberal—toleration of the plurality of political and historical cultures in Europe and the world. The Jews, by
this account, were entitled to their own cultural and national existence, either within Germany or in a Palestinian homeland of their
own.[13] Yet such a philosemite reading of Herder leaves unexplained
numerous anti-Jewish statements, which are often found in the very
same paragraphs as his more favorable remarks. This kind of unhistorical approach to Herder merely generates paradoxes, as it does

[13] The main accounts in English of Herder on the Jewish Question see him as a
philosemite, viewing him through liberal categories and removing him from the moralist and statist contexts to which he belongs. See F. M. Barnard, "The Hebrews and
Herder's Political Creed," *Modern Language Review* 54 (1959): 533–46; idem, "Herder
and Israel," *Jewish Social Studies* 28 (1966): 25–33. I. Berlin, *Vico and Herder* (New York,
1977), pp. 159f., on the Jews, is a brilliant—but to my mind misconceived—attempt to
interpret Herder as a liberal pluralist at the expense of removing him from his German context. Other strong avowals of Herder's "pro-Jewish" stance are Low, *Jews*, pp.
55–66, and A. Bein, "The Jewish Parasite," *LBIY* 10 (1964): 3–41 (p. 10: Herder was
"anything but an enemy of the Jews"). Z. Levy, "The Place of Judaism in J. G. Herder's
Philosophy of History," *Jerusalem Studies in Jewish Thought* 4 (1982): 236–78, goes to the
extreme of seeing Herder as recommending Jewish self-fulfillment in a Zionist return
to Palestine. (Herder does sarcastically remark on the project of a Jewish return to
Palestine, but it is not, as we shall see, a remark motivated by concern for Jewish fulfillment.) In general, these accounts take Herder's ambiguous remarks at face value,
even at the cost of rendering them inconsistent with his general philosophy, as will be
seen below. Other commentators to have shied away from a thorough consideration of
Herder's views on the Jewish Question include (surprisingly) J. L. Talmon, "Herder
and the German Mind," in his *The Unique and the Universal* (London, 1965), pp. 91–
118. In German, cf. L. Geiger, *Die deutsche Literatur und die Juden* (Berlin, 1910), pp.
63–80, and A. Kohut, *Gekrönte und ungekrönte Judenfreunde* (Berlin, 1913), pp. 163–79,
for useful quotations.

Only J. Katz, *From Prejudice to Destruction: Anti-Semitism 1700–1933* (Cambridge,
Mass., 1980), p. 338, enters a dissenting footnote to this rosy picture of a philosemitic
Herder.

with the statists and Kant. More than his attitude to the Jews, however, is involved here. In such cases as Herder, a reevaluation of his ideas on Judaism may supply a key to unlock certain basic obscurities in his thought that stubbornly remain enigmatic when confronted head-on. To expose what Herder really thought about the Jewish Question enables us to judge whether he really was as liberal or humanitarian as his philosophy appears to be at first sight. The Jewish Question is, in fact, a window into his mind, and it suggests that the recent tendency to see his general outlook as liberal and humanitarian is misconceived.

Herder's first major statement on Judaism appeared in the third volume of his *Ideas for the Philosophy of the History of Mankind* (1787), whose chapter on the "Hebrews" (XII, 3) provides a very mixed assessment of Jewish religion and history.[14] Herder took pains here to dissociate himself from the "lies" of the ancient enemies of the Jews (*Judenfeinde*), and he pointedly praises the Jews as a patriotic, warlike, landed people, very inventive and noble in religion, a people shaped by the great lawgiver Moses. However, from being superior in religion and law to other ancient peoples, the Jews had degenerated after the return from Babylon:

> Their religiosity became now pharisaism, their erudition a ponderous hairsplitting that gnawed at only one book, their patriotism a knavish devotion to a misunderstood old law, so that they became contemptible or ridiculous in the eyes of all neighboring peoples.

This decline was completed after the destruction of the Second Temple when they ceased to be a political and warrior nation, and lost their state along with their land. It was at this time that the Jews entered the best-known phase of their history—their involvement in finance, usury, and commerce (*Geldhandel*). This occurred because the new barbarian nations of Europe, so inexpert in civilized economics, needed moneymen to develop commerce as the Spartans needed helots. Soon the crude new states of Europe "became the voluntary slaves of their [Jewish] exploiters."

Herder, however, is not content to allow the Jews to be merely the victims of their historical misfortunes. Like Kant, he is disposed to trace Jewish moral defects back to an original and enduring national character. The ancient Jews had been happy

> to live among other peoples, a trait of their national character against which Moses himself had struggled forcefully. . . . [They had] never

---

[14] *Ideen zur Philosophie der Geschichte der Menschheit* (1784–91), ed. G. Schmidt (Darmstadt, 1966), pp. 311–16.

established a mature political culture in their own land, and so never attained a true feeling of honor and freedom. In the sciences . . . they showed more an imposed devotion than a fruitful freedom of the mind, and they were already from time immemorial deprived of the virtues of a patriot.

And now Herder introduces the common moralist condemnation of the Jews as a parasite nation:

The people of God, to whom He Himself had once granted a fatherland, has for millennia, indeed almost from its origin, been a parasitic plant on the stems of other nations; a stock of cunning go-betweens over well-nigh the whole globe, which, despite all oppression, nowhere longs for its own honor and dwelling, for a fatherland of its own.

Jewish bad character does not therefore begin with the destruction of the Second Temple in A.D. 70 and the loss of their state, but is intrinsic in their society "almost from its origin." This is the context in which Herder's admiring remarks on Moses must be seen: Moses was actually struggling *against* Jewish national character!

In the chapter of the *Ideas* headed "Foreign Peoples in Europe" (XVI, 5), Herder develops these notions of the Jews:

We observe the Jews here only as the parasitic plant that has attached itself to almost all the European nations, and draws more or less on their sap. After the destruction of old Rome, they were yet only few in Europe, but through the persecutions of the Arabs they came in great crowds. . . . During the barbarian centuries they were exchangemen, agents, and imperial servants. . . . They were oppressed cruelly . . . and tyrannously robbed of what they had amassed through avarice and cheating, or through hard work, cleverness, and diligence. . . . There will come a time when in Europe one will no longer ask who be Jew and who Christian. For the Jew too will live according to European law and contribute to the good of the state. Only a barbarian constitution may impede him from doing that or render his ability dangerous.[15]

These last three sentences have often been quoted to demonstrate just how warmly and liberally Herder was disposed towards the Jews and to show his hope for their complete emancipation.[16] But the con-

[15] *Ideen*, pp. 435–37.

[16] Low consistently interprets such statements of Herder's as those quoted above as calls for complete civil and political emancipation. He remarks, for example, that "the granting of full equality for the Jews was for Herder a natural imperative. Political

text shows that his meaning was quite otherwise. Herder sees the Jews' role as European financiers and usurers as part of a "barbarian" phase of European history. With the coming age of Enlightenment and human liberation, the Jews need no longer serve out this role and draw down persecution upon themselves. The Jew will be compelled to shed his hateful parasitical status and become subject to the laws that govern other men. Then he will contribute properly to the good of the state instead of being the financier who "enslaves" the state. Here Herder, for all his dislike of "statism," is remarkably close to the statist outlook of Dohm and Humboldt. "Only a barbarian constitution" would prevent the Jew from serving the state more usefully than he may at present, says Herder—meaning that the outdated "barbarian" constraints and discriminations, which at present frustrate that utilitarian end, are to be abolished. Herder does not mean that he is in favor of granting civil rights, merely that unenlightened "barbarian" disabilities—relics of a primitive phase of European society and culture—are to be done away with. For it is these very disabilities that channel the Jews into the very financial pursuits that are natural to them and at the same time so corrupting to their national character. In any event, the day when in Europe one will no longer ask "who be Jew and who Christian" is deferred into the distant utopian future when the Jews shall have redeemed themselves into full humanity. In other words, Herder's grand statement is nothing more than an empty utopian gesture bearing no practical significance. Like so many other German pronouncements of magnanimity toward the Jews, Herder's is really an alibi and an evasion of German responsibility.

On one fundamental issue, however, Herder differed from most German critics of the Jews, and especially from Kant. Herder certainly shared the philosopher's view that Christianity was a higher and more moral religious form than Judaism. For Herder, Judaism was fundamentally a "state religion," whereas Christianity was a free and purely moral religion.[17] But in contrast to Kant, Herder's religious sensibility led him to admire ancient Jewish Scripture. More-

---

inequality was rejected" (p. 61). It must be emphasized that nowhere in his writings does Herder call for the political equality of the Jews. His recommendation of civil equality is limited to the repeal of those legal disabilities that force the Jews into immoral financial and commercial pursuits. Barnard and Berlin also draw what seem to be unwarranted conclusions from Herder's texts. The *Encyclopaedia Judaica, s.v.* "Herder," affirms that Herder's *Adrastea* "called for the total emancipation of the Jews"; this is most certainly not so as far as the political and civil emancipation of the Jews is concerned.

[17] *Ideen*, p. 315.

over, each national culture was in Herder's eyes preciously unique, and he extended this respect for organic, historical, national cultures into the present day, to the point of admitting that modern Jewry possessed a religious and cultural validity. There was accordingly no need for—in fact, it was undesirable that there should be—a Kantian "euthanasia of Judaism." Even if Christianity were superior to Judaism, it had no right to demand its abolition.

But while Herder was willing to see Judaism survive and accepted that there was no point in having the Jews convert to Christianity (that would be false to their cultural and national character), Jewish survival raised the question: could two organic national cultures exist symbiotically in one territory? In the *Ideas* of 1787, Herder left this question unexpressed and unanswered, reserving its explicit discussion until 1802. But it is clear from the whole cultural-historical philosophy of the *Ideas* that the question must have presented a major difficulty to Herder's mind all along. This was, of course, the very same problem that taxed the German nationalists, but there was a twist to Herder's perception of it. Herder did not encounter the problem from a narrowly nationalist starting point, but was led to it by his quite contrasting cosmopolitan worldview, which allowed validity to all cultures. This eclecticism of Herder's could encompass an enthusiasm for those Hebrew Scriptures that were so repellent to the straight anti-Jewish nationalists as well as to Kant. Yet his admiration for the Old Testament should not be mistaken for friendship for the Jews, nor his acceptance of Jewish nationality for a liberal creed of cultural pluralism. As we shall see, there are good reasons for believing that Herder's insistence on the Jews remaining a separate culture and people apart from the Germans was inspired by less worthy motives than liberal respect for cultural pluralism.

The tension between Herder's admiration and fear of Jewish survival is palpable in the *Letters on the Study of Theology* (1790). Herder provocatively praises the survival of the Jews as a people, which he sees as vital to the divine plan for humanity, rather than as a Kantian anomaly. The fundamental question of theology is

> whether the history of this people is true? . . . It was and is the most remarkable people on earth. In its origin and development to the present day, in its fortune and misfortune, in its feats and faults, in its abasement and grandeur, it is so unique, so special that I count the history, the nature, the existence of this nation the most convincing proof of the miracles and Scriptures which indeed we have from them. Something like this cannot be made up, such a history with all that is connected with it—in short, such a people—cannot be feigned.

Its yet uncompleted direction is the greatest poem of the ages, which will clearly proceed until the last twist in the great, still intact, knot of all the nations of earth. . . . [The Hebrew national poetry is the Scriptures, which reflect the spirit and the history of this unique people.] . . . You see, my friend, how holy and sublime these books are to me, and how very much a Jew I am—as in Voltaire's jest—when I read them, for must we not be Greeks and Romans when we read their books too? Every book must be read in its own spirit.[18]

Yet while their Scriptures may be sublime, the Jews themselves are not. They are an unpleasing race, ironically chosen by Providence:

I do not wish you to misunderstand me and attribute the advantages of this people to its natural merit, to its lofty and virtuous national character [*Stammcharakter*], or to put them in a quite splendid role superior to all the other peoples on earth. Against this depiction speaks the content of those very Scriptures. The Jews are an obstinate, hard, ungrateful, insolent people as best described in Moses and the prophets.

The Jews are chosen to show how God tries to lead even the bad to the good. Although Herder was willing to praise the Jews as a people "obsessed with God," his general attitude to them is very jaundiced indeed and close to the stereotypes of traditional Jew-hatred.[19]

Out of distaste for political analysis, Herder was reluctant to undertake any specific discussion of the Jewish Question. He came to it only in one of his last essays entitled *Conversion of the Jews* printed in

---

[18] Herder, *Briefe das Studium der Theologie betreffend* (Frankfurt, 1790), 1:xii, 185f., 192.

[19] Herder, *Briefe*, pp. 188–91. Like Herder, the revolutionary poet Schiller admired the nobility of the ancient Jews and contrasted it unfavorably with the moral and physical squalor of contemporary Jewry. But Schiller followed Dohm in attributing this depravity to oppression. The Jews might be "diseased" as the ancient Egyptian Manetho had alleged; but that "had been the result of being forced by their oppressors to live increasingly closer together. . . . The effects developed which are inevitable in such a case . . . the greatest uncleanness and contagious diseases . . . a natural result . . . of scant nutrition and the maltreatment which people accorded them. . . . They were deprived of their holiest human rights. It is not surprising that barbarism arose among them."

In contrast to Herder, Schiller finds the solution to lie in the granting of civil rights as a prelude to the ultimate assimilation of the Jews. For the Egyptians, instead of limiting the Jews' numbers by cruelty, "a sound policy would naturally have led to their dispersal among the other inhabitants and to giving them equal rights." Schiller, "Die Sendung Moysis," in his *Sämtliche Werke* (Munich, 1910–20), 7:29–30. The text dates from 1790, not 1789 as in Low, *Jews*, p. 89. Like Herder also, Schiller later advanced ironically the idea of setting up a new Jewish state in Palestine by robbers and Jews in his play *The Robbers*, act I, sc. ii (Boston, 1902), pp. 17f. Cf. Low, *Jews*, pp. 87–92.

1802, the year before his death.[20] Part I of this essay interprets the Jewish Question as a political question, not a religious one. For Herder, the Jewish Question hinges on *how many* Jews are to be tolerated by the state:

> The Jewish race is and remains in Europe an Asiatic people alien to our region. . . . Whether [Jewish] law and the manners of thinking and living which spring from it belong in our states is no longer a dispute of religion where meanings and beliefs are under discussion, but a single-sided question of state: How many of this alien race, existing under such an alien national constitution, accustomed to such particular manners of thinking and living, pursuing certain businesses and no others—how many may be dispensed with, how many are useful or detrimental to *this* and not to any other state—that is the problem. (XXIV, 62–63)

Two points come through very clearly here. The first is the extent to which Herder sees the Jewish Question from a strongly statist point of view: how many Jews are *useful* to the state is his sole criterion. Herder does not view the question in liberal terms as one of civil and political rights; nor, more surprisingly in a thinker who is often praised for his religious principle of "humanity," does he see it in enlightened terms as an issue bearing on universal religious toleration. There is no respect here at all for the individual and his religious conscience; the Jews are merely pawns in the game of raison d'état. Evidently, when it came to the Jewish Question, Herder's much praised hatred of "the accursed state" faded somewhat, an inconsistency that raises difficulties for any attempt to make Herder into a Western liberal.[21] He simply preferred the "nation" of the German *Volk* to the "state"; both, however, excluded Jews.

The second point here is that the Jews are an alien presence in Germany, a point reinforced thus:

> For the Mosaic-Sinaitic law and the people connected to it . . . belong to Palestine and not to Europe. Since Israel in its prayers despises all the other peoples from which it is set apart, how can it be otherwise than that it is itself despised by the other nations? (XXIV, 64)

[20] *Bekehrung der Juden*, published in Herder's own journal *Adrastea* 4 (1802), reprinted in his *Sämtliche Werke*, ed. V. Suphan (repr. Hildesheim, 1967), 24:61–75 (references in text to this edition).

[21] Cf. Berlin, *Vico and Herder*, p. 158, for a very plausible attempt to read Herder sympathetically as a Western liberal. Only a full appreciation of the German context of Herder's thought—and specifically an understanding of his hostile approach to the Jewish Question—permits one to resist the elegance of this essay.

For all of Herder's alleged benign pluralism, he is here deploying the essential psychological strategy of traditional German Jew-hatred—the projection of German feelings of hatred onto the very targets of that hatred.

Herder has rejected the idea of religious conversion as outmoded and in any case a betrayal of Jewish character, and he has also ruled out any possibility of a true assimilation since Israel is an alien nation. This places the Jews in a hopelessly exposed and precarious position, without any secure identity or legal status (except, of course, for Herder's acknowledgment of a valid—if unfortunate—Jewish existence). The most that he can offer the Jews, therefore, is a partial toleration that would consist in their remaining Jews, but reforming their greedy, trade-oriented national character. For he sees, like Kant, that there is a danger in having large numbers of commercial Jews within a state, useful as some may be:

> Since the business activity of the Jews has been recognized for more
> than three thousand years, and since the influence that this has had,
> and still unchangingly has on the character of this nation, is revealed
> in its whole history, what is the purpose of vague discussions—for in-
> stance, on the rights of mankind—if the question is purely: How
> many of this foreign race may be permitted to pursue their business
> in this European state without detriment to the native population? For
> that such an unrestricted mass of these may corrupt an ill-organized
> state is proven unhappily by many sad historical examples.[22] . . .
> Trade is the profession of the Jews, since they are incompetent for
> war and agriculture. . . . Trade divides them from the artists as it does
> from the citizens. (xxiv, 64–65)

Even their own rabbis acknowledge the danger: Simone Luzzatto in 1638 recommended to Venice that six thousand would be a good number to be permitted to settle there, large enough to be of use to the government, but small enough "to prevent the crimes of the Jews, and for their law not to be hostile to humanity" (xxiv, 66).

But what if the Jewish Question might be solved by having the Jews at long last return to their ancestral Palestine? Herder quotes a sympathetic proposal made to this effect by the English writer David Hartley, which had appeared in German translation in 1772. But then Herder adds his own comment in a mocking tone:

> Good luck to them, if a Messiah-Bonaparte may victoriously lead
> them there, good luck to them in Palestine! But it will be difficult for

---

[22] Herder casually dismisses the successful Dutch case of toleration as proving nothing, so different is Holland from other countries.

this richly competitive nation to live in a narrow Palestine if they cannot there take over the general middle trade of both the old and the
new world. For the old world would be convenient to their land. Fine,
sharp-witted race, wonder of the ages! One of the brilliant glosses of
their rabbis yokes together a complaining Esau and Israel [Jacob].
Both suffer from the kiss, but they cannot separate themselves. (xxiv,
67)

Amazingly, this passage has been mistaken for a proto-Zionist declaration. In reality, it is scarcely warmer towards Jews than were those
SS circles which in the 1930s thought that the solution to the Jewish
Question might consist in removing Germany's Jews to Palestine.
There is a definite unpleasantness here in both the vocabulary and
the sentiments. A "fine, sharp-witted race" (*feines, scharfsinniges Volk*)
is not meant in a complimentary way. In Palestine, Herder believes,
this fine race will not be content to rest in peace, but will just intensify
their old commercial habits and use their position to control trade
between the Levant and the west.

In fact, the Palestine solution is for Herder no solution at all. As he
allusively suggests in speaking of Esau and Jacob's embrace, Jews and
Europeans are too entwined with one another to achieve any easy
geographical separation. So if not emigration to Palestine, then what?
The only way out of the quandary is to redeem the Jews into honor
and humanity, to "moralize" them and make them "noble." This is
the subject of part II of Herder's article, which declares that "it is the
duty of the Europeans to make good the guilt of their predecessors
and to render again suitable and worthy of honor those [Jews] who,
through them, became honorless. How is this to be achieved?" (xxiv,
69).

Herder is not, however, as benevolent as he seems. Disarmingly following in Dohm's footsteps in ascribing to Christians some of the
blame for Jewish national character, Herder insists that first and foremost "we must abolish the sources of honorless profit and cheating
that we opened, and still open, to the Jews in ill-organized states."
Herder bitterly attacks those honorless Christians who place Jews in
public positions where they may indulge their greed; those ministries,
departments, and universities controlled financially by Jews are "Pontine Marshes." He affirms generously: "Political conversion begins
with an unjust end if it affects only Jews and not Christians." But then
he posits a coercive approach eschewed by Dohm: "The harshest punitive laws here are for the Hebrews' own welfare" (xxiv, 70).

Herder's second proposal for the ennobling of the Jews again recalls Dohm. All laws, he says, that force the Jews into dishonorable

financial trades "demonstrate the continuing barbarism of the state that allowed these laws because of barbaric times." Such laws only deprave the Jews further, yet the Jew is definitely capable of moral reform, as Lessing's *Nathan the Wise* shows. Here and there, Herder indicates, one finds noble Jews; not all Jews are Shylocks (xxiv, 70ff.).

But—Herder's third point—such noble Jews are still exceptions. "If the greater part of the nation do not yet freely have this gentleness, what may lead them to it? Morality and culture." Herder here becomes seemingly humanitarian, urging a program of national education that would put Christians together with Jews in the same school classes. "Communal education of the soul unites men of all times, circumstances, and races." Who thinks of Spinoza's and Mendelssohn's works as being written by Jews?

In a magnificent, often quoted passage, Herder glimpses the "purely human" Jew of the future:

> What a prospect it would be to see the Jews, that so sharp-witted race [!], dedicate themselves to the culture of scholarship, to the welfare of the state that protects them, and to the generally useful purposes of mankind, to see them purely humanized [*rein-humanisiert*] in their occupations and ways of thinking. Strip away the old national prejudice, throw away the customs that do not belong to our time and constitution—even to our climate; let them work not as slaves in a coliseum, but as the fellow-workers of enlightened races on that greatest and most beautiful coliseum, on the building of knowledge, the collective culture of mankind. Not on the bare mountains of Palestine, that narrow ravaged land, but everywhere their Temple will spiritually rise up from its ruins; all nations shall honor with them, and they with all nations, the Creator of the world. . . . Not through the concession of new mercantile advantages will they be led to honor and virtue; they shall raise themselves there only through purely human [*rein-menschliche*] intellectual and civil merit. Their Palestine is there everywhere they live and work nobly. (xxiv, 73–75)

This humanitarian rapture contains not a word about the need for mundane political emancipation. Herder has already excluded the Jews from political rights by barring them from public financial office. The most that is promised here is the rescinding of certain legal disabilities that effectively force the Jews into the unhealthy "money" trades. And even here there are restrictions. "New mercantile advantages"—what in Western liberal terms would be called civil rights and emancipation—are airily dismissed by Herder. What the philosopher conceives of as being true "emancipation" is very obvious and indeed he states it quite explicitly. It is the human (*rein-menschlich*) emancipation of the Jews, that is to say, their "ennobling" from immoral into moral human beings. The idea is to reform the Jews, curing them of their money corruption and emancipating them into enlightened society, just as Spinoza and Mendelssohn had emancipated themselves. But these humanly emancipated Jews of Herder's would not be burdened with civil and political rights, any more than Moses Mendelssohn himself had been.

There remains at the heart of Herder's alluring proposal a pernicious fallacy—or perhaps deception would be a better word. For Herder, the Jews, even when ennobled and moralized, remain Jews, belonging to an alien nation with its own national religious culture, its members lacking political rights not only as a nation, but as individuals. This is a far cry from any properly liberal or humanitarian solution. Herder envisages the continuation of two national cultures within the same land, but German culture will be the master. Clearly, political rights are to be allocated according to membership in that master culture, rather than according to membership in a liberal German state.

Did Herder believe that the Jews could obtain "tickets of admission" to German culture? It has often been argued by his liberal apologists that Herder was no crude racist of the German nationalist school. Certainly, his sense of what was "German" and what was "Jewish" stemmed from an enlightened cosmopolitan vision opposed in spirit to German chauvinism. But at the same time, Herder's sense of the cultural singularities of "Germanness" and "Jewishness" convinced him that the two phenomena were incompatible. In theory, culture may not be racially determined (that is, biologically based) in Herder's eyes, yet national character is so deeply ingrained by tradition and by religion ("imbibed with mother's milk"), that it might as well be racially or biologically transmitted. The extraordinary ability of Moses, Spinoza, and Mendelssohn to transcend Judaism would only have served to confirm Herder's suspicion that the eventual assimilation of the Jews into Germanness—into "pure humanity"—was something that could not take place for a very long time indeed, requiring as it did a feat of genius.

———

Herder's attitude to the Jewish Question reveals that his attractive principles of national cultural pluralism and cosmopolitan humanity do not belong to the Western liberal tradition, but rather must be understood in the context of the German philosophical revolutionary tradition. He held to the essentially illiberal German conviction that the Jews were far too alien and distinct a nation ever to become "Germans." All that Herder conceded was that, with proper coercion and instruction, they might become enlightened human beings while remaining "Jews." Human emancipation—that great revolutionary ideal—went hand in hand in the modern world with depriving the the Jews of commercial, civil, and political rights. Only in a utopian Europe of the safely remote future would no one inquire "who be Jew and who Christian." Herder was most assuredly no liberal emancipationist; his idealist emancipationism belonged to the realm of revolutionary enlightenment.

The myth of Herder as a liberal pluralist and, indeed, a mortal enemy of "the state," is further belied by his ruthless application of the principle of raison d'état to the Jewish Question and by his abrogation of religious toleration except where it suited the utility of the state. Little sympathizing with the Jews as individuals with rights, any benevolence that Herder bestowed on them was merely an illusory refraction of his attitude that they were simply objects for the use of the state. For all his vaunted aversion to the state, Herder used statist concepts to restrict Jewish rights as naturally as did the Prussian statists. This should not be surprising in view of Herder's agreement with the statists' overriding desire to replace the old-style barbarian, ill-organized state with a new kind of rational state attuned to the revolutionary principles of enlightenment and humanity.

If Herder was not a "liberal," neither was he a "humanitarian" in the customary English meaning of the word. Here again, Herder's attitude to the Jewish Question sheds much light on what exactly he meant by the "principle of humanity" and may warn the modern liberal reader against too wholehearted an embrace of Herder as the great humanitarian. For him, "humanity" was a kind of secular enlightened religion, governed by the abstract principle of reason. Herder's idea—and indeed much of the German idea—of "humanity" had nothing in common with the emotional humanitarianism of the English reformers, which stemmed from compassion for the oppressed individual and for oppressed peoples and classes. *Humanität* meant the rational development of the human mind and character (self-redemption through educational *Bildung*) and its extension into the rational state. The German idea of humanity, like the German idea of freedom, must not be misconstrued in Western liberal terms.

Herder loved humanity, but he was no humanitarian. The dangers of this German kind of "humanity" for the Jewish Question were incalculable. The principle of humanity seemed only to confirm that the Jews suffered from irrationality and vice, lacked the qualities essential to be true human beings, and could be redeemed only by a revolutionary transformation of their national character—by their "pure humanization." The prejudiced moral premise that the Jews had to redeem themselves into humanity became the theoretical foundation of revolutionary antisemitism. "Pure humanization" meant the destruction of Jewishness for the sake of humanness. "A pure humanized Jew is, however, no Jew," was Houston Stewart Chamberlain's satisfied comment on this fundamental formulation of Herder.[23]

## HEGEL: "HISTORY" AND THE JEWISH QUESTION

Most of the apparent contradictions in the thinkers analyzed in this book are merely intellectual mirages. Only one major figure, it seems, embodies a genuinely bifurcated position on the Jewish Question—and that is Hegel.

Hegel's early writings—which, it must be remembered, he took pains to see remained unpublished in his lifetime—conform to the basic Kantian idealist and moralist critique of Judaism. Judaism is seen as the epitome of an unfree psyche that had to be redeemed by revolution—first by revolutionary Christianity, and now in the modern age by revolutionary German philosophy. Hegel never repudiated this position, which indeed was quite consistent with the main elements of his mature philosophy. But neither did he publicly emphasize it: the critique of Judaism remains underplayed and largely implicit in his later philosophy of religion. Hegel's explicit attitude to Judaism and the Jewish Question is, in fact, to be found not so much in his philosophy of religion as in his philosophy of history and his philosophy of law.

It was Hegel's historical philosophy that provided revolutionary antisemitism with one of its theoretical pillars, namely the supposition that the Jews had fulfilled their historical purpose in antiquity, that they were now no more than a Ahasverian "ghost-people" without land or living spirit, and that they must now "die" and dissolve into the ashes of history. Only thus could the Jews become "free"; the final revolutionary redemption of Jewish history was to be the redemption of Ahasverus—extinction.

But while Hegel supplied Jew-hatred with this powerful philosophical illustration of the Wandering Jew, his philosophy of law and the state led him away from revolutionism into an almost "liberal" position on the Jewish Question. Hegel found himself defending the Jewish right to political emancipation on the ground that the Jews were

[23] H. S. Chamberlain, *Die Grundlagen des neunzehnten Jahrhunderts* (Munich, 1906 ed.), 1:145.

human beings like any other citizens. Of course, Hegel was not really a liberal on this score; he interpreted the equality of human beings from the standpoint of the state which, if it were rational and free, should not discriminate between its Jewish and Christian members. Hegel did not argue that rights were implicit in the individual, but rather that the rational state obliged itself by its own principle of reason to give equal rights to all its human members. Nevertheless, it is notable that Hegel's support for the Jews seems to have been influenced by genuinely humane feelings, unlike the professed goodwill of so many of his contemporaries and disciples.

These varied elements of moralism, historicism, and statism—each of which is internally valid in its own line of argument and yet at odds with the others—make perhaps for a genuine paradox, an unresolved antinomy, in Hegel's attitude to the Jewish Question. Had he lived long enough, he might have been able to straighten things out, perhaps by elucidating his central philosophy of man and the state. As it was, Hegel's formulations served only to provide his less subtle followers of both left and right with a palette of new justifications for Jew-hatred.

---

The writings of the young Hegel eagerly espoused Kant's philosophical sneer that Judaism was not truly moral because it entailed obedience to the external commandments of a remote God, rather than hearkening like Christianity to man's inner urges to love, freedom, and morality.[24] Such was the line taken in Hegel's *Life of Jesus* (1795), which put Kantian ethics into the mouth of Jesus. In other early essays, Hegel portrayed Jesus not as divine redeemer, but as the preacher of a pantheism of "love" countering the ethic of "domination" practiced by the Jews.[25] The Jews were hostile to a "Nature" (meaning both human nature and the world of nature) that they could not understand and to which they could relate only by possessing and dominating it. But it was this very lust for power and domination, this materialistic denial of emancipating love, that made the

[24] N. Rotenstreich, "Hegel's Image of Judaism," *Jewish Social Studies* 15 (1953): 33–52; idem, *The Recurring Pattern*, pp. 274–80; Fackenheim, *Encounters*, pp. 89–96, 153–69; Katz, *From Prejudice to Destruction*, pp. 68ff.; Low, *Jews*, pp. 274ff.; *HAS*, 3:182ff., 513f.

[25] The early writings are printed in Hegel, *Theologische Jugendschriften*, ed. H. Nohl (Tübingen, 1907). Some are translated by T. M. Knox in Hegel, *Early Theological Writings* (Chicago, 1948). The latter omits *Das Leben Jesu*, which is now available in Hegel, *Three Essays 1793–1795*, trans. P. Fuss and J. Dobbins (Notre Dame, 1984), see especially p. 127.

Jews servile and unloved beings. By rebelling against a Nature that was essentially beneficent, the domination-seeking Jews had willfully blinded themselves to Christ's natural gospel of love and freedom. The notion of a political messiah, which made them reject Jesus, had prevented them from moving on to an inner, genuinely moral freedom independent of external commands.

More than that, it was the very nature of Judaism—"Jewish consciousness" itself—that blocked the way to love. "The teaching of love failed to overcome the whole fate of Judaism. . . . The Jewish multitude were bound to wreck His attempt to give them a [new] consciousness of something divine."[26] Deficient in freedom, addicted to domination, and unable to embrace love, the Jews thus doomed themselves to a perpetual parasitism among the new healthy, living, and loving nations of the world:

> All the conditions of the Jewish people, including the wretched, abjectly poor, and squalid state they are still in today, are nothing more than the consequences and developments of their original destiny—an infinite power that they desperately sought to surmount—a destiny that has maltreated them and will not cease to do so until this people conciliates it by the spirit of beauty, abolishing it as a result of this conciliation.[27]

Only when the Jews abolish their "destiny" and rejoin Nature by destroying Judaism shall they be redeemed:

> The fate of the Jewish people is the fate of Macbeth who stepped out of nature itself, clung to alien beings, and so in their service had to trample and slay everything holy in human nature—and had at last to be forsaken by his gods (since they were objects and he their slave) and be dashed to pieces on his faith itself.[28]

Here is the kernel of the later critical attacks on Judaism by Feuerbach, Marx, and the other Young Hegelian radicals. For the young Hegel, the Jews' inexorable destiny is rooted in that servile, fetishistic Jewish consciousness of "egoism" that had compelled the Jews to re-

[26] See Hegel's essays on "The Positivity of the Christian Religion" (1795–96) and the "Spirit of Christianity" (1798–99) in his *Theologische Jugendschriften*, especially pp. 243–60. (Cf. *Early Theological Writings*, pp. 9, 68ff., 177ff., 182, 253ff.) C. Taylor, *Hegel* (Cambridge, 1975), pp. 58–64, treats these early texts as a critique of Christianity and neglects their indictment of Judaism, but he does remark (p. 498) of Hegel's later writings that in them "the whole negative side of his judgement on the religion of unhappy consciousness is discharged into Judaism."

[27] *Theologische Jugendschriften*, p. 260; *Early Theological Writings*, pp. 199ff.

[28] *Theologische Jugendschriften*, p. 260; *Early Theological Writings*, p. 201.

ject Christ's teaching of love and that still renders them parasites, loveless and unloved, among the nations. They must abandon this "animal existence" and become free and human in a very rapid historical process. There is in this early Hegelian concept of a servile Jewish consciousness more than a hint of the old Christian theme of the perpetual servitude of the Jews. If Hegel allows the Jews a way of escape from this servitude through their human emancipation, the solution is not in the end so different from the Christian path of conversion.

In his mature writings, however, Hegel replaced his Kantian moralist argument against Judaism with a more typically historical one of his own based on the dialectic.[29] Judaism, he now claimed, had been superseded by the movement of the world spirit from the ancient to the modern Christian world, and in the process the Jewish people had been left stranded outside the current of world history. The Jews were seen as incapable of historical development, a "fossil nation," a "ghost-race." Isolation from true life-giving history thus rendered the Jews a "parasite race" whose only access to freedom and redemption lay in their disappearance from a historical stage on which they no longer had a role. In the eyes of Hegel, the old theological vice of Jewish "stubbornness" acquired a new dimension—the irrational refusal of the Jews to join the rubbish heap of history. Freedom from history can be achieved only by abandoning those traits and practices that preserve the Jews as a separate people, that is, by their desertion of the Law and their forswearing of legalism and ritualism. In this secular interpretation, stubbornness denoted Jewish "isolation" and "particularism"—that infuriating refusal to assimilate that so irritated many of the Jews' self-declared friends in the new age of emancipation. But this tactic scarcely provided Hegel with any convincing explanation of the very mystifying fact that the Jews had indeed survived.

Had Hegel and the Young Hegelians been able to lay aside their residual prejudices, their ingenuity would surely have permitted them to find an apology for Judaism that observed the terms of their own dialectic and at the same time resolved the anomaly of Jewish survival. The Jewish disciple of Hegel, Nachman Krochmal (1785–1840), for instance, used Hegelian concepts to explain the survival of the Jews that so perplexed the philosopher. Krochmal argued that the Jews are an eternal people who have developed historically

[29] See H. Liebeschütz, *Das Judentum im deutschen Geschichtsbild von Hegel bis Max Weber* (Tübingen, 1967), chap. 1. Hegel discusses Judaism incidentally in the *Aesthetics*, the *Lectures on the Philosophy of Religion*, the *Phenomenology of Mind*, and the *Philosophy of History*.

through a sequence of life cycles different from those of other peoples subject to the Hegelian dialectic of history. This privileged "cyclism" is due to the fact that Judaism is the purest form of monotheism and so is equal to the Idea or Spirit itself. All other histories, including Christian German history, are merely particular examples of Spirit; Judaism alone is universal Spirit. Indeed so powerful is the Spirit in Judaism that the Jewish people alone of all peoples have survived without the existence of a state! By this elegant argument Krochmal was able to turn the weakness of Jewish history into a strength, so solving the puzzle of Jewish survival into modern times without the apparently indispensable apparatus of a state.[30]

Hegel's mystification about the Jews' lack of interest in being redeemed may have led him in his later years to soften considerably his attitude towards Jewish "fanaticism of stubbornness"; he even admitted it might better be termed "an admirable firmness." The formal reason he gave for this revision was that the Jews had to remain stubborn in their particularity because of Judaism's profound understanding of divine transcendence. Their religious insight necessarily prevented their integration into a Christianity that proclaims the union of God and man through Christ. It is a theological irreconcilability that Hegel sees mirrored in the Jews' social isolation from Christians over the centuries. (Here Hegel was prevented by Christian presuppositions about Judaism from appreciating the extent to which Jewish theology actually sought areas of union between God and man, such as the Covenant.)

Hegel came also to admire the poetic fantasy of the putatively "enslaving" Old Testament that had inspired Jewish firmness. Herder, too, had admired the Bible's poetry, but mainly for its heroic epic qualities; Hegel's interest, however, stemmed more from its moral content. Far from merely depicting a tyrannical relationship between man and God, the Hebrew Scriptures now seemed to Hegel to have opened the way to "true morality and integrity."

This positive reassessment of Jewish character—together with his own developing theory of the state—led Hegel to become an explicit supporter of Jewish civil rights. He denounced not only the medieval crusaders who had massacred the Jews, but also their modern German successors who sought to punish continuing Jewish stubborn-

---

[30] For an account of Krochmal's *Guide to the Perplexed of Our Time*, published in Hebrew in 1851, see S. Avineri, *The Making of Modern Zionism* (New York, 1981), chap. 1; N. Rotenstreich, *Jews and German Philosophy* (New York, 1984), pp. 143–51. The most notable critique of this aspect of Hegel from the Jewish point of view is Samuel Hirsch's *Die Religionsphilosophie der Juden* (1842). Cf. N. Rotenstreich, *Jewish Philosophy in Modern Times* (New York, 1968).

ness by denying civil rights to the Jews. Repudiating the notion that the Jews were an "alien" nation within the modern German states, Hegel ruled out national character as a valid moral or political argument in discussion of the Jewish Question. At the University of Heidelberg in 1818, while the student *Burschenschaften* of the other German universities were loudly barring Jews from membership, Hegel influenced his students to open their *Burschenschaft* to Jews. His main pupil there, the philosopher Friedrich Wilhelm Carové (1789–1852), indeed remained a consistent supporter of Jewish rights on clear Hegelian philosophical grounds. In 1837 Carové declared that "the emancipation of the Jews is the universal problem of the emancipation of humanity itself," and when Hegel's self-proclaimed "Young Hegelian" followers, led by Bruno Bauer and Karl Marx, launched their "critical" attacks on Judaism in 1843–45, Carové stayed a loyal philosophical defender of Jewish rights. Nevertheless, even for Carové the Jews remained an alien nation. Arguing for the admission of Jews to the Heidelberg *Burschenschaft*, he appealed: "Is it not the most beautiful part of German national character to honor the rights also of *foreigners?*" And in 1819, when the students under Carové's leadership took up arms to protect the Jews during the Hep-Hep riots, they were careful afterwards to insist that they had been motivated "by respect for law and justice" rather than by any "love for the Jews."[31]

Carové grounded his defense on Hegel's own principles in the *Philosophy of Right*, written in 1818–19 in the period immediately before and after the Hep-Hep riots. Here Hegel had openly scorned the anti-Jewish spoutings of the academic mentor of the *Burschenschaften*, Jakob Fries—and by implication those of Kant himself—as "superficial pap" unworthy of the name of philosophy.[32] The Jews, Hegel insisted, must be given civil rights. It was actually foolish and unphilosophical to obstruct the emancipation of the Jews, for to do so showed a basic ignorance of the nature of law and of the state:

---

[31] Carové, "Emanzipation der Juden," *Phoenix* 3 (1837): 390–99 *passim*, 450–66 *passim*, 474–75. He participated in the "critical" controversy of the Bruno Bauer school with his "Schriften, betreffend die Religion und die Emanzipation der Juden," *Theologisches Literaturblatt* (1843): 1177–1221, and his book *Über Emanzipation der Juden* (Siegen, 1845), which argued for complete religious freedom and indifference. In 1819 Carové took up arms to defend the Jews of Heidelberg against the anti-Jewish rioters. Cf. E. Sterling, *Judenhass* (Frankfurt, 1969), pp. 90f., 93f., 149; idem, "The Hep-Hep Riots in Germany 1819: A Displacement of Social Protest," *Historia Judaica* 12 (1950): 105–42; O. F. Scheuer, *Burschenschaft und Judenfrage* (Berlin, 1927), pp. 10–16.

[32] Hegel, *Philosophy of Right*, trans. T. M. Knox (Oxford, 1952), pp. 5f., 28. For Fries, see the following chapter on Fichte.

The opponents of the Jews ignore that they are first of all human beings and that this is not a shallow, abstract quality. To exclude the
Jews from civil rights . . . the state would have misunderstood its own
basic principle.[33]

Yet if Hegel supported the Prussian Edict of Emancipation and
publicly defended Jewish students, his support arose out of his general theory of the state and that created a difficulty. For Hegel, "civil
society"—the stage of society in which man was not a free, genuinely
social man, but merely one who obeyed his own selfish interests and
the laws imposed by external authority—was most aptly symbolized
by Judaism, the religion of divinely imposed Law. The higher form
of the state, however, would make men free and genuinely social in a
regime of reason and love, just as Christianity had superseded Judaism. Hegel, therefore, came back indirectly to his youthful Kantian
view that Judaism was ethically inferior to Christianity; but he now
embodied this view in a grand philosophical-historical system that always required that Judaism be interpreted as a superseded phase of
world history.

Although there might appear at first sight to be a contradiction
between Hegel's later sympathy towards Judaism and his critical attitude, intellectually he was nevertheless quite consistent.[34] Both his
support for Jewish emancipation and his condescension towards Judaism were argued from a single source, namely his philosophy of
man and the state. His combination of dislike for Judaism with advocacy of Jewish rights proved typical of many of his self-styled
Young Hegelian disciples. Unfortunately, so intensely did these disciples develop the potential for a radical critique of Judaism contained in Hegel's philosophy, that their animosity towards Judaism
made their pro forma support of Jewish rights seem somewhat bewildering to their Jewish opponents, as we shall see in later chapters.

Even if he himself did not press it, Hegel's critique of Judaism was

[33] *Philosophy of Right*, p. 169, paragraph 270, footnote (cf. p. 134). See the clear analyses by S. Avineri, "A Note on Hegel's Views on Jewish Emancipation," *Jewish Social
Studies* 25 (1963): 145–51, and *Hegel's Theory of the Modern State* (Cambridge, 1972), pp.
17–24, 119f., 170f.

[34] Low, *Jews*, p. 278, remarks on a certain contradiction in Hegel's writings but does
not try to explain it.

Hegel's familiarity with such Jews as the idiosyncratic Heinrich Heine and the clown-
ish Heinrich Beer—a curious choice of acquaintance for such a subtle and self-aware
person as Hegel—may well be a psychological manifestation of a deep dissociation in
his attitude towards Judaism and Jews. For these curious friendships, see the texts
translated in Heine, *History of Religion and Philosophy in Germany*, ed. P. L. Rose (North
Queensland, 1982), pp. 127ff.

of fundamental importance for the history of modern antisemitism up to the present day. For Hegel formulated a concept of "human emancipation" that embraced the twin elements that reappear constantly in the revolutionary critique of Judaism. First, there was the idea of Jewish "lovelessness." Hegel took over from Kant the prejudice that Judaism was essentially an immoral religion, but he reinterpreted this as part of a systematic concept of "egoism." Thus, Hegel in his earlier writings characterized Jewish religion as one in which excessive self-love (egoism) and the instinct to dominate had driven out true social human love and produced a religion of lovelessness.

To this imputation of egoistic lovelessness, Hegel added a second historical element, namely his conviction that Judaism was obsolete and that its only way to redemption lay in its "destruction." Here again the basic concept of loveless egoism played a large part. For the peculiar survival of Judaism was viewed as the result of an *egoistic* refusal to be "destroyed," to merge with the new peoples of modern Europe, to rejoin history, to love humanity. The lineaments of the secularized myth of Ahasverus are evident in Hegel's philosophical conception of Judaism.

Still, even if Hegel did adumbrate the main themes of the new mythology, he stopped well short of subscribing to the new ideology of Jew-hatred. He himself made a more serious and sympathetic effort to understand Jews and Judaism than had Kant. More importantly, although he indicated that Judaism was a religion of materialism, Hegel never tried (except in his youthful works) to link his ideas of Jewish egoism and domination to the doctrine of the economic selfishness and parasitism of the Jews on which Kant, Herder, and Fichte had fixed. Unfortunately Hegel's followers turned out to be less scrupulous; in the writings of such literary men as Karl Gutzkow and Heinrich Laube, and in the political and philosophical works of Moses Hess and Karl Marx, it became commonplace to assert blankly that the main manifestation of Jewish egoism and domination was to be found in the Jews' involvement with money. This was a logical enough extension of Hegel's views on egoism, but whether the responsibility for this later tendency should be laid on Hegel is open to question. Like his student protégé Heine, Hegel also might have ended up abandoning this plausible prejudice in his later years.

# The German Nationalists and the Jewish Question: Fichte and the Birth of Revolutionary Antisemitism

IN 1793—the year in which Kant published the first of his moralist attacks on Judaism, the year of the Revolutionary Terror in France—the specter of revolutionary Jew-hatred appeared before the alarmed eyes of the German Jewish rationalist Saul Ascher (1767–1822). It manifested itself in an anonymous radical defense of the events in France entitled *Contribution to the Correction of the Public Verdict on the French Revolution*, whose author was soon revealed to be the erstwhile Kantian philosopher Johann Gottlieb Fichte (1762–1814), then going through a Jacobin phase before his final epiphany as the prophet of German nationalism. Despite their shared sympathies with the French Revolution, Ascher recognized something new and dangerous in Fichte's tract, and in the following year he published a reply, *Eisenmenger the Second*. (The title refers to the early eighteenth-century Jew-hater.) Like Moses Mendelssohn ten years before, he warned that the old Christian anti-Jewish prejudices were giving way to a new kind of secular hostility towards the Jews:

> There is evolving before our eyes a quite new species of opponents armed with more dreadful weapons than their predecessors. . . . If the Jewish nation had until now political and religious opponents, it is now moral antagonists who are ranged against them.[1]

These new moral enemies of Judaism, observed Ascher, "all hold themselves to be rational or noble-minded . . . and they believe it" (p. 34). The ancestry of their ideas may be traced back to the critical philosophy of Immanuel Kant, but it had been left to his disciple Fichte to systematize Kant's adumbrations into a new philosophy of Jew-hatred:

[1] Saul Ascher, *Eisenmenger der Zweite* (Berlin, 1794), pp. 35, 77 (page references in text are to this edition). For his career as a rationalist see E. Littmann, "Saul Ascher: First Theorist of Progressive Judaism," *LBIY* 5 (1960): 107–21; W. Grab, "Saul Ascher: Ein jüdisch-deutscher Spätaufklärer zwischen Revolution und Restauration," *Jahrbuch des Instituts für Deutsche Geschichte* 6 (1977): 131–80. Cf. Moses Mendelssohn's preface to Manasseh Ben Israel's *Rettung der Juden* (1782), quoted above, chap. 7, notes 1f.

A new epoch of Jew-hatred begins with Fichte's *Contribution*. . . . I may honor the founder of this new product of human lucubration with the name Eisenmenger II. . . . Fichte builds a quite new road. . . . What progress the science of Judaism has made! (pp. 32f.)

Judaism, he says, will never raise itself to the principle of a sole true church and consequently the Jews, as members of that faith, can never be good human beings. In this perspective the author of the *Contribution* has delivered to humanity a powerful reprimand. (p. 77)

The critical philosophy [of Fichte's] *Critique of All Revelation* sees Judaism as the antinomy of its critical principle of religion. . . . According to this, the rightness of the idea of Jew-hatred may be deduced a priori. . . . Through his deduction of the concept of Jew-hatred, the eternal dispute over whether the Jew is to be tolerated or persecuted has been enlarged. (pp. 78f.)

We see now from which source Eisenmenger II has constructed his principles of Jew-hatred. . . . The sole guilt in my opinion falls upon Eisenmenger II, who occupied himself in constructing out of the system of his great teacher Kant the principle from which he could develop for himself a consequential system of intolerance. (pp. 80f.)

Fichte has shown that the religious basis of Jew-hatred must be relinquished. . . . As to the political basis, Fichte has argued for this ecstatically but not proven it philosophically. Authors of this ilk who want to demonstrate the truth of Jew-hatred from principles must embark upon just as contradictory a road as those who until now have sought to confirm their Jew-hatred from empirical knowledge. Eisenmenger II has only the immortal merit of being the first to have opened this road. . . . If Fichte should have such a successor as he himself has been to Eisenmenger, then the best of luck to my nation and to the whole of humanity! (pp. 90ff.)

The novel deductive principles of Jew-hatred that Fichte had incorporated into his system of revolutionary freedom arose out of his belief that man was essentially moral and free.[2] But the aristocracy,

[2] On Fichte's attitudes to the Jews, see E. L. Schaub, "J. G. Fichte and Anti-Semitism," *Philosophical Review* 49 (1940): 37–52, which, however, fails to discern the deductive principles of Fichte's Jew-hatred. J. Levy, *Fichte und die Juden* (Berlin, 1924), and A. Low, *Jews in the Eyes of the Germans: From the Enlightenment to Imperial Germany* (Philadelphia, 1979), pp. 143–54, conclude that the later Fichte recanted his prejudice. Low (p. 47) argues that Fichte criticized his own earlier anti-Jewish views as "exaggerated and one-sided." However, Fichte was not referring here "expressly" (*pace* Low) to the Jews, but to his general enthusiasm for atheism and the French Revolution as proclaimed in the 1793 *Contribution*. There is no indication in any of Fichte's writings or letters that he ever abandoned his hostility to Judaism. J. Katz, "A State Within a State: The History of an Anti-Semitic Slogan," in his *Emancipation and Assimilation: Studies in*

the church, and the army all acted to obstruct the revolutionary achievement of this freedom and the redemption of man and human society. Foremost among these enemies of revolutionary freedom for Fichte, writing as a Jacobin in 1793, were the Jews:

> In the bosom of almost all the nations of Europe there spreads a powerful state driven by hostile feelings that is continually at war with all the others, and that in certain states terribly oppresses the citizens. I speak of Jewry [*Judentum*].[3]

This "state" of Jewry is redoubtable, not because it is a powerfully united territorial state, but because it is "founded on a hatred of all humankind." Fichte is not routinely repeating Tacitus's condemnation of the Jewish hatred towards all other peoples; far more originally, he is discovering in that notorious Jewish "hostility" the negation of his own new, revolutionary, philosophical principle of morality and freedom. The Jews have cut themselves off from the European peoples in the past and this has led them into the barrenness of a separate existence, devoid of love and inspired only by selfish egoism and hatred of humanity.

This egoism has been sharpened, according to Fichte, by two factors. One is religious: the ritual exclusiveness imposed on the Jews by their religion prevents them from entering into a full loving social communion with their Christian neighbors. "They are a people excluded by the strongest human bond of all—by religion—from our meals, from our pleasures, from the sweet exchange of good cheer from heart to heart." The other factor is economic: "Judaism has condemned itself—and is condemned—to a petty trading that enfeebles the body and closes the mind to every noble feeling."

The other main principle of revolutionary Jew-hatred is deduced from the basic axiom that the Jews are cut off as enemies from humanity by their egoism and loveless hatred: so evil, so hostile and

---

*Modern Jewish History* (Farnborough, Hants., Eng., 1972), p. 63n., also asserts without foundation that Fichte later changed his attitude; but cf. the same author's *From Prejudice to Destruction: Anti-Semitism 1700–1933* (Cambridge, Mass., 1980), pp. 57f. and notes thereto for an apparent reversal of his earlier finding.

A hostile appraisal of Fichte—correct in its conclusions but not adequately analyzed—is to be found in L. Poliakov, *La causalité diabolique* (Paris, 1980), chap. 6. (See also his *HAS*, 3:180ff.)

For Fichte's thought in general, see J. L. Talmon, *Political Messianism* (London, 1960), pp. 177ff.; L. Krieger, *The German Idea of Freedom* (Chicago, 1972; repr.) pp. 176ff.

[3] This and following quotations come from Fichte, *Beiträge zur Berichtigung der Urtheile des Publicums über die französische Revolution*, ed. R. Schottke (Hamburg, 1973), pp. 114ff.

dangerous is the "Jewish essence" to mankind that "Jewishness" must be annihilated if human freedom is to triumph.

There are, Fichte and his successors agree, two main ways to eradicate the moral deficiency of Jewishness that is so deeply ingrained, so instinctive in Jews. One course is voluntary and calls for the Jews to redeem themselves from their loveless isolation and overcome their hatred of humanity by a voluntary accession of love. But, says Fichte,

> the Jew, who overcomes the strong—one might say insurmountable—barriers that lie before him and attains to a universal love of justice, humanity, and truth, is a hero and a saint. I don't know whether there has been or is such. I will believe it when I see it.

The other course of Jewish redemption is an imposed solution—and this is what Fichte duly proposes, albeit jestingly:

> As to giving them civil rights, I see no way other than that of some night cutting off their heads and attaching in their place others in which there is not a single Jewish idea. To protect ourselves from them I see no means other than to conquer for them their promised land and to pack them off there.

Though Fichte flippantly raises the twin solutions of expulsion and extermination, the tone and the context suggest that he did not mean his words to be taken literally, any more than did Herder his own notion of shipping the Jews off to Palestine. Moreover, Fichte also insists here that the Jews are to be granted basic human rights (as distinct from civil ones) and these presumably would have been sufficient to save German Jews from the rigors of his modest proposals. But there is nevertheless something disturbing in the use of death as a metaphor for the solution of the Jewish Question, if only because when jokes are made about murder there is usually present an emotional ambivalence that is close to wishful thinking. "Cutting off their heads" might seem to be no more than playful exaggeration, but it was to have sinister echoes in later times. Wagner would speak vaguely of the "destruction" of Judaism and joke about setting fire to a theater full of Jews; but soon after he would warmly welcome the real-life murders of Jews that were taking place in the Russian pogroms. And Hitler would casually note in *Mein Kampf* that holding down a few thousand Jewish heads under poison gas in World War I might have made the war worthwhile. It should be remembered similarly that at the very time Fichte was being so amusing, real heads were falling under the Paris guillotine in the furtherance of revolutionary virtue.

Whether or not Fichte's remark was meant to be purely figurative, it established a fundamental axiom of modern Jew-hatred that unified revolutionary Jew-hatred with the parallel rising school of nationalist Germanic Jew-hatred. Jewishness had to be annihilated, whether by the voluntary efforts of the Jews themselves or by external compulsion, whether by kindness or by violence.

---

It is often assumed that drastic solutions and racist theories originated exclusively with the German nationalist antisemites of the right. This assumption has led many commentators to conscript Fichte as a crude nationalist whose anti-Jewish remarks had their source in patriotic bigotry. Yet this is to mistake the essential revolutionary element in Fichte's thinking. Onto his Kantian moralist distaste for Judaism Fichte had grafted a French Revolutionary moralism that defined the "citizen" in terms of revolutionary virtue: only a moral being was capable of being such a virtuous citizen. Relying on Kant's a priori ethical definition of the Jew as the negation of freedom and morality, Fichte in 1793 constructed a *political* definition of the Jew as a being inherently unsuitable for citizenship and civil rights. Kant's moralism now served as the springboard for a new revolutionary, political approach to the Jewish Question.[4]

A man of great intensity of feeling and absolute moral certitude, Fichte was prone to ill-considered outbursts and by 1794 he seems to have thought better of his remarks of the previous year. This does not mean that he reversed his anti-Jewish opinions but simply that he thought it against the public interest to continue to voice them publicly. Fichte never openly or privately retracted his anti-Jewish comments in the *Contribution*, but neither did he renew the attack in his subsequent writings. The Jews are conspicuously absent from his utopian socialist treatise *The Closed Commercial State* (1800), although its extensive discussions of the nature of money and trade cried out for elaboration of the *Contribution*'s theme of Jewish involvement in commerce. More strikingly still, in his major nationalist work of 1807, the *Addresses to the German Nation*, Fichte pointedly omitted any reference to the "alien" Jews, even when describing the "self-seeking" (*Selbstsucht*) that had overtaken the German character. Yet in the 1793 *Contribution*, "self-seeking" had implicitly been taken to be supremely

---

[4] There are some parallels in French and German revolutionary definitions of Jews, but the French versions lack the philosophical and statist foundations of the German. And, of course, the moralist approach to citizenship did not prevent the French granting equal rights to Jews in 1791, even if Napoleon effectively abrogated them. It took little to persuade Napoleon of the alienness and immorality of the Jews. See F. Kobler, *Napoleon and the Jews* (New York, 1975); *HAS*, 3:226–30; S. Schwarzfuchs, *Napoleon, the Jews and the Sanhedrin* (London, 1978). See above, chap. 6, n. 19.

characteristic of the Jews, a theme hammered home by Fichte's nationalist and revolutionary colleagues alike. These mysterious silences about Judaism in discussions where it should have been centrally relevant—indeed even required by the argument—are difficult to explain. Perhaps like Wagner after him, Fichte relied upon the native instincts of his audience to supply the awareness that purging the German character of "self-seeking" meant purging it of Jewishness. At any rate, Fichte after 1793 chose to remove his antisemitism from the context of merely *political* revolution on the French model to a somewhat higher German philosophical plane.

One fruit of this was his introduction into European consciousness of one of the main ideas of racial antisemitism—the "Aryan Christ"—which appears in his philosophical work of 1804–6, *Characteristics of the Present Age*.⁵ Carried away by his vision of a natural pristine *ur*-Christianity represented by St. John's Gospel, a religion of human freedom, Fichte decried Judaism as a "degeneration" of the original true religion of mankind into a corrupted form that had been borne into the Judaized Christianity of St. Paul. In this effort to de-Judaize the origins of "authentic" (as opposed to Pauline) Christianity, Fichte raised the possibility that Christ was not actually of Jewish descent as the other "Jewish" gospels (including Luke!) portray Him:

> In John it remains wholly doubtful whether or not Jesus was of Jewish origin at all. . . . That Judaism was once the true religion is wholly denied by John, but asserted by Paul.⁶

This bizarre doctrine does not impress one as the thought of a mind neutral towards Judaism.

---

Two episodes often adduced to prove Fichte's "neutrality" towards the Jews need to be critically examined. As rector of the University of Berlin, Fichte in 1810 intervened in a case of harassment

⁵ Fichte, *Die Grundzüge des gegenwärtigen Zeitalters*, ed. A. Diemer (Hamburg, 1956), pp. 102ff., lecture 7; L. Poliakov, *The Aryan Myth* (repr. New York, 1977), pp. 101, 305; *HAS*, 3:18off. One basis for this postulate of the "Aryan Christ" has been a Talmudic reference to "Jesus the son of Pantera," Pantera or Pandera being the name of a Roman soldier based in Palestine. The futility of this theory is demonstrated by J. Klausner, *Jesus of Nazareth*, trans. (London, 1925), pp. 22ff., 233, who shows that "Pantera" actually derives from the Greek *parthenos*, making the Talmudic name an ironic reference to "Jesus the son of the Virgin."

⁶ Fichte, *Grundzüge*, pp. 182, lecture 12. This doctrine did not prevent Fichte from commenting in the same work on the superiority of Judaism to other ancient religions, noting that "during their dispersion (under the Assyrians) the Jews were emancipated from their former rude superstitions and elevated to better conceptions of God and of the spiritual world."

of a Jewish student named Joseph Leyser Brogi, who had been challenged to a duel. When Fichte moved against Brogi's tormentor, however, he did so not out of any pro-Jewish feeling or even a belief in justice, but rather because of his own aversion to dueling as a form of student disorder. Fichte consequently suspended the main offender from the university for a brief time, but also voted to imprison the hapless plaintiff Brogi for eight days. The renewal of the baiting a month later offended Fichte by its contempt for the university authorities. He then sentenced the main baiter to fourteen days in jail, while poor Brogi received another eight days. Fichte's support of justice for the Jews was in this case somewhat peculiar.[7]

The second episode concerns Fichte's membership in the Christian-German Dining Club, which met at Berlin in 1810–12. The statutes of this club excluded Jews, and when Clemens Brentano read a bitterly anti-Jewish satire to its members he was cheered and congratulated. As a member, Fichte presumably subscribed to its aversion toward Jews. But in January 1812 he read some verses to a meeting that seemed to take exception to the ridiculing of "Jews" and "Philistines." Yet here again one must be careful of imputing to Fichte a liberalism that he did not possess. What he objected to was the trivializing of the high moral mission of the club, which was to promote German human values against such inferior ethical forms as Judaism and Philistinism. By descending to ridicule such forms, said Fichte (anticipating Nietzsche's later dislike of vulgar antisemitism), one risks bringing into ridicule one's own high ideals.[8] Fichte certainly disliked vulgar, petty Jew-hatred; but there is no reason to believe that he had forsaken his more noble enmity to Judaism, or indeed that he developed a sympathy for Jewish civil rights. He seems not to have reacted to Hardenberg's Edict of Emancipation, a somewhat surprising silence considering both his acquaintance with Hardenberg and his own new prominence as both a national and cultural prophet in Prussia.

---

The difficulty involved in establishing Fichte's precise attitude to the Jews—of saying whether his is merely a "spiritual" as opposed to a "practical" antisemitism—is actually only a special aspect of the

---

[7] See M. Lenz, *Geschichte der Königlichen Friedrich-Wilhelm-Universität zu Berlin* (Halle, 1910), 1:410–17; X. Leon, *Fichte et son temps* (Paris, 1922–59), 2, ii, 195–209.

[8] Fichte, "Am 18. Januar 1812," in his *Sämtliche Werke* (Berlin, 1845–46; repr. 1965), 8:468–71. Low, *Jews*, pp. 151ff., interprets Fichte's verses as pro-Jewish! For the *Christlich-Germanische Tischgesellschaft* (on which there is surprisingly little modern literature), see, for instance, R. Aris, *History of Political Thought in Germany from 1789 to 1815* (repr. New York, 1965), pp. 401ff. Also above, chap. 6, n. 25.

more general problem of interpreting Fichte's "nationalism." Hostile Western critics have sought to blame Fichte for the rise of aggressive German political nationalism; Fichte's defenders have (like Herder's) replied that their hero was no militarist or political chauvinist, but rather preached a nationalism that was cultural and spiritual. Yet to divide Fichte's outlook into one or the other of these categories is false; his attitude was a universal amalgam of a "Germanness" that was simultaneously political and cultural, militaristic and pedagogical. Fichte's nationalism was soaked in moral and revolutionary values that defy any "liberal" categorizing.

The same may be said of the argument as to whether Fichte and Herder were racist or antiracist thinkers. Certainly neither of them advocated a "racial" concept of nationalism. Both seem, in fact, to have rejected a biological definition of "the German nation," preferring to see "Germanness" as something shaped by culture, history, tradition, and spirit. But this does not mean that they were therefore liberals who dismissed any thought of there being "national" differences between Jews and Germans. We shall be led to this liberal conclusion only if we subscribe to the liberal conception that racial and nonracial categories are mutually exclusive. For Fichte and Herder, the "national" spirit was intrinsically "racial," even if not so in the biological sense. Their distinction between "racial" and "cultural" (or "ethnic") was, analytically speaking, merely a technicality. This may become clearer if it is understood that in practice Fichte's definition of the German or Jewish "nations" might just as well have been "racial" (in modern language), so much did he envisage the Jews as a separate alien nation with an alien culture that could not be transcended except by "cutting off their heads."

These conceptual complications affect also the analysis of the German revolutionary nationalism inspired by Fichte. This movement of political and national liberation is often characterized as "racist," but at this stage of its development it was actually informed by a fundamental ambivalence about the biological idea of Jewish "race." As we shall see, its spokesmen (such as Fries) were able to speak in what seems to the modern reader to be thoroughly racist language about the racial contrast between Germans and Jews, and yet also seem to be saying that if the Jews can destroy their own Jewishness—that is, their racial character—then they may be accepted as Germans. As Jakob Fries put it, "the Jew in the Jew must be done to death." This kind of ambiguity of language—so central to modern revolutionary Jew-hatred—has led to a great deal of sterile argument as to whether or not its users meant their words to be taken literally or metaphorically. But to insist on a simple answer is to miss the whole ambivalence that is built into the mental structure of writers like Fichte and Fries or Arndt and Jahn. The reality is that they are—in modern terms— racists and nonracists at the same time, often hazily unaware themselves (for all their violent bluntness of speech) of whether they are advocating a physical or merely metaphorical destruction of the Jews. Until a fully biological theory of race had been formulated by about 1860, this ambiguity about "nation," "race," and "culture" could not be resolved, and it pervades all the varied theorizing that flourished before 1860.

The most public and rancorous manifestation of the revolutionary nationalist spirit of Fichte broke forth in the student *Burschenschaften* fraternities that appeared after 1815. Although their immediate impetus came from such "Germanomaniacs" as E. M. Arndt and Friedrich Jahn, the logical capacity for development into dangerous nationalism and antisemitism inherent in Fichte's doctrines made them extremely influential. Significantly, Fichte's leading disciple, the philosopher Jakob Fries (1773–1843), took a prominent role in the formation of these intolerantly nationalistic and anti-Jewish associations.[9] Very often described as freedom-seeking "democratic" groups, the *Burschenschaften* had, in fact (as Saul Ascher noted), taken up the French ideal of liberty and Germanized it so that it became a peculiarly German revolutionary myth embodying primitive nationalistic and Teutonic enthusiasms.[10]

For these romantically minded German students, revolutionism and nationalism fused together into a great revolutionary myth of German redemption that took its real inspiration from Fichte's vision of German liberation, a liberation, as one enthusiastic student put it,

> not only from the Napoleonic conquest of 1806, meaning simply from a political, exterior situation, but also from our spiritual inner slavery . . . from the bondage of Egypt.[11]

The powerful emotional swell of this myth encompassed even those Jewish students whom it was meant to exclude. Writing in the

---

[9] See *HAS*, 3:380–91; O. F. Scheuer, *Burschenschaft und Judenfrage* (Berlin, 1927). Very useful indeed is J. G. Legge's little-known *Rhyme and Revolution in Germany . . . 1813–1850* (London, 1918).

[10] Saul Ascher, *Die Germanomanie* (Berlin, 1815). Cf. G. Steiger, *Urburschenschaft und Wartburgfest* (Leipzig, 1967) for Ascher's polemic with the Wartburgers. In general, see P. Wentzcke, *Geschichte der deutschen Burschenschaft* (Heidelberg, 1919), vol. 1.

[11] Quoted in the important article by U. Tal, "Young German Intellectuals on Romanticism and Judaism—Spiritual Turbulence in the Early Nineteenth Century," in *Salo Wittmayer Baron Jubilee Volume* (Jerusalem, 1974), 2:919–38, at p. 920.

aftermath of the *Burschenschaft* festival at the Wartburg in October 1817, one such Jewish student gave vent to both the splendor and misery of the event for him as a revolutionary German Jew:

> Never in my life have I been asked so often, so intensively, so persistently, about my being a Jew, as during the last week. It was the week . . . of that great event at Wartburg. . . . Some pitied me for being doomed to be a Jew, others accused me; some insulted me, others praised me for it . . . but all my comrades were constantly aware of it. Oh, how deeply was I disappointed, how deeply wounded, frustrated, humiliated, how much in pain, in despair—and now, ever since then, how perplexed, how bewildered, how hopeless am I. . . . Didn't we all believe that these days, when the light of such great men as Fichte, Jahn, or Arndt brightens our life, are days of a total renewal of man, of Germanic man, days of moral regeneration, of national unity, of a complete and final redemption of our soul and our mind, of mankind, of a complete return to the womb of our entire existence, to nature.[12]

The Jewish Question, in fact, was central to the revolutionism of the Wartburg. The seminar papers and diaries of German students of these angry years reveal a startling intensification of Fichte's revolutionary hostility into an intellectual and emotional hatred of Judaism that demanded its total extirpation from German life. In the mouthings of these revolutionary students of 1812–19 there are shocking glimpses of the real ancestry of Nazi antisemitism, including even the "stab in the back" theme. One anguished soul howls:

> The shameful confederation against Prussia which, as everybody knows, was made possible by the typically treacherous Jewish espionage, makes me feel as if limbs were torn from my own body. . . . I now swear that my whole life will be dedicated to the resurrection of the Reich.[13]

Another writes: "The Jewish emancipation [of 1812] was the destruction not only of Prussia but of the whole German nation, the totality of the *Volk*."[14] Later antisemitic writers paid homage to these *Burschenschaften* (and the Hep-Hep riots that they provoked in 1819) for their critical contribution to the maturing of modern revolutionary *and* nationalist hatred of the Jews.[15]

Far from being a "liberal" opposition against Metternich's new re-

[12] Quoted ibid., p. 919.
[13] Quoted ibid., p. 926.
[14] Quoted Tal, "Young German Intellectuals," p. 924.
[15] Cf. ibid., p. 923.

actionary European order, these student associations represented a revolutionary reaction impregnated for the most part with a powerful streak of Jew-hatred that emerged prominently in the Wartburg Festival. The only real exception to this general intolerance was the Heidelberg *Burschenschaft*, which under the influence of Hegel and Carové admitted Jews and pressed for civil rights. When the conservative dramatist August von Kotzebue (like Hegel, a supporter of Jewish civil rights) was assassinated by a student in 1819, the murder was portrayed as a patriotic racial cleansing and not just a liberal action against the authoritarianism of Metternich. In the aftermath of this assassination the Hep-Hep riots against the Jews erupted in August 1819 and led immediately to Metternich's imposition of the repressive Karlsbad decrees the following month. The German revolutionary student movement for "freedom" was far too imbued with nationalist Teutonic feelings to be categorized as a "revolutionary" movement in the French libertarian sense, or as some sort of "democratic" opposition. As August von Kotzebue had informed his friend Saul Ascher in 1818, the Wartburg Festival had been no democratic event, but rather one inspired by Teutonic revolutionism.[16]

The paradoxical character of the *Burschenschaften* appears quite clearly in the idiosyncratic thought of their immediate spiritual begetter, Ernst Moritz Arndt (1769–1860). Arndt's tract of 1815 on *The German Student State* laid down the philosophy of the *Burschenschaften* and made it clear that Jews were to be excluded on the ground that they belonged to a different race and nation.[17] Yet, at the same time as he happily denies any civil rights to the Jews, Arndt strongly advocates such liberal political rights as freedom of the press. Even more perplexing for a simple interpretation of Arndt is his contradictory "racial" conception. Arndt identified each nation as a separate race, and he excoriated the French and Poles—as well as the Jews— as the curse of Germany. Drawing on the analogy of animal breeding

[16] W. von Kotzebue, *August von Kotzebue* (Dresden, 1881), pp. 164f., letter of 1 February 1818, quoted by E. Sterling, "The Hep-Hep Riots in Germany 1819: A Displacement of Social Protest," *Historia Judaica* 12 (1950): 105–42. See also C. Rabany, *Kotzebue: Sa vie et son temps* (Paris, 1893), pp. 111–44; Scheuer, *Burschenschaft*, pp. 12–15. For the background, see F. G. Eyck, "The Political Theories and Activities of the German Academic Youth between 1815 and 1819," *Journal of Modern History* 27 (1955): 27–38; L. S. Feuer, "Terrorism and Suicidalism in the German Student Movement," in his *The Conflict of Generations* (New York, 1969), chap. 2, pp. 54–75; K. H. Jarausch, "The Sources of German Student Unrest 1815–1848," in *The University in Society* (Princeton, 1974), 2:533–69, which last seriously underrates the anti-Jewish aspects of the *Burschenschaft*.

[17] E. M. Arndt, *Über den deutschen Studentenstaat*, in his *Schriften an und für seine lieben Deutschen* (Leipzig, 1844–45), 2:235–93. Cf. Low, *Jews*, p. 155.

to argue for the need for purity of race, he regarded as sinful the degeneration of noble species through cross-breeding. To protect the Germans from such degeneration, he wrote in 1814,

> one must prohibit and prevent the importation into Germany of Jews from abroad. . . . The Jews as Jews do not fit into this world and this state, and therefore I do not want their number to be unduly increased in Germany. I also do not wish this because they are an alien race and because I desire to keep the Germanic race as pure as possible.[18]

But then he blithely advocates permitting those Jews now in Germany to assimilate by conversion:

> Experience shows that as soon as they abandon their disconcerting laws and become Christian, the peculiarities of the Jewish character and type rapidly grow indistinct, and by the second generation, it is difficult to recognize the seed of Abraham. . . . I don't belong to those who hate the Jews as Jews by all means, or hold them to be a people wicked by nature.[19]

Though he would deny the Jews civil rights until they should have assimilated, Arndt insisted that in the meantime they should be protected and defended from further malice, dishonor, and dehumanization. From this composite picture of Arndt's outlook, it is evident that it is not possible to draw simple conclusions about the separate or opposed natures of "racist" and "nationalist" thought in this volatile and complex phase of their development.[20]

While Arndt and Jahn provided the blunt emotional thrust for the anti-Jewish stance of the *Burschenschaften* that animated the Hep-Hep riots, the academic framework of revolutionary and nationalist student Jew-hatred was prepared by a series of pamphlets published by sympathetic professors. The mixture of arguments used by the authors (some of the lines were mutually contradictory) testifies to the fact that nationalist Jew-hatred was still in a germinating stage and had not yet settled into a formally racist cast. The campaign was launched in 1815 by Friedrich Rühs's pamphlet, *On the Claims of the*

[18] E. M. Arndt, *Ein Blick aus der Zeit auf die Zeit* (Frankfurt, 1814), pp. 180–201. See Low, *Jews*, pp. 153–65; A. G. Pundt, *Arndt and the Nationalist Awakening in Germany* (New York, 1935); H. Kohn, "Arndt and the Character of German Nationalism," *American Historical Review* 54 (1949): 787–803.

[19] Arndt, *Blick.*

[20] The same goes for Jahn, who also cannot be reduced to the simple category of "racist." See *HAS*, 3:334ff.; H. Überhorst, *Friedrich Ludwig Jahn 1778–1978* (Bonn, 1978).

*Jews to Civil Rights in Germany*, which, invoking Fichte's authority, proclaimed that the Jews were an entirely different people from the Germans with alien values, beliefs, and behavior, and should therefore be denied political rights.[21] But for all his German nationalist adversion against the Jews, and his belief that national character was natural to the Jews rather than acquired as the result of persecution, Rühs was traditional enough to maintain that genuine conversion to Christianity sufficed to give the Jews entrance into German life and enabled them to unite with the German people.

This did not satisfy Jakob Fries, who felt Rühs's critique was somewhat too narrowly religious and doctrinal. Fries preferred to supply a more authentically secular theory of Jew-hatred. Like his master Fichte, Fries held that the highest values of Christianity had been absorbed into a sublimely secular "Germanness." In his *Endangering of German Welfare and Character by the Jews* (1816), Fries insisted that because of this secularization, Jewish reception into the body of the German nation could not depend on religious conversion alone, but on a wholehearted adoption of German culture and values, above all, the love of moral freedom.[22] The solution to the Jewish Question had to emerge from the twin processes of freedom-seeking revolution and German nationalism.

Fries was emphatically a believer in a "German revolution" purified of French liberal ideas and Jewish parasitism alike. Fancying himself a "champion of the oppressed," Fries glorified the Germans as a "natural people" removed from the artificiality of commerce. He thus interwove ideals of freedom and social protest with a potent Jew-hatred founded on the economic activity of the Jews as a "commercial caste." Fries's work combines abstruse philosophical criticism of Judaism with vulgar insults to Jewish commercial character, which led to its actually being read aloud in beerhalls.[23]

Full of references to the Jews as "bloodsuckers" and the like, Fries's polemic is the first extensive working-out of the classic principles of moral and revolutionary antisemitism set down by Kant and Fichte.

[21] Rühs, *Über die Ansprüche der Juden an das deutsche Bürgerrecht* (Berlin, 1816). See Tal, "Young German Intellectuals," pp. 931ff.; Katz, *From Prejudice*, pp. 76ff.; idem, *Out of the Ghetto* (Cambridge, Mass., 1973), pp. 199f.; S. Stern-Täubler, "Der literarische Kampf um die Emanzipation in den Jahren 1816–1820 und seine ideologischen und soziologischen Voraussetzungen," *Hebrew Union College Annual* 23 (1950–51): 171–96.

[22] J. Fries, *Über die Gefährdung des Wohlstandes und Charakters der Deutschen durch die Juden* (Heidelberg, 1816). See E. L. T. Henke, *Jakob Friedrich Fries* (Leipzig, 1867), pp. 153ff., 158. Cf. Katz, *From Prejudice*, pp. 81ff.; Low, *Jews*, p. 111; *HAS*, 3:301.

[23] See Sterling, "Hep-Hep Riots," p. 116, quoting Sigmund Zimmern, *Versuch einer Würdigung der Angriffs des Herrn Professor Fries auf die Juden* (Heidelberg, 1816).

Even though the nationalistic and racist animus is obvious through-out, it is subordinated to these higher idealistic principles. Thus, Fries reproaches the Rühs school for implying that there was "a racial quality in this people" (*Rasse im Volk*) that might forever bar them from full civil rights! For Fries, the "humanization" of the Jews through the destruction of the Jewish commercial caste—combined as in Rühs with the abandoning of their hateful religion—would secure the admission of the Jews into German life.

Like Fichte, Fries confessed himself anxious to preserve the human rights of the Jews and he condemned their unjust persecution by "Christians." But his prescriptions for dealing with the Jews before their final redemption raise a question about what he meant by "human rights." Fries was intent on banishing Jews back to the ghetto as well as controlling their numbers by limits on marriage. And where Fichte might have been jesting, Fries was in earnest about the ultimate sanctions to be used. If the Jews fail to reform themselves, then they are to be expelled. And he threateningly intoned:

> This scandal [of Jewish exploitation of Germans] will not come to an
> end without dreadful acts of violence if our government does not halt
> the [Jewish] evil quickly.

Fries even called for the "radical extermination of the caste of Jews"; but, of course, he later disarmingly (under police investigation in 1819) insisted that what he had in mind was the annihilation of "Judaism" or the Jewish "nation" or the "Jewish commercial caste," rather than of individual Jews.[24] Nevertheless, it is clear that Fries's "extermination of the caste of Jews" entailed their physical reduction, even if the means stopped short of murder as he claimed.

If the vagueness of Fichte's notions were already becoming more defined in Fries's words, so, too, were the racial implications coming into focus. In 1817 Fries instigated the nationalist students' Wartburg Festival, whose program included a ceremonial burning of Saul Ascher's squib against *Germanomanie* (1815) to the incantation "Woe to the Jews."[25] Two years later these nationalist calls for metaphorical extermination and woe produced the Hep-Hep riots of 1819 in which

---

[24] E. Sterling, *Judenhass: Die Anfänge des politischen Antisemitismus 1815–1850* (Frankfurt, 1969), p. 147.

[25] Ascher, *Die Germanomanie*. He later wrote: "They probably burned my *Germanomanie* because in it I said that all men are made the same way as Germans." (*Die Wartburg-Feier* [Leipzig, 1818], p. 34.) Cf. C. Brinkmann, *Der Nationalismus und die deutschen Universitäten im Zeitalter der deutschen Erhebung* (Sitzungsberichte der Heidelberger Akademie der Wissenschaften, Phil.-Hist. Klasse, 32, Abhandlungen no. 3 (Heidelberg, 1932), p. 67; *HAS*, 3:390; Scheuer, *Burschenschaft*, pp. 12–16.

some measures of a rather more physical nature were inflicted on numerous individual Jews and not just on the "religion" or the "community." The distance from incitement to violence—and later to policy—was not great. When it came to practical realities, Jakob Fries and his student followers stood ready to translate Fichtean revolutionary ideals into action.

---

Fichte's apotheosis in the public consciousness of modern Germany as the founding spirit of "Germanness" means that he bears a large responsibility for the rise of both revolutionary and nationalist Jew-hatred. One may try to absolve Fichte from being himself a hater of Jews by arguing that this contribution was perhaps involuntary, that it was not his fault if his followers read into his nationalism a hatred of Jews that was not there. But this excuse does not reach the heart of the issue, which is that it was Fichte who explicitly made the first attempt to introduce a new kind of revolutionary Jew-hatred into politics, one whose influence was not restricted to the left-wing advocates of Jacobin revolution, but who powerfully affected the new generation of believers in a "German revolution" whose politics cannot be conveniently categorized as "left" or "right." The practical meaning of this vision of the "German revolution" did not take long to materialize, and when it did, the anti-Jewish element that Fichte had inserted into it in his *Contribution* appeared all too prominently.

But if the ideological content of Fichte's German revolutionism was to prove itself dangerous, the cultural and psychological consequences of his doctrine of revolution were perhaps even more disastrous in the long run. For Fichte brought to bear on the Jewish Question the emotions and mythological power of a new secular religion of human redemption. Thus, his *Contribution* disowned the petty "hot" Jew-hatred of earlier generations, but in its place proclaimed—in very vague terms—a revolutionary mythology of Judaism as the supreme expression of self-interest, the secular equivalent of the original sin from which mankind had to be redeemed. In the course of the great transformation of German thought from the theological to the secular, certain constants may be seen beneath the apparent intellectual shift. One of the most enduring is precisely the demonological conception of the Jew that easily survived the process of secularization. Fichte inherited the old Christian perception pattern that saw the Jew as something simultaneously metaphorical and actual, and also something central to the understanding of the universe. For Fichte, Judaism was a Kantian parable of the need for human moral regeneration; but, at the same time, Fichte saw that Judaism played a role in the revolutionary drama of modern man because the Jews represented the practical, as well as the spiritual, resistance to political and social revolution.

This dual aspect of Judaism as moral metaphor and social reality was what made it possible for Jewishness to become as central and ubiquitous an obsession in the new secular mythology of political redemption in modern Germany as it had been in the theological universe of Christian Europe. In the Gospels, Judaism might have been intended as a universal myth of human rejection of the good; but at the same time it was always remembered in later centuries that it had been real-life Jews who had demanded the crucifixion of Christ, and that their descendants formed a nation that still rejected human redemption. So too in the new European secular mentality: Judaism could now function as a universal myth of human egoism and rejection of moral freedom, while in everyday life Jews were always easily identified as the actual practitioners of egoism in politics and commerce. Such an unstable fusion of a metaphor with its actual referent renders Judaism perhaps the most pregnant myth of the European mind, one that has survived two thousand years of theological and secular transformations. It would be naive to think that it should suddenly cease to be so in the course of a few recent decades (unless, that is, it can be shown that the raw emotions that conjured up the intellectual superstructures have vanished from the psyche).

When Fichte claimed in 1793 that he was no Jew-hater, that his attack on "Judaism" was devoid of "private animosity," anger, or hatred, he was putting forth a claim to an anti-Judaism that was cool, detached, based on "objective" facts—and all the more dangerous for its pretense at having cast loose from the emotional and psychological moorings of conventional Christian Jew-hatred. With justice Saul Ascher could see Fichte as the progenitor of the national revolutionary antisemitism of Arndt, Brentano, and Jahn, lamenting "the savage and awful tone in which Fichte, one of the architects of the new teachings, at the end of the eighteenth century stormed forth against Judaism and Jews."[26]

[26] See Ascher, *Die Germanomanie*, pp. 14, 27, 47ff. for Fichte's influence.

# PART THREE

Young Germany: Literary Revolutionism
and the Jewish Question

# Revolutionary Judaism and the German Revolution: Börne and Heine

Börne is like a Jewish wolf and changeling, or

one of the masks of the Wandering Jew that

are nowadays popping up everywhere . . .

those same fatherlandless types [like Börne

and Heine] who in their cosmopolitan way

wander around until the Last Judgment. . . .

This Wandering Jew has in the shape of

friend Heine reached the highest degree of

blasphemy against God and the Cross . . . and

Börne follows on his heels.[1]

—Cruciger, *Newest Wanderings and Adventures*

*of the Wandering Jew under the Names of Börne,*

*Heine, Saphir, and Others* (1832)

RHINELAND Jewry produced four of the most eminent exponents of revolutionism—Ludwig Börne, Heinrich Heine, Moses Hess, and Karl Marx.[2] All four also made critically important contributions to the theory of revolutionary antisemitism, each goaded on by an itching consciousness of the fact that his Jewishness, no matter how much it was rejected or suppressed or nullified by conversion, prevented him from being a fully normal and true German.[3] This "em-

[1] Cruciger (Friedrich von der Hagen), *Neueste Wanderungen: Umtriebe und Abenteuer des Ewigen Juden unter den Namen Börne, Heine, Saphir u.a.* (Friedrich-Wilhelmstadt/Berlin, 1832), pp. 3ff.

[2] Cf. H. Liebeschütz, "German Radicalism and the Formation of Jewish Political Attitudes during the Earlier Part of the Nineteenth Century," in *Studies in Nineteenth-Century Jewish Intellectual History*, ed. A. Altmann (Cambridge, Mass., 1964), pp. 141–70; M. Schneider, *Die kranke, schöne Seele der Revolution: Heine, Börne, das "Junge Deutschland," Marx und Engels* (Frankfurt, 1980).

[3] See now S. Gilman, *Jewish Self-Hatred* (Ithaca, N.Y., 1986); Michael A. Meyer, *The*

barrassment" at being Jewish is often termed "Jewish self-hatred" and its dynamics are quite well known. It fed on the psychological need to become a member of the dominant culture of the social environment and so had a special relevance to the phenomenon of German revolutionism, which seemed to promise a road to freedom out of Jewishness. Overcoming the old barriers that blocked the way forward into German society, the new creed of revolution would render obsolete the social discrimination of the ancien regime as well as discrediting the anti-Jewish prejudices of Christianity. Even more valuably, revolutionism would destroy the new obstructions being raised by German nationalism, itself a variant of revolutionism, but one impregnated with antisemitism.

Börne and Heine summoned the German revolution to vanquish the antisemitic ghosts of German nationalism. *Their* German revolution was but a species of the universal revolution of all humanity, and so could not embody a Jew-hatred that was, by their definition, against the spirit of true humanity. In the pursuit of universal revolution Marx and Hess went even further, to the point of repudiating even the very notion of a "German revolution," dismissing the "German ideology" as nothing but a reactionary ploy.

Conservatives like Heinrich von Treitschke reviled these Jewish revolutionists as the journalistic agitators who had betrayed German nationalism—that true German conservative revolution—by contaminating it with French and Jewish ideas of revolution. Treitschke damned Börne "as the first to introduce into our journalism the brazen manner of speaking about the Fatherland irreverently, like an outsider who does not belong to the same Fatherland."[4] But the real disappointment of Jewish revolutionism arose from their fellow German revolutionists. The German spirit of revolution lost its potency when it came face to face with "Jewish noses," as Hess put it. Heine gradually escaped the delusion that the German revolution was the true solution to the Jewish Question; Börne remained trapped within it. But together they had framed a revolutionary critique of Jewishness that became the basic intellectual currency of the revolutionary discussion of the Jewish Question. Upon their equation of Jewishness with money and philistine capitalism, Börne and Heine constructed an apparently self-evident allegory of capitalist society. It entailed the

*Origins of the Modern Jew: Jewish Identity and European Culture in Germany 1749–1824* (Detroit, 1967), especially pp. 145ff.

4 Heinrich von Treitschke, *Unsere Aussichten* (1879), in *Der Berliner Antisemitismusstreit*, ed. W. Böhlich (Frankfurt, 1965), p. 13. For his attacks on Heine and Börne in his *Deutsche Geschichte im neunzehnten Jahrhundert*, vols. 3 and 4 (1885–89), see A. Dorpalen, *Heinrich von Treitschke* (New Haven, 1957), pp. 266, 268.

destruction of Jewishness as the key to the human emancipation, not only of the Jews themselves, but of the whole corrupt European world that they symbolized.

## BÖRNE: JEWISH REDEMPTION THROUGH GERMAN REVOLUTION

Fichte declared that he knew of no Jew who had yet transcended his Jewish nature. But one Jew was, according to Richard Wagner, to achieve such a redemption from the burden of Jewishness, from the curse of Ahasverus:

> We must mention one other Jew [in addition to Heine] who appeared among us as a writer. From his isolation as a Jew he came seeking redemption among us. He did not find it and had to discover that he could gain it only through *our* being redeemed and ourselves becoming truly human. But to become a true human being along with us the Jew must cease to be a Jew. Börne ceased to be a Jew. But even Börne shows us how this redemption cannot be achieved in complacency or in easy, indifferent comfort. It is attained only as with us—through sweat, privation, and the depths of sorrow and suffering.[5]

This Jewish paragon was Ludwig Börne (1786–1837), born Judah Loew Baruch—the great revolutionary patriot and apostle of German freedom in the Metternich era.[6] Börne proclaimed his own brand of "ultraliberal" revolutionary republicanism in the brilliantly stylish *Letters from Paris* (1832–34), one of the great landmarks in the politicization of German literature. Famous both as an author of *Ten-*

---

[5] Wagner, *Judaism in Music* (*PW*, 3:100), my amended translation.

[6] A superb introduction to Börne is O. Figes, "Ludwig Börne and the Formation of a Radical Critique of Judaism," *LBIY* 29 (1984): 351–82. Useful biographies are Ludwig Marcuse, *Börne: Aus der Frühzeit der deutschen Demokratie*, 2d ed. (Rothenburg, 1968; repr. Zurich, 1977); H. Bock, *Ludwig Börne: Vom Gettojuden zum Nationalschriftsteller* (East Berlin, 1962). A chronology and bibliography are provided in the third and fifth volumes of the standard edition of Börne's writings, *Sämtliche Schriften*, ed. I. and P. Rippmann, 5 vols. (repr. Dreieich/Düsseldorf, 1977), abbreviated hereafter to *BSS*.

Other introductions are S. Liptzin, *Germany's Stepchildren* (Philadelphia, 1944), pp. 27–44 (who advances the dubious argument that Börne evolved in his later years into a stance that was more sympathetic to Judaism—this seems to be merely wishful thinking); W. Hinderer, "Die Frankfurter Judengasse und das Ghetto Europas. Der praktische Hintergrund von Ludwig Börnes emanzipativem Patriotismus," *Germanisch-Romanische Monatsschrift* (n.f.) 24 (1974): 421–29; W. Labuhn, "Die Ludwig Börne-Forschung seit 1945," *Zeitschrift für deutsche Philologie* 96 (1977): 269–86; Liebeschütz, "German Radicalism," pp. 141–70. I have not seen *Ludwig Börne 1786–1837: Ausstellungskatalog*, ed. A. Estermann (Frankfurt, 1986); I. Rippmann, *Börne-Index* (Berlin, 1985).

*denzliteratur* and as a blazing political orator, Börne was lionized at the patriotic revolutionary students' Hambach Festival of 1832 where he was marched through the streets to the cry, "Long live Börne, long live the German Börne, author of the *Briefe aus Paris*."[7] To the Young German literary and political circles of the 1830s, Börne was the very ideal of a revolutionary patriot. Heinrich Laube, the leader of "Young Germany," recalled:

> The influence exerted by Börne on German youth was immeasurable. Since Schiller no writer had been read with such enthusiasm. . . . Börne was a dynamic power.[8]

Ironic as it was that a Frankfurt Jew should come to personify German freedom, Börne himself saw it as almost inevitable that an outsider such as he should lead the Germans to revolutionary redemption:

> I have the undeserved good fortune of being at the same time a German and a Jew, so that I can strive for the virtues of the Germans without sharing their faults. Because I was born a bondsman, I love freedom more than you do; because I was reared in slavery, I desire more warmly than you a fatherland. And because my birthplace was no bigger than the Jews' Street and abroad began for me outside the

---

[7] Letter of 28 May 1832 to Jeanette Wohl-Strauss, in *BSS*, 5:253. Metternich also greatly admired Börne's style and sought to recruit his pen to the conservative cause by offering him an imperial councillorship.

[8] Laube in his periodical *Zeitung für die elegante Welt*, 3 March 1837, quoted by Bock, *Börne*, p. 399. See below, chap. 12, for Laube. Laube first met Börne at Paris in 1833; in 1835, he tried to commit the Young Germany movement to Börne's political program (Laube, 14 September 1835, cited by Bock, *Börne*, pp. 374–80). Another Young German revolutionist, Ludwig Köhler (1819–62), conferred a near messianic status on Börne in his epic poem *The New Ahasverus* (*Der neue Ahasverus*, Jena, 1841). The preface, influenced by the Gutzkow "Ahasverus dispute" of the 1830s, depicts Ahasverus as a heartless opportunist, condemned by Jesus to wander until freedom finally reigns. In modern times, Ahasverus is involved in the French Revolution, then participates in the German "liberal" battle against the tyrant Napoleon. After Waterloo, Ahasverus turns up at the Wartburg Festival of German liberty before moving on to some convenient wars of liberation and revolution in Greece, France, and Poland. Yet despite these stirrings, the progress of freedom is constantly being thwarted and along with it the redemption of Ahasverus. The supreme freedom-fighter, Jesus himself, who had been sent on his mission by the All-Loving Father, had succumbed to the envy of a wrathful, bloodthirsty Jehovah who exacts fasting and sacrifice rather than bestowing freedom. Luther had similarly failed to emancipate mankind. And now another German hero—Ludwig Börne—has again lost the battle; he from whom Ahasverus had expected redemption now lies in a grave in Paris. But the struggle for freedom is not yet over; it has now become linked with Germanic culture. Köhler, like Wagner, glimpses in the Nibelung saga the gleam of freedom. "Freedom is the Nibelung hoard."

closed gates of the ghetto, no city nor any province will suffice for me; only the whole broad fatherland will please me.[9]

Fine phrases—but behind their Olympian magnanimity and detachment it is not hard to detect a sharp note of pain and resentment. In the 1830s and 1840s Börne was the most widely read revolutionary author in Germany, but his Jewishness, like that of Heine, always intruded on the consciousness of his contemporaries, whether friend or foe.

Börne's earlier career aptly summarized the unpleasant disabilities of the Jews in German society. During his youth in Frankfurt he had experienced the usual judicial insults: a passport stamped "Jew"; the obligation to give way on the street to louts who called out the magic phrase "Make obeisance, Jew"; the strict limitation on the annual number of Jewish marriages so as to prevent the increase of Jewish population; confinement within a ghetto whose gates slammed shut like a prison at sunset; a maximum of four Jewish doctors in the city; the banning of Jews from legal practice and public office; a promenade signposted "No Jews and no pigs."[10] Despite these humiliations, Jews had fought in defense of Germany against Napoleon—only to be rewarded with fresh penalties and contempt. After the French defeat of 1814–15, the old Frankfurt constitution barring Jews from civil office was restored and Börne lost his post of police actuary in the upswell of nationalist antisemitism:

> The patriots wanted a chorus that sang entirely in unison and were all dressed in the same uniforms, with the Germans as they had emerged from Tacitus's forests, red-haired and light blue-eyed. The dark Jews were a hateful contrast. . . . We were set free from the purgatory of French rule so that we might gain redemption, not into paradise, but into hell.[11]

In 1818 Börne found his own private redemption in conversion to Christianity. Conversion certainly removed the formal barriers to politics and the professions, but for Börne it was not merely an opportunistic act. Christianity satisfied a deep need in him for a universal creed that would overcome the false obstacles to "freedom" set up by the selfish particularisms of Germans and Jews alike. He longed for a religion of love that would vanquish egoism and at the same

---

[9] *Briefe aus Paris*, no. 74, in *BSS*, 3:511. Among the faults of the Germans, Börne included abject surrender to authority, parochialism, and philistinism.

[10] *Juden in der Freien Stadt Frankfurt*, *BSS*, 2:237ff.

[11] *Für die Juden* (1819), in *BSS*, 1:876, 879. My quotation conflates sentences from two different articles of the same title.

time grant him a personal affection he felt deprived of by his own family. For Börne, the change of name from Baruch and the change of religion in 1818 were means of escape from an alienation he felt to be created by the circumstances of his Jewish birth and an upbringing in which he felt (like Karl Marx) that love had been replaced by interest in money and respectability. Renunciation of Judaism—of money, of lovelessness, of the barriers to freedom—was the key to Börne's personal redemption, and this individual religious psychology must be kept in mind if his ambivalent attitude to the Jewish Question is to be understood.[12]

On the surface, Börne seems very much a staunch liberal defender of Jewish civil emancipation. He denounced the reactionaries who refused civil rights to the Jews, and he insisted that Jewish emancipation was an integral part of a revolutionary movement for German political freedom:

> I reject the separation of human rights from civil rights, of religious from political toleration, the notion that one may be had without the other. What you call human rights are mere animal rights, such as the right to seek nourishment and to eat. . . . These rights are enjoyed in the wild and in the field until one dies—and now you wish to grant them to the Jews. Political rights—these alone are human rights, for man first becomes human in civil society. He is born into it as a citizen. This is the foundation of England, France, and every free state.[13]

Here Börne's notion of freedom is solidly political, practical, liberal. Human freedom is civil freedom, human rights are civil rights, political rights. To the conservatives who withhold civil rights from the Jews on the ground that they are not full citizens conforming to the Christian constitutions of the German states, Börne would reply along with Bettina Brentano that Jewish emancipation should serve as the index of the humanity of the genuinely Christian state.[14]

But Börne's perception of the Jewish Question goes beyond seeing it merely as a matter of emancipating the Jews according to good liberal principles. The Jewish Question is for him the central paradigm for the liberation of Germany herself. The Jews without rights in their Jewish ghetto are the symbols of the German people's lack of rights in their own land:

[12] The autobiographical fragment *Ludwig Bartel* of 1802 (*BBS*, 4:7) manifests the psychological impulses that eventually came to fulfillment in his conversion. Cf. Schneider, *Die kranke Seele der Revolution*; Figes, "Ludwig Börne," p. 360.

[13] *Der ewige Jude*, *BSS*, 2:522, a point of view shared by Gabriel Riesser.

[14] Cf. A. Low, *Jews in the Eyes of the Germans: From the Enlightenment to Imperial Germany* (Philadelphia, 1979), pp. 188ff.

Is not Germany the ghetto of Europe? Do not all Germans carry a yellow star on their hats? Are not all Frankfurters now in the earlier position of the Jews? Are not the Austrians and Prussians *their* Christians?[15]

Here in their own subjection lies the reason for the Germans' oppression of the Jews:

The poor Germans! Dwelling on the lowest floor, pushed down by seven storeys of classes above them, it relieves their wretched feelings to speak of people who live still lower than they in the cellar.[16]

The German people will discover that they were designated the jailers of the Jews because jailers as well as the jailed may not leave prison. . . . Neither group is really free.[17]

See how far you get with the freedom of Germany so long as this freedom is not to be for all.[18]

In revolutionary perspective the Jewish Question is not peripheral, but the very center of the quest for German freedom.

For Börne, however, the Jewish Question has an even more pregnant significance than this, one that goes beyond Jews and Germans to affect all humanity:

You might think that the persecution of the Jews is irrelevant to patriotic concerns, that it's a trivial matter of no importance. . . . But like the earth, mankind has a dual motion, comprising a particular and a general movement. This carries us unendingly upwards, it is the fate of mankind. Everyone is marked by it. It is freedom.[19]

And here the problems begin with Börne's liberalism, because Börne has not stopped at a liberal political idea of freedom, but broadened his notion of emancipation to something grander and more nebulous: the universal freedom of humanity—moral and human liberation. Ultimately it is not liberal freedom, but the sovereign principle of human freedom—*Freiheit und Humanität*—that dictates Börne's conception of the Jewish Question as a paradigm, not just for the liberation of Germany, but of all humanity. "I don't love the Jews or Christians as Jews or Christians," he affirms, "I love them only as they are human beings [*Menschen*] and born for freedom."[20]

[15] *Menzel der Franzosenfresser, BSS,* 3:889.
[16] *Briefe aus Paris,* no. 74, *BSS,* 3:511.
[17] *Für die Juden, BSS,* 1:875.
[18] *Zwangsgottesdienst* (1819), *BSS,* 1:1004.
[19] *BSS,* 1:872f.
[20] *Der ewige Jude, BSS,* 2:537.

This sense of universal humanity led Börne to restrict his particular loyalties, whether to the Jewish people or to Germany. His concept of freedom transcended the egoism of individuals, of nations, and of religions. Even Börne's devotion to the cause of German patriotism was circumscribed by his love of universal humanity. Refusing to become a "patriotic booby," Börne asserted that "one thing gives me joy, namely that I am a Jew. Thereby I become a citizen of the whole world and need not be ashamed of my Germanness."[21] Judaism itself was thus invoked to assert a deeper love for Germany against what he regarded as the "false patriotism" and national egoism of German chauvinists, above all Wolfgang Menzel.[22] Börne's last work, *Menzel the Franco-Guzzler* (*Menzel der Franzosenfresser*) was an exuberant warning against the folly of assuming the superiority of all things German and of believing that freedom and justice were specifically or exclusively German qualities. Like Heine, Börne had a mixed view of the Germans, despising and admiring them at once.

A somewhat more perverse ambivalence, however, attached to Börne's attitude to the Jewish people. Although he was ever ready to come to their defense against egoistic Germans, Börne was always reluctant to treat the Jews as a special case and, in fact, would often distance himself from them. Jewish emancipation was necessary, not because the Jews were good or deserved it, but because it was a condition of the general emancipation of Germany and humanity. Börne indeed disliked very much what he saw as the narrow religiosity and tribalism of the Jews, what he called this dead "Egyptian mummy."[23] What appealed to him about his ancestral religion was the universalizing strain within it that was now at last overcoming its narrow nationalism:

> The nationality of the Jews has perished in a beautiful and enviable manner—it has become universalism. . . . The Jews are the teachers of cosmopolitanism and the whole world is their school. And because they are teachers of cosmopolitanism, they are also the apostles of freedom. No freedom is possible as long as nation-states rule. What divides the peoples is what unites the princes.[24]

For Börne the Jewish mission in history had been accomplished when, through their invention of Christianity, the Jews taught the world a compassionate cosmopolitanism. To this humane, universalizing Christianity Börne attached his feelings from the time of his

[21] *Aphorismen 1808–1810*, no. 41, *BSS*, 1:145.
[22] *Menzel der Franzosenfresser*, *BSS*, 3:906.
[23] *Aphorismen*, no. 164, *BSS*, 1:163.
[24] Cf. *Briefe aus Paris*, no. 103, *BSS*, 3:757f.

conversion in 1818, finally in his last years discovering intellectual ful-fillment in the Catholic socialism of the Abbé de Lamennais.

We can now see that Börne's revolutionary idea of freedom was almost religious in its purpose, with a visionary character that verged on the utopian. It was far from being conventionally liberal in the sense that Gabriel Riesser's opinions were. Riesser was interested only in the necessity of granting civil and political rights to Germans and Jews indiscriminately; he made no claim for larger, more abstract human rights. If Jews, after gaining their civil emancipation, wished to remain as "unhuman" and loveless as their Christian fellow citizens, then that was no concern of Riesser's; but it was very much Börne's concern that the Jews should go to emancipate themselves as *human beings*. Equally, for Riesser, it was not the purpose of emancipation to convert the Jews to Christianity and to destroy the basis of Jewish existence or identity. Yet this was earnestly desired by Börne.

The difference between the two Jewish "liberals" comes out very strikingly in Börne's rejection of Riesser's plan to launch a Jewish po-litical journal in 1833:

> A Jewish journal [objected Börne] is misconceived. Whoever wishes to work for the Jews ought not to treat them in isolation. . . . In order to help them we must establish a relationship between the Jewish cause and the rights and claims of universal freedom.[25]

Not surprisingly, when he was attacked *as a Jew* by the Jew-hater Edu-ard Meyer in 1831, Börne bitterly resented being defended by Ries-ser, whom he saw as one of those "special" defenders of Jewish free-dom lacking any grasp of the general issue of freedom.[26] Underneath Börne's apparently "liberal" attitude to the Jewish Question, then, we ought to be looking for a certain anti-Jewish tension formed by the revolutionary temper of his thought. And indeed a close examination of his series of writings on the Jewish Question brings to light a com-plicated structure of revolutionary ideas and assumptions that are im-plicitly anti-Jewish.

---

We find these ideas first explained in a work of 1808 that com-bines the "liberal" case for Jewish rights with an essentially anti-Jew-

[25] *BSS*, 3:757f., 2 February 1833.
[26] Gabriel Riesser, *Börne und die Juden* (Altenburg, 1832). For Börne's resentment of this aid, see *BSS*, 3:364f., 510. Cf. above, chap. 6, n. 3, and below, chap. 10, nn. 23f., 28ff., and chap. 11, n. 41.
For Meyer see above, chap. 6, n. 31; below, n. 52, and also below, chap. 10, nn. 22ff.; chap. 11, n. 41.

ish ideology in a way typical of German revolutionary thinkers. *Candid Remarks on the New Order for the Abode and Protection of the Jewry of Frankfurt* was written to defend the Frankfurt Jews in the face of the discriminatory measures reimposed on them in 1808.[27] Börne here looks at the anti-Jewish feeling that inspired these measures and finds that it is no longer the fanatical religious Jew-hatred of the Middle Ages, but a more recent enlightened kind that is basically economic in nature. This is the solution to the problem of why Jew-hatred still flourishes, despite the proscription of religious hatred by an "enlightened age":

> That this hatred has not ceased to the present day after every trace of fanaticism has faded away can be explained only through the commercial aristocracy of the Jews. Egoism indeed rises in step with intellectual enlightenment; but while better souls seek the use and profit of life in their noble self, common souls reduce it to a desire for despicable money. Since a large part of the Frankfurt merchant class may be counted among the latter category, it is only natural that such people must always persecute Jewish tradesmen as rivals. (p. 59)

Where earlier religious prejudice had at least forced the Jews to direct all their mental energy into trade and to end up as aristocrats of commerce, the modern use of religion as a cover for economic rivalry has deprived the Jews of any outlet for their energy (pp. 27f.). Worse, it has intensified the "Jewish disease" (*Krankheit*), which Börne finds to consist in

> an excessive nervous energy [*Hypersthenie*] in the desire for trade and profit. Because all their life activity is gathered towards this, the remaining parts of their organism become weakened. (pp. 55f.)

Börne's cure is the conventional liberal prescription of opening the doors to the professions, landownership, and agriculture, which will foster a healing "love of the fatherland" (p. 56). The best policy here is to destroy the "commercial aristocracy" of the Jews (shades of Fries!) by giving them "the most extravagant freedom of trade." The removal of stimulating obstacles will gradually detach the Jews from commerce and dissipate their intense "activity" (p. 61). But while

[27] *Freimütige Bemerkungen*, BSS, 1:14–72, a work rightly emphasized by Figes, "Ludwig Börne." My only dissent from Figes's excellent analysis concerns his division of Börne's thought into a pre-1830 "social" phase and a post-1830 "proto-social*ist*" phase. It seems to me that most of the mature ideas of Börne were present in embryonic form in the *Bemerkungen* of 1808, and in any event, they were fixed and elaborated in *Der ewige Jude* of 1821. (Page references in the following text are to the *BSS* edition of the *Bemerkungen*.)

Börne proposes respectably liberal measures of civil emancipation, he does so with the revolutionary aim of destroying Jewishness and he also adopts (albeit positively) the idea of a Jewish racial character:

> It is said: Because of their ingrained [*eingefleischter*] desire for profit, the Jews will never of their own free will abandon commerce; they will have to be driven out of the circle by force. But this is doubly wrong. First, new houses should be built for them before they are driven out of their old ones. Second, it is certainly not desire for profit alone that inspires the Jews to commerce. . . . Neither avarice, which delights in the power of money, nor extravagance, which rejoices in the action of money, are to be found among them. With the Jews it is more the profiting than the profit, more the cheating than the proceeds, that are at stake. For a race [*Volk*] like the Jews, whose southern origin endures still so pure in its blood and feeling, a race that is preoccupied more with fantasy than with reason, more with wit than with strength of judgment, more with fire than stamina—such a race must always be pushed to activity by its restless spirit [*von seinem rastlosen Geiste*]. Because a prescribed prejudice and an unsound policy deprive them of all the object of their activity, commerce, which is the only means of bringing peace to their spirit, has to be seized with joy and love. (p. 62)

In trying to discredit the traditional Christian economic Jew-hatred, which had been based on commercial rivalry, Börne blindly provided the rationale for a progressive *Judenhass* directed towards healing the Jews of their Mammonist disease of money-seeking. The new rationale is not simply economic or commercial, but rather a fusion of moral and economic elements that condemns the Jews for their general egoism, of which addiction to money and profit is but a particular expression. Börne even assures his Christian readers that only his personal knowledge and conditioning as a Jew puts him in a position to grasp just how far-reaching the Mammonist deformity of the Jews is:

> Egoism, which always asserts its rights in the domain of practice, is still sometimes denied in the theoretical realm. But among the Jews egoism never loses its predominance in the theoretical.

For instance, Christians may see themselves as only the footmen of a central sun such as the state. But with the Jews, even the humblest regards himself as the centerpoint of the whole world. Prussians may refer to "our army" or "our king," but the Jews speak of "the Prussian army" and "the Prussian king." Thus, "the intimate *our* is only uttered in speaking of commerce or money" (p. 28).

One has the impression that these remarks are an attempt to rationalize an adolescent revulsion against money and the commercial environment of his youth. Of a visit to the Frankfurt ghetto in 1805,
Börne wrote: "There are three things they know how to value: first,
money; second, money; and third, money."[28] Börne, of course, was
convinced he was doing something quite original and mature, that he
was taking traditional anti-Jewish remarks bearing on Jewish greed
and construing them as part of a larger, previously unsuspected picture—a progressive, revolutionary critique of Judaism that would
render obsolete the old economic *Judenhass*.

The danger of this approach was that Börne had manufactured a
new modern stereotype of the Jews as the supreme embodiments of
egoism. That Börne could lightly suggest a reform of Jewish education might help diminish the egoism of the Jews is hardly a mitigation
of the ominous stereotype he has created. Little wonder Börne's father (perhaps with the aid of the Frankfurt Jewish community) intervened to prevent the publication of these *Candid Remarks*, even
though they purported to be promoting Jewish emancipation.[29]

A year after his 1818 conversion, the outbreak of the Hep-Hep
riots forced Börne to return again to the Jewish Question, this time
in a series of articles entitled *For the Jews*.[30] In the *Candid Remarks* he
had spoken out against the economic Jew-hatred of the Frankfurt
merchants; now, in the changed circumstances of German reaction
and revolutionism, Börne turned to refute the Jew-hatred of the German nationalists. The French invasions, he admitted, had provoked
anti-Jewish feeling in Germany; in a time of heightened German national awareness the Jews had seemed obtrusively foreign and of an
alien culture. There had grown up an "operatic distinction" between
blond Germans and dark-haired Jews. The result was that the Jews
had been driven for their own self-protection to ally their financial

[28] *BSS*, 4:120f., quoted by Figes, "Ludwig Börne," p. 361.
[29] In another work of the same year, *Von dem Gelde* (1808)—published in Börne's
collected works of 1840 and so available to Wagner, as well as Marx and Hess—Börne
developed the idea that money was an expression of the egoism that filled every human being (*BSS*, 2:72–100, at pp. 75ff.). J. Toury, *Die politischen Orientierungen der Juden in Deutschland von Jena bis Weimar* (Tübingen, 1966), p. 355 (cf. p. 44), gives a col-
lation of Börne's and Marx's phrases that strongly suggests Marx's acquaintance (and
Hess's) with the writings of Börne. Given Börne's standing in revolutionary circles in
the early 1840s, it is almost inconceivable that Marx and Hess had not read him. Nevertheless, Börne, unlike Hess thirty years later in the *Essence of Money*, refrained from
identifying egoism or money worship specifically with the Jews.
[30] *Für die Juden, BSS*, 1:877–79.

power with the interests of the princes. The lesson of all this, according to Börne, is that nationalist Jew-hatred actually advantages the reactionary rulers of Germany and must be repudiated if German freedom is to flourish. Börne has here given his central theme of Jewish economic egoism a clever political twist.

In the same year, 1819, stimulated by Richard Cumberland's English play *The Jew* (1794), Börne went on to develop another aspect of Jewish egoism. Where until now he had been interested primarily in how egoism was expressed as desire for money and commercial activity, Börne now considered how Jewish egoism manifested itself in the form of lovelessness. In a review that has otherwise little to do with the content of Cumberland's play, Börne sets up the play's hero, the outwardly miserly Scheva, as a variant of the Wandering Jew, wandering from Spain to Germany—"an old sick man, rejoicing in [his] death." But then, to the usual attributes of Ahasverus—eternity, wandering, decay, and lovelessness—Börne adds what he has already identified as the specifically Jewish attribute of devotion to money:

> But "a Jew remains a Jew," says the Master of the Temple. Scheva almost adheres to his money. . . . Is money something other than the hope of pleasure . . . is it not past and future, and shall the poor Jew, who has no present, also be robbed of this? Is not money the universal grave that gathers up kings and beggars, fortunate and unfortunate, persecutors and persecuted? Is it not the social decomposition that mixes Jews and Christians into one another and abolishes their marks of distinction?

In the end, says Börne, Scheva is loveless and addicted to money precisely because he is a victim of Christian lovelessness. "How should Scheva not love money, since no one loves him or anything in him for what he *is*, but only for what he *has*."[31] In alleviating Scheva's guilt by blaming it on Christian lovelessness, Börne established the closeness of the link between Jewish lovelessness and Mammonism.

Cumberland's play had started by depicting Scheva as a Shylock-like "bloodsucker and extortionist," but one who hid his true noble "heart," which was in the end revealed to the world. A few years later Heine went back to the Shakespearian original and composed an essay which, like Cumberland, inverted the usual harsh interpretation of Shylock's character. But Börne's own *Shylock* (1828) gives a damning Mammonistic portrait of the Jew that stands in sad contrast to the warm version of Heine. Money and revenge are the driving forces in Shylock's personality. "We detest the money-devil [*Geldteufel*] in Shy-

[31] *Der Jude*, BSS, 1:286–89.

lock, we grieve for the tormented man, but we love and marvel at the avenger of inhuman persecution." But Shylock knows that his accursed lust for money is sick (*vermaledeite Geldsucht*), and in the end, he is forced to admit that love is stronger than money:

> He gives away money to avenge his people and discovers that gold is not the lord of the world as the Jew believes, but that love is more powerful than money, even in the Jew.

And, of course, Börne expands the Jewish significance of the Shylock story into a universal allegory about modern European bourgeois man:

> How Shakespeare would have portrayed *our* Shylocks, those great Shylocks with Christian decorations on Jewish frock coats! How he would have depicted those paper-trafficking Shylocks without the coats who own the flesh and blood of entire peoples with their certificates. . . . How he would have drawn those evil wretches whose God is a finance minister who commanded: "Let it be!" and there was created a papered world. . . . How Shakespeare would have disclosed the secrets of the stock exchange heart . . . [of] our Shylocks of the Old and New Testaments.[32]

Jewish "moneyness" and "lovelessness" are the mythological emblems of modern financial capitalism.

---

In 1821, when he came to present in detail his revolutionary critique of Judaism, Börne chose as his metaphor the figure of the Eternal Jew; but this time he invested Ahasverus with a new set of attributes. Börne had already touched on the Ahasverus theme in two short reviews of books on the Wandering Jew;[33] but it was Ludolf Holst's *Judaism in All Its Parts*[34]—a volume of patriotic prejudice, masquerading as an enlightened critique of Judaism—that stimulated him to write his own essay *Der ewige Jude*.[35]

From the outset, the Christian legend of the Wandering Jew seemed absurd to Börne: "It always appeared to me slanderous that the Savior, the God of Love and Reconciliation, could exact such a

---

[32] *Shylock* (1828), *BSS*, 1:499–505. (The piece was made available in the 1844–50 edition of Börne's collected works.) Richard Cumberland's *The Jew: A Comedy* was first published at London in 1794 and reprinted in *The British Theatre*, vol. 18 (London, 1808). For "heart," see pp. 12f., 25, and 65 in that edition.

[33] *BSS*, 2:456–68, dealing with literary aspects of the theme.

[34] *Judenthum in allen dessen Theilen* (Mainz, 1821).

[35] *BSS*, 2:494–538. Page references in the text are to this edition.

horrible vengeance as to curse [Ahasverus] with eternal misery."[36] He therefore transformed *Der ewige Jude* from being the personal history of Ahasverus into a catchphrase for the obsessive preoccupation of the Germans with what they see as Jewishness:

> In Frankfurt the word *Jew* is the inseparable shadow of all events, all relations, all conversations, of every ruse, every vexation. . . . Anyone who like me has observed this foolishness for twenty years, whether with anger or amusement, with disapproval or with sympathy, would exclaim—"*Der ewige Jude!*" (pp. 495f.)

For Börne, the key to this obsession is the selfishly commercial Jew-hatred of competing Christian merchants:

> Isn't it comical how those authors who hasten against the Jews first make themselves dizzy on the heights of high-blown argument seeking to prove that the sun, moon, and stars have a stake in the Jewish Question—but soon tumble from these heights into a grimy sack of soil, a sugar barrel, a banking office, or a dry-goods store? (p. 505)

But the essay goes beyond satirizing commercially motivated *Judenhass* to present Börne's deeper moral-economic interpretation of *Der ewige Jude*. He argues that the eternal Jewishness of the Jews resides in their psychological proclivity for *praxis* and commerce. It is this characteristic that is the essence of the *Ewiger Jude*. The whole essay reflects Börne's ambivalence to the Jewish Question, sneering at Jews and Jew-haters alike as expressions of a loveless egoism.[37] One should, therefore, guard against reading this essay as a liberal "pro-Jewish" statement, even though it appears to be a commendably liberal attack upon the various Christian, commercial, and nationalist species of Jew-hatred as enemies of German freedom. ("*Judenhass* is one of those Pontine Marshes that pollute the beautiful spring land of our freedom" [p. 498].)

Börne's main target, however, is not these variations of *Judenhass*, but the new rational and moral species of Jew-hatred represented by Holst's book. And here he parallels Saul Ascher's reply to Fichte thirty years before:

> All Holst's discussions are Kantified [*kantiert*]. . . . His book is properly not a practical but a metaphysical Hep-Hep. He divides the world in two parts, and calls one Judaism, the other non-Judaism. . . . Judaism is for him a sewer of stinking filth. Hatred, envy, covetousness, evil,

[36] Review of *Geschichte des ewigen Juden* (1821), *BSS*, 2:466.
[37] See especially *BSS*, 2:498, 536.

lying, brutality, godlessness, and all the other vices reside in the Jews. (p. 499)

From his noble vantage point, Holst may write in genuine outrage against the earlier inhumane Christian persecutions of the Jews, while blaming the Jews themselves for their misfortunes for having given birth to a "bloody Christianity"! Holst, being a believer in a higher, enlightened Kantian religion, prefers a more rational and humane persecution in the form of denial of civil rights; but, in any case, the Jews' own vices render them unsuited for the enjoyment of civil rights (pp. 499–506).

To Börne's mind, the true object of the present enlightened campaign of Holst and his fellows is simply to ensure the continued servitude of the Jews. Holst may claim that "he hates and can hate no Jew, for they belong to universal humanity," but the spuriousness of the argument is obvious: Holst's whole point, charges Börne, is that the spirit of rabbinical Judaism—which moves the Jews to vice—lies embedded in the very stomachs of the Jews and must be cut out. To do this, one has in practice to persecute not an abstract "spirit" but the actual Jews within whom that spirit dwells (pp. 522–25). And in practice, again, this boils down to persecuting *all* Jews, regardless of their individual character, by denying them civil and commercial rights on the sole ground of their being Jews. In the end Holst's book, argues Börne, is nothing but the old style *Judenhass* drawn from Eisenmenger with new labels on the outside (p. 528).[38]

> You do not speak as an enemy against the Jews, but you behave as one . . . and one cannot contradict deeds. . . . To live is to love, but you are the slave of your hatred. (pp. 537f., and cf. p. 498)

Not all of Holst's book could be so easily disposed of, however. One of its central themes in particular evidently worried Börne, since it was rooted in the premises of his own ambivalence towards Judaism and so could not properly be refuted without destroying his own revolutionary critique in the process. Holst had listed addiction to money and fraud as a national characteristic of the Jews ever since their occupation of Canaan, and he had (in the best revolutionary tradition) interpreted their Mammonism—consisting in usury, peddling, and stock-exchange swindling—as essentially an expression of Jewish egoism. To this Börne might reply in two ways. One was the general point that this argument, even if true, could not be used to justify hatred of the Jews and civil discrimination, because Jew-hatred itself was a form of loveless and egoistic behavior. The second point was

---

[38] For Eisenmenger's *Judaism Unmasked* (1711), see above, chap. 1.

that egoism is not restricted to the Jews and so cannot be designated as specifically Jewish:

> I don't believe that the Christian merchants are any better than the Jewish ones. They too are egoists as one can see from their business-letter style [which uses the word "have" as a synonym for "I"]. Language experts, and experts in the human heart, both know well that egoism in all ages is concealed in the verb "have." (p. 508)

Clearly Börne could not press matters too hard without weakening his own critique. And yet he obviously sensed that it was vital to refute Holst on this issue since it was generating a dangerous series of anti-Jewish arguments that implied the existence of a Jewish racial instinct to domination through money. Börne has indeed glimpsed in Holst the deadly complex of egoism, race, and Jewification that forms the structure of revolutionary nationalist antisemitism. Börne thus scorns Holst's belief that Jewish egoism and greed are *racially* inherited and almost ineradicable:

> Not wishing to deprive any Jew of his inheritance of hatred, Holst, like a loving father, resolves in his will that a Jew, even if he becomes a Christian, still remains a cheat, indeed becomes a double cheat. . . . He ordains that Jewish blood requires for its purification a threefold filtration, and only to the grandson of a baptized Jew originally married into a Christian family may political and civil rights be granted. (p. 508)

Börne also tries to ridicule Holst's related argument that this Jewish egoism is corrupting Germany in a process of "Jewification." Holst's line anticipates that of Wagner because it starts off by inquiring into the failure of the Jews to produce a creative genius in the arts and sciences. This deficiency only serves to confirm that the true Jewish aptitude is for Mammon, not Apollo. But the Jews are corrupting even commerce by usury in their quest for world domination. In their ambition to be lords of the world, claims Holst, Jews and converted Jews seek to become nobles and senators, to infiltrate government office, to manage the theater, and to manipulate public opinion. Through their control of books and above all newspapers, "the Jews aim at the complete domination of the world of thought" (pp. 515–18).

Börne airily dismisses all this talk of Jewish domination as mere hypochondriac fears, but a serious problem remains unresolved here since he has failed to dissociate himself from the basic premise of Holst's arguments, namely the identification of Judaism with Mammonism. On the contrary, Börne proceeds to assert quite vehemently this very premise in the context of advancing an authentically revolutionary critique of "Jewishness" that is intended to replace the bogus one of Holst:

> I will not defend the world of business whose Jewishness [*Judentüm-lichkeit*]—this manifestation of the money-demon, this raised fury of greed, this beautiful devil of gold—I hate in my deepest soul, whether I encounter it in the shape of a Jew, a Moslem, or a Christian. But is this Jewishness only the disgrace and guilt of the Jew? Is it not the stuffy air that forms the atmosphere of the whole world of business, maintaining life while at the same time choking that life in a deadly fashion? (p. 512)

Here Börne has accepted the stereotyping of the Jews as egoists by taking "Jewishness" as his chief metaphor for money egoism. But he has generalized the metaphor so that all bourgeois capitalist society, whether formally Jewish or Christian, is designated as "Jewish." Börne thinks that this broadening removes the specific basis for Holst's new kind of economic Jew-hatred. What Börne fails to see, however, is that in the process of trying to rescue the Jews by stamping all capitalism as "Jewish," he has made "Judaism" the archetypal metaphor for evil in modern life.

Two main factors may explain why Börne remained willfully and optimistically blind to the fact that his metaphor of *Judentümlichkeit* was opening the door to pernicious developments. Psychologically, there was Börne's discomfort with his own Jewish origins. The passage on *Judentümlichkeit* reeks of irrational hostility towards Judaism: the intensity of the attack on the "money-demon" and the actual choice of "Jewishness" as the allegory of evil betray an inner conflict and anger within Börne that all his customary nonchalance about his Jewish origins (and his conversion to Christianity) could not efface.[39] An uneasy guilt prompted this angry attack on what he took to be the cause of his own unhappiness and alienation.

The second reason seems to be intellectual, but is actually emotional again in that it stemmed from the other pole of Börne's ambivalence towards Judaism, that is, his residual loyalty to his people and his wish to redeem them both from their own bad qualities and from the hatred of their persecutors. Börne's fundamental reason for rejecting Holst's economic critique as evil was that, for all its close relationship to his own, it was nevertheless motivated by Jew-hatred.

---

[39] "If I were not myself a Jew, I would wish to say something in praise of the Jews. But *die deutsche Eitelkeit* forces me to affect a separation," *Aphorismen*, no. 24 (1808–10), *BSS*, 1:142.

Holst's concept of Jewish egoism was despised by Börne as vulgar and distorted, born of prejudice and nothing but a fraudulent rationale for a *Judenhass* that was itself symptomatic of greed and lovelessness among Christians. In effect, Börne reproached Holst for not having developed a revolutionary, "loving" critique of Judaism. The basic principle of this should be "freedom and humanity," making the question of whether a man were a Jew or a Christian irrelevant (pp. 536f.). The other principles of this critique followed naturally: It should be directed against Judaism, not against Jews. It should not deny civil rights to Jews, even if it should preach the need for Jews to emancipate themselves from egoism into full humanity. It should aim at the universal good of society, rather than serving sectional Christian self-interest. And lastly, it should be inspired by love, including love for the Jews, as opposed to the Christian egoism that foments Jew-hatred.

Holst's critique of Judaism failed to satisfy any of these criteria, but Börne saw his own critique as both morally and intellectually valid, passing all the tests of a truly humane and revolutionary solution to the Jewish Question. Most importantly, while Holst seized upon Jewish Mammonism to justify denying civil rights to the Jews, Börne insisted that the reprehensible addiction of Jews to money does not justify Jew-hatred.[40]

Doubtless Börne himself thought that his proclamation of authentic love and freedom were sufficient to render his critique safe from abuse *against* the Jews and would prevent its potentially dangerous allegory of "Judaism equals capitalism" developing into revolutionary antisemitism. But this was wishful thinking on his part. Even in *Der ewige Jude*, Börne had found himself having to defend his earlier piece *Für die Juden* from being traduced by Holst to mean that Börne damned the Jews as the evil financial allies of the repressive princes.[41] Here then was an immediate example of the dangers inherent in Börne's revolutionary economic critique (pp. 50ff.).[42] In practice, Börne's analysis had failed to rescue him from the premise of economic Jew-hatred that he shared with Holst. Börne might insist that *his* kind of critique, unlike Holst's, was neither motivated by *Judenhass* nor intended to justify it. But the genie was out of the bottle: Börne had taken an anti-Jewish concept of great potency from the arsenal of Jew-hatred and legitimated it in progressive revolutionary circles.

[40] On rights see *BSS*, 1:522.

[41] *BSS*, 2:504. Cf. *Für die Juden, BSS*, 1:876.

[42] Börne's disclaimer in *Der ewige Jude* about his earlier attack on Jewish finance is not entirely convincing in the light of his later embittered remarks against the Rothschilds as royal financiers. See *Briefe aus Paris*, nos. 58 and 72, *BSS*, 3:351ff., 482ff.

His rather tortuous warnings against employing Jewish Mammonism and egoism as pretexts for *Judenhass* were scarcely an effective control upon the pernicious use to which his idea could be put once it was firmly and respectably established in German revolutionary thinking. After all, St. Paul's advocacy of love for the Jews within the context of his own critique of Judaism had been largely unavailing.

---

Börne's later writings continued his ambivalent denunciation of both Jewish Mammonism and of the Jew-hatred based on that same premise. On the one hand, he would roundly condemn Jews for their Mammonism, which obstructed freedom. The Jews were seen as responsible for the development of the modern money system,[43] while their alliance with the July Monarchy made them priests of Moloch. "Rothschild is the high priest of Fear, that goddess upon whose altar freedom, love of fatherland, honor, and every other virtue are sacrificed."[44] Jewish banking is the enemy of "the people" (that is, the working class), the new hero of Börne's democratic revolutionism after 1830, who "alone do not bargain their whole soul and faith with accursed money."[45]

But at the same time, Börne would pursue his attacks on Jew-hatred itself as the enemy of love of freedom, excoriating in *Menzel der Franzosenfresser* the fervent German nationalist Jew-hatred that was seizing ground at the expense of the universal ideal of freedom. For Börne, in fact, there was no contradiction between his critical attitude towards egoistic Judaism and his detestation of Jew-hatred; both his outlooks were shaped by his revolutionary ideals of freedom and humanity.

For the treatment of these twin sicknesses of Jewish egoism and German Jew-hatred Börne found an exemplary prescription after 1834 in the Catholicism of Lamennais. Christianity, Börne now discovered, was a primal socialism, ordained by God and sustained by love, which in Catholicism in particular constituted a doctrine full of revolutionary faith whose power could be seen in contemporary Poland. The Reformation, Börne now averred, had corrupted Christianity by delivering religious Germany into the hands of the princes and justifying an economic individualism lethal to the soul. Political power and economic egoism had become the twin forces that to-

---

[43] Ibid., no. 70, *BSS*, 3:473.

[44] Ibid., no. 58, *BSS*, 3:351f. (and similarly pp. 482ff.). See also Figes, "Ludwig Börne," pp. 379f.

[45] *Briefe aus Paris*, no. 24, *BSS*, 3:114.

gether killed the spirit of "German freedom."[46] In Catholicism, Börne found ultimately the positive religious fulfillment of his revolutionary critique of Judaism.

———

Börne himself recognized that he never genuinely escaped from his own "Jewishness" into human emancipation. That was the real source of his ambivalence towards Judaism. For all his emancipated German and cosmopolitan pretensions, Börne remained aware of his ineradicable Jewishness in the eyes of the world, a peculiarity that baptism could not wash away:

> One may never forget that I am a Jew. . . . What a marvel! A thousand times I have experienced it, yet it seems eternally new to me. Some reproach me with being a Jew, others pardon me, still others praise me for it. But all are thinking about it. They are as though spellbound in this magic Jewish circle and not one of them can escape from it. I know full well whence comes this evil enchantment [*from the German's need to compensate for his own wretched condition by looking down on someone of even lower status*]. . . . You have scattered the salt of hate in your heart.[47]

"For long have I felt bitterly in my own self the persecution of the Jews," wrote the ostensibly emancipated Börne towards the end of his life.[48]

Still, Börne was noted for his ability to throw the pain off lightly, as in his affectedly bemused remarks about the magic Jewish circle. Heine was astonished at his rival's insouciant attitude to those writers who referred to his Jewish descent: Börne would express amusement that they couldn't find anything more damaging to his character than to accuse him of being Jewish; and he would toss off such provocative asides as the sentence that "Jesus Christ, who by the way was my relative, preached equality."[49]

Opponents, however, found it easy to harp on Börne's ancestry. Wolfgang Menzel—less venomous than some—saw that years of anti-Jewish discrimination had marked Börne's personality, but he still contrived by artful choice of metaphor to transfer most of the blame to a baneful Jewish inheritance: "The curse of his race weighed

---

[46] *Menzel, BSS,* 3:924f. Cf. Figes, "Ludwig Börne," pp. 380ff.

[47] *Briefe aus Paris,* no. 74, *BSS,* 3:510, 512.

[48] *Menzel, BSS,* 3:888.

[49] The key text of the Heine–Börne rivalry is Heine's *Ludwig Börne: Eine Denkschrift* (1840). See below, n. 63.

heavily upon him."[50] Or, as another critic less delicately put it, "The pariah-brand was stamped on his breast."[51] Eduard Meyer lamented "the many hateful qualities of the Asiatic that cannot be so easily laid aside by baptism."[52] In a neat psychological maneuver, many of his enemies projected the hatred that lay within their own hearts into those of their Jewish victims. Karl von Simrock, the Germanomaniac translator of the *Nibelungenlied*, unwittingly revealed this transference of hatred: "If I had not been enjoined by Christianity to love all men, I would have had to hate your people," he informed Börne. From his own innate hatred of the Jews, Simrock concluded that the Jews must hate him as a German![53] Nor did the Left fail in its detective powers; the revolutionary *Halle Yearbooks*, mouthpiece of the Young Hegelians, scorned Börne "as a true fanatical Jew; he knows only hatred, his mind is nothing but a joke."[54] And Wagner, who had exalted the revolutionary virtues of Börne in 1850, revised his opinion in later years and dismissed the tribune of the people as being just as bad a case of Jewishness as Heine himself.[55]

None of this outraged reaction would have much surprised Börne, who had once noted that any protest by Jews at their victimized condition is promptly denounced as arrogance by the Jew-haters.[56] Yet underneath his amused exterior, Börne must have been disturbed by the way in which this hatred of the Jews continued to simmer. In the concluding sentences of *Der ewige Jude* (1821), Börne had shown himself optimistic that the current persecution of the Jews was but the last flicker of the flame of Jew-hatred, which would soon be extin-

---

[50] Börne, quoting Menzel, in *BSS*, 3:888.

[51] *Mitternachtszeitung für gebildete Stände*, quoted in K. Spalding, "Gedanken zum Börne-Bild der Gegenwart," in *Erfahrung und Überlieferung: Festschrift für C. P. Magill*, ed. H. Siefken and A. Robinson (Cardiff, 1974), pp. 88–99, n. 22.

[52] "Börne calls himself a German, but we beg to decline him this honor. . . . Börne is a Jew . . . baptized or not, it is all the same. . . . We do not hate the faith of the Jews, but rather the many ugly peculiarities of these Asiatics, which cannot be laid aside so easily through baptism" (Eduard Meyer, *Gegen L. Börne* [Altona, 1831], pp. 5, 12f., quoted by J. Katz, *From Prejudice to Destruction: Anti-Semitism 1700–1933* [Cambridge, Mass., 1980], pp. 177f.). Börne's reply is in his *Briefe aus Paris*, nos. 58 and 59, *BSS*, 3:359–63. For Riesser's unwelcome defense of Börne, see above n. 26, and also chap. 6, n. 31; chap. 10, nn. 22ff.; chap. 11, n. 41. Cf. M. Zimmermann, *Hamburgischer Patriotismus und deutscher Nationalismus: Die Emanzipation der Juden in Hamburg 1830–1865* (Hamburg, 1979), pp. 61ff.; C. Hoffmann, *Juden und Judentum im Werk deutscher Althistoriker des 19. und 20. Jahrhunderts* (Leiden, 1988), pp. 173–76, for Meyer.

[53] Quoted in *HAS*, 3:400.

[54] Ibid., 3:400, quoting the *Hallische Jahrbücher* 2 (1839): 1347.

[55] Cf. Wagner, *PW*, 4:93, who criticizes Börne for mocking the *Burschenschaftler* assassin of August Kotzebue (cf. ibid., 165).

[56] *Der ewige Jude*, *BSS*, 2:499f.

guished eternally by the tide of universal freedom.[57] But elsewhere in the same essay and more so in later life he realized that things were not so simple. In 1831 Börne expressed his misgivings about whether the mass of Germans would really absorb the Jews after the coming revolution:

> It is bad for the Jews that in this matter as in everything else the German is ruled by his heart. Even to be just, a German must love. But it is a fact that the Jews are not loved.[58]

Ludwig Börne is the seminal figure in whose works are to be found the five main anti-Jewish themes of nineteenth-century revolutionary thought. It was Börne who set up, as early as 1808, the scheme of the two main Jewish "egoisms": *practical* egoism, which takes the form of the worship of money, and *theoretical* egoism, which manifests itself as lovelessness. To these egoisms Börne assigned mythical representations; in the case of money, the myth is that of the "money-devil" or Mammon/Moloch, while Ahasverus or the Eternal Jew becomes the archetypal embodiment of lovelessness. (These egoisms were in effect reinterpretations of a crude original Jewish egoism seen in the claim to be the "Chosen Race.")

The second theme was the projection onto modern German society of these specifically Jewish vices. While Börne saw the Jewish Question as a test of civil freedom, he less favorably interpreted Judaism as the parable of an unfree, economic, egoistic society. Crucially, Börne framed the metaphor of *Judentümlichkeit*, which became central to anti-Jewish theorizing in the 1840s. The whole loveless, selfish edifice of bourgeois capitalist society was simply "Jewishness" writ large.

Thirdly, through the metaphor of *Judentümlichkeit*, the redemption of the Jews was transformed from being merely a matter of civil emancipation into being a messianic paradigm of the redemption of all mankind. But the implication of this new ideology was that "Jewishness" affected not only the Jews themselves, but the Germans also, in the form of "Jewification." Admittedly, Börne did not press the notion of *Verjudung*—indeed he even scoffed at it in 1821—but it is intrinsic to his critique of Judaism and it also emerges in disguise in his attacks on Jewish finance as the abettor of the German princes.

Börne also reinforced a fourth theme, the idea of "destruction." Judaism or Jewishness was to be destroyed through the human eman-

[57] Ibid., 2:538.
[58] *Briefe aus Paris*, no. 60, *BSS*, 3:386.

cipation of the Jews. In effect, this was a demand for the extinction of a specific Jewish existence or consciousness—a call for the suicide of Judaism—through total assimilation. In making this demand, progressives like Börne saw themselves as doing the Jews a great favor, for they envisaged the extinction of Judaism as coming about through love. The Jews would evolve from a separate, unhappy, diseased, egoistic existence into the community of love, just as Börne himself had through revolutionary freedom and spiritual love. For Börne saw in his own individual conversion to love the hope of a general redemption of the Jews and an end to the "Eternally Jewish." As early as 1807, Börne had expounded revolutionary "destruction" as the solution to the Jewish Question: in his aphorisms of that year he wrote that "the hatred between Judaism and Christianity is necessary; for everything, in order to attain its highest life, requires the destruction [*Untergang*] of the other."[59]

The fifth and last theme that Börne bequeathed to his revolutionary heirs was his invention of a socioeconomic critique of Judaism founded on the concept of practical egoism. Where Kant (to be followed by Hegel, Feuerbach, and others) had adumbrated a religious and philosophical critique grounded in the theoretical egoism of Jewish religion, Börne's picture of Judaism as an essentially alienated, dehumanized obsession with money was taken up by Marx and Hess, not to mention Wagner. Like the two communist Jewish revolutionaries, Börne's search for love and community, his estrangement from the money culture that he thought typified Judaism, and his personal alienation from both Jewish and Christian society, led him to develop a radical economic critique of Judaism as an integral part of a revolutionary ideology based on "freedom and humanity." From this ideology there emerged the quasi-religious category of redemption, rather than emancipation, as the solution to the Jewish Question. Instead of being a matter of rational and liberal civil rights, the Jewish Question was lifted onto an abstract, almost metaphysical level where the Jews were required to transmute themselves into genuine human beings. Tragically, Börne had cleared away the old Jew-hatred only to prepare the ground for the new.

## HEINE THE IRREDEEMABLE

Heinrich Heine (1797–1856), the most ironic of European poets, was driven by a strong religious instinct that constantly found itself at odds with his incurably skeptical intellect. This tension filled

[59] *14 Sätze* (1807), *BSS*, 1:12.

Heine's poems, his essays, and his life.[60] When he had himself baptized in 1825, he commented cynically that he had done so to obtain an "entry ticket to European civilization"; soon he was writing that "I am now hated by both Christian and Jew. I much regret having been baptized. ... Isn't it absurd how scarcely am I baptized than I am cried down as a Jew?" Later, Heine remarked that he had merely "been baptized, but not converted." And yet, hardly disguised beneath this affected religious indifference and flippancy about his conversion, there is a genuine misery and guilt that he should thus have trivialized and betrayed his religious urge. After 1840, his watershed year, this urge increasingly asserted itself and impelled him to a genuine conversion to a universal religion, free of any formal church or synagogue, but so rich in Jewish ideas and feelings that he seemed to be returning at last to his ancestral religion.[61]

Heine's religious feelings were equally contradicted by his revolutionary mentality. He had early on adopted the revolutionism of the French Saint-Simonian thinkers, who had preached a messianic healing of the rift in human nature between spirit and flesh, and the corresponding rift in human society between the organic and the artificial. But in Heine's view it was in Germany that these forms of human "alienation" (*Zerrissenheit*) would be swept away in a true "emancipation of the flesh." The French Revolution was now being eclipsed by the dramatic shift in consciousness taking place in Germany. A German philosophical revolution was achieving a liberation of the human spirit that a profoundly German revolution would transform into social, human harmony. Heine's German revolution was the redemptionist program of Young Germany and the Young Hegelians. Man's divided soul would be reconciled in harmony of flesh and spirit; man would live in an organic, reconciled society in which he would no

---

[60] For recent scholarship, see N. Reeves, *Heinrich Heine: Poetry and Politics* (Oxford, 1974); J. L. Sammons, *Heinrich Heine: A Modern Biography* (Princeton, 1979). Useful too are E. M. Butler, *Heinrich Heine: A Biography* (London, 1956), and S. S. Prawer, *Heine: The Tragic Satirist* (Cambridge, 1961).

[61] On Heine and the Jewish Question, see S. S. Prawer, *Heine's Jewish Comedy* (Oxford, 1983). Cf. A. Bein, "Heinrich Heine, der Schamlose," in his *Die Judenfrage* (Stuttgart, 1980), 2:231–50. H. Bieber, *Heinrich Heine: Jüdisches Manifest* (original title *Confessio Judaica*), 2d ed. (New York, 1946), reprints the key German texts.

For convenience I cite where necessary from the recent German edition of Heine, *Sämtliche Schriften*, ed. K. Briegleb, 6 vols. (Munich, 1968–76; *HSS*), unless otherwise indicated. References are also given to two English translations: *The Works of Heinrich Heine*, trans. C. G. Leland et al., 12 vols. (London, 1892–1905); F. Ewen, *Heinrich Heine: A Self-Portrait* (Philadelphia, 1974; *HW*), which is an abbreviated version with changed pagination of Ewen's *Prose and Poetry of Heinrich Heine* (New York, 1948).

The quotations come from Bieber, *Manifest* (*JM*), pp. 68, 281; Ewen, *Self-Portrait* (*SP*), pp. 119–23; *HAS*, 3:401–4.

longer be alienated from his fellows as he was in the present political state, which was fragmented by greed and religion.[62]

Where Börne was adopted as the totem of political revolutionism in Germany, Heine's revolutionary impact was in the realm of artistic and sensual liberation. Heine himself in a scandalous posthumous tribute to his old rival Börne summed up their differences as stemming from two opposing temperaments, the Nazarene and the Hellene, the ascetic and the sensualist, the moralistic politician and the artistic revolutionary. Alas, this onslaught antagonized Heine's own circle; Karl Gutzkow rounded on him as a blackguard and Laube refused to defend him.[63] Virtually Heine's sole apologist was Richard Wagner, who praised him as "this great awakener of the German mind" so shamefully silenced by the Börne lobby. Wagner's support, however, was to be mysteriously reversed in 1850 when he extolled Börne as the redeemable Jew and anathematized Heine in *Judaism in Music*.[64]

[62] See Reeves, *Heine*, pp. 76–100, for his revolutionism; E. M. Butler, *The Saint-Simonian Religion in Germany: A Study of the Young German Movement* (Cambridge, 1926); G. C. Iggers, "Heine and the Saint-Simonians: A Re-examination," *Comparative Literature* 10 (1958): 289–308. See also my annotated version of Heine's *History of Religion and Philosophy in Germany*, ed. P. L. Rose (North Queensland, 1982).

For Heine's notions about universal revolution bringing the emancipation of all humanity, see *HSS*, 2:376; 5:742.

[63] *PW*, 3:99f. Heine's *Ludwig Börne: Eine Denkschrift* of 1840 was admired for its brilliance of style by Nietzsche and Thomas Mann. Printed in *HSS*, 4:108; definitive edition in Heine, *Historisch-kritische Gesamtausgabe der Werke*, ed. M. Windfuhr et al. (Hamburg, 1973–), vol. 2. Related texts in H. M. Enzensberger, ed., *Ludwig Börne und Heinrich Heine: Ein deutsches Zerwürfnis* (Nordingen, 1986). No complete English version of *Ludwig Börne* is easily available but excerpts are translated in *Memoirs from His Works: Letters and Conversations*, ed. and trans. G. Karpeles (London, 1910), 2:86–109.

Cf. Prawer, *Heine's Jewish Comedy*, chap. 7; Reeves, *Heine*, pp. 166–70; Butler, *Heine*, pp. 97ff.; Sammons, *Heine: A Modern Biography*, pp. 238ff.; idem, *Heine: The Elusive Poet* (New Haven, 1969), pp. 248–93; W. Kaufmann, *Nietzsche*, 4th ed. (Princeton, 1974), pp. 376ff. See above, note 49.

[64] *HSS*, 6/i:519f. (cf. 5:743). (Trans. in H. Barth, et al., *Wagner: A Documentary Study*, [New York, 1975], p. 163; *PW*, 8:147.) Wagner also defended Heine in the *Abendzeitung* issue of 3 August 1841. See my "Heine and Wagner Revisited: Art, Myth and Revolution," *Heine-Jahrbuch*, 1991, 93–122.

None of the extant accounts of the Wagner–Heine relationship deals adequately with such problems as Heine's reticence in responding to the attack on him in *Judaism in Music*. K. Richter, "Absage und Verleugung: Die Verdrängung Heinrich Heines aus Werk und Bewusstsein Richard Wagners," in *Richard Wagner: Wie anti-semitisch darf ein Künstler sein?*, ed. H.-K. Metzger and R. Riehn (Munich, 1978), describes Wagner's use of Heine but simply attributes Heine's silence to his having regarded Wagner as a mere musician. Richter in effect denies that there is a real problem about Heine's lack of response since, he implies (pp. 13f.), Wagner's attack on the poet by name appeared only in the 1869 reissue of *Judaism in Music*. Actually, Heine is attacked by name in the

The picture of Judaism that emerges from the writings of Heine's aggressively revolutionary years is an ambivalent one and it parallels Börne's own outlook in many respects. There is, of course, the usual Hegelian contempt for the Jews as a spent Ahasverian historical force:

> A mummified people [*Volksmumie*] that wanders the earth, wrapped up in its swathing of prescriptive letters, an obstinate piece of world history, a specter that bargains for its maintenance with bills of exchange and old hose.[65]

This philosophical prejudice was reinforced by an artistic distaste for Judaism as the matrix of the Nazarene spirit. Behind both attitudes it is possible to detect Heine's resentment against the whole class of wealthy business Jews (including his own family), whose prime function he saw as being the patronage of such artists as himself.

At times, Heine's hatred for the merchant class as Philistines merged into Börne-like denunciation of the wealthy as Mammonists. He despised their "counting-house morality" and inveighed: "Money is the god of our time and Rothschild is his prophet." Such feelings turned him into a revolutionary activist in 1843–44, when he befriended Marx and the two collaborated on both literary and political projects. Significantly, this was the very time when Marx was writing his essay *On the Jewish Question* (1843), which systematized the sort of incautious remarks on Jews and Mammon that Börne and Heine were wont to utter.[66]

Naturally, like Börne, Heine refused to characterize the Jews as the

---

original 1850 version. The more extensive account of the relationship by L. Prox, "Wagner und Heine," *Deutsche Vierteljahrsschrift für Literaturwissenschaft und Geistesgeschichte* 46 (1972): 684–98, also fails to consider seriously the reasons for Heine's reticence (p. 690). See also the surprising lack of interest in the problem in Sammons, *Heine: A Modern Biography*, p. 332; idem, *Heine: The Elusive Poet*, p. 417; Butler, *Heine*, p. 253; Prawer, *Heine: The Tragic Satirist*, p. 243. Cf. F. Hirth, "Wagner, Meyerbeer and Heine," *Das Goldene Tor* 5 (1950): 383–88.

[65] *Travel Pictures: The City of Lucca*, chap. 13 (*HSS*, 2:515; *HW*, 3:309). Even here a layer of sympathetic irony is present. For the "wandering" metaphor in Heine, see below.

[66] Letters of 23 August and 28 November 1823 to Moser, in *Briefe*, ed. F. Hirth, 6 vols. (Mainz, 1950–51; repr. 1965), 1:101ff., 126. *Lutetia* (31 March 1841), *HSS*, 5:355 (*JM*, p. 157; *HW*, 8:231). Cf. *JM*, pp. 17, 25. The poem *Anno 1829* attacks the "Zahlungsfähige Moral (der Krämerwelt)," *HSS*, 4:379. In 1850 Heine remarked that it was not money-fever that was the Jewish vice, but simply trading-fever. See H. H. Houben, *Gespräche mit Heine* (Frankfurt, 1926), p. 726.

exclusive embodiment of greed and he threw the charge back onto the Christians:

> The merchant throughout the world has the same religion. His count-inghouse is his church . . . his gold is his God, his credit is his faith.[67]

In 1825 he commented: "I am becoming now a true Christian, that is, I sponge on rich Jews."[68]

Again, like Börne, Heine perceived both Christians and Jews as "egoistic nationalists" pursuing only their own narrow interests. The two revolutionists preferred to support Jewish emancipation as part of the universal struggle for human liberty for all peoples:

> That I will be a defender of Jewish rights, of that I am certain. . . .
> But a born enemy of all positive religions will never champion that re-ligion which was the first to bring in its wake that disregard for people which causes so much anguish to this day.[69]
>
> What is the great task of our day? It is emancipation. Not simply the emancipation of the Irish, the Greeks, the Frankfurt Jews, and all such oppressed peoples—but the emancipation of the whole world, and especially of Europe, from aristocracy.[70]

Heine embraced Börne's hope that the revolution would dispose of a Jew-hatred that was now becoming openly economic in nature:

> Yes, sooner or later, the Jews will have to be emancipated, be it from a sense of justice, or wisdom, or necessity. Among the upper classes, an-

[67] *Briefe aus Berlin*, no. 2, 16 March 1822, *HSS*, 2:36 (*JM*, p. 9). Cf. *Lutetia* (27 May 1840), *HSS*, 5:274 (*HW*, 8:75); *Travel Pictures: The City of Lucca*, chap. 4 (*HSS*, 2:486); *HW*, 3:260.
It seems that Heine was more of an influence on Marx than the other way around. See Reeves, *Heine*, pp. 152ff.; idem, "Heine and the Young Marx," *Oxford German Studies* 7 (1972–73): 44–97, at pp. 60ff. L. Marcuse, "Heine and Marx: A History and a Legend," *Germanic Review* 30 (1955): 100–24, argues convincingly that Heine probably never shared Marx's dogmatics despite their collaboration and coincidence of revolutionary political interests in 1844.
Marx also in 1846 changed to Heine's side and persuaded Engels to retract his earlier sanctimonious denunciation of the Heine book as "the most worthless thing ever written in the German language." Cf. Sammons, *Heine: A Modern Biography*, pp. 241f.; Butler, *Heine*, p. 168.
[68] Letter of 18 December 1825 to Moser, in *Briefe*, 1:245 (*JM*, p. 64). Cf. Heine's marvelous readings of *The Merchant of Venice* in which he portrays Shylock as seeking to preserve his daughter from the lovelessness of the Mammonist Christian merchants! *Shakespeare's Maidens and Women: Portia; Jessica* (1838), *HSS*, 4:251ff. (*JM*, pp. 118–31; *SP*, pp. 424–34).
[69] Letter of 23 August 1823 to M. Moser, in *Briefe*, 1:101.
[70] *Travel Pictures: Journey from Munich*, chap. 29, *HSS*, 2:376 (*JM*, p. 79; *HW*, 3:104; *SP*, p. 563).

tagonism against the Jews is no longer due to religion. And among the lower classes, it is every day being more rapidly transformed into a social hatred of the overweening power of capital, of exploitation of the poor by the rich. The governments have at last come to the sane conclusion that the state is an organic body that cannot achieve complete health as long as one of its members, be it the smallest toe, is diseased.[71]

And he also expected the revolution to put an end to the rising nationalist Germanic Jew-hatred:

> Does German nationality suffer a loss through complete fusion with the Jews? Our nationalists, the so-called patriots who have in their heads only race, blood, and that kind of horse-breeding ideas—these stragglers from the Middle Ages will soon encounter enemies who may put an end to all their dreams of Germanic, Romanic, and Slavonic national character, so that they will no longer think of carping at the Germanness of the Jews.[72]

But in his less doctrinaire moments, Heine understood that this type of Jew-hatred was not just an aberration, but deeply entrenched in modern romantic German culture:

> [Modern] Jew-hatred began with the Romantic School, with the enthusiasm for the Middle Ages, for Catholicism, and for knighthood—and it was intensified by the Germanophiles.[73]

Nor did he dissent when his correspondent Giacomo Meyerbeer confided that

> 99 percent of readers are Jew-haters. That is why they relish, and always will relish, Jew-hatred, as long as it is administered to them with a little skill.[74]

---

Heine's Jewish sensibility opened his eyes to the dangers of the German revolution. Heine may never have envisaged the full horror

[71] *Ludwig Marcus: Denkworte* (1844), *HSS*, 5:184 (*JM*, p. 176; *SP*, p. 420). Cf. *Shakespeare's Maidens: Jessica*, *HSS*, 4:260f. (*SP*, p. 432), for his comments on economic antisemitism.

[72] *Ludwig Marcus*, *HSS*, 5:185. For other comments on the Germanomaniacs, see *Ludwig Börne*, ed. Windfuhr, 2:100, 585f. Also, *HSS*, 4:89.

[73] *Gedanken und Einfälle (Thoughts and Fancies)*, *HSS*, 6/i:652 (*JM*, p. 264; *SP*, pp. 451f.).

[74] G. Meyerbeer, *Briefwechsel und Tagebücher*, ed. H. and G. Becker (Berlin, 1975), 3:195f., letter of 29 August 1839.

of Hitler, but his famous prophecies grew out of an understanding of those passions and fears that eventually engendered the mad German Redeemer. A prophecy that Hitler almost seemed driven to act out—"Where one burns books, in the end one will burn people"—was uttered presciently by Heine in 1820, when he was still far from his mature knowledge of the German soul.[75] By 1835, however, Heine had fathomed that the violent currents of feeling that were then expressing themselves in abstract philosophical pantheism and romanticism would eventually be unleashed in political revolution. German pantheism, once freed of the restraints of German Christian piety and respectability, would fill the world with horror and admiration:

> Then Thor with his colossal hammer will finally leap forth and smash the Gothic cathedrals into fragments. . . . Thought precedes the deed as lightning thunder. . . . A drama will be enacted in Germany in comparison with which the French revolution will appear a harmless idyll.

Even if one must beware of reading too much into these utterances, there is here a startling anticipation of Jung's 1935 interpretation of Nazism as a revival of those primitive Germanic impulses that were embodied in Thor's brother god Wotan.[76]

What this German revolution would mean for the Jews was proclaimed in Heine's profound visionary statement of 1838:

> But let some day triumph Satan and that evil pantheism of which all the saints of the Old and New Testaments, and the Koran too, warn us—then shall a thunderstorm of persecution be drawn down upon the heads of the poor Jews that will surpass by far all their earlier sufferings.[77]

Heine could not have known of the conceptions of social Darwinism and scientific materialism that were to give the stamp of certainty to Hitler's pantheism. But the poet was all too aware of the role of German revolutionary romanticism in shaping the changing face of Jew-hatred in the nineteenth century.

------

Despite all his Börnerian theorizing, Heine's deeper religious instincts compelled him gradually to a revolutionary understanding

[75] *Almansor*: "Das war ein Vorspiel nur, dort wo man Bücher / Verbrennt, verbrennt man auch am Ende Menschen," *HSS*, 1:284f.

[76] *HSS*, 3:639f. (*HW*, 5:208f.). Cf. the essays *Wotan* (1936) and *After the Catastrophe* (1945), reprinted in C. G. Jung, *Collected Works* (London, 1964), vol. 10.

[77] *Shakespeare's Maidens and Women: Portia* (1838), *HSS*, 4:265 (*JM*, p. 130; *HW*, 1:400f.).

of Jews, of Jewish religion, and of Jewish history that was quite different from that of most German revolutionists. Heine was fascinated by the mystery of Jewish survival and sought its purpose:

> The Jews are a ghost who keeps guard over a treasure that was once entrusted to it. Thus sat this murdered people, this ghost-people, in its dark ghetto, and guarded there its Hebrew Bible.[78]

Neither Hegel nor Börne's Mammonist theory explained the enigmatic survival of this "inexhaustible people," this "people of the book," this "yeast of humanity." At the height of his Hellenist posturing, Heine admitted his pride at belonging to the peculiar race of Israelites that was such a volatile mixture of Mammonism and nobility, the race so eternally fruitful in ideas and that seemed to be the bearer of some strange, as yet unrealized mission for all humanity:

> The Jews are the stuff of which gods are made. . . . While some of them creep about in the filthiest mire of commerce, others ascend to the highest peaks of humanity, and Golgotha is not the only mountain on which a Jewish God has bled for the salvation of the world. . . . The world has perhaps still to expect further discoveries from them.[79]

As early as 1824, a sensitivity to the meaning of Jewish history had led Heine to voice intimations of an eventual reconversion to Judaism:

> I am moved by strange feelings as I read through those sad annals of Jewish history, so full of instruction and sorrow. The spirit of Jewish history is revealed to me more and more, and this spiritual equipment will some day stand me in good stead.[80]

For much of the next two decades, this Jewish feeling may have been submerged in his Hellenism, but it was never lost.

After 1840, two events combined to shock Heine into an accelerating rapprochement with Judaism. In May 1840, news reached Heine at Paris of the Damascus Blood Libel and he reported on it at length to the German press. There was not the slightest doubt, exclaimed Heine in imitation of the humanitarian Voltaire, that "Monsieur Crémieux, the Jews' advocate, is really pleading the cause of all humanity" against torture and superstition. But equally Voltairean were the snide remarks against the Eastern Jews with which Heine showed off his superiority: the persecutors and victims alike are unsavory and small-minded. The real issue is to demonstrate the virtue of Euro-

---

[78] *History of Religion and Philosophy*, HSS, 3:545 (*JM*, p. 107; *HW*, 5:55).

[79] *Ludwig Börne* (1840), HSS, 4:118ff. (*JM*, p. 145. Omitted from the Leland version, but partly translated in Heine, *Memoirs*, 2:100).

[80] *Briefe*, 1:172 (*JM*, p. 26).

pean justice and reason.[81] The real psychological impact of the Damascus Affair on Heine's feelings of Jewishness, however, emerged in his decision to publish his long-abandoned novel, *The Rabbi of Bacherach*, a tale of Jewish persecution in medieval Germany that had been put aside unfinished in 1824–25 just before his baptism. The resuscitation of this intensely Jewish work, which opens with curdling forebodings of a massacre triggered by the Blood Libel, marks the first great step in Heine's road back from Hegelianism.[82]

The second factor in Heine's reconversion, and the one that really brought him to his senses, was the paralysis that gradually overwhelmed him in the 1840s and confined him after 1848 to his "mattress-grave." Reconsidering his priorities, Heine rejected the Hegelian philosophical keystone of his Hellenism:

> I have given up the God, or rather the Godlessness of Hegel.[83]
>
> A great change has come over me. . . . I am no longer the Great Pagan Number 2 . . . no longer a joyful Hellene . . . I am only a poor Jew sick unto death.[84]

When he wrote the preface for a new edition of his Hegelian *History of Religion and Philosophy* in 1852, Heine indicted his old friend Marx as well as the rest of the Young Hegelians for grounding their revolutionism on the death of God:

> This cobweb Berlin dialectic cannot . . . kill a cat, much less a God. . . . I recommend the Book of Daniel to the excellent Ruge as well as to my still more deeply deluded friends Messrs. Marx, Feuerbach, Daumer, Bruno Bauer . . . those godless self-gods.[85]

Heine had cast off all his old arrogant humanism, and he had repudiated the revolutionary politics to which it gave birth as a crazy farce: "Universal anarchy, the world turned upside down, divine madness become visible," he cried in 1848.[86] In his vision of revolu-

---

[81] *Lutetia* (7 and 27 May, 25 and 30 July 1840), *HSS*, 5:267ff. (*JM*, pp. 148–57).

[82] *HSS*, 1:459ff. (excerpts in *JM*, pp. 32ff.; *SP*, pp. 259ff.).

[83] Letters of 25 January and 12 October 1850, in *Briefe*, 3:195, 232 (*JM*, p. 188, for former only; *SP*, pp. 212, 216). Cf. *Confessions*, *HSS*, 6/i:474f. (*SP*, p. 210; *Memoirs*, 2:251).

[84] *Berichtigung* (*Correction*), *HSS*, 5:109 (*JM*, p. 187; *SP*, p. 207). Cf. *Romanzero*, "Epilogue" (1851), *HSS*, 6/i:18off.

[85] *History of Religion*, preface to 2d German edition (1852), *HSS*, 3:510 (*HW*, 5:xliii), repudiating atheism. Reprinted in the *Confessions* of 1854, *HSS*, 6/i:479. This preface and other texts relating to Hegel are collected in my edition of the *History of Religion*.

Heine refers to Daumer's views on Hebrew religion in a conversation of 1850 (Houben, *Gespräche mit Heine*, p. 690). Cf. *HAS*, 3:410–15.

[86] Letter of 9 July 1848 to J. Campe in *Briefe*, 2:151.

tion, Judaism was something to be preserved, not destroyed. The eternal Ahasverian life of the Jews had a revolutionary purpose:

> Moses created a nation that was to defy the centuries—a great, eternal, holy people, the people of God, which could serve as the model for all humanity.
>
> If all pride of ancestry were not a silly paradox in a champion of the revolution and its democratic principles, the writer of these lines could well be proud that . . . he is a descendant of those martyrs of Israel who gave the world a God and a morality, and who fought and suffered on all the battlefields of thought.[87]

In 1850 Heine remarked: "I make no secret of my Judaism, to which I have not returned, because I never left it."[88] Indeed, throughout his life and writings, Heine's Jewish sensibility figured in his handling of the Ahasverus myth. Ahasverus seemed an emblem of Heine's own life. In 1826 he wrote:

> I am driven passionately to say farewell to the German fatherland. It is less the desire to wander than the affliction of personal circumstances—for instance, the never-to-be-washed-away Jew in me—that drives me hence. . . . How deeply rooted is still the myth of the Wandering Jew! In the calm forest valley, the mother tells her children the hair-raising tale, which brings the little ones closer to the hearth in fear. Outside it is night, the posthorn sounds, and Jewish peddlers travel to Leipzig for the fair. But we who are the heroes of this legend don't even know it. No barber can shave away the white beard whose edge had blackened with time, becoming youthful again.[89]

This unsettling passage fixed Heine's self-awareness of himself as a permanent Jewish outsider, and at the same time rooted his sensibility in Jewish history.[90]

Ahasverus never deserted Heine's imagination. Take, for example, the detail of Ahasverus's blackening beard. Twenty-five years after, it reappears in the *Romanzero* poem "Jehuda ben Halevy," again as an emblem of Jewish eternal vitality:

---

[87] *Confessions, HSS,* 6/i:480f. (*JM,* pp. 256f.; *SP,* pp. 413f.).

[88] Houben, *Gespräche mit Heine,* p. 668.

[89] *Briefe,* 1:284.

[90] For the Wandering Jew (and his abstraction) as a recurrent poetic theme see the editorial comments in *HSS,* 1:730, 751f., 774; 6/ii:118. (Passing references ibid., 5:1031f.; 6/i:664.) *The Rabbi of Bacherach* is of course a Wandering Jew, compelled to wander by the Christian massacre of his community. Cf. Reeves, *Heine,* pp. 122, 132.

A pilgrim [Ahasverus] had visited Toledo and told of Jerusalem and the Holy Land. . . . While he speaks, his silver white beard blackens once again . . . and youthens . . . his eyes looking forth as though out of a thousand-year melancholy.[91]

And the *Doktor Faust* of 1851 resurrects the "Wandering Jew with his eighteen-hundred-year-old beard whose white hairs at their ends blacken as though become young again."[92]

This beard is not a petty literary detail, but rather a complex metaphor for the Jews and Judaism. It is firstly a symbol of that permanent quality of Jewishness that cannot be shaved or washed away by the individual. At the same time, the blackening beard is a symbol of the eternal race of the Jews, an eternally youthful and vigorous race, always renewing itself. Such pride in a perpetually regenerating Jewish race was a triumphant reversal of the prevailing Hegelian contempt for the Jews as a lifeless historical fossil race. The Ahasverian beards of the Jews betoken their providential mission for revolutionary humanity:

[They gave the world a God and a morality] . . . Yet the deeds of the Jews, like their individual essence, are still unknown to the world. Some think they know the Jews because they can recognize their *beards*, which is all they have ever revealed of themselves. Now as during the Middle Ages, they remain a *wandering mystery*, a mystery that may perhaps be solved on the day that the prophet foretells . . . when the righteous who have suffered for the good of humanity shall receive a glorious reward [emphasis added].[93]

Heine has transformed the Wandering Jew from a myth of pessimism to one of optimism, and at the same time converted it from a Christian myth into one of Jewish messianic hope. The wandering Jews are righteous and will be redeemed, perhaps by God or perhaps by revolution. Their eternity of wandering is not a divine punishment, but a glorious mystery in this Heinean transformation.

---

[91] *HSS*, 6/i:138f. (*HW*, 12:22). The blackening beard also appears in the earlier description of the Wandering Jew in *The City of Lucca* (1831), *HSS*, 2:515 (*HW*, 3:309).

[92] *HSS*, 6/i:391 (*HW*, 6:281).

[93] *Confessions*, *HSS*, 6/i:481f. (*SP*, p. 414). Cf. the conversation of 1847 with Balzac and Eugène Sue (author of the celebrated novel *Le Juif errant*) in which Heine asserted that the Jews are entitled to immortality because of their discovery of "monotheism, the minimum of religion, the divine quantum: Therefore, the Jews are never to be rooted out, they will never die out, they are never to be warred upon" (Houben, *Gespräche mit Heine*, p. 518; cf. p. 814).

For Heine's earlier Hegelian view of the wandering Jews—"a mummified race who wander the earth"—see *The City of Lucca*, quoted above, n. 65.

Yet there is also a darker side to the legend. Heine remained acutely conscious of the tragic significance of the Ahasverus myth as a metaphor of Jewish history. *The Rabbi of Bacherach*, for instance, portrays its hero as a representative of the age-old suffering of the Jews in exile, insecure strangers in foreign lands, a wandering up-rooted race.[94] And in a moving passage in his 1838 essay on *Portia*, Heine allusively fuses the Wandering Jew with Shylock, who is seen in the synagogue on the Day of Atonement giving vent to

> utterances of agony [over the loss of his daughter to the Christians], such as could only come from a breast that held shut within itself all the martyrdom that an utterly tormented race had endured for eigh-teen hundred years.

And this whole episode is but a dream observed by another wander-ing Jew—Heine himself, the "wandering haunter of dreams."[95]

The Wandering Jew, however, was for Heine more than a particu-lar Jewish symbol: it was a universal metaphor of humanity. Ahas-verus wanders through Heine's poems as an intimation, not only of the eternity of Judaism, but of mankind's ghostly immortality, of the antiquity of human wisdom, of the world-weariness of the human race—a personification of poetic melancholy. The Wandering Jew was for Heine an "old god" of the Germans who had taken on, like the other powers and forces of man and nature, a Christianized iden-tity. In *Elemental Spirits* Heine had written:

> To the two Christian personalities of Christ and the Devil, the people have added two other figures, as immortal and as indestructible, namely Death and the Wandering Jew. The Middle Ages have thus bequeathed to modern art these four figures as colossal personifica-tions of Good and Evil, of Destruction and Man.[96]

Ahasverus was thus the mythological image of all mankind in search of a redemption. The Wandering Jew was, in essence, the universal revolutionary.

[94] Reeves, *Heine*, p. 122.

[95] *Shakespeare's Maidens: Portia*, HSS, 4:264ff. (*HW*, 1:398–401). Heine calls himself here the "wandelnder Traumjäger."

[96] *Elementargeister* (*Elemental Spirits*), French version, HSS, 3:1015. Cf. Heine's praise of Quinet in *Lutetia* (1 June 1843): "When I read *Ahasverus* or other poems of Quinet, I feel entirely at home and think I hear the nightingales of my homeland. . . . He is one of us, he is a German" *HSS*, 5:492 (*HW*, 8:438).

Quinet in turn admired Heine's Mephistophelean genius. Like Schubert in his in-spired settings of Heine's verse, Quinet appreciated the subtle poison underlying the apparent innocence of his lyrics.

Heine's thinking on the Jewish Question reached its critical point during the 1848 revolutions. Then the tension between, on the one hand, his revolutionary and personal antipathies to Judaism, and on the other, his growing Jewish sensibility, was finally resolved by his abandoning of the revolutionary faith and return to those Jewish values that he denied he had ever forsaken. After 1848, Heine saw the Jews as the key to the redemption of all humanity, but in a way different from that envisaged by Börne and company. The young Heine had interpreted Judaism as an allegory of the alienation of body and soul, as well as being symbolic of the stifling money ethos of bourgeois society. By 1848, though, Heine had progressed beyond this idealistic cant and now grasped that Judaism represented something more profoundly human than could be found in his earlier creed of philosophical humanism. Judaism now signified mankind's reaching out for an absolute unattainable by a flawed humanity. Yet in the process of this aspiration great things come about: intellectually, in the monotheism of Moses that is man's highest conception of the absolute; socially, in the vision of a just state advocated by Moses and the Hebrew prophets; and morally, in the ideal of the righteous man. The Jews now embodied for Heine the nobility of man. "Human redemption" was no longer a catch formula of the "cobweb Berlin dialectic" of the German revolutionists; human redemption now meant taking a road to civilization pioneered by the Jews.

In 1848, Heine renounced the radical religion of revolution for the "liberal" one of "Judaism." That same year, his erstwhile friend Richard Wagner succumbed entirely to the revolutionary faith and discovered the creed of revolutionary antisemitism. The 1848 conversions of Heine and Wagner are thus distorted mirror images of one another, each focused around the central point of "Judaism." For Heine, Judaism denoted the highest ideals of revolutionary humanity; for Wagner, Judaism symbolized the cesspool from which the revolution had to redeem humanity. When Wagner understood this, he had no choice but to suppress his earlier defense of Heine and write the apotheosis of the poet's great adversary, Börne, with which *Judaism in Music* ends. Börne had managed to redeem himself into German humanity; but Heine had remained irredeemably Jewish by turning the revolution into Judaism.

# "Young Germany—Young Palestine": The *Junges Deutschland* Controversy of 1835

T HE MOST publicized progeny of the revolutionary preachings of Börne and Heine was the famous (verging on notorious) literary movement known as "Young Germany" (*Junges Deutschland*). For a brief few years in the 1830s Young Germany formed the vanguard of both literary and political "modernism" in Germany, and indeed achieved a succès de scandale culminating in its proscription by the federal parliament in 1835.

Young Germany is generally seen as a liberal movement very much in favor of Jewish emancipation. There is no doubt that two of its most prominent personalities, Gutzkow and Laube, did support the civil emancipation of the Jews and were in that sense "pro-Jewish." But in real terms this simple categorization is deeply misleading. While Gutzkow and Laube may have been "liberal" as far as Jewish civil and political rights were concerned, both were hostile to the idea of Jewishness and Judaism. This was no accident, but sprang from the very source of their political and philosophical outlook, which was not liberal, but rather revolutionist. Although Laube greatly moderated his opinions into a safer liberalism later in life, both he and Gutzkow in the 1830s and 1840s held a redemptive concept of revolution that they sought to portray in literary terms. They saw the revolution not as narrowly political, but as a sensual healing of the alienation of the human spirit that had been rendered "inorganic" by the corruption of civil society. For them "civil" freedom was a desirable first step towards this cosmic aim, but such a political emancipation was in itself an inadequate redemption. They wanted a revolutionary redemption—the human "emancipation of the flesh," as their catchphrase had it. The implication of this revolutionism for the Jewish Question was that while the civil emancipation of the Jews was to be striven for, the true redemption of the Jews required the destruction of their Jewishness and their ascent into the truly human and the truly German.

The name "Young Germany" was coined (in imitation of Laube's political novel, *Young Europe*) by Ludolph Wienbarg, who dedicated his *Aesthetic Campaigns* (1834) to "Das junge Deutschland." Two main themes are usually taken to be characteristic of the school. There was, first and foremost, a devotion to *human* emancipation. They shared a preoccupation with *Zerrissenheit*, that inner alienation of man caused by a discordance between his sensual and spiritual instincts. Like Heine, they translated this discomfort into a Saint Simonian campaign for the emancipation or redemption of the flesh, which was to be restored into a more healthy balance with the spiritual aspect of human nature. But where Heine openly rejoices in the sensual, the pedestrian novels of the Young German writers merely laboriously hint that the redemption of the flesh may involve a sensual liberation.

Their other proclaimed theme, *political* emancipation, was scarcely more adventurous in reality. Critical as they were of both Christianity and the authoritarian state, the Young Germans seemed to be properly "liberal" advocates of such social reforms as the emancipation of the Jews and of women; enthusiastic modern scholarship has seen in their writings the continuation of the "liberal" political *Tendenz* championed by Börne.[1] There are, however, reasons for suspecting that the Young Germans were never the true heirs of Börne and Heine in literature or politics. It has been argued indeed that Young Germany was neither a political nor a literary movement, but rather an "ideological" one.[2] Its members were very much a group of second-rate writers in thrall to an ideology of revolutionism, writers by accident rather than by vocation. As Wagner, once sympathetic to Young Germany, observed, the ideology was "modernism," a revolutionary critique of established principles in religion and politics, a vaguely ethical ideology whose true political content was very tenuous indeed.[3]

---

[1] See E. M. Butler, *The Saint-Simonian Movement in Germany: A Study of the Young German Movement* (Cambridge, 1926); J. L. Sammons, *Six Essays on the Young German Novel* (Chapel Hill, 1972); H. Boeschenstein, *German Literature of the Nineteenth Century* (London, 1969); J. Hermand, *Das Junge Deutschland: Texte und Dokumente* (Stuttgart, 1966); U. Köster, *Literarischer Radikalismus: Zeitbewusstsein und Geschichtsphilosophie in der Entwicklung vom Jungen Deutschland zur Hegelschen Linken* (Frankfurt, 1972); H. Koopmann, *Das Junge Deutschland* (Stuttgart, 1970); W. Dietze, *Junges Deutschland und deutsche Klassik* (Berlin, 1957); *Reallexikon der deutschen Literaturgeschichte*, ed. P. Merker, et al., 2d ed. (Berlin, 1958), 1:781–97.

These conventional treatments completely fail to take account of the movement's attitude to the Jewish Question. Only H. H. Houben, *Gutzkow-Funde* (Berlin, 1901; hereafter *GF*), pp. 145–280, treats the question in detail as a central issue. (Cf. also his *Jungdeutscher Sturm und Drang* [Leipzig, 1911].) Can one really define Young Germany without reference to the Jewish Question, considering that Heine and Börne were taken as the patrons of the movement?

[2] C. P. Magill, "Young Germany: A Revaluation," in *German Studies Presented to L. A. Willoughby* (Oxford, 1952), pp. 108–19 (which also fails to mention the Jewish Question).

[3] Wagner was a member of the group and very close to Laube, but eventually repu-

At no time were the Young Germans of the 1830s truly political "liberals"; they were simply voicing their moral imperatives in what they took to be apt political terms.

This defect of liberal conviction is confirmed by their shifting attitudes towards the Jewish Question. Although they took up for a time the cause of Jewish emancipation, Gutzkow and Laube could deliver themselves of some nastily anti-Jewish remarks whenever it suited them. Such ambivalence prevents one describing them as consistently liberal in any true sense of the word, even though on occasion their conclusions agreed with those of such authentic liberals as Gabriel Riesser, as we shall see. The prevailing tendency of characterizing Young Germany as a movement simply favorable to Jewish emancipation, let alone Jews and Judaism, seems to be very much misconceived.

"It needed two Jews—Heine and Börne—to overthrow the old ideology and shake all illusions," declared Gutzkow in 1839.[4] Modeled though the movement may have been on the two Jewish writers, neither really belonged to Young Germany. Heine, however, found himself cited as its leader in the federal decree of December 10, 1835, that banned its members' publications. The ban had been provoked by the publication of Gutzkow's novel of ideas, *Wally, the Doubtress* (1835), which appeared to preach the need for sexual emancipation, a message quickly denied (to no avail) by its author. One of the most influential German reviewers, Wolfgang Menzel, resentful of the success of his former protégé Gutzkow, had in October 1835 denounced *Wally* as rank immorality. The ensuing public outcry resulted in the eventual imprisonment of many of the leading lights of Young Germany. This might have remained a purely literary feud were it not for the fact that Menzel invoked anti-Jewish prejudices as a useful weapon for his attack. From its inception, Young Germany was therefore damned by its opponents as "Young Palestine," a Jewish conspiracy against German literature and morals, a plot engineered by those idols of Young Germany, Heine and Börne. In his article Menzel chose to label the anti-Christian, "immoral" element in *Wally* as "Jewish." The Jews—and Heine—were thus dragged into a bitter political and literary dispute where Judaism became identified with immorality. So was revived an irrelevant but insistent argument in the political struggle for Jewish civil emancipation: should such an immoral class

---

diated it. See his essay, "Modern" (1878), *PW*, 6:45f. Cf. *MLE*, pp. 98, 101 (80, 83); *CWD*, 1:646.

4 K. Gutzkow, *Jahrbuch der Literatur* 1 (1839): 14, quoted in *HAS*, 3:405.

as the Jews have any more claim to civil rights than the criminal class?[5]

Menzel had not always been an enemy of the Jews. In an article of 1833, he had indeed spoken out against Jew-hatred and defended Heine and Börne from the calumnies of Cruciger's *Newest Wanderings*:

> If such minds as Heine's and Börne's err in certain respects, yet there is still so much nobility in them, so much poetic fire . . . that even the most exalted judge will rise to pay homage to their genius. . . . The literary rabble who scream Hep-Hep should rightly be thrown out the door. . . . Men will rejoice a century hence in Heine's magnificent fantasies and no longer stupidly enquire whether the man's morals should not be improved and his politics inspired with more loyalty.[6]

Menzel pointed out that Goethe had also been condemned for "immorality." He also used a humanitarian argument to defend Jewish writers:

> The old rabbi who was burnt with all his family in his own house might be thought fortunate in comparison with a present writer of Jewish descent who, no matter how intelligent, how humane, how elevated above all prejudice he may be, is still hounded by the dogs of all our Christian-German capitals, who damn him to a lifelong murder of the soul. Lessing's wisdom, so worthy of love, has been ignored. . . . How are wisdom and love of humanity to enter into our people where such demagogues of mob wisdom and such reason-preachers are confounding the natural sense of what is noble and righteous. The fight against these demagogues, I hold to be the sacred duty of a German, a Christian, of a man of the nineteenth century. If we do not at last

---

[5] Cf. Heine, *Sämtliche Schriften*, ed. K. Briegleb (Munich, 1968–76), 5:20; *Memoirs*, ed. G. Karpeles (London, 1910), 2:23–35.

[6] This and the following quotation from *Literaturblatt* of 1833, quoted in *GF*, pp. 196f.

For Cruciger's *Neueste Wanderungen* of 1832, see above, chap. 9.

On Menzel and the Jews, see L. Geiger, "Die Juden und das Junge Deutschland," *Allgemeine Zeitung des Judentums* 24 & 25 (1906): 282–85, 295–98; J. Toury, *Die politische Orientierungen der Juden in Deutschland von Jena bis Weimar* (Tübingen, 1966), pp. 1–46; A. Low, *Jews in the Eyes of the Germans: From the Enlightenment to Imperial Germany* (Philadelphia, 1979), pp. 257ff.; J. Katz, *From Prejudice to Destruction: Anti-Semitism 1700–1933* (Cambridge, Mass., 1980), pp. 179ff.; I. and G. Österle, "Der literarische Bürgerkrieg: Gutzkow, Heine, Börne wider Menzel," in *Demokratische-revolutionäre Literatur in Deutschland: Vormärz*, ed. G. Mattenklott (Kronberg, 1974), pp. 151–85.

In general, see E. Schuppe, *Der Burschenschaftler Wolfgang Menzel: Eine Quelle zum Verständnis des Nationalsozialismus* (Frankfurt, 1952), especially, pp. 102ff.; *HAS*, 3:386f.

restore undiminished their human rights to the Jews, we deserve to lose ours for eternity.

But suddenly in 1835 Menzel changed his mind about the irrelevance of morality to literature. He erupted in rage against his former colleague Gutzkow as well as Goethe himself. Young Germany was now denounced as a Jewish venture and its leading lights, notably Laube and Gutzkow, smeared as being of Jewish descent or closely affiliated with Jews. In his article "Immoral Literature," Menzel took care to insist that it was not the Jews he was attacking, but rather the Young Germans for their acceptance of Jewish immorality. To the Jews themselves, Menzel offered a veiled warning:

> I would very much like to know what advantage the Jews expect in the delicate matter of their emancipation from these literary lackeys of Young Germany. For one hears everywhere that the so-called Young Germany is really a Young Palestine; and besides there is generally blamed on Judaism in the public mind all the loathsomeness that lies in the boundless importunity, in the truckling to French fashion, in the malicious yet impotent hatred towards things German and Christian that preoccupies the new propaganda from Frankfurt.[7]

Menzel asserted he was giving this advice in a spirit of helpfulness. If the Jews became tarred with the sins of Young Germany, how could they hope to obtain public support for their own emancipation?

> I have the right to grieve over this pernicious diversion from the highway made by honest men's struggles to the emancipation of the Jews. For it is known to all with how much warmth I have always supported that cause.

Pursuing this line, Menzel a few weeks later even appealed to Heine and Börne themselves to join him in the struggle against "the filth and Jew-pitch of this literary rabble [Young Germany]."[8] But in January 1836, Menzel used Heine's influence on Young Germany as the supreme proof of the movement's Jewishness:

> From Heine the whole mischief has issued. . . . He first combined Jewish antipathies and French ideas to foster ridicule of Christianity and morality and German nationalism and virtue, popularizing the emancipation of the flesh . . . and appealing to the Great Republic of the Future. He was the first to make up all this into the fruitful theme

---

[7] Quotations from "Immoralische Literatur," *Literaturblatt* (26 October 1835), quoted in *GF*, pp. 200f. The "Frankfurt propaganda" is Gutzkow's projected *Deutsche Revue*.

[8] Review of *Wally* in *Literaturblatt* (11 November 1835), quoted in *GF*, p. 200.

that the Young Germans have ever since played through in all its variations.[9]

Heine's admirer Gutzkow especially brought to the movement "the disorganizing [that is, anti-organic] talent, the corroding and consuming intellect that Heinrich Leo marks down as characteristic of Judaism." Elsewhere Menzel commented that Young Germany was "a Jewish republic of vice newly set up by the firm Heine and Co."[10]

Not surprisingly, Menzel felt obliged to clear up some of the public's misconceptions about his ideas on the Jewish Question in a review headed "Writings on Jews" (1837). Here Menzel declared that Jews should not be excluded from civil rights, which belong to all rational subjects who obey the law. He recognized, too, that the "notorious" defects and blemishes of Judaism were but the consequence of the age-old oppression of the Jews. Nevertheless, Menzel reserved the right to "condemn pitilessly the new literary Jews' school of Heine and its insolent immorality."[11] The review appears to be a sincere attempt by Menzel to rescue himself from crass Jew-hatred and to restrict his attacks on the Jews to their alleged role in the Young Germany affair. Yet there is also here an element of instinctive aversion of the Jews that reappears in the works of those Young Germans like Laube and Gutzkow whom Menzel was denigrating. It seems as though the earlier Menzel had forced himself to defend Jewish emancipation against his deepest inclinations. Deprived of the usual means of expression of these feelings, Menzel was allowing his aversion to the Jews to emerge in what he thought was a strictly circumscribed and reasonable area that allowed him to remain easy in his conscience about his prejudice against the Jews. As far as anti-Jewish feelings were concerned, perhaps the gulf separating Menzel from his Young German adversaries was not as great as they believed.

Even though Menzel had resisted to a degree the anti-Jewish indoctrination of Friedrich Jahn's patriotic German youth bands, in the end Jahn's phobias against the Jews and the French asserted themselves in Menzel's characterization of Young Germany as a Franco-Jewish plot, carried out by the "Israelitic-French party."[12] Twenty years later, the Young Germany affair still aroused Menzel's venom:

[9] Review of *Die Jeune Allemagne* (see below), *Literaturblatt* (January 1836), quoted in *GF*, pp. 200f., 205.

[10] Quoted in *GF*, p. 202.

[11] "Schriften über Juden," *Literaturblatt* (September 1837), quoted in *GF*, p. 206.

[12] *Literaturblatt* (November 1837), quoted in *GF*, p. 206. For Menzel's career in the student movements, see *HAS*, 3:386f.; Schuppe, *Menzel*, pp. 11ff., 102ff., 195.

"Young Germany's physiognomy was fashioned from Paris by means of the debauchery of enervated Jew-boys."[13]

Menzel had come, in fact, to believe in the reality of the Eternal Jew. The image could apply to individuals; Börne was dismissed with the comment, "Still, Jew remains Jew."[14] It could equally apply to the Jewish people: "The Wandering Jew is Judaism itself," observes Menzel in his survey of German poetry. "His wanderings refer to the dispersal of the Jews after the destruction of Jerusalem. . . . In Ahasverus is personified the Jewish people." But more than a symbol of Judaism, Ahasverus is, for Menzel, one of the two central metaphors of the Christian-German mind, the other being Faust:

> But where Ahasverus flees life . . . Faust seeks to make the desire of the passing moment eternal. . . . Ancient Judaism goes ever wandering like a ghost through the Christian world. . . . Death and the devil—the former in the shape of Judaism, the latter in the form of paganism—press in on the kingdom of Christ.[15]

Menzel must have been gratified when a local poet in 1838 caught on to his ideas about Ahasverus and the "Israelitic-French party" and brought out a piece entitled *Ahasverus and Bonaparte*, explaining that the Wandering Jew had protected Napoleon in order to embarrass the Christian nations of Europe, and that in turn Napoleon had provided a front to conceal Jewish plans for the domination of the continent.[16]

The Franco-Jewish plot very much featured in the literary polemics of the 1830s about Young Germany. The most provocative of these was Paul Pfitzer's anonymously published pamphlet *Die Jeune Allemagne in Deutschland* (Stuttgart, 1836) whose very title designated Young Germany as a French movement within Germany.[17] Praised by Menzel, this clumsily written outburst proclaimed that Germany

[13] Menzel, *Deutsche Dichtung* (Stuttgart, 1856), 3:467; see *GF*, pp. 202, 206, for similar remarks.

[14] Menzel, *Denkwürdigkeiten* (Leipzig, 1887), p. 195, quoted in *GF*, p. 198.

[15] *Deutsche Dichtung*, 2:202f. Like Gutzkow, Menzel condemned those who made Ahasverus the symbol of a new Promethean era (*Literaturblatt* [1838], quoted by A. Soergel, *Ahasver-Dichtungen seit Goethe* [Leipzig, 1905], p. 84).

[16] Alexander von Württemberg, "Ahasver und Bonaparte," in *Lieder des Sturms* (Stuttgart, 1838), pp. 216–19, reprinted in his *Gesammelte Gedichte* (Stuttgart, 1841).

[17] Geiger, "Die Juden und das Junge Deutschland," p. 283, seems to be using secret reports to Metternich to identify the author as Paul Pfitzer, brother of the literary figure Gustav Pfitzer. Katz, *From Prejudice*, p. 180, however, follows V. Eichstädt, *Bibliographie zur Geschichte der Judenfrage* (Hamburg, 1938), 1:216, in making the publisher of the pamphlet—S. Liesching—also its author. Cf. *GF*, pp. 202f.

was losing its capacity to perform its heroic moral task for it was beset
by

> cowardice swollen by the lowest kind of egoism, by money and plea-
> sure. . . . Material interests have defeated honor and moral strength,
> that lever of progress. . . . True art and science, inseparable from
> freedom and bearing fruit only through public life, yield to the din of
> industry. . . . A foreign morality now threatens German morality,
> which is the foundation of German freedom. (pp. 9–11)

"The hysterical propagandizing of French virtue" has meant the
"moral suicide of Germany" and it is now time for the Germans to
rid themselves of the "Gallic poison" of French intellect, morality,
and religion:

> a people of the deepest religious feeling that may provide a strong an-
> chor for its inner and outer existence. . . . French values may only
> cover the furrows of inner alienation and hide the inner sickness of
> the art. . . . There are no true organic elements here, only dissipating
> ones lacking the strength to create a great character whether good or
> bad; a blind, restless striving, a bitter resentment of the calls of hu-
> manity, an unreserved hatred of sacrifices . . . but the greatest enthu-
> siasm for the sensual, the piquant, the lecherous. (pp. 15f.)

French values and morals pretend to be organic and to heal the inner
alienation of man, but are, in fact, negative and utterly destructive of
human—and German—nature.

The agents of this moral decay within Germany were, of course,
the Jews:

> What a field for treacherous prophets of the future. . . . Who could
> they be, these fatherland-shy hybrids? . . . Are they Germans? No, our
> people has, despite its poverty, too much shame . . . conscience and
> feeling for inner right. . . . Could they be French? It is too soon. They
> still have to learn our language, literature, and ways. . . . No, it must
> be men to whom duty and humanity have granted civil rights, men
> whose determination has been steeled through the bitterest fates,
> whose acumen has been refined through countless struggles, men of
> whom a lurking cleverness and thousand-hued talent might have
> made anything—except that which a hard-won emancipation requires,
> that is, to de-nation themselves so that they cease to be what their his-
> tory, their religion, their innermost nature, their future demand they
> be—Jews. (pp. 19f.)

The root Jewish vice of negation has forced them to adopt all those
devices of intellect and deceit that are the antithesis of the organic:

Their outstanding characteristic, which is attributable to the persecutions that we have been guilty of visiting upon them, is negation. . . . [With their partners in negation] Frenchmen and Jews are stoking an unholy fire that is consuming our best sap, the secret inheritance of our inner national feeling; they are poisoning our purity of heart . . . making the corroding intellect [in H. Leo's phrase] the sole director of our thought.

Money, above all, is the negation of nobility:

They are in possession of great means, thanks to their diabolic instinct for precious metals and most lately their magical gift for creating gold out of paper. But the Jew lives in the clearest awareness that he can acquire only the name and never the essence of any race [*Nationalität*] other than his own. And he can pursue his policy of conquest not through iron, which is available only to whole true men, but only through the smuggling of moral frauds of all kinds. To the Jew without a fatherland, love of fatherland must seem foolishness. (pp. 20f.)

Pfitzer concluded by secularizing one of the major myths of medieval Jew-hatred:

It was told in darker times how the Jews poisoned the wells and how thousands of Jews consequently fell victim to the revenge of the people. Such lies have now become truth. . . . The poisoning of our rising national feeling, that highest endeavor, has become the aim of the oriental party. . . . This is to poison the sources of all that is beautiful and saving in life, art, and literature. (pp. 26–27)

The final verdict in this literary survey (which fails to mention any literary names) is that Young Germany's productions "are famous not through talent, but simply because of the moral sterility of the times . . . and those traitorous interests that are at work winning greater riches" (pp. 28–29).

These themes were repeated, albeit in muted language, in Hermann Marggraff's 1839 analysis of Young Germany, *Germany's Latest Literary and Cultural Epoch,* which saw the movement as essentially Jewish in its origins, even though it thought Menzel went too far in denouncing Jewish writers as literary Shylocks lusting after Christian flesh.[18] Marggraff conceded that the Jews were really seeking legitimate rights rather than revenge and for this purpose had recruited the aid of Young Germany, whose politics centered on the "emanci-

[18] H. Marggraff, *Deutschlands jüngste Literatur- und Culturepoche* (Leipzig, 1839), pp. 251–64.

pation questions" of the age. Still, in return for rights, the Jews must acquire moral and civil virtue:

> They must throw off their arrogance, their forwardness, their garrulous pushiness, their tendency to look for gain, turning all—even friendship and the most inner relationships—to mere utility. They must renounce their middleman attitude and behavior, their wisecracking and taking lightly what Christians hold sacred. (p. 256)

Though Marggraff insists he "is speaking here not of the rabbis and other serious and worthy oriental aspects of Judaism, but only of those Jews changed through modern life," he spoils this liberality by observing that he could no more allow a traditionally educated Jew than a Moslem to hold office in a Christian state (p. 257). Again ambivalently, Marggraff praises Jewish family life, but also condemns the ghetto for making Jews "dangerous enemies of human society, like wild animals" (pp. 257ff.). He takes a rather severer view of Jewish national character than had Dohm:

> Rashness and acrimony of understanding, already seated in the Jewish national character, were intensified in their peculiarly oppressive relations with Christians. To this national bent and burden, the Jews owe their cutting wit. While other peoples in similar circumstances became surly, gloomy, even stupid, the Jews' quick-flowing oriental blood turned them to a national passion for wit. . . . But their wit was not always based on honor or integrity. (p. 260)

Wit and skepticism were thus the instruments of Jewish revenge on oppressive Christianity, and Young Germany had been enlisted as their ally. Marggraff speculates that a secret society of Jews and Christians exists that would be happy to replace Mozart and Schiller with Meyerbeer and Heine. Yet, despite the positive contributions of Börne and Michael Beer, the literary production of Young Germany has been baneful: Heine's *History of Religion and Philosophy* is singled out as mere brash egoism. The Young Germans are for Marggraff neither Christians nor Jews, but men dedicated to their own egoism instead of to their country. This much is apparent to those nobler Jews who have become imbroiled in the current literary dispute.[19]

---

Jewish replies to Menzel and Pfitzer were not lacking. Börne devoted his last and most brilliantly amusing work to a repudiation of

[19] To be sure, Marggraff (p. 423) did also accuse the non-Jewish Hegelians of "egoism."

*Menzel der Franzosenfresser* (1837), the devourer of Frenchmen and Jews, who had dismissed as "Jews" all those German writers who happened to like French culture, damning for this vice the whole of Young Germany even though there was not a Jew in it![20] A more respectably moderate reply came from one Jacob Weil in his *Young Germany and the Jews* (1836).[21] Young Germany, Weil pointed out, had no Jew among its membership, since Heine and Börne were both Christians and even opponents of Judaism.

Weil reproached Menzel for having betrayed his own previous efforts for the rightful claims of the Jews and turning to the publication of mad allegations such as he had earlier condemned. To accuse the Jews of immorality and so lacking true German feeling is indeed "un-German and un-Christian" (pp. 6–8). As to Pfitzer's charge that the Jew cannot redeem himself because he cannot cease to be a Jew, Weil replied that this pernicious statement confuses Jewish religion and nationality. The Jews are a religion, not a race, and they can change, indeed have changed. In any case,

> their religion commands them to love their neighbors and to obey unhesitatingly the laws of the state. Their innermost nature is, as anatomists may tell, no different from that of other human beings; and of their future they expect—redemption [*Erlösung*]. (p. 9)

To Pfitzer's call for the Germans to chase out Jews and Frenchmen, Weil retorted that "there is scarcely anything of Christianity in Jew-hatred, just as there is scarcely a jot of true Germanness in hatred of the French." Calumnies against the Jews as having no love for the fatherland are shameful (as Menzel had earlier admitted); so, too, the stamping of the Jews as a republican or revolutionary class is absurd (pp. 10f.).

Weil's answer to Pfitzer was somewhat piecemeal in that it consisted of specific rejoinders to various points. Gabriel Riesser, however, provided a more rigorous refutation based on general moral and legal principles. A prominent Jewish lawyer and the leading spokesman of Jewish emancipation, Riesser had already had experience of literary-political controversy in defending Börne (rather redundantly) from the chidings of Eduard Meyer in 1832. What particularly had aroused Riesser's ire was Meyer's insistence that the Jews were not only a separate religion, but a separate nation, recognizable by their bad personal qualities, within Germany: "We do not hate the faith of the Jews . . . but rather the many ugly peculiarities of these Asiatics,

---

[20] L. Börne, *Sämtliche Schriften*, ed. I. and P. Rippmann (Dreieich, 1977), 3:953f.

[21] J. Weil, *Das Junge Deutschland und die Juden* (Frankfurt, 1836).

which cannot be laid aside so easily through baptism."[22] Some noble Jews there might be, but Meyer held that these were rare exceptions to the rule of Jewish national character. Even without the aspersions, this talk of Judaism as a nationality would have offended Riesser, who based his demands for Jewish emancipation on liberal principles of politics, particularly the separation of church from state, of religious from political matters.[23] The Jewish Question was for him an essentially constitutional and juridical question rather than a social or moral one. Denying the "nationhood" of the Jews, Riesser insisted that Judaism was merely a confessional religion and that it was unjust and unconstitutional to deny its adherents political rights. The Jews were "fully German," being "Germans of Mosaic or Israelite confession." The German Jews' status as members of the Jewish religion had nothing at all to do with their status as citizens of the German states and could not be used to refuse them political rights. That the Jews were fully German was, for instance, proven by their services in the war against Napoleon. For Riesser, then, Jewish emancipation was the acid test of the liberal German state. Jews had the right as Germans to demand, not just petition for, emancipation—and should not be required to apologize for their religion, to reform it, or to convert in order to obtain their rights.

As far as the Jews were concerned, Riesser deemed opportunistic conversion and baptism to be despicable courses of action. He remained committed to Jewish solidarity and declared himself loyal to a "Judaism," which retained within it the eternal ideas of "reason and freedom." Judaism lived as a tradition, a historical consciousness, "an idea rooted in a race."[24] Yet Riesser's liberal reasonableness concealed some thorny contradictions.

He never seems to have found any difficulty in rejecting the separate "nationhood" of the Jews while accepting that they had a distinctive national and religious tradition.[25] Loyal to that tradition though Riesser may himself have been, his devotion to liberal principles

[22] E. Meyer, *Gegen Ludwig Börne* (Altenburg, 1830), pp. 12ff., quoted by Katz, *From Prejudice*, p. 178. See above, chap. 6, n. 31; chap. 9, nn. 26, 52.

[23] Riesser replied to Meyer with *Börne und die Juden* (Altenburg, 1830), reprinted in his *Gesammelte Schriften*, ed. M. Isler (Frankfurt, 1867–68), 4:303–28. See below, chap. 11, n. 41.

[24] Quoted by M. Rinott, "Gabriel Riesser: Fighter for Jewish Emancipation," *LBIY* 7 (1962): 11–38, p. 20. Riesser is blind to the contradiction.

[25] H. M. Graupe, *The Rise of Modern Judaism: An Intellectual History of German Jewry 1650–1942* (Huntington, N.Y., 1978), pp. 190ff., argues that Riesser looked at "confessional religion" through Christian spectacles, adopting Christian concepts of "church" and "religion," and destroying the Jewish idea of religion as a *national* covenant with God. A confessional religion of Judaism, stripped of its basis in Jewish nationhood, is unlikely to endure.

forced even him ultimately to regard the disappearance of an independent Judaism as desirable. At the Frankfurt Parliament of 1848, where he was vice-president and a member of the delegation that offered the German crown to the king of Prussia, Riesser postulated that the assembly's legal and constitutional reforms would promote Jewish assimilation through the encouragement of Jewish-Christian marriages, and hence eventually abolish religious divisions within the state.[26] Why Riesser thought that mixed marriages should be any less reprehensible than baptism, which he sharply condemned, is not clear; intermarriage as much as baptism meant the demise of Jewish solidarity. Riesser may have demanded the right of the German Jews to be emancipated without precondition of being converted to Christianity. But in the end his assimilationist program required a destruction of Jewish identity, loath to acknowledge or even perceive this though he may have been.

The correctness of Riesser's mind, his devotion to principle, and the propriety of his behavior were such that even an antisemite like Treitschke could posthumously commend him as "a German man in the best sense of the word . . . utterly different from Heine and Börne and other ferments of decomposition."[27] Praise like this, however, is never disinterested. It is also poisoned because it cannot be received without also accepting the axiom that only by ceasing to be a Jew does the Jew become respected. Riesser had repudiated conversion as a means by which the Jew might win respect from the German, and it is likely that he would also have recognized Treitschke's judgment as a condescending avenue of Jewish self-destruction.

To a man of Riesser's probity, the whole Young German polemic—especially Menzel's crassness—was rebarbative. In October 1837 Riesser told a friend: "I share your distaste for the new ways of this literary clique [Young Germany]."[28] And later:

> I have a distaste for the whole polemic . . . founded as it is on hate and envy and political fear. . . . The quarrel is pursued on all sides with harm to humanity, to rightfulness, and to honorable feelings.[29]

Menzel's crudeness was especially revolting:

> Menzel used Jew-hatred as a weapon against his literary foes, as he used the political fears of the rulers in a similar war. He threw the Jews, like a stone, at the heads of his opponents. . . . His enemies sur-

[26] Speech of 29 August 1848, quoted by A. Bein, *Die Judenfrage* (Stuttgart, 1980), 2:222.

[27] *HAS*, 3:409.

[28] Riesser, *Gesammelte Schriften*, 1:246, quoted in *GF*, p. 207.

[29] Letter of May 1838, in Riesser, *Gesammelte Schriften*, 1:279, quoted in *GF*, p. 207.

vived, but on the other hand, he enriched Jew-hatred with a new, until now, unheard of element, through the accusation of immorality
and so provided a new poison.

Menzel had turned Young Germany into a Jewish conspiracy in order
that it might become hateful; the only result, however, was to foment
hatred of the Jews rather than of the Young Germans:

> A magic formula has been devised whereby any opponent can be dis-
> credited simply by denouncing him as a Jew. All things hateful in pol-
> itics, art, or religion are proclaimed to be Jewish. . . . We have Jewish
> hatred, Jewish possession, Jewish impudence.[30]

Stung by Menzel's continual "poisonous and unjust invectives
against the Jews," Riesser in 1842 published a sharp counterattack in
the second volume of his *Jewish Letters for Defense and Understanding*.
Menzel was sternly rebuked for tyrannically confusing the categories
of art and morality. Young Germany is a literary movement and
should be permitted to proceed with its artistic experiments, unhin-
dered by a puritanical morality. Menzel, charges Riesser, has
whipped up the whole artistic quarrel out of personal animosities.
Besides, the accusation that Young Germany is a Jewish movement at
all is a wild delusion. Heine, for example, is a baptized Christian, and
no longer a Jew, according to Riesser's definition of Judaism as a confessional religion rather than a nation.[31]

Menzel's careless involvement of the Jews in the affair of Young
Germany had, however, opened a Pandora's box of woe that was not
to be easily closed by the efforts of Riesser. Within a few years, indeed, Riesser found himself defending the Jews from the barbed remarks of Young Germany itself in the person of Gutzkow.[32] Whatever the strategies of self-delusion employed by Menzel and his rival
Gutzkow to reassure themselves that they were not haters of the Jews,
the fact remains that both Young Germany and its opponents made
the Jews their scapegoats. This new kind of Jew-hatred is the hidden
logic underlying an otherwise apparently nonsensical polemic. As far
as Gutzkow and Menzel were concerned, Riesser's liberal logic was
quite irrelevant.

[30] Letters of 1837–38 in Riesser, *Gesammelte Schriften*, 1:237; 4:133. *GF*, pp. 199–210,
gives a good account. Low, *Jews*, pp. 257–60, is confused, as are its references.

[31] *Jüdische Briefe zur Abwehr und zur Verständigung*, in *Gesammelte Schriften*, 4:10ff., 14,
40ff., 120ff., etc. See *GF*, pp. 207ff.; Geiger, "Die Juden," pp. 296f. For Riesser's criticism of Gutzkow, see below, chap. 11, n. 41.

[32] *GF*, pp. 275ff.

# Karl Gutzkow's "New Ahasverus": Lovelessness, Egoism, and the Redemption of the Flesh

WITH the publication of *Wally, the Doubtress* in 1835, Karl Ferdinand Gutzkow (1811–78) sprang into public notoriety and sparked the campaign against Young Germany. Though denounced as a celebration of Heinean sensualism, the real focus of *Wally* is the Jewish Question. The conventional forms of Christianity and Judaism alike are seen to be not only superstitious, but obsolescent. The Jewish Question has arisen because of Christian oppression on the one hand and Jewish apartness on the other; in the new religious age, it will be solved by intermarriage, which will finally break down the barriers and redeem the Jews. This is conveyed in the rather artificial novel by the marriage of its most sympathetic character, the Jewess Delphine, to the hero Caesar.[1] Assimilation, therefore, is the road to redemption and can take place only with the weakening of the old religious ignorance and superstitions of both sides. This condescension towards traditional religion reeked of the Hegelian critique of religion, and indeed Gutzkow had studied under Hegel at Berlin in 1830.

However, it was not Hegel who was denounced as the source of Gutzkow's radicalism but rather the Jews. The anonymous pamphlet *The Ban on Young Germany* accused Gutzkow of reviving the eighteenth-century rationalist critique of Christianity with a Jewish accent, and scorned him as a Jew-sympathizer, the biographer of the Rothschilds, and the friend of literary Jews. His literary work was taken to be typically Jewish, dealing as it did with Jewish characters and evincing in its attack on religion and morality that "talent for the destruction of the organic and that corroding and consuming intellect that are the marks of Judaism." The rift between Gutzkow and his former mentor Menzel was thus taken as the result of the novel-

---

[1] The basic source for Gutzkow is H. H. Houben, *Gutzkow-Funde* (Berlin, 1901; hereafter *GF*), especially pp. 144–280, dealing with the Jewish Question. Neither Houben nor A. Low, *Jews in the Eyes of the Germans: From the Enlightenment to Imperial Germany* (Philadelphia, 1979), pp. 262–68, succeed in making sense of his tangled attitudes towards Jews. The Jewish Question is omitted from J. Dresch, *Gutzkow et la Jeune Allemagne* (Paris, 1904); E. M. Butler, *The Saint-Simonian Religion in Germany: A Study of the Young German Movement* (Cambridge, 1926), chaps. 14–19; E. W. Dobert, *Karl Gutzkow und seine Zeit* (Bern, 1968).

ist's essential Jewishness, which had so rightly been excoriated in Menzel's famous review of *Wally*.[2]

Needless to say, Gutzkow was not in the least Jewish. In his youth he had grown up in an atmosphere that was intensely hostile towards Jews, who had been seen as "traitors" and "bloodsucking usurers." In his maturer years, under the influence of his better instincts, he tried to suppress this childhood indoctrination, which he saw as part of the education of Christian German children in general. He reinterpreted his experience, so that he now saw a pride even in the lowest Jew, "a feeling of kindred with his forefathers" and a deep kinship with the rest of his people.[3] Gutzkow, however, never completely eradicated his ingrained childhood prejudices against the Jews. The power of these emotional fears and the inevitable failure of his honest efforts to subdue them by the exercise of a humane reason were to be a personal tragedy for Gutzkow. Only when the self-devouring conflict between the two sides of Gutzkow's personality is appreciated can sense be made of his ever contradictory utterances about the Jewish Question. Heine remarked on the violence of this split attitude:

> Gutzkow is possessed by a demon. Against his own will, he throws dung. Me, for instance, he wants to praise, but he can't do anything better after building me up with praise than blot it with the old Menzel sort of dirt in speaking of my Jewishness.[4]

It was Börne's revolutionary literature that encouraged Gutzkow to question his own Jew-hatred and seek its resolution in the destruction of the Jews by assimilation:

> I confess that in my early student years I did not like Heine because he was a Jew, and that eight years ago a dagger was plunged into my heart when I heard that my adored Börne was also a Jew. But I believe that it is our rightful nature to abandon all anti-Jewish fanaticism. . . . Through literature, I came to tolerate the race and to sacrifice my interests to an inner fusion with a race that is no longer a race, and no longer should be.[5]

[2] Anonymous, *Votum über das Junge Deutschland* (Liesching, Stuttgart, 1836); *GF*, p. 201.

[3] *Ludwig Börne's Leben* (1840), quoted in *GF*, pp. 248ff. Cf. passages from the memoirs *Rückblicke* and *Aus der Knabenzeit* quoted in *GF*, pp. 149–54.

[4] Letter of 7 January 1839 to Laube, quoted in E. Elster, "H. Heine und H. Laube," *Deutsche Rundschau* 134 (1908): 77–90, p. 88. Cf. H. Heine, *Memoirs*, trans. G. Karpeles (London, 1910), 2:73–83.

[5] *Götter, Helden, Don Quixote* (1838), quoted in *GF*, pp. 148f. Cf. *Rückblicke*, in *Werke*, ed. R. Gensel (Berlin, 1910), 9:53. For similar passages, see *GF*, p. 147.

Like Börne himself, Gutzkow turned Jewishness into a revolutionary asset, making Judaism the symbol of the lack of political freedom in Germany. "Only perhaps out of Judaism could there arise so genuine and welcome a reaction against our ideology, which had forged itself the chains of a new slavery"; Jewish redemption was thereby identified as the centerpiece of a general revolution in Germany.[6] This was the idea that underlay Gutzkow's adulatory biography of Börne (which was published in 1840)—in stark contrast to Heine's scandalous memoir.

Reacting against his own childhood prejudice, Gutzkow sought out Jewish fellow students as friends, among them Joel Jacoby and Berthold Auerbach.[7] A little later, he began to frequent the celebrated literary salon run by the Jewess Rahel von Varnhagen at Berlin:

> Berlin Jewry has the highest significance for German culture in general and particularly for art and literature. . . . Conservatively oriented [and] an elegant ghetto, the Jewish literary society of Berlin was then an exclusive group, guarding and preserving classical traditions, as well as embodying the continuously agitated ferment of the age.[8]

The ambivalence in this passage is characteristic of the man said to have coined the phrase: "Many of my best and dearest friends are Jews."[9]

Jewish themes soon appeared in Gutzkow's writings, notably in his story "The Sadducee of Amsterdam" (1843), which was later reworked into his famous play *Uriel Acosta* (1846). But these "Jewish" works are not at all "pro-Jewish." The heroic Jewish deist Acosta achieves freedom by abandoning Judaism and Jewishness.[10] Jewish religion is also condemned in his 1835 article "Jewish Theology," which uneasily combines the liberal view of Riesser that Judaism is merely a religious confession with the Hegelian critique calling for its

---

[6] *Vergangenheit und Gegenwart* (1839), in *Werke*, 8:93, quoted by H. H. Houben, *Jungdeutscher Sturm und Drang* (Leipzig, 1911), p. 101.

[7] *GF*, pp. 158–77, gives details of his Jewish friendships, including Jacoby (pp. 154ff., 210ff.) and Auerbach (pp. 175ff.). See below for his quarrel with Jacoby, whom he accused of being a police informer and also full of *Judenschmerz* (*Das Kastanienwäldchen in Berlin*, *Werke*, 8:33).

[8] *Rückblicke*, *Werke*, 9:72, quoted in *GF*, pp. 165f. Cf. Low, *Jews*, pp. 255, 307.

[9] Writing in 1842 (reference in n. 42, below), quoted in *GF*, pp. 277–80.

[10] Gutzkow decried its label as a "Jew-play": "A play in which everyone is a Jew is, in effect, a play in which no one is a Jew." The play is neither a plea for Jewish emancipation nor a defense of Judaism. Cf. *GF*, pp. 173, 337, 442; C. A. Lea, *Emancipation, Assimilation, and Stereotype: The Image of the Jew in German and Austrian Drama 1800–1850* (Bonn, 1978), pp. 49ff.

destruction. Gutzkow insisted on the separation of church and state and the consequent granting of full civil rights to the Jews. The Jewish Question was to be solved as a political issue. But Judaism itself had been superseded by historical change and was now but a ghost-religion; only its naturalistic and ethical teachings remained valid. "Leave behind on Mount Sinai your revengeful God, the anthropomorphic Jehovah," Gutzkow exhorted the Jews, whose religion he scorned as a "rotten and decayed residue." "Let the Jews desert this relic of Judaism and join other faiths in a world religion."[11]

This call for a philosophical reform of Judaism and the accompanying emphasis that the "Jews were a people that are no longer a people" may have been acceptable in part to Riesser and Auerbach. But they would scarcely have welcomed the extent of the reform that Gutzkow had in mind, and which he spelled out in his pseudonymously published *Zeitgenossen (Contemporaries)* of 1837. Here it became fairly plain that Gutzkow wanted not a compromise from Judaism, but a surrender.

*Zeitgenossen* is a survey of the main political and cultural questions preoccupying Germany.[12] The section on the Jews begins quietly enough, but already an anti-Jewish stereotype lurks in the statement that the Jews are "a people who use the moment to profit only the individual or his friends or kindred. Here and there one is reminded of times of darkest barbarism." To reassure any alarmed sensibilities in his Jewish readers, however, Gutzkow quickly adds that it is "oppression that has isolated human beings of Jewish faith from the purifying and refreshing winds of progress in public life."[13] Now, in the aftermath of the Enlightenment, Jews may properly claim full civil equality without further discrimination on the old grounds of religion. "An awakened humanity recognizes in these civil rights their general rights as human beings." In the past, when religious divisions were real, it was right that "the Jews should not have purchased redemption [*Erlösung*] from their yokes at the price of their religion and nationality." But now that dogmatic religion is waning and social boundaries of class are weakening under the influence of trade, the Jews may join the Christians in their enjoyment of culture and love. The Jews, says Gutzkow, are willing at last to modernize themselves,

---

[11] *GF*, pp. 176ff.

[12] *Die Zeitgenossen* was published under the English pseudonym of "E. Bulwer-Lytton" at Stuttgart in 1837. Reprinted under Gutzkow's own name as *Säkularbilder* in 1846. The latter edition contains important changes and also omits material present in the original essay, which is quoted here. Jews are discussed in *Zeitgenossen*, 2:207–35. Cf. *GF*, pp. 224–33.

[13] *Zeitgenossen*, pp. 208f.

abandoning old traditions for enlightenment and money. They are ready for emancipation. After they have won freedom, the rough edges can be rounded out, but in the meantime those edges are no longer any justification for denying emancipation. All over Europe the Jews are gaining redemption and Germany must be no exception.[14]

Apart from his peculiar opening remark, Gutzkow so far has used fair and rational words that leave no doubt about his outright support for the emancipation of the Jews. It is when he begins to list the obstacles to Jewish emancipation that one's unease about that remark hardens. Gutzkow's suppressed emotional hatreds well to the surface as he lectures the Jews on their own share of the "guilt" for continued discrimination against them by Christian Germans. Here the faint line of a new Jewish stereotype flares up into a lurid portrait:

> The Jews themselves bear part of the guilt. . . . It is not [Christian] intolerance alone that enrages some of our contemporaries against the freeing of the Jews. Without doubt there is a certain loathsomeness that we cannot get used to among the Jews. The Jew has an unlovable character, over-affectionate towards everything that bears his name, cold and repellent against all that does not affect his own ego [*Ich*]. . . . They greet without sincerity, they speak with one another without looking at each other. . . . These faults can also be found among Christians, but they become conspicuous in a circle where a single feeling pervades with binding force the whole life of the group, the feeling of a unitary situation and hope.
>
> For the strongest friend of emancipation cannot deny that the Jew, with rare exceptions, is crude and heartless, a man of abstract, refined ideas. . . . Their youth are brash, importunate, frequently unashamed. They do not adopt our customary fine and gentle considerations. Their girls are slovenly. Those Jews of finer taste and feeling admit . . . that Jewish drive is not suited for culture and humanity. . . . Art and science are assessed by the standard of money; the spirit of usury yet swells forth from the pores of the most elegant manners. Everyone must exaggerate to succeed among them; if one has knowledge, one has to bond it with arrogance; an artist has to affect an unendurable brilliance; wit has to be used to wound pitilessly.
>
> Any Jew of insight and dignity . . . must confess with shame that the Jewish condition . . . [born of] having lived so long under persecution . . . can be overcome only by [excessive] competitiveness.[15]

[14] Ibid., pp. 210ff.
[15] Ibid., pp. 213ff. Houben, *GF*, pp. 224ff., tries to excuse Gutzkow, but most readers

Here are the classic features of the noble-minded nineteenth-century stereotype of the Jew: egoism, heartlessness, lovelessness, Mammonism. But beneath the high-minded intellectual and moral argument against the Jews there lies a reservoir of primitive embittered emotion. The energy and impetus of Gutzkow's sentences are clearly generated by hidden anger and hatred.

Gutzkow seems to have sensed this himself, for when he published a similar passage under his own name in the *Säkularbilder* of 1846, he toned down some of the more vicious remarks:

> What follows is subject always to the excuse that the Jews owe their insufferable manners to their oppression. The greatest part of the Jews is motivated by desire for quick and usurious earnings.
>
> Christians are base enough, but their commerce is not marked by such a methodical conspiracy to cheat. The Jews disdain no means of making a rich profit from their often dirty businesses. The most dubious practices, which one would not experience at the hands of other people in business, is experienced at the hands of the Jews. For through their naturally nervously excited character they are more exposed to the ridiculous than are Christians. The cleverest and most cultivated Jewish salon-lady has an air that can soon be pierced by the keener observer; the elegant, wealthy tradesman who boasts of the market value and golden frame of his painting, even the beautiful one who sings of the nightingale and the rose, all have a certain peculiar tang that offends us. One concludes that behind this over-varnished cultural appearance, the racial characteristics [*das speziell Nationale*] of the Jews have not been surrendered. For their religion demands a social apartness that is repugnant to our feelings in the highest degree. . . . Only the Jews preserve a society of their own . . . instead of allowing intermarriage between Christians and Jews. Therein lies the impediment to emancipation. It is tactless of the Jewish advocates of emancipation to want to solve everything at one leap and at the same time to think that our nerves are without feeling. . . . In a word, I am with the most sacred determination in favor of the equality of Jews and Christians. But the way in which this equality is moved has something distasteful and importunate about it. Thus, I have never found any of their advocates of emancipation admitting that Judaism is for us a moral issue, and that the question is not one of law, but rather of feeling and the deepest sensitivities.[16]

---

of the passage will react strongly to the emotional spleen that Gutzkow vents under the pretext of a "rational discussion."

[16] *Zeitgenossen*, pp. 216f. Cf. *GF*, p. 225.

Despite Gutzkow's rhetorical stratagem, there is no mistaking the surge of hostility here. After the initial token justification that Christian oppression promoted the growth of unpleasant traits among the Jewish race, Gutzkow roundly blames Jewish faults on the Jews themselves. Emancipation is seen as a matter of concessions by Christians rather than arising out of the *rights* of all German subjects. If the Jews seek a swift emancipation, they are told off for being pushy and insensitive to the feelings of their oppressors. And throughout there is the absolute belief in an essential antagonism—not just a difference—between the Jewish and German character. The gratuitous sneer at Gutzkow's patroness—the Jewish salonière Rahel von Varnhagen—exposes the real resentment underlying this purportedly rational analysis.

As a progressive, however, Gutzkow does not pass up the opportunity to condescend to the less enlightened opponents of Jewish emancipation. Thus, the proponents of the "Christian-organic" state who demand that all its citizens be Christians are ridiculed as idealists who do not realize that the whole nature of the state has changed in modern times. Not religion, but trade, industry, and finance are the new principles of the state. On the other hand, those "realists" who would allow piecemeal emancipation of the Jews according to *political* circumstances are acting unjustly; why open the door and then block further advancement of the Jews? (Gutzkow's own objections to the rapidity of emancipation are based on *moral*, not political factors; one should not press hard on behalf of unregenerate Jewry, particularly in the face of a Christendom that has not yet overhauled its own morals and feelings.)

Another group of Christians opposed to Jewish civil rights are those governed by unjustified fears of a takeover by moneyed Jews indifferent to true religion and without a sense of public duty. Finally, there is the argument that if the Christians were at the Jews' mercy, the Jews would never emancipate such a people of opposed character and religion. These slanders are reminiscent of Gutzkow's own characterization of the unpleasing traits of the Jews and so he concedes that "there is something of the truth" in these charges.[17] But he is still constrained by the demands of humanity, and he therefore goes on to argue that, notwithstanding, the Jews are entitled to emancipation.

Emancipation, he suggests, will scarcely shake the foundations of Christian society. After gaining rights, the Jews will no longer be an immigrant race, but would be fully settled in Germany. Freedom

---

[17] *Zeitgenossen*, pp. 217–21.

would guide the Jews away from their haggling instinct and direct them to the higher professions, where they would no longer be a danger to truly German life. The more honest financiers among the Jews would cooperate with German business to promote prosperity. "Emancipation would enjoin upon them the right and the duty to end this immorality and compel them to work."[18]

Should the Jews have to "emancipate themselves" before they can be politically emancipated? Here Gutzkow admits that part of the reason why the Jews are not "free and noble spirits" is that the Christians, by denying them political emancipation, have made them so. "All this can only be the result of isolation. Their excesses, as well as their deficiencies, come from oppression." If one continues this oppression by insisting that Jews become Christians, then one is blocking the new religious impulse of reform within Judaism, which is now "opening the way to a higher, spiritual emancipation" and so allowing the Jews to redeem themselves spiritually as their critics demand. "Those Jewish vices that so repel us Christians are now gradually coming to disgust the Jews themselves." The spirit of reform will break down the Jewish outlook that comes from having been "a people apart."

Here Gutzkow confronts again his deep-seated repugnance to Jews: will assimilation be able to overcome the rift between Jewish and German nature? Or are the Jews inescapably alien?

> It is always objected against the liberation of the Jews that we have an insuperable feeling against taking into the inner circles of our society a caste whose peculiarity is so repulsive to us.

His answer to this is scarcely convincing. All those Jewish peculiarities—their accents, their unusual manners ("the greatest impediment to emancipation"), their ways of speaking and thinking, their intellectual abstraction and their destructive wit, their pursuit of money, their egoism—all these are kept alive "only through isolation." Give the Jew free access to all trades and professions, all clubs and societies, and his bad character will soon dissolve.[19]

Commendable as this appeal for emancipation is, it did not sit well with Gutzkow's emotional prejudices and he deleted it from the later editions of *Zeitgenossen*.[20] Even here, he cannot keep the charity alive for long and he soon reverts, as in the earlier part of his essay, to recrimination against the Jews themselves who are not, he charges,

[18] Ibid., pp. 221–28.
[19] Ibid., pp. 224–28.
[20] Cf. Houben, *GF*, p. 230, who ingenuously thinks it was omitted because Gutzkow had already given the essence of the passage.

doing enough to speed the process of assimilation. Again he reminds his readers that the Jews do not understand that the question is for the Christians a moral rather than a political one. They have to be persuaded that Jewish emancipation will endanger neither Christianity nor the state, nor "German blood." And how may Christians be persuaded of this as long as Judaism continues to be a closed-off phalanx? The Jews must give good faith of their *moral* commitment to assimilation by destroying the rotten vices "of an old and stubborn Judaism." (Note how the old Christian charge of Jewish "stubbornness" now receives a secular meaning; it no longer refers to a stubborn rejection of Christianity, but of modernity!)

Assimilation is the real solution to the Jewish Question and intermarriage between Jews and Christians is the main avenue to this assimilation (as it was in *Wally*). To attempt to preserve a separate Jewish "caste" would nullify the whole purpose of emancipation, which should seek to unite the Jews in the deepest way with other Germans, sharing their language, their nation, and their fatherland. If this is to happen, the Jews must also abandon their peculiar customs that set them apart—their dietary laws, their observance of a Saturday sabbath. Exchanging their old Asian homeland for a Western fatherland, they must abandon their ancient superstitions. In all this, opines Gutzkow, the current reform movement within Judaism is playing an important role. But there will be a price to pay if the Jews do not reform themselves. Here Gutzkow's advice verges on a threat: "The Christians are no fools and will not make you an offering if you have nothing to give them in return. Hearken to this warning!"[21]

And here Ahasverus at last makes his appearance. For if the Jews finally do achieve true redemption through emancipation and assimilation, Christ's prophecy will be fulfilled:

> The Jews wander and find only shelter among you. . . . [Yet] they have been long amongst us and strive to merge with us. Thus must now be exactly fulfilled the word of Christ that the Jews would wander in error for eternity and they should remain scattered over the whole earth. Pious Christian souls fear that emancipation might deny this prophecy of Christ in an outrageous way. But in fact emancipation would for the first time directly split the Jews apart from one another, who until now have simply been scattered, and would fulfill the curse that was foreseen by Christ, namely that the Jews should cease for all eternity to be a people.[22]

[21] *Zeitgenossen*, pp. 229–33.
[22] Ibid., pp. 233–35.

It would be mistaken to take *Zeitgenossen* as a warmly pro-Jewish document; critics who have done so have been obliged to dismiss its anti-Jewish remarks as being simply a matter of Gutzkow's wrongheadedness.[23] This excuse misses the boiling emotion that produces these utterances and so cannot make any real sense of Gutzkow's convoluted attitude towards the Jews. In Gutzkow's case, a virulent prejudice is hardly masked by being phrased in the rationalistic clichés deployed by the Young Germans and Young Hegelians in the manufacture of their new stereotype of the Jews. For Gutzkow (as well as for Wagner writing in 1848–50), loveless and egoistic traits are so ingrained in the Jews as to have become almost racially inherited characteristics—"almost" inherited, because both Gutzkow and the author of *Judaism in Music* still accept that exceptional Jews could with effort redeem themselves from the curse of their Jewishness.[24]

For Gutzkow, the "destruction" of Ahasverus and the Jewish people would be the final achievement of emancipation, and here we may begin to grasp the real idea lying behind his apparent confusion of prejudiced and enlightened thinking about the Jews. Gutzkow believed that the pressing need for the destruction of Judaism would be satisfied through emancipation. In Gutzkow's mind, emancipation is, therefore, not merely the assertion of his reasonable and humane side; it is more fundamentally his method of dealing with that peculiar Jewish essence which he always found so repugnant. Only in this double perspective does Gutzkow's desire for emancipation become comprehensible.

---

Ahasverus did not appear by accident at the end of *Zeitgenossen*. The first printing in 1836 of Goethe's fragment on the *Wandering Jew* (1774) had kindled fresh literary interest in the figure who was now taken up by Jewish writers.[25] Ahasverus figured in the epilogue to Auerbach's *Spinoza* in 1837, and in the same year, achieved notoriety

[23] Houben, *GF*, strenuously apologizes for Gutzkow; Low, *Jews*, is perplexed at the contradictions in Gutzkow, but tends to be sharper in judging him than is Houben.

[24] Wagner was well acquainted with Gutzkow at Dresden in 1847–48, though the two were antagonistic. Later Wagner jeered at Gutzkow as "the glory of the madhouse." See the amusingly contradictory accounts in Gutzkow, *Rückblicke* (1875) (in his *Werke*, 9:284–88) and Wagner, *MLE*, pp. 388–92 (321ff.). Cf. also *CWD*, 1:492 (1 June 1872); E. Newman, *The Life of Richard Wagner* (repr. Cambridge, 1976), 1:475–78; see also Wagner's comments in *PW*, 1:xvii, 5:9, 46, 174, 222, 6:89, 133, 139; *SB*, 2:549ff., 555, 4:311.

[25] G. K. Anderson, *The Legend of the Wandering Jew* (Providence, R.I., 1965), pp. 168ff.

in Joel Jacoby's *Klagen eines Juden (A Jew's Lament)*.[26] This ignominious work comprised a series of pathetic Ahasverus poems calling for the self-extinction of the Jews as a nation. Where the European nations are young in spirit, nothing can rejuvenate the weary spirit of the Jewish race:

> Lord, let us go home. We are weak, we are tired, we yearn for the final vault. . . . Only if the Jews are allowed to perish as Ahasverus himself wishes may they be borne up into the stream of history and progress. But such a redemption is open only to some who may perhaps become true Germans. The whole Jewish people cannot thus be assimilated. "Extinguish scorn and hate from your heart, and do not begrudge us the grave."

Redemption into German humanity is open only to a select few. Accordingly, Jacoby himself soon converted to Catholicism. As he had percipiently observed, there was really no hope for the Jews: the revolution might emancipate them, only to guillotine them the very next day as capitalists.[27]

Though contemptuous of both Jacoby and his work, Gutzkow was enthusiastic about his choice of Ahasverus as a theme.[28] "What a theme," he exclaimed, one that bore upon the whole religious isolation and obsolescence of Judaism, one that covered, too, "the political and social existence of the Jew."[29] "Ahasverus," Gutzkow asserted, "is a living idea of the age." But Gutzkow welcomed Ahasverus only as a negative symbol. He reacted wildly when the journal *Zeitung für die elegante Welt*, reviewing Julius Mosen's epic poem *Ahasver* (1838), charged that the poem was not "modern" enough in that it failed to interpret the Wandering Jew as a symbol of the unmerited sufferings

[26] Written in 1835 but first published anonymously at Mannheim in 1837. Reprinted, Berlin, 1838. See Anderson, *Legend*, p. 220; *GF*, pp. 154–58, 210–21, 233; S. Liptzin, *Germany's Stepchildren* (Philadelphia, 1944), pp. 49ff.; A. Soergel, *Ahasver-Dichtungen seit Goethe* (Leipzig, 1905), p. 60; E. Sterling, "Jewish Reaction to Jew-hatred," *LBIY* 3 (1958): 103–21, especially pp. 106, 121. Jacoby saw no end to Jewish misery, though he believed that the whole world itself had become the "Wandering Jew." See above, chap. 2, n. 28, and below, chap. 18, n. 2.

[27] Quotations from *GF*, pp. 210–23; Liptzin, *Stepchildren*, pp. 49ff.; Sterling, "Jewish Reaction," p. 106. Jacoby was much distressed by Frederick II's forbidding the Jews to bear Christian names.

[28] See *GF*, pp. 210–33. Gutzkow and Jacoby had studied together under Hegel at Berlin in 1830. But by 1837, Gutzkow was portraying Jacoby as a police informer in the novel *Seraphine*.

[29] Review of *Klagen* in the literary supplement to *Telegraph für Deutschland* (henceforth *TfD*; 1837), quoted by *GF*, p. 233, from the reprinted text in *Götter, Helden* (1838), pp. 319f.

of the Jews that could be redeemed by emancipation.[30] In a furious essay in August 1838, Gutzkow expounded a plan for a thoroughly modern Ahasverus of his own (*Plan for an Ahasverus*).[31] "The legend of the Wandering Jew," he began, "is a living idea of the age" and requires a modern literary treatment, but not one that reduces it either to a general allegory of redemption or a specific parable of Jewish suffering and subsequent redemption. In Gutzkow's hands, Ahasverus emerges not as a symbol of redemption, but as an indictment of human lovelessness, while remaining, as in the Christian legend, a representative of Jewish stubbornness and the curse the race carries. The essence of the legend demands that an eventual end be put to the wanderings of Ahasverus and also that he represent in some form the Jewish people itself. There is thus something both universally human and particularly Jewish about Gutzkow's understanding of Ahasverus, but he insists it not be confused with the recent poetic portrayals of the Wandering Jew, which he believes are deeply unsatisfying as well as obscure and false. These accounts tend either to see the Wandering Jew as a parable of Jewish civil emancipation, or to give Ahasverus a missionary and redemptive status that quite betrays the essence of the myth:

> He is portrayed as a martyr . . . and believed to be fulfilling a mission that will end when Christ Himself asks his forgiveness. In all this, the emancipation of the Jews and the reform of Christianity play a great role. . . . Dreams of this sort, unclearly conceived, more felt than formed, are dawning in the heads of young Christian and Jewish poets. (pp. 155f.)

Gutzkow acknowledges that Ahasverus is Judaism itself and that he was cursed by Christ for his scoffing at redemption. But how to interpret this in "modern" terms without destroying the traditional fabric of the myth? The solution lies in a modernistic reinterpretation of

[30] *Ahasver: Episches Gedicht* (Dresden-Leipzig, 1838). Mosen had taken Ahasverus not just as the representative of Judaism, but as the Promethean bearer of redemption to all of suffering humanity. Pardoned by Christ and purged of Jewish egoism, this romantic hero would now wander for the sake of mankind, not just the Jews. He was in fact an emancipated Jewish citizen of the world. Cf. Anderson, *Legend*, pp. 218ff.; Soergel, *Ahasver-Dichtungen*, pp. 76–83. (Wagner owned a copy of Mosen's works, according to C. von Westernhagen, *Richard Wagners Dresdener Bibliothek 1842–1849* [Wiesbaden, 1966], p. 98.)

[31] *TfD* (August 1838), nos. 124, 128, reprinted in his *Vermischte Schriften* (Leipzig, 1842), 2:154–70. (Page references in text refer to this reprint.) See also *GF*, pp. 235–40; Soergel, *Ahasver-Dichtungen*, pp. 61ff. Low, *Jews*, pp. 261ff., confusingly telescopes Gutzkow's various writings on the theme. (Gutzkow later referred to the traditional Ahasverus in *Uriel Acosta*; see *GF*, p. 302.)

Ahasverus's original sin, which has been transmitted to present-day Jews:

> Is Ahasverus's crime merely against Christianity? In the negative answer to this question lies the whole solution and the possibility of a modern Ahasverus. Ahasverus's crime was the basest lovelessness. He offended not as a Jew, but as an egoist and opportunist who valued things by their success, who thus jeered at Christ: "Are you God's son who cannot even carry your cross." The Jews were not damned to wander over the earth because they were not Christians, but because they lacked the stirrings of moral, noble, beautiful, human feeling, because they lack love, because they with the despising mocking spirit of this race [*Partikularismus*] sneered at misfortune. They committed a crime, not against Christianity, but against humanity!
>
> To portray Ahasverus as . . . a martyr is a distortion of the legend. Ahasverus is the Jew in his futile materialism, a cobbler who . . . ridicules passing greatness and nobility because it is experiencing misfortune and cannot move mountains and can be defeated with Brabant thalers. Ahasverus is the Jew in that he has been excluded from taking part in the call of history, the Jew precisely in his incapacity to have a mission. He is the shameful part of Judaism—its loveless, partisan, sneering, destructive aspects—he is exactly all that which still most hinders emancipation. Though Ahasverus after a two-thousand-year wandering now may . . . find himself taken as the representative of "modern consciousness," even so he is still the old hateful Jew who yet believes that sun, moon, and stars all move for him, and that Goethe, Schiller, Herder, and Hegel must all be judged according to their views on emancipation. He is the same Jew who now seeks to extort emancipation by his letters and seals, by his millions, . . . by his claims on human rights, . . . importunately, noisily, scoffingly. This is the modern Ahasverus as he still constantly trades and haggles among us, as he jeers in literature, dissolving the organic. This is the disgusting, self-reinforcing part of Judaism, that part which is always celebrating itself, this is Ahasverus who has now in our poems transformed himself into a great man and a missionary of the future.
>
> Oh, I could give you an Ahasverus! I would combine the secrets of Judaism with the hopes of Christianity. I would not reproach the Jew for not being a Christian, but I would show the Jew what it was in him that prevented him from becoming a Christian! . . . Christ did not curse him for not believing . . . but because he was without heart. . . . How much higher stands the pagan Pontius Pilate in this regard! And I would show, too, that there is a metaphysics in the legend and that therein the whole fate of Judaism lies expressed. (pp. 157–59)

What a lethal modernization of Ahasverus this is—and what an eruption of suppressed anger fills its furious language!

Ahasverus's shame is next put into a Hegelian perspective by Gutzkow. Despite his presence at each of the historical junctures of European modernization—the Renaissance, the Reformation, the invention of printing, the age of exploration, the discovery of gunpowder—Ahasverus has remained apart from these events. He has not become part of the "modern." But now at last Ahasverus and the Jews can become modern, at least philosophically, if they embrace the religious criticism of their creed and essence offered by the Young Hegelians. The redemption of Ahasverus, like the redemption of modern German Jews, requires not political emancipation, but a human emancipation:

> Ahasverus must understand his crime, first from a moral, then from a philosophical point of view. . . . He need not be baptized, for he baptizes himself. . . . Christ demands from him not worship as God, but only recognition of humanity and that loving surrender which, even if the Jews were [civilly] emancipated, will not be achieved by them unless they emancipate *themselves* [that is, humanly]. . . . I am not against Jewish interests . . . but I want to see Jewish achievement, not eternal Jewish misery. (pp. 160f.)

Yet, in practice, Gutzkow is as skeptical as Fichte about the Jews' capacity for such self-redemption into humanity:

> Ahasverus has the worst deed in history to his name. . . . And the eternal Jew remains loveless, cold, egoistic, apart from others and increasing in insolent pride as he wanders through history . . . until at the Last Judgment . . . he will finally admit that . . . a king can be great without money. And Christ will transform him into a gold coin that is no longer legal tender. This will be Ahasverus's hell. (p. 162)

This tasteless joke about Ahasverus's devotion to money highlights Mammonism as a Jewish vice and so completes the constellation of Jewish defects conjured up by the progressive thinkers of the 1830s. Egoism is the source of all these defects. From it stem greed for money, materialism, and Mammonism on the one hand, and, on the other, lovelessness, coldness, cruel humor. That egoism is reflected on a national scale in the "particular" feeling as a people apart that the Jews have of themselves. If one looks at this strange race from outside, it is no wonder in Gutzkow's mind—and that of Christian Europe in general—that the Jews should, because of their refusal to join their fellowmen, have to pay the penalty of eternal wandering and being perpetual outsiders. In Gutzkow's picture, Ahasverus, by his jeering at Christ, personifies the lovelessness of the race, and at the same time he represents the wandering fate that will affect the Jews as long as they fail to free themselves from their Jewishness.

Gutzkow's conception of the redemption of Ahasverus foreshadows Wagner's central idea that Jewish redemption must consist in "self-destruction" and indeed he coins the very word for it—*Selbstvernichtung*:

> Ahasverus is the tragic consequence of Jewish hopes. There is embodied so painfully in this individual just that which the Jews wish collectively for themselves. There is in Judaism despair because though they would gladly die, they cannot. Certainly, the stubborn clinging to life by the Jews is a tragedy among their misfortunes. A messianic hope, which cannot be relinquished by even the most enlightened and purified Jews, tethers them to a bleak existence. . . .
>
> For Judaism has never had the urge to self-destruction [*Selbstvernichtung*]. It has always been greedy to preserve and maintain itself for a triumphant future. Ahasverus's tragic fate is not his violent and unsuccessful search for death, but rather his exhausted dusk-watch, his outliving of himself, his obsolescence. Time itself always remains young: new peoples arise, new heroes, new empires. Only Ahasverus stays on, a living corpse, a dead man who has not yet died.[32] (pp. 164–66)

Gutzkow vehemently denied that he was a Jew-hater and insisted that he was speaking only of the "evil side or part" of Judaism. Certainly, he has nothing to say about Jewish virtues in this essay. Rather, the most revealing aspect of the text is its automatic and unreflective construction of a Jewish stereotype. Christians are not stereotyped, but allowed to be innocent until proven guilty. However, in charging the Jews as a whole people with egoism and lovelessness, Gutzkow automatically presumes the individual Jew to be guilty unless he prove himself to be a "good" human being. This is the perverse logic of Gutzkow's Jew-hatred. In this light, Gutzkow's pious utterance that "he has a great hope of the younger generation of Jews" must appear not only as so much cant, but, much worse, a statement of his innermost conviction that the vast majority of Jews are evil and incapable of redemption.

Such an outburst as Gutzkow's could not go unanswered. Ludwig Philippson's *Allgemeine Zeitung des Judenthums*, in decrying recent attempts to force the rich diversity of Jewish history within the symbol-

[32] Gutzkow is generally omitted from studies of Wagner, despite their acquaintance and their parallel handling of the Ahasverus myth.

ism of a single old cobbler, scorned the recent efforts of Gutzkow et
al. for a "new Ahasverus" as "merely the work of proud fools who
without knowledge of reality and without desire for serious study of
the theme present their chimera as history and wisdom." The anonymous critic (probably Philippson himself) roundly took Gutzkow to
task for his liberal pretensions:

> We can only regard this as the work of those false priests of freedom
> who would concede to their fellowmen not an inch of that freedom
> which they claim for themselves. . . . Know, ye prophets of freedom,
> . . . that you are its bitterest enemy.

Even if Gutzkow were right that there persists in Judaism a "base,
antihuman" aspect created by Christian persecution, his remedy is
indignantly rejected. "We can never be such traitors to ourselves as to
give up the good, the spiritual, the divine qualities of Judaism . . . in
order to acquire those few rights that time and Christian love will
grant us."

The reviewer did not mince words when it came to exposing the
philosophical bigotry in Gutzkow's apparently pro-emancipationist
stand:

> Gutzkow wants to emancipate us, but to do so in a way that will de-
> stroy and tear us apart beforehand. He does not mean that we should
> not be emancipated, indeed he demands it. . . . But he plunges a knife
> in our heart, makes us phantoms without essence, murders all our ef-
> forts and hopes, stamps on all our endeavors and then announces—"I
> emancipate you!" . . .
>
> We Jews do not really wish to be deified or to be paraded as para-
> gons of virtue. Our many faults and weaknesses should in God's name
> be exposed to us. But he who makes us into devils, who depicts us as
> opportunity men and creatures of materialism, who reproaches us as
> always being deficient in love and being of the most loveless essence
> (though bereft of love himself!) . . . misjudges and slanders us. . . . Yet
> he claims to be the defender of our emancipation! We may well ex-
> pose him as a public liar and counterfeit![33]

Gutzkow replied with a *Postscript*, which began by emphasizing how
much he had written over the years in support of Jewish emancipation. But, he said,

---

[33] Anonymous, "Ahasver, Gutzkow und Juden," *Allgemeine Zeitung des Judenthums*
(Sept.–Oct. 1838): 460–61, 472–73, 484–85. Cf. *Auf der Suche nach der jüdische Erzähl-
literatur: Die Literaturkritik der "Allgemeine Zeitung des Judentums" 1837–1922*, ed. H. O.
Horch (Frankfurt, 1985).

the question is not so much whether the Jews should be made equal, but rather how, once they have achieved the civil freedom that will come to them sooner or later in the German states . . . they may be integrated as fruitfully as possible in Christian society.[34]

While refusing to be identified with Christian opponents of emancipation, Gutzkow still insisted that he was right to sympathize with the anti-Jewish tenor of the legend of the Wandering Jew:

> The legend of Ahasverus is a general verdict on Judaism. I tried only to give the legend a meaning in the light of the aberrations and deficiencies of Judaism.

And he then somewhat speciously justifies his criticism of certain Jews (who turn out to be rather numerous):

> Instead of reproaching me for Jew-hatred, one should have asked oneself why it was that a man who had supported the Jewish cause should now be angry at the Jews. I would answer: my article is not aimed against the community of Jews but, firstly, at certain recent Jewish writers who, angry at the so long delayed emancipation, throw themselves back on the "fate" of Judaism [as represented by Ahasverus]. . . . Secondly, it is directed at those philosophers . . . who give all scholarship a Jewish coloring and may be said to hate Christ. Thirdly, against those Jews who believe they should be granted civil equality because of the idea of religious indifference.[35] . . . Fourthly, against those who because of the obstacles to emancipation presented by bigots and the mass of Christian people, because of the shameful discrimination in everyday life against the Jews, because of the course of history . . . demand of Christendom that it apologize to Judaism. Fifthly, against those who, as though sitting in Noah's Ark, open the window and ask year to year: "Are we yet emancipated?" and then close the window, without any interest in the rest of the world . . . whose only standard for interpreting the history of Germany is that under Napoleon they were free, but that in the current age, which they hate, they are oppressed. I do not harm the interests of Judaism but I attack those who among the leadership of the Jews work for a dangerous separation, press quarrels, incite passions, and only block reconciliation through their anger. They call upon Christian feelings for emancipation not always rightly nor gently enough. They overrate

[34] "Nachtrag" (postscript to article on Mosen), in *TfD* (1838), no. 130, cited here from the reprint in *Vermischte Schriften* (1842), 2:171–77. Cf. *GF*, pp. 241ff.

[35] "Religious indifference"—does Gutzkow mean here the state's nonpreference for a particular religion, or has he in mind the equal validity of religions in philosophical perspective?

the influence of enlightened Christians over unenlightened ones. They rush through historical development. Concern with emancipation makes them feel indifferent towards their own fatherland.

Gutzkow's apologetic method is magnanimously to concede rights to the Jews while forbidding them themselves to ask for those rights!

Replying to another attack, Gutzkow again took refuge in his claim that he was always a defender of emancipation, who was criticizing only the Jewish literary tendency to pervert Ahasverus into a myth for Jewish emancipation, so betraying its Christan essence:

> I repeat: Ahasverus is a Christian, not a Jewish myth. Let it remain pure . . . or abandon it as a conception of dark times. If you wish to develop it, then you must retain its original essence. . . . Goethe made the magician Faust a philosopher imbued with the vision of our own age. . . . But this is quite different from modern Jewish writers' handling of Ahasverus . . . who seek to make him the bearer of higher ideas. . . . It is a Christian legend and must be treated with respect for the spirit it expresses. The Jewish Question, the question of the day, finds no allegory in Ahasverus. . . . The matter of emancipation would best be managed by letting the myth sleep. . . . The introduction by modern Jewish poets and singers of Jewish suffering [*Judenschmerz*], of the theme of emancipation into the legend can only entangle them and arouse opposition among those Christian temperaments who have no wish to grant Judaism a mission or Ahasverus a future.[36]

Two years later Gutzkow was able to redeem his liberal reputation somewhat when the Heine–Börne scandal erupted. Heine's dissection of the character of the recently deceased Börne was generally regarded as a libertine's assassination of a moral hero. Not the least person to be outraged was Gutzkow, whose own reverential biography of Börne had been held back by Heine's publisher. Gutzkow, however, published it a few months later in a supplementary volume of the complete works of Börne, prefaced by an attack on Heine. The biography itself emphasized Börne's Jewishness, and especially admired Börne's own misgivings about Jewish emancipation:

[36] "Noch einmal Ahasver," *Zeitung für die elegante Welt* (Oct. 1838). Gutzkow's reply in *TfD* is reprinted as the second part of his "Nachtrag" in *Vermischte Schriften*, 2:175–77. In the late *Rückblicke*, he observed that "ten years after [my student period], the Jewish agonizing [*Judenschmerz*] of the Ahasverus tragedy went against my Christian-German spirit . . . [and so I opposed] the sentimentalized *Judenschmerz* interpretation of Ahasverus, while striving for Jewish emancipation" (*Werke*, 9:54).

The Jewish ancestry of Börne was decisive for his later intellectual development. . . . Yet his integrity caused him to have little sympathy for the recent efforts for Jewish emancipation in Frankfurt.

It was partly that [Börne] was vexed by the one-sidedness of an affirmation of freedom [such as Jewish emancipation], which was aristocratic in its concern for a single class of men: he saw that all mankind lay in chains and fetters. And [his reluctance to espouse Jewish emancipation] was also due in part to the fact that he understood the inner organization of Jewish society well enough to be afraid that the spirit of money-seeking, the purely material aims of the majority of Jews, would unite with the drivers of humanity and rule over the mass of the people. . . .

Börne had no interest in the lately common but excessive emphasis on race [*Nationalität*] and virtuous separation; rather, he wished for a fusion, a complete Germanizing of Judaism. . . . Above all, . . . their cause was bound up with the hopes of the entire German people and with the freedom of the whole of mankind.[37]

Gutzkow's kinder mood towards the Jews did not last, however, and by 1841 he was involved in renewed controversy, this time with the redoubtable Gabriel Riesser. The occasion was a review by Gutzkow of a book by their mutual friend Salomon Steinheim on the civil status of the Jews of Schleswig-Holstein. This essay is a remarkable disclosure of Gutzkow's instinctive aversion to Judaism, particularly in its phrases about blood and insects:

Jewish emancipation has long been a declared principle among enlightened people. Practically, however, the question has been shaped otherwise. Here I will repeat what I have often said elsewhere, that the Jewish advocates of their own natural and civil rights are not fortunate in the tone that they strike in debates. . . . They forget that the status of the Jews in Germany is a consequence of prejudice. Certainly prejudice is something that all enlightened men might struggle against, but it cannot be rooted out as quickly as Riesser, Steinheim, and others imagine. . . . [Nonetheless] we Christians should definitely see in the Jews nothing but the heirs of a thousand-year-long wretchedness, a pariah-caste of helots. Our upbringing and religious education have endowed us with an idiosyncrasy [*Idiosynkrasie*] against Judaism that we cannot suppress in ourselves overnight. . . . It takes a

---

[37] The life of Börne was first published in 1840 and reprinted in Gutzkow's *Gesammelte Werke* (Frankfurt, 1845), vol. 6. The quotations come from that volume, pp. 36f., 41f. See also *GF*, pp. 247–52.

greater heroism to master ourselves as quickly as those advocates wish. We are no heroes, at least in the mass. . . .

Dr. Steinheim would say: How rooted is this hatred, how rotten this prejudice. Certainly so. For this evil hatred was infused into us Christians as soon as we learned to read. With our first religious instruction in the Bible we saw Christianity stringently divorce itself from Judaism. The Jewish boys we knew . . . appeared ridiculous to us with their provocative peculiarities. . . . We knew that the Jews ate their own particularly slaughtered meat and could not share our food. In short, the aversion of Christians to the Jews is a physical-moral idiosyncrasy against which one can only struggle with great difficulty as do those who feel a revulsion towards blood or insects. It is shameful that we have to confess this, but it is so for the present and it may only disappear after emancipation. The shame consists in the prejudice of our parents, the carelessness of our teachers, the thousand-year curse of history. We know cases where Christians might have Jews as their most intimate friends, and yet these Christians will never allow to all Jews what they have granted gladly to some individuals.

In the second part of this review, Gutzkow turned from "idiosyncrasies" to more concrete motives for Jew-hatred. Anticipating a later view of antisemitism as a reaction to economic "modernism," Gutzkow points to the fear of Jewish competition on the part of the local craftsmen and rural population. With their international Jewish trading connections and access to outside Jewish capital, the Jews are bound to ruin local manufacturers. Gutzkow, however, carefully distinguishes his consequent defense of "Christian interests" from that of conventional Jew-haters:

It is our shame that the Jews have been treated until now as villains. . . . But now the Jew should be freed of all persecution under which he lives to the degradation of both his and our humanity. Work now through education against Jew-hatred. Grant to the Jew that freedom to choose his profession and advance how and where he wishes. But take these steps with care for Christian interests. Do not intensify Jew-hatred through rapid laws from above, but, for instance, in Holstein open up one city, one profession at a time to them. . . . The Jewish Question cannot be solved with a stroke of magic.[38]

[38] Gutzkow's review of M. Steinheim, *Meditationen* (Altona, 1841), in *TfD* (March 1841), nos. 47 and 48, pp. 182–84, 191–92 (quoted in part, with transposed paragraphs, by *GF*, pp. 264–69). Gutzkow naturally (p. 191) reproaches the "egoism" of the Jews in claiming rights for themselves instead of being concerned with those of their oppressed fellow Germans.

In a sequel to this piece, Gutzkow tried further to escape from his innate anti-Jewish feelings with this curious rationalization:

> The prejudice against the Jews springs not from an evil heart, not from an unsuppressible hatred and zeal for persecution. . . . I have not defended the prejudice of Christians, but have only portrayed it as a deeply rooted, ingrained feeling that can be eradicated neither by jest nor by ridicule, nor by passionate demonstrations of human law, but rather must be laid hold of with a spirit of real resistance so as to weaken it and subdue it to our better reflection.

The psychological strategy here was to blame such antagonism on the Jews' own separationist behavior. Because their dietary laws, religious rituals, and social clannishness have made the Jews into an isolated caste, it is natural that they should be suspected and hated by the people among whom they dwell. And it is because they form a caste that Gutzkow feels justified in opening to them all the professions but two: public education and state officialdom.[39]

It was Gutzkow's quasi-racial characterization of antisemitism as a *physisch-moralische Idiosyncrasie* that Steinheim seized on in his reply to Gutzkow's review of his book. Even in his early novel *Wally*, said Steinheim, friend Gutzkow had sought "to derive moral principles from the physical body." The novelist's attitude to the Jews in *Wally* had been favorable and hence he had there distinguished in the warmth of one of its Jewish characters a

> naturalness that is a species characteristic of the Oriental. . . . Character here depends on the Jewish racial psychology [*Stammespsychologie*], which clearly has a physical basis [*körperliche Grundlage*].

This racial fallacy of Gutzkow's, benevolent as it was in *Wally*, later led the novelist into claiming a "naturally endowed antipathy and attraction between Christians and Jews . . . and the naturally promoted divisions of races [*Volksverschiedenheiten*]." Although Steinheim took pains to excuse his friend from any imputaton of the vulgar and primitive racism of the Germanic enthusiasts, he reproached him for using concepts applicable to the animal world in discussing human nature (words reminiscent of Heine) and called Gutzkow "more fanatical than a religious fanatic" for adopting such wild ideas.[40]

---

[39] Gutzkow, "Für die Juden," *TfD* (Aug. 1841), no. 134, pp. 533–35, which prefaces Steinheim's rejoinder. Here as elsewhere Houben (*GF*, pp. 269–72) is far too lenient to Gutzkow, whom he portrays as a good friend of the Jews.

[40] M. Steinheim, "Einige Worte der Erläuterung über die Besprechung meiner Meditationen im Telegraphen," *TfD* (Aug. 1841), nos. 135–38, pp. 539–40, 542–44, 546–48, 551–52.

Steinheim was right to perceive the latent racism in Gutzkow's early theme of the "emancipation of the flesh." The Jewess in *Wally* might represent the fleshly "naturalness" of the "oriental species"; but if that "naturalness" were intrinsic to Jews, why should the endemic vices of egoism and lovelessness not be so, too? As we have seen, Gutzkow struggled to deny this corollary, arguing strenuously that Jewish vice was the result of a thousand years of oppression and isolation: he could never see the contradiction in his argument. Ultimately, racial antisemitism and the emancipation of the flesh shared the same materialist premise. Both were rooted in the physical body, but where free love was a positive revelation of that premise, hereditary Jewish vice was its negative aspect. (The same ideas are also encountered frequently in Wagner.)

Steinheim's identification of a racist element in Gutzkow's outlook is all the more telling because it appeared in what was intended to be a defense of the novelist from Ludwig Philippson's charge of Jew-hatred. Gutzkow, Steinheim insisted, had never subscribed to the "monstrous" racism of the Germanomaniacs, who demanded racial purity and separation. Nor had Gutzkow ever deserted the cause of Jewish emancipation, which indeed he had adopted as the best way of ending the isolation of Jews from German culture. Despite his unfortunate propensity to a biological racism, thought Steinheim, Gutzkow believed wholeheartedly in the assimilation of the Jews into German race and culture. The new racial beliefs, unlike the older separationist ones of the Germanomaniacs, might well coexist with an acceptance of Jewish assimilation into Germany!

Steinheim also naively accepted Gutzkow's pretext for engaging in tales of Jewish vice: "Gutzkow writes only to designate and explain, not to justify [Christian prejudice against the Jews]," suggested Steinheim. This was an ingenuous conclusion that other critics found hard to accept since Gutzkow's "descriptions" of Jewish vice had been done with such gusto. Steinheim did, however, demur from Gutzkow's charge of egoism against Jewish emancipationists: "They fight for emancipation out of hatred for prejudice, not for purely selfish interests." Steinheim did not quite see that the charge of egoism was the keystone of Gutzkow's whole approach to the Jewish Question: Jewish "isolation" and "separation" stemmed from the Jews' national egoism.

Gabriel Riesser was not in the least deceived by Gutzkow's tortuous apologetics, which he took to task in the famous *Jewish Letters for Defense and Understanding* (1842). Equality, thundered Riesser, demands not the destruction of subjective prejudice, but comes simply from a judgment about *political* injustice. Gutzkow's current arguments about the need to erase Christian animosity to the Jews before emancipation can be fully attained are nothing but cowardice. Worse, they amount to a defense of prejudice. After all, in *Wally*, Gutzkow had not been as respectful of the sensibilities of ordinary Christians as he was now about those of Christian Jew-haters. And yet, even though Gutzkow paints this Jew-hating prejudice in glowing colors *con amore*, his portrait of it is nothing but a lie and a caricature.

Riesser exposes the contradiction of Gutzkow's exaggeration of a prejudice that he affects to abhor. How can Gutzkow despise the Jewish community and yet exempt from it those Jews he chooses to have as his close friends? Then again, how can Gutzkow exhort the Jews not to embitter the debate on Judaism after he himself has written provocatively on the sensitive matter of Ahasverus?[41]

Gutzkow's deaf reply in the *Telegraph* of 1842 simply dismissed Riesser's haste for emancipation (as well as his personal criticism) as symptomatic of

> that irredeemable vice [of egoism] that is encountered even in the best
> of Jews. . . . When someone friendly says something about Judaism,
> the Jews suddenly take offense and turn on those they once loved.

Accusing Riesser of this sort of egoism, Gutzkow scorns the emancipationist's protest as a one-sided travesty of what he had actually intended to be a defense of the Jewish cause. Far from defending Christian prejudice, as Riesser alleges, Gutzkow claims to be lamenting it. But then he presents a series of the most aggravatingly subtle insults under the guise of a self-righteous solicitude:

> The Jews have pursued the emancipation debates with such exaggerated touchiness that discussion with them is impossible. . . . If anyone
> calls, regretfully enough, the prejudice of Christians in general
> against Judaism an "idiosyncrasy," they take offense.
>
> I sense well enough the source of this sensitivity. A wound smarts at
> the slightest touch. Christian writers certainly must be more restrained and considerate . . . but in these debates one cannot have regard for the most trivial and insignificant things as Riesser does. Otherwise the whole debate will become petty and nothing but a
> conversation between hysterical women.

[41] Riesser, *Jüdische Briefe*, 2:12 (May 1841; first published in 1842), in his *Gesammelte Schriften*, ed. M. Isler (Frankfurt, 1867–68), 4:260–96. Cf. Houben, *GF*, who reproaches Riesser for misjudging Gutzkow's good intentions and quotes some earlier statements of Riesser's to illustrate the latter's alleged unfairness. Houben himself seems to be seriously misjudging the whole matter. (For Riesser, see above, chaps. 6, n. 31; 9, nn. 26, 52; 10, nn. 23f., 28ff.).

> I am so fearful of writing on the subject that I have promised my-
> self never to write on it again. The words will be misunderstood. . . . I
> dare no longer to write the word "Jew" because I tremble lest it be
> taken as offensive. Many of my dearest and best friends are Jews. I
> have often said to them: "Would that all Jews were more like you, and
> Christians as I." But these Jews are aggrieved at being regarded as ex-
> ceptions.

Gutzkow is here spectacularly missing the point: all Christians, good
or bad, have political rights; Jews have to be especially good to earn
those rights. (When Auerbach, one of these good Jewish friends of
Gutzkow, was told, "Would that all Jews were like you," he replied,
"Yes, would that all Christians were like me.")

Finally, Gutzkow resorted to a somewhat academic distinction, insisting that Christian prejudice is "not a prejudice of hatred, but one
of religion." Only when the Christian religion itself had been reconstructed might the rift between Christian and Jew be bridged by education and humanity. He ended with the smug pronouncement:

> To reply point by point to Riesser would be foolishness and would
> only broaden the gulf which it is our first duty to narrow. Even if such
> a distinguished man as the honored advocate of his fellow Jews does
> not have self-control, I do.[42]

This was Gutzkow's last specific analysis of the problem of Jewish
emancipation, but he returned to Jewish themes in his literary writing. The famous play *Uriel Acosta* (1846)—Gutzkow's "Jew-piece" as it
became known—seemed to many to be the nineteenth-century sequel
to Lessing's *Nathan the Wise*. In truth, however, it was far from being
a proclamation of the humanity of Judaism. Though sympathetically
portraying some of its Jewish characters, it was really an allegory in
Jewish costume of contemporary problems: the problems of social reaction; of political censorship; of superstitious religion; of the non-
organic wholeness of society; of lovelessness; and the problem of Judaism as an obsolete religion in the modern world. It was
emphatically *not* about the problem of Jewish civil emancipation.

---

In his memoirs Gutzkow implied that he had initially adopted
the Jewish cause because it was in tune with his own feelings of unhappiness and persecution:

---

[42] *TfD* (1842), no. 4 (quoted in *GF*, pp. 277–80). Houben quite misses the offensive
nature of these remarks.

The curbing of my own Christian-German feeling went so far as outright sympathy with the rising literary mode of the so-called "Jewish-
piteousness" [*Judenschmerz*] of the grieving Ahasverus. I candidly
adopted as my own this subjective problem of humanity and worked
enthusiastically for the cause of emancipation.[43]

As far as he understood, Gutzkow did everything that was humanly
possible to overcome his own instinctive Jew-hatred. He fought for
Jewish emancipation, he befriended individual meritorious Jews,
even married a Jewess. But still the Jews were against him. They completely failed to understand his lofty critique of Judaism as having
been made egoistic and loveless through millennia of isolation.
Hence, reasoned Gutzkow, the fault must be in those modern German Jews who criticized him; the fault was not in himself. Two other
arguments strengthened this conviction that he was in the right. First
of all, the rational and humane part of his character, he believed, had
suppressed the original hatred within him, which had been incul-
cated by parents and teachers. And secondly, during 1837–42, he
had succeeded in transferring that same Jew-hatred from himself to
the mass of Germans, thereby doubly absolving himself of an irrational prejudice against the Jews. When he spoke of the difficulties of
Germans in purging themselves of Jew-hatred, Gutzkow was project-
ing (perhaps justly) his own difficulties in this regard upon his fellow
countrymen.

Eventually, however, these psychological strategies failed and the
intense feelings they had allayed boiled over into raving paranoia. In
1858, he poured scorn on his old friend Berthold Auerbach's *Black
Forest Village Tales*,[44] and in 1865, he attempted suicide in the belief
that he was being pursued and persecuted by Jews.[45] There followed
a series of stays in mental asylums. Still, there is evidence of Gutzkow's increasing sympathy for the Jews. In 1862, Gutzkow welcomed
Moses Hess's fantastic revolutionary prophecy in *Rome and Jerusalem*
and, at the same time, deprecated Bruno Bauer's surrender to the
instinct of racial separation.[46] And in his later autobiographical writings of 1871–75, there appeared a warmth of feeling towards the
Jews that turns the belittling sneers of the 1837 *Zeitgenossen* about

[43] *Rückblicke* (1875), quoted in *GF*, pp. 223f.

[44] For the Auerbach quarrel of 1858–59, see below, chap. 13, n. 21.

[45] *GF*, p. 280, however, sees this simply as a manifestation of a long-term paranoia
unrelated to Gutzkow's earlier writings on the Jewish Question! For the attempted suicide see P. Bürgel, *Die Briefe des frühen Gutzkows 1830–48: Pathologie einer Epoche* (Bern,
1975), pp. 55, 93; Lea, *Emancipation*, pp. 52ff.

[46] *Unterhaltungen am häuslichen Herd* (Leipzig, 3. Folge, Bd. 2, 1862), p. 716. See below, chap. 18, n. 60.

Jewish literary salons of Berlin into the fulsome statement that such salons showed that "the Jews are born with a sense of honorable respect."[47]

Yet this belated retraction could scarcely repair the damage done to the Jews by Gutzkow's contribution to the formulation of revolutionary antisemitism: his insistence that there existed a specifically Jewish Ahasverian character—a vicious one—from which the Jews must redeem themselves before they can be truly German, truly human.[48]

[47] *Rückblicke, Werke*, 9:73. See *GF*, p. 166.

[48] Perhaps Gutzkow thought that his later grotesque satire *Die ewige Jüdin* (in *Die schöneren Stunden*, Stuttgart, 1869) made amends.

# Heinrich Laube: Revolutionary German Art and Jewish Mammonism

HEINRICH Laube (1806–84), Gutzkow's fellow leader of Young Germany, had a far more profound impact on the development of German revolutionism and revolutionary antisemitism than his colleague.[1] For it was Laube who developed the ideals of literary revolutionism that directly influenced his intimate friend Wagner in the two decades before 1848. Laube not only invented the idea of a revolutionary German art, but also exposed its anti-Jewish corollaries. Indeed, the two central ideas of Wagner's *Judaism in Music* came from Laube: firstly, that the Jewish artistic spirit was itself sterile, and secondly, that the Jews had degraded German revolutionary art by introducing the Jewish commercializing spirit into it.

Together Laube and Wagner had eagerly pursued the possibility of joining art to revolution in the 1830s. The Polish revolt of 1831 had inspired them to embark on a revolutionary overture and opera on the subjects *Polonia* and *Kosciuszko*. They believed ardently in a "politics of the future," in a universal republic of freedom in which love would reign and property be abolished. For them, the revolution was not merely political, but a great sensual regeneration that would shatter the fabric of bourgeois society and conventional morality. Laube expounded this vision in his novel *Young Europe* (1833) and in his edition of Wilhelm Heinse's classic utopian novel *Ardinghello* (1838), as well as in the influential *Zeitung für die elegante Welt*, which he edited for two short spells in 1833–34 and 1843–44; echoes of it resound in Wagner's early operas *Forbidden Love* (1836) and *Rienzi* (1840).[2]

---

[1] General accounts are E. M. Butler, *The Saint-Simonian Religion in Germany: A Study of the Young German Movement* (Cambridge, 1926), chaps. 9–13; K. Nolle, *Heinrich Laube als sozialer und politischer Schriftsteller* (Münster, 1914); H. H. Houben, *Heinrich Laubes Leben und Schaffen*, which introduces Laube's *Ausgewählte Werke in Zehn Bänden* (Leipzig, 1906). Houben, "Laube und die Juden," *Allgemeine Zeitung des Judentums* 70 (1906): 497–500, deals mainly with Laube's later moderated views. Cf. *Allgemeine deutsche Biographie* (Leipzig, 1875–1911), 51:752–90.

[2] For Laube's collaboration with Wagner and the latter's early revolutionary themes, see Laube, *Erinnerungen* (printed in his *Gesammelte Werke*, ed. H. H. Houben [Leipzig, 1909], vols. 40–41), 1:400–4, and "Nachträge," pp. 292–94; and the references by Wagner in, *inter alia*, *MLE*, pp. 85f., 98, 101ff., 193, 277, 388ff., 434; *PW*, 1:9, 292ff.; 8:55ff.; *SB*, 1:50, 82, 89, 102, 160, 190, 227, 251, 352, 409; *CWD*, 2:210f.

In promoting this sensualist artistic revolutionism, Laube and Wagner found Heine's "rehabilitation of the flesh" more to their taste than Ludwig Börne's puritanical revolutionism. The coming "organic age" would dissolve the empty formalism of bourgeois marriage, which was so hostile to spontaneous "life feelings." The "loving philistinism" of marital fidelity would be overcome by the revolutionary morality of the true artist.[3] Little wonder that Laube and Wagner were united in these years in admiration of Heine. From 1833, Laube corresponded with the poet and they became personal friends at Paris in 1839–40, when Wagner was introduced into the circle. Laube nevertheless retained an admiration for Börne, and was taken aback by the manuscript of Heine's acerbic memoir of 1840. After its appearance in print, relations between Laube and Heine cooled somewhat, and they did not meet again until 1847.[4]

Doubtless Laube found Heine's own revolutionary critique of Judaism congenial in 1839–40, though they did not much discuss the question at the time. (Writing much later, Laube simply commented that "nothing in Heine—except perhaps his flat feet—recalled the type of the Jewish race.")[5] Like Heine and Gutzkow, Laube automatically supported Jewish emancipation. But though he did not discuss the Jewish Question in detail until 1847, the structure of literary revolutionism that he shared with Heine and Gutzkow was permeated with hostility to Judaism, even if it were not overtly expressed. This is clear from Laube's early writings on Jewish themes.

These evince the characteristic ambivalence of Young Germany. First writing of the Jewish Question as a theater critic at Leipzig in 1832, Laube approved one play solely on "pro-Jewish" grounds:

> It is a mirror of the un-Christian drive of the Christians against the Jews for the last eighteen hundred years, described by the Saint-Simonians' expression: "The Jews crucified Christ and for eighteen hundred years after that the Christians have crucified humanity in one people, the Jews."[6]

But a year later, his *Reisenovelle: Triest* balanced this sympathy with a stinging attack on "Jewish money-doings."[7] The 1835 novel, *The War-*

---

[3] See Butler, *Saint-Simonian Religion*, pp. 235ff.

[4] Laube, *Erinnerungen*, 1:53, 210, 390ff., 417f., 424. E. Elster, "H. Heine und H. Laube," *Deutsche Rundschau* 135 (1908): 91–116, pp. 102f., dates Wagner's introduction to December 1839. Cf. Wagner, *MLE*, p. 221; *SB*, 1:381.

[5] Laube writing in 1868, quoted in H. H. Houben, *Gespräche mit Heine* (Frankfurt, 1926), p. 572. On the lack of discussion of Judaism then, see Laube's *Erinnerungen*, 1:414.

[6] Quoted by Houben, "Laube und die Juden," p. 497. Cf. H. Laube, *Theaterkritiken* (Berlin, 1906), I:xxxvi f.

[7] Quoted from Houben, *Laubes Leben*, p. 72; Nolle, *Laube*, pp. 47ff.

*riors*, combined these opposing views. Set in revolutionary Poland, it portrayed two contrasting types of Jew. The old orthodox Manasse is dirty and hates the Christians who persecute his people. He is a trading-Jew, full of anger and without compassion or love for others. He loves only that which is his own, namely, his own son. Here we have the Ahasverus stereotype: loveless, egoistic, greedy. By contrast, the son Joel represents the modern, liberal, enlightened Jew, inspired with high ideals and full of compassion for all his countrymen, whether Christian or Jew. But while Joel tries to shake off the chains of the old Judaism that cling to him, his efforts to join the Polish nation are repulsed. Full of *Judenschmerz* at being excluded from progressive society, he is thrown back onto the old despised rag-and-bone Judaism. In the end, however, he finds redemption by death on the battlefield of Polish freedom.[8]

These are fairly conventional Young German notions, but in 1847 Laube suddenly launched a twofold attack on the theme of the threat of Judaism to revolutionary art. The first tack he took was to insist that the Jewish spirit itself was wholly alien to the instinct for beauty that animated genuine revolutionary art. After visiting Paris in the spring of 1847, Laube reported that the Jewish actress Rachel Félix had demonstrated that the abstracted bodiless roles of French tragedy were especially suited to interpretation by Jews:

> From the outset Jewish essence is abstract and solely intellectual, from the outset it is completely and wholly hostile to the visual and to plastic expression. This hostility stems from an innermost feeling of aversion. The Baal cult, which rendered God flesh, was repulsive to Hebrew instincts [which expressed themselves in the power of the intellect]. . . . What a rich unity [of intellect] in the Old Testament, but equally what formlessness!
>
> In the Old Testament, the race was young and creative, but the Talmud which followed is only a labyrinth of splintered intellect. . . . An immensity of skills and talents were bestowed on the Jewish people as a substitute for a fatherland, but a talent for the plastic, in the special meaning of the word, for the beautiful, is not among them. This is partly because that earthly putty of spiritual creation, a fatherland, has been lost to them. They may achieve combinations in the arts with great success, for they are extraordinarily gifted, but real creation—to

[8] *Die Krieger* (1835; pub. Mannheim, 1837). Cf. J. L. Sammons, *Six Essays on the Young German Novel* (Chapel Hill, 1972), pp. 115ff., assessing Laube as probably the most talented of the Young German novelists; Nolle, *Laube*, pp. 46f.; *HAS*, 3:405.

Like Gutzkow, Laube wants the Jews to assimilate and therefore abandon their hope of a national messiah and reestablished Jewish state (*Gesammelte Werke*, 2:39, 294f., cited by Nolle, p. 48).

create new forms, to embody life, heart, and soul in new creations—of
that they are incapable.[9]

It is precisely this racial difference, this intellectual peculiarity of
the Jews, that leads Laube to argue vigorously for the emancipation
of the unusual and talented Jewish race:

> [In Paris] no one bothers to mention Demoiselle Rachel's Jewish descent. Where the Jew is emancipated, he is also nationalized. Why do
> we hesitate to take such a necessary step that humanity and good
> sense alike present to us? The French are after all not ignorant of the
> division between human races, between Eastern and Western peoples;
> they are made aware in many ways of the consequences of this division even if their newspapers are not full of it. But though they speak
> much of it in conversation, they are always more polite and human
> than we when they do so. . . .
>  As it has occurred easily with the French, so may the emancipation
> of the Jews be beneficial for us Germans. We stand perhaps in greater
> need than the energetic French of a sharp leavening. The pungent
> Jewish spirit has become the leavening of the world; what a bad policy
> it would be to let this leavening always ferment in complete isolation!
> Its good work is done only when it is mixed with another food. Every
> hour of delaying a measure that is in the end wholly necessary is a
> loss. The preaching of conversion is thus an error. Conversions will
> take place only really after we have been united.[10]

Despite the warmth of his support for emancipation, Laube had by
now become sharply hostile towards "Jewishness." In June 1847, he
(somewhat condescendingly) wrote to Heine that he was intending
soon "to grapple bloodily with Jewish shortcomings, and to refute
possibly in your case the Jewish element."[11] His announced vehicle
for this was to be the preface to his new play *Struensee*, and the personal target was to be the Jewish composer Giacomo Meyerbeer, who
was conveniently also in Heine's bad books at the time. The overriding theme of this notorious preface was to be the Jewish commercialization of an authentically German revolutionary art.

The basic facts of the *Struensee* affair are as follows: Michael Beer,
Meyerbeer's brother, had written a tragedy *Struensee* based on the life
of the Danish statesman of that name. Heine fulsomely reviewed it in

---

[9] *Paris 1847*, report of April, in *Gesammelte Werke*, 35:92f.

[10] Ibid., pp. 126f. The leavening argument is later repeated, but applied to culture
rather than just to German society, in *Erinnerungen*, 1:413. See below.

[11] Letter of 11 June 1847, in Elster, "Heine und Laube," *Deutsche Rundschau* 136
(1908): 445.

1828, but gave the game away with the barbed remark: "As long as Beer lives, he will be immortal."[12] After Beer's death in 1833, *Struensee* disappeared from public sight and so Laube could facilely claim to have conceived his own play of the same name independently. Laube's *Struensee* was first performed at Stuttgart in 1844 and then in Dresden the following February. But its anticipated Berlin opening was delayed by the intervention of the Beer family at the Prussian court, resulting in the performance of Beer's version instead in the capital in September 1846. The Beer play was subsequently mounted at Dresden in October 1846. Frustrated by his lack of success at Berlin, Laube had his own play printed at Leipzig in late 1847, and attached to it a vitriolic preface against Meyerbeer and his family. Soon afterwards, in January 1848, Laube did have his play put on at Berlin, but only for a very short run—as he later alleged, because its leading actor was suborned for another production of the Michael Beer version.[13]

These complications offered plenty of scope for grievance, real or imagined. Laube affirmed that he had casually informed Meyerbeer of his planned play on *Struensee* in the naive hope that the brother's own interest in the theme might result in a collaboration of some kind. (Here Laube contradicted his assertion elsewhere that he had come upon the subject without being aware of the Michael Beer version.) The approach backfired when Meyerbeer reacted like a Jewish tradesman rather than an artist:

> Poetic imagination and invention do not form part of the daily competition between merchants. . . . Perhaps it might have been otherwise with Michael Beer. . . . But the brother had grown great in the sumptuous bustle of competition that is Parisian operatic life and evidently believed that he had to turn into cash a sort of family entail on the Struensee theme. My idea stunned him speechless. . . . I could hardly finish my sentences, so excited was he to arrange for the two Struensee dramas to be mounted together on the stage. From that moment

---

[12] Houben, *Gespräche mit Heine*, pp. 137, 205. The review is in Heine, *Sämtliche Schriften*, ed. K. Briegleb (Munich, 1968–76), 1:430ff. (cf. pp. 817ff.).

[13] The production history of Beer's *Struensee* is given in Houben's introduction to the play (Laube, *Gesammelte Werke*, 24:7ff.) and in his *Laubes Leben*, pp. 181ff. In November 1844, Laube had informed Heine of Meyerbeer's "intrigues" at Dresden (Elster, "Heine und Laube," p. 202). For a missing letter of January 1845 from Meyerbeer inquiring about the staging of his brother's play at Dresden, see Meyerbeer, *Briefwechsel und Tagebücher*, ed. H. and G. Becker (Berlin, 1960–), 3:796. The play was actually produced there in October 1846. See *Briefwechsel*, 4:112, 122, 238, 254, 524f., 540, which shows Meyerbeer fully aware of the anti-Jewish embitterment of Laube and his "Young German coterie."

> began the maneuvering against my play at Munich and Dresden and elsewhere.[14]

Laube airily declares he was naive about all this, but he makes up for it by a comment reminding his readers of the Jews' part in crucifying Christ:

> Meyerbeer hastened in person to Herod and Pilate, and applied all means to destroy my play. . . . This so-called liberal man, who in Paris had declared himself so valiantly for the defense of artistic priority, engineered it so that one management wrote to me explaining the Meyerbeer literary-historical logic [that old plays always preempt new ones on similar topics]. (p. 17)

Though Munich and Dresden were blocked, the Berlin royal theater accepted Laube's play, but suspended it for two years for fear of offending the Danes (even though the Laube version was far less political than its rival). The government in the end agreed to a performance in late 1846; Meyerbeer countered by having the Beer version put on in advance of the new one (p. 20).

At this point, Laube expressly identifies Meyerbeer's business instinct as essentially Jewish, and he forges links between the Philistine, artificial, commercialized culture of Paris and the quintessential Mammonism of the Jews. This is done in a passage that must be seen as the matrix of Wagner's essay *Judaism in Music* and deserves to be quoted *in extenso*:

> An alien element has surged recently into all our ways, including our literature. This is the Jewish element. I emphasize that it is an alien element, because the Jews are as much today as they were two thousand years ago an oriental nation totally separate from us. I belong in no way to the opponents of Jewish civil emancipation. On the contrary, I rise to the most radical emancipation possible. I find deeply imperfect any emancipation that does not open all conceivable paths. For as fellow human beings, the Jews have all claims to human, that is to say, civil rights. That which bothers us about the Jews, namely their foreignness, can be transformed only by a thorough ingathering [*Einheimsung*] of them among us. Nonemancipation leaves the Jews in a

[14] Laube's preface to *Struensee* is in his *Dramatische Werke* (Leipzig, 1847), 4:9–47. Page references in the text refer to this work. He modified the account in his later *Memoirs* (*Erinnerungen*), for example, admitting that, contrary to his claim of 1847, his *Struensee* was more political than the Beer version. In the *Memoirs* Laube also tries to cover up his prior knowledge of Beer's play, whereas he seemed to say in 1847 that he already knew the work. (The fact that Laube's play was first staged in 1844 has led Nolle, *Laube*, p. 48, to misdate the preface to 1844 instead of 1847.)

perpetual state of beleaguerment, and the beleaguered remains an enemy, defending himself instinctively with the best weapons, above all with his very own racial character itself, that which is so natural to the Jew and so fiercely hostile to us. Thus, we are actually preserving that essence of the Jew that is so thoroughly repugnant to us. All the innermost values of life that struggle against us so shrilly in a hundred ways will, through our half-defense, be kept going intact in the character of the Jews. *Either we must be barbarians and root out [austreiben] the Jews to the last man, or we must assimilate them.*

The latter alternative must inevitably come to pass, and therefore it is our sacred duty repeatedly and unrelentingly to expose what in their innermost life values does not go well with us, to show what both we and they, according to our powers, must soften, *even though no one can completely change themselves.*

A certain indefinable quality of alien Jewishness is under discussion here, a quality that has pushed itself importunately into the German literary world. The readiness of every author in whatever field to adduce a crowd of Jewish views may be taken as proof of my opinion that the drive of the Jewish impulse is hazardous to our own national qualities. This Jewish quality is already a deeply spreading attitude of Berlin Jewry. Among the Berlin Jews, there appear more than elsewhere highly gifted and genial human beings. They flourish especially in Berlin, or show themselves and gravitate there. For Berlin, more than any other city, offers opportunity; it has a propensity to the giddy, merely witty, remark; it respects a merely mechanical intellectual current; it is more a camp than a city—at least its character as a capital derives much more from an imposed, rather than from an inner sense of site and landscape. And for this reason there has not developed in the majority of its inhabitants the strong feeling of an organic life that is inherently suspicious of the foreign. One, therefore, draws thence from the rest of Germany the unique, the profitably brilliant. Consequently, in this city there is a brilliant Jewry *which in the nature of things cannot, even in its best accomplishments, attain an organic German character*, here in Berlin where Jewry is able to develop most freely.

From these general elements of Jewishness, and from Berlin Jewry in particular, stems that tactic of Herr Meyerbeer which he has introduced into our literary world, and which we reject as repulsive in its foreignness. The German way, when two authors have handled the same theme, is quite different. I would not say that jealousy is always absent. Sadly, we good Germans are feeble humans like other nations. Sadly, there is certainly among artists an envy that is a vile inheritance of human nature and against which one must struggle, an envy which, even it if may not be surmounted, can be suppressed. Latterly this has occurred among Germans. It thoroughly disgusts us all to pursue haggling in matters of art and knowledge in such a manner that so-called [commercial] competition—the very word is insufferable in literature—might arise to our detriment. If an encounter occurs between two living writers, as there is here between a living and a deceased one, let each seek to prevail, but let each take care to shun the demand that the other be repressed. Such an encounter creates a spurious strife between a living author and one long dead; such an encounter engenders and produces the naked destruction of the living writer. Certainly, to carry on by all available means the cause of a dead author remembered only by his family and not by the literary and artistic world—all that is an alien element in German literary life. It is that Jewish element which we do not want to adopt into the ambit of our literary life.

For nobility and sensibility to be trampled down among our poets, that would be far more evil than if the market-crying, goods-hawking style were to ruin the solid mercantile practice of our German trade fairs.

Only because of its significance for literary life do I think this *Struensee* rivalry worth mentioning. And to demonstrate by an example what I wish to make understood as the rejection of the Jewish factor in literature, I cite the name of a Jewish author among us who has already completely overcome in himself this factor that is so repugnant to us. This writer is Berthold Auerbach. He is expressive testimony that the sacrificing Jew may thoroughly nationalize himself as German among us. To be sure, this will not happen easily in the superficial bustle of big-city life. Gabriel Riesser and others, whether anticipating or following Auerbach, have shown that this nationalization of the Jew is not Auerbach's purely personal achievement, but a general possibility for truly refashioned Jewish characters. (pp. 21–26; emphasis added)

This forceful passage anticipates all the main themes of *Judaism in Music*. In both works, Meyerbeer is the chief target (though not named by Wagner). The Jews are taken to be a "foreign element" within Germany, with a dissonant culture that is alien and inorganic. Most importantly, they have corrupted German art by introducing the Mammonist commercial spirit into its life. In both essays, there is a strong element of racial thinking, but the idea of race is still inchoate. Laube and Wagner both allow the possibility of exceptional Jews redeeming themselves into true freedom: Wagner singles out Ludwig Börne, while Laube exalts Gabriel Riesser and Berthold Auerbach.

Wagner was, however, far more mealymouthed than Laube about the issue of Jewish redemption in general. Where Laube honestly spelled out the alternatives as "expulsion or assimilation," and then insisted that only assimilation was conceivable, Wagner did not state the alternatives until 1869, when he reissued *Judaism in Music*—and then he evaded giving a straight answer as to which alternative he preferred.[15]

There can be no doubt that the *Struensee* preface directly influenced Wagner's revolutionary antisemitism. Wagner had attended the Dresden première of *Struensee* in February 1845 and remained on intimate terms with Laube, who was based in nearby Leipzig. Moreover, in 1847, Laube was trying to repeat his play at Dresden in the face of an intended restaging there of the Beer version. The staff of the Dresden theater—including Wagner—could not have failed to be aware of the scandal and of Laube's feelings. Finally, in February 1848, Laube accompanied Wagner to the funeral of the latter's mother at Leipzig and commiserated on

> the unbearable burden that seemed to us to lie like a dead weight on every noble effort made to resist the tendency of the time to sink into utter worthlessness.[16]

These are words that might well have come straight from the *Struensee* preface; there is no need actually to mention the Jewish nature of the "tendency of the time to sink into utter worthlessness," since Laube's whole structure of ideas here is essentially and fundamentally anti-Jewish.

Laube, however, claimed that his attitude towards the Jews was really quite positive. The *Struensee* preface, after all, preached the as-

[15] *Erklärungen* (1869), *PW*, 3:121. E. Sterling, *Judenhass* (Frankfurt, 1969), p. 198, n. 103, unfortunately leaves Laube's opinion in doubt by omitting his statement that emancipation is inevitable; the passage is therefore taken simply as evidence of his racial notions. (Like Wagner, Laube had in the 1830s rejected a narrowly "German" revolution; this may have helped weaken their concept of race in 1847–50. Cf. Nolle, *Laube*, p. 40.)

A further parallel is Laube's proposal for a revolutionary "national German theater" run "by the people" and not the princes, such as Wagner envisioned in 1848–49 (*Struensee: Einleitung*, pp. 11ff.; *PW*, 7:320ff.).

[16] *MLE*, p. 434. Wagner dined with Laube after the 1845 Dresden première of *Struensee* (*SB*, 2:419), and attended the opening of another Laube play in 1846 (Houben, *Laubes Leben*, p. 187).

J. Katz, *From Prejudice to Destruction: Anti-Semitism 1700–1933* (Cambridge, Mass., 1980), pp. 182ff., 192, and idem, *The Dark Side of Genius* (Hanover, N.H., 1986), pp. 19, 26, 126, mentions the parallel between Laube's and Wagner's thinking, but appears unaware of the closeness of their connection in 1847. More details will be found in my forthcoming book, *Wagner—Race and Revolution*.

similation of the Jews and insisted that emancipation be enacted at once to help achieve this. And in the same month that he published the preface (November 1847), Laube followed up the constitutional principles involved by denouncing the "Christian-German state" that was being advocated by the Prussian conservative Friedrich Julius Stahl, a state in which full political rights would be restricted to Christian Germans, though Jews would be legally tolerated.[17]

Nevertheless the violence of Laube's stereotyping of Jewish Mammonism in the preface obscured any possible benevolence. No less offensive was Laube's call to the Jews to transcend their foreignness and redeem themselves from their Jewishness; this seemed tantamount to demanding the symbolic suicide of Jewish nationality, as had been suggested by Joel's redemption in *The Warriors*. The *Struensee* preface indeed provoked in 1847 a bitterly ironic protest in the literary journal *Europa*. Here Heinrich Landesmann dismissed Laube's complaint "about Meyerbeer's lack of piety towards him," and he mocked Laube as "the long-awaited Messiah of the Jews," to whom he affected to bring redemption. From such friends as Laube, advised Landesmann, the Jews should ask God to protect them. He then challenged Laube as to what precisely was so "foreign" about the Jewish artistic mind. The moving spirits of modern German literature were the Jews Heine and Börne, whom Laube himself strove to imitate: if they were alien to German feeling, so, too, must Laube be. In fact, critics had found Laube's *Struensee* not to be "German in its meaning or essence." Landesmann also commented sarcastically on how patronizing it was of Laube to assent to two meritorious exceptions from his general damnation of Jewish nature: Auerbach, who had achieved "self-emancipation"—and Riesser, a remarkable case where "a Jew has become a human being."[18]

---

Once the immediate grievance of the *Struensee* affair had passed, Laube's equable—and opportunistic—character settled him into a more moderate position. One facet of this was the collapse of the 1848 revolution, which effectively cured him of his revolutionism. He repudiated his former colleagues in a tract that even the disillu-

---

[17] Laube, "Das Christenthum und die Constitutionen zur Vermittlung," in *Monatsblätter zur Ergänzung der Allgemeine Zeitung* (Nov. 1847): 513–22. For Stahl, see below, chap. 19, n. 7.

[18] Hieronymus Lorm (Heinrich Landesmann), "Das literarische Dachstübchen: Heinrich Laube als Messias der Juden," *Europa* (Karlsruhe, 1847): 450–54.

Wagner may have known this article. He was a former contributor to the journal. (see E. Newman, *The Life of Richard Wagner* [repr. Cambridge, 1976], 1:221).

sioned Heine found extreme. Abandoning his youthful utopian political fantasies as those of "a liar or a dangerous fool," Laube inveighed against the "literary adventurers" and "radical enthusiasts" of 1848. Like Heine, he now rejected the "philosophical jargon" and "radical politics" of the *Halle Yearbooks*.[19]

But while Laube had become disillusioned, Wagner's revolutionary faith was intensified by the events of 1848–49. By the time that *Judaism in Music* appeared in 1850, Laube was no longer interested in the antisemitic ideas of art and revolution he had helped to shape. There was little contact between the two former close friends for nearly twenty years. Then, in 1868, a bitter quarrel arose between them over Wagner's failure to help Laube acquire an appointment at the Munich court theater. It may be no coincidence that it was in the aftermath of this that Wagner suddenly felt driven to reissue his *Judaism in Music* in January 1869 against the advice of all his friends. What seemed to Wagner to be Laube's current monetary attitude to artistic activity may well have triggered the composer's memory of the original *Struensee* attack on the Jewish commercialized approach to art, reminding him of the need to renew that lesson by reissuing his own essay. It was, in a way, an indirect attack on the now lapsed Laube.[20]

This estrangement from the apostle of revolutionary antisemitism no doubt inclined Laube to come to the defense of his fellow Wagner-victims after 1869. In his later *Memoirs*, Laube recalled that

> on Wagner's return to Leipzig [1842], I collected money for the impoverished young artist and obtained a contribution from the Jew Axenfeld. . . . But later, when Wagner had pronounced his ban against the Jews, [Axenfeld] seized me by the coat-buttons and cried: "For this are we now thieves and murderers? For this did the Jew from Brody press a contribution into your hand for this promising artist, so that he might now be despised by the high and mighty Wahnfried?"[21]

The Jewish writer Berthold Auerbach, who had been on close terms with both Laube and Wagner in the 1840s before becoming the butt of Wagner's anti-Jewish comments, was now warmly defended:

---

[19] Laube, *Das erste deutsche Parlament* (1849), in *Gesammelte Werke*, vol. 36, especially pp. 152ff. Despite his disapproval, Heine kept up a friendly correspondence, printed in Elster, "Heine und Laube." Cf. *Erinnerungen*, 1:329ff.; Nolle, *Laube*, p. 74.

[20] For Wagner's quarrels with Laube, see *The Diary of Richard Wagner: The Brown Book*, trans. G. Bird (London, 1980), pp. 161ff.; Newman, *Life of Wagner*, 1:274f.; *CWD*, 1:159, 308, 447, 509, 727, 2:834. Cf. Laube, *Erinnerungen*, "Nachträge," pp. 298f.

[21] *Erinnerungen*, "Nachträge," p. 294.

One cannot forget in mentioning the name of Auerbach that he was a
passionate German who took up the national development of our fatherland with the most active sympathy. He was certainly evidence
against those of the modern age who wish to exclude the Jews from
our national community. He was compelling evidence that the Jew
could merge perfectly with a nationality that did not originate from
Palestine.[22]

Meyerbeer, too, was now defended against Wagner's libels. Laube
recalled him as having "painstaking conscientiousness" in manner
and art alike. "He was a thinking man and held enlightened opinions
on all subjects." What a remarkable contrast there had been between
Meyerbeer's contentment and the recklessness of his protégé Wagner.[23] Laube conceded that Meyerbeer had "introduced to an extraordinary degree the practice of industrial business into literature."
But Laube no longer took Meyerbeer's commercializing instinct to be
symptomatic of Jewishness; instead, it was ascribed to his "Parisian
ambience."[24] Laube, however, still maintained that Meyerbeer's Jewish experience pervaded his operas: Meyerbeer may have been
"above all an artist and undoubtedly possessed of the greatest talents
. . . a musical talent of the highest order," but much of his art clearly
"stemmed from the synagogue."[25]

The offensive tone of the *Struensee* preface is completely absent
from Laube's *Memoirs* of 1875–83. There is no longer any demand
for the extrusion of Jewish influence in German art, no angry condemnation of the "foreignness" of Jews. Indeed, Laube now presented the Jewishness of Meyerbeer's art as a positive contribution to
German art, a much needed leavening for German culture:

> I have always been quite indifferent about whether a distinguished
> man be a Christian or Jew, Moslem or pagan. I would argue only that
> certain productions of art require national peculiarities if they are to

[22] Ibid., 2:370, 374. Laube also (2:140) mentions Riesser as "a wonderfully warm
heart . . . a divinely Christian Jew! Our best orator [at the Frankfurt Parliament]."

[23] *Erinnerungen*, 1:399–404. Cf. Meyerbeer, *Briefwechsel*, 3:187, 209, 212, 271, 299,
696f. Meyerbeer met with Laube and Wagner in November 1839 (p. 209).

[24] *Erinnerungen*, 1:404f.; "Nachträge," pp. 345–48, 367. In a passage written in 1882
(2:161–64), Laube attributes the difficulties of producing *Struensee* at Berlin to the "political" character of the play; this section omits all mention of Meyerbeer's intervention,
which is, however, well chided in the first volume of these memoirs (1:404f.) published
in 1875.

[25] *Erinnerungen*, 1:400–405. Laube recalled that "to the very end Meyerbeer was a
Jew, and as such remained mistrustful whether emancipation [in Germany] would really take place. He committed himself, therefore, to the French; to them, a Jew was not
suspect, but a human being like any other, he thought."

satisfy our artistic taste. Thus, a Jew could not create a Schillerian drama for us, nor could he easily become a good sculptor, given the ancient Hebrew abhorrence of visually portraying God. Poetry and music are the real preferences of the Jews. But even this prejudice is now being somewhat upset, and who knows all the things this historical leavening might give birth to that are novel and useful.[26]

Laube no longer insisted on the total abandoning of Jewish culture through assimilation; now he accepted that Jews were as entitled as Christians to preserve national individuality in their art.[27] Of course, there is a certain degree of cant in these *Memoirs*: "I have never had any prejudice against the Jews," Laube wrote, forgetful of the bitterness of the *Struensee* preface.[28] Nevertheless, by the 1870s Laube's *Memoirs* and his essays in the Vienna *Neue Freie Presse* played a prominent role in advancing a "liberal" defense against the revolutionary antisemitism of Wagner and his disciples. Laube remarked pointedly:

> Our century angers the dogs, at least in Vienna. And the enemies of the Jews say: "It's the fault of the Jews, who are always frightened of the dogs." But I say: No. My own dog is at fault. He bites, but he wears a proper muzzle.[29]

The irony was that it was Laube's own essay of 1847 on the Jewish Mammonist threat to a revolutionary, redeeming art that had armed Wagner with the weapons for his own more enduring hatred.

[26] Ibid., 1:413f. This is far more explicit about the positive contribution of Jewish leavening to German culture than the similar passage in *Paris 1847* quoted earlier.

[27] Again, there is a subtle difference between Laube's attitudes of 1847 and those of his later memoirs towards the persistence of Jewishness in German art and society.

[28] *Erinnerungen*, "Nachträge" (1882–83), p. 253.

[29] Ibid., p. 441.

# CHAPTER 13

# Berthold Auerbach: Reconciling Jewishness and Germanness

"THE FIRST Jew I ever met with whom I could discuss the whole subject of Jewishness with a hearty lack of inhibition," was how Wagner remembered Berthold Auerbach (1812–82), the best-known German-Jewish writer of the nineteenth century after Heine.[1] Auerbach sought throughout his life to erase the deleterious aspects of Jewishness by two strategies. Firstly, he envisaged Judaism as an integral part of a universal religion of humanity, consisting of reason, social love, and progress. Applying Young Hegelian reasoning, he tried to prove the continuing validity of Judaism by showing that it was still contributing to the "true and universal messianic reign of rational religion":

> My highest wish [he wrote in 1832] is to fuse Mosaism with Hegelian philosophy. . . . The spirit of humanity, earlier manifested in Moses, remains eternally the same in Hegel.[2]

Auerbach's second strategy was to interpret the idea of *Volkstümlichkeit* (German national character) so as to harmonize the twin Jewish and German elements both in his own character and in German

---

[1] *MLE*, pp. 392f. The best study of Auerbach is J. Katz, "Berthold Auerbach's Anticipation of the German Jewish Tragedy," in *Hebrew Union College Annual* 53 (1982): 215–40. Cf. A. Bettelheim, *Berthold Auerbach: Der Mann, sein Werk, sein Nachlass* (Stuttgart-Berlin, 1907; henceforth *AM*); idem, "Der Nachlass Berthold Auerbachs in Schwäbischen Schiller-Verein," in *Schwäbsicher Schiller-Verein: 6.ter Rechensbericht* (1902), pp. 3–53; idem, "Berthold Auerbach," in *Allgemeine deutsche Biographie* 47 (1903): 412–19; M. Zwick, *Berthold Auerbachs sozial-politischer und ethischer Liberalismus* (Stuttgart, 1933); S. Liptzin, *Germany's Stepchildren* (Philadelphia, 1944), chap. 5; M. Pazi, "Berthold Auerbach and Moritz Hartmann," *LBIY* 18 (1973): 201–18; idem, "Berthold Auerbach und seine revolutionäre und literarische Tätigkeit," in *Revolution und Demokratie in Geschichte und Literatur: Festschrift für Walter Grab*, ed. J. H. Schoeps and I. Geiss (Duisburg, 1979), pp. 355–74; D. Sorkin, "The Invisible Community: Emancipation, Secular Culture, and Jewish Identity in the Writings of Berthold Auerbach," in *The Jewish Response to German Culture*, ed. J. Reinharz and W. Schatzberg (Hanover, N.H., 1985), pp. 100–119.

[2] Letter of 24/27 December 1832, printed in Auerbach's *Briefe an seinen Freund Jakob Auerbach: Ein biographische Denkmal* (Frankfurt, 1884), 1:16 (henceforth *BA*).

Despite his admiration for his friends D. F. Strauss and F.-T. Vischer, Auerbach had little time for the other Young Hegelians: in 1839, he dismissed as trivial the "Hegelian gypsy-jargon of the *Hallische Jahrbücher*" (*BA*, 1:36). Cf. *AM*, pp. 60, 141, 166, 335, etc.

society. In his novel *Poet and Merchant* (1840), Auerbach insisted that its hero remain *both* a Jew and a German, for to do otherwise "would tear out his life roots"[3]

> Our source is Jewishness. . . . But source water can feed only a poor stream. To become rivers, we must take up from right and left the brooks issuing from that German nationality [*Volkstum*] amidst which we live.[4]

In his most famous work, the popular *Black Forest Village Tales* (1843–54), Auerbach combined his strategies by recounting stories that showed how the natural German *Volkstümlichkeit* of country folk disposed them to brotherly love and humane religious toleration of the Jews living among them. Despite the widely favorable welcome given to these tales, their attempt to reconcile Jewishness and Germanness aroused only the contempt of antisemites, including Wagner himself, who had come to see through Auerbach's personal affectation of wearing German country clothes as a mere sham to cover an ineradicable Jewishness. At the end of his life, confronting the mass Antisemites' Petition of 1880, Auerbach himself recognized the failure of his great project to revolutionize the Jewish Question by means of the very German *Volkstümlichkeit* that was so often the bitterest enemy of the Jews.

---

In the 1830s Auerbach first came to notice with two works aimed at correcting what he took to be Young Germany's mistaken hostility to Judaism. The first was a rebuttal of Menzel's double attack on Young Germany and Judaism alike as seedbeds of immorality (*Judaism and Contemporary Literature*, 1836), while the second was an intellectual novel, *Spinoza* (1837), tracing the evolution of philosophical religion and freedom of thought and featuring the appearance of a positively drawn Ahasverus.

Unusually for Auerbach, *Judaism and Contemporary Literature* admitted that a "demonic Jew-hatred was endemic among Germans."[5] It was perhaps partly this frank admission of German intransigence, so damaging to his case for reconciling Jewishness and Germanness, that led Auerbach to exclude the booklet from the collected editions of his works compiled during his middle years of optimistic self-de-

---

[3] *Dichter und Kaufmann*, quoted by Zwick, *Liberalismus*, p. 22. (Liptzin, *Stepchildren*, p. 92, slips in misdating this novel to 1836.)

[4] Letter quoted by Zwick, *Liberalismus*, p. 19n.

[5] *Das Judentum und die neueste Literatur* (Stuttgart, 1836). Page references in text to this edition.

lusion as to the kindly disposition of Germans towards Jews. At the time of publication, however, the author was so satisfied with his work that he sent a copy of it to his good friend Gabriel Riesser, with whose characterization of Judaism as a confessional religion (and not a nationality) he completely agreed.[6]

Auerbach acknowledged that a new literary epoch had arisen with Heine's "rehabilitation of the flesh," which represented a revolutionary synthesis of poetry, philosophy, and politics. But Auerbach rejected Heine's claim that the new sensualism was a return to man's true nature. Arguing on Hegelian grounds, he accused Heine and Young Germany of being regressives who did not understand that spirit was superior to flesh. Since history is the rise of spirit, a philosophy such as sensualism (which strives against spirit) must be regressive. If history is the process of fulfillment of human nature, it follows that sensualism must not only be antihistorical, but also against nature. Heine wanted to redeem mankind from the shackles of superstitious religion by means of a shabby Saint-Simonian philosophy; but he completely failed to grasp that such a redemption required a new higher form of religion based on spirit and taking account of revelation:

> History allows no back-stepping. The step of revealed religion has taken place and left its footprint indelibly in history. We cannot go back, we must go forward. . . . But the new spirit may not be forced into the old forms. The new spirit must instead create for itself a new form. . . . Sensualism was born of the excited muddy waters of the times and is to be buried with them. . . . Philosophy and politics, private and public life, Christianity and Judaism stand with their whole higher content and historical evolution against all sensualist unnaturalness. (p. 15)

Auerbach's debt to Young Hegelian ideas of history and spirit are evident here, but his desire to justify Judaism as a valid religious philosophy goes against the mainstream of the "critical" school, which saw Judaism superseded by Christianity as a higher manifestation of spirit. The author, however, discreetly tries to set Kant, Hegel, and the Hegelians to rights about the "content and historical evolution of Judaism." Jewish history and religious development did not come to an end with the destruction of the Temple and rise of Christianity, as most contemporaries seem to believe. Rather a new spiritual content

---

[6] Letter of January 1836, *BA*, 1:25. Auerbach later claimed he excluded *Das Judentum* from his collected works because of "its affected, fashionably modernistic" style (viz., its Heinean style). See *AM*, p. 88.

was given to the Jewish messianic idea by the later Pharisees and Talmudists. Furthermore, the end of the Temple rite and the Jewish state were of the greatest importance religiously, for only when Judaism had lost its original theocratic political connection could it become a "pure" religion and ascend to a higher degree in the history of spirit.

Much of this "purity," however, had been lost, for the price of survival of the religion in the face of medieval Christian hostility was the hardening and rigidifying of rabbinical Judaism. For the intellectual spirit and essence of Judaism to be vindicated in the modern age required the redemption of the Jews from their status of a pariah nation. Political emancipation has indeed allowed the Jews to throw off their besieged mentality and a great flowering of religious thought has taken place. This Jewish reformation has revived the true spirit of the religion while remaining true to its central idea of "revealed Deism." In the nobility of its idea of spirit and in its capacity to evolve historically, Judaism, therefore, has not been displaced by Christianity as so many have assumed, but rather maintains its validity in the present age (pp. 16–20).[7]

Auerbach next analyzed how the dominant German attitude to the Jews was now shaped, not so much by Christianity, as by what he terms "practical liberalism." This is to be seen on several levels of sophistication. The lowest level is that of the bourgeoisie, a narrow-minded class on whom the words "Jew" and "Yid" have an electric effect. They feel free themselves only if they have slaves below them (words reminiscent of Heine). A superior class of the bourgeoisie, however, call the Jews "Israelites" and pretend to favor them as kin:

> On first acquaintance they tell you how many fine Jews they know but they never forget that you are a Jew. Their general love for mankind enables them to respect the humanity in a Jew, but this patronizing relationship only flatters their complacency. Should, however, a Jew act freely and independently with the whole manner of an individual personality in their presence, or oppose their ideas, immediately there breaks forth the traces of a merely concealed Jew-hatred. (p. 26)

The periodicals and books of this class of "liberalism" are full of fine humanitarian phases: "We want the Jews to be free and have civil

---

[7] Auerbach answers Hegel's dismissal of Judaism as superseded by Christianity by citing Spinoza as the genius who had raised Judaism to a higher sphere that was commensurable with Christianity. Spinoza's pantheism, which united God and nature, was really a transformation of the original Jewish monotheism. And, said Auerbach, Hegel himself had admitted this when he blamed the failings of Spinoza's philosophy on his Jewishness (pp. 41–45).

rights." But always there is the demand that in return the Jews will have to conform. The Jews will have to work in public offices on *their* sabbath and utter cheerful amens to Christian litanies. When it suits, however, this liberal class is quick to damn the Jews with the phrase "Only a Jew could do that . . . lie, betray, cheat. . . ." None of this hypocrisy is surprising in a bourgeoisie who, addicted to industrialism and materialism, have lost the inner meaning of religious life and pursue an "Americanism undermined by German elements" (pp. 24–30). No wonder then that practical liberalism has given birth to its own brand of "theological rationalism," which has destroyed the poetry of religion. This school of biblical textual criticism seeks to discredit Judaism as a religion following error in the shape of spurious scriptural texts; it therefore encourages resistance to granting civil rights to the Jews who show themselves to be irrational in their devotion to a bogus Old Testament. Auerbach's reply is blunt: "The Jew-hatred of so many theological and political rationalists" is not at all rational but rather based on a subjective passion that goes against both reason and history (pp. 30–33). A truly civilizing "education" (*wahre Bildung*) must combine reason and passion (pp. 34ff.).

Auerbach's examination of the pretences of "practical liberalism" is devastatingly frank. Most readers of the time would have found it too savagely Heinean, and it was no doubt this section that Auerbach judged in later years to have been too "piquant" for re-publication.

The last section of Auerbach's booklet argues that the blaming of Young Germany's amorality on Judaism is misconceived, for authentic "Jewish" sensualism is quite opposed to that of the Young Germans. "The productions of the so-called Young Germany display a sensualist-radicalism that threatens to poison all the healthy parts of our national life"—but this has nothing to do with Judaism (p. 47). Heine and Börne—the axis of Young Germany—were born Jews, but have since converted. Börne's commitment to Judaism seems solely to lie in his argument that Jews are neither better nor worse than Christians and should be granted civil rights. Heine, however, is quite otherwise. He is a modern Prometheus, a prophet of the rehabilitation of the flesh who denounces Judaism and Christianity alike.[8] It is this doctrine, argues Auerbach, that has been carried forward by Gutzkow and Young Germany. Rather subtly, however, Gutzkow has inquired into the impact of Heine's moral and political revolution upon the internal religious development of Judaism. He believes Judaism to have been suddenly torn apart from its inner and outer history and now, awakened to new life and loosened from history, to be

[8] Auerbach was split in his opinion of Heine: "Heine is a phenomenon—a poet and an archscoundrel." See *BA*, 1:324; 2:404, 406.

relinquishing its old basic ideas. Gutzkow, observes Auerbach, is calling for Judaism to adopt a new spiritual idea, namely, the "emancipation of love." But why should pure Judaism have to dance attendance on Gutzkow's Heinean cult of sensualism, a cult born of a few paltry Saint-Simonian notions?⁹ "The religion of Judaism," thunders Auerbach, "like Christianity, stands under the banner of the struggle against sensualist extravagance" (pp. 49f.). Morality and the sacred are fundamental concerns of Judaism. Moreover, it is absurd of the Heine cult to think of Judaism as outmoded. It can satisfy the needs of men in different historical periods for it is not only an eternal, but a constantly evolving religion. "The union of faith and science is for Judaism not a merely ephemeral need of the times, but an eternal decree." Nor is Judaism a dogmatic creed like Christianity. Its sole dogma is the unity of God, which gives Judaism its inner essence and philosophical coherence. For Auerbach, therefore, Judaism is an eternal religion, but also a dynamic one. Its worth is proven by its production of a host of admirable Jewish thinkers and personalities in contemporary Germany, above all, Riesser (pp. 50ff.).

What can such an excellent religion as Judaism have to do with Heine's Young Germany? Menzel's charge is nothing but "a literary quarrel unjustly confused with a quarrel against the Jews." The Young Germans are no more "Jewish" than their eighteenth–century anti-Christian predecessors such as Voltaire, as Menzel well knows. Yet, just as a charge that the Jews had desecrated the Host could lead to a massacre of the Jews in the Middle Ages, so in this "enlightened century" can a false accusation such as Menzel's against the Jews trigger a modern crusade (pp. 54–57).

While *Judaism and Contemporary Literature* was being printed, Paul Pfitzer's Francophobic *Die Jeune Allemagne* appeared and Auerbach added an afterword to refute it:

> The contents of this piece seem to be too laughable to upset one, yet it does this for it shows us once again the protean nature of that Jew-hatred that we so often have to combat. . . . The Jew-hatred of 1835 is now founded on the Jews' betrayal of virtue and their self-abandonment to sensualist adoration of the French. . . . The modern enemy of the Jews preaches Jew-hatred not for the old reasons, nor because Börne and Heine are Jews, but rather because Young Germany are Jews, and because, above all, all Jews are Young Germans. (p. 65)

Auerbach ends with a heartfelt statement on the profound injustice of the accusation that the Jews are not loyal and virtuous Germans:

⁹ Though Auerbach confessed he had earlier "found many of my own ideas" in Gutzkow's article on Jewish theology (*BA*, 1:23).

> We rely on the living morality of the German nation. Yes, we respect
> and love German virtue and the German heart, for it is also our mo-
> rality and our heart. I express the cheerfully confident conviction and
> feelings of our whole younger generation of Jews when I remark:
> Test us in the fire ordeal of danger, and there you will find us pure of
> all dross of egoism and refined immorality. Give us the fatherland to
> which we belong through birth, morals, and love, and cheerfully we
> will lay down our goods and blood on its altar. Forget us and spare us
> the sorrows that embattle you because you so often join the demon of
> Jew-hatred to your efforts for the fatherland. (p. 67)

Auerbach had grasped that the main thrust of Jew-hating had become the charge of egoism, whether financial or moral egoism. And
he believed that this continuation of Jew-hatred was contaminating
the very feeling of Germanness that should eradicate it.[10]

Despite his onslaught on its "sensualist-radicalism," Auerbach came
to be on good terms with Young Germany's leading representatives.
He had already known Gutzkow well since 1835 and the two were on
cordial terms; and at Leipzig in 1845, Auerbach was befriended by
Laube, who in his memoirs speaks warmly of the acquaintance.[11] It
was in these years that Wagner held his conversations on Judaism
with Auerbach at Dresden. Auerbach was always amiable, and, besides, his *Spinoza* seemed to be near enough in the Young German
mold.

Published at Leipzig in 1837, *Spinoza* expounded the central place
that the philosopher, both as a Jewish religious thinker and as an advocate of human freedom, held in Auerbach's "religion of humanity."
But as in the booklet on Young Germany, the problem of Jew-hatred
looms large in *Spinoza*. One of the Jewish characters admits that in
the eyes of their enemies, the Jew will always remain a Jew:

> They have imbibed with mother's milk hatred and a bad opinion
> against the Jews; you waste your love on them. What good they ex-
> tend to you they count only as an exception. If you strive for money
> and honor, they will say: "That's a Jewish greed of money and honor."
> If you don't have much regard for either, then they say: "He has
> something of a Christian moderation and contempt for earthly
> goods." They find it incomparably charming if you jeer at Jewish silli-
> ness. But if you want to make an impression on one of their preju-
> dices, even if they themselves had long since cast aside their mockery,

[10] My analysis here differs from the accounts in *AM*, pp. 88–104, and Zwick, *Liberalismus*, pp. 101f.

[11] Laube, *Erinnerungen*, "Nachträge" (*Gesammelte Werke*, vol. 41), ed. H. H. Houben
(Leipzig, 1909), pp. 370–74; *BA*, 1:23, 289; *AM*, pp. 99, 182f., 205.

you may not do it and you do not do it. You, "the pushing, importunate Jew." . . . Heaven would sooner kiss earth, and fire and water unite like brothers, than that a Jew and a Christian should embrace in a true, inner, all-oblivious love and unity. And if you be baptized, the first offense that it removes is the old, Jewish Adam in you.[12]

Auerbach counters this pessimism with a statement that "love and knowledge are more enduring than hatred and prejudice" and will in the end prevail. But the main correction to this negative image of the *Ewiger Jude*—"the old Jewish Adam"—is the appearance in the epilogue of Ahasverus himself, transformed into a positive image of humanity and progress as well as of Jewish redemption.[13] In a dream, Ahasverus reveals himself to Spinoza as the archetype of the exiled wandering Jewish people, the symbol of Jewish persecution. The Jews can only be redeemed from persecution and suffering by the political freedom that Spinoza's revolution in thought will bring. Spinoza is the redeemer who will remove the curse of the Wandering Jew from all Jews, and thanks to him the Jews will eventually regain and rebuild Jerusalem in the new age of the "religion of humanity." Auerbach would later furiously disown the nationalist Zionism of Moses Hess, but in 1837 he was willing to espouse a Zionism that was rooted in ideas of universal humanity and redemption. Thus, with a dying kiss, Ahasverus hails Spinoza, not only as the redeemer of the Jews, but "the redeemer of the world." In Auerbach's mind, Ahasverus had transcended a narrow identification with Jewish redemption to become the symbol of world history.[14] But the novel's transfigured Ahasverus was not much to the liking of Gutzkow. In his Ahasverus polemic of 1838 the critic took to task such "Jewish" transformations of an inalienably Christian legend. Gutzkow demanded a loveless Ahasverus; to depict him otherwise would be to strip away the whole mythological aura of the figure.[15]

———

The German romantic folklorists had always distressed Auerbach by the manner in which they had corrupted *Volkstümlichkeit* with

[12] Quoted by Zwick, *Liberalismus*, p. 21.

[13] *AM*, pp. 111f.; A. Soergel, *Ahasver-Dichtungen seit Goethe* (Leipzig, 1905), p. 60; G. K. Anderson, *The Legend of the Wandering Jew* (Providence, R.I., 1965), p. 224.

[14] In Auerbach's discussion of Nicholas Lenau's *Der ewige Jude* (1833) and other texts, Ahasverus becomes one of the three great symbols of *Weltschmerz* and anguish: "Faust represents metaphysical, Ahasverus world-historical, and Don Juan social dissonance" (*Deutsche Abend*, quoted by Soergel, *Ahasver-Dichtungen*, p. 77).

[15] Auerbach approved of Mosen's *Ahasverus*, which had been the pretext for the 1838 polemic of Gutzkow. See *AM*, p. 116.

anti-Jewish feelings. "The Jew in the Thorn" in Jakob Grimm's fairy tale collection had pilloried Jewish greed and taken satisfaction in the hanging of the thieving Jew. *The Boy's Magic Horn* (1806) of Arnim and Brentano had included an unsympathetic portrait of the Wandering Jew that reflected the Jew-hatred of the editors. It was to show that Jews were part of a universal humanity and as such were consistent with German *Volkstum* that Auerbach wrote his *Black Forest Village Tales* (1843–54). Many of the earlier tales abound in allusions to the good relations existing between peasants and Jews in a state of nature, as it were. Thanks to the popularity of this work, it seemed for a while that German folklorists did not have to be necessarily anti-Jewish.[16] Admired by Menzel, the *Tales* were welcomed by Grimm as the work of a true *Volk*-German; much later, Auerbach's friend, the novelist Gustav Freytag, praised them as a "redemption from salon literature . . . portraits from German *Volkstum*." At court, the German Crown Prince would greet the author with the words: "Well, my dear Auerbach, how are things in the German woods?" Only Heine was sour enough to complain to Laube about their "wretched sentimentality" and "religious and moral insipidity."[17]

For all his popularity, however, feeling against Jews in Auerbach's home region prevented him being elected to the German Parliament of 1848.[18] From early on Auerbach had been aware of how a widespread and latent Jew-hatred threw into jeopardy his whole "religion of humanity." His personal relationships, especially those with Gutzkow and Wagner, brought this home forcibly in the latter decades of his life. Despite a long-standing acquaintance since 1835 and even a period of collaboration with Gutzkow at Dresden in 1846–47, there was always a barrier between the Jew and the German. In December 1851, Auerbach wrote:

> With Gutzkow I can have no real sympathy, and, while all the contradictions in our natures may be peaceably reconciled, I know for cer-

---

[16] In 1867 Auerbach recalled how he had been enchanted by Grimm until "Der Jude im Dorn" "wounded him to the heart" (*BA*, 1:338). The Ahasverus theme occurs in "Das Leiden des Herrn," in *Des Knaben Wunderhorn*, ed. A. von Arnim and C. Brentano (Heidelberg, 1806), 1:143. For the fuller depiction of Ahasverus in Arnim's *Halle und Jerusalem*, see above, chap. 2. Cf. Anderson, *Legend*, p. 195; A. Low, *Jews in the Eyes of the Germans: From the Enlightenment to Imperial Germany* (Philadelphia, 1979), p. 171. Sympathetic echoes of Ahasverus are heard in the *Black Forest Village Tales*, according to Bettelheim, *AM*, p. 175.

[17] *AM*, pp. 157, 336; A. Bettelheim, "Auerbach," *Allgemeine deutsche Biographie*. For the Heine remark, see Pazi, "Auerbach and Hartmann," p. 206n.

[18] Pazi, "Auerbach and Hartmann," p. 207n.; *AM*, p. 433; S. Baron, "The Impact of the Revolution of 1848 on Jewish Emancipation," *Jewish Social Studies* 11 (1949): 195–248, at pp. 227f.

tain that he would above all never forgive straight out the Jew in me. But let it pass.[19]

After Gutzkow's death in 1878, Auerbach sadly concluded:

> The main reason for this barrier was that Gutzkow had always been within himself an enemy of the Jews. In this respect he was part of that phenomenon which has perhaps been possible only in Germany whereby one may be a free radical in politics and religion and still maintain an opposition against the Jews. In Gutzkow's case it happened that he suspected everywhere cliques and networks in quite the same way as Richard Wagner, believing that he had not been promoted by the Jews, indeed, even that he had been hindered. Already in 1834 Gutzkow had shown this hostility and it remained always so. As he once openly acknowledged in his writing, he had been shocked to hear that Ludwig Börne was a Jew.[20]

An open break had occurred in 1858–59 when Gutzkow harshly wrote of his friend's impoverishment of rich folk themes and later publicly snubbed the writer at a Schiller festival; but this did not prevent Auerbach from kindly receiving his errant critic in 1869 when symptoms of the latter's madness were by then evident.[21]

Soon Gutzkow was joined, however, by conservative critics who felt no need to dissemble their dislike of the Jew in Auerbach. In 1860, Auerbach had chosen to settle at Berlin, which he saw as the future capital of a united Germany. This provoked the Prussian conservative journal, the *Berliner Revue*, to publish a belated review of one of his political writings of 1849 under the title "Berthold Auerbach as the Court-Jew," a mocking reference to his aristocratic patrons. Referring to Auerbach's *Vienna Diary 1848* as being of "undoubtedly oriental inspiration," the anonymous reviewer (probably the Young Hegelian Jew-hater Bruno Bauer) concluded that if Auerbach's liberal opinions constitute "the loyalty of a court-Jew, what is to be expected of the common Jews [*Volksjuden*]?" Wounded, Auerbach wrote privately: "So I am now the court-Jew Auerbach. . . . How miserable it is when one has worked with all one's soul for the good of the *Volk*

[19] *BA*, 1:85 (27 December 1851). Cf. *BA*, 1:23, 411; *AM*, pp. 230, 257, 270, 365; Zwick, *Liberalismus*, pp. 103f.

[20] *BA*, 2:385 (17 December 1878).

[21] Ibid., 1, 122ff. Also the later comments: "A pity to see such a talent so fumbling," *BA*, 1:411 (1869); "There was, and is in Gutzkow a striving for truth—but he lacks love," *BA*, 1:213 (1874); Gutzkow, *Verirrungen der Dorfgeschichte* (1858) and *Schillerfestspruch* (1859) in his *Werke* (Berlin, 1910), 10:153 and 95ff., respectively. Cf. *AM*, pp. 257, 270. See above, text at chap. 11, n. 44.

that one should have to submit to this."[22] Two years later, another conservative review, the *Kreuzzeitung*, managed a more elegant sneer when Auerbach made the opening speech of the Fichte centenary celebration before an audience of four thousand. The *Kreuzzeitung* "found the weak spot" in Auerbach's eulogy by pointing out his silence about Fichte's notorious Jew-hatred! Yet Auerbach had originally intended, he says in a letter, to object in his speech to "Fichte's *terrorism*, especially concerning the Jews." Only he had refrained so as not to seem to be approaching every subject "from a Jewish perspective." This public reticence, which persisted throughout his career, even when he was most provoked and alarmed, irreparably damaged Auerbach's ability to combat the rising tide of Jew-hatred.[23]

Another assault on Auerbach's hopes for *Volkstümlichkeit* was the Zionist program proposed in 1861–62 by Moses Hess in his *Rome and Jerusalem*. Hess met the racist challenge head on by acclaiming the Jews as a *Volk*; he accepted the coin of the Jew-haters who scorned the Jews as a race apart, but he turned the coin over onto its positive side. The Jews were hailed as a progressive and benevolent race, whose persecution was attributed to their lack of a homeland. Only restoration of the Jews to the land of Israel could put an end to Jew-hatred. Hess founded his Zionism, therefore, on the idea of a Jewish race or nationality, a notion repugnant to Auerbach.

Hess and Auerbach had been close friends from 1839 to 1845, but their friendship cooled for ideological reasons. For the liberal Auerbach, the better sort of bourgeoisie was the vehicle of history and would grow with *Bildung* to become the embodiment of humanity. "The bourgeoisie is the core and fruition of all healthy state and *Volk*-life. The free and educated bourgeoisie is the highest flower of the peaceful development of mankind."[24] To Hess, "the communist-rabbi," this attitude was a betrayal of the struggle for human redemption. In 1845 he reprimanded Auerbach.

> You seek to idealize the disinherited, dehumanized people. . . . But you should have entered with me the cottages of the wretched and have exposed the dreadful secrets of depraved humanity [*Menschheit*]

[22] Anonymous, "Berthold Auerbach als—'Hofjude,' " *Berliner Revue* 23 (1860): 393–95. Written by Bauer, according to E. Barnikol, *Bruno Bauer: Studien und Materialen* (Assen, 1972), p. 351 (see below, chap. 15). Auerbach's remark is in *BA*, 1:149 (25 December 1860).

[23] *BA*, I, 1:230 (29 May 1862). Cf. Pazi, "Auerbach and Hartmann," p. 212. Gutzkow had cunningly undermined attempts at Jewish self-defense by objecting that the Jews had a "disposition to subordinate *everything* to the Jewish Question"—another example of Jewish egoism.

[24] Quoted by Zwick, *Liberalismus*, pp. 72f.

. . . and so have worked for the redemption of humanity [*Erlösung der Menschheit*] instead of writing another sort of fairy tale for winter evenings.[25]

This was bad enough but when Hess tried in 1861 to renew the friendship and sent his friend the manuscript of his Zionist blueprint *Rome and Jerusalem*, Auerbach reacted with outrage. The argument that the destiny of German Jews belonged with Jews elsewhere rather than with the Germans quite unhinged Auerbach, whose whole life was dedicated to constructing an identity for himself as a Jew *within* German life. "Who made thee a prince and a judge over us?" exploded Auerbach in biblical Hebrew in a scathing letter that Hess later quoted in his book. Auerbach informed Hess that *he* preferred *his* "homeland" of humanity and German language to Hess's "subjective" (that is, irrational) alienation within Germany. Fearful of the damage and pain that would be inflicted, Auerbach begged Hess not to publish his erroneous idea about the Jews being a distinct race or nationality. The manuscript—"this curiosity"—was returned to Hess only half-read, so disgusting did Auerbach find it. Auerbach's personal insecurity blinded him to the humanitarian vision of *Rome and Jerusalem* which, far from preaching racial hatred, saw the ethnic independence of all peoples as the path to a universally just world.[26] Hess was stricken by the "cold shower . . . this rejection of a half-read work written with my heart's blood." It was not, he told Auerbach in a final letter, the "German-hating work" his friend believed it to be. Their friendship was now ending in sorrow, but Hess still pleaded for a reconciliation (which never came about).[27]

In the "Fourth Letter" of *Rome and Jerusalem* (1862), Hess interpreted Auerbach's "reticence" as typical of the generation of liberal Jewish emancipation. This generation had failed to understand that religious reform of Judaism would never eradicate a Jew-hatred that was based on the fact that the Jews were a separate race. (The Germans object "less [to] their peculiar beliefs than their peculiar noses.")

> Progressive German Jews seem to think that they have sufficient reason for turning away from the Jewish national movement. My dear old friend, Berthold Auerbach, is disappointed with me. . . . He com-

[25] Moses Hess, *Briefwechsel*, ed. E. Silberner (The Hague, 1951), p. 111. The correspondence began in January 1839.

[26] Letter to Hess (8 April 1861), in Hess, *Briefwechsel*, pp. 375f. (Hess's letter accompanying the manuscript to Auerbach is not printed in this exchange.) Cf. E. Silberner, *Moses Hess: Geschichte seines Lebens* (London, 1966), pp. 388f., 393f. Cf. Liptzin, *Stepchildren*, pp. 93ff.

[27] Letter of 25 November 1862, in *Briefwechsel*, pp. 417f.

plains bitterly about my attitude and finally exclaims: "Who made thee a prince and a judge over us?" (Exod. 2:14). It seems that on account of the hatred that surrounds him on all sides, the German Jew is determined to estrange himself from Judaism as far as possible, and endeavors even to deny his race.[28]

Some of this is unjust to Auerbach, who never denied that he was a Jew and often publicly stated the fact. But, despite his courage, there is no doubt that the violence of Auerbach's reaction revealed his insecurity as a Jew in German society as well as his fear that his basic conception of a friendly German *Volkstümlichkeit* was wrong.

Auerbach shunned Hess and his Zionist solution completely, yet the curious thing is that in 1861 he was leaning to his former friend's view that Jews were inherently different from Germans. Unlike Hess, however, he tried to minimize the difference, seeing it merely as something that would be removed by gradual social assimilation: "Alsatian Frenchmen are like baptized Jews. To become true Frenchmen, they need three generations, as do baptized Jews," Auerbach wrote to his cousin in September 1861.[29] And a few weeks later: "That the Jews have now become among the various peoples so nationally minded is a most important theme. I should like at some time to portray in a large novel the whole of Jewish life."[30]

Auerbach doubtless thought to subordinate this "nationalism" of the Jews to their universal mission for humanity. On an abstract level, there was therefore a kinship between Auerbach's and Hess's visions of the Jewish role in achieving universal love and justice. But "humanity" was too fuzzy a concept to have practical application to Jews in a real and hostile world. Something more than "humanity" was needed to defend the Jews from Jew-hatred. Auerbach was blind to this reality. Hess's seemingly utopian proposals based on "race" turned out to be the ones that were realistic.

---

From now until his death in 1882, Auerbach's assurance about the place of the Jews among the German *Volk* was severely tested by the rise of organized political antisemitism, but he tried for a time to whistle in the dark. When he spoke at a banquet in October 1869 in honor of Adolphe Crémieux, the defender of the Damascus Jews in the 1840 Blood Libel case, Auerbach showed renewed confidence in the German destiny of the Jews as their redemption:

[28] *Rome and Jerusalem*, trans. M. Waxman, 2d ed. (New York, 1945), pp. 51f.
[29] *BA*, 1:178 (7 September 1861).
[30] *BA*, 1:190 (24 October 1861).

> The mission of the Jews . . . is to become in France full Frenchmen, in
> Germany full Germans and so on. Their mission lies in establishing
> political life and nationality in their higher meaning, not on race [*Blut-
> abstammung*], but on mind [*Geist*].[31]

Though he was distressed by the Franco-Prussian War of 1870–71,
Auerbach welcomed the subsequent unification of Germany for its
exaltation of patriotism ("the richest source for moral and artistic inspiration") and he hoped, for a time, for a new "Church of Humanity" that would bring together German Jews and Christians in salvation.[32] This self-dedication to the ideal of German patriotism led
Auerbach in 1872 to take an idiosyncratic attitude to the attempt of
a Jewish group to organize the emigration of one hundred thousand
Romanian Jews to America. Much as he deplored the persecution of
these Jews, Auerbach would not tolerate this sort of voluntary "expulsion." It would, he believed, only encourage Jew-hating dema-
gogues in other countries to seek a similar solution to *their* Jewish
questions. More positively, it must be made clear that Jews were patriots, "rooted in their native soils." Jews have a patriotic, as well as a
cosmopolitan, instinct and to weaken that instinct through encouragement of mass emigration would make gypsies of them.[33] The implication here was that settlement in Germany "had opened the gates
of love and life" and redeemed the Jews from being gypsies, as Auerbach had pointed out in an earlier letter;[34] to reverse this would be
to revoke the redemption of the Jews.

    Within a year of the mass emigration issue, Auerbach was com-
pelled to recognize that Jewish avowals of patriotism were useless in
the face of virulent Jew-hatred. In his home capital of Stuttgart there
were outbreaks of violence in 1873 against Jewish shopkeepers, while
persecution of the Jews continued to flare in eastern Europe. Auerbach became convinced that the papacy and clergy were anti-Jewish
and aiming at a return of the ghetto.[35] However, it is from late 1875
that a marked concern with a renewed Jew-hatred within Germany

---

[31] *BA*, 1:407 (15 October 1869).

[32] Zwick, *Liberalismus*, pp. 89ff.

[33] *BA*, 2:122ff. (6 October 1872). Auerbach is also rather worried by the financial
costs of this mass emigration. Cf. Pazi, "Auerbach and Hartmann," p. 213; Liptzin,
*Stepchildren*, pp. 92f. In 1878 Auerbach supported the Berlin Congress's suggestion of
rights for the Romanian Jews (*BA*, 2:349).

[34] *BA*, 1:338 (20 April 1867).

[35] For the eastern persecutions see *BA*, 2:144. "All blood can become poison and
venom, as the practice of what calls itself the *religion of love* shows." See Pazi, "Auerbach
and Hartmann," p. 213, for the Stuttgart riots, though there is little evidence of Auerbach's reaction.

becomes evident in Auerbach's correspondence. The Viennese Catholic paper *Vaterland* has printed, wrote Auerbach, a piece of "total Jew-hatred. There has sprung up a quite new and evil antagonism to the Jews":[36]

> A new hatred of the Jews rages *in flagrante delicto* and gathers on all sides. . . . If savage peoples are fanatical, that is at least a natural anger. But Christianity excels all religions in its written incitements to persecution. Or at least the Christians who write do this. Before me lies a pamphlet, "The Destructive Influence of Judaism on the German Empire." The author knows that he lies, and still he does it. So I must turn again to solidarity with my own people [*Stammesgenossen*].[37]

While Auerbach was in this mood, the Billroth affair broke out. The Viennese surgeon Theodor Billroth, a friend of Auerbach's, published in late 1875 an article on "Teaching and Studying in German Faculties of Medicine," which questioned the wisdom of having what he regarded as too great a number of Jewish students in German medical schools. Disowning the modern Jew-baiters, Billroth acknowledged that there were many fine spirits among the Jews, but

> despite all my consideration and personal sympathies, it is very clear to me that within myself I am ever as deeply aware of the gulf between pure German and pure Jewish blood as a Teuton would be aware of the gulf between him and a Phoenician.[38]

Following the press outcry against these remarks, Billroth sent a copy of the article to "The German Poet, Berthold Auerbach." Auerbach could hardly believe his eyes:

> I have been good friends with Billroth. . . . Only recently in September we spent half a day together at Aussee very pleasantly, and yet even then the man had already a poisonous feeling in his soul against the Jews. One can be totally wrong about people.

What stung was the repetition of Hess's allegation that the Jews were in truth a separate race from the Germans, no matter how much they may dwell among one another. For it led, thought Auerbach, to a racist materialism that denied the essence of humanity:

---

[36] *BA*, 2:258 (3 October 1875). Pazi, "Auerbach and Hartmann" (pp. 213, 216) dates the change in Auerbach to 1873; Liptzin, *Stepchildren* (p. 93) with 1875 is nearer the mark.

[37] *BA*, 2:263f. (4 November 1875).

[38] Quoted in *AM*, p. 361. See accounts in Zwick, *Liberalismus*, pp. 105f.; Liptzin, *Stepchildren*, p. 96; Pazi, "Auerbach and Hartmann," p. 216.

It is right and necessary to fix the basic form and enduring roots of man by using concepts of descent, selective breeding, and racial separation. But man exists not only as blood and brain, muscle and nerves. "He does not live by bread alone," he is, above all, also a human being. . . . He is not only a political animal, but also a religious being in the broadest sense. There never was and never will be a human world without a governing nonmaterial principle.[39]

This pushed Auerbach to his first public attack on Jew-hatred since his Young German polemic of 1836. This time it took the form of an open letter to Billroth. On 1 January 1876 he wrote:

I must today revise the Billroth article. I seem to have begun the New Year with a good deed. The newly awakened *furor teutonicus* against the Jews mystifies me. I should like to know the seed of it. Can it be that it stems from the awakened self-confidence of the Germans? But Jew-hatred existed in the times of oppression of Germany and was especially strong during the years of reaction 1812–30. Where then does it come from?[40]

The letter, published in early 1876, was blunt about Billroth's distinction between Jews and their fellow Germans on the ground that they lacked a common history:

Is it conceivable for an Englishman to demean himself thus . . . telling Disraeli that he is just an English-speaking Jew who happens to have been born in England? . . .

It is idiosyncratic of you to remark that the Jews are incapable [unlike Germans] of martyrdom. . . . You must know that the history of the Jews, the gifted and the not-gifted, is an eighteen-hundred-year martyrology, which has not ended even today. Or do you believe that it is no martyrdom to have to explain even today to a man of your profession that we are not just Jews who happen to speak German, who happen to have been brought up in Germany, that we think of ourselves completely as Germans?

You say that Jews had no part in the romanticism of the Middle Ages. But how did the peasants participate in that. . . . You banish us into the exile of foreignness and refuse to understand that the history of Judaism in Germany has passed through all the stages in the development of German culture. The Jews were imbued with German val-

[39] Auerbach's initial reaction in *BA*, 2:266 (15 December 1875). Later thoughts in *BA*, 2:270 (12 January 1876).

[40] *BA*, 2:269 (1 January 1876). The article had been sketched—with the usual misgivings—on 25 December (*BA*, 2:267).

ues before your compatriots, the Slavs and the Wends, were Germanized. . . .

Have you considered the consequences that will come as the natural
result of your assertion of racial hatred [*Rassenhass*]?⁴¹

Auerbach's alarm broke out again with the launching of the great
"Antisemitic Campaign" of 1879–81. In November 1879 he cried:
"This is incitement to murder and pillage, and still we have to put up
with it!"⁴² It brought him finally to doubt the beneficence of a German culture that had produced such "absolute German master-
pieces" as Lessing's *Nathan*, Goethe's *Faust*, and *The Magic Flute* of
Mozart:

> But one is now ashamed, and must be ashamed, to speak of "absolute
> Germanness," for the possibility and practice of Jew-baiting are a de-
> feat and pollution of the German spirit. Is it still the *Volk* of human-
> ity?⁴³

In 1876 Auerbach had noted "how few men are completely *free* in
their perception of the Jews";⁴⁴ and now he observed this symptom
of nonredemption to have affected even such luminaries of German
culture as Hegel and Goethe, the latter of whom "never managed to
rid himself of an animosity towards Jews picked up in his Frankfurt
days."⁴⁵ This residual prejudice was now erupting: "One can only despair. In the freest there is an arrogance and hostility towards the
Jews that awaited only the occasion to come to the light of day."⁴⁶

As the antisemitic campaign gained momentum, however, Auerbach was relieved to find that the Jews did indeed have defenders
among the Christians, including the prominent pathologist Rudolf
Virchow and the historian Theodor Mommsen.⁴⁷ The German em-
press herself was alerted to the peril by Auerbach personally and be-

⁴¹ Quoted in *AM*, pp. 361f. Auerbach misses the point that the peasants participated
passively as Christians in medieval romance. He should rather have mentioned the
Jewish romance-poetry of the Middle Ages. Cf. Zwick, *Liberalismus*, pp. 105f. (Pazi,
"Auerbach and Hartmann," p. 216, seems to be in doubt about the date of the open
letter's publication.)

⁴² *BA*, 2:412 (8 November 1879). Cf. 2:409, 412, 419, 421, for his agonizing on the
matter.

⁴³ *BA*, 2:422 (2 January 1880).

⁴⁴ *BA*, 2:270 (5 January 1876).

⁴⁵ *BA*, 2:432 (31 May 1880), on Goethe. Hegel failed to condemn "the barbarism in
the streets" of the Hep-Hep pogroms (*BA*, 2:396; cf. Zwick, *Liberalismus*, p. 100). Even
Spinoza is criticized for his "unfree" bitterness towards his own religion (*BA*, 2:262; 21
October 1875).

⁴⁶ *BA*, 2:427 (19 March 1880).

⁴⁷ *BA*, 2:425–27, 430 (February–March 1880).

gan to show an active interest in Jewish charities in 1881.[48] When the theologian Ignaz von Döllinger defended the Jews in Bavaria in July 1881, Auerbach began to feel that at last the Christians were beginning to see Jew-hatred as a great *Christian* problem, not a Jewish one.[49]

The case of Heinrich von Treitschke, however, had given Auerbach a fright he could not get over quickly. Auerbach had known and admired the historian since 1871, but in 1875 he found in one of Treitschke's works "a certain antipathy against the Jews, a remarkable symptom."[50] When Treitschke assumed the intellectual leadership of the antisemitic campaign with his articles in the *Prussian Yearbooks* of 1879–80 popularizing the slogan "The Jews are our misfortune," Auerbach saw him as practicing "an infamous Jew-baiting."[51] "It is sad to see how such a man as Treitschke has sold himself to the rabble," wrote Auerbach, who gave up going to his dining club "in case I encounter him there and be unable to greet him."[52]

To the friend who had shown him the offending publication Auerbach mourned:

> Why do you send me Treitschke's article? It is an explosive, illegal in international law, and has shattered my heart. That we should have worked for so long only to witness such barbarity from a cultivated, serious-minded German. . . . If I for once should obtain repose, then I should summon just once the whole religious-political gang before the court of logic and humanity and let them total up what their Christianity and Germanness are.[53]

For his part, Treitschke's opinion of Auerbach was predictable. While acknowledging the initial success of the *Black Forest Village Tales*, Treitschke sneered that when the novelty had worn off, "one noted that some of the peasants were nothing more than disguised Jews."[54]

Treitschke's incitement duly gave birth to the Antisemites' Petition of 1880, which called for restricted Jewish immigration and exclusion

[48] *BA*, 2:452f. (26 March 1881).
[49] *BA*, 2:467, 469 (27 July, 12 August 1881). Cf. *AM*, p. 376.
[50] *BA*, 2:242 (24 April 1875). Ibid., 2:266f. (15 December 1875), mentions a similar sentiment in one of Treitschke's speeches (*BA*, 2:63). Cf. Pazi, "Auerbach and Hartmann," p. 216.
[51] *BA*, 2:417 (29 November 1879). See A. Dorpalen, *Heinrich von Treitschke* (New Haven, 1957), pp. 241–48.
[52] *BA*, 2:425 (17 February 1880); 2:427 (24 February).
[53] Quoted in *AM*, p. 373.
[54] Treitschke, *German History in the Nineteenth Century*, quoted by Pazi, "Auerbach and Hartmann," p. 217n. For his insistence on racial hatred while disdaining antisemitism, see Dorpalen, *Treitschke*, pp. 241ff.; Low, *Jews*, pp. 369ff.

of the Jews from government posts and certain judicial and teaching positions. The petition was a little to extreme for Treitschke, but he only faintly damned it and this was taken to be his way of praising it.[55] Conceived around July 1880 by Bernhard Förster, the petition circulated rapidly and ended up with a quarter of a million signatures.[56] So virulent was the agitation by the autumn that Rudolf Virchow initiated a two-day debate in the parliament of 20 and 22 November in an attempt to quell the tide of hatred. The crisis can be followed in Auerbach's letters: On 11 November 1880, he writes:

> I have slept scarcely an hour the whole night. Yesterday evening's *National-Zeitung* published the text of the petition to Bismarck against the Jews. That we would still have to experience this! I saw it coming, I have repeatedly warned and admonished about it. When I returned here in January, I wished to organize a large convention which, through correspondence and personal approaches to the most eminent men of learning, politics, and high office, would energetically settle once and for all the newly aroused Jewish Question before the evil devours further. . . . I was laughed at by some, regarded as a crank and an oddity by others. . . . I foresee the most dismal future. There is a hope that a group of perceptive Christians who yet know what humanity is will step forth against this petition and the whole infamy. But it is too late. . . .[57]

But Mommsen and others did come to the defense of the Jews, and Auerbach cheered up for a while:

> One can again be joyful to see that the cause of the Jews is not just their's alone, but also the cause of freedom and humanity. What we have long and ever wished and hoped for—that we Jews should not have to defend ourselves but that Christians should take the initiative—has happened and for the best. One may now once more work peacefully and live in the knowledge that one is living among our true compatriots and work for them. . . . The agitation against the Jews could be a blessing.[58]

[55] Dorpalen, *Treitschke*, pp. 245ff.; M. Meyer, "The Great Debate on Anti-Semitism—Jewish Reaction to New Hostility in Germany 1879–1881," *LBIY* 11 (1966): 137–70. Relevant texts are edited by W. Böhlich, *Der Berliner Antisemitismusstreit* (Frankfurt, 1975). Cf. L. Dawidowicz, *The War against the Jews* (New York, 1975), pp. 36ff.; P. J. Pulzer, *The Rise of Political Antisemitism in Germany and Austria*, 2d ed. (London, 1988).

[56] R. S. Levy, *The Downfall of the Anti-Semitic Parties in Imperial Germany* (New Haven, 1975), pp. 21ff., comments that the idea of the petition came to Förster during the Bayreuth Festival of August 1880. However, Wagner had been approached on the matter by Förster by 6 July of that year (*CWD*, 2:506).

[57] *BA*, 2:438f. (11 November 1880).

[58] *BA*, 2:440 (14 November 1880).

The illusion did not survive the debate of 22 November:

> In vain have I lived and worked! That is the crushing impression I
> have received from this two-day debate in the House. And if I say it
> again, there is perhaps nothing so wholly evil, no fact so horrifying,
> than that such savagery, such lies, and such hatred are still possible.
> And even if one should meditate day and night to shape the pure and
> beautiful and make that the work of our whole soul, yet the soul is
> flooded with horror and loathsomeness. Thus vanquished, how can it
> be redeemed? The shame of the fatherland must be shared and en-
> dured.
>
> Yesterday afternoon I was in the parliament. The sitting lasted
> from eleven in the morning until six o'clock and I entered an already
> highly excited emotional atmosphere. It was a wrestling-match with
> most embittered gnashing of teeth. . . . What is [my literary work]
> against this great devastation of the soul? I console myself with the
> hope that all this will be healed within months, but the awareness of
> what still lies within the Germans and can unforeseen explode, that
> cannot be blotted out.[59]

Auerbach's despair was palpable in the succeeding months:

> It is no small thing to have to be permitted to say that one no longer
> belongs to the Germans and is without a fatherland. Yet I have wit-
> nessed this at first hand, I who for forty-six years have worked to the
> best of my strength for the German people and am second to no man
> in my patriotism.[60]
>
> To have to fight for all those things one believed had already been
> won by fighting, and in my old age with expiring strength, that is bit-
> ter. Would that I live no longer through this time. . . . It breaks my
> heart, I, to whom Jakob Grimm once said: "Your writings are so
> through and through German, that you might be a direct descendent
> of Hermann"—I, who have all my life felt for Germany, suffered and
> struggled for her, should suddenly be an "alien"? There are no words
> for my sorrow. My tower of ideals has crashed. I am shattered.[61]
>
> I am not supposed to be German after all! The shame of it no
> longer lets me sleep.[62]

With its presentation to Bismarck in April 1881 the petition lapsed

[59] *BA*, 2:442 (23 November 1880). Auerbach missed the first day of the debate
(2:441; 20 November).

[60] *BA*, 2:452f. (26 March 1881).

[61] Letter to K. Franzos, quoted by Zwick, *Liberalismus*, p. 108; Pazi, "Auerbach and
Hartmann," p. 217.

[62] Remark to Mauthner, quoted by Zwick, *Liberalismus*, p. 110.

from view, but it left a detritus in the form of the nationalist Unions of German Students, which were fiercely antisemitic. In July 1881, these held a meeting on the Kyffhäuser mountain, reminiscent of their nationalistic Jew-hating predecessors who had gathered for the Wartburg Festival in 1817. "The Jews," commented Auerbach on the Kyffhäuser affair, "were the foremost concrete object of attack in the onslaught against that liberalism which was born of humanity."[63]

And now Wagner came back to haunt Auerbach. The two men had been acquainted at Dresden in 1846–47, where Wagner had at the time written fulsomely of his Jewish friend as "a splendid poet."[64] Even as late as 1859, Wagner had sought Auerbach's promotion of the manuscript of *The Ring* poem.[65] But by 1865–67 things were beyond repair. In his manuscript memoirs, Wagner included a vicious character assassination of his erstwhile friend. Auerbach became the preeminent example of how the Jew could never aspire to membership of the German *Volk*. Beneath his apparent "German" ingenuousness there operated a typically Jewish cunning, the enemy of all naturalness. Seen through by Wagner, Auerbach had reverted to type, to the "usual Jewish fidgetiness," to whining and pure opportunism. No defenses were left to him: if Auerbach sought the granting of civil rights, he was condemned by Wagner for subordinating everything to the Jewish Question (a charge Gutzkow also had thrown at his Jewish critics).[66]

In 1869, in his *Explanations* to the second edition of *Judaism in Music*, Wagner at last ventured to publish—though with circumspection—some snide observations on Auerbach.[67] Though he was not actually named, the tone of these comments was almost enough to provoke Auerbach to a public rejoinder, but in the end he restricted himself, as usual, to only private expressions of distaste:

> I don't know what I should do. I cannot be at ease. I would like to give Richard Wagner a public answer, and I believe I could give him a

[63] *BA*, 2:466 (18 July 1881). P. J. Pulzer, *Rise of Political Antisemitism*, 1st ed. (New York, 1964), p. 255 (at p. 96, he slips in dating the presentation of the petition to 1882).

[64] For details, see P. L. Rose, "One of Wagner's Jewish Friends: Berthold Auerbach and his Unpublished Reply to Richard Wagner's Antisemitism," *LBIY* 36 (1991): 219–28. Cf. J. Katz, *The Darker Side of Genius: Richard Wagner's Anti-Semitism* (Hanover, N.H., 1986), p. 47.

[65] *MLE*, p. 439.

[66] *MLE*, pp. 391ff.

[67] *Erklärungen zur Judentum in der Musik* (1869), *PW*, 3:120.

blow he would not lightly get over. But that would be for me really
pointless. . . .

Even more astonishing than the tenacious preservation of the Jews
in history are the tenacity and changing themes of Jew-hatred. . . .

Wagner speaks of me. You know that in Dresden we were often and
much together and also corresponded later. Certainly he now speaks
very well and back-slappingly of me, but even there I may be of use to
him. . . .

I believe I must speak out . . . [but] I am not styled for polemic. . . .
Yet this affair leaves me no peace and takes up all my thought.[68]

Considering he had not seen Wagner's spiteful remarks in the manuscript of *My Life*, Auerbach's perception of the composer's malice
was most astute.

Now in December 1880 Auerbach saw the "Master" as the true
source of the new Jew-hatred:

Richard Wagner was the first to acknowledge himself as a Jew-hater
and he proclaimed Jew-hatred to be quite compatible with culture
[*Bildung*]. So flowed together many different currents, to which was
added the anxieties of the sons of minor officials lest the Jews gain
access to those official careers reserved previously for themselves.[69]

The Berlin *Ring* cycle of May 1881, mounted by the Jewish impre-
sario Angelo Neumann, brought Auerbach's agonizing about Wagner to a head. The public patronage by Berlin Jews of the notorious
Jew-hater was simply too much for Auerbach, who finally took up the
challenge to pen a tract against Wagner that he had evaded in 1869.
The manuscript *Richard Wagner and the Self-Respect of the Jews* is dated
2 May 1881, but yet again Auerbach's nerve was to fail him, and he
was to leave the essay unpublished among his papers.[70] Its main
thrust, however, typically of the altruistic Auerbach, is not against
Wagner—the composer's antisemitism is taken as given—but against
those Jews who fool themselves into attending Wagnerian perfor-
mances by claiming that it is all for their own self-improvement. Jewish

[68] *BA*, 1:394f. (12 March 1869).
[69] *BA*, 2:443 (6 December 1880).
[70] *Richard Wagner und die Selbstachtung der Juden*, manuscript in the Auerbach-Nach-
lass, Deutsches Literaturarchiv, Schiller-Nationalmuseum, Marbach-am-Neckar. The
title is listed in Bettelheim, "Nachlass," (1902), p. 52, but no other reference has appeared in the Wagner or Auerbach secondary literature. Pazi, "Auerbach and Hartmann," p. 212, states that "his answer to Wagner was never published or even drafted";
this is true only of the earlier intended reply of 1869.

For the complete text and translation, see Rose, "One of Wagner's Jewish Friends."

Cf. Auerbach's conversations with Eduard Hanslick in 1879 (*BA*, 2:404).

self-respect should not permit Jews to honor Wagner and his operas, asserted Auerbach, for the man is inseparable from his Jew-hating ideology. The article is, nonetheless, more a cry of anguish than a serious analysis, and unfortunately fails to address the central problem of how far Wagner's Jew-hatred is embedded in the operas and whether this is somehow communicated subconsciously to the audience. Nevertheless, Auerbach's essay does show how well he had grasped the Master's evil influence on the antisemitic campaign despite Wagner's self-righteous pretence of standing apart from the "vulgar Jew-baiters" as he termed them.[71]

---

The events of 1880–81 remorselessly forced Auerbach to acknowledge that Heine's mistrust of the Germans had, after all, been well placed. In those years Auerbach had to concede with grief that the Germans did not want to share their fatherland with the Jews, and he had to admit that, for all his personal successes, his own effort to integrate Jews and Germans had been a general failure. All that was left was humanity, and in his last work, a commemorative lecture on Lessing—the original apostle of German-Jewish friendship—Auerbach exhorted the Jews to live by humanity even if the Germans did not:

> I see how the religion of love has been perverted so that it incites hatred and envy and other base passions against the Jews. I see how the search for truth has been falsified so that it denies the facts that lie open before our eyes. I see the miserable destruction of feelings. But I fear much less the eventuality that a decay of the soul will take permanent root in the German people of Christian descent. Men of understanding and honesty will not rest and the brave will become ashamed so that the so-called Jewish Question will be set right and thereby all hatred against the Jews be hatched out. What is at present hidden will become clear. I fear far more that among us Jews bitterness will set in. . . . Do not let your misfortunes and the wickedness of

[71] Wagner delightedly welcomed the Russian pogroms of April 1881 as "an expression of the strength of the people" (*CWD*, 2:705, 14 August 1881). Two weeks after writing his essay against Wagner, Auerbach confided: "I cannot tell you how the Jew-baiting in Russia makes me despair. . . . What a grim riddle is posed by the renewal of this abominable vulgarity. I mean that such an epidemic, such a poisoning of souls, has never yet been seen" (*BA*, 2:458, 15 May 1881). In 1879 Auerbach had reacted to reports of a Blood Libel pogrom with his article "Cannibal Easter." See Zwick, *Liberalismus*, pp. 109f.

others rob you of your love of mankind. There is God, and the spirit of humanity will triumph.[72]

In the end, however, Auerbach relinquished even his hope that the Germans would in the distant future relent and repent their hatred of the Jews. On 17 December 1881 he wrote the numbed words: "I would welcome death. There is nothing left for me to do and nothing left for me to hope for."[73]

Auerbach had placed his hopes for the redemption of the Jews in their solidarity with the German people of whom he devoutly believed the Jews were a part. A century of emancipation, however, had not vindicated this conviction. Quite the reverse. The farther emancipation progressed, the more abrupt and incensed became the opposition to the Jews, and the more loudly proclaimed their allegedly irreducible apartness from the Germans. The road to redemption had turned into a cruel deception. Auerbach died at Cannes, far from his homeland, on 8 February 1882. He died in the awareness that revolutionary antisemitism had defeated his search for redemption through the German *Volk*.

[72] *Der Genesis der "Nathan"* (Berlin, 1881), quoted in Zwick, *Liberalismus*, p. 111; Liptzin, *Stepchildren*, p. 98.

[73] *BA*, 2:477 (17 December 1881). Cf. Pazi, "Auerbach and Hartmann," p. 218.

# PART FOUR

# Young Hegelianism: The Philosophical and Social Revolutionists on the Jewish Question

# CHAPTER 14

# Judaism as Molochism: The Philosophical and Socialist Revolutionary Critiques of Judaism, 1836–1844

THE NEW mythology of rational human "freedom" of the nineteenth-century German philosophical humanists took its inspiration from the writings of Kant and Hegel. While never repudiating Christianity outright, both Kant and Hegel had undertaken the task of clearing away the philosophical and religious rubble that obstructed the road to reason and freedom. After their critique of religion had done its work, there might remain a purified Christianity, but of Judaism—that fossilized remnant of a primitive and impure stage of human progress—nothing should survive. Ahasverus, the eternal Jew who had outlived his proper span, was the perfect symbol of a Judaism that stubbornly and irrationally refused to acknowledge its meaninglessness, first in the Christian and now in the modern humanist age. The process of history itself demanded the extinction of Judaism and the Jews, for the religion and the nation had both long been shattered and exhausted and must seek a grateful release through death. The instrument of this redemption was to be the sharp weapon of the "critical philosophy."[1]

The "critical philosophy" inspired the philosophical revolutionism that dominated German radical thinking in theology, philosophy, and politics in the decades before the revolution of 1848. In this atmosphere an extraordinarily intense development of hostile "critical" thinking on the Jewish Question took place in the 1840s, above all in the seminal years 1843–44, when the dual "philosophical" and "socialist" critiques of the Jewish Question crystallized in the course of the "Bruno Bauer controversy." The critical mythology generated by these discussions changed the Jews from being the deniers of God's Son to being the negators of human freedom and morality, of humanity, and reason itself. It thus became rational and liberating to be

---

[1] For the contribution of Left Hegelianism to antisemitism see R. Wistrich, *Socialism and the Jews* (London, 1982), pp. 15–45. I cannot agree with Wistrich's view (pp. 15ff.) that Hegel was even more hostile to Judaism than Kant had been. For Kant and Hegel, see above, chap. 7.

an antisemite. This was the foundation, not just of German, but of all modern revolutionary antisemitism.

———

The Young Hegelian critique of religion found its first serious exposition in the famous *Life of Jesus Critically Examined* (1835–36) of David Friedrich Strauss (1808–74), which aimed at "humanizing" Christianity. Strauss was not as hostile to Judaism as were his fellow Young Hegelian critics. Indeed his views even influenced the new "Jewish" ideas of his friend Berthold Auerbach. Strauss went so far as to find some merit in the Jewish religion, recognizing in the prophetic tradition of the Old Testament a moral countercurrent to the Jewish legalism so disliked by Kant and the early Hegel. Nevertheless, Strauss concluded that modern-day Jews were essentially a static remnant whose religion had been rendered obsolete by the higher ethical code of Christianity presaged by the prophets.

As with Hegel himself, Strauss combined this philosophical aversion to Judaism with a belief in the need for Jewish emancipation. He did not demand the conversion of the Jews to Christianity as the precondition of their gaining civil rights, but he still expected that their full redemption would be achieved ultimately only through intermarriage and the weakening of their ritual laws, which would mean an end to their "isolation." Eventually the Jewish Question would disappear peacefully through the gentle self-destruction of a separate Jewish existence.

Strauss was certainly a humane man, yet the ugly prejudice that lay beneath the elegant sophistication of the "critical philosophy" emerged in 1848. In two articles of that year on the peasants' pogroms of the mid-1840s, Strauss blamed the Jews themselves for the riots because of their "financial dishonesty" and their "apartness" or "spiritual isolation," as he put it philosophically.[2] As long as the Jews remained a separate "organism," declared Strauss, to deny them civil rights was not religious intolerance but elementary political wisdom. Nevertheless, he was forced to recommend full emancipation as the

[2] Strauss's articles in the *Jahrbücher der Gegenwart* of 1848 are cited by I. Zlocisti, "D. F. Strauss über Judenverfolgung und Emanzipation," in *Der jüdische Student* 2, no. 1 (1905): 10–14. See J. Carlebach, *Karl Marx and the Radical Critique of Judaism* (London, 1978), pp. 99ff. M. A. Riff, "The Anti-Jewish Aspect of the Revolutionary Unrest of 1848 in Baden and Its Impact on Emancipation," LBIY 21:27–40. None of the other recent accounts of Strauss examines the fundamental question of his attitude to Judaism, e.g., H. Harris, *David Friedrich Strauss and His Theology* (Cambridge, 1973); W. Brazill, *The Young Hegelians* (New Haven, 1970); J. E. Toews, *Hegelianism: The Path toward Dialectical Humanism, 1805–1841* (Cambridge, 1980), pp. 165ff.

only means that would free the Jews of their faults. A jaundiced view of Jewish national character permeates these remarks and places Strauss's support of Jewish emancipation almost in the tradition of Dohm and Humboldt. However, it is jarring to read his near justification of popular violence against the Jews. This departure from established opinion testifies vividly to the manner in which the sophistry of the Young Hegelians' revolutionary arguments corrupted moral sensibility. It was not a good omen for the future.

Strauss's demythologizing of religion encouraged the growth of the "anthropological" atheistic critique of his disciple Ludwig Feuerbach (1804–72), whose *Essence of Christianity* (1841) interpreted Judaism and Christianity alike as mere fetishistic mythologies: "The secret of religion is anthropology." Religion is not really man's worship of God, but man's own worship of himself in the self-projected form of an invented "God." Religious experience was a psychological illusion in which human hopes and fears were projected onto an exterior deity. According to the "anthropological concept," religion may fill a basic human need, but it lacks any "truth." These glib reductions persuaded Feuerbach that he had written a book that itself was "a world-historical event." It was indeed shocking, not only to Christian theologians, but to conservative Hegelians, who were dedicated to the reconciliation of spirit and matter by Hegel's "God of Spirit." Subsequent works, including the *Foundations of the Philosophy of the Future* (1841), announced a revolutionary materialist philosophy of the future that would reduce all existence to physical matter and finally do away with gods and souls, at last liberating mankind from its own tyrannous mental creations.[3]

Feuerbach built his theories on Hegel's historical account of the evolution of religion. All religions, thought Feuerbach, were essentially products of human egoism, but whereas paganism and Christianity moderated this egoism, turning it to purposes of beauty and intellect, Judaism exalted it. The original Jewish concept of Creation itself was the outcome of an egoistic desire for instant gratification of one's wishes, projected onto a God who would be able to create at whim. Jewish monotheism was merely the worship of egoism itself: "Egoism is essentially monotheistic, having only one thing—itself—as its objective."

Jewish egoism had recruited as its ally the principle of utilism:

> Utilism is the supreme principle of Judaism. . . . The Jews' principle, their God, is the most practical principle in the world—egoism—and

[3] See M. Wartofsky, *Feuerbach* (Cambridge, 1977); E. Kamenka, *The Philosophy of Ludwig Feuerbach* (London, 1970); K. Löwith, *From Hegel to Nietzsche* (London, 1965).

that egoism takes the form of religion. . . . The Jew makes nature merely the servant of his will . . . the abject vassal of his selfish interests, of his practical egoism. . . . God is the ego of Israel, which regards itself as the end and aim, the lord of nature.

Egoism, utilism—and domination are the marks of Judaism.

Unlike the Greeks, who had enjoyed nature sensually and intellectually, the Jews' practical domination of nature led them to adopt a more basic mode of enjoyment:

> The Jews opened their gastric senses to nature. They only enjoyed nature through their palates. . . . Eating is the most solemn act, even initiation, in the Jewish religion. . . . The Jews have an alimentary view of theology.

Christians, on the other hand, achieved in Holy Communion "an ennoblement of man's dependence on bread, wine, and water."[4]

This eccentric view of Judaism should not be surprising, coming as it does from the inventor of the German pun, *Man ist, was er isst* ("One is what he eats"). But the obsession with Judaism as a stomach religion also hints at the contemporary suspicion that Judaism included elements of ritual cannibalism. Indeed, in 1839 Feuerbach's close friend Georg Friedrich Daumer had advanced the lunatic theory that Judaism was originally a cannibal-cult that was still continued by some Jews. Daumer argued, furthermore, that early Christianity itself had tried to restore the declining ritual. These notions were taken seriously by Feuerbach, who referred to them approvingly in his second edition of *Essence of Christianity* in 1843:

> Faith sacrifices man to God. Human sacrifice belongs to the very idea of religion. Bloody human sacrifices only dramatize this idea. . . . On the human sacrifices in the Jewish religion, we refer the reader to the works of Daumer and Ghillany.[5]

[4] Feuerbach, *The Essence of Christianity*. trans. George Eliot (repr. New York, 1957), chaps. 11 and 12, and appendix, pp. 112–19, 298ff. These chapters are numbered 12 and 13 in the German edition, *Sämtliche Werke*, ed. W. Bolin, H. Sass, and F. Jodl, 2d ed. (Stuttgart, 1964), 6:133–58. On Feuerbach and Judaism, see J. Katz, *From Prejudice to Destruction: Anti-Semitism 1700–1933* (Cambridge, Mass., 1980), pp. 162ff. (whose translation is amended and partly quoted here); *HAS*, 3:413–16; Carlebach, *Marx and the Radical Critique*, pp. 104–10; Kamenka, *Philosophy*, pp. 45ff.; Wartofsky, *Feuerbach*, pp. 319ff.

[5] Appendix to *Essence of Christianity*, pp. 330f. Cf. *Sämtliche Werke*, 13:89, 383. For Molochism, see above, chap. 3.

Karl Marx warmly recommended this crazed theory in 1847: "We know that the supreme element in Christianity is human sacrifice. . . . Daumer shows that Christians have eaten human flesh and drunk human blood. . . . This history of his gives the final

Despite this indictment of Christianity, Feuerbach still accepted that

> in contrast with the Israelite, the Christian is a free spirit. . . . Jewish consciousness is circumscribed by the limits of a particular national interest from which Christians have freed themselves. . . . Christianity is the Jewish religion purified of its national egoism.[6]

Like several other Young Hegelian atheists, Feuerbach therefore strangely insisted that the Jews must convert to Christianity before being absorbed into modern European free humanity. This anachronistic insistence on conversion makes sense when it is realized how completely blinded were Feuerbach and others by the logic of their wonderful new ideology of philosophical revolution. Feuerbach was not a man of hatred; he refrained from vulgar, goading abuse of Jews, was genuinely friendly with the Jewish physician Jacob Herz, and had picked up a youthful knowledge of Hebrew from a local rabbi. But he was a reductionist in the grip of a new system and so could credulously cite as fact the Blood Libel tales about the Jews retailed in Eisenmenger's *Judaism Unmasked* when they were urged upon him by Daumer as "excellent proofs for [your] presentation of Judaism as the religion of egoism."[7]

Daumer (1800–75) used Hegel's idea of a new age of revolutionary Spirit to justify the unhinged vendetta he pursued for nearly forty years against a "Molochist" Christianity.[8] In this campaign Judaism, as the parent of Christianity, became the first victim of his hatchet. *Sabbath, Moloch, and Tabu* (1839) disclosed that the sabbath was originally the day of sacrifice to Moloch/Jehovah, and that the ritual had been spread as far as Tahiti by the ancient Jews. The Trojan War had

---

blow to Christianity." Quoted in *HAS*, 3:413, 554. (Marx reviewed Daumer's book in the *Neue Rheinische Zeitung* in 1850.) Remarkably the German communist press reissued Daumer's book with Marx's recommendation as Daumer, *Geheimnisse . . . mit einer einleitende Rede von Karl Marx* (Dresden, 1923; in the series "Wissenschaftliche Bibliothek des proletarischen Freidenkertums" of the Proletarian Freethinkers' Press).

[6] *Essence of Christianity*, chap. 12, pp. 120ff.

[7] Feuerbach, *Sämtliche Werke*, 13:89, Daumer's letter of January 1842. Eisenmenger is cited as an authority in the appendix (*Essence*, p. 299). Cf. Carlebach, *Marx and the Radical Critique*, p. 389.

[8] A. Kühne, *Der Religionsphilosoph Georg Friedrich Daumer: Wege und Wirkungen seiner Entwicklung* (Berlin, 1936); *HAS*, 3:410–13; R. W. Stock, *Die Judenfrage durch fünf Jahrhunderte* (Nuremberg, 1939; "a *Stürmer* edition"), pp. 365–86.

K. Kluncker, *George Friedrich Daumer: Leben und Werk 1800–1875* (Bonn, 1984), discusses Daumer's antisemitism, but sees it purely as a matter of his critique of Christianity. It seems to me more problematic than this and rooted in a complex feeling against Judaism *per se*. Kluncker, pp. 225f., also seems to think that Daumer's deluded musings on Judaism as a Moloch cult are worth taking seriously and still open to confirmation.

been "a struggle of enlightenment and humanity against Moloch and the regime of semitic-oriental priests."[9]

The Damascus Affair fired Daumer to pursue his own archaeological investigations. In April 1842 he excitedly informed Feuerbach that on exploring the cellars of the old synagogue at Nuremberg he had discovered an oven and old bones. He felt there was a clear correspondence between these remains and those other relics of Christian human sacrifice now to be found in the churches of the city. Daumer's letter promised to publish "unheard of, incredible things" about how

> the Jews slaughtered their own and gentile children, about the sacrifice of rabbis and the worship of their remains, about the drinking of human blood at the festival of Purim. . . . No one has an inkling of the cannibalism in the Talmud.[10]

Daumer divulged these secrets in his book *The Fire and Moloch Cult of the Ancient Hebrews* (1842), which began by asserting the truth of the Damascus Blood Libel of 1840, seeing it as evidence of an enduring Jewish ritual murder cult: the sabbath's cessation of movement symbolized the destruction of life by Moloch/Jehovah, the devourer of the firstborn. Moses (whom Daumer admired) had tried to abolish the cult by inventing the Passover festival, replacing human sacrifice with that of animals. But thanks to Solomon and the kings, the cult had survived, as the murder of Christian children at Passover proved. Even if the cult were a minority one among Jews, it still thrived on Jewish inheritance. The Damascus allegations did not appear improbable to Daumer, predisposed to the cult as even modern Jews were by the barbarism of the Old Testament. The cult's persistence

> can be doubted only by those unacquainted with the history and character of this race, or those blinded by prejudice and self-interest. . . .
> One must seriously consider that [modern] Jews, even if not Jews by belief or morality, remain Jews by ancestry.[11]

Daumer's sequel, *The Secrets of Ancient Christianity* (1847), reiterated that the medieval Blood Libels were rooted in fact, but tried to show his lack of Jew-hatred by pointing out that only a small group of "fanatical Jews" had been involved and that some Christians had also

⁹ Kühne, *Daumer*, pp. 63ff.; Stock, *Judenfrage*, p. 384.

¹⁰ Feuerbach, *Sämtliche Werke*, 13:96ff. Cf. Carlebach, *Marx and the Radical Critique*, p. 389; *HAS*, 3:413; Kühne, *Daumer*, pp. 66ff.

¹¹ Quotations in Stock, *Judenfrage*, pp. 377f., 380, from Daumer's *Der Feuer- und Molochdienst der alten Hebräer* (Brunswick, 1842), pp. 72ff.

practiced child-sacrifice. The Last Supper had been a cannibal meal.[12]

Daumer's aversion to Molochist Christianity led him in 1849 to seek vainly for a new pure Germanic religion based on "Nature," but then he suddenly found himself attracted to conventional Judaism itself, which had "done all it could to avoid such a misfortune [Christianity] issuing from its bosom."[13] He compiled a collection of the *Wisdom of Israel* in which he declared:

> What a treasury of humane, noble, and fine thought and moral teaching is contained in Jewish literature, especially in the disparaged Talmud!

The Talmud, reviled in his earlier writings, now became the source of a new universal messianic idea. More astonishingly still, Daumer attempted to join the Reformed Jewish community of Frankfurt, though he was rejected in 1855. Finally, he was publicly converted to Catholicism at Mainz in 1858, his earlier works were placed on the Index, and he acknowledged his *Secrets of Ancient Christianity* as "the summit of [my] errors."[14]

With so bizarre a personal and intellectual biography, it is questionable whether terming Daumer an antisemite has any meaning at all. Feuerbach wrote in 1851 that since 1844 he had broken off all contact with Daumer, who was "unreliable, unfree, the slave of a sick imagination."[15] (For his part, Daumer scorned Feuerbach for being "an abstract reductionist and anthropocentrist . . . an Onanist in religion.")[16] Praising the vast majority of Jews who had always tried to suppress the aberrant Molochists among them, willing to become a Jew himself, Daumer would have repudiated any charge of antisemitism. The Damascus Affair and the Blood Libels were, for him, historically proven facts. Undoubtedly, the usual proponents of the Blood Libel were Jew-haters; but, for Daumer, his affirming the historical truth about ritual murder did not mean that he was an enemy of conventional Judaism. His concern with Jewish ritual murder did not arise specifically out of Jew-hatred, but was rather the result of

[12] *Die Geheimnisse des christlichen Altertums* (Hamburg, 1847), concentrates on discrediting Christianity, but there is plenty on Judaism. Cf. Kühne, *Daumer*, pp. 69ff., 90.
[13] *Die Religion des neuen Weltalters* (Hamburg, 1849), 1:74, quoted by Kühne, *Daumer*, p. 96n.
[14] Kühne, pp. 74, 96–110. He recounts his progress in *Meine Conversion* (Mainz, 1859).
[15] Carlebach, *Marx and the Radical Critique*, p. 390.
[16] Kühne, *Daumer*, p. 76.

his search for a religious revolution that would dissolve all traditional theology and religion, those bloodthirsty enemies of humanity.[17]

The same excuses cannot be made for Daumer's disciple, Friedrich Wilhelm Ghillany (1807–76), who purposefully used the Moloch/Jehovah thesis to foment a political campaign of revolutionary Jew-hatred. His eight-hundred-page sally *The Human Sacrifices of the Ancient Hebrews* (1842) avowed virulently that the Jews continued to murder to the present day in pursuit of "their religion of hatred for all humanity":

> The blood accusation against the Jews is taken by modern people for a medieval fairy tale. . . . In fact the rite is the prescribed religion of the ancient Hebrews.

The Old Testament, Ghillany argued, consists of barely concealed rules and justifications for human sacrifice and is not fit reading for Christians or humanists. Jehovah demands the destruction of all other religions and peoples, and in his image, Judaism is a religion of hatred and his people the haters of humanity. The sacrifice of non-Jews is still carried out at Passover and human blood is required as an ingredient in the unleavened bread. The Jewish Jehovah of blood and destruction has no connection at all to the loving father of Christianity.[18]

Not only Jews but Protestant thinkers were outraged by Ghillany's work. Encouraged, he went on to apply these rather generalized libels to the concrete Jewish Question of the day. In two contributions to the Bruno Bauer controversy of 1843–44, he insisted that their human sacrifices and other abominations barred the Jews from civil emancipation. Ghillany argued that Jew-hatred was a justified defense of German humanity against the antihuman Jews, who prayed still for a restored temple in which to resume their human sacrifices.

---

[17] Daumer was also celebrated for his protection of the foundling Caspar Häuser and for his promotion of vegetarian ideas. His work on vegetarianism, as well as his *Hafis* (1845–52)—a translation of Persian poetry—were well known to Wagner. Cf. Kühne, *Daumer*, pp. 67f., 82, 124; *MLE*, p. 601; *SB*, 4:472, 476; *CWD*, vol. 1, 4 February 1869 and 29 November 1872, also pp. 657ff., 734f.

[18] Ghillany, *Die Menschenopfer der alten Hebräer* (Nuremberg, 1842), especially, "Vorwort," pp. iii ff. Cf. Stock, *Judenfrage*, pp. 393ff.

This charge has recently been adapted to anti-Zionist antisemitism. David Robarts, the Anglican Dean of Perth, Australia, wrote letters to the press in October 1982 claiming that "it was Jewish self-interest and false messianism which crucified Jesus. . . . Christians have no commitment to an Old Testament genocidal God. . . . [Israelis] have a deeply ingrained paranoia and a . . . dangerously misplaced sense of national and racial superiority." Dean Robarts sees no inconsistency in also stating that "the vast majority of Israeli Jews are settlers of non-Semitic origins."

Ghillany's *The Jewish Question* (1843) held that two fundamental ideas ruled the Jews: their racial hatred of non-Jews, and their messianic hope. Their hatred isolated the Jewish race and concentrated the evils of Judaism among them. Jewish hatred of mankind had in turn aroused universal Jew-hatred:

> Every man who has a human heart, who carries within his breast a feeling for humanity and the progress of our race, must come to be an enemy of the Jewish essence.

The messianic hope of this hateful Jewish essence was that it should dominate the world. The Jews' seizure of power would be heralded by the slaughter of non-Jews, and the recent ritual murders both in Damascus and Germany suggest indeed that their messianic age has already begun. Amazingly, this evil race is now claiming rights for itself!

> How can political rights be granted to such men, who adhere so rigidly to old inhuman prejudices, who regard us as impure like serfs and dogs, just as their ancestors did, even if they do not flaunt it to our face. It is men such as these who claim full civil rights, the right to exercise functions of government, to become the superiors of Christians, judicial and administrative officers![19]

Rights, said Ghillany, are contingent on the Jews abandoning their human sacrifices and their religion of hatred of humanity. But were they really capable of reforming themselves? This was the question treated in Ghillany's sequel, *Judaism and Criticism: Hebrew Human Sacrifice and the Necessity of a Timely Reform of Judaism* (1844). Here he dismissed attempts at "Reformed Judaism" by saying that Reformed Jews retained their hate-filled exclusiveness towards non-Jews. "Reformed Judaism" is a contradiction in terms, since Jehovah is a tribal god, opposed to humanity. The Jewish Bible is merely a catalog of debauchery, Jewish history a history of "humanity-hating messianism."[20]

With such an incorrigible people, what was to be done then? *The Jewish Question* of 1843 had anticipated Laube in placing the naked alternatives of Jewish emigration or absorption before the German reader, though rather more hypocritically:

[19] *Die Judenfrage: Eine Beigabe zu Bruno Bauer's Abhandlung über dieser Gegenstand* (Nuremberg, 1843), pp. 45ff., quoted in *HAS*, 3:414; Stock, *Judenfrage*, pp. 409ff.

[20] *Das Judenthum und die Kritik: Oder es bleibt bei den Menschenopfern der Hebräer und bei der Notwendigkeit einer zeitgemässen Reform des Judenthums* (Nuremberg, 1844). Cf. Stock, *Judenfrage*, pp. 412–14.

They have been an alien, foreign element within Germany for more than a thousand years. We must either help them towards the land of their fathers, or fuse completely with them. . . . But it would be best for Europe if they were to emigrate . . . to Palestine . . . or to America.[21]

In *Judaism and Criticism*, however, Ghillany dropped some of this transparently dishonest pretense of a voluntary "emigration":

One should not even avoid a financial sacrifice to have the Jews leave Germany and found a state in their promised land, and so free our fatherland of its foreign element. . . . For it is not only the devout dogma of theirs that alienates them from the German *Volk*, but the dishonor of Jewish character in general, that filthy essence of body and soul, that single struggle to gain money at the cost of honor, that selling of everything . . . that lack of concern for the general good. . . . These are reproaches that affect a great part of your Jewish people. I do not conceal it from you that I should like the Germans to learn to be free of a revolting oriental stamp that cannot ever be in accord with the Germanic.[22]

Ghillany's invectives provoked several spirited replies from Jewish and other authors;[23] but by 1844 the polemic had broadened into a general debate on the whole relationship between Young Hegelian revolutionism and the Jewish Question. And in this arena Ghillany himself deferred to the philosophical *enfant terrible* recognized as the leader of the anti-Jewish school: Bruno Bauer.[24]

---

The "critical" discussion of the Jewish Question in 1843–44 produced new perceptions in the sphere of political revolutionism, often in contradictory forms. Bruno Bauer's political revolutionism demanded a "free state" that would be entirely rational, and so exclude

[21] Ghillany, dedication to *Judenfrage*. Cf. Stock, *Judenfrage*, pp. 406ff.

[22] *Judenthum und Kritik*, p. 55. Cf. Stock, *Judenfrage*, p. 420.

Ghillany was one of the first to develop the idée fixe of Jewish control of the German press ("60 percent Jewish domination of the press"). Cf. *Judenthum und Kritik*, preface, p. xxi; Stock, *Judenfrage*, pp. 412ff.

[23] For example, H. S. H. [Hirschfeld], *Molochsglaube und Religionsschandung: Eine notwendige Schrift für Herrn Ghillany und die Leser seiner Werke. Eine Abfertigung der Schrift "Das Judentum und die Kritik"* (Wollstein, 1844). Other replies are listed in V. Eichstädt, *Bibliographie zur Geschichte der Judenfrage* (Hamburg, 1938), nos. 1306ff.

[24] For Ghillany's defense of Bauer, see N. Rotenstreich, "For and Against Emancipation: The Bruno Bauer Controversy," *LBIY* 4 (1959): 3–36, especially pp. 18ff.; idem, *Jews and German Philosophy* (New York, 1984), pp. 91–94.

the irrational Jews as a matter of course. In his frantic attacks on the established Prussian state, Bauer gives the impression of being a "left-wing" revolutionary, but in fact he was a revolutionist of a different sort. In his subsequent career he developed quite naturally into an antisemitic racist and aggressive German nationalist preacher of *Realpolitik*. His contemporary, Wilhelm Marr, on the other hand, was an admitted communist revolutionary in the 1840s, but, equally naturally, he also had moved into racist antisemitism by the 1860s. Both Bauer and Marr were very active in the antisemitic campaigns of the 1870s, though belonging to different formal political wings. As always, it is dangerous to apply to German revolutionism the simple "left" and "right" labels of Western liberal politics.

The most notable political revolutionism to emerge from the critical debates was, of course, the socialist school. In the first flush of revolutionary socialist consciousness, both Karl Marx and Moses Hess devised their violently anti-Jewish tracts of 1843–45. These outbursts were not purely accidental, however, but grew out of the very logic of their revolutionism, in which the Jewish Question was embedded. It was a style of revolutionism that Marx learned at the feet of his teacher Bruno Bauer. Indeed, Bauer's own critique of Judaism in 1843 had forced Marx to work out his own analysis, not only of Judaism, but arguably of civil society in general.

Yet the socialist revolutionism of the 1840s was not confined to the atheist circles of Marx and Hess and their colleague Wilhelm Marr. A form of Christian religious communism also flourished in the 1840s, led by the revolutionary Wilhelm Weitling (1808–71). Weitling tried to apply Strauss's notion of a humanizing Jesus to the social realm with his *Gospel of a Poor Sinner* (1843, published 1845), which announced that "the principle of Jesus is the principle of freedom and happiness." Christ had come to launch a revolutionary campaign against hypocrisy and materialism. Jesus as revolutionary proclaimed the kingdom of heaven, which was actually to be a human society founded on brotherhood and love. Now communism would bring this about through the destruction of the sovereignty of money. Jesus Himself was thus the founder of communism, the prophet of the abolition of property, the enemy of Mammon. The prospectus of this interesting book was enough to have Weitling arrested in Zurich for blasphemy and incitement, though in the end he was merely sentenced to a short term in prison for being a public nuisance and exiled. The 1848 revolution proved a great disappointment and he blamed its failure on its leaders—particularly the Jews—who had really represented the "old moneybags" rather than freedom. Later, when in America, Weitling would observe that the German Jews who had preceded him there were "not a favorable factor for ennobling the German element."[25]

From the start, however, the Christian element in Weitling's thought had been intrinsically anti-Jewish, based as it was on the idea that the Jews were the forces of Mammon whom Jesus' revolution was destined to smash. Weitling's case was quite a cause célèbre in 1843–44, but even before the scandal broke Richard Wagner had arrived at an identical vision of Christianity as a utopian socialist creed. In his choral work, *The Love Feast of the Apostles* in 1843, Wagner depicted a communistic society based on love, a new revolutionary form of Christianity. In 1848, with the outbreak of the long-awaited revolution itself, Wagner returned in his projected opera *Jesus of Nazareth* to this idea of a revolutionary socialist Jesus clearing away the corruption of a moneyed egoistic society and redeeming human freedom from the toils of Judaism.[26]

[25] See C. Wittke, *The Utopian Communist: A Biography of Wilhelm Weitling, Nineteenth Century Reformer* (Baton Rouge, 1950), pp. 72–84, 134ff., 169ff.; W. O. Shanahan, *German Protestants Face the Social Question* (Notre Dame, 1954), pp. 168–75; G. M. Bravo, *Wilhelm Weitling e il communismo tedesco prima del Quarantotto* (Turin, 1963).

Weitling's book appeared eventually at Bern in 1845 (*Das Evangelium eines armen Sünders*, repr. Leipzig, 1967).

Weitling's belief in the purifying destructive power of the "people" influenced Bakunin's "conversion" to revolutionism. See A. P. Mendel, *Michael Bakunin: The Roots of Apocalypse* (New York, 1981), pp. 192ff.

[26] See below, chap. 20.

# Revolution to Race I: Bruno Bauer
# and the Critical Revolution

T
HE CAREER of Bruno Bauer (1809–82) vividly demonstrates the
intimate connection between revolutionism and racism in the
German tradition. Bauer began as a radical professor preaching a
critical, rational revolution that would destroy theology and institute
a "free state"; by the 1850s he had developed this program into a
campaign for a rationalist, but reactionary revolution in Germany;
and by the 1870s he was urging an aggressive militaristic crusade that
would enable German revolutionary "freedom" to dominate Europe.

In each of these stages of Bauer's revolutionism, the Jewish Question was ineluctably present. This was inevitable, considering how
deeply Bauer's secular German revolutionism was imbued with the
basic thought patterns of that Christian theology which it sought so
fiercely to eradicate. Theological concepts such as salvation and redemption were transformed by Bauer into rationalist secular themes,
but the structure of ideas was kept intact and the emotional charge
remained. This applied especially to the fateful role of the Jews,
which had now received a new "critical" definition. The old Christian
glosses of Jewish stubbornness, sinfulness, and perpetual servitude
were given fresh new philosophical clothing. This propaganda process began with Bauer's notorious essay of 1843 on *The Jewish Question*, whose title effectively standardized the very name of the debate
on the status of Jews in Germany. As Bauer in his journalism translated his critical revolutionism successively into more and more practical political terms, he developed the concept of a coherent "political
antisemitism" that would implement the insights of critical revolutionary antisemitism in the real world. Political antisemitism, through
its media manipulation of mass radical politics and its parallel promotion of pressure groups among the elites, set the pattern of a modern populist revolutionary political culture in Germany.[1]

[1] See J. Carlebach, *Karl Marx and the Radical Critique of Judaism* (London, 1978), chap.
7; R. Wistrich, *Socialism and the Jews* (London, 1982), pp. 19–25, for Bauer's impact on
major antisemitic propagandists including Marr and Dühring. In general, E. Barnikol,
*Bruno Bauer: Studien und Materialen* (Assen, 1972); Z. Rosen, *Bruno Bauer and Karl Marx*
(The Hague, 1977); W. Brazill, *The Young Hegelians* (New Haven, 1970), chap. 5.

Bauer started out as a conventional Young Hegelian interested in the philosophical interpretation of religion, but by 1841 he had made a radical departure from this intellectual position, as well as an enforced departure from his university chair at Bonn. Rather unconventionally for a professor of theology, Bauer had demanded the abolition of religion and a "reign of critical terror" that would finally free human self-consciousness from its corrupting bondage to traditional religion. The young "Robespierre of theology" intended that the sword of this great revolution was to be the "critical intellect." As he wrote to his erstwhile student Karl Marx in 1841, "the terrorism of pure theory will clear the field."[2]

Bauer's atheistic crusade began in earnest in 1841 with a *Critique of the Synoptic Gospels* that exposed—far more stridently than had Strauss—the mythological character of the New Testament. This work, written with the arrogance that marked all of his writings, was fed with an intense scorn and hatred of Judaism that predated his conversion to "critical atheism." In *Religion of the Old Testament* (1838), written during his conventionally Hegelian phase, Bauer had taken the customary line that the ancient Jews had lacked true moral awareness and freedom, in bondage as they always were to an external deity or Law. By comparison, Greco-Roman religious consciousness had been more advanced and "human" in its awareness of man as an independently moral being capable of freeing himself. Christianity, the religion of love and freedom, had issued from classical culture, rather than from Jewish religion.[3] Bauer pursued this notion in a tract against *Herr Hengstenberg* (1839), a Protestant theologian who had erred in seeing Christianity as a continuation of Judaism and who had emphasized that the theme of love is to be found in the Old Testament. Bauer would have none of this and insisted that Christianity was a qualitatively new religion of love and freedom that had abandoned the main principles of Judaism, namely utility and egoism. Anticipating Feuerbach, Bauer saw Jewish religion merely as a means of satisfying the egoistic, selfish needs of ancient and modern Jews. Judaism, for all its weak strains of universal love in the prophetic books of the Bible, was tribal and extremely limited. It represented enslave-

[2] Quoted by J. E. Toews, *Hegelianism: The Path toward Dialectical Humanism, 1805–1841* (Cambridge, 1980), p. 317.

[3] J. Katz, *From Prejudice to Destruction: Anti-Semitism 1700–1933* (Cambridge, Mass., 1980), exaggerates Bauer's protectiveness towards the Old Testament during this first period. But see Z. Rosen, "The Anti-Jewish Opinions of Bruno Bauer 1838–43: Their Sources and Significance," *Zion* 33 (1968): 59–76 (Hebrew, with English summary, pp. iv–v).

ment to a coercive, irrational, external Law from which Christianity had freed itself.[4]

The next two years saw a critical expansion of this hostile picture. Realizing suddenly that all consciousness had to be stripped of its religious impedimenta if man were to make himself truly free of his enslavement of outside powers and images, Bauer launched an attack on Christianity. This meant that the grounds of his refutation of Judaism also had to change. In the new war against all religion, Judaism was seen as the source of disasters and errors, the evil progenitor of a bad Christianity (which was nevertheless still an improvement on its parent religion). Otherwise the argument stayed the same: the essence of Judaism remained the natural messianic spirit of the Jews, which was "oriental" in its lack of genuine moral freedom and its dependence on "God." A static Jewish essence survived into the present, unable to accept the changing tides of history. Judaism was as antihistorical as it was antihuman.

In this radicalization of Hegel's thought Bauer sought to prove that atheism had all along been the secret message of the philosopher. The new "Left Hegelianism" was proclaimed (anonymously) by Bauer in 1841 in *The Trumpet-Blast of the Last Judgment on Hegel the Atheist and Anti-Christian*, of which one chapter was devoted to Hegel's necessary "Hatred against Judaism":

> If art and rejoicing in it be the exposure of the mysteries of religion
> . . . then certainly should Hegel hate Judaism. Art resounds in man,
> freeing him from the vice of religion [present] in Judaism as in all re-
> ligions. . . . The foundation of Jewish religion, says Hegel, is fear of
> the Lord; thus is self-consciousness totally blocked . . . by a pure and
> fearful egoism . . . the egoism of Judaism. . . . The content of this reli-
> gion of egoism is "Possession, which receives here an eternally abso-
> lute justification, a divine justification." . . . Possession is irrational.
> Possession is abstract obedience, without innerness. . . . For this reason
> Hegel was a greater friend of Greek religion than of Judaism.[5]

Bauer's appreciation of the negative significance of Judaism in the struggle for human freedom induced him to spend much of 1842 reading the literature of the last century on the Jewish Question. He was subsequently able to come up with the "true solution" that had eluded all the earlier disputants. "All that the Jew-lovers and the Jews have done until now," he informed Arnold Ruge, the radical editor

[4] Cf. Rosen, *Bauer and Marx*, pp. 42ff.
[5] *Die Posaune des jüngsten Gerichts über Hegel den Atheisten und Antichristen* (Leipzig, 1841), pp. 109–13.

of the *Halle Yearbooks* (now renamed the *German Yearbooks*), "has been done as though criticism did not exist."[6] The first of these critical lucubrations appeared as "The Jewish Question" in the *German Yearbooks* in November 1842 and was immediately reissued separately in an expanded edition early the next year.[7]

By now Bauer was a "metaphysical revolutionary," possessed by a quasi-religious faith in revolution, and he saw the Jewish Question as part of the general problem of revolution and redemption. Emancipationists who sought to solve the question by specific political reforms, he pronounced, were anxious only for a "false peace." Only the emancipation of society into free self-consciousness and full humanity—to be brought about by the abolition of both Judaism and Christianity, those religious distortions of consciousness—could ensure a true pacification of the Jewish Question:

> The emancipation of the Jew in a thorough, successful and secure fashion is only possible if they will be emancipated not as Jews, that is, as beings who must forever remain alien to Christians, but rather as human beings who will not be separated from their fellow-creatures through some barriers which they falsely deem to be essential. . . .
> The emancipation problem has until now been treated in a basically wrong manner by considering it one-sidedly as the Jewish problem.
> . . . The problem of emancipation is a general problem—it is *the* problem of our age. (pp. 62f.)

As long as one treats Judaism and Christianity as equally bad in their different ways, it might be possible to argue this line without falling into Jew-hatred. Indeed, Bauer admits the Christians have their faults, not the least of which has been their keenness to persecute the Jews. But then Bauer shows his prejudice. Christian failings, he argues, pale into insignificance beside the ingrown vices of the Jews that have attracted—and almost merited—persecution by the Christians. All the various manifestations of Jewish vice can be

---

[6] Letter quoted in Katz, *From Prejudice*, p. 167. Barnikol, *Bauer Studien*, pp. 71ff.

[7] "Die Judenfrage," in *Deutsche Jahrbücher für Wissenschaft und Kunst*, nos. 274–82, (November 1842); reissued in a separate enlarged edition, *Die Judenfrage* (Brunswick, 1843). Page references in the text are to the English translation by H. Lederer, *The Jewish Problem* (Cincinnati, 1958).

See N. Rotenstreich, "For and against Emancipation: The Bruno Bauer Controversy," *LBIY* 4 (1959): 3–36; Katz, *From Prejudice*, pp. 167ff.; Carlebach, *Marx and the Radical Critique*, pp. 125–47.

For general reflections on the relationship between the anti-Christian and anti-Jewish feelings of the atheists and their associates, see U. Tal, "Anti-Christian Anti-Semitism," in *The Catastrophe of European Jewry*, ed. Y. Gutman and L. Rothkirchen (New York, 1976), pp. 90–126.

summed up in the one classic quality so long attributed by theologians to the Jews, and that is stubbornness. Of course, Bauer is not interested in the old Christian idea of Jewish obstinacy, but rather in the new advanced Kantian and Hegelian theories that interpret Jewish tenacity under historical and moral headings. On this critical basis Bauer now finds the Jews to be guilty of two things: they have stubbornly refused to submit to the life force of historical change; and they have been unrepentant in their adherence to a code of coercive Law, which has prevented them becoming morally free. It is a stubbornness that has been nurtured by both their history and their religion. The result is an enduring and impermeable Jewish "spirit" or "essence":

> The basis of the stubborn Jewish national spirit is its inability to de-
> velop with history. This explains the quite unhistorical character of
> that nation, and it is due in turn to its oriental nature. Such stationary
> nations exist in the orient . . . where man does not yet know that he is
> free and gifted with reason. . . . The [coercive irrational] Law has
> fenced the Jews off from the influences of history. (pp. 12f.)

Bauer's starting point is the claim that Judaism has been privileged in its immunity from "criticism." While Christians are expected to give up their prejudices against the Jews, the Jews are not expected to reciprocate:

> The heart of Judaism remains untouched. . . . Are the Jews to suffer
> no pain? Are they to have equal rights with those who fought and suf-
> fered for the new world? As if that could be! As if they could feel at
> home in a world which they did not help to make, which is contrary to
> their unchanged nature! . . . Nobody who has not gone through the
> flames of criticism will be able to enter the new world which will soon
> come. . . . If the criticism seems harsh, or really is harsh, still it will
> lead to freedom and nothing else will. (pp. 2–4)

It is the stubborn refusal of the Jews to change—"their clinging to their nationality and their resistance of the movements and changes of history"—that has provoked universal hostility to them. They are, therefore, to blame for their own misfortunes (p. 5). Their stubborn, irrational fight against "the first law of history"—that is, change and progress—has promoted one of the most deadly features of Judaism—its exclusiveness. The Jews have always hated other nations, says Bauer, and their grasp of reality has now become so warped by their false Jewish conception of themselves as the chosen race that even if given complete freedom now, they will always ruin it as long as they remain Jews. "Therefore, they are of necessity oppressed and their suffering is incurable" (p. 16).

Nor can this oppression be relieved by constitutional means. Because the Jew, like the confessing Christian, is first a religious believer rather than a human being and segregates himself from humanity voluntarily, he cannot be granted *human* rights. As to *civil* rights, in the unfree Christian state there are no true civil rights. The Jews already have the special civil right of being allowed to live in a Christian state without being Christians; they are privileged enough (pp. 20ff.).

Bauer now proceeds to a lengthy malicious critique of Judaism that attempts to destroy all claims of the Jews to dignity. Their Old Testament is derided as lacking the concept of love; they are scorned as cruel without being courageous in war; they are credited with exclusiveness instead of a true "national feeling." The Law itself is dismissed as a shambles because the Jews do not bother to obey it. Bauer's box of critical tricks enables him to perform some clever sleight of mind, but it is not difficult to see that what is at stake here is not the truth, but rather Bauer's hunger to defame and destroy his opponents. As with so many sophisticated works of Jew-hatred, it is the intent rather than the formal content that is important. Specific refutation is pointless.

How is the Jew to redeem himself from this quagmire of failure and become free? Baptism is no answer, for it merely imposes a less evil form of religious consciousness. Nor is there any point in trying to "humanize" Judaism. As long as one accepts even a humanized, universal Moses, the acceptance of an external Law of the Ten Commandments is entailed and with it the denial of real freedom. The reform of Judaism is, therefore, just as much a futile contradiction in terms as "reformed Jehovism" had been for Ghillany. The criticism of Judaism must mean its destruction, not its reform:

> There can be no doubt about what the Jew has to do—beside us and with us—if he is serious in his wish for freedom. . . . He has to make the cause of humanity his own. . . . He has to tear up by the roots the idea that he is the only one oppressed. (pp. 97f.)

But Bauer makes sure his readers understand that the Jewish feeling of caste and their narrow-mindedness together conspire to render such a self-redemption virtually impossible (pp. 106ff.). Moreover, Bauer remarks for good measure, "we have yet to describe the sophistry of the Jews which makes it impossible for them to accept freedom sincerely even if it were to be given to them" (p. 113).

Bauer's "Jewish Question" contains many harbingers of the main themes of later antisemitism. Jewish essence is dismissed, à la Wagner, as sterile in the arts and sciences because these are not considered to be "practical" pursuits (pp. 11, 52). Egoism and utility are seen as general principles of civil society, but are nevertheless principles that have become in the form of usury the special domain of the Jews (p. 10). The specter of Jewish world domination through financial power is raised (p. 123).

But perhaps the most sinister theme is the new radical argument against the liberal state. Jews and Christians, alleges Bauer, can never coexist, for their respective religious consciousnesses are exclusive of one another. Only a totally new revolutionary "free state" based on universal human liberation (that is, philosophical atheism) can bring the Jews emancipation, a state from which irrational Judaism and Christianity must disappear, leaving only "human beings." Only human beings can grant and receive human rights and so, as long as there remain Jews and Christians as such, no real rights can exist (pp. 21ff., 56ff.). Thus, all hopes for Jewish advancement in the current liberal state are cut off; any such rights as they are granted are merely "special" and "legalistic" and are given at the pleasure of the government. The redemption of the Jews, therefore, may only consist in the self-destruction of their identity as Jews in the coming rational "free state."

There flow from this revolutionary position the wellsprings of a new river of Jew-hatred, that is, hatred of the Jews as the embodiment of the liberal capitalist state. For as long as the Jews are seeking only liberal toleration and equal rights, they are acting true to their role as parasites. "They have struck roots in the gaps and crevices of society and have entrapped the victims of the element of insecurity of civil life," remarks Bauer just after mentioning the Jewish specialization in usury. Liberal emancipation is nothing but a paltry emancipation intended to consolidate egoistic Jewish interest, a legalistic emancipation that rebels against the law of historical change that drives man on to true human liberation. Jewish emancipation is, in fact, the enemy of German political freedom! As we shall see, Marx did not take long to recognize the significance of these hints of Bauer's about the connections between Judaism and capitalism.

A few months after the appearance of "The Jewish Question," Bauer's dedication to the revolutionary "free state" led him to contribute an article to the collection of radical and socialist manifestoes entitled *Twenty-One Folios from Switzerland* (1843), which also included inflammatory theoretical calls to revolution by such firebrands as Moses Hess, the "communist rabbi." Bauer's piece, "The Capacity of Present-day Jews and Christians to Become Free," elaborated his earlier opinion that Jews could never become free in the Christian—or for that matter, the liberal—state, but only in the totally "free" state.[8] "The demand of the Jews to be free [through the granting of civil rights] is as meaningless as that of blacks to become white; it is a demand to stay unfree." All religious consciousness must be shed by those who join the "free state." To attain "freedom," the Jews must first criticize themselves out of existence.

Not surprisingly, the Jews have far less capacity than the Christians to become free, according to Bauer. Besides overcoming their prevailing Jewishness, the Jews have to progress through two stages—firstly, to abandon their Law and Judaism; secondly, to acquire and then transcend a Christianity that is itself on the point of critical dissolution into atheism and free humanity. A new consciousness, and not baptism, is the Jew's entry ticket to European culture. "Nothing is impossible for man," Bauer concludes optimistically, but his magnanimity scarcely masks the fact that he has enlisted historical, theological, economic, and political pretexts to prove that the Jew is an inferior man and citizen to the Christian. The tempting prospect of redemption in the free state that Bauer holds out to the Jew is merely a cruel logical joke. The article is simply a text on resentment.

*Twenty-One Folios* was promptly banned by the Swiss censor for its radicalism. So also was a more violently antireligious treatise, *Christianity Unmasked*, in which Bauer took upon himself the writing of the critical riposte to Eisenmenger's *Judaism Unmasked*, which the incapable Jews had failed to write themselves. "Very extremist" was how he described this critical effort to destroy all religion. In blasphemous pages of searing arrogance, Bauer disposed of Christianity as the religion *par excellence* of hatred, exclusiveness, and self-love. While the Jews receded into the background of the polemic, they were still held ultimately responsible for the evil of Christianity because it was they who had engendered it and endowed it with its most noxious qualities.[9]

The intervention of the Swiss censor Bluentschli during June and July 1843 in the matters of *Twenty-One Folios, Christianity Unmasked*, and also Weitling's *Gospel of a Poor Sinner* (with its revolutionary, socialist Christ) had the effect of creating lively discussion all over Ger-

---

[8] "Die Fähigkeit der heutigen Juden und Christen, frei zu werden," in G. Herwegh, ed., *Einundzwanzig Bogen aus der Schweiz* (Zurich, 1843), pp. 56–71.

[9] The edition was destroyed, but Barnikol was able to reprint the work from the few surviving copies as *Das Entdeckte Christentum im Vormärz. Bruno Bauers Kampf gegen Religion und Christentum und Erstausgabe seiner Kampfschrift* (Jena, 1927). See idem, "Bruno Bauers Kampf gegen Religion und Christentum und die Spaltung der vormärzlichen preussischen Opposition," *Zeitschrift für Kirchengeschichte* 46 (1927–28): 1–34. Bauer implied his intention to write the treatise in *The Jewish Problem*, p. 89.

many about their themes even if the books could not be had.[10] Though always denying that he was prejudiced against the Jews and pretending merely to be explaining the facts "critically," Bauer's sensational writings had by the end of 1844 aroused a sharp controversy in which he found himself under attack from Jews, Christians, and liberals alike; only communists like Hess and Marx could really sympathize with his projected free state. But Bauer was soon to tire of his radical socialist bedfellows, and after the debacle of 1848, he found a new wrinkle to his revolutionary struggle against Judaism.[11] Having dismissed the "entire revolution of 1848 as a fraud," Bauer gravitated towards the Prussian conservative circle led by Hermann Wagener and became a scathing, though often anonymous, contributor to such publications as the *Berliner Revue*, where he denounced Berthold Auerbach as a "court-Jew," commented on "German Patience and Jewish Audacity," and related "Disraeli's Napoleonism and the Jewish Character in his Novels."[12]

Bauer's switch from revolution to reaction was not as real as it seems. He had never been a socialist, nor a liberal (although he had many supporters in those camps as a result of his dismissal from his chair), and he had in any case kept very vague his ideas about the exact nature of the longed-for revolutionary free state. Bauer's was really a destructive, anarchic intellect that had latched onto religion— particularly Judaism—as a rich subject for critical dissection and abuse. Lacking all moral integrity, Bauer would cheerfully rationalize any position that pandered to his own prejudices. (David Strauss commented that "Bauer was a scoundrel in every possible respect.")[13] Bauer might justify his apparent move to the "right" by arguing that the differences between Young Hegelian and Prussian conservatives were merely superficial. In what was essential—namely, the rejection of the liberal state—both "critic" and "conservative" were in fast agreement. This was especially evident in the case of their attitude to one of the central tests of the liberal state, the Jewish Question. By attacking the Jews, Bauer was continuing his criticism of the liberal state, just as were, in their own way, his newfound Christian conser-

[10] See Barnikol, "Bauers Kampf," pp. 5–8; idem, *Das Entdeckte Christentum im Vormärz*, pp. 10ff. There is a chapter on Weitling in Bauer's *Complete History of the Party Conflicts in Germany 1842–1846* (Berlin, 1847), 3:30–63. He despised Weitling's fantasies as messianic delusions, but Feuerbach was enchanted by them (see above, chap. 14).

[11] Marx's polemic against Bauer, *The Holy Family* (1845), observed that "Bauer's belief in Jehovah has been transformed into a belief in the Prussian state." The early date is significant for Bauer's long-standing tendency to the antiliberal reaction.

[12] "Berthold Auerbach als Hofjude," *Berliner Revue* 23 (1860): 393–95 (see above, chap. 13). See Barnikol, *Bauer Studien*, pp. 347–53, for the various articles.

[13] Quoted by Toews, *Hegelianism*, p. 289.

vative friends, who also repudiated the emancipation of the Jews. Bauer, however, was cunning enough to refrain from stating in his later articles that once Judaism had been disposed of, Christianity would have to follow it on the road to oblivion. Bauer's association with the Prussian conservatives was thus rationalized as the pursuit of his revolutionary principles of the free state and antisemitism.

The radical conservatives took quickly to Bauer's anti-Jewish views and indeed Hermann Wagener himself enlisted Bauer as his advisor in a pseudonymous tract, *The Jews and the German State*, which became a classic document of Jew-hatred and went through more than twenty editions in the next half-century.[14] What helped to smooth this marriage, however, were certain important changes that had taken place in the minds of Bauer and German conservatives alike after 1848. The Prussian conservatism of the 1840s had been dominated by the "Christian state" constitutional theories of Friedrich Julius Stahl, which proposed that Jews had only to be baptized to become full citizens of the constitutional state. The reaction, led by Hermann Wagener and his friends, now regressed to an earlier Germanic tradition, strong at the beginning of the century, which held that Jews and Germans were so intrinsically different in their history and character that the Jews could never truly become part of the Germanic state. Germanness (*Deutschtum*) lay outside the reach of Jews, baptized or not. Race was thus made the foundation of the new phase of revolutionary antisemitism launched by Bauer and his conservative allies in the 1850s.[15] Bauer had preached a genuine racist concept as early as 1853 in his *Russia and Germanism*, in which he had argued that racial mixing (as long as it did not involve Jews) is essential for giving a *Volk* the "moral and intellectual elasticity necessary to attain world dominion." At that time, Russia alone had seemed to have this quality and Bauer contrasted her to the spurious world dominion attempted by the English and French, who were governed by Jewish thinking and Jewish money and led by the Jew Disraeli and the secret Jew Napoleon III.[16] With the rise of Bismarck, however, Bauer transferred his admiration from Russia to Germany, seeing the Germans alone as possessed of the proper racial character needed to form a true *rational* master nation.

[14] *Die Juden und der deutsche Staat* (Berlin, 1861), author variously given as "J. Nordmann" and "H. Naudh." See Katz, *From Prejudice*, pp. 213ff. (see below, chap. 18, n. 55). Moses Hess saw Bauer's hand in the tract.

[15] Barnikol, *Bauer Studien*, pp. 347ff.; W. O. Shanahan, *German Protestants Face the Social Question* (Notre Dame, 1954), pp. 272–80, 363ff.

[16] *Russland und das Germanentum* (Charlottenburg, 1853), cited by Barnikol, *Bauer Studien*, pp. 317f.

Bauer's new racial outlook emerged most abusively in a long article that he wrote for Hermann Wagener's *State and Social Dictionary* in 1862, and which was reissued as a separate booklet the following year under the title *Judaism Abroad*.[17] It was a catalog of all the vices that made the Jew the enemy of "the true human being of the future." The general interpretation of Jewish "stubbornness" was rehearsed from Bauer's 1843 *The Jewish Question* but in even more hateful terms. (About this earlier work, however, Bauer now remains reticient, probably because its incidental sneers at Christianity would not have been welcome to some of his new conservative audience.) Jewish stubbornness and exclusiveness and the refusal to join the freedom-giving tide of history have produced the peculiarly unhappy Jewish psychology. Isolation from the real world as it changes and progresses has generated the characteristically Jewish combination of pride and bitterness; the Jew is proud to be apart from the world of the gentiles, but bitter at being excluded from it.

But now Bauer introduces the fundamental racist principle that physical characteristics determine—or at least are indissociable from—the mind. Thus, their stubbornness and their unique psychology are innate to the Jews; their different bodies and blood evince their peculiar passions and intellect. Bauer devotes pages (pp. 10ff.) to enlarging on Jewish physiognomy and how it betrays their repellent mental characteristics. One of his less offensive remarks refers to the "fire in the Jew's eye that is restless and piercing; there is neither stability nor steadfastness there." Like Wagner, Bauer turns unpleasing Jewish speech traits into the result of Jewish oral physiognomy and at the same time views them as the symptom of a degenerate mentality.

According to Bauer, genuine mixture of the Jewish and German races is impossible, for where the Jews are involved, it is a one-way process: Europeans can be "Jewified," but the Jew cannot be truly Germanized:

> His flesh and blood and the rest of his personality protect the Jew
> [from being Germanized]. . . . The life and soul of the Jews are totally
> cut off from ours. . . . The Jewish race has in reality a different blood
> from that of the Christian peoples of Europe, a different body and a
> different constitution, different feelings and longings. And with this

[17] *Judentum in der Fremde* (Berlin, 1863). Page references in text to this edition. Originally printed in *Staats- und Gesellschafts-Lexikon*, ed. H. Wagener (Berlin, 1859–67), 10:599–692. See N. Rotenstreich, *Jews and German Philosophy* (New York, 1984), pp. 101–7, for Bauer's transition to racism; idem, "The Bruno Bauer Controversy," pp. 32–36. For the book's impact, see Katz, *From Prejudice*, pp. 213–18.

different physical body goes that alienation to which the race was doomed not just since the fall of Jerusalem, but since the very beginning of its existence. (pp. 8f.)

This is the *racial* meaning of Ahasverus, whose crime is now seen to predate his scorning of Christ. The crime of Ahasverus had afflicted the Jewish people from their origin as a race and was eternal, permitted no redemption except physical destruction.

Almost despite himself, however, Bauer still admits that the Jews have undergone a historical development (naturally for the worse) since the time of Christ. For since Ahasverus and his people have begun their wanderings, their character has degenerated even further because they have become parasites without a fatherland of their own. And as universal parasites, they have sought to dominate their hosts and the whole world in a struggle for world dominion for which they strive by cultural, moral, and political subversion. Identifying the Jew as the subversive revolutionary demon was a congenial theme to conservatives. But Bauer, of course, was not abandoning his own idolatry of revolution. For Bauer, as for Wagner, the "Jewish revolutionism" of Börne and Heine was, unlike the true "German revolutionism" of Fichte and himself, a negative, unhealthy, force.[18]

Using Ahasverus as his primary symbol, Bauer smoothly associates the sick revolutionary instincts of the Jews with that psychological alienation and restlessness which are the result of their refusal to accept the verdict of history:

> The embitterment that has taken possession of the Jewish soul since antiquity is to be seen in their revolutionary disposition and agitation against Christianity and the whole Christian world order. . . . The Jew, the *Ewiger Jude*, the purest and most unadulterated representative of the ancient world, the bearer of anger and chagrin at a two-thousand-year-long history that has been made without him and against his will, is thus the friend of every revolution. . . . For the anger and vexation of the Jew there is no healing or appeasement. The *Ewiger Jude* cannot be helped. He is ashamed equally of the antiquity and the blood that give him his pride and revolutionary right. He is, therefore, proud of being a Jew and yet ashamed of being a Jew and being called a Jew. (pp. 1–3)

[18] Cf. the image of Ahasverus as Jewish revolutionist in Cruciger's *Newest Wanderings* of 1830 (above, chap. 9). Wagner also condemned the false "Judeo-French" revolutionism of Börne as compared with the authentic German revolutionism of the *Burschenschaften* in *What Is German?* and *German Art and German Politics*, PW, 4:92f., 165f. See below, chap. 20.

We may call the Jew eternally young, observes Bauer, but he is really an exhausted old youth (pp. 18f.).

Nevertheless, this exhausted race of wandering Jews hopes for its redemption by revolution. For them the age of revolution is "the labor pains of the messianic time, an unmistakable harbinger of their world dominion." Revolution has been the specialty of the Jews; since antiquity they have been a "virus of disintegration" and now they seek the destruction of the national solidarity of their hosts. But even this they do not bravely, but exploitatively and insidiously, through their satire ("the repulsive insolence of Börne and Heine"), their cosmopolitanism, their pacifism, the class war that they foment—and "the mixture of racial blood." They are an antirace, alienated from humanity and incapable of organic life, capable only of exterminating the organic life of the healthy German nation. Indeed, through the dissolution of their own religion over the years, the Jews are no longer really a nation at all, but a deadly "dust living in the pores of healthy organisms."[19]

If the Jews were for Bauer an absolutely unassimilable element in Germany, what was to be the solution to the Jewish Question? Firstly, as the radical conservatives argued, one should immediately revoke the emancipationist legislation that removed the barriers to public office. "Let not the offices of dignity and conscience," intoned Bauer, "degenerate into business pursuits." But were the Jews, if they could not be assimilated, to be expelled from Germany? (We are back with the grim alternatives explained by Laube.) Bauer's answer to this problem was his usual cynicism. Let their selfish business minds serve the interests of German society: "The Lord of this world needs the Jews in order to accomplish His finite and profane objectives. . . . Were it not for the Jews, all of us would have to take their place!" (p. 77).

Bauer's adherence to the concept of race was not purely arbitrary. On the contrary, racial theory was the logical fulfillment of two of Bauer's long-standing intellectual concerns. One of these was his Kantian characterization of Jewish religion as "oriental" in that it was based on an unfree subservience to an external God or Law.[20] Judaism, an Asiatic religion, seemed to have been smuggled into a Europe where it did not belong. With it came all those particularly Jewish habits and vices that were the epiphenomena of the religion. The

---

[19] Cf. J. L. Talmon, *The Unique and the Universal* (London, 1965), pp. 153ff.

[20] *The Jewish Problem*, p. 60, for instance, remarks on the oriental character of the Jews.

philosophical critique of "oriental" religion, therefore, was one factor that guided Bauer to his racial theory.

The other factor was Bauer's atheistic materialism. Given the fact that materialism reduced spirit and religion to matter, one should not be surprised to find Bauer reducing the "oriental" essence of Jewish religion to something immanent in the physical body of the Jew. In *Twenty-One Folios*, Bauer had compared the Jew's desire to remain Jewish and be free with a black's wish to become white.[21] Now, in *Judaism Abroad*, the metaphor became a physical statement of race: "The Jew is a white negro, with a larger brain than the black." This natural propensity of materialism to lead often to racism can be seen at work also in the thought of Karl Marx, who was himself enamored of the phrase "the white negro." As Tocqueville was to explain repeatedly to no avail in his correspondence with Gobineau, racism and materialism are intimately linked with one another.[22]

Bauer's *Judaism Abroad* signaled the arrival of a new phase of revolutionary antisemitism where nearly all future discussion of the Jewish Question was established on a racial basis. It was not by coincidence that 1862–63, the years of Bauer's tract, saw also the publication of two other books that advanced strongly racial analyses of the Jewish Question—one by Wilhelm Marr following in the footsteps of Bauer, the other by Moses Hess taking a fervently pro-Jewish stand. But neither of these writers was to succeed in inaugurating a widespread public debate on the Jewish Question. It was only after Richard Wagner's reissue of *Judaism in Music* in 1869 and the unification of Germany in 1870–71 that the writings of Bauer and Marr finally attracted German public interest. (Hess's *Rome and Jerusalem*, however, had to wait another twenty years for its impact to become felt thanks to the activities of Theodor Herzl.)

Where the antisemitism of *Judaism Abroad* had been aimed at the Prussian conservative opposition to the liberal state, the context of Bauer's Antisemitic Campaign polemics of the 1870s was the "world-political" struggle between the new German Empire and the other great powers. *Disraeli's Romantic and Bismarck's Social Imperialism*, published in 1882, the year of Bauer's death, developed an argument first outlined by Bauer in 1853 in his *Russia and Germanism*.[23] Analyzing the "racial secret" of Disraeli's novels, Bauer argued that they

[21] Bauer, "Fähigkeit," p. 57.

[22] A. de Tocqueville, *The European Revolution and Correspondence with Gobineau*, trans. J. Lukacs (New York, 1959), pp. 221ff. Cf. D. Paul, " 'In the Interests of Civilization': Marxist Views of Race and Culture in the Nineteenth Century," *Journal of the History of Ideas* 42 (1981), 115–38, especially pp. 128ff.

[23] *Disraelis romantischer und Bismarcks sozialistischer Imperialismus* (Chemnitz, 1882), pp. 33–63. Cf. Barnikol, *Bauer Studien*, pp. 393–407. For the remarks of 1853, see above.

contained the essence of Jewish racial ambitions, which had become manifest in British imperial policy, a policy based on money and debased Jewish concepts of national heroism. Nor was it accidental that Disraeli was a Conservative leader: "The Toryism of the Jews lies in their blood," while for their part the Tories' addiction to bishops leads them to subscribe through their new leader to the growth of the "Church of Jerusalem," which sees Jesus as a Semitic Jew (pp. 54f.). Disraeli has smuggled into a receptive England all the aims and tactics of an "Asian or oriental world power"; England "is now fulfilling political and Semitic dreams."

This extension of racial theory to the discussion of current international affairs was promoted by a new periodical, the *Internationale Monatsschrift*, which Bauer's publisher, Ernst Schmeitzner of Chemnitz, brought out in 1882. Bauer was clearly the inspirer of this journal and his hand is to be seen even in the style of many of its articles. It was revolutionary and antisemitic and earned Bauer the title of "the father of antisemitism" from the Jewish writer Ludwig Philippson. The *Internationale Monatsschrift* did not long survive the death of its progenitor in 1882.[24]

Among its aims was the promotion of the revolutionary meaning of Richard Wagner's work. One contributor invoked Bauer's axiom that Judaism had been an "unhealthy ferment in ancient religion" to prove that modern Judaism was equally baneful to the new Wagnerian "religion of art."[25] Bauer himself in his Schmeitzner publication, *Bismarck's Era* (1880), praised Wagner as the prophet of the death of the old bourgeois gods and the herald of a new revolutionary order.

> A new man has been produced, a new spirit . . . a new circle of gods, a new heaven, and a new world order. . . . Our contemporary world senses [this change] as a *Götterdämmerung*, and our premonition of the nearing crisis reveals part of our inner anxiety. . . . Richard Wagner's dramatic picture has impressed this on our contemporaries. . . . The artist has energetically grasped that which stirs the soul of our modern life.[26]

Bauer had been friendly since 1854 with Cosima Wagner, who doubtless influenced her husband in the 1870s to keep abreast of the phi-

[24] *Internationale Monatsschrift* (Chemnitz) 1 (1882). Cf. Barnikol, *Bauer Studien*, pp. 425ff.; Carlebach, *Marx and the Radical Critique*, p. 147.

[25] E. Schläger, "Die Bedeutung des Wagner'schen *Parsifal* in und für unsere Zeit," *Internationale Monatsschrift* 1 (1882): 495–512; E. Wolfart, "Zur Würdigung Richard Wagner's," ibid., 537–61, 601–30. Cf. Barnikol, *Bauer Studien*, pp. 426f., 429.

[26] *Zur Orientierung über die Bismarck'sche Ära* (Chemnitz, 1880), pp. 183f. Cf. Barnikol, *Bauer Studien*, pp. 383, 392ff.

losopher's racist and political writings.[27] Indeed, Bauer was invited to contribute to Wagner's own revolutionary journal, the *Bayreuther Blätter* (also published by Schmeitzner). Had it not been for the deaths of the respective editors in 1882 and 1883, the connections between the two Schmeitzner antisemitic journals—the one cultural, the other political—would certainly have prospered.

━━━━━

In his trajectory from philosophical to racial antisemitism, Bruno Bauer had a dramatic impact on three successive phases of the development of modern revolutionary Jew-hatred. In 1843, his *Jewish Question* established the revolutionary left-wing hostility to Jews, which still flourishes today; in that year Bauer, himself not a socialist, inspired the communists Karl Marx and Moses Hess to produce outbursts that saw the Jews as the embodiments of soulless, antihuman capitalism. Then, twenty years later in 1862–63, Bauer presided at the birth of the racist campaign against the Jews, which took up the scattered references of the early decades of the century to the "oriental Asiatic" character of the Jewish race as being alien to Germany. These allusions were now molded into a serious theory that was able to draw on the philosophical refinements of the Young Hegelians. And finally, twenty years after that, in 1880–82, Bruno Bauer was present at the full maturing of this theory into practice with the Antisemitic Campaign. *The Jewish Question* (1843), *Judaism Abroad* (1863), and Bauer's last political writings of 1880–82 are all ugly landmarks in the rise of a revolutionary and rational antisemitism in Germany that cut across the traditional political distinctions of "right" and "left."

[27] Bauer was friendly with Cosima from the time she was the wife of Hans von Bülow. See Barnikol, *Bauer Studien*, pp. 553ff., 560; Hans von Bülow, *Briefe und Schriften* (Leipzig, 1896–1908), 2:253, 300ff., 312ff., 4:157, 328, 8:379, 393; R. Graf Du Moulin-Eckart, *Hans von Bülow* (Munich, 1921), pp. 256f. Two of Bülow's letters to Bauer are now believed to be in the USSR, according to information from the International Institute of Social History in Amsterdam, which holds Barnikol's notes.

For references to Wagner's reading of Bauer between 1873 and 1882 and other connections see *CWD*, 1:682, 2:620, 755, 879, 1108. Bauer's article, "Luthers Optimismus und Pessimismus" was printed in *Bayreuther Blätter* 4 (1881): 285–90.

CHAPTER 16

# Revolution to Race II: Wilhelm Marr and the Antisemitic Revolution

THE FIRST German to popularize the term "antisemitism" as the watchword of a fully racist Jew-hatred began his career as a revolutionary atheistic disciple of Bruno Bauer. Wilhelm Marr (1819–1904), the son of the Hamburg theatrical director Heinrich Marr, spent his twenties in exile as a political agitator in Switzerland.[1] There he had founded the revolutionary democratic movement known as Young Germany, modeled on the politically activist Young Italy of Giuseppe Mazzini rather than on the original literary Young German group formed by Gutzkow and Laube in the 1830s.[2]

Marr's task in Switzerland was twofold: to advance the causes of revolution and of atheism. By nature intensely antiliberal, Marr did not mean by revolution the acquisition of liberal rights and constitutional government, but rather a revolutionary "free state" of the Young Hegelian kind.[3] Proclaiming the "cult of the individual" Marr called for the achievement of "democracy and all its consequences." This brought him into uneasy alliance with the communists, including Wilhelm Weitling, but Marr was more an anarchist than anything and his main motive was a revolutionary hatred of all religions. Communism seemed to him merely a "social theology," an inversion of Christianity.[4] His ambition was to have every worker become "a per-

---

[1] M. Zimmermann's valuable new biography, *Wilhelm Marr: Patriarch of Anti-semitism* (New York, 1986), based on the Marr manuscript memoirs in the Hamburg Staatsarchiv, appeared after the completion of the present chapter. See also Zimmermann, *Hamburgischer Patriotismus und deutscher Nationalismus: Die Emanzipation der Juden in Hamburg 1830–1865* (Hamburg, 1979), pp. 102–99, 215–28, for Marr's political career. Also idem, "Two Generations in the History of German Antisemitism: The Letters of Theodor Fritsch to Wilhelm Marr," *LBIY* 23 (1978): 89–99; "Gabriel Riesser und Wilhelm Marr in Meinungsstreit . . . 1848–1862," *Zeitschrift des Vereins für Hamburgische Geschichte* 61 (1975): 59–84. Cf. A. Bein, *Die Judenfrage* (Stuttgart, 1980), 2:166ff.; J. Katz, *From Prejudice to Destruction: Anti-Semitism 1700–1933* (Cambridge, Mass., 1980), pp. 207ff. (who slips in dating Marr's birth to 1818 in Magdeburg).

[2] Marr, *Das Junge Deutschland in der Schweiz* (Leipzig, 1846), pp. 71ff. Visiting Laube in April 1845, Marr found him "a man of talent, though not the man for our plans," and viewed him as merely the leader of a Heinean literary coterie (ibid., p. 300). Much later, however, Marr admitted that his two revolutionary mentors had been Börne and Heine (Zimmermann, *Wilhelm Marr*, pp. 131, 135f.). See below.

[3] Marr, *Das Junge Deutschland*, pp. 206, 230.

[4] Ibid., pp. 30ff., 33, 46, 51, 118ff. (For Weitling, see above, chap. 14.)

sonal enemy of God" and he advocated an atheistic "religion of the future" derived from Feuerbach and Bauer.⁵ He adopted the code name "Bauer" in his political activities,⁶ and when Bauer's *Christianity Unmasked* was banned by the Swiss authorities, Marr issued an anonymous polemic in 1843 entitled *Unmasked and Masked Christianity in Zurich*, which was itself immediately destroyed by the government. It was indeed Marr's atheistic crusade rather than his politics that led to his expulsion from Switzerland in 1845.⁷

Marr must have been well aware of the Young Hegelian critical arguments against the Jews. Surprisingly, however, there is scarcely a trace of Jew-hatred in the early works describing his atheistic mission with Young Germany.⁸ When he wrote of the specter of "society" as "the new Moloch to whom human beings are sacrificed," Marr did not try to suggest that Moloch (nor Mammon) had a Jewish connection.⁹ Indeed, he even quotes a Swiss report referring to himself as Marr "the ultraradical, under the protection of our local Jew—and pagan—friends."¹⁰

Yet hints of later developments are present. In a chapter of his *Young Germany* (1846) headed "The Volk," Marr explained that in the *Volk* the idea of the collective becomes real flesh and blood, but that the species is produced by the individual. "The *Volk* as understood by our philosophers, poets, and politicians until now has been a ghost but should . . . [as in Feuerbach's vision] be a sublime, radiant, majestic form," that is, a material form comprised of physical individuals. Though Marr is using *Volk* and "species" here in a basically economic sense, such a materialist understanding of *Volk* could later be developed into a biological idea of species and race.¹¹

When the Parliament of 1848 proved not democratic enough for Marr's radical tastes, he dismissed the liberal hopes of German unity

⁵ Ibid., pp. 131ff., 137, 203.

⁶ Ibid., p. 206. E. Barnikol, *Bruno Bauer: Studien und Materialen* (Assen, 1972), pp. 558f.

⁷ Anonymous [i.e. Marr], *Das entdeckte und das unentdeckte Christentum in Zurich und ein Traum . . . vom Antichrist* (Bern, 1843). See E. Barnikol, *Das Entdeckte Christentum im Vormärz* (Jena, 1927), pp. 17–27.

⁸ Barnikol, *Das Entdeckte Christentum*, p. 22n., sees an anticipation of Marr's later antisemitism in the phrase "unsere heilige 'pasanteife' Religion" in Marr's *Das entdeckte Christentum in Zurich*, p. 16.

⁹ *Das Junge Deutschland*, pp. 131ff.

¹⁰ Ibid., p. 344.

¹¹ Ibid., pp. 109–15. There are some faint hints of materialist and racial struggle: Marr sees Nature in Switzerland as being engaged in an "eternal struggle" (ibid., p. 1) and describes the Swiss citizenry as being a mixture "without respect to racial division" (*Racenunterschied*, p. 26).

as "Germany's curse."[12] Soon there followed veiled suggestions that
Judaism was to blame: "The unity of Germany is a dream. Freedom
lies in the individual. . . . Outside the individual lives the tyrannical
Jehovah, despotism." The Jewish Jehovah was the enemy of German
freedom.[13] A few years later, in 1852, Marr's views on race emerged
more explicitly:

> By itself the division of races [*Racenverschiedenheit*] can have no abso-
> lute claim to authority. For, just as horses and the like can be im-
> proved through the interbreeding of races [*Racenkreuzung*], so can the
> mixing of the separate human races by turned to advantage. . . . The
> law of harmony most fittingly awards hegemony to the Caucasian
> race, not for political, but simply for physiological reasons, as a pass-
> ing glance comparing the skull of a European with that of a Negro
> teaches us. . . . The brow is the central site of nervous activity and na-
> ture has remarkably endowed the peoples of Caucasian race in this re-
> spect. . . . Contact between the [Caucasian] peoples is a natural pro-
> cess of development that is rooted in the universal substance of
> humanity.[14]

Most nineteenth-century definitions of "Caucasian" tended to exclude the Jews although they were white-skinned, but did Marr include the Jews in this race? In the context he refers to the Caucasians
as comprising the Latin, German, and Slav peoples; but in 1862, he
saw the Jews as "being of a strongly prevailing Caucasian character"
(see below). In any event, Marr's main animus was against the black
races and very soon afterward he had a chance to put his theories
into practice when he moved for seven years to Central America.
There he is said to have engaged in the slave trade.[15]

These may have been racial straws in the wind, but after a quarrel
with Gabriel Riesser and the Hamburg liberals, Marr finally grasped
the torch of Jew-hatred with both hands.[16] In June 1862, when a fellow democrat asked him to support Jewish emancipation in Bremen,
Marr retorted with a violent open letter to the press:

> Leave me in peace. The scales are falling more and more from my
> eyes about the Jewish Question. . . . I will have nothing more about it.
> . . . If the Jews want to live in our fatherland and enjoy equal rights
> with us, they must erect no ecclesiastical or political state within a

---

[12] Quoted by Zimmermann, "Riesser und Marr," p. 67.
[13] Marr, *Anarchie oder Autorität?* (Hamburg, 1852).
[14] Ibid., pp. 116f.
[15] Zimmermann, *Hamburgischer Patriotismus*, p. 225.
[16] Zimmermann, "Riesser und Marr," p. 78.

state. But the question goes deeper. I believe Judaism, because it is a
racial particularity [*Stammeseigenthümlichkeit*], is incompatible with our
political and social life. It must, because of its inner nature, seek to
build a state within a state.

"The Jews," averred Marr, "will not destroy with their so-called
emancipation the instinctive revulsion of the people towards them."[17]

A public outcry against Marr's letter from Jews and non-Jews alike
only incited him to rewrite in the space of two days a "philosemitic"
pamphlet, which he had kept in his desk for some months. The original draft had commended the Reform Jews of Hamburg for their
readiness (unlike their Orthodox brethren) to assimilate. "Once my
philosemitism burst out," he recalls in his *Memoirs*, "I wrote a pamphlet and left open the title. I argued there for the complete fusion
of the Jewish and the Aryan."[18] A Jewish friend advised him to leave
the text unpublished as it would be misunderstood and result in
charges of Jew-hatred. But Marr had been stung by the reception his
open letter received from the Reform Jews, and he broadened the
pamphlet into a general attack on all forms of Judaism. For the first
time Marr invoked racial arguments to deny the Jews the capacity for
assimilation. Thus did the revolutionary democrat openly become a
Jew-hater.

The *Jews' Mirror* (*Der Judenspiegel*) appeared on 22 June 1862, and
went into five editions within a few months, even though it was
openly despised by establishment circles. Riesser did not deign to reply, while even the anti-Jewish conservative press expressed disapproval of Marr's arguments as too radical and personal.[19] Marr in
effect jumbled two different revolutionary currents, one formed of
"enlightened" Voltairean sneers at the barbarism of the Old Testament, the other being the more recent Feuerbach/Bauer critique of
"Jehovism" as an anthropological illusion. The result was then enliv-
ened by a constant carping at the "exclusiveness" and "peculiarities"
of the Jews in the manner of Gutzkow. It was observed that justice
demanded Judaism be treated as "critically" as had been Christianity,
and Marr insisted that he "harbored no hatred against any Jews, for
all the world knows I have intimate friends among them. But I hate
Judaism [*Judentum*]."[20]

[17] Letter to *Courier an der Weser*, June 1862, quoted by Zimmermann, "Riesser und
Marr," p. 79. Cf. idem, *Hamburgischer Patriotismus*, pp. 222f.
[18] Marr, *Memoiren*, Staatsarchiv, Hamburg, MS Familie-Marr, V:70, quoted by Zimmermann, *Hamburgischer Patriotismus*, p. 220.
[19] Ibid., p. 225.
[20] Marr, *Der Judenspiegel*, 5th ed. (Hamburg, 1862), pp. 11f. (preface). Page references in text are to this edition.

To Marr, the paramount aim is the destruction of *Judentum* and the best means to this end is assimilation. On the religious level this will take place either through baptism or simply through the abjuring of Jewish religion (which would be more congenial to an atheistic radical). But the true assimilation process would take place at social and racial levels and finally redeem the Jews from their self-imposed burden of Jew-hatred:

> Past Jew-hatred appeared on the surface to be of a religious character, but in reality it was a naturally based aversion to the inherent peculiarities of the Jews, which were the very negation of our life. . . . So long as these peculiarities are not removed, any sympathy for the Jews is by nature impossible (pp. 36f.).

The Jews, "the chosen race," of course, bear the responsibility:

> Historically the Jews have no right to reproach us. The "Chosen People of God" . . . have committed horrible deeds on a massive scale against other peoples; Christians have committed such acts against Jews only "in detail." . . . Politically, they have just as little right, as long as they refuse to relinquish their "nationality." . . . The religion of Judaism is really too specific-national-Jewish. (p. 37)

"The aversion against the Jews that is found everywhere," declares Marr, "has its origin in the essence of Judaism. This aversion is but reality" (p. 42). That essence is manifest in the hateful peculiarities of the Jews—ostentation, greed, money-mindedness, exaggerated manners—all of them "oriental" traits (pp. 43f.).

For Marr the source of these vicious peculiarities lies in the Jews' false sense of "nationality," which has led to a racial separation that reinforces both their peculiarities and their exclusiveness. However, this self-imposed separation of the chosen race has been a dreadful error, because the Jews are not a true race at all. Marr believed that the ancient Jews were not a true *Volk* but rather an agglomeration of different peoples (*Stämme*) as symbolized in the myth of the twelve sons of Jacob. With Moses at their head, "the so-called Jews—a mixture of descendants of different *Völker*—were expelled en masse from Egypt." In the Promised Land miscegenation continued to be the rule and resulted in a people who comprised a mixture of racial physiognomies rather than a pure race (pp. 31–34). It was only after the Romans destroyed the Second Temple and exiled the Jews that they resorted to a close-knit "exclusiveness" to preserve their identity and set themselves up as the pure, chosen race, forbidding intermarriage. The Jews, however, retain the stamp of their origin as "a mixed people, of a strongly prevailing Caucasian character" (pp. 44–46).

The isolation of the Jews, abetted by their enthrallment to an abstruse theology, has produced a visible degeneration of this mixed race. It is no wonder, therefore, that there has arisen a deep natural enmity between Jews and Germans:

> Jewish ways of life and . . . the physiology of Jewishness have waxed. Against these our aesthetic and physical sensibility has reacted. It is a law of nature that we cannot deny by means of all kinds of abstractions. We have sought to carry ourselves away with phrases . . . we have artfully induced a general sympathy, but one which we cannot accept as long as a real and pregnant animosity of flesh and spirit exists between Jew and non-Jew, both implicitly and explicitly. (pp. 35f.)

In order to heal the rift, Marr now holds out a magnanimous vision of Jewish redemption by ennoblement of the race. The only way to reverse the pernicious degeneration of the Jews and to redeem them from their fate is "fleshly assimilation," that is, the physical fusion of Jew and German through intermarriage. It was only "Christian monkist fanaticism" that forbade the intermarriage of Christian and Jewess in the Middle Ages and so ensured the continuation of the unfortunate specific Jewish type:

> Climatic and various local factors may have altered that type, but these factors cannot operate absolutely; they may only modify extremely. An Indian cannot in all generations lose his Indian character, nor a Negro his Negro character. Just as little may that sport of Western peoples that one calls a *Jew* abandon his character. The ennoblement of the Jews, that is, their emancipation, must forsake the realm of the abstract and pass over into a concrete fleshly interbreeding [*Vermischung*]. Jehovah works no more miracles. (pp. 47f.)

For Marr, racial redemption and emancipation can only come about through full miscegenation:

> Rapprochement and assimilation with your Western fellow citizens is unavoidable, and it must happen that the crossbreeding process, which before existed among Jewry in Egypt, must begin again . . . this time for the strengthening and ennobling of your people. . . . This is a solid emancipation, one based on science, and a naturally and firmly standing emancipation that we offer you, an honorable emancipation, not a crying Jewish grieving. (p. 51)

(It was a process that Marr himself tried to set in motion by marrying consecutively three women of Jewish ancestry!)[21]

---

[21] Zimmermann, *Hamburgischer Patriotismus*, p. 222.

Marr's "philosemitism" consisted here of offering the prospect of racial "ennoblement" to the Jews; but it was the usual poisoned offer of the revolutionists. What Marr required in return was the suicide of Jewry, both as a religion and as a people. To join the Germans, the Jews must first abjure themselves. This was the price of redemption, but would it be rendered?

> The crux is whether the Jews can in their totality surrender their pretensions to be the chosen race and assimilate with Western peoples . . . whether their "peculiarities" can be rooted out. . . . In the light of what we have seen in North America we do not despair of the possibility of such an assimilation. (p. 57)

Racial redemption then is the general solution, but what of the practical issue of Jewish civil rights? Marr makes full political rights conditional upon the disappearance of the Jewish community proper, or "state within a state" as he terms it:

> Jews have as men the right . . . to participate in the general right of voting. . . . But in a free state, the state has the right to demand guarantees that its officials do not decay back into Jewry. . . . Jewry as such can give no such guarantees. . . . A much better way is to "emancipate yourselves." . . . Give up your particular community membership for a state-citizenship. . . . Abolish your temples and make your worship a purely individual affiliation. . . . With the dissolution of the bonds of community, civil prejudice against your people will end. (pp. 50f.)

Those who feel they must have a religion can worship purely privately. But those who give up "all formal connections with Judaism will be welcome among us" (p. 54), Marr patronizingly assures his audience:

> Every Jew who strives for this ruthlessly, honorably, and earnestly, is our friend. . . . The dissolution of their social-ecclesiastical-national community bonds is the first step towards the equality of the Jews. (p. 58)

Complete renunciation of the Jewish community is necessary if one is to enter the German community as a friend, for "the difference between Germans and orientals is still too great in race for us to accept deserters without some security" (p. 54).

Marr has only sharp words for what he sees as the false political emancipation of the Jews that has been under way. He repudiates those "fanatics of free conscience" who wish to grant the Jews rights unconditionally (p. 5). As for the Jews, Marr notes that where they had been ultraradical in the struggle for Jewish rights, they have since joined the forces of reaction, possessed as they are by that urge to exploit every situation for self-advantage so characteristic of Judaism (p. 38). Let the Jews now with the aid of the *Jews' Mirror* (which Marr has held up to them) seek a true emancipation by the method he has detailed and "thus will they be able to reach full civil equality among us" (pp. 52, 56).

The real problem, however, is that the Jews "remain imprisoned in Judaism" and it is this from which they need redemption (p. 48):

> You, as Jews, are an incompetent people, persecuting and persecuted, despising and despised, a vexatious and vexed people, and will remain so as long as you remain "Jews." (p. 52)

For their own good the Jews must escape from the Judaism that attracts only persecution from other peoples:

> You want human rights and still remain the special children of Jehovah. My dear people, that can't be. . . . If you want equal rights with others in a state, you must *assimilate* in every part with the state . . . and not treat it as a business enterprise. (p. 53)

Nevertheless, Marr was willing to grant some civil rights to those who stuck to Judaism as a private religion. Such Jews may be called citizens, may engage in all kinds of business and enjoy all manner of possessions. But they may not hold public office unless, like any other foreigner, they are willing to "Germanize" themselves (p. 58).

"Assimilation," then, for Marr would be the redemption of Ahasverus and of the Jews, those "modern nomads" who must above all surrender their "gypsy-like" existence and become true Germans (pp. 45, 59). Like Laube in 1847, Marr reduced the Jewish Question to the bald alternatives of assimilation or emigration. It was not the Germans' fault, canted Marr, that the Jews had come from Palestine to Germany (p. 36) and now that they were here were rightly reluctant to emigrate to their original homeland to form a model state (p. 52). Marr thus agreed with Laube that assimilation was preferable to emigration, but, of course, the assimilation he envisaged was far more extreme than Laube's.

The *Jews' Mirror* therefore consisted of two sets of arguments that reinforced each other. Marr combined a *revolutionary* critique of Judaism with a *racial* argument in demanding the spiritual and physical suicide of the Jewish people, which was to be their redemption. The revolutionary argument sounded the keynotes of humane Wagnerian hatred of *Judentum*: "Judaism must end if humanity is to begin" (p. 54). "The emancipation of the Jews lies in themselves—*self-emancipa-*

*tion from Judaism!*" (pp. 42, 55). Intelligent Jews realize that "it is fatal for them to be a Jew . . . , that is, that very small number who are truly free human beings and . . . are no longer Jews" (p. 36). Critical arguments underpin this revolutionary antisemitism, which (as Wagner observed in 1869) was not to be confused with the vulgar medieval Christian sort of Jew-hatred. Marr remarks:

> It is a lie to say the Jews have become as they are through persecution. They were persecuted because they were as they are. In the Middle Ages, it was done by means of crude violence, in the modern world by objective *Kritik*. (p. 57)

Marr's critical argument merges easily into a racial one. The uneasiness that exists between Jew and Christian does not have its origin in any

> religious Jew-hatred that cannot exist among enlightened men. Its cause is rather a sort of antagonism of essence, which one might call chemical. This cannot be contained and it induces a decomposition of the [social] body by what may be termed an inorganic process. The morals, behavior, and manners of true Jews are not compatible with ours for any length of time. Our ears bristle at the sound of the Jewish wheedling voice [*Mauscheln*] and our eyes are averted from the sight of their alien appearance. . . . No matter how much we twist and turn, we always come back to the point where we must face the fact that it is not this or that Jew, but Jewishness [*Judentum*] itself that is disgusting to us. (pp. 40f.)

The major appeal of a racist "chemical" argument to Marr lay no doubt in its ability to satisfy his atheistic materialism. Marr believed that Jew and German were utterly alien to one another in essence, the Jews being an "oriental" bastard mixture of races (pp. 44, 54). But Marr's concept of "oriental" did not go beyond the common anti-Jewish use of the term of the 1840s. In 1862, Marr's biological determinism had still not developed and his revolutionary idealism was still strong enough to make him believe that the racial emancipation of the Jews was possible, and indeed desirable. There did not yet exist for Marr a permanent racial war between Jew and German. A peace might still be achieved through the assimilation and ennoblement of the Jewish race. In this sense, the *Jews' Mirror* was indeed, in comparison with the later direction of Marr's thought, a "philosemitic" tract. But its pretense of genuine feeling for the Jews was belied by the bitterness of its language and emotion and by the sheer offensiveness of its tone.

The year 1862 marks a turn for the worse in the history of the

Jewish Question. Certainly times had changed for the better at Hamburg since the Börne–Meyer dispute thirty years before, when the emancipation of the Jews had been very much in doubt. Continued cause for optimism was found in the final ratification of Jewish rights by the German states between 1862 and 1871. Marr himself went into political eclipse for some years at Hamburg. But the economic depression and stock-exchange scandals of the 1870s stimulated a rising tide of Jew-hatred and gave Marr another chance of capturing an audience. In 1876 his *Religious Expeditions of a Philosophical Tourist* ventured a fresh critical attack on Judaism as the begetter of a Christianity that was "zealous from its birth to kill and persecute one's fellow men." Judaism and Christianity, like every religion, were a "disease of human consciousness." This philosophical idea was translated into politics by arguing that the "Jewification of mankind" had brought Germany to destruction by weakening German moral fiber and producing all the social ills of industrialization.[22] It had now become a matter of Jews attacking Germans. The anti-Christian bent to Marr's Jew-hatred put him at odds with Adolf Stöcker, the leader of the powerful new stream of Christian antisemitism, but both could agree that Jews were the symbols of the destructive creed of "Manchesterism" and the engineers of the rapid industrial and social change that was corrupting the health of organic society.

Marr's fourth marriage (to a non-Jewess) in 1877 removed the last impediment to his slide into antisemitism proper. His first three marriages to women of Jewish ancestry had disposed him to believe that assimilation by intermarriage was the solution to the racial question. But now he was at last freed emotionally to break forth with a barrage of racist antisemitism, repudiating the idea of assimilation and establishing "antisemitism" as the basic term of discourse.[23]

His opening shot was the bombastic *The Victory of Judaism over Germanism* (1879), which urged the Germans to defend themselves from a Jewish victory which, Marr affected, had already arrived.[24] The

[22] *Religiöse Streifzüge eines philosophischen Touristen* (Berlin, 1876). Cf. U. Tal, *Christians and Jews in Germany: Religion, Politics and Ideology in the Second Reich 1870–1914* (Ithaca, N.Y., 1975), pp. 246, 262ff., for Marr and the anti-Christian character of the new antisemitism.

[23] The term "anti-semitic" was actually coined by the Jewish writer M. Steinschneider in a polemic against Ernest Renan in 1860. It next appeared in 1879 with Marr's "Anti-Semites' League" and was soon adapted into such expressions as "Anti-Semitic Party," "Anti-Semitic Movement," and "Anti-Semite." The abstract term "anti-semitism" came into use soon after. See Bein, *Judenfrage*, 2:165–67. On Marr's later antisemitism see Zimmermann, *Wilhelm Marr*; Katz, *From Prejudice*, pp. 26off.; P. J. Pulzer, *The Rise of Political Anti-Semitism in Germany and Austria* (London, 1964), pp. 47–52, 297.

[24] *Der Sieg des Judenthums über das Germanenthum: Vom nicht konfessionalen Standpunkt ausbetracht*, 4th ed. (Bern, 1879).

book was an immediate best-seller, going through twelve editions in 1879 with more than twenty thousand copies sold.[25] Its success vindicated Marr's basic aim, which was to "take the Jewish Question out of the quarrels of the parties" and make it into the overriding "social issue of the age." Henceforth antisemitism was to be a central social principle in itself, instead of being an incidental issue in party politics.

Marr constructed *The Victory* around two wars. One was the "1,800 Year War" between the Jews and the Germans, which had begun with the destruction of Jerusalem; the other was the "30 Year War," the final phase of the longer struggle, which had been initiated in 1848 with the liberal emancipation of the Jews in Germany and which had produced the final defeat of the German people. Germany had been utterly "Jewified," its press, economy, social institutions, and political offices overrun by the victorious Jews. The phrases "Jewified society" and "Jewified Germany" recur monotonously and his obsession with Jewish control of the press is almost demented. The specter of the new Jewish "world power" haunts the book. For Marr the Jews are "a demonic apparition," full of intellect and elasticity. "With its Jewish spirit, this people conquers the world!" The essence of Jewish spirit was a practical *realism* that emerged in the Jews' unidealistic religion; Jewish religion was no more than a "business relationship" with Jehovah. In practice this realism has taken the form of the pursuit of money-power. Even Lessing, for all his admiration of Jewish religion, had intuitively made Nathan the Wise a banker (pp. 16–19). Driven from Palestine, these superbly equipped Jews had unleashed their drive for realism among the idealistic Germans, who had succumbed to the extent of naively inviting their conquerors in through the front door of Jewish emancipation. A Jewish "alien domination" had now triumphed in Germany.

Marr, like Constantin Frantz and Wagner, saw the Bismarckian Empire as the Jews' artifice. It had combined centralized emancipation with encouragement of the huge financial and industrial expansion, thus completing the Jewish victory. Germany has become thoroughly Jewified, "the new Palestine, the new Promised Land, the center of Semitism." Even the socialist opposition to capitalism has been subverted by the Jew Lassalle (pp. 12, 15, 22–30).

Yet all of this was inevitable and should have been foreseen. Knowing the exclusive realism of the Jews, who could really have expected ever to have assimilated them into Germany? A foreign people, their nature forbade them to assimilate. All the other settlers in German lands had assimilated, but "the tough semitic race had survived for

---

[25] Zimmermann, "Two Generations," p. 99.

eighteen hundred years . . . and was now the social-political dictator of Germany!" (pp. 15, 23).

Like Wagner,[26] Marr rhetorically pretended to chide the compliant Germans rather than blame the Jews for following their own nature:

> But I repeat . . . not the faintest Jew-hatred inspires me, less a religious hatred against the Jews. Not even a national nor a racial hatred. No people can help its "specialties."

Marr's own earlier *Jews' Mirror* was now admitted to have been a mistaken anachronism; it had been several hundred years too late to do any good:

> I harbor now not the slightest enmity against the Jews if they do not harm me personally. . . . In a war, who can personally hate the soldiers? . . . But in its inner nature dwells the fundamental consciousness of the race—hating us, or seeing us only as a people to be exploited—this is in the nature of his race and was part of the history of the ancient world. . . . He had to fight us, he had to follow his victory of 1848 with more successes and strive to drive our German world into the ground. This is the destructive mission of Judaism. (pp. 40–42)

But for all this pretended fatalism Marr was eager to sow the idea of revenge in the minds of his outraged German readers. Pointing to the financial problems besetting Germany, he opined that anti-Jewish feeling was now rising by the hour and that an explosion was inevitable. Perhaps one would soon have to protect the Jews from popular fury. This does not, however, detract from his final note of resignation:

> We have traveled so deeply into Jewification that we can no longer escape. A brutal anti-Jewish explosion can only delay, not prevent, the collapse of our Jewified society. . . .
>
> I may have erred. A social-political peace between Semitism and Germanism may be concluded. I don't believe so. . . .
>
> Speak not of confessional or racial hatred. It is the agony of our oppressed people which speaks from my pen. . . . *Götterdämmerung* has dawned for us. (pp. 44–50)

Marr saw the originality of his "antisemitism" as residing in the fact that "it was free from all confessional prejudice." Its intellectual

---

[26] E. Newman, *The Life of Richard Wagner* (repr. Cambridge, 1976), 4:600. See below, chap. 20.

achievement lay, he claimed, in having unveiled the real human motives for Jew-hatred, which had been distorted by Christianity:

> Christianity produced an apparently religious Jew-hatred. . . . But this religious aspect was idiotic. . . . The reality of Jew-hatred lay in the instinctive struggle of the [European] peoples against the actual Jewification [*Verjudung*] of society—it was a struggle for existence. . . . I take the Jews into my protection against such [Christian] religious persecution. (pp. 7–9)

With this repudiation of Christian Jew-hatred came a revaluation of the Ahasverus concept. Marr does not bring up Ahasverus by name, but one of the salient ideas of the Wandering Jew—the eternal survival of the Jews—is clearly being reversed when he observes that "to Judaism belongs the future and life, to Germanism the past and death." The survival of the Jews as a race apart, instead of being a testimony to their guilt, has become a symptom of their strength. Ahasverus has become the witness of Jewish victory, rather than of defeat and humiliation (pp. 23, 39).

In the controversy provoked by *The Victory of Judaism*, Marr sharpened his opposition to the assimilation of the Jews. *The Jewish Theater of War Operations* of 1879 reasserted that the whole question depended on race.[27] "One should not speak of [our] parading religious prejudice here where it is a matter of race; the separation between the Jews and ourselves *lies in the blood*" (p. 19). Race determines Jewish character, which *must* naturally seek to destroy Germanism. "No reproach against Jewry, I repeat. It lies in the race, in the blood, as it has since remote antiquity. The Jew *cannot* honestly sacrifice himself to us" (p. 27). For the Germans, therefore, the Jewish Question "is a question of our existence" and so "the true social question of our age" (pp. 20, 24).

Marr now admitted that the central error in his earlier writings was his failure to appreciate the true meaning of the Jewish Question. He had even mistakenly protected Jews while at school and later written in favor of Jewish emancipation. It was only in 1862 that he had departed from this superficial liberalism and taken up his pen against the Jews with the *Jews' Mirror*; but even that had been blind:

> Is it the Christian mission to redeem the Jews from their apartness? . . . When I was still imprisoned in the illusions of democracy, I demanded in my *Jews' Mirror* . . . that racial crossbreeding become the means of union and fusion. . . . For I ascribed the physical character-

[27] *Vom jüdischen Kriegsschauplatz: Eine Streitschrift*, 2d ed. (Bern, 1879), for page references given here in text.

istics of the Jews to their exclusively marrying within their
religion. . . .

But my racial-fusion theory was . . . a right fiasco. The peculiar
characters of the Jewish and German females prevents it. . . . Perhaps,
I will grant, after thousands of years this opposition [of types] will disappear in a natural way . . . but that would only make us slaves. . . .

It is a struggle between two divided races. The philosopher may
condemn the racial struggle, but that is like condemning the terres-
trial struggle between the developing forces of earth and sea that is
irksome to us. . . .

I was a rebel [against history and nature] when I preached and
wrote *for* Jewish emancipation, and I am so again today when I act
*against* it. . . . For after only thirty years of emancipation in Germany,
the Jews here have established their supremacy. (pp. 36–37)

What then is the solution to the Jewish Question if not assimilation?

Either we reconcile ourselves to the cultural-historical process of our
Jewification and resign ourselves . . . or we make good the faults of
our predecessors and win back the Jews' fatherland for them. . . .
Here they disorganize, there let them organize. (pp. 38–40)

Marr is so carried away by enthusiasm for this new solution that he
forgets to say whether the German Jews are to be forcibly expelled to
Palestine.

The emigration of the Jews to Palestine—voluntary or otherwise—
had come to seem a reasonable solution to the Jewish Question. What
had been dismissed as unthinkable barbarism by Laube in 1847, what
Wagner had timidly raised as a remote possibility in 1869, had by
1879 entered into the realm of permissible political discussion.[28]

The issue of race distinguished Marr's prejudice from an allied
current of Christian antisemitism which under Stöcker was gaining
ground in these years. In a third work of 1879, *The Jews' War*,[29] Marr
pointed out that Stöcker, by preaching the conversion of the Jews,
was missing the whole point. It was no longer the case that the Jews'
refusal of Christian redemption was the cause of Jew-hatred:

The empirical-scientific question of race . . . respecting the Jews had
already existed before the birth of Christianity. . . . This physiological
and psychological phenomenon cannot be explained away by Christian ecclesiastical abstractions. . . . Stöcker thinks it possible to improve

[28] As Marr shows (pp. 41ff.) by reprinting a speech to that effect in the Hungarian
Parliament.
[29] *Der Judenkrieg*, 2d ed. (Chemnitz, 1880; 1st ed., 1879).

the Jews. . . . But did not God, did not Providence itself, create this racial distinction?³⁰

*The Jews' War* was one of a series of *Antisemitic Booklets* (*Anti-Semitische Hefte*) published in 1879–80, years in which Marr threw himself into a flurry of activity, publishing his tracts, launching a short-lived anti-Jewish journal,³¹ and forming the Antisemites' League "for the salvation of Germany from complete Jewification."³² Its first meeting was held in Berlin in September 1879 and the league was now active in promoting the Antisemites' Petition to the Reichstag. (All this activity did not, however, spare Marr from being publicly branded as being of Jewish descent!)³³

In fact, in the new climate of political antisemitism of the 1880s, Marr soon lost much of his notoriety and was written off by Theodor Fritsch as a mere "theorist" who failed to prosper in the antisemitic political parties that his *Victory of Judaism* had spawned.³⁴ In return, Marr excoriated the way in which its new exponents had reduced antisemitism to a "racket." Even as a theorist Marr was not up to it. He never really framed any properly biological theory of race and, unlike Wagner, he failed to draw on the possibilities of Darwinism. Nor was he consistent in his attitude to assimilation; *The Road to the Victory of Germanism over Judaism* (Berlin, 1880) seemed to revert to a belief in the long-term "assimilation of this foreign element."³⁵

Marr's declining fortunes were mirrored in his relations with Wagner. Inspired by Wagner's reissued *Judaism in Music* of 1869, Marr sent him in 1870 a brochure that Cosima praised as "not at all badly written,"³⁶ while Wagner told him how much pleasure he had derived from its "new perspectives" on Judaism.³⁷ In return, Marr became an enthusiastic promoter of the Wagner claque at Hamburg.³⁸ But in

³⁰ *Der Judenkrieg*, quoted by Tal, *Christians and Jews*, p. 264.

³¹ *Die deutsche Wacht: Monatsschrift für nationale Entwicklung*, October 1879.

³² *Anti-Semiten Liga* (Statutes), Berlin, 1879, quoted by Katz, *From Prejudice*, pp. 260f.; Pulzer, *Rise*, p. 51.

³³ As, for instance, by F. Sailer, *Die Juden und das Deutsche Reich* (Berlin, 1879), p. 18, according to M. Meyer, "Great Debate on Anti-semitism," *LBIY* 11 (1966): 137–60. The family genealogy in the Hamburg Marr archives seems to disprove the charge, but the matter is not yet certain to my mind. See Bein, *Judenfrage*, 2:167.

³⁴ See Zimmermann, "Two Generations."

³⁵ *Der Weg zum Siege des Germanenthums über das Judenthum* (Berlin, 1880; the 4th ed. of *Wählet keinen Juden [Elect no Jew]*, Berlin, 1879). Cf. Tal, *Christians and Jews*, p. 264.

³⁶ *CWD*, 28 June 1870.

³⁷ Letter to Marr, 21 July 1870, Hamburg Staatsarchiv, Marr Nachlass, no. 274. (No. 273 is a letter of Cosima's of 1871; letters from Wagner's assistant Hans von Wolzogen in 1879–80 form no. 296.)

³⁸ C. F. Glasenapp, *Das Leben Richard Wagners*, 4th ed. (Leipzig, 1907–11), 5:62f.

1873, Wagner had a "horrible dream. . . . Among the figures jostling him was Marr from Hamburg, whom he did not recognize, so grand had he become."[39] Wagner's doubts grew. In 1879 Cosima remarked that Marr's *Victory of Judaism* "contains views which are, alas, very close to Richard's."[40] Subsequent tracts received from Marr were deemed "rather superficial" and "not very enlivening."[41]

But in one respect Marr was as progressive as Wagner, that is in his refusal to be accounted a mere "Teutomaniac fanatic." Marr disowned this sort of Jew-hatred as keenly as he did the religious kind.[42] In the noble racist antisemitism of Marr and Wagner, the "old empty Teutonic phrases" were replaced with a new theory of natural enmity and struggle between races, a struggle for existence between German idealism and tradition on the one hand, and Jewish realism and modernism on the other.[43] The new theory, unlike the old, was practically demonstrated by recent developments in German society. In the decades since emancipation, unwelcome economic and political structures had arisen that betokened the triumph of Judaism. These structures were especially resented by those radicals of the 1840s who were seeing their revolutionary theories bypassed by the success of liberal capitalism. How was one to explain the continued "irrational" success of Judaism and the liberal capitalist state in spite of all the predictions of the critical philosophers? "Criticism" itself was powerless to explain this paradox. A new racial theory of antisemitism was instead called in to account for the failure of the revolutionary hopes of the 1840s. The new antisemitism of the 1870s did not mean that revolutionary principles were being abandoned, merely that they were receiving their definitive clarification. As Marr wrote in 1891, "antisemitism is a socialist movement, only in nobler and purer form than social democracy."[44]

Marr insisted that it was his revolutionism that had led him to racism. The *Jews' Mirror* of 1862, he later stated, had originated in "the ultrarevolutionary outlook that I then possessed." Nor was he shy of making the ironical admission that he had embarked on his revolu-

---

Marr was overwhelmed on reading *Opera and Drama* and sent Wagner an essay on it in March 1871 (*CWD*, 8 December 1870; 13 March 1871).

[39] *CWD*, 20 January 1875.

[40] *CWD*, 27 February and 1 March 1879. Wagner, however, thought Marr's journal *Die deutsche Wacht* "well-done" (*CWD*, 22 October 1879). Marr praised Wagner in his *Sieg des Judenthums*, p. 26n.

[41] *CWD*, 14 and 21 July 1879.

[42] Zimmermann, "Two Generations," p. 99.

[43] See *Sieg des Judenthums*.

[44] Quoted by Pulzer, *Rise*, p. 47. For his attacks on *Geschäftsantisemitismus* ("the antisemitism-racket"), see Zimmermann, *Wilhelm Marr*, pp. 149, 153.

tionary path under the Jewish influence of Börne and Heine whose genius he never (unlike Wagner) tried to deny. In the 1830s (Marr recalled),

> Heine and Börne were our prophets. It is the undeniable truth that these two Jews were pathbreakers to the ideas of freedom. . . . Israel incited us in order to attain achievements for itself. This in the final analysis is the entire secret of liberal and revolutionary Judaism, in the past and in the present as well, with Judaism aspiring towards unlimited power. . . . We read Heine and Börne in secret and were excited by them.

For Marr the tragedy of modern antisemitism was that it had become a "racket" and lost its true revolutionary impulse, leaving the agenda of revolution in the hands of the self-interested Jews who directed it to their own ends. "The Jews Börne and Heine, Lassalle and Karl Marx, have remained the fathers of today's political and socialist *revolutionary movement*."[45] Marr's own brand of revolutionary antisemitism, like Wagner's, was intended to achieve a heroic feat of rescue: the revolution itself was to be redeemed from the Jews.

[45] Zimmermann, *Wilhelm Marr*, p. 136.

CHAPTER 17

# Karl Marx: Judaism as Moral Myth
# and Social Reality

K ARL Marx (1818–83) never escaped completely the fact of his Jewish ancestry. He constantly sought to persuade himself that he had transcended *Judentum*, first by baptism as an infant, then by a progressive Christian education, and later by a "human" emancipation from Christianity into universal love of humanity.[1]

It was in August 1842 that the young Marx first announced his plan of setting discussion on the Jewish Question on a new course.[2] His project was stimulated by the publication in November 1842 of "The Jewish Question" by his close collaborator of the time, Bruno Bauer.[3] But it was not until the latter half of 1843 that Marx committed his thoughts to paper in the form of a polemical review of Bauer's reissued *Jewish Question* and subsequent essay "The Capacity of Present-day Jews and Christians to Become Free."[4]

External events were also directing Marx toward a critique of Judaism. In March 1843, the head of the Cologne Jewish community approached him for help with a petition to the government for Jewish rights. "I am willing to do it," Marx told Arnold Ruge.

> However much I dislike Judaism, Bauer's view seems to me too abstract. The thing is to make as many breaches as possible in the Christian state and to smuggle in as much as we can of what is rational.[5]

---

[1] For the significance of Marx's Jewish ancestry, see M. Wolfson, *Marx: Economist, Philosopher, Jew. Steps in the Development of a Doctrine* (London, 1982); R. Wistrich, *Revolutionary Jews from Marx to Trotsky* (London, 1976), chap. 1; S. Gilman, *Jewish Self-Hatred* (Baltimore, 1986), pp. 188–208; J. Carlebach, *Karl Marx and the Radical Critique of Judaism* (London, 1978), chap. 8; N. Weyl, *Karl Marx: Racist* (New Rochelle, N.Y., 1979); A. Künzli, *Karl Marx: Eine Psychographie* (Vienna, 1966); I. Berlin, "Benjamin Disraeli, Karl Marx and the Search for Identity," in his *Against the Current* (London, 1979), pp. 252–86; A. Prinz, "New Perspectives on Marx as a Jew," *LBIY* 15 (1970): 107–24.

[2] Letter to D. Oppenheim, 25 August 1842, in *Marx-Engels Collected Works* (London, 1975–), 1:391f (*MECW*).

[3] In 1841 Marx planned to edit with Bauer and Feuerbach a series entitled *Atheistic Archives*.

[4] In *Einundzwanzig Bogen aus der Schweiz* (Zurich, 1843). See above, chap. 15.

[5] To Ruge, 13 March 1843, *MECW*, 1:400. D. McLellan, *Marx before Marxism* (London, 1970), p. 133, thinks it was the leader of the Kreuznach community who approached Marx.

Indeed, Marx was coming to dislike Judaism very much in these months, thanks to his mother's "Jewish" denial to him of his portion of his late father's inheritance.[6] Serious quarrels continued between them and, as if to disown any Jewish traits he might have inherited, Marx ostentatiously left out his new, non-Jewish bride's cash dowry in an open box during their honeymoon in June 1843 for their friends to help themselves.[7]

The crucial period of Marx's conversion from belief in "civil" bourgeois society and the rational state to humanism and thence socialism was his stay at Kreuznach from May to October 1843. The conversion is evident in the two opposed parts of his *Critique of Hegel's Philosophy of Law*. In the main body of this text, which dates from before his conversion, Marx attacks Hegel's conservative doctrine of the state and advocates revolutionary democracy; but he still accepts the core of Hegelian "civil society," that is, private property, self-interest, and the "state."[8] But at the end of 1843, that is, after his conversion, Marx wrote an *Introduction to the Critique of Hegel's Philosophy of Law* that negated what he had written earlier. Now he repudiated the self-interest of civil society and, claiming that man was essentially a "species-being," preached an ethic of social love that would destroy the egoism and self-interest on which the "state"—whether "rational," "free," or not—was founded. The egoism of private property would be abolished and human emancipation would be achieved through the proletariat, which Marx had discovered would be the agent of the revolution.[9]

The *Introduction* was the result of Marx's newfound mission for the "reform of consciousness." In his program of September 1843 for the *German-French Yearbooks* Marx had interpreted religion and society as complementary expressions of a submerged "hidden consciousness" that corrupted bourgeois society.[10] To expose and reform this "mystical consciousness" of bourgeois society—at once religious and social—became his great task; and Marx found in *Judentum* the ideal myth to convey this conversionary insight.

Judaism was uniquely suited to Marx's purposes. *Judentum* might

[6] For example, to Ruge, 25 January 1843, *MECW*, 1:397. See Prinz, "New Perspectives," for the dealings with his Dutch relatives. Cf. Wolfson, *Marx*, chap. 1.

[7] Franziska Kugelmann, "Kleine Züge zu dem grossen Charakterbild von Karl Marx," memoir printed in *Mohr und General. Erinnerungen an Marx und Engels*, 3d ed. (Dietz, Berlin, 1970), p. 294.

[8] Marx left the main text unpublished. Modern editions include *Critique of Hegel's Philosophy of Right*, ed. J. Malley (Cambridge, 1970); Marx, *Early Writings*, ed. L. Colletti (Harmondsworth, 1975), pp. 57ff.; *MECW*, 3:3ff.

[9] Printed in *Early Writings*, pp. 243ff.; *MECW*, 3:175ff.

[10] To Ruge, September 1843, *MECW*, 3:144; *Early Writings*, p. 209.

designate the religion of the Jews and at the same time represent their existence as a social-economic community. Furthermore, *Judentum* was an especially apt way of characterizing the consciousness of a bourgeois society based on money and self-interest. Feuerbach had declared that the religion of the Jews was practical egoism; but Marx would go beyond this simple philosophical assertion about Jewish egoism. He would show that the psychological alienation from true humanity that arises from Jewish religion was but the religious form of a social and economic alienation that afflicts bourgeois society at large *and* the Jews in particular as a social group. Where Feuerbach had stopped short at a purely philosophical recognition of the evils of Jewish religion, Marx went well beyond this into an understanding that *Judentum* was a myth not merely of philosophical alienation but of economic and material unhappiness.

Marx seems to have arrived at this insight into the mythological possibilities of *Judentum* around the time he described his program for the *German-French Yearbooks*. To the autumn of 1843 also belongs the great declaratory document of Marx's conversion to "humanity," the essay *On the Jewish Question*.[11] A few months later there followed the *Introduction to Hegel's Critique*, which, with its emphasis that the critique of religion was the first step to the critique of society, formed the logical sequel to *On the Jewish Question*. Indeed, both essays were published alongside each other in the first and only issue of the *German-French Yearbooks* in February 1844. Their stress on a materialist interpretation of a specific religion and society marks the first real step on the road to *The Communist Manifesto*.[12]

Nevertheless, *On the Jewish Question* has been persistently undervalued as a crucial step in the evolution of Marx's thought. Marx himself suppressed any mention of it when he reconstructed his intellectual biography in 1858. Many later commentators have been too embarrassed by its ferocious Jew-hatred to recognize the genesis of humane Marxism in such a repellent essay. Yet its emotional excitement and

[11] For the question of whether Moses Hess's *Essence of Money*—also intended for the *German-French Yearbooks*—influenced Marx's essay *On the Jewish Question*. See below, chap. 18.

[12] J. Katz, *From Prejudice to Destruction: Anti-Semitism 1700–1933* (Cambridge, Mass., 1980), pp. 170ff., finds the juxtaposition of *On the Jewish Question* and the *Introduction* "purely accidental," and asserts that anyone interested in the development of Marx's socialist doctrine can dispense with his original linkage of it to the Jewish Question. This dismissal of the role of *On the Jewish Question* seems to me to destroy any hope of understanding Marx's intellectual development. By contrast, M. Rubel (*Rubel on Karl Marx*, ed. J. O'Malley [Cambridge, 1981], pp. 107ff.) sees the *Introduction* and the Jewish essay as inseparable: "the results of a single ethical conviction."

rush of connected argument are the hallmarks of the first account of an intellectual and emotional breakthrough. This quasi-religious "conversion" at last made all clear. The puzzle of the "hidden consciousness" has been solved at a stroke; religious egoism and the practical Mammonism of private property are manifestations of "the one mystical consciousness"—and that consciousness is *Judentum*.[13]

*On the Jewish Question* consists of two separate critiques, the first a critique of Bauer's work on *The Jewish Question*, the second of the same author's "Capacity of Present-day Jews and Christians to Become Free." The lynchpin of Marx's criticism was that Bauer had misunderstood the natures of both "political emancipation and human emancipation."[14] Accordingly, Marx devoted his first critique to an analysis of political emancipation. Bauer had seen political emancipation as meaning the emancipation both of the Jews and of the state itself from their *religious* consciousness. The Jew would be emancipated politically when he loosed himself from his Jewishness, and the state would be free when it had lost its Christian aspect. According to Marx, such reasoning arose from a hopeless misunderstanding of "the state" and a confusion of political and human emancipation. Marx immediately attacked the very concept of the "state" as being unfree; Bauer's "free state" was a chimera, for the state was the paramount institution of civil or bourgeois society. The rights granted by any state were bourgeois rights, that is, civil rights and the "rights of man," and these were but the rights of the egoistic, self-interested men who formed civil society. Such rights, representing only a political emancipation, were not those true human rights, which could come only from human emancipation. Marx ended by declaring that

> political emancipation is the reduction of man to a member of civil society, to an egoistic, independent individual on the one hand, and on the other hand, to a citizen, a moral person. Only when the actual, individual man has taken into himself the abstract citizen and become a species-being . . . will human emancipation be completed.[15] (p. 234)

[13] *Introduction to the Critique of Political Economy*, 1858. But McLellan, *Marx before Marxism*, p. 141, for example, concedes that *On the Jewish Question* was the first tentative application of the doctrine of alienation in the context of economic materialism. Rubel fully admits the Jewish essay's central importance in several of his writings including his *Marx* (London, 1980), pp. 8f.; *Rubel on Marx*, pp. 107–11; *Marx without Myth* (Oxford, 1975), p. 31. J. Waldron, *Nonsense upon Stilts: Bentham, Burke, and Marx on the Rights of Man* (New York, 1988), focuses on the importance of *On the Jewish Question* for Marx's general theories of rights. Cf. M. Maidan, "Marx on the Jewish Question: A Meta-critical Analysis," *Studies in Soviet Thought* 33 (1987): 27–41.

[14] *Early Writings*, p. 216.

[15] Page references are to the (amended) translation by Colletti in *Early Writings*.

In the meantime, in the bourgeois, self-interested, individualistic state, there is every reason why forthwith the Jews should be politically emancipated without renouncing their egoistic religion. Marx thus refuted Bauer's denial of the Jewish claim to political emancipation by deploying a critique of the fundamental concepts of "the state" held by radical, liberal, and conservative alike. The foundations of Marx's later thought are evident in this critique: the insistence that bourgeois civil rights are illusory and a mere projection of the ethic of egoistic civil society; the notion of false consciousness; the call for a more profound revolution; the promise of human redemption.[16]

This distinction between "human" and "civil-political" emancipation has often been taken as one of the more novel features of Marx's essay. Yet as we have seen it was a commonplace with the Young German movement, being particularly clearly expounded by Gutzkow and, of course, by Wagner at the end of *Judaism in Music*.[17] The distinction was the basis of the very widespread revolutionary attitude that anyone who conceded the justice of civil emancipation was permitted to brand his Jewish protégés as moral, economic, and national egoists and materialists—and to demand that the Jews emancipate themselves from their Jewish vice into full humanity.

In the second critique Marx turned to the nature of human emancipation itself and, by means of the fecund myth of *Judentum*, expressed his vision of the redemption of man from alienated egoist into loving species-being. Judaism is depicted as the religion of egoism that obstructs the redemption, not only of the Jews, but of civil society in general. Giving Feuerbach's ideas an economic twist, Marx related the rise of the various egoistic consciousnesses to different stages of economic development. And he further twists Feuerbach and Bauer by insisting that Judaism, far from being abolished by Christianity, has subsumed it and through Christianity now governs civil society. Money, the Mammon of Israel, is the fetish of bourgeois society:

> What was the essential basis of the Jewish religion? Practical need, egoism. . . . These are the principles of *civil society*. . . . The god of practical need and self-interest is money. . . . Money is the jealous God of Israel before whom no other god may stand. Money debases all the gods of mankind and turns them into commodities. . . . Money has

---

[16] Carlebach, *Marx and the Radical Critique*, pp. 164ff., rightly sees this critique as far more penetrating an attack on the bourgeois state than the second critique, which is usually seen (despite its anti-Jewish tone) as more fertile.

[17] K. Gutzkow, *Vermischte Schriften* (Leipzig, 1842), 2:175, writing in 1838. See above, chap. 11.

robbed the whole world, the world of man as well as of nature, of its proper worth. Money is the alienated essence of man's labor and life, and this alien essence dominates him as he worships it. (p. 239)

Only with the abolition of this false god, which alienates man from man, will come the abolition of religion and of the civil state, and therewith "freedom."

This second critique, which has proved so pernicious in its influence, depends for its persuasive power on the ambiguity of the term *Judentum*. Marx fluctuates constantly between *Judentum* as a purely allegorical depiction of civil society and as the term for actual Jewry. On one page he can emphasize first that *Judentum* is the essence of civil society and then smoothly shift to the claim that the actual Jew's real essence is economic. The distinction between the Jew as a real person and the Jew as a metaphor is hazed over intentionally throughout the essay in such passages as these:

> The Jew has emancipated himself in a Jewish way, not only by acquiring financial power, but also because both through him and without him, *money* has become a world-power and the practical Jewish spirit has become the practical spirit of the Christian peoples. . . .
>
> We therefore recognize in Judaism the presence of a universal and *contemporary anti-social* element whose historical evolution—eagerly nurtured by the Jews in its harmful aspects—has arrived at its present peak. (p. 237) . . .
>
> Not only in the Pentateuch and the Talmud but also in present-day society we find the essence of the modern Jew . . . not only as the narrowness of the Jew, but as the Jewish narrowness of society. (p. 241)

The ambiguity is further blurred by Marx's "transformational" trick of reversing subjects to bring out new meanings. Thus, "let us not look for the Jew's secret in his religion; rather let us look for the secret of religion in the real Jew" (p. 236). This ingrained ambiguity permeating the whole text is a warning against reading the essay as merely an allegorical use of *Judentum* to designate the commercial world.[18] *On the Jewish Question* is in fact the foundation of an entirely

---

[18] Rubel, *Marx without Myth*, pp. 38ff. *Rubel on Marx*, pp. 109ff., goes so far in exculpation that he claims Marx did not reproach the Jews for their "religion." In fact, Marx repeatedly condemns the Jews for the egoism of their religious belief. McLellan, *Marx before Marxism*, pp. 141f., rather ingenuously construes the essay as mere allegory, as does E. Silberner, *Sozialisten zur Judenfrage* (Berlin, 1962).

Contemporary communists such as Hermann Ewerbeck saw Marx's essay as a full religious critique. It was first reprinted in French translation in Ewerbeck's collection of radical German religious writings, *Qu-est-ce que la Bible d'après la nouvelle philosophie allemande* (Paris, 1850), which includes extracts from Bauer, Ghillany, Daumer, and

secularized form of Jew-hatred far more systematic in its theory than the other revolutionary efforts of Bauer and company.[19]

For Marx successfully replaces the Christian dual meaning of the Jew as both actual and metaphorical sinfulness with a new myth that sees Jews simultaneously as real-life agents of egoistic capitalism and as metaphors for the whole of sinful civil society. Just as Christ's redeeming mission had earlier been resisted by the stubborn Jews, so now their tenacious, unchanged, real-life descendants stand in the way of human redemption. And, at the same time, as in Christianity, Judaism retains its power as an allegory of debased, alienated humanity. Redemption from *Judentum* will redeem mankind as it has redeemed Marx personally.

With this transformation of Christian Jew-hatred comes a fresh economic, social Ahasverus. Now the message is: Save the Jew, and save society at the one stroke by destroying *Judentum*.

> We can explain the tenacity of the Jew not from his religion, but from the human foundation of his religion, from practical need and egoism. . . .
>
> Not only in the Pentateuch and the Talmud but also in present-day society we find the essence of the modern Jew not in an abstract but in a supremely empirical form—not only as the narrowness of the Jew, but as the Jewish narrowness of society. . . .
>
> The social emancipation of the Jew is the emancipation of the Jew from Judaism. (p. 241)

The personal redemption of Karl Marx, the redemption of the Jews as a race, and the redemption of society at large are all involved in the one process—the destruction of Judaism. While this is all very well as a visionary myth, the use of a myth with real referents raises real dangers. The double meaning of *Judentum* means not only that mankind is to be released from metaphorical Judaism but also that society is to be purged of actual Jewry. Real-life Jews are doubly cursed; they are the demonic personification of capitalism *and* the actual agents who have produced capitalism with its attendant distortion of human relations and freedom.

It is noteworthy how much of the anti-Jewish baggage of Wagner is evident here. Although the two men never met, they both went through the same crucial stage of intellectual development: each of

---

Weitling. Marx admired Daumer's idiotic proofs that Jewish religion was "Moloch-mysticism." See M. Nettlau, "Marxanalekten," *Archiv für die Geschichte des Sozialismus und der Arbeiterbewegung* 8 (1919): 388–401, especially pp. 398ff. See above, chap. 14.

[19] For the intensity of this hatred see Wolfson, *Marx*, pp. 74–103; Carlebach, *Marx and the Radical Critique*, pp. 170ff.; Berlin, "Disraeli and Marx."

them began his spiritual rebirth and conversion with an essay on the question of *Judentum*; both men diagnosed the disease of modern man as *Judentum* and prescribed revolution as its treatment. Their main difference lay in Wagner's intensification of the Jewish allegory by overlarding it with a thick dose of Germanism and romanticism. Otherwise we find the same elusive shifting between real and metaphorical Judaism; the same belief that human redemption is being thwarted by the Jews, those incarnations of egoism who reject love and species-being; the same conviction that money is the root of the evils of bourgeois society and that the priests of Mammon are the Jews; the same resentment of law—especially Jewish law—as a corruption of nature; the same claim that the Jewish relation to nature is one of domination; the same indictment of a *Philistine* Jewish contempt for nature, art, and man; the same assertion that the Jews are consequently incapable of true art; the same alleged Jewish—and bourgeois—perversion of sexual relationships between man and woman; the same harping on Jewish traits, which are always seen to be bad; the same assumption that the Jews had not changed for the better since antiquity; and finally the same article of faith that the redemption of Ahasverus must be "destruction." The Jew is as much for Marx as he is for Wagner "the plastic demon" of mankind, shriveling all he touches, the archenemy of the "social." This could be Wagner speaking:

The god of the Jews has been secularized and become the god of the world. Exchange is the true god of the Jew. His god is nothing more than illusory exchange.

The view of nature which has grown up under the regime of private property and of money is an actual contempt for and practical degradation of nature which does exist in the Jewish religion but there only in an imaginary form. . . .

What is present in an abstract form in the Jewish religion—contempt for theory, for art, for history, for man as an end in himself—is the actual and conscious standpoint, the virtue, of the man of money in general. The species-relation itself, the relation between man and woman, etc., becomes a commercial object! Woman is put on the market. . . .

The ungrounded and unfounded law of the Jew is only the religious caricature of ungrounded and unfounded morality and law in general, of the purely formal rites with which the world of self-interest surrounds itself. Here too the supreme relation of man is the *legal* relation, the relation to laws which apply to him not because they are the laws of his own will and nature but because they *dominate* him and because breaches of them would be avenged. (p. 239)

"Judaism could not create a new world" (p. 240); for Marx, that was the task of the proletariat; for Wagner, that of the artist.[20]

Marx's powerful tract outdoes even *Judaism in Music* in its capacity to generate hatred for *Judentum* and it has remained the chief source of socialist antisemitism, even inspiring in 1972 a curious defense of Auschwitz by the leftist terrorist Ulrike Meinhof:

> Auschwitz meant that six million Jews were killed, and thrown on the waste-heap of Europe, for what they were: money-Jews. Finance capital and the banks, the hard core of the system of imperialism and capitalism, had turned the hatred of men against money and exploitation, and against the Jews. . . . Antisemitism is really a hatred of capitalism.[21]

The high road to human redemption leads only too often through the defile of Jew-hatred.

True, in *The Holy Family* of 1845 Marx tried to emphasize the purely allegorical meaning of *Judentum* and moderated his prejudice against real Jews as "hagglers," but it took him decades to overcome

---

[20] There are many parallels between the two. Both were fearful of their Jewish descent, both were driven by "rancour and irritation" (as Marx's wife said of her husband [*MECW*, 3:579]), both were archegoists who hated egoism ("Marx professes communism, but he is the true believer in egoism," said Ruge with a hint of antisemitism [quoted by Wolfson, *Marx*, p. 75]).

Wagner and Marx never met, but they moved in the same revolutionary circles frequented by Mikhail Bakunin, Georg Herwegh, and August Röckel. C. von Westernhagen, *Wagner* (Cambridge, 1978), 1:133, facilely dismisses the impact of Marxian ideas on Wagner on the ground that the Dresden catalog of Wagner's library contained no political texts. But Heine's *Ludwig Börne*, which Wagner certainly read, does not appear in the catalog either. Arguments based on omission from the Dresden library list must be treated with great caution. (M. Gregor-Dellin, *Richard Wagner* [Munich, 1980], regards the "Marx–Wagner problem" as still unresolved.)

Marx seems ignorant of Wagner until he was delighted by a performance of *Tannhäuser* in 1869, which made Wagner his "favorite composer" (Kugelmann, "Kleine Züge," pp. 297f. The questionnaire here listing Wagner is not the same as that printed in D. McLellan, *Karl Marx: His Life and Thought* [London, 1973], p. 456). But by 1876 Marx was irritated enough by the Wagner Bayreuth boom to scorn the Wahnfried goings-on as suitable material for an "Offenbach libretto." See S. Padover, *The Letters of Karl Marx* (Englewood Cliffs, N.J., 1979), pp. 310, 312.

[21] G. Watson, "Race and the Socialists," *Encounter* (Nov. 1976): 15–23, p. 23; D. Paul, " 'In the Interests of Civilization': Marxist Views of Race and Culture in the Nineteenth Century," *Journal of the History of Ideas* 42 (1981): 115–38, at pp. 127ff.; R. Wistrich, *Socialism and the Jews* (Rutherford, 1982); idem, *Hitler's Apocalypse: Jews and the Nazi Legacy* (London, 1985).

his Jew-hatred, which often emerged in disgusting remarks.[22] Unable to accept his own Jewishness, he was ever bitterly provoked by the Jewishness of his socialist fellows, particularly Lassalle, whom he derided as "a Jewish nigger."[23] But in the eyes of his non-Jewish socialist fellows, Marx never lost the taint of Jewishness. Proudhon and Bakunin saw no difference between "a Marx and a Rothschild"; both belonged to the same parasitic "race of leeches."[24] In 1878 Karl Eugen Dühring, attacking "the Jew Marx," gloated over this "racial conflict in the International," which he attributed to "Bakunin's revulsion against the Jewish blood of Marx." This racial insult stung Marx to the heart: unable to answer for himself, he left it to Engels to write the *Anti-Dühring* and combat the antisemitism that the two friends had fostered for so many years.

It may be that this wound drove Marx to reconsider his attitude to Judaism. In his last years Marx seemed to hint at a softening of his hostility to Jews. He advised his family to turn to the Jewish prophets rather than freethinkers for inspiration, and he befriended the Jewish historian Heinrich Graetz.[25] Perhaps Marx was belatedly following the path of his intimate friend Heine, who might well have agreed with the theorist's anti-Jewish attitude during the period of their collaboration in 1844, but by 1848 had recognized the vacuity and injustice of the revolutionary critique of Judaism.[26]

[22] *MECW*, 4:87ff., 94ff., 106ff. See Carlebach, *Marx and the Radical Critique*, pp. 174ff, for *The Holy Family*. For sample remarks see M. Geltman, "Socialist Anti-semitism," *Encounter* (March 1976): 92–94; (Aug. 1976): 95–96.

[23] W. H. Chaloner and W. O. Henderson, "Marx/Engels and Racism," *Encounter* (July 1975): 18–23, at p. 19.

[24] Silberner, *Sozialisten*, pp. 390ff.; G. Lichtheim, "Socialism and the Jews," *Dissent* (July–Aug. 1968): 314–42, especially pp. 332ff., 338.

[25] Prinz, "New Perspectives."

[26] Heine, 2d preface to *History of Religion and Philosophy in Germany*, ed. P. L. Rose (North Queensland, 1982), pp. 1–7. See above, chap. 9.

# CHAPTER 18

# Beyond Ahasverus and Moloch: Moses Hess's Subversion of the Revolutionary Myths of Judaism

Moses Hess (1812–75)—the "communist rabbi" and the founder of Zionism who helped convert Marx, Engels, and Bakunin to revolutionary socialism—was one of the very few in the nineteenth century to reprimand his good friend Marx for his diatribe *On the Jewish Question*. Marx, said Hess, "ought to be ashamed of joining the German racist enemies of the Jews and insulting his ancestors in their graves."[1] This basic disagreement arose from the utterly contrasting characters of the two Jewish communists, which carried through into their political ideas. Where Marx claimed scientific proof of the victory of socialism and relied on logical demonstration, Hess regarded socialism as a matter of ethics and justice, concepts which in his later works he saw as constituting also the essence of Judaism. Moreover, unlike Marx, who used his universal ideals to denigrate Judaism, Hess openly despised the invocation of grand humanitarian ideals to abolish the true historical reality of individual cultures and nations. This sensitivity to the question of nationality moved Hess in his late work *Rome and Jerusalem* to announce that the redemption of humanity would be attained by the liberation of the Jews, not through their disappearance as a nation, but rather by their emancipation once more into the dignity of nationhood. The Jewish Question was, indeed, the "last nationality question." This final transformation of the Jewish Question subverted (for those few willing to listen) the whole edifice of the revolutionary critique of Judaism that, ironically, the young Hess had been so active in constructing with Marx and the Young Hegelians in 1843–45. From the very start, however, Hess was moved by profoundly Jewish sympathies that put him out of step

---

[1] Manuscript quoted by E. Silberner, *Moses Hess: Geschichte seines Lebens* (Leyden, 1966), p. 559 (*SGL*). In general, see S. Na'aman, *Emanzipation und Messianismus: Leben und Werk des Moses Hess* (Frankfurt, 1981); S. Avineri, *Moses Hess: Prophet of Communism and Zionism* (New York, 1985); idem, *The Making of Modern Zionism* (London, 1981), chap. 3; I. Berlin, "The Life and Opinions of Moses Hess," in his *Against the Current* (London, 1979), pp. 231–51; J. Frankel, *Prophecy and Politics: Socialism, Nationalism, and the Russian Jews 1862–1917* (Cambridge, 1981), pp. 7–28.

with his fellow Young Hegelian revolutionaries but at the same time allowed him to transcend their rather mechanical systematism.

Hess's first book, the anonymously published *The Sacred History of Mankind* (Stuttgart, 1837), had attempted an interpretation of the role Judaism might play in a modern secular revolutionary world. It was in a sense a response to the despair expressed about Judaism and Jewishness by Joel Jacoby in his *Lamentations of a Jew* of the same year, and Hess actually begins with a quotation from Jacoby.[2] The book is permeated with the new revolutionary spirit abroad in Germany, but it is also shot through with a deep sympathy for the modern quandary of Judaism exemplified in an extreme form by Jacoby. Hess, however, sees a way out of the apparent cul-de-sac, one for which he draws on the inspiration of two other perplexed Jews, Spinoza and Heine.

For Hess, as for Heine in the 1830s, the Jewish Question is an intensified case of the general problem of human alienation (*Zerrissenheit*). But Hess also perceived that Judaism, as well as being part of the problem, was also the key to its solution—an insight that was to come to Heine only after his "conversion" of 1848. Both Heine and Hess agreed in 1837 that the general solution to alienation was "the religion of love," a precept that they both preferred to derive from the Saint-Simonians rather than the Young Hegelians, whom it appears that Hess had not yet read. But Hess was ready to trace the "religion of love" back to Spinoza and to understand it as essentially a modernized and secularized—"revolutionized"—form of Judaism. The modern revolutionary age itself was thus to incorporate "Jewish" traits and structures. This "Judaization" of revolution—and of Hegel's thought—was something that was not likely to appeal to Young Hegelian and Young German apostles of revolution. It marks Hess as an outsider within the German revolutionary tradition.

Yet *The Sacred History of Mankind* gives the appearance of being very much in the Young Hegelian mold, adding as it does a visionary dimension to Hegel's concepts of reason, history, and spirit. Hess here interprets the history of mankind as a "sacred" process of spirit, which culminates in the final "organic" unity of the human species in the Third Age of the spirit. A "New Jerusalem" will be created in the heart of Europe in which inherited property will be abolished and free love reign between man and woman. This universal emancipa-

---

[2] Reprinted in Hess, *Philosophische und sozialistische Schriften 1837–1850*, ed. A. Cornu and W. Mönke, 2d ed. (Vaduz, 1980; *PSS*). Hess signs himself "A Disciple of Spinoza" and (p. 33) quotes Heine's *History of Religion and Philosophy in Germany,* though (p. 466) he had not yet read the radical German philosophers. (For Jacoby, see above, chap. 2, n. 28, and chap. 11, n. 26).

tion is to be accomplished by the triumph of a Spinozan "religion of love" over the egoism promoted by "money aristocracy." But here Hess departs from the usual Young Hegelian tracks; he refrains from stigmatizing Judaism as the archreligion of egoism. He does, however, see Judaism as having been superseded by Christianity, although in turn that was itself being replaced by the Spinozan religion of love with its Jewish connotations.

Hence the ambiguity of Hess's depiction of the Ahasverus motif in the later sections of this work. There is first of all what appears to be the conventional depiction of the lifeless ghost of the Wandering Jew:

> Life when [organically] sundered may carry on for some time, but God is no longer its essence. History furnishes us with . . . two major and cautionary examples. We are terrified when we behold them as if we had seen some nocturnal spirits. Both have long since fallen into the grave. One appears to us only as an airy mist, the other like a rigid corpse. They are the Jewish people, a spirit without life—and the Chinese, life without spirit.[3]

But to counter this typically Young Hegelian view of a lifeless Ahasverian Judaism, spent both as a race and as a religion, Hess concludes with a final vision of the revolutionizing potential that Judaism still holds for the rest of humanity. Judaism contains the germ of the messianic utopia of the future because, unlike Christianity, it embodies the secret of how to unite religion and politics, matter and spirit, something that is impossible in Christianity:

> We speak of the old sacred *Volkesstaat*, which long ago fell, but which in the emotions of its dispersed members still flourishes today. In the Jews, in this despised race true to its own customs which after a long sleep has again awakened to a higher consciousness, which by degrees begins to end the inconstant wandering to which it had been condemned until it saw His face again—in the Jews, I believe, their old Law lives again, a more vivid testimony of their sacredness than any other historical monument, an even truer testimony than their Holy Scriptures, a more eloquent one than their ancient deeds of freedom. This people was called from the beginning to conquer the world, not like pagan Rome, through force of arms, but through the inner strength of its spirit. It wandered, like a spirit, through the world that it conquered, and could not be destroyed by its enemies because it is impalpable. Now has this spirit penetrated the world, now does it seek a constitution worthy of the ancient mother. This new sacred constitution will rise again transfigured. From the old world fallen into chaos,

[3] *Heilige Geschichte*, in *PSS*, p. 72. Cf. pp. 54ff., 58, 62, 66ff., 72.

the genius of mankind will break surface, as from a tide driven by the spirit of God.[4]

The redemption of this wandering spirit-race of Jews will be achieved by their assimilation into the European peoples. Then the Jewish teachings of Jesus and Spinoza will guide the Europeans into the New Jerusalem. The redemption of Ahasverus is therefore the key to the European revolution.

For Spinoza is the prophet of revolution and it is through him that the revolutionary essence of Judaism will live again. Though traditional Judaism may, as the Young Hegelians say, be obsolete—a spirit without a body—the redeemed Jews will donate their fertilizing spirit to the new revolutionary "body" of the European peoples. Judaism, because of what Hess sees as its intrinsic vision of social harmony and justice, represents the true spirit of revolution.

The brilliant originality of Hess's approach may seem to verge on eccentricity, but that is so only if one regards it through the conventional lens of Christian European historiography. He has taken the revolutionary spirit and reinterpreted it within Jewish rather than Christian categories; he has insisted that Jewish history is not marginal, but rather central to world history; he has rejected the Hegelian characterization of Judaism as the religion of egoism and made it instead the religion of love; and he has, on the mythological level, accepted the Ahasverian allegory of Judaism but turned it inside out so that it represents the eternal fertility of Judaism, rather than being a symbol of its irrelevance.

Three years after this first book, the Damascus Blood Libel of 1840 confronted Hess with both the Jewish Question and the problem of his own Jewish identity. Later, in 1862, he recalled:

> Twenty years ago an absurd charge from Damascus against the Jews circulated in Europe and a bitter but justifiable grief welled up in all Jewish hearts because of the crassness and credulity of the Asiatic and European mobs ready today, as two thousand years ago, to lend ear to every calumny against the Jews. At that time I was in the midst of my socialist strivings, but the realization came to me for the first time very sharply that I belonged to an unfortunate, slandered people, forsaken by all the world, scattered in all lands, but a people not yet dead. Even though I then stood far from Judaism, my Jewish patriotic feelings found expression in a cry of pain, which nevertheless was soon again

[4] Ibid., pp. 73f.

smothered in my breast by the greater pain that the European proletariat aroused in me.[5]

In 1840, however, Hess had been forced to conclude that a Jewish
national feeling of solidarity was sorely lacking, particularly after an
unfortunate personal experience later that year:

> The manner in which this persecution of the [Damascus] Jews has
> been understood in enlightened Germany must be reckoned to mark
> a turning point in Judaism. It shows only too well how, despite all the
> education of the Western Jews, there exists between them and the Eu-
> ropean peoples still as great a division as there was during the most
> lamentable religious fanaticism. . . . Yet Jew-hatred has remained a
> riddle to our educated German Jews. . . . Did I not myself have the
> unpardonable stupidity to send a musical setting of "The Free Ger-
> man Rhine," this German Marseillaise, to its author, Nikolaus Becker
> . . . only to find that this German gentleman not only answered my
> patriotically glowing letter in an icy tone, but on the back of his letter
> in a disguised hand added "You are a Jew."[6]

Jewish national consciousness was too weak to protect the Jews
against this racial antagonism. In another text of 1840, Hess compared the Jews with the Poles, who seemed to him to have a future
(despite the partition of Poland) precisely because their national feeling lived on. The weak reaction of the Jews to the Damascus Affair
appears to have convinced Hess that they were so deficient in national consciousness as to have lost any independent future.[7] The
only solution to the Jewish Question, therefore, lay in the victory of
a universal religion and the total assimilation of the Jews. With the
disappearance of Judaism, Jew-hatred would vanish, too. At this
point, Hess seems to have had no inkling of the possibility of an independent Jewish state.

This assimilationist line, born of a pessimistic appraisal of the national consciousness of the German Jews, was extended in Hess's next
work, *The European Triarchy* (Leipzig, 1841), brought out by Feuerbach's radical publisher Otto Wigand. The Jew-hatred revived by the
Damascus Affair impressed Hess that pious hopes for a civilizing "religion of love" were not enough. In 1840–41, he therefore developed

[5] *Rom und Jerusalem*, 2d ed. (Leipzig, 1899), Brief V, pp. 18f. (*RJ*).

[6] Ibid., pp. 20f.

[7] "Polen und Juden," manuscript in Central Zionist Archives, Jerusalem, Hess Papers (indexed as MS B. 228 in E. Silberner, *The Works of Moses Hess: An Inventory* [Ley-
den, 1958]). Cited by Avineri, *Making*, p. 40. See R. Michael, "Vier unveröffentliche
Manuskripte von Moses Hess," *Bulletin des Leo Baeck Instituts* (Jerusalem) 7 (1964): 312–
44. See also below.

a new "philosophy of action," which would secure the social emancipation of Europe by means of a messianic pan-Europeanism implemented by England, France, and Germany. In this European redemption, the Jews had a unique part to play, having been led to the west by Providence, where they had acted as a fundamental principle of historical change and progress:

> The Jews must exist as a goad in the life of Western man. . . . They are the ferment of Western man, from the beginning called upon to represent the principle of movement. When the time comes, the Jews will cast their leavening on mankind.[8]

The "wandering" of the Jews, from being a curse, has been transformed into a symbol of the very principle of history, of becoming, of movement. (This insight was to be developed dramatically in Hess's later writings.) Their dynamic "fermenting" role in the new Europe would release the Jews from the static curse of Ahasverus, a curse that Hess now saw (with some theological modification) the Christians as sharing:

> Do not be so contemptuous of the Wandering Jew. Do not forget that your hope of the second coming of the Lord is like the Jewish hope in the messiah. But it is true that the Jews since relinquishing their idea of the future and producing Christ have remained unsouled mummies. The curse of stagnation afflicts ever the children of Israel and like a ghost they have wandered since then through the world of the living, which is animated by the spirit of God. They cannot die nor rise again from the dead. The rejuvenating principle of Judaism—the belief in the messiah—is extinct and their hope for redemption, which they have truly misconceived, has been shriveled into a bald abstraction. But is it otherwise with the Christians' hope in the triumph of Christ? . . . The rejuvenating hope of the Christian Church is equally extinct.[9]

Hess has here generalized the Young Hegelian allegory of the Wandering Jew into an allegory of European society. Ahaverus now represents a stagnation in human affairs that must be overcome. The redemption of Ahasverus, therefore, is of universal rather than merely Jewish significance. "The emancipation of the Jews is an integrating moment in the emancipation of the spirit."

This cosmic perspective informs Hess's attitude to even the narrower issue of the civil emancipation of the Jews. The key civil right

[8] *Die europäische Triarchie*, in *PSS*, p. 130.
[9] Ibid., pp. 130f.

becomes that of civil marriage between Jews and Christians, for this
is the road to the total social assimilation of the Jews and the victory
of love:

> The Jews lack the . . . most essential thing for their equality if they are
> not granted besides their civil rights that right of civil marriage [with
> Christians], which is the means of their emerging from their sepa-
> rated social isolation. What would emancipation benefit them if in life
> they remain as before exposed to the slow torture of hatred and con-
> tempt?[10]

Surrendering now all hope for Jewish national survival, Hess goes to
the extreme of urging "educated Jews to escape their nationality," to
marry Christians and not bring their children up as Jews.[11] With intermarriage, wrote Hess in an article in Marx's *Rheinische Zeitung* in
1842, "the national and every separate characteristic of the Jews"
would vanish.[12]

It is important to notice that Hess means the soft "destruction" of
Judaism to be achieved through intermarriage (he himself married a
Christian) and not through conversion. This rejection of conversion
is most significant. Conversion appeared to Hess to be denying the
Jew's historical identity and personal consciousness; the false new
identity acquired would satisfy neither the convert nor his fellow Germans for whom the enlightened, baptized, or revolutionized Jew still
remained a Jew withal. "We still hear some speaking of Jewish 'race'
[*Nationalität*] as something that stands in the way of emancipation.
But please tell me, what may the enlightened Jew do in order to escape from his *Nationalität*?" In Hess's opinion, there was only one way
out and that was intermarriage. This was the only genuine path to
the destruction of traditional Jewish identity, not only in the eyes of
the Germans, but also for the Jews themselves, who would thereby
acquire a genuine new revolutionary identity by assimilation among
the peoples of the world.

Hess's call for the destruction of "Judaism" was sincerely motivated
by a keen desire to abolish the existence of Jew-hatred itself. Since
the Jews, he reasoned, no longer had the will to form an effective
nation of their own, their continued existence as an exiled ghost-race
must always stir the hatred of their reluctant hosts. Hess arrived at
this conclusion from a fundamentally different direction than had
the Young Hegelians; indeed, he started from opposing premises

---

[10] Ibid., p. 143.

[11] Ibid.

[12] *Rheinische Zeitung*, 31 May 1842, quoted by E. Silberner, *Sozialisten zur Judenfrage*
(Berlin, 1962), p. 184.

and aims, notably a desire to vindicate the equal rights of Judaism and rescue its revolutionary vision. There was no whiff in Hess of his colleagues' shameful program of eradicating an inferior and vicious Judaism. Nevertheless, Hess shared with them the same practical conclusion of the "destruction" of Judaism, and no doubt his somewhat oracular and nebulous style concealed the uniqueness of his revolutionary conception from the eyes of his fellow revolutionists.

In any event, Hess was now very much in the radical camp. He was on intimate terms with Marx from 1840, met Gutzkow in 1842, read Feuerbach and Bauer, and was published by Otto Wigand.[13] As Hess informed his skeptical friend Berthold Auerbach, the revolutionists were making an immense and fundamental contribution to "our struggle for the Jews" by reducing the Jewish Question to a basic philosophical principle of self-consciousness.[14] What this meant in reality was that Hess had slipped for the best of intentions into the trap of revolutionary antisemitism.

Like Marx, Hess expected, however, to escape the quandary of Bruno Bauer's crudely anti-Jewish revolutionism by the panacea of "socialism." Hess was well aware of the peril; he had contributed two of his own pieces to *Twenty-One Folios from Switzerland* (Zurich, 1843) in which Bauer's "Capacity of Present-day Jews and Christians to Become Free" appeared. But unlike Bauer's purely atheistic approach, Hess veers to a revolutionary critique of Judaism that is avowedly socialist in character. This is made clear in Hess's main essay here, "Philosophy of Action," where a distinction is made between truly social acts and the egoistic acts of bourgeois society. Here, for the first time, Hess specifically identifies bourgeois society and egoism with *Judentum* and, furthermore, sets this attack in the context of "Molochism," one of the most dangerous and emotionally charged themes of the new Jew-hatred, one given new life by the Damascus Affair and the notorious books on Jewish human sacrifice published by Daumer and Ghillany in its aftermath.[15]

Hess follows Daumer and Ghillany in alleging the identity of the Jewish Jehovah with Moloch, the god of human sacrifice, an egoistic, all-consuming god who is still active in modern life in both a symbolic and a real form:

[13] Moses Hess, *Briefwechsel*, ed. E. Silberner (The Hague, 1959), p. 80 (*HB*).
[14] To Auerbach, 27 July 1842, in *HB*, p. 98.
[15] For these titles, see above, chaps. 14 and 15. Cf. J. Carlebach, *Karl Marx and the Radical Critique of Judaism* (London, 1978), pp. 123, 394.

> The essence of religion and politics consists in absorbing the real life of the real individual by means of an abstract universal that is in reality nothing. . . . That is the conception and also the history of this noble pair of sisters, religion and politics. And Moloch is their archetype. Human sacrifices form everywhere the keynote of divine *and* state service. "Absolute spirit," which celebrates its realization in the "state," is an imitation of the Christian God who allowed his firstborn son to be crucified. . . . The Christian God is an imitation of the Jewish Moloch-Jehovah to whom was sacrificed the firstborn to conciliate Him; with Him the *juste-milieu* Age of Judaism came to terms by means of money, the firstborn being "redeemed" and animals instead of men being sacrificed. *The original slaughtered sacrifice was everywhere man* and, if he later sought to be "delivered" or "redeemed," yet he remained sacrificed in a figurative sense as long as religion and politics existed and is just so sacrificed today.[16]

There is a crucial double transformation here. It is not just a matter of human sacrifice being replaced by money or animal sacrifice—a humanitarian development. Rather, real human sacrifice has been replaced by the sacrifice of humanity itself to money, its apparent substitute! In the liberal "Age of Judaism," Moloch has metamorphosed into Mammon, blood into money.

In an essay written later in 1843 but not printed until 1845, Hess took the money–blood theme to extremes. *The Essence of Money* began by advancing a Rousseauesque morality, albeit in gruesome terms:

> What God is for theoretical life, money is for practical life. . . . Money is the hallmark of our slavery, the brand of our servitude. . . . Money is the coagulated blood and sweat of those who market their inalienable property, their real wealth—namely, their life activity—in exchange for something called capital in order to feed cannibalistically off their own fat. . . . Make no mistake; not only we proletarians but also we capitalists are the victims who suck our own blood, consume our own flesh. . . . The money we consume, for which we work, is our own flesh and blood, acquired, looted, and consumed by us in its alienated form. We are all, to be honest, cannibals, predatory animals, bloodsuckers.[17]

The host to this mass of alienated, egoistic men living off the metaphorical "blood" of money is the "Christian peddler-world" of bourgeois Europe. But Hess cannot remain there and, seduced by the

---

[16] *Philosophie der Tat*, in *PSS*, p. 215.

[17] *Über das Geldwesen*, in *PSS*, pp. 334f. Adapted from Carlebach, *Marx and the Radical Critique*, p. 115.

Young Hegelian revolutionary critique of Judaism, he goes on to characterize bloodthirsty Christian Europe as essentially "Jewish."

This denouement is led up to via a congealed series of metaphors about carnivorous animals and blood, which uncannily anticipates Wagner's later ideas on vegetarianism and blood:

> We find ourselves at the culmination of the social animal world; we are now social beasts of prey—complete, conscious egoists who in the free competition of the war of all against all . . . sanction a money thirst of the social beast of prey. We are no longer herbivores, like our gentle ancestors . . . we are bloodsuckers. . . . Man enjoys his life in the form of money in a brutal, bestial, cannibalistic way. Money is social blood, but alienated, spilled blood.
>
> In the natural history of the social animal world, the Jews had the world-historical mission to develop the beast of prey in mankind and have now completed their task. The mystery of Judaism and Christianity has been revealed in the modern Jewish-Christian peddler-world. The mystery of the blood of Christ, like that of the ancient Jewish reverence for blood, appears now finally unveiled as the mystery of the beast of prey.[18]

But in the modern Jewish-Christian peddler-world the old blood mystery of the beast of prey has lost its poetry and been reduced to prosaic moneymaking. Christian priests are now the mere hyenas of the "money-state," although the kings remain its lions.

And here Moloch makes his appearance, for both money and Jehovah/Moloch are seen as Semitic inventions:

> Money coagulates to form dead written characters. . . . The invention of money and the alphabet are ascribed to the same people who also invented the Jewish god. . . . The alphabet . . . must have been invented by the inventors of Moloch.[19]

It is no accident that Moloch, the blood cult, money, and egoism should all have their matrix in Judaism.

Hess was no doubt trying in this essay to rescue Jews from the Blood Libel allegations of the Damascus Affair by insisting that the Jewish interest was in metaphorical blood rather than real Christian blood. But *The Essence of Money* nevertheless remains shocking for its invocation of an emotional anti-Jewish metaphor that lay deeply embedded in Christian consciousness. After all, the blood of Christ to which Hess refers was itself seen as having been shed by the guilty

[18] *PSS*, pp. 345f. Cf. Carlebach, *Marx and the Radical Critique*, p. 123.
[19] *PSS*, pp. 346f.

Jews. And even on a metaphorical level, the essay strikes a distinctly anti-Jewish note. For, though the modern "social animal world" is seen as jointly Jewish and Christian, Hess singles out the Jews from among its denizens for special mention—"beasts of prey, bloodsuckers, Jews, money-wolves."[20] Hess's revolutionary defense of the Jews was perhaps more dangerous for them than were the older superstitious libels. The Blood Libel had modulated into a Money Libel more appealing to a revolutionary age.[21]

Whence did Hess derive his blood–money metaphor? Ludwig Börne in his *On Money* of 1808 had denounced the money aristocracy of modern society and understood that money was the concrete expression of a prevailing egoism.[22] But in that essay Börne had mentioned neither the Jews nor blood. Heine, on the other hand, held a bitter personal hatred of the Jewish money aristocracy to which his own uncle's family belonged, and he had denounced "money as the true religion of the day and its god." The poet won Hess's admiration for his outspokenness on the subject when the two men became friends at Paris in 1842 (soon after Wagner's departure).[23] Certainly, when Hess rehearsed his bloody "animal world" imagery in 1850, he did so in the context of supporting Heine against Börne:

> The Börne fanatics [he told Alexander Herzen] felt themselves fatally wounded [by Heine's *Ludwig Börne*] and they rush like shot boars upon the hunter—and while the game still bleeds, the hunter shoots again and expertly at more dangerous game, at lions and hyenas, at the kings and priests of the social animal world.[24]

Heine also impressed Karl Marx at Paris in 1844. But while Marx's own *Jewish Question* parallels Hess's *Essence of Money* on the central notion of a "Jewish peddler-world," Marx is more circumspect on the matter of "blood" and refrains from the more vivid imagery of his fellow communist. Even in 1847, when commenting enthusiastically on Daumer's book on Judeo-Christian human sacrifice, Marx emphasized its anti-Christian significance rather than dwelling on its Jewish aspect.[25]

[20] *PSS*, p. 346.

[21] Na'aman, *Emanzipation*, p. 140, and Avineri, *Making*, p. 40, admit its ferocity. Silberner, *SGL*, p. 189, seems to underrate its dangers.

[22] L. Börne, *Sämtliche Schriften*, ed. I. and P. Rippmann (Dreieich, 1964), 1:76. See above, chap. 9. It does not seem to have been previously pointed out that both Börne and Hess may have derived the equation of blood with money from the Hebrew idiom *damim*, where the plural of "blood" also means "money."

[23] *SGL*, pp. 19ff., 36, 56, 152ff.

[24] *HB*, p. 241, letter of February 1850.

[25] Cf. Na'aman, *Emanzipation*, p. 140. Avineri's generally admirable *Moses Hess* seems

Was it Marx or Hess who first expanded the allegory that made the modern bourgeois world a specifically "Jewish" peddler-world? Hess's *Essence of Money* appears to have been written at the end of 1843 and submitted to Marx for inclusion in the *German-French Year-books* soon after. Did Marx, as some critics have suggested, draw on Hess's idea as the inspiration for his own *On the Jewish Question*, which appeared in the first and only issue of the *German-French Yearbooks* in early 1844? The odds seem to be against this. Marx had written his own essay, as far as can be ascertained, at Kreuznach in the autumn and its ideas are related to those in other key documents of the period written before he could have received Hess's script, which probably arrived in November or December 1843. In any event Marx scheduled Hess's essay to appear in the second issue of the *German-French Yearbooks*; had Marx had in his hands the draft of the Hess article before writing his own piece, it seems likely he would have published the works together as companion analyses in the journal's first issue. (This is not to deny that Marx might well have used Hess's piece to polish his own essay.) In any event, the *German-French Year-books* were suppressed after the inaugural issue and Hess's *On the Essence of Money* eventually appeared elsewhere in 1845.[26]

---

The Damascus Affair and Becker's slur had reminded Hess forcibly of the dangerously anomalous position of the Jews in Germany. His answer in *The European Triarchy* and *The Essence of Money* was to seek the redemption of the Jews from this peril by means of the panacea of socialism. But even in 1840 Hess had glimpsed another, far more revolutionary solution to the Jewish Question. The unpublished essay of that year entitled *Poles and Jews* lamented the

to me in his discussion of *Geldwesen* (chap. 5, pp. 131f., 156f.) to neglect the context of the "Blood" debates of the 1840s. Moreover, although Hess certainly damns the Christian money world in this essay, it is difficult to agree with Avineri that Hess primarily identifies bourgeois capitalism with capitalism in contrast to Marx's use of "Judaism" as the main allegory. Hess makes it clear that the "Christian God" stems from the Jewish Jehovah of blood and money.

[26] Avineri, *Making*, pp. 40f., follows earlier writers including Silberner and McLellan in suspecting that Hess's essay strongly influenced Marx's *Zur Judenfrage*, as does also Z. Rosen, "Moses Hess' Einfluss auf die Entfremdungstheorie von Karl Marx," in *Juden im Vormärz und in der Revolution von 1848*, ed. W. Grab and J. H. Schoeps (Stuttgart, 1983), pp. 169–98. Carlebach (*Marx and the Radical Critique*, pp. 110–24), however, disagrees, finding Hess's ideas more in evidence in Marx's *Economic and Philosophical Manuscripts*. But most of Carlebach's argument is based on comparison of Hess's *Geldwesen* and the first part of *Zur Judenfrage*, whereas the real parallel lies in the second part of the Marx essay.

failure of German Jews to understand that Jew-hatred was too ingrained in the German mind to allow them the easy integration they
longed for. A strong national consciousness might have given the
Jews, as it did the partitioned Poles, hope for a future independent
existence; but the helpless reaction of the Jews to the Damascus
Blood Libel proved that they had lost their national identity.[27] Could
the Jews ever recover their national consciousness and redeem themselves? For a time in that same critical year of 1840 Hess dreamed of
a messianic "restoration of the Jews" in Palestine but soon got over
this "pious hope." Not only did the Jews lack the two main attributes
of real existence—a land and a language—they had also effectively
renounced their nationality. "How can the political rebirth of a people happen without a free and strong will—and the will is here entirely lacking." Consequently, Hess felt himself forced to a solution of
the Jewish Question that was assimilationist and saw the Jews' best
hope lying in the triumph of socialism, which alone would ensure
their final integration into German society.[28]

But twenty years later Hess came back once more to the great problem. This time, following through his own logic, he argued that the
Jews did indeed have a national future, and that it consisted in the
restoration of their own nation-state in their own ancient land of Israel:

> Here I stand again after a twenty-year estrangement in the midst of
> my people. . . . A thought that I believed to have been forever stifled
> within my breast stands again vividly before me . . . the thought of my
> own race, inseparable from the Holy Land and the Eternal City, from
> the birthplace of belief in the divine unity of life and the future
> brotherhood of all men.
>
> For years this thought buried alive pounded in my locked breast
> and demanded release.[29]

Three things prepared the ground for Hess's conversion to faith
in the restoration of a Jewish state. In the late 1850s Hess's immersal
in scientific and anthropological studies had begun to work a change
in his outlook, awakening him to the unity that lay beneath the apparent diversity of creation. Seeking to unify the realm of human
existence with the external world of natural forces, Hess looked for
an explanation of why nature divided mankind into varied races:

[27] For this essay, see above, n. 7.

[28] E. Silberner, "Der junge Moses Hess im Lichte bisher unerschlossener Quellen
1812–1840," *International Review of Social History* 3 (1958): 43–70, 239–68, quoted at
pp. 264ff.

[29] *RJ*, Brief I.

What were the national, and the social, purposes of such a diversity of races?

The event that catalyzed this abstract interest in race into a more practical interest occurred in 1859. In that year, the national unification of Italy suddenly opened Hess's eyes to the connection between his racial investigations and the movements of national liberation afoot in Europe. He suddenly realized that the racial idea had until now been monopolized—and *perverted*—by the German nationalists. They had perverted racial thinking into a theory of "racial domination." Always aware of the necessity of racial harmony, Hess abhorred "racial domination," particularly that exercised by Germans against Jews. But now the rebirth of the Italian nation appeared to Hess as a portent of the downfall of the "racial dominations" that had hitherto marred European history.[30]

The final inspiration for Hess's vision of a Jewish state in Israel was the publication of Ernest Laharanne's *The New Eastern Question: Reconstitution of Jewish Nationhood* (Paris, 1860), which demonstrated how a new conjunction of European international politics had made such a state feasible. This was an argument that appealed to Hess who had (since his *European Triarchy* of 1841) been a believer in the messianic potential of the European states system.[31] As Hess was to emphasize, his new Zionist vision, far from being a betrayal of his earlier universalist and socialist ideas, was in fact the culmination of perceptions that he had first dimly expressed in *The European Triarchy* and *The Sacred History of Mankind*.[32]

These three developments prepared the ground, but the real impulse of the climatic *Rome and Jerusalem* was Hess's sudden inspiration in 1861 that the Jews were a reborn, living race. In 1859 Hess had accepted the Jews as a "primal race" but excluded them as a factor in the new racial era of the newer mixed races of France and America. However, a family death in February 1860 seems to have inspired Hess with the revelation of the new messianic role of the Jewish race in modern Europe.[33]

The whole thrust of Hess's *Rome and Jerusalem* (published in 1862) was to prove that the apparent conflict between the universal socialist drive of mankind and the specific needs of the Jewish people was purely illusory. By a feat of intellectual imagination Hess succeeded in this powerful work in totally transforming the "Jewish Question"

---

[30] *RJ*, Vorwort. "Rome" here refers to the liberation of modern Rome from the papacy.

[31] Several pages from Laharanne are reproduced in *RJ*, Brief XI.

[32] *RJ*, Brief V.

[33] *HB*, p. 368. See *SGL*; Silberner, *Sozialisten*, pp. 185–97; Frankel, *Prophecy*, p. 25.

so that the redemption of the Jews was no longer to be granted them by the rest of humanity; instead, the redemption of all mankind was made to depend on the redemption of the Jews. Jewish redemption stemmed not from the destruction of Ahasverus, but rather from his final vindication! Ahasverus may not be mentioned by name, but his presence is palpable throughout *Rome and Jerusalem* as Hess remorselessly demolishes the paramount symbolism of the classical myth of the Eternal Jew that depicted the Jews as a wandering, immortal ghost-race redeemable only by destruction and death.

Hess stood on its head the Hegelian truism that the Jews as a nation were a spent historical force. Contrary to accepted wisdom, dead races could rise again, as the resurrection of Italy, Greece, and Poland showed in modern times:

> To the peoples believed dead . . . who now must affirm their national rights belongs the Jewish race, which not for nothing has for two thousand years defied the storms of world history . . . and turned towards Jerusalem.[34]

What was the purpose of this Jewish survival? Hess sought the answer in a dramatic rewriting of Hegel's concept of world history. From Hegel's dead race irrelevant to human progress, the Jews are turned into a dynamic race and one of the two driving forces in both world history and social life.[35] The Greeks and the Indo-Germans represent the *structural* principle of "nature," of "being," of beauty, and of contemplation, but the Jews are portrayed as embodying the complementary principle of historical change and progress, of "becoming," the *social* principle.[36] Indeed the Jews were more than just the people of "history"; they were the bearers of "organic unity." They had been present at the inauguration of each era of human progress and had produced Christ as a symbolic link between the "historical" and "natural" principles, one of the great steps in humanity's progress.[37] Christianity, however, had not thereby rendered Judaism obsolete.[38] Because of its doctrinal rigidity, Christianity itself was eventually endangered by the growth of those national and humanitarian feelings that marked the newest stage of human development and that had also been ushered in by another Jew, Spinoza. In this latest stage in

[34] *RJ*, Vorwort.

[35] "The Aryan and the Semitic are the two complementary factors conditioning historical life and the equally important facts of social life" (Hess, *Dynamische Stofflehre* [Paris, 1877], quoted by Silberner, *Sozialisten*, pp. 190ff.).

[36] *RJ*, Brief II.

[37] *RJ*, Briefe VI and IX.

[38] *RJ*, Brief V.

the sacred history of mankind, Judaism was coming into its own again, being flexible in dogma and open both to modern philosophical and practical ideas.[39] Now the resurrection of the Jews would usher in the messianic climax of mankind's sacred history, "the world-historical sabbath."[40]

Hess's whole concept of race was positive and humane. The main source of his theoretical idea of "race" as an ethnic and cultural group was Ernest Renan's *General and Comparative History of Semitic Languages* (Paris, 1855).[41] He does not cite Gobineau's *Essay on the Inequality of Human Races* (Paris, 1853–55), whose insistence on the superiority of the Aryan race would have repelled him.[42] Hess totally repudiated any principle of racial supremacy and sincerely insisted on the unique role each race had to play in the growth of humanity, contributing its own individual qualities to human progress. Above all, in the final synthesis of world history the tension between the two primal races, the Jews and the Germans, would at last be resolved harmoniously.[43]

Although Hess believed in the endurance of racial character ("members of a race possess the instincts of their race"),[44] he never preached that faith in the unchanging purity of racial stock that so obsessed the Germans. In 1859, indeed, Hess had seen the future as belonging to the racially mixed peoples of France and America rather than to the relatively unmixed German and Jewish races.[45] In 1862, however, he argues strenuously that the Jews, though not racially pure, nevertheless in breeding with other Aryan and Mongol races reproduced the "Jewish type unaltered." According to *Rome and Jerusalem*:

> The Jewish race is fundamental and original and reproduces itself in its integrity despite climatic influences. . . . The Jewish type is indestructible.[46]

Hess comes close here to a biological idea of race and indeed later he preached that "Darwinism is the general principle of the law of progress."[47] But Hess was no reductionist; he understood race as a com-

[39] *RJ*, Brief VII.

[40] *RJ*, Brief X.

[41] Renan is mentioned in *RJ*, Epilog 1 (p. 109). See above, chap. 1.

[42] *SGL*, pp. 404ff.; Silberner, *Sozialisten*, pp. 190ff.

[43] *RJ*, Epilog 1.

[44] *Dynamische Stofflehre*, p. 34, quoted by Silberner, *Sozialisten*, pp. 190f.

[45] *HB*, p. 368. Cf. Frankel, *Prophecy*, p. 25.

[46] *RJ*, Brief IV, and Epilog 1. Cf. *SGL*, p. 407. See below, n. 87.

[47] Title of manuscript of 1868, listed in E. Silberner, "Zur Hess-Bibliographie," *Archiv für Sozialgeschichte* 6–7 (1966–67): 241–314, no. 192.

plex mixture of ethnic inheritance and cultural tradition solidified over thousands of years, and he totally rejected the crude "blood" thinking of the German racists.[48] Skeptical himself of the racial purity of the Jews, Hess had no hesitation in condemning the German idea of "racial purity" as absurd and unscientific. He confronts honestly the commonplace of German life that Jews are Jews, baptized or not, and he turns it from a negative prejudice into a positive argument for Jewishness. In the "Seventh Letter," Hess observes:

> A Jew belongs by his ancestry to Judaism, even if he or his parents have converted. . . . I have noticed that this is the common practice. The baptized Jew remains a Jew, however he may chafe against it.

In present-day Germany this "racial" quality of Jewishness, however, had acquired an unpleasant significance because of the prevalence of the pernicious German ambition of "racial domination" over Hess's ideal of "racial harmony." This obsession raised the Jewish Question in Germany to a centrality in political debate absent in other countries. Indeed the instinct for racial domination evinced in their attitude towards the Jews would eventually lead the Germans, thought Hess, into a racial war against the nations of Europe, especially the French. In 1859 and again in 1870 Hess predicted a general European coalition against German military domination:

> Then we shall see . . . what will become of those millions of "German swords" that are now being brandished. It will come to this in the end, mark my words.[49]

In 1840, as Hess now recalled in *Rome and Jerusalem*, he himself had been carried away in the wave of fervent German patriotism against the French. It was only the insulting remark by Nikolaus Becker on Hess's setting of "The Free German Rhine" that alerted him to the essentially negative spirit of that patriotism:

> I took Becker's Hep-Hep [anti-Jewish remark] as a personal insult . . . but the insult was not at all personal. One cannot be at the same time a German enthusiast and a friend of the Jews. . . . Such enthusiasts love in their fatherland not the state, but racial domination. . . . The German wants to possess his fatherland for himself exclusively. We will always remain strangers among the nations, which might well

---

[48] "Life is a unity," though a direct product of race (*RJ*, Brief IX). Spirit, society, and race are all indissolubly linked (*RJ*, Brief IV, p. 12). Hess believed that the "primal races" had a simultaneous origin, rather than sharing common descent from a single ancestral race. See *RJ*, Brief IX, and Epilog 1.

[49] *HB*, pp. 366, 368, quoted by Frankel, *Prophecy*, p. 22.

emancipate us out of humanitarianism or justice, but will never respect us as long as we ignore our own great national tradition.[50]

Assimilation had not been able to overcome the innate antagonism of the Germans. As long as the Jews remained bereft of their own land there would always be a Jewish Question, especially in Germany, where an extreme sensitivity to questions of race guaranteed that they would ever be persecuted as an alien race:

> Even baptism will not redeem the German Jew from the nightmare of German Jew-hatred. The Germans hate less the religion of the Jews than their race, less their peculiar beliefs than their peculiar noses. Neither reform, nor baptism, nor education, nor emancipation will completely open up for the Jews the gates of social life. . . . Jewish noses cannot be reformed, nor black, curly, Jewish hair be turned through baptism or combing into smooth hair. The Jewish race is a primal one, which has reproduced itself in its integrity despite climatic influences. The Jewish type has remained the same through the course of centuries. . . . Baptism in the great sea of Indo-German and Mongolian races has not enabled the Jews to betray their race. The Jewish type is indestructible.[51]

Hess saw through the whole delusion of German revolutionary thought, realizing that as far as the Jews were concerned German racism informed even "humanitarian" attitudes. When Hess had sent the manuscript of *Rome and Jerusalem* to his revolutionary publisher Otto Wigand, that philosophical bookseller had been appalled by its assertion of Jewish nationalism. "I will not publish your observations and views under my signature. The whole text goes against my purely human nature," Wigand had replied.[52] Hess subsequently observed:

> "The pure human nature of the Germans" is the nature of the pure German race, which rises to the conception of humanity in theory only, while in practice it has not succeeded in overcoming its natural sympathies and antipathies. . . . German antagonism to Jewish national aspirations has a double origin. . . . Jewish national hopes are antagonistic to the *theoretical* cosmopolitan tendencies of the Germans. But in addition, the German opposes those aspirations of the Jews because of his racial antipathy, from which even the noblest and most enlightened Germans have not yet emancipated themselves. That

[50] *RJ*, Brief V. See above.
[51] *RJ*, Brief IV.
[52] *HB*, pp. 376f, 2 May 1861. Cf. *RJ*, Brief IV.

German, whose "pure human" conscience revolted against publishing
a book advocating the revival of Jewish nationality, published books
preaching hatred of Jews and Judaism without the slightest remorse
despite their motive—that is, inborn racial antagonism—being essentially opposed to the "pure human conscience." Of his racial prejudice
the German has no clear awareness; he sees in his instincts as in his
spiritual effort not German, nor Teutonic colors, but "human tendencies." He does not know that he follows the last only in theory while in
practice he clings to his German instincts.[53]

In 1858 Wigand had felt able to publish a work by A. Geiger that
insisted that the Jewish and German races instinctively repulsed one
another and that reason and good sense were unavailing in the solution of the Jewish Question. For Hess this selective blindness of Wigand's was proof that in Germany racial antagonism and racial domination triumphed above all ideals of racial harmony. The Germans
could only understand "pure human instincts" in the guise of "pure
Germanism."[54]

Hess's alarm at the open emergence of German racial Jew-hatred
was confirmed by the appearance in 1862 of revolutionary books by
Bauer and Marr, which unmistakeably signified a shift from a purely
philosophical to a racial critique of Judaism. Bauer had also been a
leading light of Wigand's stable of revolutionary writers. His *Judaism
Abroad* especially disturbed Hess, who also assumed him to be the author of an anonymous, ruthless racial attack circulated widely the
same year. *The Jews and the German State* (Berlin, 1861, and later editions by "H. Naudh") amply confirmed the intensity of German racial
antipathy to the Jews and thus hardened Hess's conclusion that emancipation or assimilation would never solve the Jewish Question in
Germany.[55] Behind the book's Christian-German flavor, Hess perceived the pen of a "speculative atheist and revolutionary," whom,
however, he declined to name.[56] (This was not the first time Hess had
criticized Bauer without naming him; even in the collection *Twenty-
One Folios from Switzerland*, to which he and Bauer had contributed,
Hess had criticized "one of those Hegelian rationalists in whose rational state there will be no rights for Protestants, Catholics, and
Jews.")[57] In 1843, however, Hess had not grasped that the true mo-

[53] *RJ*, Brief IV.
[54] *RJ*, Note III.
[55] See above, chap. 15, n. 14. Cf. J. Katz, *From Prejudice to Destruction: Anti-Semitism
1700–1933* (Cambridge, Mass., 1980), p. 213.
[56] *RJ*, Nachschrift, p. 202.
[57] Hess, "Socialismus und Communismus," *PSS*, p. 209. For his subsequent critical
remarks, see *SGL*, pp. 123, 127, 130, 207, 246, 434.

tive of Bauer's anti-Jewish essays lay in racial hatred rather than merely in an excess of rationalism.

Despite his pessimism, however, Hess still held out a slim hope that the Germans could reform themselves and that an eventual reconciliation would avert the "final catastrophe."[58] The reaction to Hess's book by Karl Gutzkow, who had known him since 1842, would have given him grounds for such hope.[59] Reviewing *Rome and Jerusalem* jointly with *The Jews and the German State*, Gutzkow characterized both treatments as "original." He declared himself repelled by Bauer's surrender to instincts of racial separation, but admired Hess's book as a "stimulating combination of rabbinical learning and fantastic revolutionary prophecy."[60] Other reactions were discouraging. The book provoked a violent response from Hess's old Jewish friend Berthold Auerbach, who was convinced that the Jewish Question was in fact being solved by the growth of a humane liberalism actively integrating the Jews into German society. Yet here was Hess prophesying racial antagonism and so jeopardizing the gains already made in Germany towards the emancipation of the Jews. Auerbach had received a manuscript of *Rome and Jerusalem* before publication. Like Wigand, however, he had refused to read more than half the text. He told Hess that he preferred the "homeland of spirit and German language" to his friend's "subjective unhappiness." "Who made thee a prince and a judge over us?" he demanded.[61] Hess was heartbroken by Auerbach's "rejection of a half-read work written with my heart's blood," and insisted that it was not at all a "German-hating work."[62]

Though he admired with Auerbach the ability of such German spirits as Lessing to "rise through education above common prejudice to the highest moral plane,"[63] Hess was convinced that the public life of Germany was too flawed to allow a peaceful solution of the Jewish Question:

> The Germans have so long and so profoundly demonstrated to us that our Jewish race is an obstacle to our "inner emancipation" that we have finally believed it and devoted everything to showing ourselves worthy of blond "Germanness" through the disavowing of our ancestry. . . . But it didn't help Meyerbeer at all that he so anxiously

[58] *RJ*, Briefe VI and XII, Epilog 4–6.

[59] *SGL*, p. 142.

[60] Gutzkow, in *Unterhaltungen am häuslichen Herd* (Leipzig, 3. Folge, Bd. 2, 1862), p. 716, quoted by *SGL*, pp. 434, 716.

[61] *HB*, pp. 451, 375 (Auerbach to Hess, 8 April 1861).

[62] *HB*, pp. 417f., 25 November 1862. For this episode, see *RJ*, Brief IV. Cf. *SGL*, pp. 57–60, 101, 106, 350, 388f., 393, 399. For Auerbach, see above chap. 13.

[63] *RJ*, Brief VI.

avoided treating any Jewish subject in an opera. He did not thereby escape German Jew-hatred. The good *Augsburger Allgemeine* seldom mentions his name without adding in parentheses: (Properly Jacob Meyer Lippmann Beer). Nor did it help the German patriot Börne to have his family name Baruch baptized away.[64]

Liberal emancipation would not do; it ignored the twin facts of German racial hatred and Jewish racial identity. The root of the problem was that liberals wrongly assumed that the Jews were a religion and not a nation. If through civil emancipation Jews were to lose their historical national identity, they should only acquire a false German identity and consciousness, which must leave them unhappy and appear to the Germans as a deception:

> Why deceive ourselves? The European nations have always regarded the existence of the Jews among them as an anomaly. We shall always be strangers among the nations, though they may out of feelings of humanity and justice grant us emancipation.[65]

Liberal emancipation is therefore a false redemption.

Only a genuinely revolutionary solution was possible, one that transcended domestic constitutional debate in Germany about the legal status of the Jews. The solution was a restored Jewish state that would be of global and not merely Jewish interest. For, as the solution to "the final national question," the new Israel was the harbinger of the messianic age in which all races would live in harmony and universal redemption be attained. This new Israel would reflect the final fruition of the two great revolutionary forces, the racial and the social. It would reveal to the world the secret that had eluded Hess's erstwhile socialist fellows—the secret that the racial domination of the Germans towards the Jews was the last obstacle not only to racial harmony but to socialism:

> Forms of social life, like spiritual attitudes to life, are typically and originally creations of race. The whole of history until now has been driven by racial struggles and class struggles. The racial struggle is the primary one, the class struggle the secondary. . . . Thanks to the great French Revolution, which destroyed every racial domination in its midst, racial antagonism is today coming to an end. With that the class struggle will come to an end. The equality of all social classes will fol-

[64] *RJ*, Brief VI. The Meyerbeer reference suggests a tilt at Wagner. Hess certainly knew of Wagner's antisemitism by the time of the 1869 reissue of *Judaism in Music*. Reviewing Wagner's *Rienzi* at Paris in the late 1860s, Hess mischievously remarked that "it is often reminiscent of *The Jewess* and other operas which today Wagner attacks with great animosity" (quoted by *SGL*, p. 579).

[65] *RJ*, Brief V.

low in step with that of all races and is consequently merely an academic question for social economy.[66]

The German instinct for racial domination, however, was still strong and Hess believed it only realistic to admit that a "race war" would be necessary to make the Germans social and humane. Were France and Italy to be conquered in this war, Hess presciently comments, a

> police state would be imposed on the German people, not to mention the Jews for whom something far worse would be in store than befell them after the German War of Liberation . . . when they were excluded from civil rights.[67]

In recognizing the vitality of racial feeling, good and bad, among the peoples of the world, Hess parted company with his socialist friends. Socialist claims to humanitarianism were just as vapid as Wigand's claim to idealism. They all produced misery by shutting out reality:

> In antinational humanitarian theoretical aspirations I see more idealism than actuality. We inhale so much spiritualistic love potion [*Liebesduft*] and humanistic chloroform that we, in our intoxication, become insensible to the sorrow that the continued antagonism of the great human family brings about in real life. . . . Our present national aspirations, far from excluding the humanitarian, rather presuppose them because they are a healthy reaction against the leveling tendencies of modern industry and civilization, which threaten to kill every powerful organic vital instinct through an inorganic mechanism. . . . I only wanted to make comprehensible why I cannot become reconciled with those "universal" strivings for humanity that erase every distinction in the organism of mankind with a few misunderstood concepts of "freedom" and "progressing," only to build altars of license and ignorance.[68]

---

Hess's exposure of the cant of "humanitarianism" and "idealism" signaled his general subversion of the revolutionary critique of Judaism in *Rome and Jerusalem*. The work in fact dismantled the three major foundations of the critique: the belief that the Jews were a sterile ghost-people; the charge that they were a race of egoists; and the designation of the Jews as the archsymbol of the alienation of modern life.

[66] *RJ*, Epilog 5.
[67] Ibid.
[68] *RJ*, Brief IX.

## THE GHOST-PEOPLE

For Hess the Jews had become a living, dynamic, primal race, an organic fusion of life and spirit in constant regeneration. They were not the eternally lifeless race of the Ahasverus myth but were eternal because they embodied a vital principle of Western man, the historical principle of "becoming" itself. Their redemption could not be attained by the death wished upon them by the Christian-German tradition, a death that the revolutionists had merely reformulated. Jewish redemption rather should mean the vindication of the Jews' racial principle of "becoming" and its reconciliation with the Indo-German principle of "being."

By thus discovering in the "eternity" of the Wandering Jew a *vital*, not a *ghost*, principle, Hess shattered the mold of the revolutionary argument against Judaism. The Jews were no longer required to make themselves into true human beings before they could be redeemed; nor did their redemption depend upon the prior emancipation of the rest of humanity. The redemption of the Jews became now the restoration of lost Jewish nationhood and, with Ahasverus restored to his own land, the redemption of the whole world would be at hand. The Jews would become once more the "messianic race" for mankind as they had previously been with Moses and Christ. If any curse remained upon Ahasverus, that was the responsibility not of the Jews but of the Germans, whose desire for "racial domination" led them to refuse redemption to the Jews except through self-destruction of their Jewishness. Disparaging the Jewish religion as dead legalism, German revolutionists felt that for Jews to forsake it would be no sacrifice. But this scorn of Judaism was totally mistaken. Judaism was the great humanitarian religion of the world, not just the national religion of the Jews. It had given birth to the prophets of humanity, Christ and Spinoza. Judaism was indeed the highest religious affirmation of the organic, the life-affirming, the creative instinct of mankind.[69] Judaism was thus a universal religion, though it was not a universal church in that it did not seek converts from outside the Jewish race:

> I believe that the national essence of Judaism not only does not exclude humanitarianism and civilization but has them as its necessary consequences. The Jewish people was until the French Revolution the sole people in the world which had a religion that was both national and supranational. Through Judaism the history of mankind has become a sacred history of humanity, that is, a unitary organic process

[69] Ibid.

of development, which, beginning with family love, will not be completed until all mankind has become a single family.[70]

The Ahasverian eternity and inability of the Jews to die (*Unsterblichkeit*) is thus transformed by Hess from a curse into a testimony to the eternal vitality of Jewish national and humane ideals.

## THE RACE OF EGOISTS

Hess's Ahasverus was no wandering ghost, nor was he the archegoist, that other cliché of the German revolutionary tradition. Just as Hess reversed Young Hegelian principles by making the undyingness (*Unsterblichkeit*) of the wandering Jews a guarantee of the redemption of mankind rather than an obstacle, so he revoked the revolutionary identification of egoism and inhumanity with Judaism and instead made Judaism the epitome of humanity and love. The Jews now became the race of love who will destroy the egoism of the world and thus redeem it!

The basis of this Jewish claim to love is a family love (which Wagner rejected as utterly inferior to the sexual love that he saw as the redeeming force of the world):[71]

Your grief over your dear departed one [Hess told his sister-in-law] ripened my decision to strive for the national rebirth of my people. Love such as yours, which, like maternal love, springs from the blood, and yet is as pure as the spirit of God, such a pure and infinite love of family only a Jewish heart can feel. Only the Jews had the healthy instinct to subordinate the love of women to mother love. . . . This love between generations is the natural source of that intellectual love of God, which, according to Spinoza, is the highest to which the spirit can aspire. From the unconquerable fount of Jewish family love arise the redeemers of the human race. "Through you," says the divine genius of the Jewish family in its self-revelation, "will all the families of the earth be blessed." Every Jew has within him the stuff of a messiah, every Jewess that of a *mater dolorosa*.[72]

You may see plainly the source of the Jewish belief in immortality; it stems from our family love. . . . The living faith in the continuity of the spirit in organic history grew out of the Jewish family. These flowers of Judaism, whose root is Jewish family love and whose stem is Jewish patriotism, this fairest blossom of our national historical religion, has shriveled up [with Christianity] into the belief in the atomis-

[70] Ibid.
[71] Cf. Silberner, *Sozialisten*, pp. 191ff., and Wagner, *PW*, 8:314f.
[72] *RJ*, Brief I.

tic immortality of the isolated soul. . . . Only in the Jewish family has it
survived. . . . But after Descartes, the last Christian philosopher, there
arose out of Judaism [through Spinoza] in its original strength the belief in the Eternal in nature and history which is a bulwark against all
spiritual egoism and materialistic individualism.[73]

Having so scorned the Christian dream of personal immortality as
simple egoism, Hess was able to throw the charge of Jewish selfishness back upon those modern German idealists who had falsely imposed it on the Jews. It was now Schopenhauer and Bruno Bauer
who stood accused of "spiritual egoism" and "materialist individualism." Already in 1844–45 Hess had denounced Bauer as an egoist:
"Philosophical humanism is the same as theoretical egoism."[74] Now
he took issue with Wagner's idol Schopenhauer and the cult of renunciation and annihilation of the will with its trappings of ancient
Indian wisdom:

> In temperate abstinence from the pleasures of life the scriptures of
> both world-historical races discovered the way to holiness and re-
> demption. . . . But among the Indo-German race this abstemiousness
> . . . degenerated into a total renunciation and denial of life as in Brah-
> minism and Buddhism. . . .
>
> The ancient Indian wisdom has rediscovered its purest expression
> in our century in a pure-blooded German, Schopenhauer, who is
> known to every educated person. . . . To renounce life [and will] in
> order to attain holiness is nothing other than contemplative egoism.
> Every effort for a better existence . . . appears to this contemplative
> egoism as pure silliness. For it seems only to perpetuate the natural
> order, the crude, elemental, inorganic unspiritual struggle, the war of
> all against all. But this materialist, antisocial attitude lies behind all re-
> actionary social movements. Schopenhauer has evidently bequeathed
> his property to the Berlin fighters [Bauer et al.] against the people.[75]

The family love and national love of the Jews render nonsensical
the allegation that they are a race of egoists:

> Nothing is more alien to the spirit of Judiasm than the egoistic salva-
> tion of the soul of the isolated individual, which is the chief concern
> of religion according to modern ideas. Judaism never separates the
> individual from the family, the family from the nation, the nation
> from humanity, humanity from the whole of organic and cosmic crea-

[73] *RJ*, Brief IV.
[74] Hess, *Die letzten Philosophen* (1845), *PSS*, pp. 382f. (For trans., see below, n. 92.) Cf.
*SGL*, p. 204.
[75] *RJ*, Note II.

tion, and that creation from the Creator. Judaism has no other dogma
than His unity. This dogma does not depend on a rigid, externally
imposed and so a dead and sterile creed, but rather is sustained by a
living creative confession that is ever regenerating itself out of its own
spirit. This is rooted in family love, flowers into patriotism, and bears
its ripe fruits in the regenerated human society of modern times. . . .
Judaism is above all a nationality whose history, outlasting millennia,
goes hand in hand with that of humanity.[76]

The central Jewish viewpoint, which never separates the individual
from his tribe, his nation from mankind, and creation from the Creator, inspired Hess to offer a final profound transformation of the
Ahasverian myth. The "undyingness," the eternity of the Jews was,
insisted Hess, related to their basic idea that immortality was not an
egoistic matter of the individual soul, but a collective hope relating to
the race as symbolized by the Messiah:

> The Jewish notion of immortality is inseparable from the national be-
> lief in the Messiah. . . . The latest manifestation of the Jewish spirit
> concerning life and death is contained in Spinoza's teaching. It will
> have nothing to do with that sickly, atomistic immortality that dis-
> solves into dust the unified life, sometimes spiritually, sometimes ma-
> terially, and raises the egoistic "every one for himself" to be the high-
> est principle of religion and morality. No people is further removed
> from this egoism than the Jews. Among them rather the fundamental
> principle of collective responsibility was always fully accepted. . . . Ac-
> cording to the fathers, the bourgeois principle of every man for him-
> self was branded as common vice.[77]

"Material individualism," that is, the cult of money, was the other
side of this "spiritual egoism." Here again Hess repudiated the common coin of anti-Jewish currency. It was, however, a coin he had earlier readily accepted himself; from 1841 Hess had abandoned traditional Judaism to its fate because he felt it had decayed into a barren
code of egoistic, practical "utility" whose disappearance would benefit
the human race. In *The Essence of Money* (1843–45) he had gone to
the extreme of characterizing Judaism as the ethic of the "social animal world" of the bourgeois capitalists. But *Rome and Jerusalem* turned
all these unpleasant stereotypes inside out. That the Jews were "parasites" in Germany was not due to their innate egoistic vice, but to the
simple fact that they were deprived of a homeland. This deficiency
forced the Jews into membership of the "social animal world," which

[76] *RJ*, Brief II.
[77] *RJ*, Brief III.

was not their creation nor peculiar to them, but was a universal phenomenon that arose out of the insufficiency of land in earlier epochs. Land was indeed the key to social conflict; to hold land against hostile peoples meant that military ruling classes had had to be set up:

> Social man needs, like plants and animals, an ample free soil. The parasitical system through which man wins life by the exploitation of others has certainly played a great role in the historical development of mankind until now and is by no means peculiar to the Jews. So long as science and industry were in their infancy, the soil that a nation acquired was never for long able to sustain its inhabitants; the peoples had either to fight and enslave each other or in their own midst institute ruling and slave classes. But the social animal world, which lives on man's exploitation of one another, is coming to an end as modern science and industry take over the world. The civilized peoples are readying themselves for the general exploitation of nature by means of the achievements of science. Science no longer needs and will therefore prevent the intermediacy of any parasites and will therefore prevent them coming into being.[78]

For more strikingly still, Judaism has now become the very archetype of "species-being," that is, of social love. The biblical sabbath laws and the jubilee and fallow years are viewed in socialist terms and the Mosaic code construed as "social and democratic" in contrast to the opportunistic individualism of Christianity.[79] In Hess's mind, the primal-racial mission of the Jews is to teach mankind the ideas of God and morality and to "free workers from the tyranny of exploitative speculation."[80] Jews, therefore, instead of being the henchmen of capitalism become its tamers. As Hess wrote subsequently, there had been no bourgeois class domination in Jewish communities, which had been social and democratic in spirit for centuries. "Their national spirit is of the justest, the most egalitarian . . . and so to speak the most modern."[81] A healthy, organic unity was the theme of Judaism, one suited to restoring balance to the present era. "Judaism is neither one-sidedly materialistic, nor one-sidedly spiritualistic; body and spirit here merge into one another." The Jews are no longer the corrosives of organic society; they stand revealed as the restorers of an organic unity that had been lost in the Christian, capitalistic, egoistic society of Germany.

[78] *RJ*, Brief XII.
[79] Cf. Avineri, *Making*, p. 44.
[80] *RJ*, Epilog 4.
[81] Remarks of 1862–64, quoted by Silberner, *Sozialisten*, p. 193.

Hess was fully aware how radically his dramatic racial interpretation might transform the accepted terms in which the Jewish Question had been discussed in the half-century since Börne and Heine.
The *Epilogue* to *Rome and Jerusalem* begins with an explicit effort to
reassess Heine's categories of Hellene and Nazarene in the light of
Hess's new racial understanding. And in 1866, as if recognizing the
original context of his racial ideas, Hess wrote an unpublished *Dialogue from beyond the Grave between Heinrich Heine and Ludwig Börne*, in
which he allowed his two Jewish forerunners to expound his own
views on the German instinct for racial domination and the inevita-
bility of the race war that it would provoke.[82] (Heine, of course, had
not originally construed these labels in a racial sense, but had devised
them to designate the opposing artistic and moral personalities of
mankind. However, after his reconversion to a visionary Judaism in
1848, Heine had extolled Israelite-Nazarene moral character as the
central and continuing contribution of the Jewish race to freedom
and history.)[83]

## SYMBOLS OF ALIENATION

Hess's ultimate refutation of the revolutionary case against
Judaism was to show that the radicals were guilty of the very sin they
attached to the Jews, namely, "speculation" and alienation. It was the
diagnosticians of alienation themselves—Bauer and Marx—who were
truly alienated!

"Speculation," argued Hess, besets the entire gamut of German
life, ranging from intellectual discussion to economic behavior:

> Philosophical and political speculation, managed by intellectual and
> material capitalists both, practice their domination over scientific *and*
> industrial labor. These two kinds of speculative activity, which seem so
> different in appearance, are identical in their function. . . . Natural
> scientists and socialists today work with more or less awareness and
> energy for the final liberation of humanity, for the emancipation of
> labor from speculation.[84]

In the new era, racial domination would first disappear and then
there would come into being

[82] *Dialogue d'outre-tombe entre Heinrich Heine et Ludwig Börne sur la liberté individuelle et
la question allemande*, printed in E. Silberner, "Ein unveröffentlicher Dialog von Moses
Hess," *International Review of Social History* 10 (1965): 455–70.

[83] *RJ*, Epilog 1.

[84] *RJ*, Epilog 5, "The Last Antagonism."

a free association of all productive forces in which the hostile opposition between speculative capital and productive labor would vanish together with that between philosophical speculation and scientific labor.[85]

Intellectually, the revolutionary school of "philosophical humanism" itself represented a merely speculative tradition and was consequently an "inorganic," alienating tendency. The "speculative atheism" of Bauer and his fellows destroyed by its one-sidedness the unity of body and spirit. The result was the gulf between speculation and labor that was manifest in the disconnections of modern life. Only by fusing philosophical and social "speculations" with true productive "labor," whether in industry or science, could the divisive dualism be reconciled and made organically whole again. The revolutionists had mythologized Judaism as the symbol of this fundamental and corrosive alienation that afflicted modern life; for them, Judaism was the epitome of intellectual and economic speculation. But for Hess, Judaism was transformed into the paradigm of the organic unity of body and spirit, and became the ethos and myth that would open the road to the redemption of all mankind in an organic, truly social, paradise. Hess had thus dissolved the whole substance of the revolutionary critique—all too late.

Hess's whole vision of Judaism and of the redemption of the modern world was focused on an Israel that he never saw: his plans to visit the Holy Land with the Jewish historian Heinrich Graetz in 1872 fell through for financial reasons. He died in Paris in 1875, his vision still unachieved, with the evidence of race war all around. As for *Rome and Jerusalem*, its reception disappointed him. The main reaction seems not to have been anger but apathy. The book did not attain a wide readership and was scarcely cited. A few Jewish writers, notably Heinrich Graetz, appreciated Hess's vision, but the founder of modern Zionism. Theodor Herzl, came across the book only after formulating his own ideas. Nevertheless, Herzl paid tribute to Hess's prophetic power, exclaiming that "everything was there."[86]

Hess's last wish was for the publication of his *Dynamic Theory of Matter*, which proclaimed the unity of all creation from rocks and plants to men and races. Coincidentally, this was the time at which Richard Wagner had also come to that final understanding of race and its role in the unity of all creation that inspired the Good Friday Spell of

[85] *RJ*, Brief XII.
[86] R. Michael, "Graetz und Hess," *LBIY* 9 (1964): 91–121.

*Parsifal.* But Wagner's was a far less loving and generous inspiration than Hess's. The whole Wagnerian notion of race and redemption was based on hatred of the Jews: the triumph of the Aryans was the message of *Parsifal.* From similar starting hopes of revolutionary redemption, both men had arrived at racial conclusions that in some ways coincided: both held that Jews remained Jews—"the Jewish type" endured despite generations of miscegenation;[87] both preached racial awareness as a healthy reaction against materialism;[88] both predicted that the reality of race would produce a race war in Europe. But how opposed were their ethics! Wagner insisted that his racial idea was based on love. But that was merely idealistic garb for the instinct of racial domination that Hess so bitingly descried everywhere in German revolutionary thought. Wagner ran true to revolutionary form in excluding the Jews from the festival of redemption; they could be redeemed only by destruction. Hess, on the other hand, cast them in the role of protagonists in the drama of cosmic redemption. Where Hess gloomily saw the German victory in the Franco-Prussian War of 1870–71 as a sign that the epoch of racial war ("the last catastrophe") had begun, Wagner welcomed that victory (even if he soon became disillusioned that the new German Empire was betraying its idealistic antisemitic mission).

What in the end divided the two revolutionists was an irrational hatred of the Jews, which blinded Wagner to any possibility of comprehending Hess's central belief that had been received from the late Heine: the belief that the Old Testament Jews had made the critical revolutionary advance in human consciousness by their awakening of the instincts of social justice and humanitarian feeling, a revolution furthered by such later Jews as Jesus and Spinoza. That Jews remained Jews through the generations was a curse for Wagner, but a blessing for mankind in the eyes of Hess.

The immensity of the Jewish contribution to humanity was used by Hess to overthrow at last the most emotionally charged bulwark of the revolutionary critique of Judaism, the charge of Molochism and Jewish addiction to the sacrifice of humanity and human beings. In his "Philosophy of Action" (1843), his *Essence of Money* (1843–45), and his letter about Börne in 1850,[89] Hess had conceded the revolutionaries' gloating pretense that the Jewish Jehovah was merely a bloodthirsty Moloch in disguise. In *Rome and Jerusalem*, however, Hess had disavowed this radical shibboleth. Now he observed that all ancient

[87] *RJ*, Brief VII. See above, n. 46.
[88] *RJ*, Brief IX.
[89] See above, n. 24 (*HB*, p. 241).

peoples had practiced human sacrifice; but the great humanitarian achievement of the Jews had been to abolish it in favor of animal sacrifice. Jehovah's origin among the blood-devouring Semitic gods was no longer seen as shameful. Rather it was the revolutionary achievement of the Jews to have transcended the cult of Moloch! Hess saw modern Judaism as having passed beyond the cult of animal sacrifice thanks to the moral teachings of the prophets and rabbis.[90] In one of his last essays, "A Characteristic Psalm (LXXXII)," published in 1873, Hess finally cast off the spell of Moloch that had bewitched him. After frankly admitting that Jehovah had emerged from among the Semitic gods ("God judgeth among the gods"), Hess went on to praise even those savage gods as superior to those of the Indo-German mythologies because in these Semitic deities a primitive ethic of justice and humanity had been present. It was this moral ethic that Jehovah had come to personify and demand from the Jews:

> What does it matter if the Semites located their gods in the stars . . . that they offered human sacrifices to the sun and the stars, served Baal and Moloch (sacrifice after all was also customary with the Aryan cults)? What does all this matter if the foundation of their divine cults was a seeking after right, justice, and humanity—things for which the gods of the most developed Aryan mythology, the gods of Greece, scarcely grieved? What would the social world have become without the Semitic gods?[91]

This was Hess's subversion of the Moloch/Jehovah equation devised by the revolutionists of the 1840s as a new Blood Libel suitable for the age of progress and enlightenment.

———

Hess was undoubtedly the most incisive and subtle critic of the Young Hegelians among whom he moved. In his mind, Young Hegelianism was in essence a secularized version of a triumphalist Christianity from which it sought revolutionary redemption. The Young Hegelian mentality was in fact swamped by Christian consciousness: Bauer and company, far from bringing a revolutionary liberation to mankind, were simply writing another chapter in the history of Christian theology. Thus, the German revolution in philosophy was no revolution at all, for it perpetuated the Christian split between

---

[90] *RJ*, Brief XI, Note VIII. Cf. *SGL*, pp. 421ff.

[91] "Ein charakteristischer Psalm," *Monatsschrift für die Wissenschaft und Geschichte des Judentums* (1873), reprinted in Hess, *Jüdische Schriften*, ed. T. Zlocisti (Berlin, 1905), pp. 124–27. Cf. Michael, "Graetz and Hess," pp. 119ff.

matter and spirit, man and society.[92] The Archimedean fulcrum outside Young Hegelianism that afforded Hess his ability to discern its
weaknesses was his own Jewishness, which he converted into a fundamental critical principle. Judaism, in Hess's hands, gave the lie to
the basic premises of the Young Hegelians—to the claim that Judaism
was an obsolete religion that must yield first to Christianity and now
to revolutionary Hegelian philosophy, to the allegation that Judaism
was the embodiment of egoism, to the verdict that a dead Judaism
must be destroyed. Hess found now for a revived Judaism a new and
crucial fructifying influence in human history, discovering in Judaism not a moribund theology, but instead the essence of a revolutionary philosophy of the future of humanity.

Nor did Hess stop at this fundamental subversion of the principles
of German philosophical revolutionism. He also demolished the
foundation of German liberal emancipationism by insisting that the
Jews were not merely a religion as Riesser and friends alleged, but
rather a nation or "race." What ultimately forced Hess to this recognition was his experience of the potency of cultured German prejudice against the Jews in an age of ostensible civil emancipation. Hess
more than any other thinker grasped the intractability of the Jewish
Question in German history. He sought a genuinely revolutionary solution that would escape the deadly ambivalence of the conventional
solutions of the German revolutionists. By seizing the nettle of "race,"
by facing the "social facts," by going back to the principles of "national character" that had informed the original discussion of the
Jewish Question in the years of Dohm, Fichte, and Humboldt, Moses
Hess overthrew the theoretical foundations of the approach of the
German revolution—in all its radical, liberal, and national guises—to
the Jewish Question. And with this subversion came a new revolutionary mythology in which the meaning of Ahasverus was turned
inside out and the old nightmare of Moloch exposed to the withering
effect of common sense.

[92] Cf. Hess's 1845 article, "The Recent Philosophers," trans. in L. Stepelevich, *The
Young Hegelians* (Cambridge, 1983), pp. 359ff.

# PART FIVE

# The Revolution and the Race

# The Chosen Race and the Revolution: Constantin Frantz's Revolutionary Christian Federalism

T HE NEW racist "antisemitism" of the 1870s was built on the connection between *race* and *revolution* urged unremittingly by such
luminaries as Marr, Bauer, and Dühring. The three were rabid atheists and bitterly anti-Christian, and it might be tempting to conclude
that modern revolutionary antisemitism has little to do with Christianity. Yet Christianity itself was being revolutionized from within in
these years so as to engender powerful new currents of revolutionary
Jew-hatred. At Berlin, the court chaplain Adolf Stöcker preached a
"Christian socialism" impregnated with hatred of Judaism; although
he rejected the biological racism of Marr and company, Stöcker nevertheless understood that the Jews were a "race" and that the "revolution" had to destroy Judaism. Stöcker achieved a certain notoriety,
but a more lasting foundation for the twentieth-century Nazi fusion
of race and revolution was being prepared in the 1870s by Richard
Wagner and Constantin Frantz, whose visions of German revolution
drew on the notion of a resurrected and transfigured German Christianity. For Wagner and Frantz, as for Bruno Bauer, the Jewish Question defined the revolution; all were united by their detestation of
Jewish civil emancipation as the corrupting symptom of a rotten, unfree, bourgeois liberal state. The institution of an authentically German revolutionary "free" state, whether Christian or atheistic, meant
liberation from Judaism—and that meant the destruction of Judaism.

    The paths of the revolutionary atheist Bruno Bauer and the
revolutionary Christian Constantin Frantz (1817–91) repeatedly in-
tersect at the crossroads of Jew-hatred.[1] Like Bauer, Frantz partici-

[1] P. Lauxtermann, *Constantin Frantz: Romantik und Realismus im Werk eines politischen
Aussenseiters* (Groningen, 1978); J. Philippson, "Constantin Frantz," *LBIY* 13 (1968):
108–19; L. Sauzin, "The Political Thought of Constantin Frantz," in *The Third Reich*
(New York/London, 1955), pp. 112–47; E. Stamm, *Konstantin Frantz' Schriften und Leben*
(I, 1817–56; II, 1857–66; Heidelberg and Stuttgart, 1906–30 [*Stamm I* and *Stamm II*]).
Idem, *Ein berühmter Unberühmter: Neue Studien* (Konstanz, 1948), affects that Frantz's
line of thought has nothing to do with the Third Reich. Stamm's prewar writings, how-

pated in the "critical" attack on Judaism in 1843–44 and later figured in the "conservative" antisemitism of the early 1860s, and finally (though skeptically) in the "political" antisemitism of the 1870s. Frantz ended up in the camp of Bauer's *Internationale Monatsschrift* group, which related "antisemitism" not only to the internal problems of German society, but to the "modern" problems of international politics and rival imperialisms. Frantz's ideas, however, were more original than the dulled sloganizing of Bauer's later style. And in contrast to Bauer's vague invocation of a "free state" that would abolish the churches and penalize the Jews, Frantz always offered an apparently coherent political philosophy and specific policies. It was a philosophy founded on a grand vision of first German, and then European, federal unification. The revolutionary task of the German race was to civilize the world and establish peace in Europe.

To the modern reader, there are obvious contradictions within Frantz's vision of a global Christian federation: he combined European federalism with fervent German nationalism; democratic monarchism with socialist measures; pacifism with aggressive German expansionism in the east; and a moral tolerant Christianity with abomination of the Jews. But to Frantz—as to his close friend of two decades, Richard Wagner—these contradictions vanished in the brilliant aura of a "new Christianity" promising universal love, freedom, and peace. Frantz's metapolitical utopia provided a "politics of the future" (his own phrase) that could match Wagner's "art of the future" as a revolutionary chart to redemption.[2]

---

ever, had argued that Frantz's thinking was quite compatible with that of Hitler and acclaimed the "confluence of National Socialism and German racial strength." In 1948, of course, it was more politic to stress the role of Frantz as a spokesman for European union. Cf. Stamm's collection of texts (which includes the anti-Jewish passages), *Das grössere Deutschland* (Breslau, 1935).

See also Kurt Waldheim's 1944 Vienna thesis (written during his leave from the Wehrmacht High Command in the Balkans), *Die Reichsidee bei Konstantin Frantz*, discussed by R. Herzstein, *Waldheim: The Missing Years* (New York, 1988), pp. 116–17, 214f., 279. The last pages of the thesis glorify the Third Reich as the culmination of Frantz's idea of European federalism. Like Stamm, Waldheim's supervisor A. Verdross was able, after the war, to exploit apparent paradoxes in Frantz to represent a non-Nazi outlook. Cf. G. A. Craig, "The Waldheim File," *New York Review of Books* 23, no. 15 (9 Oct. 1986): 3–6.

Frantz's letters have been printed as *Briefe*, ed. U. Sautter and H. Onnau (Wiesbaden, 1974), which includes the Wagner correspondence earlier printed in part by H. von Wolzogen as "Constantin Frantz an Richard Wagner," *Bayreuther Blätter* 29 (1906): 114–36; 53 (1930): 2–5. Frantz himself spelled his given name with a "C."

[2] Cf. C. von Westernhagen, "Wagner und das Reich," *Neue Wagner-Forschungen*, ed. O. Strobel (Karlsruhe, 1943), pp. 43–73, for the two thinkers' relations. I hope to deal with the Wagner–Frantz connection in a future article.

Frantz came under the Young Hegelian spell in 1839 and he later became a militant member of Bruno Bauer's "Free" circle at Berlin. Writing in the group's journal *Athenaeum* in 1841, Frantz declared: "Organize these masses, or they will organize themselves—but for battle!"[3] Then, suddenly, in 1843, he was converted to Christian idealism and repudiated the Hegelianism of Strauss and Feuerbach in his *Foundations of a True and Really Absolute Idealism*, which was meant to be a refutation of atheism:

> In a fortunate hour [he later told Wagner], I read John 17, and suddenly I felt as though scales had fallen from my eyes. . . . At one blow, not only Hegelianism but the whole of rationalism was for me dead.[4]

But in abandoning rationalist Hegelian revolutionism, Frantz did not shed his Young Hegelian antisemitism. (He had refused to avail himself of Spinoza's "Jewish" critique of atheism.)[5] Instead, Frantz sought to frame a revolutionary indictment of Judaism that would simultaneously discredit the Hegelian rationalists. His vehicle for this strategy was to be the Ahasverus mythology.

*Ahasverus or the Jewish Question* (1844) advanced a critique of the liberal theory of the state that attacked the theory at its weakest salient point, namely the principle of Jewish political rights.[6] But Frantz went beyond the reactionary "Christian-German" denial of citizenship to non-Christians. He also showed himself dissatisfied with the prevailing use of Jewish immorality as a reason for denying rights to the Jews. Frantz instead proposed a rigorous philosophical demonstration of the inadmissibility of Jewish rights in a true German state. He claimed to have discovered the "inner spirit" of the state, an organic essence rooted deep inside the fabric of the state, determining its nature and development. This inner spirit manifested itself supremely in religion, which expressed the national spirit and essence of the collective population constituting the state. Culture, art, and politics itself were lesser expressions of the spirit. The "liberal" state that disregarded this inner spirit was laughable, a rationalist state without reality and lacking vigor and endurance, a state that had lost the nature of a state and must soon collapse. The chief sign of a state

---

[3] Cf. Lauxtermann, *Frantz*, pp. 11ff.; Philippson, "Frantz," p. 112.

[4] Letter to Wagner, 8 February 1867, in Frantz, *Briefe*, pp. 60f.

[5] *Grundzüge des wahren und wirklichen absoluten Idealismus* (Berlin, 1843), p. 33; *Über den Atheismus. . .* (Berlin, 1844), for his strictures on Feuerbach. (Cf. *Stamm I*, p. 29.)

[6] *Ahasverus oder die Judenfrage* (Berlin, 1844). Page numbers in the text refer to this edition. Cf. *Stamm I*, pp. 59–65.

that had lost its religious essence was its emancipation of the Jews, those same Jews who rejected the whole moral, political, and religious authority of Christian Europe.

Frantz blamed not only the liberals for their pernicious encouragement of Jewish emancipation; he also excoriated the revolutionary Hegelians for their rationalism and materialism, which exalted the general ideal of "emancipation":

> It is amazing that so many fail to see how rationalism in its consequence is the same as atheism. . . . All rationalism leads on to materialism. . . . The younger sect of the Hegelian school who seize on the practical [political] sphere decline willfully into materialism. . . . (p. 15)
>
> The end of all emancipation is materialism, and consequently it must be concluded that Jewish emancipation cannot be permitted. (p. 36)

Against the sterile and dangerous radicalism of the Young Hegelian rationalists, which was based on "self-seeking," Frantz avowed that a true revolutionism had to be religious in essence. Only such a "religious radicalism" represented a "true love of humanity" (p. 41). Liberals, Young Hegelians, and Jews alike were therefore the targets of Frantz's *Ahasverus*—the liberals and Hegelians because they denied the religious essence of the state, the Jews because they embodied an ineradicably hostile religious essence to that of Christian Germany.

Frantz began by explaining how through its inner religious spirit the state becomes at once moral and transcendent. This religious state has nothing to do with "Jewish" ideas of theocracy and divine right. The religious state is rather the authentic expression of a *Volk*, which unites to form the state:

> A people [*Volk*] is shaped by the collective sharing of its God. And in that the members of a *Volk* have a consciousness of one and the same God, there arise among them, equally collectively, moral convictions and conditions, government and law. The first moral society was founded by the gods; states have a divine origin and are founded neither by contract nor by oppression. (p. 16)

Thus, religious idealism entails Germanic idealism. And this transcendent idealism—the deepest morality of the German people—demanded the exclusion of the Jews. "The Jew proper can be the citizen of naught but a Jewish state—and if not of a Jewish state, then of no state at all" (p. 19). This is because "through their mere existence as Jews" the Jews reject Christianity and the Christian state, just as they had rejected Christ Himself, so shutting themselves off like Ahasverus from redemption and history "for the whole of the future":

> They can form neither a people nor a state, nor can they decompose
> themselves through mixture into the Christian peoples and states.
> They can neither live nor die, and from this fate no earthly power can
> redeem them. . . .
> Emancipation is an empty word. Not only is it inadmissible in itself;
> it would also be unsuccessful. Jews always remain Jews and are
> thereby in their innermost being excluded from Christian history.
> (pp. 27f.)

It is because of their ingrained sense of "chosenness" that the Jews can never really be emancipated:

> The Jews may only achieve a deceptive appearance [of emancipation]
> because they can never forget what is promised to them and that they
> are descended from Abraham. . . . It is not to be expected that the
> whole or greater part of the Jewish people will be converted to Christianity. Jews shall remain Jews to the end of days. . . . But they will,
> through the world-historical penance that has been imposed upon
> them, gradually be softened and confess, on the last day, their infidelity. (pp. 27f.)

If the Jews are neither to be emancipated nor baptized, what is to be done with them? Frantz restrains himself and settles for a reluctant toleration that will exclude them from civil and political rights:

> Through their own guilt, the Jews have excluded themselves from the
> community founded by Christianity, and no one can ever free them
> from that punishment which they must bear through a higher necessity. But it does not befit Christians to worsen their situation through
> harshness and oppression, as though to execute the judgment of
> world history upon them.
> The Jews by rejecting Christian authority cannot have any right of
> citizenship. Further, having come into the Christian state as aliens, it is
> completely at our wish what they should be granted. The Jews in the
> Christian state are fundamentally rightless. . . . All that may be
> granted to them they enjoy only under the title of human love, fairness, and grace.
> The Jews stand in the protection of the state as passive members of
> the state. Their persons and property are protected by the common
> law and the police. . . . Offices of state . . . cannot be held by Jews. For
> such government comprises the essence of Christian authority. . . .

> Military service is a duty that arises out of citizenship. . . . Jews may
> not serve . . . but must pay a financial due. . . .
>
> In return for the place the state grants them, Jews must pay protec-
> tion money. . . .
>
> Because marriage is a powerful institution of the state and . . . as-
> sumes a community of belief, it is automatically understood that no
> marriage between Christian and Jew is to be permitted.
>
> The Christian state will allow free religious worship to the Jews.
> (pp. 29–34)

In the course of this sanctimonious gloating Frantz often gives
away his own hypocritical bad faith. For instance, he condemns Jewish rejection of Christianity while justifying Christianity's rejection of
Judaism: "The Christian, however, does not reject Judaism, but
rather acknowledges it as the assumption of Christianity" (p. 30).

For the liberal "humanitarian" doctrine of Jewish emancipation
Frantz has only contempt:

> It is an empty argument to say that Jews and Christians of separate
> religious callings . . . that the human being as such ranks higher than
> the Jew or the Christian. . . . Cannot the Jew [they say] be a good hu-
> man being; shall one deny the Jews their humanity? . . .
>
> But social morality is supplied only by a positive religion, not by an
> idea. . . . Anyway, the idea of humanity, as far as it has any meaning
> at all, is subsumed in positive Christianity. (pp. 38f.)
>
> Jews and Christians remain eternally in their innermost natures di-
> vided from one another. If one tries to unite them within one state,
> that state will be revealed to have lost its inner reality and to have be-
> come merely an outward arrangement.

Only the "lies of liberalism" would pretend otherwise (pp. 45–56).

Frantz ends with a description of Ahasverus as the political and
religious metaphor of the Jewish people:

> There is the saga of Ahasverus the Wandering Jew who, because he
> had turned away the savior from his dwelling-place, was cursed to
> wander the earth and to seek death but not find it until he should en-
> counter the savior once more. The Jewish people itself is the Wander-
> ing Jew. It turned away the savior and so dispersed itself over the
> whole earth, finding rest nowhere. That people desires to blend itself
> among the peoples of the world and thus kill its own existence as a
> people—but it cannot. This people received the promise of a messiah
> and the faithful Jew guards that promise to this day. But that messiah
> will appear when the destiny of mankind has been completed. Then

> shall the Jews accept and recognize that the messiah is verily the re-
> turning Christ. And then shall Jews and Christians unite under the
> one messiah. Until then, in the world and in the realm of time, this
> coming together is impossible. (p. 47)

Frantz has here fused the Young Hegelian conception of Ahasverus
with the Christian view. But he departs from his fellow revolutionists
in his denial of the Jew's ability ever to be worthy of being emancipated into the German state. That will only happen at the Last Judgment. At least Frantz was more honest than Bauer in that he never
extended a false promise of redemption to the willing Jew.

Despite its superficial similarity to the ideas of the Christian-Germans and other conservative thinkers, Frantz's conception of the
state as once political and religious in essence is quite revolutionary.
Such conservatives as Friedrich Julius Stahl (1802–61) saw religion as
merely one element supporting the legal-constitutional edifice of the
state, but for Frantz, the very essence of the state was religious.
Again, the ruthlessness with which Frantz ruled out any possibility of
Jewish redemption went beyond most conservative opinion. Stahl, for
instance, agreed about the badness of the Jews:

> A divine sense of harmony and order is natural to the German people
> . . . but Jews lack these life principles. They lack the moral impulses
> . . . honor, self-reliance.

But for Stahl (himself a baptized Jew), baptism—and with it the ennobling status of citizen—washed away these sins:

> These notorious Jewish traits of treachery, greed, hatred of Chris-
> tians, all have their origin in status, not in character. Sooner or later,
> when the Jews' status changes, these features will also disappear.[7]

These "tribal characteristics" cannot be held as valid reasons against
the naturalization of the Jews as long as they are willing to convert to
Christianity.

Frantz was deeply averse to the "legal" conservatism of the Stahl
school and he developed the revolutionary principle of "federalism"
to express his own contrary romantic vision of German conservativ-
ism. Impatient of Stahl's advocacy of a return to the medieval legal-

---

[7] See R. A. Kann, "Friedrich Julius Stahl: A Re-Examination of His Conservatism,"
*LBIY* 12 (1967): 55–74, especially pp. 67ff., quoting Stahl's *Der christliche Staat und sein
Verhältnis zu Deismus und Judenthum* (Berlin, 1847). (See above, chap. 12, n. 17.)

In her otherwise clear account Philippson ("Frantz," pp. 113f.) makes Frantz into a
more or less normal German conservative. But his antisemitism is radical even in 1844.

constitutional state with its divine right monarchy, its provincial estates and its state church, Frantz called for a true "federal" German
state composed of regional governments, a living union animated by
a corporate, organic spirit. This sort of "German federalism" would
be profoundly respectful of the historical essence of each of its member states and yet be a socially reforming and progressive organism.
Thus would the forces of change and tradition be reconciled. The
German revolutionary utopia would be formed of popular "social
monarchies," all inspired by a reborn Christian spirit that would heal
the rifts caused by confessional strife and war.

Stahl—in whom Frantz discovered "Jewish theocratical features"
such as divine right and the state church idea—had no inkling of such
a "German idea" as revolutionary federalism. Frantz found Stahl's
whole doctrine thoroughly "un-deutsch." A Jew by birth and a lawyer
by profession, Stahl was interested only in the technicalities of the law
rather than in the spirit and attitude that good German laws were
meant to express. No wonder Stahl had no solution to the central
problem of the day, the problem of German unification. Only an understanding of the German mind and spirit guided one to the truth
that Christian federalism was the sole solution to the German problem. The Germans were a unique people, personifying the federal
spirit that rose above mere divisions of states such as Austria and
Prussia. The supranational character of the Germans should be a
beacon to Europe and light the way to a future federation of Central
Europe in which war would be abolished. German diversity was a microcosm of the whole of humanity, which would itself be federally
united by the Germans, who, Frantz had proclaimed in *Ahasverus*,
"had replaced the Jews as the people of God."

This utopian vision transcended traditional party lines and put
Frantz well beyond the pale of normal German conservative politics.
For a time it seemed that the antisemitic conservatism of Hermann
Wagener's *Berliner Revue* would satisfy him, as it did Bruno Bauer.[8]
Indeed, in 1858 Frantz contributed his article on "The Politics of the
Future" to Wagener's journal.[9] But the *Berliner Revue* group remained tied to those Prussian military and church traditions that repelled Frantz; the *Revue*'s solution to the German problem was
merely a brutal extension of Prussian militarism. Eventually, Frantz
was to renounce both Prussian conservative politics and his post in
the civil service. His anonymous *Critique of All Parties* (1862) declared

[8] Cf. *Stamm II*, pp. 40, 67.

[9] "Die Politik der Zukunft" appeared in the *Berliner Revue* in 1858 and was reprinted
at Berlin the same year. A posthumous collection of his political writings was entitled
*Die deutsche Politik der Zukunft*, 2 vols. (Celle, 1899–1900).

in effect that he was no longer a conservative at all and bade farewell to all party labels. Henceforth, he would be a revolutionary outsider, preaching a realistic federal utopia.[10]

---

In 1865 Frantz at last discovered a kindred German revolutionary spirit who could understand his great plan:

> Frantz expounds what I have felt to be the right and true German politics [Richard Wagner told King Ludwig of Bavaria]. He has written to me that the chords of my music have unveiled to him the shape of the German future.[11]

In the course of their rapturous correspondence, Frantz insisted on his vision of the Germans as the new, revolutionary chosen race:

> The German nation represents the heart of the wholly new system of peoples [*Völkersystem*] and the engine of progress. It is certainly the chosen people of the Christian era, just as the Jewish people was that of the pre-Christian age—that once so highly favored and then so deeply rejected people because it had rejected the messiah who had been born among it for the sake of the whole world. The messiah has now based his empire in German hearts. The Holy Roman Empire was its first form, followed by the Empire of the Son, and now by that of the Holy Spirit.[12]

Wagner paid tribute to his new friend in the opening of the 1867 series of articles *German Art and German Politics*, which Frantz had inspired.[13] The following year, Wagner dedicated a new edition of *Opera and Drama* to his admirer. He hailed Frantz as the perfect political counterpart of his own revolutionary art, which had called for the "destruction of the state." Thanks to Frantz, Wagner now understood the real meaning of his formula.

> Who can measure the depth of my astonished joy when you cried to me in recognition of that so misunderstood second part of my refractory book: "Your foundering [*Untergang*] of the state is the founding

[10] *Kritik aller Parteien* (Berlin, 1862). Frantz's large literary production on Germany's federalist mission includes *Untersuchungen über das europäische Gleichgewicht* (Berlin, 1859). See *Stamm II*.

[11] Letter to King Ludwig II, 8 January 1866, in *König Ludwig II und Richard Wagner: Briefwechsel* (Karlsruhe, 1936–39), 1:281f. See C. von Westernhagen, *Wagner* (Cambridge, 1978), pp. 356, 367, 370, 377, 395, 541; *Stamm II*, pp. 237–81.

[12] Frantz, *Briefe*, p. 41, to Wagner, 26 January 1866.

[13] *Deutsche Kunst und deutsche Politik*, in *PW*, 4:37. Cf. E. Newman, *The Life of Richard Wagner* (repr. Cambridge, 1976), 4:94ff.

of my German Empire!" Seldom can there have been so complete a
mutual supplementing . . . as there has been here on the broadest basis between the politician and the artist. The German spirit . . . has
brought us both to perception of the grand mission of our people.[14]

However, Frantz's detestation of the actual German Empire set up
by Bismarck led to a cooling of relations with Wagner, especially between 1871 and 1877.[15] Even Frantz's violent antisemitism in these
years was not enough to reconcile them. In books such as *National
Liberalism and the Domination of the Jews* (1874), Frantz venomously attacked Bismarck's "parody of a Reich" run from Berlin, the center of
the Jewish campaign to dominate all Europe through the modern
forces of capitalism, rationalism, centralism, and militarism which
had together corrupted the "religious" foundation of the true German Empire. Christianity, which unified all Europeans across nation-
alities, was in decline, while Judaism, the most extreme form of exclusive militaristic nationalism, was in the ascendent and had instituted,
thanks to Bismarck, "the German Empire of the Jewish Nation." Jewish emancipation had unleashed the essential Jewish urge to dominate and exploit, and this had contaminated the German spirit itself.
The "exploitative German Empire" represented merely a "national
liberal ideal of pseudo-Germanness."[16]

How to defend Germany and Europe? Frantz agreed with Fichte
that, since Jewish heads could not be replaced simply with new ones,
the best plan would be to pack the Jews off to Palestine. But if they
stay in Germany, they must be severely curbed. Kant and Fichte had
rightly complained that it was "misplaced humanity" to tolerate the
Jews (p. 48)—therefore, "subject them to an alien law: restore them

---

[14] *PW*, 2:4f. (*PW*, 2:7, misdates the dedication to 28 April, but see *König Ludwig und
Wagner*, 2:10). The phrase *Untergang des Staates* is discussed in *PW*, 2:201, 205. The
preface to the second edition is in *GSD*, 8:195ff. Frantz was delighted by the tribute
(Frantz, *Briefe*, pp. 59f., 64ff.).

[15] There was tension as early as August 1866 arising from Wagner's admiration of
Bismarck's victory over Austria. It made for some unpleasantness during Frantz's
week-long stay at Triebschen that month (*Stamm II*, p. 265). Cf. Frantz, *Briefe*, pp. 60f.
They later broke off correspondence between 1871 and 1874. For details see my forthcoming article.

[16] *Der Nationalliberalismus und die Judenherrschaft* (Munich, 1874), pp. 63f. (reprinted
in his *Blätter für deutsche Politik und deutsches Recht: Gesammelte Aufsätze aus den Jahren
1873–1875* [Munich, 1880]). Page references in text to original edition. See Sauzin,
"Political Thought," pp. 144f.; Philippson, "Frantz," pp. 114ff.; P. J. Pulzer, *The Rise of
Political Anti-Semitism in Germany and Austria* (New York, 1964), pp. 76ff.; W. Kamp-
mann, *Deutsche und Juden* (Heidelberg, 1963), pp. 233ff.

Frantz's other works of the period include *Die Religion des Nationalliberalismus* (Leipzig, 1872); *Die preussische Intelligenz und ihre Grenzen* (Munich, 1874); *Die Untergang der
alten Parteien und die Parteien der Zukunft* (Berlin, 1878). (Wagner found the last "very
admirable and absorbing." *CWD*, 7, 8, and 13–15 November 1877.)

to the ghetto." Of course, Frantz's conscience insisted that Christians should not use force to do so. But how else could it be done?

In this book Frantz also gives the Ahasverus myth a new twist: it stands now for the evil principle of selfish nationalism of chosenness, the opposite of international federal brotherhood.

> Ahasverus . . . is Jewry itself. . . . The Jew must die in himself—and this he cannot do, because he will not give up his claim that he is God's chosen. (pp. 62f.)

Frantz never availed himself, as Bruno Bauer and others did, of the refined scientific and cultural concepts of "Jewish" or "Semitic" race that emerged in the 1860s and after. His idea of "race" remained rooted in the earlier vague conceptions of the age of Fichte. Thus, he held that baptism and assimilation were no solution to the Jewish Question, not because of the biological racial immutability of the Jews, but because they were as incapable of being converted before the Last Judgment as Ahasverus was of dying. The reason for this was more than merely biologically "racial" or "national." The secret of persisting Jewishness lay rather in the unique ability of the Jews to have fused nationality and religion together, and it was this indissoluble compound that preserved for eternity the essence of Jewish race and Jewishness itself:

> Were it merely their oriental ancestry that produced the peculiarities of the Jews, it would have been affected in the course of so many centuries by mixture of blood and climatic influences. And were it only their religion that were responsible . . . it would not have maintained itself in the face of the irresistible influences of Christian civilization. . . . But since Jewish religion is inseparably bound up with Jewish nationality . . . the Jew always remains in the core of his being a Jew, for whom Germanness or Frenchness is merely something accidental. (pp. 9f.)

By this analysis, Frantz managed to avoid the reductionist materialism of racial antisemitic arguments, while depicting the Jews as essentially irredeemable. This was his means of retaining that element of revolutionary idealism in antisemitism which he believed the political antisemites of the Second Reich had sacrificed.

---

As Wagner gradually acknowledged the "Jewishness" of Bismarck's "German" Empire, his relations with Frantz warmed again. Wagner's *What Is German?* (1878) solicited Frantz's aid in defining the form of an authentic "German politics." Frantz obliged with an essay for the *Bayreuther Blätter* accusing the Second Reich of betraying German history and German idealism to the Jews. The Reich was a Jewish Empire, based on materialism rather than on moral power. Prussia had abandoned her role of defending the empire from the Slavs by her alliance with Russia for the sake of hegemony in Germany. Yet a German Empire cannot be a nationalistic Prussian *Kaisertum*; it must rather be a comprehensive federal pan-German Reich that includes Austria—and excludes Jews:

> The new German national spirit now being concocted and pretentiously making its debut must appear loathsome in the extreme when it is actually *Jews* who are its loudest cheerleaders. . . . Really, if we want to become ever so German-nationalist, we should first of all kick out the Jews who have lodged themselves like a tapeworm in our national body, destroying and sucking dry the innermost life-germs of the German race [*Volksthum*]. . . .
>
> Christianity will grant the German spirit complete expression in the future. . . . As with German music, the German idea of justice will spread itself over the whole globe. . . . A *Kaisertum* of the German spirit will thus arise. This is the only *Kaisertum* that has a future, the only one that can truly elevate the nation. . . .
>
> But instead of this we have set up a little German military empire. . . . Neither international nor social organization is promoted by it, only *disorganization*.[17]

Bismarck's Empire is a social corpse and a threat to international peace, forcing Europe into a condition of "permanent readiness for war."

Only a federal union, beginning in Germany and spreading to Europe, will save peace. A new Germany must be animated by a new, revolutionary German politics:

> A genuinely German political science must be developed . . . one recognizing that Germany is a suprastate and supranational essence. . . . The so-called current Reich is nothing more than a completed *state*. . . . Here lies the crux of the whole German Question. . . .
>
> Everything comes together here: in order to become truly German, politics must rise above itself. It must be elevated into *metapolitics*. . . . Thereby our Germanness will not be lost to us. On the contrary, it will make us devote our whole effort to human development that will bestow greater freedom, shaping us to greater nobility, and raising us up to the highest ideas of the human spirit.
>
> This I call *German politics*. (pp. 167f.)

[17] "Offener Brief an Richard Wagner," *Bayreuther Blätter* 1 (1878): 149–70, pp. 161, 165ff. Page references to this edition. Reprinted in Stamm, *Das grössere Deutschland*, pp. 19–37.

Were it not for the giveaway of his hatred of the Jews, one might be tempted to accept Frantz's new German and European order as a vision of the humanitarian future of a unified, peaceful Europe. But it is his treatment of the Jewish Question that gives the lie to his idealism. His German revolutionary conception of the Jewish Question shows clearly that Frantz's vision of Europe has more to do with Hitler's than that of the Common Market.

The sinister character of Frantz's revolutionary politics is also evident in his systematic exposition, *Federalism* (1879). "Federalism," he explained, was a dynamic and organic principle, the natural and historical principle of the evolution of all states. Conservatism was sterile in its effort to preserve a static past and thus deny the future. Socialism, on the other hand, rejected the claims of tradition, of the individual, and of religion. Federalism alone could mediate between social and individual principles, just as it did between national and international principles. Federalism was indeed the universal principle of humanity, for it was based on the family, on love, on peace, on religion—all summed up in Christianity.

Of course, this humanity of federalism made it necessarily anti-Jewish:

> The evaluation of the Jewish Question must be the endpoint of our whole work since the present Jewish domination is undoubtedly in itself one of the greatest obstacles to the development of federalism.[18]

Frantz insisted that his analysis was not to be classed as one uttered by "a medieval obscurantist and fanatical Jew-baiter," but was rather grounded in the revolutionary philosophy of federalism. The new German and European federation embodying a restored relationship between God and the whole of humanity can have no place for Jewish essence and spirit because these are fundamentally at odds with those of all other nations, above all, Christian nations. The innermost Jewish conception of themselves as the "chosen race" sets them eternally apart from all others and is at the root of their determination to exploit and dominate their neighbors. And here Frantz reinterprets his 1844 Ahasverian metaphor in the context of federalism and its antithesis, the "chosen race" idea. Ahasverus is the symbol of Jewish chosenness and apartness and of the Jews' refusal and incapacity to integrate into the "new Europe" of Christian federalism. The Jews will not enter Frantz's new ideal Reich, but are doomed to wander like Ahasverus through a world that hates them.

[18] *Der Föderalismus* (Mainz, 1879), pp. 352–71, on the Jewish Question. Page references to this edition. Cf. Philippson, "Frantz," pp. 106ff.; Sauzin, "Political Thought," pp. 129ff.; Lauxtermann, *Frantz*, pp. 193ff.

In the meantime, until the new Reich comes into being, the misguided process of emancipation and equality must be reversed. The Jews may retain "human" rights, but must remain the foreigners they are without political and civil rights, without citizenship, though under the protection of the state. For the Jews are indeed alien to Germany both by religion and by nationality. The Jewish national character has received a "natural imprint" through centuries of wandering and parasitism, which means that despite all their efforts at a superficial assimilation, Jews cannot lose their identity. "Even if they eat pork, can that really change so much the essence of their being?" The Jews remain an exclusive "nationality," a chosen race of exploiters, parasites, and dominators. Frantz significantly declines to discuss the effect of baptism, but it is clear from his argument about the inseparability of Jewish religion and nationality that he believes the Jews incapable of sincere conversion to Christianity, bound as they are by their own Jewish inherited character.

For Frantz, then, it is a hostile Jewish "nationality" that rejects both the federal principle itself and its Christian matrix; therefore, Jewish "nationality" must be excluded from the German federation of love and peace. Thus, in Frantz's mind there is no contradiction between his advocacy of discrimination against the Jews and his proclaiming of an ideal state in which there will be peace and justice for all its true members:

> So long as the Jews regard themselves as the chosen race standing high above other peoples . . . so must they be considered henceforth an essentially antifederalist element within the Christian world . . . a powerful obstacle to international federation. . . . There is no help against their so-called Golden International except through [*our own*] international organization. And so we see ourselves led through the Jewish Question to a new and still greater problem. (pp. 369f.)

*Federalism* swept Wagner off his feet: "A complete solution to the problems of the world such as I consider to be the only correct one." He even read it at night for insomnia.[19]

---

Like Bruno Bauer, Frantz dabbled increasingly in speculation on international politics in his later years, and his last work, *World Politics* (1883), was published under the aegis of Bauer's *Internationale Monatsschrift*.[20] Some of Frantz's predictions were quite prescient, es-

[19] See the entries in *CWD*, 30 June, and 2–6, 7, 9, 13, 14 July 1879. Wagner found a current pamphlet by Wilhelm Marr "superficial" by comparison.
[20] *Die Weltpolitik*, 3 vols. (Chemnitz, 1882–83), 3:108–29, on the Jewish Question. Page references to this edition. See Philippson, "Frantz," pp. 108ff., and Sauzin, "Po-

pecially his forecast of the rise of the United States and Russia as superpowers and the accompanying decline of Britain. He also prophesied a revolution in Russia that would threaten Europe. To counter this, Frantz proposed that Germany annex eastern Europe, drive the Russians out of the Baltic, and liberate the Ukraine. The word *Lebensraum* is missing, but the rest of the German dream is there: Prussian arms would open the way to a German "cultural colonization" achieved by the "free and peaceful immigration of Germans" and the spread of the idealistic "German spirit." Naturally, this *Drang nach Osten* was to be undertaken in the name of peace and the prevention of war. "Only a big blow to Russia will end these perpetual preparations for war [and terminate] the current armed peace." Rightly directed, Prussian arms, together with the German spirit and European federalism, would create the "Thousand-Year Peace" of the new Reich. There would be a single world economy with social justice for all; armaments and tariffs alike would vanish.

Frantz insisted that this vision of a Kantian perpetual peace had nothing to do with narrow German nationalism. Germany was a part of Christian Europe; *Deutschtum* was merely the ideal expression of the universal truth of Christianity that alone could rise above the warring divisions of European states. But Germany could only find her Christian vocation if she first freed herself from that Jewish domination that signified the defeat of Christian peace and love.

Equally remarkable in *World Politics* is Frantz's prophecy of the future ferocity of revolutionary antisemitism. Like Wagner, Frantz was cynical about the quality of the political antisemites of the 1870s. Frantz was willing to praise Adolf Stöcker and company for at least awakening the Berlin public to the Jewish Question, but he could not understand the liking of the "present so-called Antisemitic agitation" for Bismarck, who had "prostituted" Germany before the Jews at the Congress of Berlin. Frantz, therefore, followed Wagner in refusing to sign the Antisemites' Petition of 1880:

> I did not assent to the current petition, which was forwarded to me for signature, because it appeared to me to be ironic that such a petition should be addressed to Bismarck. (pp. 108ff.)

In Frantz's view, "Antisemitism" was not a sufficiently clear concept to meet the Jewish threat that, he reiterated, drew its strength from the peculiar Jewish fusion of race and religion:

> Their religion and race are inseparable, and herein consists Jewish essence. To regard the Jews either solely as a race or as a religious

---

litical Thought," pp. 137ff., for useful summaries of the general arguments. (Cf. Frantz's letter of 1878 to his publisher E. Schmeitzner in *Briefe*, p. 100.)

group would be like wanting to regard water as only hydrogen or oxygen. . . . To separate one element from another transforms concrete Jewish essence into an abstraction. To speak now of Semites and Antisemitism is a misunderstanding that arises out of treating the Jews solely as a race: Semites can be Moslem Arabs or Syrian Christians. . . . The art of dividing in practice the two constituent elements of Judaism has not yet been found, nor ever will be. For that reason, Jews will remain largely and wholly Jews until the Last Day, because they are something yet more than Semites. . . . (pp. 110ff.)

The Jewish Question is even more of an international than a national question. As cosmopolitans, the Jews command the whole world through the stock exchanges. Polish, German, and French Jews are primarily Jews because that is their race [*Nationalität*]. Polish feeling, German or French feeling cannot enter his soul . . . as long as he remains a Jew, that is, as long as he feels himself to be a member of the chosen people. (pp. 112f.)

The Jews, therefore, do have an international principle of their own: their cosmopolitanism. And it is this that makes them such a threat to Frantz.[21] Their cosmopolitanism rivals his federalism, Jewish chosenness rivals German chosenness. This Jewish threat must be removed from the European stage, and here Frantz utters his chilling prediction:

It is certain, a priori, that the press and money power of the Jews, and their growing takeover of public offices, will produce such a repellent environment that finally there will be an outbreak of popular rage whose signs can already be discerned today. It will be a tragically sad way of solving the Jewish Question, but the train of things must proceed. I mean that one should consider how long misfortune can be prevented. Against a great popular movement, the police and even the army would be unable to protect the Jews. . . .

Where the first blow will be struck—the place from which the movement will rapidly spread abroad—is the German Reich. Here Jews may amount to only 1.5 percent of the population compared to 10 percent in eastern countries; but the German Jews are far richer and occupy a higher social position. (p. 115) . . .

---

[21] Stamm, *Unberühmter* (1948), was naturally unwilling to deal with the central problem of Frantz's antisemitism, though his earlier *Das grössere Deutschland* (1935) had been less reticent. In *Unberühmter*, p. 138, however, Stamm managed to mention Frantz's prediction of "a great Jewish catastrophe in central Europe"—but refrained from noting that Frantz was one of the incendiaries who kindled the antisemitic fuel of that Holocaust. The capacity of German authors for honest—and often enough opportune—self-delusion is extraordinary.

Very possibly the great Jewish catastrophe in prospect for Central Europe will on its outbreak strike also France and England. Out of the whole of Europe a huge exodus will occur, because no one anywhere will put up with them any longer. Who knows where they will move, how far they will be scattered and strewn around the world without ever finding a settled place. (p. 117) . . .

Is it not a premonition that from their earliest history the Jews have been wandering from one land to another. . . . A wandering people whose fate it is to be scattered among other peoples and wander the world. They themselves are Ahasverus, to whom no peace is granted, not even the peace of the grave, because he cannot even die—*le juif errant*. That myth certainly has deep meanings. (p. 118)

And there is another meaning that Frantz now gives to Ahasverus. The Ahasverian survival of the Jews has a purpose: "It appears that Judaism must play a part in the inner economy of world history." Hateful as it is, the destructive criticism of Ahasverian Judaism holds up a mirror to Christian society of its own failings. Jewish participation in war and finance is a reproach to similar Christian participation; Jewish cosmopolitanism is an indictment of the lack of federal internationalism among Christians; and Jewish nationalism "exposes the Jewishness of our own nationalism" (pp. 124–28).

Frantz's transformation of Ahasverus from a traditional Christian myth into one equipped to fill the psychological demands of a new utopian revolutionary Christianity was completed in his later writings. Its main lines, however, had been present in his *Ahasverus or the Jewish Question* of 1844, which he described in *World Politics* as being "certainly a youthful work, and done much too abstractly, but even then it had contained the crux of the question."[22] That youthful product of the Young Hegelian disputes on the Jewish Question had already intuited that the Ahasverus problem was not about how the Jews might be redeemed. The problem had been stood on its head: it was henceforth the problem of how the new chosen people, the Germans, might be redeemed from Ahasverus.

[22] *Weltpolitik*, p. 118. An interesting psychological interpretation could be placed on Frantz's description of his diplomatic travels of the 1850s: "So should I have wandered around lands *ad infinitum* very much like the Wandering Jew" (quoted from his papers by *Stamm II*, p. 7).

# Richard Wagner: Prophet of Revolutionary Antisemitism

> Our reawakened German instinct . . . [is not
> all] a purely racial instinct . . . but something
> higher . . . something only vaguely felt by the
> *Volk* today, which might appear as instinct, but
> is really of far nobler origin and loftier aim,
> and might well be defined as the spirit of the
> "purely Human."
>
> —*Know Thyself, PW,* 4:272

A MAJOR problem stands out in current interpretations of Richard Wagner's thought. It is the "paradox" of his simultaneous acceptance of racist antisemitism and revolutionary idealism. The solution to this problem lies in an approach that draws on the general mythology of revolution, setting Wagner and his antisemitism within the context of the German revolutionary tradition. Many other Wagnerian problems stem from this false but central paradox, especially the relationship between his social thought and his operas, but the present brief chapter can sketch in only the main lines of an analysis that requires a separate volume.[1]

[1] J. Katz, *The Darker Side of Genius: Richard Wagner's Anti-Semitism* (Hanover, N.H., 1986), is now the starting point for discussions of Wagner's antisemitism, but it is flawed by its failure to consider his revolutionism and its insistence on a simple metaphorical interpretation of "destruction." Katz is also mistaken in his arguments that (1) Wagner was a "philosemite" until 1850 (pp. 1, 20f., 57) and (2) that the Nazis were the first to read antisemitic meanings into Wagner's operas. (Cf. John Deathridge's review, "Talk of Destruction," *Times Literary Supplement* [14 November 1986], and the subsequent exchange of 9 January 1987, p. 37, and 23 January 1987, p. 85.)

Katz's book seeks to repudiate the most lively recent German critic, Hartmut Zelinsky, whose works insisting on the centrality of antisemitism to Wagner's creative work and their contribution to Nazi mentality have generally met with a barrage of personal abuse rather than any sustained critical discussion. See H. Zelinsky, *Richard Wagner: Ein deutsches Thema 1876–1976,* 2d ed. (Vienna–Berlin, 1983); "Die 'Feuerkur' des Richard Wagner oder die 'neue Religion' der 'Erlösung' durch 'Vernichtung,' " in *Richard Wagner—Wie antisemitisch darf ein Künstler sein?,* ed. H.-K. Metzger and R. Riehn (Musik-

In 1848 Richard Wagner (1813–83) experienced a dramatic conversion to the revolutionary faith. He had, of course, been long involved in revolutionary circles. Heinrich Laube and he had been very close friends, and Laube had introduced him to Heine at Paris in 1840. The impact of this Young German environment emerges in Wagner's youthful operas and texts, which emphasize the redemption of the flesh and revolutionary freedom. In the early 1840s Wagner pursued his contacts with Young Germany at Dresden, where he became acquainted with Karl Gutzkow and Berthold Auerbach. There he also extended his revolutionism by discussing Young Hegelian and socialist ideas with his intimate friend August Röckel. The influence of Wilhelm Weitling's naive revolutionary communism informs the text of his 1843 choral work, *The Love Feast of the Apostles*.[2] Wagner was, therefore, a revolutionist before 1848, but not a seriously committed one. The same may be said of his attitude towards Jews. Before 1848, occasional remarks in his letters show that he had absorbed the structural antisemitism implicit in Young German and Young Hegelian revolutionary thinking, which equated money-egoism with Judaism. Wagner even self-mockingly accuses himself of a constant egoistic need for money; asking for a loan, he laughs off

Konzepte 5) (Munich, 1978), pp. 79–112; "Rettung ins Ungenaue: Zu Martin Gregor-Dellins Wagner-Biographie," in *Richard Wagner: Parsifal*, ed. Metzger and Riehn (Musik-Konzepte 25) (Munich, 1982), pp. 74–115; "Spiegel-Gespräch über den *Parsifal*," in *Richard Wagner: Ein deutsches Ärgernis*, ed. K. Umbach (Reinheim, 1982), pp. 38–52.

L. Stein, *The Racial Thinking of Richard Wagner* (New York, 1950), is still useful despite its liberal preconceptions about "racism." See also T. W. Adorno (*In Search of Wagner*, trans. [London, 1981]). Treatments of Wagner's Jew-hatred are to be found in the two extended biographies: R. W. Gutman, *Richard Wagner: The Man, His Mind, and His Music* (New York, 1968), a brilliant description despite its occasional leaps in the argument; and Ernest Newman's standard *Life of Richard Wagner*, 4 vols. (London, 1937–47; repr. Cambridge, 1976), which fully acknowledges the fact of Wagner's antisemitism while writing it off as a peculiarity of German character. Succinct accounts are given in the two admirable short biographies by B. Millington, *Wagner* (London, 1984); J. Deathridge and C. Dahlhaus, *The New Grove Wagner* (London, 1984).

For a critical survey of approaches to the antisemitism problem in recent Wagner scholarship (often downplayed) see J. Kerman, "Wagner and Wagnerism," *New York Review of Books* (22 December 1983): pp. 27–37. Kerman points out that, unlike most cases where an artist is unjustly blamed for his later influence, Wagner's is unusual in that he consciously tried to create a mythology that would remain active after his death.

The usual apologies for Wagner's Jew-hatred are refuted in P. L. Rose, "The Noble Anti-Semitism of Richard Wagner," *The Historical Journal* 25 (1982): 751–63, at p. 754. I deal with the problems posed by the nonappearance of Jews in the operas and other issues in my new book, *Wagner—Race and Revolution* (New Haven and London, 1992).

[2] *PW*, 8:277ff. Wagner wrote the *Love Feast* a few weeks before the arrest of Weitling made headlines. For Weitling, see above, chap. 14.

"this accursed Jewish scummery" (*das verfluchte Judensgeschmeiss*).³ But he had not made this antisemitism a dominating concern. He was quite willing in this period to support and befriend Jews such as Samuel Lehrs. All this was to change after 1848; thereafter, any connection with Jews was conducted without exception in a purely exploitative and privately contemptuous fashion.

It was Laube's *Struensee* that began the process of Wagner's conversion. In November 1847, the *Struensee* preface introduced a more bitter and overt antisemitic tone into the writings of the Young German school. The Jews were seen as the enemies of Laube and other German artists through their introduction of commercialized values into German art.⁴ In February 1848, at the funeral of Wagner's mother, Laube commiserated with his friend, conflating the sadness of the hour with their general resentment and despair at the state of German art:

> On the way to the station, we discussed the unbearable burden that seemed to us to lie like a dead weight on every noble effort made to resist the tendency of the time to sink into utter worthlessness.

And, as the *Struensee* preface made clear, this "worthlessness" consisted in the flowering of "Jewish" values. Wagner's only remedy was to "plunge dully and coldly into the only thing that could cheer and warm me, the working out of my *Lohengrin* and my studies of German antiquity."⁵

Then came the shock of the 1848 revolution. For a year and a half Wagner fell into a rapture of revolutionism, endlessly arguing and rushing around with Bakunin and Röckel and inciting armed resistance. In an ecstatic article entitled *The Revolution*, Wagner proclaimed revolution as a new Christian revelation, bringing redemption to all by its destruction of bourgeois law and capitalism:

> I am Revolution, I am the ever-fashioning Life, I am the only God.
> . . . The millions, the embodied Revolution, the God become Man . . .
> proclaim to all the world the new Gospel of Happiness!⁶

---

³ *Sämtliche Briefe* (Leipzig, 1967–), 1:177f. (henceforth *SB*)—this despite Katz, *Darker Side*, p. 21: "Nothing in his letters and other statements during the previous decades presages anti-Jewish sentiments"; and p. 57, "Remarks of this kind (*ironic jocular ones about Judaism and money*) are not found in his statements dating from earlier decades." Cf. *SB*, 1:178, 378f., 388, 397, 399, 405, 410f., 521, 523.

⁴ For Laube's *Struensee*, see above, chap. 12. Katz, *Darker Side*, p. 19, discusses the analogy between *Struensee* and *Judaism in Music*, but fails to notice the vital connecting link to be found in *Mein Leben*.

⁵ Wagner's mother died on 9 January 1848.

⁶ *The Revolution*, in *PW*, 8:232f., 236–38.

An impassioned speech to the Dresden Patriotic Club in June 1848 was specific about how money obstructed the emancipation of humanity:

> God will light us to the rightful law to put [the revolution] into practice. And like a hideous nightmare this demonic idea of Money will vanish from us with all its loathsome retinue of open and secret usury, paper-juggling, percentage, and banker's speculation. That will be the *full emancipation of the human race*, that will be the *fulfillment of Christ's pure teaching*.[7]

Wagner developed this idea of a revolutionary new Christianity in the opera text *Jesus of Nazareth* (1849), which depicted Jesus as redeeming men from the materialism of the

> Roman world . . . and still more, of that [Jewish] world subject to the Romans. . . . I saw the modern world of the present day as a prey to the *worthlessness* [!] akin to that which surrounded Jesus.[8]

Wagner presented here in socialist revolutionary language the kernel of Kant's critique of Judaism. Enslaved to the "Law," the Jews had rejected Jesus' message of "love"; Jewish egoism and lovelessness had led Judas to betray Him. The Jews preferred "power, domination and above all, the protection of property" against love. Jesus was thus the symbol of revolution, opposed by the loveless forces of property and law, symbolized by "Judaism." Wagner had in effect modernized the original anti-Jewish bias of the Gospels by turning the Jesus story into a myth of secular revolutionary antisemitism.[9]

This fundamental antisemitic principle that Judaism is the enemy of revolution runs through the famous series of revolutionary treatises written by Wagner in 1849–50: *Art and Revolution, Artwork of the Future*, and *Judaism in Music*. All three aim at the revolutionary destruction of the Jewish characteristics of money-mindedness, lovelessness, and egoism in art and society alike. In *Art and Revolution*, for example, Jesus and Apollo are seen as being subjected by Mammon, the "god of the 5 percent": "Our god is Gold, our religion the pursuit of wealth." Mammon's Jewish devotees may not be named as such in the text, but they are silently present in its whole mythological structure.[10] In *Artwork of the Future*, written a few months later, Wagner does name the "Jewish-oriental theory of Nature's subservience to human utility"—which had been adopted by Christianity—as the

---

[7] *Vaterlandsverein Speech, PW*, 4:136ff.
[8] *Communication to My Friends, PW*, 1:378–80.
[9] *PW*, 8:298f., 303f.
[10] *Art and Revolution, PW*, 1:59, 65.

source of Christian religious strife. Christianity must be freed of this Jewish influence of utility, domination, and egoism, and renovated by Greek ideals of beauty and enjoyment. This religiously inspired "art of the future" means a return to the true racial spirit of the German *Volk*, for the spirit of the *Volk* is the source of all art. Wagner's concept of *Volk* is thus not merely a racial concept, but a revolutionary one.[11]

In the essay *The Wibelungen* (1848–49), Wagner explained the connection between his ideas of the German race and revolution. The essay interprets medieval German history in the light of the ancient Nibelung myths, but it does so by invoking the modern revolutionary concepts of property and power. The Nibelung saga is seen as a poetic reflection of an archaic German form of kingship based on property; the "Nibelung hoard" persists to the present day in the form of capitalist property and possession. This alienation of the human spirit and flesh will be swept away by the revolution. In 1848 Wagner attempted to depict this fusion of German myth and revolution in his plans for the Nibelung opera *Siegfried's Death*, which eventually became *Götterdämmerung*.[12] Thus, the *Ring* cycle originated, not as an atavistic nationalistic reversion to German mythology, but as a great revolutionary project. Moreover, Wagner began to compose the music for the work in August 1850, the very same month that he wrote *Judaism in Music*. To observers ignorant of the relationship between Wagner's revolutionism, his Germanism, and his antisemitism, this may appear purely coincidental. But once the relationship is understood, then the virtually simultaneous composition of the Nibelung music and the antisemitic tract suggest that Wagner had finally reached a state of psychological readiness to break forth with his new vision in different spheres.[13]

*Judaism in Music* is usually misinterpreted as a sudden outburst of spleen, triggered by a controversy in the musical press over Jewish musicianship. In its present form, the essay does indeed date from August 1850. But in fact Wagner's systematic antisemitism and a first

---

[11] *Artwork of the Future*, PW, 1:143, 147, 177ff., 207ff.

[12] *Die Wibelungen*, PW, 7:261, 295. The editor of *PW* attributes the first version of the essay to 1848. (The original idea of *The Ring* is be found in an 1848 sketch: *Der Nibelung-Mythus als Entwurf zu einem Drama*.) The attempted recent re-dating of *The Wibelungen* to 1849 seems to me to be due in part to a misconceived opposition between Wagner's "revolutionary" and "Germanic" outlooks in 1848–49, as in Deathridge and Dahlhaus, *New Grove Wagner*, p. 33. This is not to deny Deathridge's argument that the artistic plan of the *Die Nibelungen* (PW, 7:299ff.) and *Siegfrieds Tod* predate the historical explanation of *Die Wibelungen*.

[13] The first sketch of the *Götterdämmerung* music is dated 12 August 1850. See Deathridge and Dahlhaus, *New Grove Wagner*, p. 171.

essay on the subject date from nearly two years before, from the time of his conversion to a fiery revolutionism. This is proven by a neglected but crucially important letter written to him by his estranged wife in 1850. Under the stress, first of his revolutionary activity at Dresden in 1848–49, and then of his flight to Paris, Wagner's marriage had cracked. In a letter to Minna, Wagner blamed the estrangement on Minna's inability to understand his revolutionism.[14] Minna replied on 8 May 1850:

> Only during the last *two years*, ever since you turned to miserable politics . . . have I been unwise enough not to avoid violent scenes with you. . . . One thing was clear in my simple mind—that nothing good would come to you from revolutionary activity. . . .
>
> [I used to be] happy in the knowledge that you were close to me while you created *all* the *beautiful* things . . . you always made me so happy, sang and played almost every new scene for me. But since *two years* ago, when you wanted to read me that essay in which you *slander* whole *races* that have been fundamentally helpful to you, I could not force myself to listen, and ever since that time you have borne a grudge against me, and punished me so severely for it that you never again let me hear anything from your works.[15]

The significance of this letter is clear. Wagner's antisemitism was not suddenly created out of thin air in 1850, nor was it a trivial or aberrant opinion. It sprang forth in 1848 out of his conversion to the revolution and it remained a major foundation of his revolutionary art and philosophy thereafter.

A general failure to appreciate this often leads to *Judaism in Music* being mistakenly read as a purely racial treatise.[16] It is, however, actually part of the constellation of revolutionary essays of 1848–50,

[14] See Wagner, *Selected Letters*, ed. S. Spencer and B. Millington (London, 1987), p. 194.

[15] The letter is translated in *Letters of Richard Wagner: The Burrell Collection*, ed. J. N. Burk (London, 1951), pp. 290f. It was cited first by Gutman, *Richard Wagner*, p. 135, then by Rose, "Noble Anti-Semitism," p. 754. Katz, *Darker Side*, p. 52, also quotes the letter without, however, appearing to appreciate its crucial significance for the dating and context of Wagner's conversion to a systematic revolutionary antisemitism.

[16] Katz's *Darker Side* neither examines the role of antisemitism in the revolutionary treatises of 1848–51 nor gives any "revolutionary" context for the antisemitism of *Judaism in Music*. Zelinsky, "Rettung," pp. 82ff., sees *Judaism in Music* as part of the cycle of revolutionary writings, as does O. D. Kulka, "Richard Wagner und die Anfänge des modernen Antisemitismus," *Bulletin des Leo Baeck Instituts* (Jerusalem) 4 (1961): 281–300, who argues for the connection between Wagner's "messianic-revolutionary" ideas of 1848–51 and his antisemitism. D. Borchmeyer's 1983 "Jubilee" edition of the *Dichtungen und Schriften* excludes *Judaism* and other antisemitic works as irrelevant aberrations.

and embodies major revolutionary as well as racial elements, just as do the early *Ring* sketches. The Jews are seen as the negation of the true artistic spirit and the representatives of bourgeois values. Judaism is the embodiment of the bourgeois money-egoist spirit. As Wagner later confessed to Liszt:

> I felt a long-repressed hatred for this Jewish money-world, and this hatred is as necessary to my nature as gall is to the blood. An opportunity arose when their damnable scribbling annoyed me most, and so I broke forth at last.[17]

Wagner explained at the outset of *Judaism in Music* that he was preaching a new revolutionary approach to the Jewish Question and he poured scorn on the outdated liberal emancipationist solutions of his own past:

> Our liberalism was a not very lucid mental sport. . . . We went for the freedom of that nation [*Volk*] without knowledge of that *Volk* itself, nay, with a dislike of any real contact with it. So our eagerness to level up the rights of the Jews was rather much more stimulated by a general idea, rather than any real sympathy; for with all our speaking and writing in favor of the Jews' emancipation, we always felt instinctively repelled by any actual, operative contact with them.
>
> Here then we touch the point that brings us closer to our main inquiry; we have to explain to ourselves the *involuntary repellence* possessed for us by the nature and personality of the Jews, so as to vindicate that instinctive dislike which we plainly recognize as stronger and more overpowering than our conscious zeal to rid ourselves thereof. Even today we only purposely fool ourselves when we think necessary to hold immoral and taboo all open proclamation of a natural repugnance against the Jewish nature. Only in quite the most recent times do we seem to have reached an insight that it is more rational to rid ourselves of that strenuous self-deception so as instead quite soberly to view the object of our violent feeling and bring ourselves to understand a repugnance which still abides with us in spite of all our liberal utopias. To our astonishment, we perceive that, like good Christians, we have been floating in the air and fighting clouds.[18]

Wagner was proposing a revolutionary approach based on the instinctive German racial aversion towards Jews! At one stroke, he thus got rid of the contradiction that had so troubled critics as different as

[17] *Correspondence of Wagner and Liszt* (London, 1897; repr. 1973), 1:145f., letter of 18 April 1851.
[18] *PW*, 3:79–81.

Gutzkow and Humboldt: the contradiction between their support of Jewish emancipation and their persisting dislike of Jews. Wagner now explained it all by explaining that this aversion was real, was moral, and was rational!

Wagner next showed how the Jewish concept of art as a form of commerce further validated his justification of the rightness of anti-semitism (note the Hess-like reference to blood):

> [All] is turned to money by the Jew. Who thinks of noticing that the guileless looking scrap of paper is slimy with the blood of countless generations? What the heroes of the arts . . . have invented . . . from two millennia of misery, today the Jew converts into an art-bazaar. . . .
>
> We have no need first to substantiate the Jewification [*Verjudung*] of modern art. It springs to the eye. . . . If emancipation from the yoke of Judaism appears to us the greatest of necessities, we must hold it crucial above all to assemble our forces for this war of liberation. But we shall never gain these forces by merely defining the phenomenon [of Judaism] in an abstract way. This will be done only by accurately knowing the nature of that involuntary feeling of ours which utters itself as an instinctive repugnance against the Jew's prime essence. Through it, through this unconquerable feeling—if we admit it without prevarication—there must become plain to us *what* we hate in that essence. . . . Then we can rout the demon from the field . . . where he has sheltered under a twilit darkness . . . which we good-natured humanists ourselves have conferred on him.[19]

Wagner thus demonstrated his axiom that German repugnance towards Jewishness and Jews is in fact the "liberating" revolutionary principle that will redeem German art and politics alike from money and egoism.

In all this it is vital to be aware of the context in which Wagner is thinking, especially the arguments of Laube's *Struensee* preface. This immediately points up Wagner's indebtedness to Laube for his major themes about the essential racial inability of the Jews to create beauty in new forms and their introduction of commercialized values into German art. It is not coincidental that Meyerbeer is the real target of both Laube's and Wagner's pieces. Even so, Wagner went much further than Laube in that *Judaism in Music* contains a vastly strengthened idea of racial determinism.

Knowledge of a second suppressed context is also necessary for comprehension of the ending of *Judaism in Music*, this time Heine's 1840 critique of Ludwig Börne. After damning Heine as the spirit of

[19] *PW*, 3:82.

Jewish negation, Wagner's final paragraph turned in an encomium
of Ludwig Börne as the shining example of a Jew who could be redeemed into true humanity by the revolutionary faith.

> Yet another Jew must we name who appeared among us as a writer.
> From out of his isolation as a Jew he came among us seeking redemp-
> tion. He found it not and had to learn that *only with our redemption, too,
> into genuine humanity*, would he ever find it. To become man at once
> with us, however, means firstly for the Jew that he must cease to be
> Jew. And this had BÖRNE done. Yet Börne of all others teaches us
> that this redemption cannot be reached in ease and in cold indifferent
> complacency, but costs—as cost it must for us—sweat, anguish, want,
> and all the dregs of suffering and sorrow. Without once looking back,
> take ye your part in this regenerative work of deliverance through
> this self-destroying bloody struggle; then are we one and unsepa-
> rated![20]

This marked a volte face in Wagner's attitude to Börne. In 1841 Wagner had been almost alone in taking Heine's side *against* Börne; now,
in *Judaism in Music*, he turned viciously on Heine and extolled Börne
as the redeemable Jew—the one Jew Fichte had never expected to set
eyes upon!

But it is the final lines that have largely mystified commentators.
Here Wagner linked Börne directly to Ahasverian redemption of destruction in his famous closing sentence, so enigmatic without an
awareness of the whole Ahasverian mythology:

> But remember, only one thing can redeem you from the burden of
> your curse—the redemption of Ahasverus: *Destruction [Untergang]!*

"Destruction" here was meant largely in the metaphorical sense,
but as always it carries the implicit possibility of physical removal.[21]

---

[20] *PW*, 3:100 (rev. version). For Wagner's 1841 defense of Heine, see H. Barth et al.,
*Wagner: A Documentary Study* (London, 1975), p. 163.

[21] Katz, *Darker Side*, pp. 45, 125, 126, sees "destruction" as merely metaphorical without considering the German revolutionary context that endowed it with a crucial ambivalence; he believes Wagner's "destruction" to have become physical in meaning only
at the hands of the Nazis. L. J. Rather, *The Dream of Self-Destruction: Wagner's Ring and
the Modern World* (Baton Rouge, 1979), pp. 88–102, 167–80, also argues for the harm-
lessness of Wagner's metaphor, which was "perverted" by the Nazis. Neither Katz nor
Rather have dealt seriously with Zelinsky's charge that, at least in the later writings,
"destruction" bears a literal meaning and that there is a real link between Wagnerian
and Nazi ideology. See especially Zelinsky's essays "Die 'Feuerkur,' " *loc. cit.*; "Rettung";
and especially "Richard Wagner's *Kunstwerk der Zukunft* und seine Idee der Vernichtung," in *Geschichtsprophetien im 19. und 20. Jahrhundert*, ed. J. H. Knoll and J. H.
Schoeps (Stuttgart, 1984), pp. 84–106.

Cf. *CWD*, 21 November 1880: "Richard says of himself that he is the plenipotentiary
of destruction—this he sees increasingly." See H. Zelinsky, "Der *Plenipotentarius des Un-*

RICHARD WAGNER 367

By 1869, when he reissued the piece, Wagner was willing to be more explicit. His added *Explanations* put the question of whether the Jews should be destroyed through "assimilation" or "expulsion," that is, the alternatives originally put by Laube in the *Struensee* preface. But whereas Laube had emphatically decided in favor of assimilation, Wagner coyly declined to state his own preference, and took refuge in the ambiguity of the relationship between politics and art by evasively remarking that he was unacquainted with the (political) forces needed to effect a solution.[22]

One typical historical comment on Wagner's career has been that "Wagner is the first example of the baffling transition from the atheistic, social radicalism of a barricade fighter in 1848 to extreme racist antisemitism and to poetry of the pagan Germanic myth."[23] The transition ceases to be baffling when knowledge of the varied contexts of

*tergangs," Neohelicon* 9 (1982): 145–76. Cf. Nietzsche's "We Must be Destroyers," *The Will to Power*, trans. W. Kaufmann (New York, 1968), p. 224.

[22] Wagner certainly approved of the Russian pogroms (CWD, 11 and 14 August 1881).

I find it difficult to understand Katz's thinking on the question of "practical measures." *Darker Side*, pp. 69, 91, 110, reports Wagner's remarks on expulsion, burning, etc., but then seems to say that he disclaimed these measures: "[he] shrank from the consequences. . . . The Master did indeed poke the fire, but he let others burn their fingers in it" (pp. 113f); "Still, fleeting notions concerning possible action against the Jews are indication enough of the consequences that can follow from the passionate negation of Jewish existence. In this sense Wagner's mentality and way of thinking are indeed an anticipation of future horrors" (p. 119); "It is difficult to acquit him of responsibility for subsequent objectively unforeseeable consequences" (p. 128) (yet Wagner seems to have foreseen expulsion clearly enough!); "Wagner's restraint [*sic!*], his shrinking from the practical consequences of his way of thinking . . . shows he was aware of the problematic aspect of the situation" (p. 132). One is left somewhat confused here whether Wagner actually wanted to expel the Jews or not. The source of this reluctance to admit that Wagner's conception of "destruction" (even if only in his later years) could be genuinely practical lies in Katz's methodological principle that one must not read later Nazi thinking back into Wagner; hence Wagner must be made out to be uncomfortable about thinking nastily practical thoughts about getting rid of the Jews. Yet, as Deathridge's review ("Talk of Destruction") points out, there is no reason to think that Wagner ever felt any moral qualms about his theoretical or his practical antisemitism. It should be remembered that in the 1869 addendum to *Judaism in Music* his only reservation about expelling the Jews was whether it was practically and politically possible—the question of whether it would be moral to do so never seems to have entered his mind.

It is also difficult to know how to take Katz's surprising statement (p. 110) that Wagner's essays had "no decisive impact" on the emergence of the antisemitic movement of the 1870s. The trail of major and minor antisemites to his door recorded in Cosima's diaries shows how he had become the personification of public antisemitism thanks to the reissue of *Judaism in Music* in 1869.

[23] J. L. Talmon, *The Myth of the Nation and the Vision of Revolution* (London, 1981), p. 208. Curiously Talmon neglected to point out that Wagner's understanding of revolution was not liberal.

*Judaism in Music* is brought to bear on the problem: the contexts of Laube's *Struensee* and Heine's *Ludwig Börne*; of the Ahasverus mythology; of the systematization of Wagner's antisemitism in his revolutionary conversion of 1849; of the place of *Judaism in Music* in Wagner's cycle of revolutionary essays; of the relationship between the antisemitism of the *Ring* and the revolutionary essays.

———

Wagner's antagonism to the Jews—and especially to Meyerbeer—was sharpened by his experiences at Paris following the collapse of the Dresden revolution in 1849. At Paris he was painfully disillusioned by the ostensibly more successful revolution there, which he believed to have been commandeered by the capitalists and Jews:

> Paris had the most depressing effect on me. The motto, *liberté, égalité, fraternité*, was still to be seen on all the public buildings . . . but, on the other hand, I was alarmed at seeing the money men making their way from the bank with their long money-sacks over their shoulders.[24]

To show the connection between capitalism and Judaism, Wagner juxtaposed this passage to an account of how he entered a music shop and found there Meyerbeer, who had been trying to hide. Dishonesty was common to both the Parisian capitalists and the Jewish composer. For Wagner, the only antidote to this false revolutionism of Frenchmen, capitalists, and Jews was an authentic German revolutionism.

Because Wagner provided his blueprint for German unification in the 1860s—the decade when he was most in thrall to the king of Bavaria—several misconceptions have obscured its revolutionism. Instead, debate has flourished around three false problems. Did Wagner, it is asked, desert his revolutionary beliefs of 1848–50 for reactionary monarchism under the patronage of Ludwig II? Did Wagner support a military "power state" or a purely idealistic spiritual movement? Did he abandon his belief in revolution for a belief in race? All three "problems" dissolve when Wagner's idea of the German revolution is understood rightly.

---

[24] *MLE*, p. 250. Wagner was at this time under the influence of Bakunin and Proudhon, who were both intensely antisemitic. See *MLE*, pp. 78ff., 452, 488, 491–99, 509; E. Silberner, "Two Studies on Modern Anti-semitism: I. The Jew-hatred of Mikhail Bakunin," *Historia Judaica* 14 (1952): 93–106; idem, *Sozialisten zur Judenfragen* (Berlin, 1962), pp. 54–64, 390ff. (Surprisingly Silberner does not mention the connection with Wagner.) A. P. Mendel, *Mikhail Bakunin: Roots of Apocalypse* (New York, 1981), pp. 206, 264, 330f., 354, 381–85; G. Lichtheim, "Socialism and the Jews," *Dissent* (July–Aug. 1968): 314–42, at pp. 323, 338; *HAS*, 3:322, 373–79, 547.

For Wagner, the mission of the German spirit was "to restore the purely human itself to its pristine freedom." Germany was the vehicle of revolutionary human freedom. In the 1860s Wagner realized that German politics had lost sight of this great aim, thanks to the spread of Jewish capitalism and Jewishness in general, which had caused "our princes to quite unlearn an understanding of this German spirit." On the other side, the concept of revolution itself had been de-Germanized over the preceding half century. Wagner lamented this in his essay *What Is German?* (1865; published 1878), while observing that it had been "reserved for Börne the Jew to sound the first challenge to the German's sloth." But in doing so Börne provoked a profound misunderstanding of the German *Burschenschaft* concept of revolution and perverted it into a French—and Jewish— liberal idea of revolution:

> The misunderstanding that prompted the Austrian chancellor Metternich to deem the aspirations of the German *Burschenschaft* identical with those of the bygone Paris Jacobin Club and to take hostile measures accordingly—that misunderstanding was most advantageous to the Jewish speculator who stood outside seeking nothing but his personal profit. This time, if he played his game well, that speculator had only to swing himself into the midst of the German *Volk* and state to exploit and in the end, not merely to govern it, but downright make it his own property. . . . There soon also arose adventurers to teach the downtrodden German national spirit to apply French maxims to the estimates of its governments. The demagogues had now arrived indeed; but what a doleful afterbirth! Every new Parisian revolution was promptly "mounted" in Germany; naturally, since every new spectacular Paris opera had been mounted forthwith in the court theaters of Berlin and Vienna, setting a pattern for all Germany. I have no hesitation about styling the subsequent revolutions in Germany entirely un-German.
>
> "Democracy" in Germany is purely a translated thing. It exists merely in the "press" and what this German press is one must find out for oneself. But untowardly enough, this translated Franco-Judaeo-German Democracy could easily borrow a handle, a pretext, and a deceptive cloak from the misprised and maltreated spirit of the German *Volk*. To secure a following among the people, "Democracy" aped a German mien, and "Germanness," "German spirit," "German honesty," "German freedom," "German morals" became catchwords disgusting no one more than him who had true German culture, who had to stand in sorrow and watch the singular comedy of agitators from a non-German people. . . . The astounding lack of success of the

so loud-mouthed movement of 1848 is easily explained by the curious circumstance that the genuine German found himself and his name suddenly represented by a race of men quite alien to him . . . these Democratic speculators.[25]

In *German Art and German Politics* (1867–68) Wagner repeated his view that the authentic German revolutionism of the *Burschenschaften* had been betrayed and misunderstood as just another outbreak of French revolutionism. In 1819, the judges of Kotzebue's student assassin could not believe that the young Sand had acted purely instinctively out of the urgings of the "German spirit" in the conviction that his target was "the corrupter of German youth and the betrayer of the German *Volk*." Sand's Germanness was so natural that it enabled him to accept torture and death, conduct incomprehensible to Jewish revolutionists. "It was a clever Jew, Börne by name, who first made merry at this deed; nor did Heine, if our memory serves us, allow it to escape his wit."[26] Yet it is the German spirit of the *Burschenschaften* that would revolutionize the ugly face of current authority and bureaucracy in Germany (pp. 60–62).

Wagner invoked Constantin Frantz for his principle that a new form of revolutionary German politics was required, one freed of Judeo-French democratic materialism, one rising above the divisions of German parties into monarchists and republicans. The new German politics would defy conventional labels to achieve a revolutionary union of the German king and the German race. The old Prussian-style state, based on expediency, power, and war, would be destroyed:

> We finally admonish a genuinely redeeming inner union of the German princes with their peoples, and their imbuement with the true German spirit. . . . (p. 50)
>
> The rebirth of the German spirit . . . will ennoble the public spiritual life of the German *Volk*, to the end of founding a new and truly German civilization, extending its blessings even beyond our frontiers. . . . (p. 63)
>
> We have appealed to neither aristocratic nor democratic, to neither liberal nor conservative, neither monarchical nor republican, to neither Catholic nor Protestant interests; but in each demand of ours we have relied on nothing but the character of the German spirit. . . .
>
> This will allow us, as touching the social basis of the state, to take that

[25] *PW*, 4:165f. The Börne remark is in *PW*, 4:165, but not in the original 1865 text (which is often harsher than the later version) in *König Ludwig II und Richard Wagner: Briefwechsel* (Karlsruhe, 1936–39), 4:5ff., 26–34. It is quoted extensively by Newman, *Life of Wagner*, 3:475ff.

[26] *PW*, 4:46ff., 92f. Page references in text are to this edition.

absolutely conservative standpoint that we will call the idealistic, in opposition to the formally realistic. (p. 129) . . . The greatest relation,
that of king and *Volk*, embraces all the relations like it. . . . To give this
German spirit a fitting habitation in the system of the German state
. . . is tantamount to establishing the best and only lasting constitution.
(p. 135)

For the Wagner of the 1860s, the racial idea of the *Volk* did not
supersede the revolution. Rather it deepened the revolutionary concept. (In his *State and Religion* of 1864, Wagner had indeed anticipated the charge of abandoning the revolution by explaining that he
had simply shed the simplistic socialist remedies of 1848–51.)[27]
Wagner's claim that his new German state would be "defensive-ide-
alist-conservative" rather than "aggressive-revolutionary," not a conventional power state but an ideal society, is apt to mislead innocent
readers.[28] His new state was not meant to be revolutionary in a
French sense. Rather, in a profounder, German way, it aimed at a
redemptive liberation of the Germans and all humanity. This vision
hearkened back to the Prussian educational and moral renaissance of
Fichte's *Addresses to the German Nation*.[29] And here again we come to
the central problem of ambivalence and ambiguity in the German political tradition. It is misconceived to separate the ideal and the practical into rigid compartments and ask in which one of them Fichte or
Wagner belongs. The whole point is that the tradition's two elements
are fused with one another in an eternal ambiguity, just as in Jewish
history the question of whether the Jews are a people *or* a religion is
misconceived. To ask, then, whether Wagner is thinking about a political or an ideal revolutionary state misses the essential point. Sometimes he is thinking more of the ideal elements, sometimes of the
practical, but he always conceives of the revolution as a fluctuating
synthesis of the ideal and the real. Fichte's and Wagner's almost mystical conception of revolution is not the precise, practical conception
of Western liberalism.

Nor was Wagner's attitude to war that of a liberal pacifist. During
the Franco-Prussian War of 1870–71, he urged Bismarck to raze

---

[27] *PW*, 4:5, 7. Contrast Deathridge and Dahlhaus, *New Grove Wagner*, p. 52: "Wagner
was exchanging his former progressive views for a reactionary vision of *Deutschtum* and
German supremacy." Katz, *Darker Side*, p. 63: "Denying his former democratic leanings
. . . Revolution and democracy, he maintained, were foreign to the German folk-
spirit." Such statements arise out of a basic misconception of Wagner's revolutionism,
assuming it to be rooted in the Western liberal-democratic tradition.

[28] *PW*, 4:123. Cf. "Was ist Deutsch?" in *König Ludwig und Wagner*, 4:19f., 26, 28f., 32
(pp. 19–26 and 29–32 are omitted from the 1878 version in *PW*).

[29] See above, chap. 8.

Paris to the ground and was anxious lest the impending bombard-ment of the city be averted by a premature armistice. Later, the ide-alist remarked how "glad he was that he had gone through the war with feelings of joy."[30] Such statements are not merely those of an unstable personality, but rather reflect the intrinsic instability and ambiguity of the German revolutionary tradition.

Of course, Wagner's enthusiasm for Bismarck faded when the chancellor also betrayed the German revolution (in addition to failing to provide sufficient patronage for Bayreuth). Then Wagner joined with Frantz in deploring the Jewishness of the new empire, which had turned out to be just another *real-politischer* state, rather than a truly revolutionary German one:

> Bismarck is creating German unity, but he has no conception of its nature. . . . His conduct is a disgrace for Germany . . . his decisions have brought forth from the Jews a petition of thanks.[31]

Bismarck's speech against the Antisemites' Petition of 1880 proved that he had "a pact with the Jews."[32]

---

In the 1870s Wagner achieved a new ideological rigor in his rev-olutionary antisemitism by means of the emergent biological doctrine of race. The two main influences on which he drew were, first, the strictly biological ideas of Darwinism (which was spreading rapidly in German thanks to the popularizing work of Ernst Häckel and oth-ers), and, second, the cultural racial ideas of Gobineau (which in the light of Darwinism were taking on an implicitly biological flavor). To his sophistication of his basic ideology of race and revolution, Wagner gave a new name: regeneration.

This "regenerative" racist antisemitism of the 1870s and 1880s has often been dismissed as an aberration and as senile raving.[33] But in fact its fundamental moral argument (as opposed to its pseudoscien-tific "racial" superstructure) goes back to the early 1850s, when he came under the influence of Schopenhauer. Nietzsche observed that "Wagner's hatred of the Jews is Schopenhauerian," and indeed one of the Schopenhauerian elements that Wagner drew on was the con-

[30] Cf. *CWD*, 18 August 1870, and the nasty tone of the other entries for July to September 1870. Also 8 November 1878. Cf. T. Schieder, "Richard Wagner, das Reich und die Deutschen nach den Tagebüchern Cosima Wagners," *Historische Zeitschrift* 227 (1978): 571–98.

[31] *CWD*, 16 December and 15 July 1878.

[32] *CWD*, 10 November 1881. For Wagner's refusal to sign the petition, see Rose, "No-ble Anti-Semitism," pp. 759ff.

[33] See for instance, Newman, *Life of Wagner*, 4:654.

cept of an "Aryan Christianity" (adumbrated by Fichte).[34] Wagner's *Parsifal* and its accompanying racial essays invoked the idea of a non-Jewish Jesus in seeking to divorce Christianity entirely from its Jewish roots and "the huge perversion of the Semite-Latin Church."[35]

By this time Wagner had come to appreciate that the greatest Semitic perversion of Aryan Christianity was the murder of animals for meat, a practice promoted by the Jewish God Jehovah, which symbolized the Jewish cult of power and domination over humanity, and indeed all Nature. The Aryan Christ had sacrificed his own flesh and blood as expiation "for all the sin of outpoured blood and slaughtered flesh." But His sacrifice had been betrayed by the church, which made European man a "beast of prey, encouraging him to kill not only animals but men through religious warfare." And here Wagner discovered a new twist to the "Blood Libel" that had evaded the ingenuity of his predecessors such as Daumer and Hess:

> Blood at last, and blood alone, seemed fitted to sustain the conquerors' courage. . . . Attack and defense, want and war, victory and defeat, lordship and thralldom, all sealed with the seal of blood; this from henceforth is the History of Man. The victory of the stronger is followed close by enervation through a culture taught them by their conquered thralls; whereon, uprooting of the degenerate by fresh raw forces, of blood-thirst still unslaked. Then, falling lower and lower, the only worthy food for the world-conqueror appears to be human blood and corpses.

Thus, in Wagner's modern world, the mass slaughter of animals in a Parisian abattoir has its counterpart in the mass carnage of human beings on the battlefield.[36] War, the glorification of the state, the "daily bloodbath of animals . . . for luncheon feasting upon the limbs of murdered household animals," the purchase of land by money in the bourgeois state—all these activities are but different manifesta-

[34] Nietzsche, *The Gay Science*, chapter 99 (*Werke*, ed. G. Colli and M. Montinari [New York–Berlin, 1967–], 5:ii, 132). On Schopenhauer's antisemitism (which invokes the mythology of Ahasverus), see H. W. Brann, *Schopenhauer und das Judentum* (Bonn, 1975); A. Low, *Jews in the Eyes of the Germans: From the Enlightenment to Imperial Germany* (Philadelphia, 1979), pp. 321–27; N. Rotenstreich, *Jews and German Philosophy* (New York, 1974), pp. 179–200. R. Hollinrake, *Nietzsche, Wagner, and the Philosophy of Pessimism* (London, 1982), pp. 59, 129ff., appreciates the significance of Schopenhauer's antisemitism both for his general philosophy and for its influence on Wagner, but the issue is strangely ignored by B. Magee, *The Philosophy of Schopenhauer* (Oxford, 1983).

[35] See *Herodom and Christendom* and *Religion and Art*, PW, 6:280ff., and 232, respectively.

[36] PW, 6:225–28. For an echo of Hess's bloody capitalist "beasts of prey," see PW, 6:203 (and CWD, 9 September 1879): "The Pentateuch has won the day, and the prowling has become the calculating beast of prey."

tions of the essential Jewishness that has corrupted the original purity of Aryan Christianity.[37]

True redemption from these Jewish horrors meant the racial redemption of Aryan blood itself to its original purity. German blood itself had to be cleansed of its three contaminants—loveless marriage, the eating of meat, "and above all the degenerative mixing of the heroic blood of noblest races with that of former eaters of humans, now trained to be the business-agents of society."[38] The Jews are the obstacle to revolutionary human redemption, not just metaphorically but by reason of their very physical blood, which never fades through commixture (as Wagner had pointed out in *Know Thyself*). It is absurd to think that Wagner, as he penned these words, did not realize that some very physical action would have eventually to be taken to cure this physical problem of Jewish "blood."

Wagner's last unpublished essays of 1882–83 linked these later racial ideas of intermarriage and degeneration with his longtime revolutionary hatred of bourgeois marriage as loveless and perverted by Jewish motives of property and domination. His very last essay (which he died writing at Venice in February 1883) was intended to resolve finally the problem of the role of sexual love in the evolution of races of noble blood. *On the Feminine in the Human* explains that the "deterioration of the human races" occurs because man meddles in the natural choice of mates by introducing the consideration of property and possession; such is bourgeois marriage. Yet in its nobler form marriage founded on true love exemplifies

> man's power over Nature, and is called divine. It is the fashioner of noble races. . . . It is certain that the noblest white race is monogamous at its first appearance in saga and history, but marches towards its downfall through polygamous intercourse with the races which it conquers.[39]

The great revolutionary object of Wagner's "Regeneration" was to remove "Jewish" qualities of power and possession from marriage and so restore the German Aryan race to its original heroic purity, a purity based on the marriage of heroic lovers.

---

Wagner's idea of the German revolution always spilled over into the political. In 1851 Wagner had declared that his idea of revolution went far beyond the political:

[37] *PW*, 6:234.
[38] *PW*, 6:284.
[39] *PW*, 8:396ff. Cf. *CWD*, 2:1010, and entries for 26 and 30 January 1883.

> I am neither a republican, nor a democrat, nor a socialist, nor a com-
> munist, but—an artistic being; and as such, everywhere that my gaze,
> my desire, and my will extend, an out-and-out revolutionary, a de-
> stroyer of the old by the creation of the new.[40]

But this destructive revolutionism could not be contained as neatly
within the world of art and spirit as Wagner here pretended. A few
months later he betrayed himself in a private letter:

> My entire political creed consists of nothing but the bloodiest hatred
> for our whole civilization, contempt for all things deriving from it,
> and a longing for nature. . . . No one in France knows that we are *hu-*
> *man*, except perhaps Proudhon, and even he not quite clearly. But in
> all Europe I prefer dogs to these doglike men. Yet I don't despair of a
> better future; only the most terrific and destructive revolution could
> make our civilized beasts "human" again.[41]

In 1865 Wagner carefully explained the German meaning of revolution, how it had been stabbed in the back in 1813, and his own
crucial messianic role in bringing about its resurrection:

> In the year 1813 in Germany it was different . . . it was a fervent sa-
> cred cause. . . . That was hope! A Germany was supposed to come
> into being. What that was supposed to be was shown after victory and
> betrayal. Then came the *Burschenschaft*. The League of Virtue was
> founded. All so fantastic that no human being could grasp it. Now it
> is *me* whom no one grasps. I am the most German being. I am the
> German spirit. Question the incomparable magic of my works—com-
> pare them with the rest and you can for the time being say no differ-
> ently than that—it is *German!*[42]

In 1879 Wagner attempted to summarize the revolutionary significance of his career in an autobiographical memoir written for American readers. It is a remarkable story that brings together the threads
of the German revolutionary tradition that have been analyzed in this
book. Its central theme was to present Wagner's crowning achievement in making himself the prime force in fusing together the fundamental elements of revolution and Germanness.[43]

[40] Newman, *Life of Wagner*, 2:245, quotes these unpublished sentences from the *Communication to My Friends* of 1851.

[41] Letter to Kietz, 30 December 1851, in *Letters of Richard Wagner: The Burrell Collection*, p. 187; *Selected Letters*, p. 243.

[42] *The Diary of Richard Wagner: The Brown Book*, trans. G. Bird (London, 1980), p. 73,
11 September 1865.

[43] "The Work and Mission of My Life," *North American Review* nos. 223–24 (Aug.–

Wagner began with "Germanness." Because of its intrinsic "ideal-ity," "German" culture was superior to all others and was being spread by the growing strength of "German blood" in England and America. However, he recalled, in his youth that same German cul-ture had been jeopardized by a web of cultural tendencies "entirely foreign to the German race":

> A web that glittered with two changing colors, the sallow hue of the Restoration . . . and the red hue of revolution, in the new and equally French sense of "Liberty." The interweaving and arrangement of these two textures seemed to me to be undertaken by a third foreign constituent of our national life—that Jewish element whose influence was continually on the increase. How different had been the future of German culture as Young Germany might have imagined it in the pe-riod in which I was born. (pp. 111f.)

Instead of an authentic German culture and politics, there flourished an alien combination of French "reaction" and "liberal revolution," promoted by the even more alien "Jewish element," which was so fun-damentally opposed to the whole idea of a "German revolution."

Despite this unpromising climate (Wagner continued), the student *Burschenschaften* tried to assert a true German revolutionary feeling, only to have its cry of "German freedom" mistaken by the German princes for an outburst of French liberal revolutionism (pp. 114f.). Ironically, even other German revolutionaries began to adopt this "French idea of revolution," abandoning the cause of "German" rev-olutionary freedom. This foreign revolutionism had also been stamped into a moribund German literature by the Young German movement, which Wagner had joined with his friend Laube, only to find it led by the Jews Börne and Heine, members of that "race of mediators and negotiators whose influence was from this time to spread its truly 'international' power more and more widely over Ger-many." Jewish musicians too had betrayed the revolutionary idea in their works. There was Meyerbeer's fake "revolutionary" music of *Les Huguenots* and Mendelssohn's detouring of "the tempests of revolu-tion" into soothing salon music. (The same went for Schumann's tasteful German genre pieces, which embodied only a vague "Ger-man" element.) Thus had German revolutionary freedom degener-ated in the first half of the nineteenth century (pp. 119ff.). Intui-tively, says Wagner, he had utterly rejected this process; his *Rienzi* was full of "revolutionary fire," but had lacked the crucial element of

---

Sept. 1879): 107–24, 238–58, especially pp. 111–12. (Subsequent page references in text are to this source.)

"Germanness." This he had finally achieved with his discovery of the ideal forms of "German legend," which he incorporated into his "German operas" from *The Flying Dutchman* onwards. At last he had been able to envision a truly German form of revolution and its artistic expression: "A new world opened before me" (pp. 121ff.).

Summoned back to Germany by the success of *Rienzi*, Wagner had expected great things, but his years at Dresden in the 1840s brought him increasing disillusionment with the state of German culture and politics, as well as personal frustration with the bourgeois Philistine world on which he depended:

> There was no general audience to which I could turn for sympathy with my aims. The German people had not yet rediscovered its own nature, although *German freedom* and *German unity* were becoming more and more the current phrases of its political enthusiasm. (p. 240)
>
> For the mere sake of earning a living I should have to keep my true nature and opinions behind a detestable mask of hypocrisy and social conventionalism. . . . I was utterly foreign to this world, both as an artist and as a German. In the midst of this bitterness against the existing condition of things, I found myself amid the general revolutionary spirit which was growing. (p. 241)

But Wagner had been disappointed by the resulting revolution, whose party factionalism overwhelmed the true German revolutionary need for human freedom:

> The only element in history which had always attracted and inspired me had been this effort of the race to mutiny against the tyranny of a traditional and legalized formalism. . . . I saw that this idea of mine, as to what should be the essential motive of a revolution, was utterly misunderstood by the politicians (p. 242). . . . Only some great revolution of humanity at large could make the true liberty of the individual possible; and only a revolutionary movement in such a sense, with such a motive, could be of any saving worth to a true art. (p. 244)

In this passage Wagner united the two key ideals of the German "race" and the "revolution." Wagner's *human* revolution would achieve the destruction of Judaism, that antithesis of all that was human, noble, and ideal—the antithesis of all that was, in a word, "German." This was his vision of the German revolutionary future, which always, by its very nature, brought him back to the Jewish Question: "It is distressing to me always [he confessed in 1878] to come back to the theme of the Jews. But one cannot escape it if one looks to the future."[44] Without the solution of the Jewish Question, there could not in fact be a German revolution.

―――――

Hitler admitted only one real precursor—Richard Wagner. Much of the literature on the "Wagner-Hitler" connection, however, has missed the essential common link between the two figures, namely, their revolutionary mentality.[45] What attracted Hitler was Wagner's revolutionism, which encompassed both revolutionary antisemitism and a vision of a German revolution. Jewish revolutionism was for Hitler, as much as for Wagner, a false form of revolution that was completely hostile and alien to Germany. How could it be otherwise since the Jews were "led by nothing but the naked egoism of the individual" and lived as parasites on all other nations?[46] Echoing Wagner's *German Art and German Politics*, Hitler attacked the false freedoms of both liberal democracy and Marxist socialism as mere Jewish fronts for the destruction of true German freedom. The so-called "German revolution" of 1918 had been a Jewish plot, a false revolution from which Germany had to be liberated by National Socialism. National Socialism, however, was not a conventional political party, but a "movement" (again echoing Wagner) that went beyond monarchy and republicanism in being a transcendental embodiment of the German spirit. This movement would produce a true German revolution, bringing a *German* state, a *German* democracy, and *German* freedom.[47] Such were the conceptions of German revolutionism that would have formed Hitler's projected book of the 1920s, *Die German-*

[44] *CWD*, 28 November 1878.

[45] Cf. J. Matter, *Wagner et Hitler* (Lausanne, 1977). Ultimately both shared a quasi-religious vision of Aryan racial redemption, as is evident in the Hitler monologue on *Parsifal* reported by H. Rauschning, *Gespräche mit Hitler* (1940), 2d ed. (Vienna, 1973), pp. 216f. (The late Winifred Wagner confirmed in correspondence to me that for Hitler, *Parsifal* was a religious experience.) Perhaps Newman, *Life of Wagner*, 4:638f., has the best word on the similarity of characters. Discussing Wagner's desperate letter of 22 November 1881 trying to persuade Ludwig II of the morality of antisemitism, Newman comments that it "exhibits the fanaticism and sophistry of the German anti-semite of all epochs . . . [a] charming specimen of Hitlerism avant la lettre."

[46] Hitler, *Mein Kampf*, trans. R. Manheim (Boston 1943; repr. 1971), pp. 300–29, especially pp. 302 and 327. At p. 305 Hitler cites Schopenhauer's antisemitism.

[47] Ibid., pp. 333–35, 344, 346. See also A. Hitler, *Sämtliche Aufzeichnungen*, ed. E. Jäckel and A. Kuhn (Stuttgart, 1980), p. 622 ("German democracy"); p. 779 ("deutschen Germanischen Revolution"); p. 1042 ("Germanische Revolution"); and p. 1052 ("the national revolution has broken out," on occasion of 1923 putsch). Hitler acknowledges three "truly great Germans": Luther, Frederick the Great, and Wagner (ibid., pp. 1032–34; cf. p. 240).

*ische Revolution.*[48] And in this vision of German revolution the Jewish Question occupied a central place, as Hitler explained to an acquaintance in 1922:

> My object is to create first-rate revolutionary upheavals, regardless of what methods and means I have to use in the process. Earlier revolutions were directed either against the peasants, or the nobility or the clergy, or against dynasties . . . but in no case has revolution succeeded without the presence of a lightning rod that could conduct and channel the odium of the general masses.
>
> With this very thing in mind I scanned the revolutionary events of history and put the question to myself: against which racial element in Germany can I unleash my propaganda of hate with the greatest prospects of success? I had to find the right kind of victim, and especially one against whom the struggle would make sense, materially speaking. . . . I came to the conclusion that a campaign against the Jews would be as popular as it would be successful. . . . They are totally defenseless and no one will stand up to protect them.[49]

[48] Hitler drew a frontispiece for the "first volume" of this projected book, reproduced from Bundesarchiv, Koblenz, NS 26/64, by W. Maser, *Hitler's Letters and Notes*, trans. R. Manheim (London, 1974), p. 281.

[49] Conversation with Josef Heller, 1922, quoted by G. Fleming, *Hitler and the Final Solution* (Berkeley, 1984), pp. 28f. For the quasi-religious character of Nazi revolutionism, see U. Tal, "On Structures of Political Theology and Myth in Germany prior to the Holocaust," in *The Holocaust as Historical Experience*, ed. Y. Bauer and N. Rotenstreich (New York, 1981), pp. 43–74. From R. Melson, "Revolutionary Genocide: On the Causes of the Armenian Genocide of 1915 and the Holocaust," *Holocaust and Genocide Studies* 4 (1989): 161–74, it may be deduced that political revolutionary crises are responsible for turning the ideology of revolutionary antisemitism into practical revolutionary genocide.

# AFTERWORD

THOUGH afterwords to new editions are a useful way of answering one's critics (and this one is no exception), the subject of this book and its implications are so grave, as well as tendentious, that I think it necessary to say a few words to clarify certain of its arguments which were misunderstood by some reviewers of the first edition, whether through my own fault or theirs.[1]

1. "Revolutionary antisemitism" is a coinage of mine that was devised to illustrate the deep structure of the German secular antisemitism that in the eighteenth century replaced the religious or merely social prejudice of earlier periods. Of course, like any general historical category, it tends to lump together phenomena in an undifferentiated way that provokes a critical reviewer to remark that it is just too broad a term to be of much use. But its very comprehensiveness, its transcendence of the normal boundaries of intellectual and political definition, is precisely the point that I was trying to make. There was a deep structure beneath all the obvious political and intellectual variations of German culture that I chose to call "revolutionary" in the same sense that both the early Christianity of St. Paul and the utopian socialism of Henri de Saint-Simon's "New Christianity" were "revolutionary." Each of these movements of moral regeneration sought to create a "new man," a restored and redeemed humanity. This messianic humanism was a general European impulse of the age of revolution, but it seems undeniable to me that the most coherent and self-conscious pursuit of the revolutionary ideal of a new humanity was undertaken by the German thinkers who were profoundly influenced by Christian theology and sensibility and sought to translate this powerful archetype of intellectual and emotional perception into a secular context. Whether one looks at Kant, Marx, Humboldt, Herder, or Wagner, they are united in their striving to construct a new "pure humanity," variously based on reason or love, that would constitute a revolution in human nature and human history alike. It was this revolutionary mentality, this deep structure,

[1] Among the more interesting—if sometimes critical—reviews of the first edition may be cited those of Anthony Quinton (*New York Review of Books*, 7 November 1991), Robert Alter (*New Republic*, 20 May 1991), Glenn Sharfman (*Shofar*, Winter, 1992), William Kluback (*Midstream*, April 1991), Geoffrey Wheatcroft (*Times Literary Supplement*, 3 January 1992), C. M. Clark (*The Historical Journal* [Cambridge], December 1991), and Deborah Hertz (*Journal of Modern History*, forthcoming. I have much to disagree with in this last review.).

that the book seeks to describe by investigating the "mythology" that both shaped and was shaped by it.[2] (I may say in passing that I was surprised that no reviewer took up what seemed to me a fertile distinction between the "morphology" and "analogy" of this and other antisemitic mythologies.)

Naively speaking, of course, no one would say there is much wrong with this German humanist aspiration; after all, if everyone were to act more reasonably or lovingly the world would no doubt be a better place. One is forced to ask, though, at which stage the purity of the original vision is debased. Is it with Hegel's apparent idolization of the Prussian state founded on reason? Or is it Nietzsche's slightly crazed (as I believe it must seem to any sensible person) notion of the amoral superman as the personification of a new purified humanity? Or does the tradition remain unsullied until Hitler began to preach his version of pure humanity that was rooted in the murder of those less than purely-human races, a murder smiled upon by his "Almighty Providence"?

2. This brings me to the second point, that of the specificity of modern German history. I have unashamedly tried to reintroduce into the discussion of German history a concept of national character that has virtually disappeared from the conceptual vocabulary of academic writing on Germany in the last twenty years. Granted, there were often ill-founded denunciations of German character by Western historians in the first sixty years of this century, but now the baby—the kernel of historical explanation—has been thrown out along with the bathwater of anti-German prejudice. This process has developed to the grotesque point where the British authors of a lively book entitled *The Peculiarities of German History* have seen fit to devote barely half a page to what any commonsense observer must see as one of the major peculiarities of German history, namely antisemitism. The reunification of Germany in 1989 may, however, lead to what Conor Cruise O'Brien has called a more "realistic" interpretation of German history, one free of the need to whitewash nineteenth-century German culture out of deference to the political realities of the Cold War. Margaret Thatcher's celebrated Chequers seminar of 1990 on German history and the German national character, in which six Anglo-American historians participated, signalled the need for a reevaluation of the issue. One might dismiss this as a politicized

[2] In pursuing this approach to nineteenth-century culture this book is really a continuation of the works of the late J. L. Talmon, who died before he was able to undertake an extended study of the role of the Jewish Question in the development of German political messianism. I was exposed to Talmon's somewhat charismatic teaching when he was a visitor at St. Catherine's College, Oxford, in 1963.

throwback, but disciplines outside history, particularly sociology, have seen a restoration of the category of national character as a meaningful subject of academic discussion in the last decade, and I would guess that the same will happen in historical circles once the prevailing fashion for "value-free" and allegedly objective analysis has faded.[3]

3. Careful as I was in this book to avoid any expression of mindless anti-Germanism, one critic has accused me of replacing the notion of the Eternal Jew with that of the Eternal German.[4] This sort of moral equalizing (of which one hears too much in the last few years in other political—especially Middle Eastern—contexts) seems to me ignorant and misguided; the Jews did not—and do not—call for the murder of the German people. In any case, let me emphasize here that the situation in Germany has been radically transformed since 1945 when, under Allied supervision, more Western liberal ways of thinking and forms of social responsibility were introduced in order to neutralize the attitudes analyzed in my book. The recent "historians' controversy" has shown how a strong authentically liberal counter-current to the dominant essentially illiberal mentality has become more genuinely rooted in German life than ever before.[5] It was precisely this kind of countercurrent that failed to achieve a recognized status in German political culture in the early nineteenth century and became increasingly marginalized until Hitler's contemptuous dismissal of its political rump in 1933. The question for the future is whether the more dangerous aspects of German political culture, now in their usual camouflage of respectability and arrogant unreflectiveness rather than in the insane colors of Nazi ideology, will in the end choke the seeds of genuine liberal feeling that have flourished since 1945. As is well recognized now in Britain at least, the German Question is not yet settled.

4. One of my main purposes in writing this book was to examine

[3] This may take some time, to judge from the rather hysterical reaction by R. Robertson in *German History* 9 (1991): 385–86, who seems to have been rendered momentarily unable to read on account of his outrage at my approach. He indicts me for quoting "a statement by Ulrike Meinhof, which he mistranslates and distorts in a way that it is charitable to call slovenly." Had Mr. Robertson been more in control of himself, he might have noticed that my translation of the Meinhof statement (p. 304) was taken with acknowledgement from another source. The reviewer seems to have been particularly irritated by my (I thought) self-evidently true remark that Marx's *Zur Judenfrage* founded a tradition of socialist antisemitism.

[4] J. F. Harris, *American Historical Review* 97 (April 1992): 571–72.

[5] A.J.P. Taylor's preface in the 1950s to his famous book *The Course of German History* despaired of ever reeducating the Germans and recommended instead protecting oneself from them. Nevertheless, in his last years he considerably revised this opinion.

German mentality and look at national character in a more subtle historical way than has usually been the case. Another concern was the history of German antisemitism. As I read more in the subject, it became clear to me that the Jewish Question as it emerged in Germany was really an attempt to conceptualize the German Question itself: What did "German" really mean? Was there a German people? Was there an authentic German culture? Should a German political nation become actual? What was Germany's place in Europe? These agonized attempts at German self-definition resulted in a disturbingly negative definition: they defined as "Jewish" whatever was "non-German," hence, the emotional intensity invested in the Jewish Question by Germans earnestly in search of their own identity. They had to discover and extrude whatever was not German in order to be left with the pure distillate of Germanness. Since the brutal solution of the Jewish Question by Hitler, German efforts at self-identification have had to seek replacements for the now-missing Jews in the guises of "guest-workers," "East Germans," and "political refugees," though the ideological discussion of these substitutes has not attained the rigorous intellectual and political development evoked by the Jewish Question in the course of the last two hundred years. In that sense, Germany has ended one era of its history, the era in which the German Question was the Jewish Question, as suggested by the new title of this book. One can only hope that the emotions and self-inflicted desperation that drove the discussion of the Jewish Question have been purged.

5. The relationship of the nineteenth-century German antisemitic mentality depicted here to the Holocaust has vexed several readers. Perhaps I should have made myself clearer here, but I intentionally wished to leave matters a little obscure and tentative (even if attentive readers of the dedication might have been able to divine my feelings on the matter). Obviously, one cannot assume simply that German antisemitism produced in a direct and inevitable way the mass-murder of the Jews. The connection needs to be demonstrated very carefully and analytically, and with special attention to the changing historical contexts that set the world of the nineteenth-century antisemites apart from that of the barbarized warfare and politics of our century. There were anti-Jewish writers of the book's period who would have been appalled by the results of the logical application of their ideology by Hitler, as indeed there may have been the occasional Nazi who regretted too rough a treatment of the Jews. The historical problem, however, is why it was that German antisemitism, rather than that of any other society, produced the movement and

the means for physically implementing the "destructionist" mentality. We cannot say just that it was an accident that German and not, say, Polish or French antisemitism brought about the Holocaust and shrug off further discussion. For a fire to burn, there must be tinder and fuel. Only if an entire culture were permeated—not always malevolently—with antisemitic sensibility could it allow itself to initiate and participate in such a process as the Holocaust. I tried in this book to delineate a peculiarly German corruption of the whole spectrum of intellectual and political culture—even of "pro-Jewish" opinion— by a habit of thinking and feeling that was profoundly anti-Jewish. In other countries, ideals such as "humanity" and "freedom" would often inhibit the growth of antisemitism (even though many liberal individuals might themselves continue personally to harbor anti-Jewish sentiments), but in Germany the highest expression of these ideals actually fostered the spread of an antisemitic mentality. When one defines "pure-humanity" and "freedom" as the exact opposite of "Jewishness," then one is morally and intellectually bound to become an antisemite in a basic sense, even if one might actually be sympathetic to Jews as individuals or as a people. I have tried in this book to show how German political and intellectual culture of the nineteenth century was soaked in this mentality to an extraordinary degree, and how this was the precondition for the Holocaust. Of course, if the defeat of 1918 had never occurred, it is arguable that Jewish assimilation would have continued at an accelerating pace and that Hitler would never have come into power. In this happy scenario there would have been neither Second World War nor Holocaust, and the antisemitic mentality might well have vanished into the mists of time as merely a historical curiosity. One must certainly allow a large degree of historical contingency in accounting for the Holocaust, but the other unavoidable side of the coin is formed by the historical context of modern German antisemitism. To regard German antisemitism as just one of many antisemitisms and disconnect it in any substantial way from the explanation of the Holocaust is to fall into a most serious historical error. There was a Holocaust, unique both historically and in moral experience, and it cannot be understood in terms that are exclusively contingential any more validly than it may be interpreted as the inevitable outcome of two centuries of German antisemitism or two thousand years of Christian antisemitism. Without the impact of these two antisemitisms, there would certainly have been no Holocaust, just as without the contingential cloak of twentieth-century mass-warfare, even Hitler might not have been able to implement physically the nineteenth century's dreams of the destruction of Judaism.[6]

*Since the completion of the first edition, there have been several notable publications on the subject including:*

Almog, S. *Nationalism and Antisemitism in Modern Europe 1815–1945*. Oxford, 1990.

Almog, S., ed. *Antisemitism through the Ages*. Oxford, 1988.

Bein, A. *The Jewish Question*. trans. New York, 1990.

Davies, A. *Infected Christianity*. Kingston, Ontario, 1990.

Erb, R. and W. Bergmann, eds. *Die Nachtseite der Judenemanzipation: Der Widerstand gegen die Integration der Jude in Deutschland 1780–1860*. Berlin, 1989.

Gilman, S. L., and S. T. Katz, eds. *Anti-Semitism in Times of Crisis*. New York, 1991.

Gilman, S. L. *The Jew's Body*. Baltimore, 1992.

James, H. *A German Identity 1770–1990*. London, 1989.

Langmuir, G. *Toward a Definition of Antisemitism*. Berkeley, 1990.

Levy, R. S. *Antisemitism in the Modern World: An Anthology of Texts*. Lexington, Mass., 1991.

Manuel, F. E. *The Broken Staff*. Cambridge, Mass., 1992.

Oberman, H. A. "The Stubborn Jews: Timing the Escalation of Antisemitism in Late Medieval Europe," *LBIY* 34 (1989): xi–xxv.

Poliakov, L. *Histoire de l'antisemitisme*, vol. 5, is to appear in 1993.

Preissler, D. *Fruehantisemitismus in der Freien Stadt Frankfurt und im Grossherzogtum Hessen (1810 bis 1860)*. Heidelberg, 1989.

Pulzer, P. *Jews and the German State: The Political History of a Minority, 1848–1933*. Oxford, 1992.

Wistrich, R. *Antisemitism: The Longest Hatred*. London, 1991 (companion text for a television series).

My own *Wagner: Race and Revolution* (New Haven and London, 1992) elaborates some of the problems involved in tracing continuities between nineteenth-century antisemitism and Nazi antisemitism.

---

[6] For an attempt to explain the divergence between German and Italian attitudes to the Holocaust in terms of divergent national cultures, see J. Steinberg, *"All or Nothing": The Axis and the Holocaust, 1941–1943* (London, 1990). The peculiarity of German extremist solutions is evident in John Röhl's forthcoming biography of Kaiser Wilhelm II which contains fascinating material on his destructionist rhetoric, both in regard to the Chinese and the Jews; during the 1920s he called presciently for the mass-gassing of the latter. Even if the bizarre character of the Kaiser is taken into account, it is significant that for the German people he represented what was respectable political discourse.

Earlier titles that should have been cited include:

Arendt, H. *Antisemitism* (Part 1 of *The Origins of Totalitarianism*). New York, 1968.

Aronsfeld, C. C. *The Text of the Holocaust: A Study of the Nazis' Extermination Propaganda 1919–1945*. Marblehead, Mass., 1985.

Craig, G. *The Germans*. New York, 1982.

Dahrendorf, R. *Society and Democracy in Germany*. London, 1967.

Stern, F. *The Failure of Illiberalism*. New York, 1972.

# INDEX

Ahasverus, the Wandering Jew, 23–43,
51, 52, 56, 116, 135, 138n, 147, 148–
49, 157, 161, 167–69, 177, 193, 194–
202, 213, 231, 232n, 274, 291, 302,
303, 308, 309, 311, 320, 328–31, 337,
343, 345–47, 351, 353, 357, 366. *See
also* antisemitic myths: destruction;
Jews and history
alienation. See *Zerrissenheit*
anti-Judaism. *See* antisemitisms
Antisemites' League, 288n, 293
Antisemites' Petition, 225, 242–44, 293,
355, 372
Antisemitic Campaign of 1879–81, 240,
241–43, 246, 276–77, 278, 355
antisemitic myths, 4, 23–29, 51–58;
Ahasverus (*see* Ahasverus); blood, 7, 8,
21, 46–50, 313–17, 365, 373–74 (*see
also* Blood Libel); chosen race, xvi, 11,
41, 157, 267, 283, 345, 353, 354, 356;
Christian, 3–10, 23–24, 51–58; continuity and transformation of Christian
and secular myths, 20–21, 24–25, 28,
42, 46, 51–58, 229, 251–52, 263, 267,
361; deicide, 3, 4, 10, 51, 52–53, 258n,
373–74; destruction, xvii, 5, 6, 23, 28–
35, 57, 96, 109, 111, 116, 157–58, 194,
220, 268, 274, 303, 366 (*see also* destruction of Judaism: means of, syno-
nyms for; German ambivalence); domination, 3, 6, 9n, 110–11, 116, 151,
253–54, 269, 274, 289, 303, 361, 374;
egoism, 19, 27, 29, 48, 51, 55, 96–97,
116, 119, 132, 139, 145, 146n, 147–48,
152–53, 157, 180, 190, 197, 198, 206–
7, 213, 230, 234n, 253–54, 258n, 264,
269, 297–303, 308, 313–17, 329–33,
359, 361, 364–65, 378; exploitation,
6–7, 129; Germanization of, 8; ghost-
race, 24–25, 29, 109, 112–13, 142,
161, 168, 195, 265, 308, 311, 312, 320,
328–29 (*see also* Ahasverus; Jews and
history); internationalist, 352–57; Jewification (*Verjudung*), 4, 40–43, 151,
157, 288–90, 365; legalism, 3, 19, 96–

97, 252, 265, 267, 275, 303–4, 328;
lovelessness, 19, 27, 29, 51, 55, 116,
147–48, 190, 196–99; Mammon, 45–
46, 47, 51, 145, 147, 150, 151, 153,
154, 157, 161, 165, 198, 216–17, 218,
223, 261–62, 280, 299, 300–301, 303,
361; Moloch, 45, 46–50, 51, 52, 154,
157, 251–62, 280, 313–17, 335–36;
moneydom, 3, 5, 18–19, 48–50, 94, 97,
145–46, 147–48, 150, 151, 161, 179,
198, 300–304, 359, 361, 364; *odium hu-
manitatis*, 3, 5, 119, 258, 267; parasitism, 3, 18–20, 40, 94, 99, 111, 112,
116, 129, 274, 305, 331, 332, 354, 378;
philistinism, 26, 123, 161, 216, 377;
secularization of, 10, 23n, 24–25, 46–
50, 55, 94, 116, 130–31, 179; stubbornness, 4, 5, 10, 24, 25, 27–28, 29,
55, 112, 113, 193, 196, 263, 267, 273;
utilism, 253–54, 264, 361; wanderers,
24–25 (*see also* Ahasverus)
antisemitism: misconceptions of, 11; and
racial theory, 11–15, 21–22, 124–25,
206–7, 272–78, 282–87, 292, 294–95,
341, 356 (*see also* race); as a term, xviii,
279, 288n, 342, 355; as universal, xvi,
51
antisemitisms, xvi, 21, 51–58, 92, 290–91
(*see also* morphology and analogy); anticapitalist, 18–20, 34–35, 48–50, 152–
53, 163, 304, 305, 313–17, 368; anti-
Zionist, xvii *n*, 52, 52n, 258n; Christian, 3–10, 26, 46, 131–32, 145, 149,
261, 287, 288, 292, 341, 353; conservative, 271–73, 342, 347, 348; continuities between Christian and secular, 10,
11, 20–21, 24–25, 26, 27, 46–50, 55–
58, 130–31, 261–62; economic, 3, 9,
18–19, 129, 144–45, 146, 147, 149,
153, 162, 290; Enlightened, 9–10, 56;
French, 13, 48n; German, xv–xvi, 41–
43, 56, 57, 238–39; Jewish, 18–19,
135–79; left-wing, xvii, 278; literary,
171–84, 185–86, 211–20, 364–65;
Marxist, xvii, 304–5; nationalist, 17–